Fiona and Adam

Wishing you many years of peace and happiness together

with love from
Rhona and Geoff Waters

Betha Colaim Chille

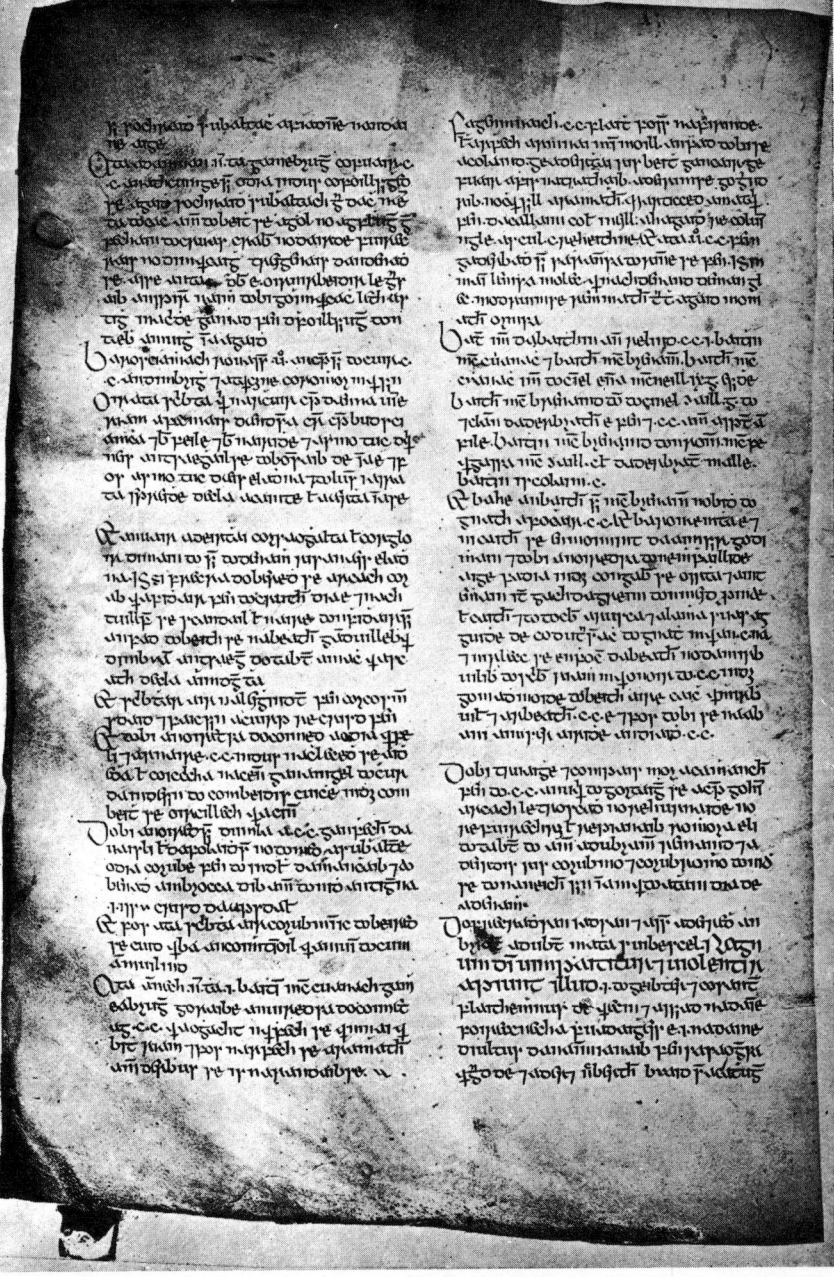

FACSIMILE PAGE OF RAWLINSON B. 514 FROM WHICH THE PRESENT LIFE OF COLUMCILLE IS EDITED.

BETHA COLAIM CHILLE
Life of Columcille

Compiled by Maghnas Ó Domhnaill in 1532

Edited and translated from manuscript Rawlinson B 514
in the Bodleian Library, Oxford,
with introduction, glossary, notes, and indexes by

A. O'KELLEHER
and
G. SCHOEPPERLE

SCHOOL OF CELTIC STUDIES
DUBLIN INSTITUTE FOR ADVANCED STUDIES

This reprint 1994

ISBN 1 85500 173 X

First published by the University of Illinois, 1918

Reprinted by
Dundalgan Press Ltd

TABLE OF CONTENTS

Table of Contents	vii
Preface	ix
Introduction	
I. The Tradition of Columcille as Manus O'Donnell Found it	xiii
II. Life of Manus O'Donnell	xxxiii
III. Manus O'Donnell's *Life of Columcille*	
Style	xxxix
Sources	xlvi
Language	xlviii
Spelling	li
Manuscript	lii
IV. Chronological Outline of the Life of Columcille*	liii
Table of Matters of the English Translation	lvii

	Sections	
Text and Translation		
The Foreword of Manus O'Donnell	1- 21	1
Of the Life of Columcille in Erin	21-202	11
Of the Life of Columcille in Iona	202-315	201
Of the Assembly of Druim Ceat	315-355	339
Of the Voyage of Columcille's Clerics	355-356	383
Of the Last Days of Columcille	356-377	403
A Comparison of Columcille with Other Holy Men	377-394	427
Of the Virtues of Columcille and of Miracles after his Death	394-435	435
Glossary		457
Index of Persons		484
Index of Places		478
Index of Matters		490
Index of First Lines of Quatrains		512
List of Chapters of the English Translation		515
Errata		516

---

*Otherwise known as Saint Columba.

PREFACE

Of the following *Life of Columcille*, written by Manus O'Donnell in 1532, the first 157 sections were edited and translated by the late Richard Henebry, and sections 157 to 232, by A. O'Kelleher, in the *Zeitschrift für Celtische Philologie* III-V, IX, and X, during the years 1901 to 1914.

The work was thus progressing with exceeding slowness when, in 1916, it received an unexpected impetus. In June of that year the attention of the Irish Fellowship Club of Chicago was drawn by President James of the University of Illinois to the importance of encouraging Irish studies in American universities, and by one of the present editors to the great number of Irish manuscripts still inedited. The Hon. John P. McGoorty, who presided at the meeting, invited the co-operation of persons interested in Irish studies, both within and outside the Irish Fellowship Club, to act upon these suggestions. A society was organized under the name of the "Irish Foundation of Chicago", to membership in which all persons interested in Irish studies are eligible. The aim of the Foundation is to foster the publication of Irish texts in America by offering academic stipends to train scholars in the Irish language and to enable scholars already trained to devote themselves to the work of editing.

The first fellowship was shortly afterward established. The Foundation guaranteed to the University of Illinois a stipend of twelve hundred dollars to enable a Research Fellow in Gaelic to give his entire time to the editing of Irish manuscripts. Rev. A. O'Kelleher, of the parish of SS. Peter and Paul at Great Crosby, and Lecturer in the University of Liverpool, was offered the appointment in November, 1916. He came to Illinois at once and has since that time devoted himself exclusively to the work of editing. Under the generous auspices of the Graduate School of the University of Illinois it has been possible to publish this *Life of Columcille* after somewhat less than two years of his tenure of the fellowship.

William Caxton, who performed a task similar to that of the present editor when he first made accessible to English readers the *Golden Legend* of Jacobus de Voragine, prefaced his work with an account of the circumstances of its making which the present belated editor of the

Golden Legend of Manus O'Donnell may cite as a brief history of his own case:

"And forasmuch as this said work was great and over chargeable to me to accomplish, I feared me in the beginning of the translation to have continued it, because of the long time of the translation, and also in the imprinting of the same, and, in manner half desperate to have accomplished it, was in purpose to have left it after that I had begun to translate it and to have laid it apart, ne had it been at the instance and request of the puissant, noble, and virtuous Earl[1], my lord William, Earl of Arundel, which desired me to proceed and continue the said work, and promised me to take a reasonable quantity of them when they were achieved and accomplished, and sent to me a worshipful gentleman[2] . . . which solicited me, in my lord's name, that I should in no wise leave it but accomplish it, promising that my said lord should during my life give and grant to me a yearly fee, that is to wit, a buck in summer and a doe in winter, with which fee I hold me well content. Then at contemplation and reverence of my said lord I have endeavored me to make an end and finish this said translation, and also to have imprinted it in the most best wise that I could or might, and present this said book to his good and noble lordship, as chief causer of the achieving of it."

The Gaelic Fellow at the University of Illinois owes "the buck in summer and the doe in winter" that have sustained him through the present task to the donors to the Irish Foundation of Chicago and to them the editors present this book as chief causers of its achieving.

The present text has been edited from a photograph of a portion of MS. Rawlinson B 514, kindly lent us by Prof. Meyer. In interpreting the verses in the text the work of previous editors, especially that of the late Whitley Stokes and the personal suggestions of Prof. Meyer have been helpful. Dr. Reeves' edition of Adamnan's *Vita Sancti Columbae* has been of great assistance in drawing up the notes. The more obvious contractions in the text have been silently extended; the others are printed in italics. Contractions which had been wrongly extended in the *Zeitschrift* have been corrected without comment. For example, in paragraph 11, *tims* (with a dash over *s*) had been extended to *timacht*. *Timacht* is a ghost word; the text should read *timsaig* as it is now printed. In the manuscript, groups of words are habitually run together; the members of these groups have been printed separately in our edition.

---

[1]*Leg.* Irish Foundation of Chicago.
[2]*Leg.* Edmund Janes James.

In the translation an effort has been made to preserve the simplicity of style characteristic of the original, and to confine the vocabulary as far as possible to words that would not have sounded strange to the ears of the author's English-speaking contemporaries. If the narrative seems abrupt, lacking in logic, burdened with repetition, and even the syntax at times halting, let the reader remember that it is exactly these qualities which endear to us the style of O'Donnell's English contemporaries, and which were characteristic of the English as well as of the Irish prose of his day.

And now we take leave of this book, concurring in the spirit of the editor of that other *Golden Legend,* who beseeches

"all them that shall read or hear it read to pardon me where I have erred or made fault, which, if any be, is of ignorance and against my will, and submit wholly of such as can and may, to correct it, humbly beseeching them so to do, and I shall pray for them unto Almighty God . . . . that it profit to all them that shall read or hear it read and may increase in them virtue, and expel vice and sin."

A. O'KELLEHER
G. SCHOEPPERLE

University of Illinois
June, 1918

---

[1] Valuable help in connection with the *index rerum* has been given by Mr. L. C. Raines (University of Illinois, 1918), who has also prepared the index of first lines of quatrains. We are indebted to Miss Alice Blumle for arranging alphabetically the words of the glossary, and indices of personal names, places and tribes.

INTRODUCTION

I.

THE TRADITION OF COLUMCILLE AS MANUS O'DONNELL FOUND IT.

In Columcille's lifetime, three thousand men, it is said, laid down their lives in the battle of Cooldrevny to save for him a little book into which he had copied the psalms. It was the magic of his presence that made the few leaves of sheepskin precious. For later generations, that knew the fiery spirit of the saint only by hearsay, they had little power to stir the soul. And so, in order that men might still share the sense of power and beauty which the touch of the saint had given in his own time even to such common things, his psalter was covered, in the twelfth century, with a shrine of "silver under gold" that should be eloquent to all of the preciousness of the thing it hid. The jewels upon it dazzled the eye with their flaming beauty; the carved figures of saintly heroes kindled the mind to thoughts of holy deeds, and the censer swinging from its side gave forth sweetness that seemed an earnest of heavenly airs. The shrine was borne thrice round the host before every battle, and the relic received the name *Cathach*, Battler. For, if it was a pure cleric that bore it on his breast, the battle was always won. Thus even until the exile of Domnall O'Donnell in the cause of the second James, the memory of the saint could still work wonders among men.

In the tradition of Columcille, the genuine records of the saint are almost as completely hidden as his psalter by its golden case.[1] Like the book-shrine which covered the ancient vellum, the present *Life* is overlaid with a thousand poetic incidents gathered from pagan and Christian times. In the legendary, as on the richly adorned *Cathach*, many figures are traced by memories of other lands and other times. It is encrusted with episodes familiar in the lives of other saints, in romances of troubadours and Arthurian knights, of the Fianna, the Ultonian heroes and the gods, in stories of druids and in folk-tales.

---

[1] An adaptation of one of the ancient Irish book-shrines, the Book of Dimma, forms the seal of the Irish Foundation Series reproduced on the cover of the present volume in the edition of the Irish Foundation Series.

In the miracles, prophecies, and visions of Columcille, there is much that is of familiar hagiographical pattern. Those who loved his memory, like those who treasured that of other saints, would permit their favorite to yield to none in sanctity and power. Fair traceries from the shrines of many another holy man are borrowed to deck that of the beloved patron. There are stories of the holy men that were Columcille's friends, and of those who were his teachers and pupils.[2]) Visits to France and pilgrimages to Rome have been added, and other practices conforming to the habits of saints of later date. Local legends explain the origin of land grants and taxes which readers of the *Life* were paying—or neglecting to pay—to Columcille's successors. Many an anecdote testifies to the genuineness of relics in this place or that— the Golden Leaf in Iona, the Red Stone of Gartan, and not a few others.

Many a miracle of Patrick or of Bridget, of the apostles and of Hebrew prophets, is told and retold of Columcille.[3]) Was he not like them in life and in works, and what the others did, should not he do also? And so Columcille, like other saints, strikes fountains from rocks, blesses stones and salt to heal maladies, illumines dark places with his hands, and by a thousand miracles already told a thousand times of other holy men, proves that indeed "there hath not come patriarch nor prophet, nor evangelist, nor apostle, nor martyr, nor confessor, nor virgin, that we may not liken Columcille to him or set him in some degree of perfection above all of them."[4])

Columcille is thought of as doing knightly service[5]) for Christ, even as Cuchulainn and Finn did service for their lords, or Tristan and Lancelot for their ladies. The same warmth of feeling breathes in this as breathes in the secular tales of the Middle Ages. The delicate tracery of detail which elaborates the narrative of the saint is of a piece with that which we find in the tradition of the heroes of romance. Take these closing words from an account of one of his miracles, for example:

> And Columcille left as its virtue upon that flagstone that whoso in sorrow should drink water therefrom, his sorrow should go from him... And the Flagstone of the Sorrows is the name of that flagstone to this day.[6])

---

[2] See Index of Personal Names.

[3] See Index of Matters, under land, taxes, topographical legends, relics etc.

[4] § 393. Of the incidents discussed in this Introduction, only the six indicated in the notes are found in Adamnan's *Vita Sancti Columbae*.

[5] *ridirecht*.

[6] § 109.

It is of the same pattern as the story in the twelfth century *Tristan* of the fairy bell from Avalon, the bell with sound so clear and soft that as the knight Tristan heard it he was soothed, and his anguish melted away, and he forgot all that he had suffered for the Queen. "Such was the virtue of the bell and such its property," says the poet, "that whosoever heard it, he lost all pain."[7])

Another romantic incident in our legend is the story of the children of the King of India,[8]) who for the tidings they heard of Columcille, conceived love for him though far away, and set out on the sea seeking him.

Just such adventurers are they as the troubadour Jaufre Rudel, prince of Blaia, who fell in love as did so many other heroes, with a Princess Far-away whom he had never seen. It was for the good he had heard of her that he loved her, his Countess of Tripoli. The pilgrims that returned from Antioch had brought him tidings.

> And for the desire he had to see her, he . . . went on the sea. And in the boat a heavy sickness fell on him, so that they that were with him in the ship deemed that he had died. But it availed them thus much that they brought him to Tripoli and bare him to an inn as one dead. And they let wit the Countess. And she came to him and took him in her arms. And when he knew it was the Countess, seeing and hearing and smelling returned to him. And he praised and thanked God that He had sustained life in him until he had seen her. And then he died in her arms. And she caused him to be buried right worshipfully in the Temple House of Tripoli.[9])

The children of the King of India who set out in quest of Columcille, die, like the troubadour, of weariness of the sea and ocean. They too are borne to land, and when the dear object of their quest comes to lament them, they rise from death "as folk that had been asleep". But for them, as for the troubadour, "there is no respite from a second death", save to look for a brief space upon the beloved.

> And Columcille charged that they be buried right worshipfully, and bade a little chapel of a temple be built over them.

Innumerable Irish manuscripts contain the colloquy of Patrick with Ossian, who long centuries after the coming of the saints, dragged

---

[7] J. Bédier, *Tristan et Iseult*, trans. by H. Belloc, London, 1913, p. 136; *Le roman de Tristan par Thomas*, Paris, 1902, I, 219.

[8] § 113.

[9] C. Appell, *Provenzalische Chrestomathie*, 1907, p. 189. *Cf.* O. Moore, *Jaufre Rudel and the Lady of Dreams*, Publications of the Modern Language Association, XXIX, 4.

on an unblessed existence, lamenting the old days.[10]) *In the Life of Columcille* also there are survivors of the Fianna. We are told that

> it was not alone the saints of Erin and patriarchs that did foretell the coming of Columcille, but Finn MacCumaill himself, the time he loosed his hound Bran against the deer at the river Sennglenn. And the hound pursued not the deer across the river of the glen. And all marvelled that that hound, the which had never let her quarry from her, should do this thing. And then Finn betook himself to his gift of knowledge, and prophesied that Columcille should one day bless the place, and make it a sanctuary.

And knowing that the spot is to be thus sanctified, the hound dares shed no blood there.

There is another reminiscence of the Fianna in the story of a giant skull that was brought to Columcille. And it was revealed to the saint that it was the skull of the old pagan, Cormac mac Airt, High King of Erin, father-in-law to Finn.

> And the skull related that albeit his faith had not been perfect (the old pagan had of course never heard of Christianity), yet such had been the measure thereof, and his keeping of the truth, that, inasmuch as God knew that Columcille would be of his seed, and would pray for his soul, he had not damned him in very truth, albeit it was in sharp pains that he awaited the prayer of Columcille.

The incident furnishes at once a miracle of the saint, a tribute to his pedigree, and a pleasant intermingling of Christian and pagan tradition. The saint's generosity and his miracle are the point of the story for the hagiographer.

The story of the reapers' ox, the whole of which was devoured at one meal by the "mighty old warrior of the men of Erin that was with Columcille that time", is such an incident as is often found in prose and verse in the tales of Patrick.[11]) There is always an aged warrior of the Fianna, Ossian or another, living on, half-starved, among a pigmy generation.

The secular tales of the voracious survivor of the Fianna run somewhat as follows:

> The blind old warrior, guided to the hunt by a little boy, sets his dog upon the deer and brings down seven of the heaviest stags. These he carries

---

[10] The stories that follow are cited from §§ 42 and 131. *Cf.* also W. J. Rees, *Lives of the Cambro-British Saints*, Llandovery, 1853, *passim*, for references to Arthur.

[11] § 212. *Cf.* J. G. Campbell, *Leabhar na Feinne*, p. 38, *Mu Shealg dheirinnich Oisin.*

on his back to the hill and boils in a giant kettle of his father Finn, which lay buried in a certain pool. "Now, lad," said Ossian to his grandson, "stay the length of a hand away from me, lest I eat you as a morsel of it. If I get my fill today I shall be young and hale again."

But when the lad saw that there was little prospect that the old man would desist while a morsel remained, he seized a piece secretly for his own small gullet. And for lack of that bit Ossian must still go hungry and weak.

Perhaps the most striking bit of hero-story story imbedded in the saint's life is the account of the nag that weeps the approaching death of the saint. The horse of supernatural powers has a long line of forbears in Greek, Germanic and Slavic,[12] and there is a similar incident in the story of the death of the Irish champion, Cuchulainn.

When the Ulster hero is about to enter his last fight, his charioteer Laeg goes to harness his steed. But the Gray of Macha rebels. Word is brought to Cuchulainn that "though all the men of Conchobar's fifth were round the Grey of Macha, they could not bring him to the chariot." Cuchulainn himself goes to him and makes the endeavor.

And thrice did the dumb beast turn his left side to him. Then Cuchulainn reproached his horse, saying that he was not wont to deal thus with his master. Thereat the Grey of Macha came and let his big round tears of blood fall on Cuchulainn's feet. And Cuchulainn leaped into the chariot and drove it suddenly southwards along the Road of Mid-Luachair. Cuchulainn was wounded to death in the battle. And he went to a pillar-stone in the plain and put his girdle round it, that he might not die seated or lying down, but that he might die standing. Then his foes drew near all around him, but they durst not go to him, for they thought he was alive. Then came the Grey of Macha to Cuchulainn to protect him so long as his soul was in him and the hero's light out of his forehead remained. The Grey of Macha wrought the three red routs all around him. And fifty fell by his teeth and thirty by each of his hoofs. The hosts of Ulster, hastening to rescue the hero, meet the faithful beast streaming with blood.

Then went the Grey of Macha and laid his head on Cuchulainn's breast. And Conall said, 'A heavy care to the Grey of Macha is that corpse'.[13]

The horse that foretells the death of Columcille is an old nag that drew the milk cart for the monks.[14] Columcille is returning from the field where he has gone out to bless the hay ricks, and he sits down by the way to rest.

And there drew toward him a white nag . . . and shed a shower of

[12] When Achilles sets out for his last battle, Xanthus, his swift-footed steed, warns him that the fatal day draws near when he must die. See also M. A. Potter, *Four Essays,* Cambridge, 1917, p. 109 ff.

[13] Abridged from *Rev. Celt.,* III, 175 ff.

[14] § 362. *Cf.* Adamnan, *Lib.* iii, *cap.* 23.

bloody tears upon his cheeks, and for a long time he lamented in this wise, as a man that biddeth farewell to a beloved comrade and hath no hope to see him again.

The poor old nag appears only for a moment at the close of the *Life,* and even this brief indulgence in feeling is begrudged him by the jealous Diarmaid, who has no appreciation of the prerogatives of the horse as an epic hero. The terms of the blessing that the saint gives the beast are equally a violation of the epic tradition.

> And it came to pass by virtue of that blessing that the nag mended and did more service for the brethren the while he lived than did other nags a great number.

There is no room in the laborious, ascetic years of the saint for a high-mettled horse such as is the comrade of the worldly hero. Cuchulainn had tamed the Grey of Macha in his youth, lured to a trial of strength by the beauty of the proud water-horse that reared his head above the shining lake. The young Columcille is bent on no such contests. The sea-beasts that appear upon the waters in our legend he has no thought of taming. He signs them with the cross and they disappear.

Gods as well as heroes make their appearance in the stories of the saints. The Cyclopean MacCuil, in the *Life of Patrick,* would appear to be a survival of the mythical MacCuil, husband of Banba, who with his brothers, MacCeacht and MacGreine, shared the rule of Ireland at the coming of the Milesians.[15])

In the *Life of Columcille* there is also a god surviving. Mongan mac Fiachna is a rebirth of Manannan, ruler of the sea.[16]) He comes to the holy man where he has sought a solitary place for prayer by the brink of Loch Foyle.[17])

> And Columcille had not been long there when he beheld a passing beautiful youth coming toward him across the lake, as if he were treading on the earth or ground. And there was a golden sandal on his foot, and whichever foot he set down, it was thereon the sandal was.
>
> "Who art thou?" asks Columcille, "or from what land or country hast thou come, or who is thy king or lord, or on what God dost thou believe?"

---

[15] MacCuil, having tempted the saint in vain, is himself converted, and as a penance is set adrift in a boat of skin, without oar or rudder. In the end he reaches the Isle of Man and becomes a bishop there. W. Stokes, *Tripartite Life,* Index, *s. v.* MacCuil; J. B. Bury, *Life of St. Patrick,* 207, O'Curry, *Mss. Materials,* 447.

[16] Nutt and Meyer, *Voyage of Bran.* See Index, Mongan mac Fiachna.

[17] § 87.

"I myself am mine own Lord, and in the gods of idolatry put I my faith."

The colloquy that follows is one of those contests between Christianity and paganism which are a favorite theme in the tradition of Irish saints. Mongan gives proof at once of his quickness of wit:

"It is strange to me," saith Columcille, "if thou art a king or the son of a king, that thou art thus alone."

"Thou art thyself alone, O cleric," saith the youth. "And wit thou well, there would be twenty hundred of followers with me here, if it were but my pleasure," saith he. "And I tell thee I am Mongan mac Fiachna, the son of the King of Ulster, and it was to match skill and knowledge with thee that I came."

Mongan's skill is shape-shifting, and his knowledge is the store of unnatural natural science and geography which delighted the readers of the mediaeval bestiaries and Mandeville's *Travels*. The saint listens to the marvels which Mongan relates with courteous deference; but on the next day, when his own turn comes to display "skill and knowledge", he overwhelms his rival by folding him under his mantle and revealing to him Hell with its torments, and Heaven with its delights. Thus druidism is confounded and Mongan brought to the Faith, to be the third of Columcille's dear sons on his breast on the Doomsday and safe from the fire of doom.

As the story of Mongan shows, the relations between saint and pagan are not always conceived as hostile. Columcille's meeting with Bec mac De is a similar friendly encounter of wit. Even the hagiographer conceded that "Bec had the gift of prophecy from God, albeit he was a druid. And he made no false prophecy ever".[18]) The genial saint, foreknowing that the good Bec is about to die, goes to him to persuade him to Heaven if he may. He deftly traps him into making two false prophecies, for only thus, he knows, can he convince him that his time has come. The professional mind is not infallible, but it can usually be trusted to see its mistakes when they are pointed out. And Bec is no exception.

Columcille saluted him, and entered into a friendly converse with him.

And he said: "Great is thy wisdom and knowledge, Bec mac De, in the tidings thou givest to other folk touching their deaths. Hast thou knowledge also of when thou shalt thyself die?"

"Thereof I have knowledge in sooth," saith Bec. "There be yet for me seven years of life."

"A man might do good works in shorter space than that," saith Colum-

---

[18] § 129. In the illustrative extracts, passages in parentheses are the editor's.

cille (prompting his pupil in friendly wise). "And knowest thou for a surety that thou hast so much of life still?"

Then was Bec silent for a space and thereafter spake he to Columcille and said, "I have not. It is but seven months of life I have."

"That is well," saith Columcille, "and art certain thou hast still so much of life to come?"

"I am not," saith Bec (awake at last to the drift of the saint's questions), "and this is a token, O Columcille. I cannot withstand the prophecy thou has made. For thou didst foretell that I should make two false prophecies ere I should die. There is left me but seven hours of this same day," saith he, "do thou assoil me and give me the sacrament."

Many, in the *Life of Columcille,* are the bits of pagan knowledge and practice that the folk have credited to their saint, such "skill and knowledge" as Mongan and Bec might have boasted. We find Columcille exorcising the evil spirit lingering in the unblessed milk pail;[19] raising a favoring wind for each of the two who set out in contrary directions;[20] hearkening, as he sits by the shore, to the prophecy which the wave reveals to him.[21]

Again and again O'Donnell pauses to point out to his readers that God subdued in a supreme degree the elements of Nature to Columcille.[22] Already Adamnan had dwelt upon his power over winds[23] and waves.[24] At his wish a storm prevents the over-zealous pilgrims from disturbing his household in their grief.[25] The earth rises[26] or sinks at his word;[27] it quakes at his death. Water[28] and fire[29] are equally powerless to injure his belongings.

We are told also of Columcille's knowledge of "science", science just such as Mongan's,

> of the place of the sun and the moon and of the higher elements ... and all the properties whereby the sun giveth light to the moon and the stars of

---

[19] § 284.

[20] § 283.

[21] § 104. For an interesting article on *The Celtic Church and its Relations to Paganism,* by W. J. Watson, see *Celtic Review,* Vol. X, p. 263.

[22] §§ 77, 97, 268, 340-1, 365-6, 376, 433.

[23] § 294. Cf. Adamnan, *Lib.* ii, *cap.* 34.

[24] § 281. Cf. Adamnan, *Lib.* ii, *cap.* 12.

[25] § 375. Cf. Adamnan, *Lib.* iii, *cap.* 23.

[26] § 159, 341.

[27] § 340-1.

[28] §§ 134, 433. Cf. Adamnan, *Lib.* ii, *cap.* 8. See also Index of Matters, *s. v.*

[29] §§ 77, 268. Cf. Adamnan, *Lib.* ii, *cap.* 7.

the firmament, and of the numbering of the stars and of the ebb and flow of the waters and the sea. . . . And he knew the secrets of Rochuaidh, that is a beast that is in the sea,[30]) and when it speweth to landward it is in sign that there will be sickness and disease in every land that year. And when it belcheth upward it is in sign that there will be great storms that year and many deaths among the birds of the air; and when it disgorgeth downward into the sea there will be many deaths among the fishes and the beasts of the sea.[31])

On his arrival in Iona, with *sang froid* that would do credit to a druid, Columcille declares to his little band of faithful followers that if their faith is to take root in the new soil, the blood of one of them must sprinkle it.[32]) It is the old pagan belief that foundations must be laid in blood. Such words do not shock us when we hear them from the wizard Merlin in the romances of Arthur, but they sit strangely upon the lips of a Christian saint.

Those that have made the legendary are versed in the whole elaborate system of imitative and sympathetic magic belonging to the older pagan world. Indeed it would be strange if it were otherwise. By the labor of observation and thought for untold ages men had drawn up an elaborate body of knowledge. According to its principles they practiced upon the elements to subdue them to the needs of man. The Christian saints could supersede the druids only by manifesting greater power over nature than they.

Incidents found all over the world in popular tradition and many times before incorporated into literature are wrought into the tracery on this shrine of O'Donnell's. For, although the lives of Irish saints were worked up in the cells of ecclesiastics and the palaces of nobles, they are full of the warm life of the folk. And the folk admires two virtues only, strength and shrewdness. The folk-hero evades a difficulty by a trick, where a less nimble-witted protagonist would prefer to succumb and preserve a superior degree of moral rigidity. In many of the tales in our legendary Columcille is pictured as a typical folk-hero. Of Tory and again of Aran he asks—we cannot believe altogether guilelessly—only so much of the island as he may cover with the width

---

[30] § 366.

[31] § 78. *Cf.* § 216. Columcille shows that the milk which the druids have boasted of drawing from an ox is really blood, and himself restores the weakened animal to strength, § 285, *Cf.* Adamnan, *Lib.* ii, *cap.* 17; he defies the wind the druids raise against him and sets sail in spite of it, §§ 294-5, *Cf.* Adamnan, *Lib.* ii, *cap.* 34.

[32] §§ 205-6. *Cf. e. g.* Geoffrey of Monmouth, *Historia Regum Britanniae, Lib.* vi, *cap.* 17.

of his hood or his mantle. One would think that the crabbed old despots would have been warned by Virgil's tale of how Dido, by a like ruse, befooled the Carthaginians. But in each case the owner grants the request, being, apparently, ignorant of the classics and not so canny as an owner should be. The mantle of course spreads over the whole of Tory, and the venomous hound which the angry king sets upon the saint is destroyed by the sign of the cross. In Aran, Enda is quick enough to seize the hood before it can commit him to much loss, but the wrtched island suffers to this day from its lack of Columcille's blessing.[33])

Columcille shows the same shrewdness in getting himself out of difficulties as he shows in getting Oillil and Enda into them. On his departure for Iona, the saint had taken a vow "to leave Erin and to behold her no more, her food and her drink to eat not or to drink, nor to see her men or her women, nor to tread on the soil of Erin forever".[34]) The vow is impressive at the time of making, but like many another, it brings difficulty in the sequel. For how, having taken such an oath, was Columcille in his later years to journey with the King of Alba to the Assembly of Druim Ceat to work good there?

Or was it perhaps for the very purpose of creating a difficulty and then triumphing over it that the weavers of Irish tradition added this touch to the history? Certainly they were not at a loss for an answer to the charge that he had broken his vow. For, on his arrival at the Assembly, we find Columcille with a sod of the soil of Alba under his feet, and cere-cloth over his eyes, so that "he beheld not man nor woman of Erin, as he had promised aforetime".[35]) And he bore with him from Alba sufficient of food and of drink, so that "he partook not of the food nor the drink of Erin the while he abode there".[36])

It is from just such a dilemma that the folk-tale delights to extricate itself. The heroine who has been bidden not to come on foot nor on horseback, not on wheels nor by water, not dressed nor undressed, can still find a way of coming. If she is sworn not to appear either naked or clothed, riding or driving, in the road or off the road, by day or by night, she nevertheless appears, and not one of the injunctions is disobeyed.[37]) A similar story is told of the princess Grainne, daugh-

[33] § III, 156.
[34] § 180.
[35] § 320.
[36] § 320.

[37] Bolte and Polivka, *Anmerkungen zu den Kinder-und Hausmärchen der Brüder Grimm,* II, 349-373. Students of folk-lore have termed the heroine of this widely spread tale the shrewd peasant girl (*Das kluge Bauernmädchen*).

ter of the High King of Erin, Cormac mac Airt, in some of the best known tales of the Fianna.[38]) And here we find it in our *Life* told of a royal saint.

It is of the essence of art that therein "the senses predominate over the intelligence"; the artist never insists upon the intellectual aspect of an experience, but interprets it in terms of image and sound. The folk, like the artist, translates the general into the particular, the abstract into the concrete.[39]) Of this O'Donnell's *Life* preserves some interesting examples, of which we cite but the following:

The proverb "I'm going to meet Death and Death is coming every day to meet me", which survives in modern times, is thus translated into narrative in a charming anecdote in O'Donnell's *Life*. Even the names are given. It is Crimthann o Coinneannta that Columcille sees running past the eastern end of Loch Bethach.[40])

> The saint cries out, "Lo, the youth runneth toward the sod of his death, and do ye seize him, and suffer him not to reach that sod."
> His followers are quick to obey his command, but it is in vain, for the sod itself comes running toward them, and when it comes under the feet of the youth, he dies. The saint restores him for a brief space, but the miracle is perfunctory; the point of the story is the quotation that ends it:
> "Three little sods that cannot be shunned;"
> As they say in the proverb:
> "The sod of his birth and the sod of his death,
> And the sod of his burying."

By the same transmutation of figurative to literal significance, the three gifts which Columcille asks of God: Virginity, Wisdom, and Prophecy, become three fair shining maidens.[41]) They approach the

---

[38] In a tenth century dialogue it is her sister that is sharp at answering the traditional set of riddles, *Tochmarc Ailbe ingine Cormac hui Chuind la Find hua mBaiscne*. Meyer, *Fianaigecht*, xxiv; cf. *Leabhar na Feinne*, p. 151. In later tradition Grainne herself evades the traditional injunctions of the type here discussed. J. F. Campbell, *West Highland Tales*, p. 40; ib., *Leabhar na Feinne*, pp. 153, 154; J. G. Campbell, *The Fians*, pp. 52-3.

[39] The learned Father H. Delahaye, S. J., in his book on the *Legends of the Saints*, trans. by Mrs. V. M. Crawford, London and New York, 1907, p. 49, deplores this fact. "Among the people," he says, "the senses predominate over the intelligence, and owing to the lethargy of their brains, they are unable to rise to an ideal conception, but stop short at the matter, the image, the sound."

[40] § 110. Cf. H. Morris, *Seanfhocla Uladh*, Dublin, 1907, p. 85.

[41] § 66. The basis of this story is the following passage in the Old Irish *Life*, "Then Columcille offered himself to the Lord of the Elements, and he begged three boons of Him, to wit, chastity, and wisdom, and pilgrimage. The three were fully granted to him." *Lismore Lives*, p. 25.

ardent young ascetic and clasp their hands about his neck and give him three kisses. The Irish story-teller cannot resist adding a touch of humour to the allegory.

> "That lover of chastity, to wit, Columcille," he says, "turned a wry face and an ill-visage upon these maidens." (Are we not told that the anxious saint kept his back turned even upon his mother?[42]) "And he put from him their kisses . . . , for he thought it was for sin they came to him."

He accepts the situation only when he has been convinced that the maidens are none other themselves than the very Virtues, and that their designs are honorable wedlock. The polygamous character of the bond does not seem to trouble our hagiographer.

Not in all cases in the present *Life*, however, have the "interior workings of grace" been translated into palpable results. In the little story of the blessed thought that Brigid had on going over the plain of Liffey, they claim full validity in their ideal form.

> If hers were the power over that plain, she thought, she would give it to God Almighty. And that blessed thought of Brigid's was made known to Columcille in his Abbey Church at Swords, and he cried with a loud vice, "It is as much for the virgin to have that thought as to bestow the plain."[42a]

Tradition, which translates dreams into visions, and allegory and proverb into actual incident, depicts character by illustrative incidents. The traits of Columcille's character to which time has accorded the most minute and loving elaboration are his love of books and poetry, and his love of Ireland. These we shall now examine somewhat in detail.

We have a hint of Columcille's love of books in Adamnan, where we are told of his solemnly confiding the copying of the psalter to Baithin at his death.[43]) The Old Irish *Life* declares that he copied three hundred books with his own hand.[44]) In Irish tradition his departure for Scotland, which is regarded as the tragedy of his life, hangs upon his passion for a book. The chief cause of the battle of Cooldrevny, we are told,[45]) and of his consequent exile from Ireland, was that he had copied, without the owner's permission, a psalter which belonged to St. Finnen. His defence, as given by O'Donnell, is curiously modern:

[42]§ 411.
[42a]§ 107.
[43]Bk. III, ch. 23; also in O'Donnell, § 362.
[44]*Lismore Lives*, § 956; also in O'Donnell, § 394.
[45]Cf. *infra*, p. ——, note.

"I contend," saith Columcille, "that the book of Finnen is none the worse for my copying it, and it is not right that the divine words in that book should perish, or that I or any other should be hindered from writing them or reading them or spreading them among the tribes. And further I declare that it was right for me to copy it, seeing there was profit to me from doing in this wise, and seeing it was my desire to give the profit thereof to all peoples with no harm therefrom to Finnen or his book."[46])

The story of the books which Columcille begged from Lon of Kilgarrow is another tradition of his passion for learning. The old miser, warned of the saint's coming, hides the books away from him, and Columcille relieves his feelings by the polite formula to which we grow accustomed in hagiographical literature:

"It is my will, if God suffer it, that thy books be of no avail to any other after thy death for ever."[47])

The terrified bibliophile, expecting a curse on himself to follow the curse on his books, hastens to present them to the saint as a gift. It is a truly Irish counterstroke. Columcille, hoisted with his own petard, has reason to wish the miser a long life.[47])

There is no mention in Adamnan of Columcille as a poet, or of any special fondness on his part for poets or poetry. But Irish poets seem to have early fathered their verses upon saints and heroes, probably from artistic instinct rather than with intent to deceive. As Ossian became the poet of the Fianna of Ireland, so Columcille became the poet of her saints. Besides his Latin poems, the *Altus Prosator*, its complement the *In te Christe*, and the *Noli Pater*,[48]) twenty-six Irish

---

[46] P. 179, § 168.

[47] § 221. Thus the prose account. The verses and the memorials quoted to support it suggest no connection with Columcille.

> "Dead is Lon
> Of Kilgarrow. O great hurt!
> To Erin with its many tribes
> It is ruin of study and of schools."

The books, we are told, are still in Iona. And "there hath not come any change or defilement or dimness upon those letters, but from the time Longarad died there was none in the world that could read a word in those books forever."

The story, as given by O'Donnell from the *Calendar of Oengus*, seems to be an effort to explain the fact that certain books, said to have belonged to one Lon of Kilgarrow of whom the poem testifies the renown, were indecipherable to a later and perhaps less learned generation.

[48] Bernard and Atkinson, *Irish Liber Hymnorum*, London, 1898, I, 62-90. The present *Life* gives an account of the composition of these hymns. *Cf. infra*. §§ 77, 216.

poems ascribed to him have been edited.[49]) Many more are still in manuscript. There are some fifteen in one of the O'Clery manuscripts preserved in the Burgundian Library at Brussels. By far the largest collection is one made in the middle of the sixteenth century and contained in MS. Laud 615, in the Bodleian Library at Oxford.[50]) In the present *Life* over two hundred quatrains are quoted as fragments of longer poems, and half of them are attributed to Columcille. They are in Old Irish, "very hard Gaelic made by the poets of the Gael",[51]) as we are told in the foreword of the *Life*; and O'Donnell has had "passing great labor"[52]) to paraphrase them.

Our author has incorporated into his *Life* the Irish satire *Imthecht na Tromdaime, The Departing of the Importunate Company*, in which Columcille has the rôle of aiding the bards when they are wandering about, desperate and disgraced, after being driven from the roof of the hospitable Guaire in quest of the *Cattle Raid of Cualnge*. Columcille leads the bards to the tomb of Fergus and fasts with them to prevail on God to raise up the dead hero to narrate the tale. To be sure Columcille and the High Bard who composed his elegy were both dead before the importunate company ever entered Guaire's great hostel.[53]) Yet here we find him still alive and rendering assistance to his obituarist's successor. Considerations of chronology are subordinate in tradition to consideration for the fitness of incident to character. And so powerful is the traditional idea that Columcille is the patron of poets, that this story of poets in distress is drawn to him as iron to a magnet.[54])

It is indubitable that the bards exploited the Irish love of praise and sensitiveness to reproach, and the story of Columcille's intervention in their behalf at the Assembly of Druim Ceat[55]) has better claim to be accounted history.[56]) Columcille's arguments in their favor are an interesting mediaeval *Defence of Poesy*. They are three. There is the social argument, vulnerable enough, alas, to a modern mind:

---

[49]Listed in the *Bibliography of Irish Philology and Printed Literature*, by R. I. Best, published by the National Library of Ireland, Dublin, 1913.

[50]Reeves' *Adamnani Vita S. Columbae*, lxxix.

[51]§ 8.

[52]§ 10.

[53]§ 338. Cf. *Imtheacht na Tromdhaimhe*, ed. O. Connellan, in *Trans. of the Ossianic Society*, Dublin, 1860, pp. 3-33.

[54]Cf. Delahaye, *Legends of the Saints, op. cit.*, pp. 17-19.

[55]Cf. *infra*, §§ 332-40. The citations that follow are from § 332.

[56]*Irish Liber Hymnorum*, II, 224-5; J. T. Fowler, *Vita Sancti Columbae*, xxi; Plummer, *Vitae Sanctorum Hiberniae*, cii.

"Folk would have no shame nor any largesse except they had those like the poets unto whom to give largesse for fear of their reviling and their scoffing verses, even as there would be no charity or alms-giving save there be found poor folk unto whom to do charity and give alms."

There is the theological argument, ingenious as only an Irishman could make it:

"Even God in truth made purchase,
Thrice fifty psalms he bought from David;
Gave him fortune in earth's dwelling,
To his Heaven-born soul gave Heaven."

And finally, there is the personal appeal to the love of fame, the desire for worldly immortality:

"The praises endure, and the treasure and riches that are given for them perish . . . and since all the world is but a fable, it were well for thee to buy the more enduring fable, rather than the fable that is less enduring."

There are numerous instances in O'Donnell's *Life* of Columcille's own weakness for poets and poetry. Once, in his youth, when a group of bards approached him and he had nothing to give them, he was seized with such shame that the sweat streamed from his brow. He put his hand to his face to wipe it away, and by the mercy of God it was made a talent of gold in his palm.[57] Another time, when they come to him asking refreshment, water is changed to wine in answer to his prayer, and an angel reveals to him goblets hidden by the folk of old in a great barrow near by.[58] His indulgence to kinsmen is the weakness which he confesses of himself to explain the fragile chair of crystal which Baithin has seen in a vision prepared for him before the Lord.[59] O'Donnell further accounts against him his weakness to poets.[60] When he heard the poets praising him at the Assembly of Druim Ceat,

"There came upon him such exaltation of mind and heart that the air above him was filled with evil spirits. And Baithin rebuked him sharply, and said it were more fitting for him to give heed to the judgment of God than to worldly praise."

And although, according to our hagiographer, he sorely repents his sin,[61] he is the next moment ready to promise heaven in reward for a eulogy.[62]

[57] § 80.
[58] § 81.
[59] According to *Lebar Brecc*, cited by Stokes, *Lismore Lives*, 303.
[60] §§ 123, 334. *Cf.* Plummer, *V. S. H.*, cii.
[61] §§ 334-5.
[62] § 336.

The second important elaboration of *motif* to which we would draw attention in O'Donnell's *Life* is Columcille's love of Erin and his prophecies of the sorrows that are to come to her.

Adamnan devotes the whole of one of the three divisions of his *Life of St. Columba* to what he calls the saint's prophecies. But almost all of them are concerned with miscellaneous events which took place within a day, or a few days, of his words, and might more correctly be termed instances of second sight. Columcille tells his household of the approach of guests before they appear. He is conscious of danger threatening friends at a distance. Looking at a man, he knows his hidden sin, his coming destiny, his place of burial.[63])

But as time passed Columcille's prophetic gift became, in the memory of the people, a power more and more far-reaching, and more and more closely associated with his love for Ireland. This tendency is perceptible in two prophecies cited by O'Donnell in poetic form. He prophesies that strangers will come to Cluaine and, having destroyed his church, carry off its stones to Bun Sentuinde.[64]) He foretells that his remains will be carried away from Iona by Viking plunderers.[65]) Opening the coffin in mid-ocean and finding in it no treasure, the robbers will cast it once more into the sea, whence it will be borne miraculously by the waves to Downpatrick. This latter prophecy is one of the many indications of the rivalry between Ireland and Iona for the honor of the saint's preference.[66]) In O'Donnell's *Life*, as we should expect, since two-thirds of it is based on traditions collected in Ireland, it is Ireland that comes off victor.

In some of the verses in the *Life*, Columcille punctiliously shares his blessing:

> "One half upon Erin sevenfold,
> One half upon Alba in like wise."[67])

But his sentiment is not always so impartial. Of Erin he makes many a verse of praise:

> "Wise are her clerics, melodious her birds,
> Beautiful her women, gentle her elders,
> Generous her rich folk without greed;
> Good her king for abundance of gifts.
>   . . . .

---

[63]Such also are most of the prophecies in the present *Life*. See Index of Matters, *infra*. Cf. Plummer, *Vitae Sanctorum Hiberniae*, Oxford, 1910, clxx-i.
[64]§ 90.
[65]§§ 371-3.
[66] Reeves, 312-318.
[67]P. 293, § 278.

> Plentiful in the West the fruit of the apple-tree,
> Many kings and makings of kings,
> Plentiful the luxurious sloes,
> Many oaks of noble mast."

But of Scotland:

> "Many here the lanky chiels,
> Many diseases here and distempers,
> Many those with scanty clouts,
> Many the hard and jealous hearts."[68]

And for him the conclusion of the whole matter is:

> "Better death in stainless Erin
> Than life forever in Alba."[69]

Of late development without doubt are the prophetic passages which cite no verses in their support. One of these is of the destruction of Tara:

> "And he said that many as were her hosts and her legions, and many her feasts and her banquetings, ... yet in the end of time she should be waste and desolate, and there should be in her nor lords nor rulers. And he made that same prophecy of Cruachu and of Aillend and of Emain Macha."[70]

O'Donnell's *Life* contains two prophecies of the foreign yoke. One is the little story of Columcille's three pets:

> "And it happed that the wren ate the fly and the cat ate the wren. And Columcille spake by the spirit of prophecy, and he said it was thus men should do in a later time: the strong of them should eat the weak... And Columcille said that the while the Gael of Erin were thus, the power of foreigners should be over them, and whenever right and justice were kept by them, they should themselves have power again."[71]

In the second passage also it is for the sins of the Gael against the weak, and especially against chapels and churches, that "they shall be driven from the land of their fathers to the glens and mountains and the rough places of Erin by the might and strength of strangers and foreigners". Here also there is the promise that the power of the foreigners shall wane. But in this passage their downfall shall come about as a punishment for their own iniquity, rather than as a result of the renewed virtue of the Gael.

[68] P. 285, § 275.
[69] P. 283, § 275. *Cf.* also §§ 183-93, 265-80.
[70] P. 125, § 126.
[71] § 118.

"And when there shall arise strife and division among the foreigners themselves, and they shall do after the Gael in respect of treachery, and in respect of kinsmen slaying each other, and in respect of wrong-doing and injustice against the chapels and churches of Erin, then shall God give back again to the Gaels their strength and their might."[72])

Thus, in centuries of sorrow, the Irish looked back upon the great lover of Ireland, who with his deeper vision may indeed have grieved, even in the midst of happy days, for the darker ones that were to come. And thus did the human heart, in prostrate Erin as in suffering Israel, justify the ways of God to man.

The tradition of Columcille's love for Ireland grew with time. The most interesting expressions of it cluster around his departure for Iona and his homesickness during the thirty-four years which he spent there.

Adamnan's record of his leaving Ireland is the sober statement:

"In the second year after the battle of Cuil Dremne, and the forty-second of his age, being desirous to make a journey for Christ from Ireland to Britain, he sailed forth."[73])

The account in the Old Irish *Life*,[74]) which O'Donnell has copied at an earlier point in his narrative,[75]) similarly represents Columcille's going to Britain as a voluntary mission. A desire to devote himself to missionary labors is altogether what we should expect of a sixth century Irish saint. The impulse led Columbanus, Gallus, and many another to cross the seas and found monasteries in foreign lands.

But there is an inconspicuous chapter in Adamnan's *Life*[76]) which may point to a further reason for Columcille's exile. It is an account of a synod in Teltown in Meath at which, as his biographer says, "St. Columba was excommunicated . . . for some venial and so far excusable matters". As to what these matters were Adamnan preserves what may be an intentional vagueness. The point of the story for Adamnan is that the excommunication is not carried out. St. Brendan of Birr,

---

[72]§ 127. A number of similar prophecies among the collection in MS. Laud 615 are mentioned by Reeves, *Vita Sancti Columbae*, p. lxxix, note 1. *The Prophecies of St. Columkille*, by N. Kearney, Dublin, 1856, consists in part of material from late mediaeval tradition, in part of modern writings. See Reeves, *loc. cit.*, lxxx.

[73]Adamnan's *Second Preface*, Reeves, p. 9, and notes.

[74]*Lismore Lives*, § 1000.

[75]§ 100.

[76]This passage is discussed in Reeves, lxxiii-v; J. T. Fowler, Adamnan's *Vita S. Columbae*, lxi-lxiv.

in obedience to a vision, venerates the offender and prevails upon the assembly to withdraw its sentence. Irish tradition connects Columcille's departure for Iona with a similar censure pronounced upon him by his fellow-ecclesiastics following the battle of Cooldrevny, which had been fought at his instance.

> And the saints of Erin fell to murmuring against Columcille, and they condemned him for all the folk that were slain in those battles of his making. And by the counsel of the saints of Erin, Columcille went then to Molaise of Devenish to accuse himself thereof. And this was the sentence Molaise laid upon him, even the sentence the angel had laid upon him afore, to wit, to leave Erin and to behold her no more, her food and her drink to eat not or to drink, nor to see her men nor her women, nor to tread on the soil of Erin forever.[77])

In relating the story of Columcille's protracted sojourn in Iona, the Irish faced a dilemma. Should the Scotch be allowed to boast that their Irish saint had chosen of his own will to spend the best part of his life among them? On the other hand, to represent him as having been condemned to depart from his own country by an Irish synod would redound neither to Ireland's credit nor to his own.

The Irish accounts, therefore, which O'Donnell follows, represent his sojourn in Iona as an unwilling exile. But it was self-imposed. It was a penance suggested by his own heart, or, as tradition puts it, by the voice of an angel, confirmed, it is true, but only in the sequel, by the advice of his confessor. His departure thus takes on the character of tragic necessity. But it was an inward necessity, no ignoble outward pressure[78]) to shame either Ireland or himself. And what openings there were in it for lays in praise of Ireland, and heart-broken lyrics of farewell.[79])

> "This is why I love Derry:
> For its level fields, for its brightness,
> For the hosts of its white angels,
> From one end to the other.
>
> . . . .

---

[77]§ 180.

[78]Even if we are disposed to consider that Columcille's departure for Iona was in some way due to ecclesiastical censure, it is clear, as Reeves has pointed out, that in leaving Ireland he severed no ties, surrendered no jurisdiction. His congregations remained in their various settlements, still subject to his authority, and he took with him no more than the prescriptive attendance of a missionary leader. *Vita Sancti Columbae,* lxxv.

[79]*Cf.* esp. §§ 183-202; 275-9. On Irish homesickness, *Cf.* Plummer, *Vitae Sanctorum Hiberniae,* cxxiii.

>   They find no room on the land,
>   For the number of good gentle angels,
>   Nine waves distant therefrom,
>   It is thus they reach out from Derry.
>
>   . . . . .
>
>   Derry of Oaks, let us leave it
>   With gloom and with tears, heavy hearted;
>   Anguish of heart to depart thence,
>   And to go away unto strangers."
>
>   . . . . .
>
>   ... the parting of body from soul
>   Is the parting to me from my kinsfolk."[80]

Lest his sorrow should seem too remote from our common grief, he is depicted as accepting the situation with only a very human degree of amiability. He grumbles at Molaise who laid the penance on him, and reflects with some satisfaction on what Ireland is losing by his departure.[81] He is piqued that his kinsmen have not interfered more vigorously to prevent it.[82] He even falls into a passion at the poor fellow who does him the questionable favor of pushing off the boat which is to carry him away.

> And when Columcille and his saints were entering into the boat, there was a certain man in the port with a forked staff in his hand. And he set the staff against the boat to push it off from land.
>
> When Columcille saw this he said: "I leave upon thee the gift of unwilling exile by reason of the help thou hast given me in leaving Erin for exile, and to those after thee that have a forked staff I leave the same gift forever."[83]

By virtue of the tradition of his banishment, Columcille has become the patron of Irish exiles. As such he is perhaps the most dearly loved of the Irish saints. The flagstone on which he was born is worn by emigrants who come and sleep upon it the night before their departure from Derry, in hope to bear a lighter heart in their exile across the sea.[84]

---

[80] The preceding quatrains are from §§ 183, 184, 191, 190.
[81] § 181, p. 185.
[82] § 191, p. 195.
[83] § 187.
[84] D. Hyde, *Literary History of Ireland*, p. 179; Reeves, lxviii; J. Healy, *Ireland's Ancient Schools and Scholars*, 293.

II.
LIFE OF MANUS O'DONNELL.

The man who undertook, in the early sixteenth century, to make the *Life of Saint Columba* which follows, was no nameless scribe, devoting to it a starved youth or an obscure old age. He was the eldest son of the aged Hugh O'Donnell, one of the great chieftains of Ireland, Lord of Tirconnell, and he completed the work while he was still full of the fire and pride of life, his youth not yet behind him, the great moments of his life still to be quaffed. Even as he dictated the pages of this work, he must have broken off more than once to receive a messenger announcing some new depredation of the O'Neill or bearing a flattering bid for friendship from Henry, Monarch of England and Defender of the Faith. And while the nameless scholars whom he had bidden "put into Gaelic the part of the *Life* that was in Latin, and make easy the part that was hard Gaelic",[1]) were left busy making ready their translation against his return, he was leading his clan on an expedition to reduce some rival chieftain or setting off to collect with the sword the rents and tributes which the family claimed in Connaught.[1a]

In the sixteenth century, Ireland, like Germany and Italy, was still torn by the feuds of petty chiefs. The idea of national unity was as yet unborn. Each chieftain was supreme lord in his own domain, and allied himself with others only in temporary union, now with one, now with another, for the purposes of the moment. The Anglo-Normans in the colony founded by Henry II had adopted the language of the surrounding clans, and the Anglo-Norman barons, such as Kildare, had recognized that the Irish clan system offered greater independence of the English Crown, and rejected English customs for Irish ways. Only in the vicinity of Dublin and in the large seaport towns like Waterford and Galway, where the Anglo-Norman element preponderated over the native, did the English preserve even the vestiges of dominion. From time to time efforts were made, by such acts as the Statute of Kilkenny, to separate English settlers from "Irish enemies". But the sphere of English influence became more and more contracted, and from an act passed at Drogheda in 1494, it is evident that in the beginning of O'Donnell's century the English name and English power counted for little in Ireland.

---

[1] P. 7, § 10, *infra*.
[1a] *Cf.* § 94 *infra*.

> As the marches of the four shires be open and not fensible in fastness of ditches and castles, by which Irishmen do great hurt in preying the same: it is enacted that every inhabitant, earth tiller and occupier in said marches, to wit, in the county of Dublin, from the water of Auliffy to the mountain in Kildare, from the water of Auliffy to Trim, and so forth to Meath and Uriel, as said marches are made and limited by Act of Parliament, held by William Bishop of Meath, do build and make a double ditch of six feet high above ground at one side, a part which mireth next unto Irishmen, betwixt this and next Lammas, the said ditches to be kept up and repaired as long as they shall occupy said lands, under pain of forty shillings, the lord of said lands to allow the old rent of said lands to the builder for one year under said penalty.[2])

From this and similar enactments relating to the double ditch (*palus*, fence or enclosure) the expression "Pale" came into use about this time, to designate the boundary of English territory. The ditch, however, was inadequate. The citizens of the Pale were forced to pay "black-rent" to the neighboring Irish chieftains for the privilege of holding their land in peace. The Irish chieftains on the other hand were able effectually to prevent incursions into their own territory.

The establishment of the vast possessions of the Butlers, Geraldines, and Burkes, and the rise of some clans and decline of others had greatly altered the physiognomy of Ireland from what it was at the time of the Norman Conquest, but in Ulster the country presented in the reign of Henry VIII much the same aspect as before Strongbow. The two great lords of the North were the O'Neill and the O'Donnell. Both were descended from the famous Niall of the Nine Hostages, who ruled all Ireland at the beginning of the fifth century. The O'Neills or Kinel-Owen traced their pedigree to Owen (Eoghan), and the O'Donnells or Kinel-Connell, to Conall Gulban, both sons of Niall. The O'Donnells held sway over Tirconnell, including the modern county of Donegal, and the territories of Inishowen, Kinel-Moen, and Fermanagh. They also claimed the overlordship of northern Connaught, and were constantly making raids into that district in the effort to bring those tribes under their control. The territory of the O'Donnells bordered on that of the O'Neills of Tyrone, who were continually at feud with them to win back the overlordship of Inishowen, Kinel-Moen, and Fermanagh.

Henry VIII undertook to reconcile these and equally conflicting interests in other parts of Ireland under the power of the English Crown. He refused to listen to the counsellors who advised subduing Ireland by force and "planting" the whole country with English set-

---

[2]Cited by R. Dunlop, Notes to Poole's *Historical Atlas*, xxx.

tlers. He wished, as he said, "to heal the great decay of that fertile land for lack of politic governance and good justice." His idea was to bind the independent chiefs of the Irishry to him by conferring honours upon them, and through them to rule the whole Irish community in the interests of unity and peace. He would rest the monarchy on an aristocracy of Irish origin, and without violent or dangerous change, it would make its benefits felt through all ranks of the people."[3])

In pursuance of this policy Henry appointed Kildare deputy, and far from insisting upon his observing English customs, allowed him to marry his daughters to Irish chieftains, and to levy coyne and livery like an Irish chieftain, in defiance of the English law. Kildare was even said to have encouraged the Irish to make inroads upon the Pale. He finally overstepped the limits of Henry's indulgence and was summoned to London on a charge of treason. During his absence his son Thomas Fitzgerald, whom he had left in Ireland as Vice-Deputy, hearing that his father had been treacherously served, led an expedition against the Pale. For several months the English dominion in Ireland was in peril. Skeffington, whom Henry now appointed to replace Kildare, succeeded in putting down the rebellion, and "Silken Thomas" Fitzgerald surrendered to his successor, Lord Leonard Grey, in 1535. The rebel was executed and the House of Kildare struck down by a sweeping act of attainder. Of the ancient family only one was saved, a child of twelve years, afterward Gerald, the eleventh earl. He was carried away secretly and concealed in the woods of Offaly.

The severity shown to the House of Kildare exasperated and alarmed the Irish chiefs. The steps taken by Henry to introduce the Reformation into Ireland added religious to racial grounds of discontent. The result was the first Geraldine League (1537), in which the O'Neills, the O'Donnells, the O'Briens of Thomond, and other powerful clans combined in an effort to restore Gerald to his earldom.[4])

Of the rebellion of "Silken Thomas" and the events which followed, the author of our *Life* was no passive spectator. Acting as deputy for his father during the latter's absence in Rome, 1510-11,[5]) he had distinguished himself in his defence of Tirconnell against the

---

[3]W. O'Connor Morris, *Ireland, 1494-1905*, revised by Robert Dunlop, *Cambridge Historical Series*, 1909, pp. 67-8.

[4]*Calendar of State Papers, Ireland*, 10 July 1539, p. 49. Cf. P. W. Joyce, *A Short History of Ireland*, London, 1911, Part III, Chap. XVI-XIX (inclusive).

[5]*Annals of the Kingdom of Ireland by the Four Masters*, Years 1510-12, p. 1308, p. 1312.

O'Neill.[6]) After 1530, broils with his family[7]) had led him to withhold his support from his father and league himself with the O'Neill.[8]) In the year 1527 he had completed the castle of Lifford on the river Foyle[9]) and there, five years later, finished the present *Life of Columcille*.[10]) The book was written among scenes connected with the saint by a thousand associations, and its author was bound to him by ties of blood as well as admiration. "Derry of Oaks", and "truly fair Loch Foyle", "beloved Raphoe with its acorns", and "delightful Drumcliffe of my heart" were no mere names to him; he had no doubt listened to stories of Columcille from the lips of "old people and historians" there. He had probably seen the Cowl at Kilmacrenan with his own eyes and touched the miraculous flagstones with his hands. In the *Annals of the Kingdom of Ireland by the Four Masters* we are told in an entry under the year 1531, that "the name and renown of Manus O'Donnell had spread not only through all Tirconnell, but through territories beyond." One wonders how much his great work on the *Life of Columcille* contributed to the warrior's renown, and how far it influenced "the successors of Columcille" to choose him above his brothers to succeed his father in the chieftainship in 1537.[11])

When Henry VIII undertook to punish the House of Kildare in 1535, O'Donnell was in the prime of life. As his book shows us, he was not without racial pride; the presence of foreigners in Erin held a sting for him.[12]) He had had a long apprenticeship in struggle and had succeeded in establishing himself in the supremacy which he felt to be his just place. The force of circumstances had proved to him that the adjustment of differences with the O'Neill was not impossible, and for some years, we may imagine, between 1535 and 1540, he hoped that the old feud[13]) between the Kinel-Connell and the Kinel-Owen might be forever buried, the House of Kildare established in the suzerainty of Ireland, and the clans united for the overthrow of English rule.

In the year after the execution of Lord Thomas Fitzgerald and his own inauguration as chief of his clan, Manus O'Donnell married Lady Eleanor McCarthy, who secretly held under her protection her nephew, the twelve-year-old Gerald Fitzgerald, heir to the earldom of

---

[6] *Ibid.*, Years 1512-30, *passim*.
[7] *Ibid.*, Year 1531, pp. 1404-7.
[8] *Annals of the Kingdom of Ireland by the Four Masters*, Year 1536, p. 1426.
[9] *Ibid.*, Year 1527, p. 1390.
[10] See *infra*, § 13.
[11] *Annals of the Kingdom of Ireland by the Four Masters*, Year 1537, p. 1438.
[12] See *infra*, §§ 90, 118, 127, 354.
[13] See infra, § 277, p. 291.

INTRODUCTION   xxxvii

Kildare. The English viewed this alliance with anxiety. "The late Earl of Kildare's sister is gone to be married to Manus O'Donnell. Young Gerrot Dalahide and others are gone with her, which I like not. I was never in despair in Ireland until now," was the news which Sir William Brabazon wrote to Gerald Aylmer and John Allen on the fifth of June, 1538.[14])

To destroy the Geraldine League the Deputy Lord Leonard Grey at once directed all his energies. He succeeded in breaking down the power of the chiefs, nearly annihilated the Geraldines, and restored the English power.[15]) In 1539 Manus O'Donnell and Con O'Neill were defeated at Lake Belahoe[16]) in Monaghan. In 1540 O'Donnell sent his submission[17]) to the King, and in 1542 he wrote asking for the gold chain which was the symbol of fealty to the English Crown.[18]) O'Neill and the other leading Irish chiefs yielded shortly afterward.[19])

Thus ended the brief hour of Manus O'Donnell's national aspiration. Modern historians take another view,[20]) but the Irish bard who witnessed these events has for the chieftains only words of contempt and shame.[21])

> "Fooboon upon you, O hosts of the Gael,
> Not one more of you survives,
> Foreigners dividing your territory,
> Your similitude is to a Fairy (*i. e.* unsubstantial) Host.
>
> . . . . . .
>
> The race of the O'Briens of Banba under Morrough,
> Their covenant is with the King of England;
> They have turned, and sad is the deed,
> Their back to the inheritance of their fathers.
>
> . . . .

---

[14]*Calendar of Carew Manuscripts,* 5 June 1538, p. 140, No. 121.
[15]*Calendar of State Papers, Ireland,* pp. 50-1.
[16]*Annals of the Kingdom of Ireland by the Four Masters,* Year 1538, p. 1452.
[17]*Calendar of State Papers, Ireland,* 20 June 1540, p. 54.
[18]*Ibid.,* 22 April 1542, p. 62. *Cf.* 29 August 1541, p. 60; 9 Sept. 1542, p. 64.
[19]*Ibid.,* 17 Dec. 1541, Nos. 46-7, p. 61; 1 Sept. 1542, Nos. 73-4, p. 64.
[20]Historians seem to agree that the policy of conciliation of Henry VIII had a beneficent influence in Ireland, and that if his successors had not broken with it, the tragic course of Irish history might have been averted. *Cf.* W. O'Connor Morris, *op. cit.,* p. 82. Similarly P. W. Joyce, *op. cit.,* p. 388. See, however, A. S. Green, *The Making of Ireland and its Undoing,* London, 1913, p. 358, note 1.
[21]Cited by A. S. Green, *op. cit.,* p. 355.

> O'Neill of Aileach and of Emania,
> King of Tara and of Tailltean,
> They have given for the earldom of Ulster
> Their kingdom submissively and unwisely.
>
> . . . .
>
> O'Donnell of Ath-seannagh,
> Who never refused combat or hardship,
> (To Ireland great is the misery)
> He has failed, Manus O'Donnell!
>
> Fooboon on the foreign-grey gun!
> Fooboon for the yellow chain!
> Fooboon for the Court without any English!
> Fooboon for Shane(?), O Son of Mary!
>
> . . . .
>
> O misguided, withered host,
> Say henceforth naught but Fooboon!"

The remaining years of O'Donnell's life were not without difficulties. The feud with the O'Neill was soon renewed, and carried on with the old bitterness.[22] His son Calvagh took up arms against him in 1548,[23] and although at first defeated, succeeded in 1555, with the aid of troops gathered in Scotland, in ravaging Tirconnell and taking his father prisoner.[24] His son Hugh was leagued with his grandson Shane O'Neill in the invasion of Tirconnell in 1557.[25] It is the same story that is recorded of more than one father and son in Irish annals, the same story that had been told of a Hugh and a Manus O'Donnell a generation before: on the one side a broken old man, the subject of England; on the other a spirited youth, leaguing himself with the rebel O'Neill. Later in life this younger Hugh O'Donnell, like Manus his father, and Hugh his grandfather, reverses his position, and combines with the English to crush the hereditary enemy of his clan.[26]

Under the year 1563, we find the following entry in the *Four Masters:*

> "O'Donnell (Manus . . .), Lord of Tirconnell, Inishowen, Kinel-Moen, Fermanagh, and Lower Connaught; a man who never suffered the chiefs who were in his neighborhood . . . . to encroach upon any of his superabundant

---

[22]*Annals of the Kingdom of Ireland by the Four Masters,* Year 1544, et seq.; *Annals of Loch Cé (Rolls Series),* II, 345.

[23]*Ibid.,* Year 1548, p. 1504.

[24]*Ibid.,* Year 1555, p. 1541.

[25]*Ibid.,* Year 1557, p. 1553.

[26]*Ibid.,* Year 1567, *Calendar of State Papers, Ireland,* 28 April 1567, p. 331.

possessions, even to the time of his disease and infirmity; a fierce, obdurate, wrathful, and combative man toward his enemies and opponents, until he had made them obedient to his jurisdiction; and a mild, friendly, benign, amiable, bountiful, and hospitable man toward the learned, the destitute, the poets, and the ollaves, towards the [religious] orders and the church, as is evident from the [accounts of] old people and historians; a learned man, skilled in many arts, gifted with a profound intellect and the knowledge of every science, died on the 9th February, at his own mansion-seat at Lifford, a castle which he had erected in despite of O'Neill and the Kinel-Owen, and was interred in the burial place of his predecessors and ancestors at Donegal, in the monastery of St. Francis, with great honor and veneration, after having vanquished the Devil and the world."[27])

[27]The editors have pleasure in thanking Prof. A. C. Cole, of the University of Illinois, who read this section of the Introduction in manuscript and made helpful suggestions.

III.
MANUS O'DONNELL'S LIFE OF COLUMCILLE.
STYLE.

Adamnan had divided his *Vita Sancti Columbae* into three books, prophecies, miracles, and angelic apparitions. He had not given us a biography, but an exposition of the chief ways in which the grace of God was manifested in the saint. Our author, on the other hand, instinctively a story-teller, has followed the biographical lines of the Old Irish *Life*, adding materials from other sources, incidents from Adamnan, and local legends, ancient poems, and "stories scattered wide apart each from other in the ancient books of Erin", such as the *Imthecht na Tromdaime*, and the very extensive *Echtra Clerech Choluimb cille*.

In some passages we can compare his version with older Irish texts from which he has drawn, and find it an almost literal reproduction. Even the language in these passages betrays archaic words and idiom characteristic of the older text and foreign to O'Donnell's habitual style. But the extant copies of these older tales are not the copies that O'Donnell used.[1]) Now O'Donnell's version lacks some incident which appears in our manuscript of his source; now he has a poem

[1]*Cf. e. g.* § 355 with *Echtra Clerech Choluimb cille*, from Y. B. L., *Rev. Celt.,* xxvi, p. 132-134.

which is lacking in it.²) Now the one has introduced from other sources a traditional prophecy, the other a local legend.³)

The verses "in very hard Gaelic made by the poets of the Gael" O'Donnell has wisely quoted in the original Old Irish, introducing them to substantiate his own delightful paraphrases in modern Irish prose. For those who can understand the verses they add lyric quality and richness of detail. Those to whom they are obscure can omit them without losing anything of the story.

In the account of Columcille's life in Iona and in the story of his last days and death, O'Donnell follows Adamnan closely, incorporating also, however, all that is given on the subject in the Old Irish *Life*.

The following outline will give an idea of the arrangement of O'Donnell's *Life* according to sources:

Chapters	Contents	Sources
I.	Foreword, §§ 1-21	
II-XV.	Life in Erin, §§ 21-202	Old Irish *Life* and Irish traditions⁴)
XV-XVII.	Life in Iona. §§ 202-220	Old Irish *Life* and Irish traditions
XVII-XXVI.	Life in Iona, §§ 220-314	Adamnan's *Vita*
XXVI-XXX.	Druim Ceat, §§ 314-355	Irish traditions
XXXI.	*Voyage of Columcille's Clerics*, § 355	*Echtra Clerech Choluim Cille*, etc.
XXXII-XXXIII.	Last Days, §§ 356-377	Adamnan's *Vita*
XXXIV.	Comparisons with others, §§ 377-394	
XXXV, XXXVI.	Virtues and posthumous miracles, §§ 394-435	Irish traditions

Sources

At the beginning of the *Life*, O'Donnell gives an account of his method and purpose.

---

²*The Vision of Adamnan* is interpolated in the Y. B. L. version, p. 138, ¶ 14; 158, ¶45. O'Donnell has incorporated the poems from other sources. Cf. e. g. § 355 with *Rev. Celt.*, p. 136, ¶ 7, 8.

³O'Donnell tells how the Golden Leaf that was cherished as a relic in Iona and the Golden Cowl at Cill mic Nenain were brought home by the clerics from marvellous islands, § 355 h. The Y. B. L. tells how the last words of the island-king before their departure were a prophecy of the coming of foreigners to subdue Erin, *loc. cit.*, pp. 164-6.

⁴See section on Sources for list of these.

"Be it known to the readers of this *Life* that it was Manus O'Donnell . . . that bade put into Gaelic the part of this *Life* that was in Latin, and bade make easy the part thereof that was hard Gaelic, to the end that it might be clear and easy of understanding to all."[5])

It appears from this statement that the young lord of Tirconnell did not himself undertake the task of translating those of his sources which offered linguistic difficulties. The following paragraph, however, makes clear that his *Betha Coluimb Chille* was the work of himself and no other. He says:

"And he collected and assembled the part thereof that was scattered throughout the ancient books of Erin, and he set it forth with his own lips. And passing great labor had he therewith. And much time did he give thereto, conning how he might put each part thereof in its own fitting place as is writ here below."[6])

Like many other mediaeval writers, O'Donnell thinks of the traditions which he has collected as a fragment of a once complete and perfect whole. "Be it known," he says, "that this *Life* was lost a long while since." The idea that some of the materials which he incorporates are of late growth does not seem to occur to him. He accounts for what he considers the paucity of the writings which remain as due to the destruction wrought by the Vikings. The materials which he uses he classifies roughly under three heads.

"Naught thereof was to be found save small parts of the book that holy Adamnan made in Latin, and another part in very hard Gaelic made by the poets of the Gael, and still another part in stories scattered wide apart each from other in the ancient books of Erin."[6a])

But whereas he has incorporated the whole of the Old Irish *Life*, he has used only a small portion of Adamnan's. This bears out his statement that of the Latin work he had access to a part only. That he would have used more of it if he had had it is hardly doubtful, since he refers to it repeatedly as his most valuable authority.

It appears that the manuscript of Adamnan's *Life* which O'Donnell used was akin to Codex D, and thus belonged to what is known as the shorter recension of Adamnan's work.[7]) There are numerous indications of this throughout the text. When O'Donnell's reading differs

[5] § 10.
[6] § 11.
[6a] § 8.
[7] The conclusion of Reeves (*op. cit.*, xii) are without foundation; for the passages which he mentions as being in O'Donnell's *Life* and on which he bases his reasoning are in fact not in it. He seems to have been misled by Colgan.

from Reeves' text it invariably agrees with the variants cited by Reeves from D. For example, in the incident as related by Adamnan, the saint, while waiting on the shore for a coble (*caupallum*, a six-oared boat), beholds a sea monster preparing to swallow his messenger. Forthwith he makes the sign of the cross and the beast withdraws. In O'Donnell's version, the translator, faithfully following Codex D, represents the saint as commanding the messenger to swim across the water to fetch a horse (*caballus*).[8])

It is where we can compare O'Donnell's version with Adamnan's that we gain the most interesting evidence of his gift of narrative style. The long compound sentences of the Latin, with their complicated structure, are infinitely less vivid than the short simple Irish ones. Adamnan's sentences are comprehensive and sonorous, but they trail off into repetition or insignificance. O'Donnell has contrived by the mere shifting of the position of the details and the excision of weakening periphrases to make the little stories dramatic. We might cite numberless cases where the helpless expository style of Adamnan is transformed by a touch into dramatic narrative. Here is one chosen at random:

> Quidam juvenis de equo lapsus in flumine, quod Scotice Boend vocitatur, mersus et mortuus, viginti sub aqua diebus permansit; qui, sicuti sub ascella, cadens, libros in pelliceo reconditos sacculo habebat, ita etiam post supra memoratum dierum numerum est repertus, sacculum cum libris inter brachium et latus continens; cujus etiam ad aridam reportato cadavere, et aperto sacculo, folium sancti Columbae sanctis scriptum digitulis, inter aliorum folia librorum non tantum corrupta sed putrefacta inventum est siccum et nullo modo corruptum, ac si scriniolo esset reconditum.[9])

[8]For instances in which the Irish text does not translate *Adamnan* with absolute accuracy, see footnotes to the following edition. An interesting example is the translation in § 238, "Colman Liath" (Colman the Grey) for Adamnan's "Colman *Canis*". It is impossible of course to tell whether O'Donnell's manuscript was corrupt and read *Canus,* or whether the translator mistook *Canis* for *Canus.*

[9]A certain youth fell from his horse in the river which is called the Boyne, and sank and died, and remained under the water for twenty days; he, as he had books enclosed in a leathern satchel under his armpit, and thus falling, was also found so, after the above-mentioned number of days, holding between his arm and his side the satchel with the books; and when his dead body was brought to the dry ground, and the satchel opened, a leaf written by the holy fingers of St. Columba was found dry and in no wise corrupted, as if it had been kept in a casket, among the leaves of other books that were not only corrupted, but even putrified. Reeves, *Adamnan, Lib.* II, viii, Translation of J. T. Fowler, *Prophecies, Miracles, and Visions of St. Columba* London, 1895. *Cf.* the story as told in O'Donnell, § 433.

Would any reader, having been told that a man had fallen with books enclosed in a leathern satchel under his armpit, and having remained in the water twenty days, been found in the same position, need to be again informed that when found at the expiration of the above mentioned number of days, he was holding the satchel with the books between his arm and his side?

O'Donnell follows his source faithfully, but he tells the story in fewer words, retouching the clumsy mass of detail and subduing it to simplicity and grace.

> "There was a certain man in Alba long while after the death of Columcille that was going on a stream or across a river, bearing a satchel of books upon his back. And he fell and was drowned. And after the space of twenty days, his body was found, and when it was lifted, the bag also. And—no marvel—all the books that were in that bag were decayed and rotted, save only one, to wit, a leaf from a book that Columcille had written with his holy blessed hand."

With all his care to follow his sources faithfully and to "put each part in its own fitting place", our author has made blunders. Sometimes, following out his purpose to include all the records available to him, he fails to notice that what he takes to be different events are really accounts of the same one, narrated by his different authorities with slightly different details. He tells us, for example,[10]) that the mother of Columcille had a vision before his birth of a napkin whereon were a multitude of all colors and the fragrance of every fruit and every flower and every sweet-smelling thing. And the angel that brought it laid it down for a space in her sight and then he took it from her again. O'Donnell does not realize, it seems, that this vision, which he is copying from Adamnan's *Life,* is the same which he has already copied, in the preceding chapter, from the Old Irish. He has been misled by some slight differences of detail into believing that he has before him two distinct visions.[11]) He incorporates into his work narratives which for artistic purposes have represented as contemporaries of the saint persons who, from better authority, we know could not possibly have been living during his life-time.[12]) Confusion of persons

---

[10] § 46.

[11] See Index of Matters, *s. v.* doublets, for other examples.

[12] Guaire, who lived in the seventh century, appears as a contemporary of Columcille, §§ 136, 138, 157. Finnachta, who reigned 675-95, appears as offering hospitality to Columcille, §§ 136-7. Domnall, son of Aed, is represented as having reached maturity at the time of the Assembly of Druim Ceat, whereas, according to the *Annals of Ulster,* he was brought thither by his fosterers as a child, § 95. See also index. There are other minor discrepancies in regard to time, *e. g.,* § 101.

owing to other causes is also frequent.[13]) O'Donnell's nearest approach to criticism is his comment on the story of how the fiend appeared in the form of a woman with a child and declared to the brethren that were gathered around that the child's father was Columcille, who lay stretched in death before them. He relates the incident immediately after his account of the saint's return from the Assembly of Druim Ceat, and adds:

> "And Columcille lived some while thereafter, as I understand it, for surely if it had been at the time of his death that this had befallen him, Adamnan would have made mention thereof in the *Life* that he did make himself."[14])

It is clear that the moral edification that might be drawn from the stories was an important consideration to the author. It is for this he cites at the beginning of his work the texts from Gregory, Augustine, Bernard, Bonaventura, the Psalmist, and St. Paul, of which the life and character of Columcille may be considered as *exempla*.[15]) For this too he makes the long series of comparisons between Columcille and other holy men at the end of the *Life*. The prayers to Columcille[16]) and the observations on his piety and his powers interspersed throughout the biography reveal the same preoccupation.

But O'Donnell's work, like Jacobus de Voragine's *Legenda Aurea*, cannot be judged as a work of edification from the modern standpoint. Mediaeval writers made no such sharp distinctions as we do between sacred and profane. "Their favorite intellectual dish," remarks a recent editor,[17])

> "was a sort of game-pie where all sorts of wild-fowl lay simmering in the same sauce under the same crust. Samson and the Argonauts, S. Michael

---

[13]The well-known saint German has been substituted as one of Columcille's teachers for Gemmán, an otherwise obscure figure. An incident in the life of Molaise of Devenish is related in O'Donnell's version of Molaise of Innishmurry, §§ 180-1, note 177. In stories told of companions of the saint, now one, now another holy man is given the important rôle. For instance, of the three chairs which Columcille beheld before the Lord, the *Leabar Breac* tells us that it was Molaise who has the silver chair. The *Life of Laisren* says it was Laisren; and O'Donnell declares it was Baithin who was thus honored, § 75.

[14]§ 353.

[15]Similarly in the Old Irish *Life* the biography is used as an *exemplum* to illustrate the text from *Genesis* xii, 1, *Exi de terra tua et de domo patris tua, et vade in terram quam tibi monstravero*. Quoted from the Irish text, *Lismore Lives*, pp. 20, 168.

[16]§§ 15, 20, 277.

[17]G. V. O'Neill, S. J., *The Golden Legend*, Cambridge, 1914, p. 11.

and Alexander the Great, lions, bears, and unicorns, miracles and gross episodes, unseemly jests leading up to most edifying conclusions—such strangely assorted elements jostle each other in the epic or romance, the *gesta* or the *legenda,* and had the advantage of gratifying at the same time a great variety of palates while seriously offending none. We must remember that the mediaeval student could be the possessor of extremely few books. Chaucer's 'Clerke of Oxenford' was fortunate in owning so many as twenty. Each volume of such a library would naturally be prized by its possessor in proportion as it was a *multum in parvo.*"

As for our author's historical conscience, even while we read the most extravagant of the tales that adorn our *Life,* we must say of it what Carlyle has said of Adamnan's: "You can see that the man who wrote it would tell no lie; what he meant you cannot always find out, but it is clear that he told things as they appeared to him." O'Donnell follows faithfully the sources which he had before him. His style is sober and restrained. In a time when the same term served for both history and fiction it is not surprising that he has incorporated much which a later age recognizes at a glance as unhistorical.[18])

To a scientifically trained mind in a critical mood it may seem incredible that such prodigies could be narrated in good faith. But we must remember that O'Donnell is transcribing the accounts of men to whom the constant interposition of Providence in daily life was a natural part of their view of the world. Moreover it is hardly doubtful that the enthusiasm which the saint inspired in those that surrounded him was such that they saw as marvels many things that might have been explained by purely natural causes. The patriotic enthusiasm inspired in all countries by the present war has expressed itself in the creation of legends no less extravagant. Readers will recall the story of the angels that came to the rescue of the English

---

[18]The present editors have made no effort to appraise the *Life* from an historical standpoint. Historians who sift O'Donnell's *Life of Columcille* will no doubt concur with what Prof. Meyer has said in his introduction to the *Life of Colmán son of Lúachan:*

"While our biographer gives us so little trustworthy information about the saint himself, he has still compiled a work of abiding historical interest and value. For, in narrating his miracles, he conveys to us a large amount of indirect historical information. Indeed, what with its wealth of varied and picturesque incidents taken from the life and customs of the people, its many instances of religious practices and information on ecclesiastical matters generally, its topographical details, and its folklore, it will always count, next to the *Tripartite Life* and the biographies of Colum Cille, as the richest and fullest among the lives of Irish saints that have come down to us." Royal Irish Academy, *Todd Lecture Series,* vol. XVII, p. xvii.

at Mons.[19]) Moreover, in ages of doubt as in ages of Faith, hope still creates the thing it yearns for. In the first year of the war hundreds of Englishmen beheld with their own eyes trainloads of Russians transported through England to the Western Front, and innumerable letters received from Germany in 1914 bore the confession of starvation underneath the stamp. How many legends are still current! Even the hardheaded Yankees of a certain university town in Illinois have seen during the past winter in the rosy light of the Aurora Borealis the finger of God in the sky unrolling the ruddy stripes from the stars in His heaven, to presage victory to the American cause.[20])

SOURCES.

The following writings are expressly mentioned by the author as the authorities on which his *Life of Columcille* is based:

(1) Adamnan's *Life of St. Columba*, §§ 8, 10, 46, 63, 72, 192, 225, 238, 244 *(bis)*, 268, 280, 295, 312, 362 *(bis)*, 363, 367 *(bis)*, 369, 370, 375, 376, 406.

(2) St. Augustine, § 3.

(3) St. Ambrose, § 387.

(4) Verses ascribed to Baithín mac Cuanach, §§ 55, 56, 83, 138, 340 *(bis)*, 411, 423, 425.

(5) Verses ascribed to St. Berchan, § 371.

(6) St. Bernard, §§ 5, 6, 7.

(7) Verses ascribed to Brenainn of Birr, § 399.

(8) Verses attributed to St. Brigid, §§ 35, 372.

(9) St. Bonaventure, §§ 11, 18.

(10) Verses attributed to St. Caillin, § 38.

(11) Book called *Cogad Gall re Gaidelaib*, § 8.

(12) a) Verses in Gaelic attributed to Columcille, §§ 27, 53, 78, 89, 90, 110, 118, 136, 137, 138, 154, 155, 159, 171, 181, 182, 183 *(bis)*, 184, 185, 189, 190, 191, 192, 197, 200, 201, 202, 211, 221, 222 *(bis)*, 275 *(quater)*, 276, 277 *(ter)*, 278, 279, 326, 332 *(quater)*, 333, 344, 347, 348 *(bis)*, 349, 353, 366, 373, 398, 411, 423. b) Latin Hymns attributed to Columcille, namely, *Noli Pater*, § 78; *Altus Prosator*, § 216.

(13) Verses ascribed to Colman mac Coimgellain, § 344.

(14) Verses ascribed to Cormac ua Liathain, § 276.

[19] A. Machen, *The Angels of Mons* London, 1915.
[20] *Urbana Courier-Herald*, Friday, 7 March, 1918 (Urbana, Illinois).

(15) Cumaín Fada mac Fíachna's book on *The Virtues of Columcille,* § 244.

(16) Verses attributed to Dallan Forgaill, §§ 159, 179, 198, 374, 399, 400, 401, 404, 423, 426; *Amra Colaim Chille,* 364, 366 *(quater).*

(17) Verses attributed to Diarmaid mac Cerbaill, § 139.

(18) Verses attributed to Domnall mac Aeda, § 354.

(19) Quatrain ascribed to Eogan of Ardstraw, § 40.

(20) The *Feallsamh Nadúra,* § 386.

(21) Pope Gregory, §§ 2, 386.

(22) The *Lectiones* of Columcille, § 409.

(23) Lives of Bishop Eogan and Moconna, § 40.

(24) Life of Fintan mac Gaibrein, §§ 160, 249.

(25) Life of Maedoc of Ferns, § 368.

(26) Life of Munda mac Tulchain, § 161.

(27) Quatrain ascribed to Mochta of Louth, § 24.

(28) Book called *Mordail Droma Cet,* § 143; also called *Lebhar na Mordhála,* § 157.

(29) Verses attributed to Muru, §§ 50, 53, 54, 159 *(bis).*

(30) Old Irish Life, §§ 8, 10.

(31) Quatrains ascribed to St. Patrick, §§ 25, 371.

(32) Verses attributed to Scannlan Mor mac Cind Faeladh, §§ 348, 349.

(33) Sechrán Clerech Colaim Chille, § 355.

(34) Senlebair Erenn, senlebair oiris Erenn §8, senlebair Erenn § 11, senchaidhe na nGaidel § 21, lebair eli §§ 28, 164.

(35) Book called *Tromdham Guaire (bis),* § 157.[1]

---

[1]This list of sources will give us some idea of the amount of labour and research O'Donnell expended on his *Life of Columcille.* He consulted many more works of which he makes no mention. These we have endeavored to trace, as far as we have been able, with the texts and MSS. at our disposal. But the notes upon them are by no means exhaustive. As a rule, the author has followed his sources very faithfully. Cases of important divergencies have been briefly pointed out in the notes.

LANGUAGE.

In the opening pages of *Betha Coluimb Chille*, the author makes two very important statements. First of all, he fixes the date of its composition: "This *Life* was put together in the year that twelve and a score and fifteen hundred years were fulfilled from the birth of our Lord" § 13. If we regard the year 1550 as the beginning of the period of modern Irish, as seems generally accepted, the language of the present *Life* must be considered late middle Irish or rather the Irish of the transition from middle Irish to modern Irish, a most interesting period in the history of the language. In the second place, the author expressly states that his language conforms to the general usage of the age in which he lived: "Be it known to the readers of this *Life* that it was Manus O'Donnell that bade put into Gaelic the part of this *Life* that was in Latin and bade make easy the part thereof that was hard Gaelic, to the end it might be clear and easy of understanding to all" § 10. There can be no doubt, then, that the Irish of *Betha Coluimb Chille* truly represents the natural development of the language of the period in which it was composed. It follows, therefore, that it will be a very valuable contribution to the history of the language of the late middle Irish period.

The reader can see for himself that the author has faithfully carried out his purpose, for the language is, as a rule, "clear and easy of understanding to all".

We shall briefly point out where he has departed from that rule.

(1) A special feature of the present *Life* is the vast amount of early middle Irish poetry that is incorporated into the prose narrative. This the author has left intact, thereby showing his good taste and judgment. To attempt to modernize it would be to destroy its beauty and charm.

(2) The language of certain portions has been considerably influenced by the language of the older sources which the author used. This is an important fact to bear in mind for the compiler of complete paradigms of the language of the *Life*. Note especially the retention of forms with the infixed pronoun in the prose narrative, *e. g.* -s- infixed pronoun sg. 3 conusfuair 378, 8; roslenatar 382, 27; roslecsat 390, 24. -s- infixed pronoun pl. 3 rustogaib 176, 5; rosbuaildis 390, 20; rusgab 392, 12.

(3) The author occasionally uses old or early Irish forms of the

verb in his narrative, *e. g.* at *thou art* 378, 7; isat *they are* 386, 31; -bia *he will be* 116, 1. 130, 22; atbert 74, 19; aduaigh *he ate* 370, 16; -ébert (co ndébert) 188, 26; co ndeabert 378, 6; fasdó 214, 26, fosdó 314, 2; testa 148, 23, *etc.*

(4) The author sometimes uses obsolete words and phrases. Numerous examples could be quoted.

We note only one instance in the prose, of the middle Irish deponent form in-tar, -tair, namely, gabustar 142, 6. pret. sg. 3 of gaibim. In the poetry there is also only one instance, namely, rodelbusdair 74, 23.

A detailed study of the language of *Betha Coluimb Chille* is impossible in a short introduction. The most we can do is to give a general idea of its quality. That it is irreproachable as regards grammar and syntax cannot be questioned. It has a great variety of constructions, and again and again the reader is struck by the wonderful power and force with which the author has wielded his pen. See, for instance, with what ease and grace he handles the following difficult construction: Acus ar na cloisdin sin don drochduine sin do bí faré Lughaidh, adubhairt nac caithfedh se biadh no deoch 7 nach fillfedh se tar ais no co bfhaghadh se bas no co faicedh se fen C. C. 7 go labradh se riss ó bél go bél, § 236.

The *Betha* contains a host of idiomatic expressions, such as feadh radairc *as far as the eye can see* 104, 6; ar béluib *in preference to* 246, 11, *etc.* Many of these beautiful phrases have fallen into disuse in modern Irish, owing to the neglect of Irish literature during the past few centuries. They are worth reviving. Now that the whole of the text of the *Betha* is available in book form, perhaps somebody may make a study of them for the sake of enriching the modern Irish language.

A few especially interesting constructions are the following:

(1) Instances where the nominative singular is used when one would usually expect the accusative with the preposition *le*. (a) Acus Mandar mac righ Lochlann do techt coblach cogaidh don baile 420, 35. (b) Ro indiss doib a techt a tirr n-Erend lucht curaigh 388, 16. (c) Tainec Brenainn ced eli 76, 2.

(2) Instances where the genitive singular of the noun is used as an adjective. (a) conách *prosperity*. The gen. used as an adj. *blessed, prosperous*. conaich 228, 3. 446, 1. (b) enech *hospitality*. The gen. used as an adj. *generous, hospitable*. fíal degh-enigh 136, 24. duine bú droch-enigh 138, 18. duine ba degh-enich 164, 3. (c) cennsa *gentleness*. The gen. used as an adj. *tame*. d'ainmide cennsa 318, 21.

The following instances of -f- Future are worth noting: ben-

deobadh 146, 28. fut. sec. sg. 3 of bendaigim *I bless. Cf.* O. I. -bendachub *I will bless*. críchnóbadh 148, 29. fut. sec. sg. 3 of críchnaigim *I end, finish*. scribeóbha me 126, 11. fut. sg. 1 of scribhaim *I write*. fut. sec. sg. 3 scribhobadh 410, 23.¹) *Cf*. cuirebh 244, 33. fut. sg. 1 of cuirim (cuiriur) *I put, I send*. fuigeabh 116, 23. fut. sg. 1 of fagbaim *I leave*. impodhbhad 286, 9. fut. sg. 1 of impóim *I turn*. fut. sec. sg. 3 impobudh 190, 22. leceb 424, 29. -f- future sg. 3 of lecim. *Cf*. O. I. -léiciub. tóicebad 318, 40. fut. sg. 1 of tócbaim *I take*.

O'Donnell strictly observed, in accordance with classical usage, the distinction between the preposition do, which elides its vowel, and the verbal particle do, whose vowel never elides. But it is interesting to note one exception, namely, d'foighenadh 318, 10. fut. sec. sg. 3 of foghnaim *I serve*. donntaighedh 328, 19, may, possibly, be another exception.

Finally we note the following interesting collective nouns in -ech, -ach, some of which the author himself invented: cráibech *branches*, collect. of cráib. sg. d. *id*. 186, 7. énach *birds* 34, 1. 194, 21. collect. of én *a bird*. fidhach *shrubs*. sg. gen. fidhaigh 68, 36. acc. fidhach 70, 4. iarnach *irons* 368, 24. collect. of iarann. íascach *fish*. acc. *id*. 68, 32. 326, 8. collect. of íasc. oirnech *pieces*. sg. gen. oirnigh 108, 28. dat. oirnech 108, 18. seems collect. of orda *a piece*, but formed from the plural oirdne. rónach *seals* 242, 17. collect. of rón *a seal*. sméróidech 18, 6. collect. of sméróid *ember*.

Manus O'Donnell has been practically unknown as a writer for nearly 400 years, but now that his work is being published, it is to be hoped that he will receive his rightful place in literature. And that is sure to be a very high one. We regard him as the precursor of the Very Reverend Canon O'Leary, the greatest living writer of the Irish language. Like *An t-athair Peadar* he wrote "for the people", as he says in the beginning of his work, "in easy Irish, to the end that it might be clear and intelligible to everybody" (§ 10). Like *An t-athair Peadar* also he excelled in dialogue. In the dialogue between Columcille and Mongan mac Fiachna (§ 87) the wit, the humor, the playfulness, the irony of both parties, and the ebb and flow of the struggle for supremacy make the passage a masterpiece. In a few cases also, as will be seen in the next section of our introduction, O'Donnell shows a tendency toward the phonetic spelling which Father O'Leary has done so much to bring into general use.

All Irishmen will honor Manus O'Donnell as a great writer, and the men of the North will take a special pride in him, though indeed they will find little "Northern Irish" in his work. In his day there

---

[1]See *Irish Texts Society*, vol. VII, p. XXIV, *s. v.* sgribhebhuinn.

were no such things as dialects in literature. The literary language was the same all over Ireland, although the spoken language, as now, no doubt showed variations. If the language is developed on truly broad and national lines, we shall soon, let us hope, have again a literary language in Ireland.

SPELLING.

The author's spelling is, as a rule, in accordance with classical usage. But there are many cases of erratic spellings. We now regret not having corrected all the erroneous spellings of the text. Phonetic tendencies in the spelling are numerous, too numerous to be accidental. The following instances may be noted. (The numbers refer to the paragraphs). adiaidh 347, for ad diaidh; ané 298, for indé; amárach 87, 104, 360, 366, for i mbárach. báite 231, for báidhte; bethaig 399, for bethaidh; brách 98, 111, for bráth. clai 224, 240, for mod. Irish claoidheadh; claite 224, for mod. Irish claoidhte; cogús 40, 145, for cocubus; cóir regularly for comhair 156; cruaitech 421, for cruaidhtech; crúas 123, 156, 361, 395, 405, 406, for cruadhas. daíne 158, 182, for mod. Irish daoine; diaig 80, 81, 89, for diaidh; Dunadha 136, for mod. Irish Donnchadha. ecóir, eccóir 105, 127, for mod. Irish éagcóir, correctly éagóir (en-cóir). foirfe 20, 46, 64, 376, for foirbhthe; foirfecht 378, 379, 386, for foirbhthecht. gaíl (sg. g.) 156, for mod. Irish gaoil. imig (pret. sg. 3) 195, for imthigh; imigh (impv.) 263, imidh 234, for imthigh; imghetar 216, 218, 229, 239, for imthighetar; imeochadh 234, for imtheochadh. leanumh 159, for leanbh; leisin 89, for leis sin; lesscél 125, for leth-scél; leghóirecht 221, for leghthóirecht. madh regularly, ma 116, 136, 182, for mbadh. naimh (sg. g.) 75, for mod. Irish naoimh; niugh 34, for andiu; nocht 41, for anocht. orum, oram regularly for orm. pecaíb, pecuib 140, 144, 214, 246, for pecaidhibh. réitech 222, for réidhtech. saibhress 386, for saidhbhress 378; spreite 11, for spreighte. tairrgire 49, for tairngire; tairrger 275, 277, for tairnger; tamhraidh (sg. g.) 288, for tshamhraidh. údarás 72, 376, 421, for ughdarás, ugdairais (sg. g.) 241.

These examples are especially interesting in view of the present movement for the simplification of the spelling of Irish.

Finally it must be noted that, where two vowels come together, the first of which should bear the mark of length, the author almost invariably places it over the second vowel, e. g. altoír, for altóir. We have retained this peculiarity of the author's spelling in the printed text.

MANUSCRIPT.

Dr. William Reeves, in his monumental edition[1]) of Adamnan's *Vita Sancti Columbae,* Dublin, 1857, p. xxxv, describes the manuscript of Manus O'Donnell's *Betha Columcille* as follows:

"The work exists in all its original dimensions, beauty, and material excellence, in a large folio of vellum, written in double columns, in a fine bold Irish hand, and is preserved in the Bodleian Library at Oxford, where it was deposited, together with the other Irish manuscripts of Mr. Rawlinson; having previously cost that gentleman, at the sale of the Chandos collection in 1766-7, the formidable sum of twenty-three shillings. . . . The leaf measures 17 by 11½ inches. There are 60 folios or 120 pages in the *Life,* followed by 18 folios containing poems on the O'Donnell family. On the second folio is a large coloured representation of the saint in episcopal robes. The volume has a slip cover of undressed skin."

The late Dr. Henebry gives a more detailed description of this representation of the saint.[2])

"A fairly tolerable drawing in full length showing an abbot vested for mass, and bearing a mitre and crosier. He stands within a Gothic frame of scrolled foliage. The folds of the drapery are conventionalized almost to geometric symmetry, and there is a back-ground in diagonal lines of four-petalled flowers, with two large roses depending from twigs filling the spaces at each side of the head. The whole seems motived by stained-glass designs, and shows no trace of characteristic Irish intertwining."

The present edition has been made from a photograph of MS. Rawlinson B 514, kindly lent us by Dr. Kuno Meyer.[3])

[1]J. T. Fowler, *Adamnani Vita S. Columbae,* edited from Dr. Reeves's text, with an introduction on the history of the Celtic church, Oxford, 1904, contains valuable bibliographical material. We have not had opportunity to consult Gertrud Brüning, *Adamnan's Vita Columbae und ihre Ableitungen,* Bonn, 1916.

[2]*Zeitschrift für Celtische Philologie,* III, 516-7.

[3]There is a good copy in the Franciscan Convent, Dublin.

IV.

CHRONOLOGICAL OUTLINE OF THE LIFE OF COLUMCILLE.

St. Columba was born at Gartan, a district in the county of Donegal, on the seventh of December, 521.[1]) Fedlimid, his father, a member of the reigning families of Ireland and Scottish Dalriada, belonged to the clan from which the territory surrounding Gartan was named. His mother, Ethne, was of Leinster extraction, descended from the illustrious provincial king, Cathair Mor.

He was baptized by the presbyter Cruithnecan, and spent his boyhood in Doire-Eithne, a hamlet in the same territory, afterwards called Cill mac Nenain (Kilmacrenan).

He became a pupil of Bishop Finnian, in his school at Moville at the head of Strangford Lough, and was ordained deacon. He afterward studied under an aged bard called Gemman, and later under St. Finnian in the monastic seminary of Clonard. Etchen, bishop of Clonfad, ordained him priest.

Columba seems to have subsequently entered the monastery of Mobhi Clairenech at Glasnevin near Dublin, where S. S. Comgall, Ciaran, and Cainnech are said to have been his companions.

In 544 a pestilence broke up the community, and Columba returned to the north. Two years afterward Columba founded the church of Derry, and seven years later (553) the monastery of Durrow, his chief institution in Ireland. During the years between 546 and 562 he established numerous churches in Ireland.

In 561 was fought the battle of Cooldrevny, which is believed to have been, in a great measure, brought about at St. Columba's instigation.[2]) Two years later he passed over with twelve attendants to the west of Scotland, possibly on the invitation of the provincial king, Conall, lord of the Scottish kingdom of Dalriada,[3]) to whom he was

[1]This date is not certainly established, but it is correct within two or three years. The following summary is based on Reeves, *op. cit.*, lxviii-lxxvii.

[2]For a discussion of this question, see *infra*, p. XXXI. *Cf.* W. Reeves, pp. lxxiii-lxxv; J. T. Fowler, *Adamnani Vita Sancti Columbae*, lxi-lxiv. It appears that a youth who had taken sanctuary with Columcille was killed by King Diarmaid, and the saint roused his tribe to avenge the wrong.

[3]The Scottish kingdom of Dal Riada was founded by the Irish Dalriada at the end of the fifth or the beginning of the sixth century.

allied by blood. He settled in the island of Iona, on the confines of Pictish and Scotic jurisdiction, and successfully applied himself to the conversion of the Picts. During the thirty-four years (563-597) which followed, he founded a number of churches in Scotland and the isles, of which Adamnan has preserved the names of the following, *Ethica insula, Elena, Himba, Scia.*[4])

At the death of Conall in 574, his cousin Aidan assumed the sovereignty and was formally inaugurated by St. Columba in the monastery of Iona. In the following year the saint accompanied Aidan to the convention of Druim Ceat, where the claims of the Irish king to the homage of Scottish Dalriada were abandoned, and the independence of that province declared.

About the year 579 a quarrel between St. Columba and St. Comgall concerning a church in the neighborhood of Coleraine, was taken up by their respective clans and led to a sanguinary struggle. Also in the battle of Cuilfedha, near Clonard, our saint is said to have been an interested party.

St. Columba visited Ireland subsequently to June, 585, and from Durrow proceeded westwards to Clonmacnois, where he was received with the warmest tokens of affection and respect.

In 593 he seems to have had an almost fatal illness, but he recovered and lived until the year 597. In that year he died at midnight between Saturday the eighth and Sunday the ninth of June.

The following passage gives a brief sketch of the achievement of St. Columba:

"In all Irish history there is no greater figure than St. Columcille—statesman and patriot, poet, scholar, and saint. After founding thirty-seven monasteries in Ireland, from Derry on the northern coast to Durrow near the Munster border, he crossed the sea in 563 to set up on the bare island of Hii or Iona a group of reed-thatched huts peopled with Irish monks. In that wild debatable land, swept by heathen raids, amid the ruins of Christian settlements, began a work equally astonishing from the religious and the political point of view. The heathen Picts had marched westward to the sea, destroying the Celtic churches. The pagan English had set up in 547 a monarchy in Northumbria and the Lowlands, threatening alike the Picts, the Irish or 'Scot' settlements along the coast, and the Celts of Strathclyde. Against this world of war Columcille opposed the idea of a peaceful federation

---

[4]Details of two foundations of Columban churches among the Picts have been preserved in the *Book of Deer,* viz., Aberdour in Banffshire, and Deer in the district of Buchan.

of peoples in the bond of Christian piety. He converted the king of the Picts at Inverness in 565, and spread Irish monasteries from Strathspey to the Dee, and from the Dee to the Tay. On the western shores about Cantyre he restored the Scot settlement from Ireland which was later to give its name to Scotland, and consecrated as king the Irish Aidan, ancestor of the kings of Scotland and England. He established friendship with the Britons of Strathclyde. From his cell at Iona he dominated the new federation of Picts and Britons and Irish on both sides of the sea—the greatest missionary that Ireland ever sent out to proclaim the gathering of peoples in free association through the power of human brotherhood, learning, and religion.

"For thirty-four years Columcille ruled as abbot in Iona. .... After his death the Irish monks carried his work over the whole of England. A heathen land lay before them, for the Roman missionaries established in 597 by Augustine in Canterbury, speaking no English and hating 'barbarism', made little progress, and after some reverses were practically confined to Kent. The first cross of the English borderland was set up in 635 by men from Iona on a heather moorland called the Heavenfield, by the ramparts of the Roman Wall. Columban monks made a second Iona at Lindisfarne, with its church of hewn oak thatched with reeds after Irish tradition in sign of poverty and lowliness, and with its famous school of art and learning. They taught the English writing, and gave them the letters which were used among them till the Norman Conquest. Labour and learning went hand in hand. From the king's court nobles came, rejoicing to change the brutalities of war for the plough, the forge-hammer, the winnowing fan: waste places were reclaimed, the ports were crowded with boats, and monasteries gave shelter to travellers. For a hundred years wherever the monks of Iona passed men ran to be signed by their hand and blessed by their voice. Their missionaries wandered on foot over middle England and along the eastern coast and even touched the channel in Sussex. In 662 there was only one bishop in the whole of England who was not of Irish consecration, and this bishop, Agilberct of Wessex, was a Frenchman who had been trained for years in Ireland. The great school of Malmesbury in Wessex was founded by an Irishman, as that of Lindisfarne had been in the north.

"For the first time also Ireland became known to Englishmen. Fleets of ships bore students and pilgrims, who forsook their na-

tive land for the sake of divine studies. The Irish most willingly received them all, supplying to them without charge food and books and teaching, welcoming them in every school from Derry to Lismore, making for them a 'Saxon Quarter' in the old university of Armagh. Under the influence of the Irish teachers the spirit of racial bitterness was checked, and a new intercourse sprang up between English, Picts, Britons, and Irish. For a moment it seemed as though the British islands were to be drawn into one peaceful confederation and communion and a common worship bounded only by the ocean. The peace of Columcille, the fellowship of learning and of piety, rested on the peoples.''[5])

---

[5] Alice Stopford Green, *Irish Nationality*, in *Home University Library*, No. 6, Ch. III, p. 43-8.

TABLE OF MATTERS.*

I. Of the Making of this Life and of the Lineage of Columcille.

1. Of the lowliness of Columcille.
2. Of a word of St. Gregory touching lowliness.
3. Of a word of St. Augustine touching lowliness.
4. Of a word of the Evangelist Matthew touching the imitation of Christ.
5. Of a word of St. Bernard touching the imitation of Christ.
6. Of another word of St. Bernard touching the patience of the martyrs.
7. Of another word of St. Bernard touching the patience of the confessors.
8. Of the sources of this *Life of Columcille.*
9. Of the destruction of the high churches of Columcille by the Danes.
10. Of Manus O'Donnell that let put together this *Life.*
11. And set it forth with his own lips in the manner below.
12. Of his love for Columcille.
13. Of the place and time of this writing.
14. Of the spiritual weapons of Columcille.
15. Manus O'Donnell maketh supplication to Columcille.
16. Of the works of Columcille.
17. Of his poverty.
18. Of his love of God.
19. How he was a companion of Mary in suffering.
20. Manus O'Donnell maketh further supplication to Columcille.
21. Of the noble lineage of Columcille.
22. Of his mother Ethne.
23. Of God's choosing Columcille.

II. Of Prophecies concerning Columcille Made before his Birth.

24. Of a prophecy made by Mochta of Louth.
25. Of a prophecy made by Padraic to Fergus and Conall.
26. Of another prophecy made by Padraic in Domnach Mor of Mag Itha in Tirconnell.

*This table of matters is not in the manuscript. It has been drawn up by the present translators, following the 435 divisions of the original. The division into 36 chapters has been made by the translators.

27. Of another prophecy made by Padraic in Armagh.
28. Of another prophecy made by Padraic when he was nigh death.
29. Of another prophecy made by Padraic at Ess mac n-Eirc on the river Boyle.
30. More of the same prophecy.
31. Another prophecy of Padraic at Assaroe.
32. Of the labors of Padraic and Columcille for the men of Erin.
33. Of a vision of Padraic.
34. Of a prophecy of the holy Martin.
35. Of a prophecy of the holy Brigid.
36. Of the prophecies concerning the burying of Padraic and Brigid and Columcille in one tomb at Dun da Lethglas.
37. Of a prophecy of the holy Dabheooc.
38. Of a prophecy of the holy Caillin.
39. Of a prophecy of the holy Brenainn.
40. Of a prophecy of Bishop Eoghan of Ardstraw.
41. Of a prophecy of Buide mac Bronaigh.
42. Of a prophecy of Finn mac Cumaill.
43. Of a prophecy of Fedlimid Rechtmar, High King of Erin.
44. Of a prophecy of the druids of Conall Gulban.

III. *Of Visions Foretelling the Birth of Columcille and of Marvels before his Birth.*

45. Of a vision that Ethne had.
46. Of another vision that Ethne had.
47. Of a vision that an envious woman had concerning Ethne.
48. Of the intentions of God concerning Columcille.
50. Of a marvel that Columcille did in his mother's womb.
51. Of the flagstone whereon Columcille was born.
52. Of the birth of Columcille at Raith Cno in Gartan and of the Red Stone.

IV. *Of Marvels Following his Birth and of the Childhood of Columcille.*

53. Of his baptism and of the name Crimthann and how he gat the name Columcille.
54. Of the flagstone whereon he was baptized.
55. Of the first walk of Columcille.
56. Of the pilgrimage to the First Walk of Columcille.
57. Of the trout that Columcille restored to life.

58. Of the Flagstone of Chastity.
59. Of the first alphabet of Columcille.
60. Of the light that surrounded him whilst he slept.
61. How Columcille did sing the *Misericordia Domini* for his foster-father Cruithnecan in the church of the holy bishop Brugach mac n-Degadh in Raith Enaigh in Tir Enna.
62. How Columcille restored his foster-father to life.
63. Of the virtues of Columcille in his childhood.
64. How his guardian angel Axal gave counsel to Columcille and blessed him.
65. Of another advision that Columcille had of the angel Axal.
66. Of the three maidens that appeared to Columcille and how he turned upon them a wry visage.
67. How Columcille did choose for himself exile and a death through fasting.

V. Of the Studies of Columcille.

68. How Columcille went to study albeit through the graces of the Holy Spirit he was already filled with knowledge.
69. How Columcille changed the water into wine.
70. How Columcille left Master Finnen and went to Master German [Gemman] to follow his studies, and how he cursed the evil man that slew the maiden.
71. How Columcille builded his bothy at the church door in obedience to Master Finnen of Clonard. And of the grinding of the meal.
72. How Brenainn of Birr defended Columcille against the bishop that had put a ban upon him.
73. How whilst he was studying with Mobi Clairenech he moved the bothies by miracle to the east side of the stream.
74. Of a quarrel betwixt Columcille and Ciaran the son of the Wright.
75. Of Cainnech, Comgall, and Columcille and of what they would have the church filled withal. And of the yellow plague that Columcille forbade to cross the stream.
76. How Columcille received priestly orders at the hands of a holy bishop that was ploughing in Cluain Foda in Meath and of the miracles that Columcille did. And of a prophecy he made.

VI. Of the Labors of Columcille in Derry and Tirconnell.

77. How Columcille received the girdle of Mobi and was given the town of Derry by Aed mac Ainmirech. And how he burned it and how he made the hymn *Noli Pater indulgere* to protect the grove.

78. How the Lord chid Columcille because he fed but an hundred of poor men each day. And how Columcille set forth the nature of the beast yclept Rochuaidh.
79. How Columcille gave compensation to the churl for the wood that he had cut down.
80. How God saved Columcille from the satire of the poets.
81. How Columcille by the grace of God furnished the poets with wine and of the Barrow of the Banquet.
82. Of the death of Maelcabha and how Columcille restored him to life and of the rewards Maelcabha gave to him and to his successors.
83. Of the fish from Loch Foyle that Columcille was wont to give to his guests.
84. Of the miracle of the loaves and fishes in Derry.
85. Of the gambler and the poor man.
86. Of Columcille's Well.
87. Of Mongan mac Fiachna and his learning and how Columcille revealed to him Hell and Heaven.
88. Of a vision that Columcille had of Pope Gregory of the Golden Lips.
89. Of the oratory called Dubhreigles and the grove fast beside it.
90. Of a prophecy that Columcille made touching Bun Sentuinde and of the palace that might not be built to the end.
91. Of the wright that was drowned in the mill pond at Raphoe, and how Columcille restored him.
92. How Columcille made the young lad Fergna a master smith.
93. How Fedlimid the father of Columcille divided his land among his brothers, and how Columcille was given tithes of the land. And of the prophecies that Columcille made.
94. How Columcille restored to life the daughter of Aed mac Ainmirech, and how he told him which of the kings of Erin had been given Heaven. And of the cowl that Columcille gave to Aed.
95. Of a prophecy that Columcille made touching the lad Domnall son of Aed.

VII. *Of the Labors of Columcille in Meath.*

96. Of the church that Columcille built at Durrow. And of the sword of Colman Mor that Columcille blessed in such wise that the owner thereof might not die.
97. How Columcille blessed the apple tree in Durrow that had borne bitter apples.
98. How Diarmaid mac Cerbhaill King of Erin gave Kells to Columcille because he had been kept waiting without the door of the palace, and how Columcille gave a cowl to Aed Slaine son of Diarmaid

and made prophecies touching his death and touching the birth of the youths of Cill Scire.

VIII. Of the Journeys of Columcille in Sundry Places to Sow the Faith and in Especial of his Labors in Leinster.

99. Of churches that Columcille builded and of the successors that he left therein. And how Columcille revealed the place where Buide mac Bronaig was interred.
100. How Finnen the teacher of Columcille saw angels in his company and of Columcille's journey to Britain to sow the Faith.
101. How Columcille found the book of Gospels in the tomb of Martin at Tours.
102. Of the fiery column that was seen above the head of Columcille at Swords.
103. Of Columcille's blessing of Swords.
104. Of a prophecy that Columcille understood from the waves.
105. Of an ensaumple that Columcille gave of God's destroying much folk by reason of the sin of one.
106. Of a prophecy that Columcille made of Iarnan of Cluain Deochrach when he was a lad.
107. Of a blessed thought that Brigid had going over the Plain of Liffey.
108. Of certain journeys that Columcille made in Leinster.

IX. Of the Labors of Columcille in Tirconnell and in Tory Island.

109. Of the Flagstone of the Sorrows and how Columcille caused a certain man to forget his grief.
110. Of the youth that was running toward the sod of his death.
111. How Columcille cast his staff toward Tory and how he spread his mantle over the island and how he caused the venomous hound to die and how Oilill gave him the whole island at the last.
112. Of the Hand-Stone that was a pillow for Columcille the while he was in Tory.
113. Of the pilgrimage of the children of the King of India to Columcille in Tory.
114. Of the Waterfall of Fianan and how Columcille saved Fianan from great thirst.
115. Of the fishes that Columcille changed to stone by reason of a lie that the fishers of Bun Linded told.
116. How Ronan mac Luig[d]ech for his obedience to Columcille was

promised a son Daluch that should have lordship over the race of Conall Gulban.

117. Of a prophecy that Columcille made at Tobar Eithne at Cell mic Nenain touching Daluch and touching the waters of that well.

X. *Of Sundry Miracles and Prophecies of Columcille in Erin and of Certain Visions.*

118. Of the three pets that Columcille had; the cat, the wren, and the fly. And of a prophecy that Columcille made, likening them to the men of Erin.
119. How Columcille bound the Adversary to appear to the scholar in his own likeness, and thus saved him from fleshly sin.
120. Of the vision that Columcille related to Baithin touching the sore strait that Padraic would be in for the sake of the men of Erin on Doomsday.
121. Of a prophecy that Columcille made touching Mochuda of Rathan and the church he should build and touching his resurrection.
122. Of the ill guesting that Columcille had with Molaise of Devenish and of the miracle that Columcille did next day.
123. Of the advision that Baithin had of the three chairs afore the Lord. And in especial of Columcille's chair that was of crystal.
124. Of the answer that Columcille gave to Annadh mac Duibh Innse that inquired of him concerning the length of his life days.
125. Of how Columcille excused him to others that asked him this question.
126. Of a prophecy that Columcille made touching Tara and touching Cruachu and Aillend and Emain Macha.
127. Of a prophecy that Columcille made concerning the driving out of the foreigners from Erin.
128. How Columcille prophesied that Domnall mac Aeda and the tribe of Conall should violate the sanctuary of Termon Cumainig in Tir Eogain, and they should be stricken with distemper. And of the Well of the Conalls.
129. Of Bec mac De the druid and of the two false prophecies that Columcille foretold he should make ere his death.
130. Of the reward that Columcille gave to Ciaran son of the Wright that copied for him the half of a book of the Gospels.
131. Of a skull that was brought to Columcille at the river Boyne, and how it was revealed to him that it was the skull of Cormac mac Airt that was ancestor to Columcille, and how Columcille obtained for him the Kingdom of God.

132. How the land of Senglend Columcille was yielded to Columcille from the demons of the fog, and how he changed to fish the demons that dwelled therein. And of the sanctuary that Columcille ordained there. And of Columcille's bell Dub Duaibsech and of the stone the angel gave him.

XI. Of the Virtue of Columcille's Blessing and of his Curse.

133. Of the blessing that Columcille laid upon the south side of Assaroe, that Padraic had cursed, and upon the north side, that Padraic in his honor had blessed but partly. And of the staff of Barrann mac Muredhaigh that was returned to him by a miracle of Columcille, and of the Trough of Barrann.
134. How Columcille blessed the Ess and bound the rocks of the northern side to abase them that the fish might pass.
135. How God likened Columcille to Moses that did strike water from the rock.
136. Of blessings of Columcille whereby certain kings did get sovereignty in Erin.
137. How Finnachta mac Dunadha through the blessing of Columcille gat the sovereignty of Erin.
138. Of the blessing and counsel that Columcille gave to Guaire mac Colmain whereby he that was erstwhile churlish became one of the three men of most largesse in Erin.
139. Of the curse that Columcille laid on Diarmaid mac Cerbaill that gave wrong judgment touching the transcript of Finnen's book. And how Diarmaid lost the sovereignty thereafter.
140. Of the riches that An Sersenach gat through the blessing of Columcille.

XII. Of the Miracles and Prophecies of Columcille and of his revealing of Secret Things.

141. Of Naail son of Aonghus mac Nadfraich and of the miracle of the fishes and the flour.
142. Of a prophecy that Columcille made touching Domnall mac Aeda and touching a well that was nigh Druim Ceat.
143. Of other miracles that Columcille did in Druim Ceat.
144. Of a feast that Bishop Conall made for Columcille and how Columcille saved Colman mac Aeda and another from their secret sins.
145. How Columcille discovered the secret sin of a priest that was saying the mass in the monastery of Trefoid.

146. Of the casket that Connla the Craftsman began to fashion for Padraic, and how after many years Columcille let finish that casket by the same craftsman albeit he had been long in his grave. And of Tice of Ath Lunga that must needs give his thumb to be in that shrine of Columcille. And of the Ford of the Thumb and MacGilligan's Height.
147. Of a prophecy that Columcille made concerning a poet.
148. How it was revealed to Columcille that the priest that visited him was a bishop.
149. How Columcille prevailed on God to save the soul of the King of Erin for that he had given him an alms albeit malgre his head.

XIII. *Of the Labors of Columcille in the West of Erin and of Sundry Matters.*

150. Of three gifts that Columcille besought of God.
151. Of tidings that Columcille gave to Baithin and Brugach and Ternog touching the end of the world.
152. Of the places that Columcille blessed in the region of Brefny and of his successor in Ess mac n-Eirc on the Boyle.
153. Of a church that Columcille builded in Imlech Foda in Corann and of his successor there.
154. Of the church that Columcille builded in Druim na Macraidhe in the land of Ailill, and of the Glassan.
155. Of the ancient tomb at Ara and how Columcille revealed that the abbot of Jerusalem was buried there.
156. How Columcille begged Enna to give him a portion of the island of Ara. And of the Field of the Hood. And how Enna denied him. And of a prophecy that Columcille made.
157. How by the counsel of Columcille the bards gat from Fergus mac Roich the tale of the Cattle Raid of Cualnge, albeit he had been many years already in his tomb. And of the departing of the bards.
158. Of the fair body of Cianan that decayed not, and how Cianan stretched forth his hand from the tomb in welcome to Columcille.
159. Of the reasons why Columcille should be honored on a Thursday above every other day.
160. Of a prophecy that the lad Fintan made of the coming of Columcille to the house of his fosterer.
161. Of a prophecy that Columcille made concerning Munda mac Tulchain when he was a lad.
162. Of the journey of Columcille around Erin.

163. Of the seat in Glen Fanad where Columcille forgat his books and of Columcille's Well.
164. Of the Well of the Thorn.
165. Of the cow called Dubh na Cat and how she was found by her track in the stones as plain as her track in the earth and of Tobur na Duibhe.
166. Of the relics of Padraic that Columcille let dig up and how he gave the Bell of the Testament to Armagh and the goblet to Dun da Lethglas and the Angel's Gospel to Columcille.

XIV. Of the Exile of Columcille from Erin.

167. Of Columcille's banishment to Alba.
168. Of the book of Finnen, and of Columcille's transcript, and of the judgment of Diarmaid King of Erin and how the King bade slay the son of the King of Connacht malgre the safeguard of Columcille.
169. How Columcille sware to avenge the unjust judgment and of the death of the son of the King of Connacht.
170. How Columcille repaired him in safety to Monasterboice.
171. How Columcille made a lay what time he was alone on Sliabh Breagh.
172. How the clans of Conall and Eoghan made ready to do battle in behalf of Columcille at Cuil Dremne in Connacht and how Columcille did fast on God to obtain the victory.
173. Of the names of the kings of the clans of Conall and Eoghan.
174. How Michael the Archangel came from God to declare to Columcille that He would give him the victory but Columcille must depart beyond the seas and live forever in exile.
175. Of the cross vigil of Columcille and of Michael the Archangel.
176. Of the cross vigil of Finnen and of the routing of the King of Erin.
177. How after the battle Columcille restored the realm of Erin to Diarmaid and would not take it for himself.
178. Of the book hight the "Battler" and of the marvels relating thereto.
179. Of Columcille's farewell to his kinsmen.
180. How the saints of Erin murmured against Columcille and how Columcille sought counsel of Molaise, and how Molaise confirmed the advice of the angel.
181. How Columcille lamented that Erin should lose by his exile.

182. Of the ill welcome that Columcille gat from Mudan, and of his converse with Cruimther Fraech and of the miracle he did in his name.
183. How Columcille was loth to leave Derry.
184. Of the quatrain that Columcille made concerning the angels in Derry.
185. Of the yew tree in front of the Black Church in Derry.
186. Of Columcille's farewell to Derry.
187. Of the curse Columcille laid on him with the forked club that would have hastened his going from Erin.
188. Of the grief of the clan of Conall and the clan of Eoghan when Columcille departed from Loch Foyle.
189. Further of Columcille's farewell to his kinsmen.
190. How Odran reproved Columcille for his great sorrow.
191. Of the wailing of the men of Derry at the departing of Columcille.
192. Of the grief of the birds of Loch Foyle at his departing.
193. Of the beast that rose out of the sea and threatened the ship of Columcille.
194. How Columcille promised Heaven to him that would go to the beast in behalf of all.
195. Of him that went into the gullet of the beast.
196. Of the grief of Columcille's followers for the death of that youth and how Columcille restored him to life.
197. How when they had passed through Loch Foyle they landed in Dal Riada in Ulidia and how Columcille embraced a little child that was Colman mac Coimgellain and how he prophesied concerning him.
198. Of the number of Columcille's followers that left Erin.
199. Of the age of Columcille when he left Erin and of the number of the years of his exile in Alba.
200. Of the quatrains that Columcille made on leaving Erin.
201. Of his putting out on the deep sea.

XV. *Of the Labors of Columcille in Iona.*

202. Of their landing in Iona.
203. Of Columcille's imitation of Jesu that did also go into exile.
204. How Columcille drave out the druids that he found already in the island.
205. How Columcille offered to bestow Heaven on him that should consent to die and be buried beneath the clay of that island.
206. How Odran obtained that gift and another beside.
207. Of the churches and crosses that Columcille builded on that island and of the prophecy he made concerning it.

208. Of the order of monks he founded there.
209. Of the man that was slain by a serpent on fleeing from the words of Columcille and how Columcille restored him.
210. Of the Saxon that did hurl a javelin at one of the monks of Columcille and of the curse of Columcille.
211. Of the pilgrim that did kiss Columcille and upset his ink-horn and of the quatrains that Columcille made.
212. How Columcille gave the old warrior the ox that he was boiling for the reapers and how the bones thereof took on again flesh at the command of Columcille.
213. How Columcille sent an angel to Cainnech, bearing his staff that he had left, and the shirt of Columcille.
214. How the lepers asked alms of Columcille, and how he cleansed them of their leprosy.

XVI. Of Columcille and Pope Gregory of Rome.

215. Of the wooden cross that angels let down upon the altar of Gregory the Pope of Rome and how Gregory sent it to Columcille and how it is the chief relic of Columcille in Tory in the north of Erin.
216. How Columcille made the hymn called the *Altus* and how the clerics added thereto when they sang it before Pope Gregory at Rome and of the vision that Pope Gregory had.
217. Of the two clerics that had promised every day to rehearse the *Altus*.
218. Of the visit that Columcille made to Pope Gregory at Rome.
219. How Brandubh King of Laigin refused to make peace at the counsel of the three holy men that Columcille had appointed and how he was slain and how Columcille did save his soul from the demons. And of the brooch that Pope Gregory left to Columcille.

XVII. More of the Labors of Columcille in Iona.

220. How Columcille would have rescued from the demons the soul of Bishop Eoghan of Ardstraw but he must answer the call to nones.
221. Of Longarad of Kilgarrow and of the curse that Columcille laid upon his books.
222. How Columcille settled the dispute between the two sons of Lugaid Red Hand.
223. How a certain monk fell into fleshly sin and after into despair and of the penance that Columcille gave him.
224. Of the woman that would have tempted Columcille to have ado with her fleshly.

225. How Finnen and Irial gained certain graces of God by invoking the name of Columcille.
226. How Columcille beheld the soul of a woman borne to Heaven and a year thereafter interceding with God for her husband.
227. How Columcille knew the death of holy Brenainn albeit none had come to him with tidings.
228. How Columcille foreknew the death of Bishop Colman in like manner.
229. Of a vision Columcille had on the Hillock of Angels and how he charged the monk that had knowledge thereof to tell it to none.
230. Of the foreknowledge that Columcille had of the coming of holy Cainnech.
231. How Columcille foretold that holy Colman should come safe from the tempest.
232. Of two that asked Columcille concerning their sons.
233. How Columcille saved the monk Bera from a monster of the sea.
234. How Baithin was saved from a beast of the sea according to the prophecy of Columcille.
235. Of the prophecy that Columcille made of the sin that was done by an Irish man.
236. How Columcille warned Lughaidh not to bring that man to land and how he held converse with him in the port and of the prophecy he made concerning him.
237. Of the vision that Columcille related to Lughaidh concerning flame and fire in Italy.
238. Of another prophecy that Columcille related to Lughaidh concerning Colman Cu and Ronan.
239. Of a reaver that would have taken seals belonging to the brethren and of a prophecy Columcille made concerning him.
240. How the druids of Aedan sought to curse Columcille.
241. How Aedan sought to try the chastity of Columcille and made his daughter Coinchend to tempt him.
242. Of the shears wherewith Aedan sought to tempt Columcille.
243. How the angel charged Columcille to crown Aedan and how he would not until the angel scourged him.
244. How the prayers of Columcille won the battle for Aedan.
245. Of the prophecy that Columcille made concerning the sons of Aedan and in especial of Eochaidh.
246. How Fiachaidh came as a pilgrim to Columcille in Iona and how he gat pardon for his sins.
247. How Columcille foretold the death of Cailtean.
248. Of Aed mac Bric and how he took an old sinner with him to Heaven and how this was revealed to Columcille.

249. How Columcille foretold to Colman Eala that Findtan mac Gabrein should be his confessor.

XVIII. Of Columcille and Mochonda.

250. How Mochonda joined him to the fellowship of Columcille.
251. Of the miracle whereby Mochonda had light to make a transcript for Columcille.
252. How Columcille sent Mochonda into the province of Pictora.
253. How Mochonda destroyed a poisonous beast.
254. Of the works of Mochonda in Pictora.
255. How Columcille journeyed with Mochonda to Rome and how Pope Gregory gave him a new name.
256. How Columcille discovered the place where the holy Martin was buried and how he left Mochonda to be bishop at Tours.
257. Of the death of Mochonda.

XIX. More of the Miracles and Prophecies of Columcille in Iona.

258. Of the pilgrims that came to Columcille and how he made them monks.
259. Of the old man that came to Iona to be blessed by Columcille.
260. How Columcille blessed the kitchen knife and how thereafter naught might redden thereon.
261. How the prayers of Columcille saved his servant Diarmaid from death.
262. Of a prophecy of Columcille that he should never again behold his uncle in life.
263. How Columcille revealed unto one that came to him that his house had been destroyed.
264. Of a prophecy of Columcille to Guaire that what should cause his death was in his own company.
265. Of the crane that made a pilgrimage from Erin to Columcille in Iona and of the prophecy that Columcille made.
266. How it was revealed to Columcille that a sore sickness lay on a certain province in Erin and how he banished it therefrom.
267. How it was revealed to Columcille that a bone was broken in a certain holy woman in Clochur and how he sent one of the brethren to heal her.
268. How Columcille healed two women of a distemper of the eyes.
269. How water sprang from the rock at the bidding of Columcille and of the prophecy he made concerning the child that he baptized.

270. Of the well of evil nature that Columcille sanctified and of the healing virtues that he gave it.

XX. Of Columcille and Cormac.

271. How Columcille foretold that Cormac should die in Erin. And of an evil monk that was in Cormac's company.
272. How the danger of Cormac was revealed to Columcille and how he charged the King of the Picts to protect him.
273. How Columcille prophesied that Cormac should return from seeking the Island of the Saints.
274. Of the monsters that Cormac saw on his journey and how he was saved therefrom by Columcille.
275. How Cormac besought Columcille to suffer him to remain with him in Alba and of the love Columcille had for Erin and for the clans of Conall and Eogan.
276. How Columcille charged Cormac to go again to Erin.
277. How Cormac went again on a pilgrimage on the sea and how he returned again to Iona. And of the relic that Cormac gat of Columcille.

XXI. Of Columcille's Love for Erin and of the Miracles he Did for the Folk There.

278. Of the love that Columcille had for the clan of Conall and the clan of Eogan and of his love for Erin.
279. Of the praise that Columcille gave to the monasteries of Erin and in especial to Derry and to Kells.
280. How through the prayer of Columcille the mind of Laisren was enlumined and he no longer drave the brethren to toil and sore labor.
281. How Columcille obtained from God to still the tempest that was on the sea.
282. How another time Columcille bade the crew trust to holy Cainnech to save them from the sea and how Cainnech ran to the church with half his shoes.
283. How Columcille obtained favoring winds for twain that travelled in contrary wise.

XXII. More of the Miracles of Columcille in Iona.

284. How the Devil was hiding in the bottom of a vessel so that the milk was spilled when Columcille blessed it.
285. How Columcille confounded the druids that had drawn blood from an ox in semblance of milk.
286. How Columcille blessed the five cows of Colman.
287. How Columcille cursed the reaver that had taken the gear of Colman and how he was drowned.

XXIII. Of the Miracles of Columcille in Pictora.

288. How Columcille foretold that a certain rich man should die ere he should eat of the swine he was fattening.
289. Of a monster that would have swallowed one of the brethren and how at the command of Columcille the beast departed softly.
290. How Columcille raised up a youth from the dead.
291. How Columcille brought King Bruide to the Faith.
292. How the druid that would not give up the bondwoman at the command of Columcille was stricken with a distemper and how he was healed thereof by a stone that Columcille had blessed.
293. How by means of that stone many others were healed.
294. Of the malice that the druid sought to work against Columcille.
295. Of a like hap that befell Bishop German. And how God gave those holy men the victory over the druids.

XXIV. Of the Miracles of Columcille in Alba.

296. How Columcille entered the monastery of Da Sruth without keys.
297. Of a poor man to whom Columcille gave a stake whereon the wild beasts did impale them.
298. How through the prayers of Columcille the hatred that a certain woman bore her husband was changed to love.
299. How without nails the wheels of the chariot held together wherein Columcille was borne.
300. How through the prayer of Columcille the angels vanquished the devils that were contending for the soul of a certain monk called Brito.
301. How a wild boar that would have come near Columcille was destroyed through his prayer.
302. How the fishers that cast their net in honor of Columcille did get a great fish.

303. How by Columcille a monk was cured of bleeding of the nose.
304. How Columcille beheld borne to Heaven the soul of an Irish cleric hight Diarmaid.

XXV. *Of Visions and Miracles of Columcille in Iona and in Divers Places.*

305. How Columcille drave the devils from the isle of Etica to the monastery of Baithin in the plain of Lunge.
306. How Columcille comforted a monk hight Colman.
307. How Columcille gave aid to the souls of the monks of Comgall.
308. How at the stream called Nisa in Britain Columcille did save the soul of a good man that had not the Faith.
309. How Columcille sent an angel from Iona to save a man that was falling from a housetop in Durrow in Erin.
310. How Cainnech and Comgall and Brenainn and Cormac beheld a fiery cloud resting upon Columcille the while he said the mass.
311. Of the light that for three days filled the island of Imba where Columcille was receiving knowledge of the secrets of God.
312. How Fergna beheld a great brightness that followed Columcille in the night.
313. How Colca beheld a great light and knew not whence it came.
314. How against the command of Columcille Berchan had sight of the great light and how Columcille foretold that he should do ill deeds but be saved in the end.

XXVI. *Of Columcille's Going to Erin and of the Assembly of Druim Ceat.*

315. How Columcille went to the Assembly of Druim Ceat with the King of Alba.
316. Of the reasons wherefore Columcille went to the Assembly of Druim Ceat.
317. How Columcille went to the Assembly to defend the poets that had satirized Aed.
318. How Columcille went to the Assembly to make peace concerning Dal Riada.
319. How Columcille went to the Assembly to release Scannlan Mor son of Cenn-faeladh and of Scannlan's sore plight.
320. How Columcille went again to Erin yet brake not his oath.
321. Of the beast on the sea and of Senuch the old smith that quelled her by the prayer of Columcille and by the iron mass that was in his tongs.

322. How Columcille's boat after passing the sea sailed the river and the dry land to Druim Ceat. And of the Field of the Coracle.
323. Of the number of clerics that were in the Assembly.
324. How Conall son of Aed did incite the rabble to stone Columcille.
325. How Columcille learned that it was Conall that showed him that dishonor.
326. How Columcille cursed Conall and of the name Conall of the Bells.
327. How Domnall son of Aed rose up and did honor to Columcille and of the rewards that Columcille gave him.
328. Of the change that blessing wrought in Domnall.
329. How the Queen called Columcille a crane-cleric and of the curse that Columcille laid on her therefor.
330. How Columcille laid a like punishment upon the Queen's handmaid.
331. How Columcille went with Domnall to King Aed and how God protected them and how Aed promised to do the will of Columcille.

XXVII. *Of Columcille and the Poets of Erin.*

332. Of the judgment that Columcille gave concerning the keeping of the poets of Erin and of his praise of poesy.
333. How the poets remained and how Columcille took the poison from poesy and of the laws he made concerning the poets.
334. How the poets praised Columcille and how Columcille sinned by pride.
335. Of the smoke that rose up from the head of Columcille and of the demons that were dispersed and of the releasing of a rich priest of Tirconnell.
336. How Columcille told Dallan Forgaill not to praise him until his death and of the reward that Columcille gave Dallan for the praise that he should make concerning him.
337. Of the reward that Columcille promised to them that should commit to mind the poem of Dallan in praise of Columcille.
338. Of the sign that Columcille promised to Dallan that he should know the hour of Columcille's death.
339. How the promise of Columcille was fulfilled.

XXVIII. Of Other Miracles of Columcille at the Assembly of Druim Ceat.

340. How at the word of Columcille the earth ceased to withdraw beneath the feet of Baithin the Tall that desired to be mean of stature and uncomely to look upon.
341. How Cainnech the Short desired to be tall and how through the marvels of God and of Columcille and of himself he obtained his desire.

XXIX. Of Columcille and Dal Riada.

342. How Columcille made peace between the men of Alba and the men of Erin concerning Dal Riada.
343. How Columcille said it was not himself should give the judgment concerning Dal Riada but Colman mac Coimgellain.
344. Of the judgment that Colman gave.

XXX. Of Columcille and Scannlan.

345. Of the prophecy that Columcille made touching Scannlan Mor that was in bondage with the King of Erin.
346. How an angel brought Scannlan forth from his bondage.
347. Of a conversation between Scannlan and Columcille.
348. How Columcille blessed Scannlan and how he gave him his staff and bade him go home without fear. And of a prophecy that Columcille made.
349. How the words of Columcille were fulfilled.
350. Of all that Columcille did in the Assembly at Druim Ceat.

XXXI. Of Columcille's Returning to Iona and of the Voyage of Columcille's Clerics.

351. Of Columcille's returning to Iona.
352. How Columcille saw upon the water the bones of Brecan son of Maine that had been drowned there and how he obtained Heaven for him.
353. How the Devil in semblance of a woman with a child appeared to the brethren when Columcille was in a death swoon and declared that the child was the child of Columcille. And how Columcille rose up and rebuked her.

354. Of the prophecy that Columcille made to Suibhne touching his aiding Congall to carry foreigners to Erin and how Suibhne heeded not the words of Columcille and of the madness of Suibhne.
355. How the Fir Roiss and Mugdcrn Maighen killed Fiachra son of Domnall for the hardships he had put upon them. And how his brother Donnchad would have avenged him and of the judgment that Columcille gave. And of the two clerics of Columcille that brought that judgment and how afterwards they made a pilgrimage on the sea and came to strange islands:
the Isle of the River of Milk
the Isle of the Giant Salmon
the Isle of the Golden Leaf
the Isle of the Cat-heads
the Isle of the Dog-heads
the Isle of the Swine-heads
the Isle of Elijah and Enoch
the Isle of the Golden Cowl
and how they returned to Iona.

XXXII. *Of the Last Days of Columcille.*

356. How Columcille would have naught but broth of nettles and how Diarmaid put butter in the broth.
357. How Columcille prevailed on God to release him from his exile and how the prayers of holy men detained him yet four years.
358. How Columcille solaced the brethren that were in grief by reason of his departing from them and how he took the venom from the serpents that were in the island.
359. Of a prophecy that Columcille made touching an angel that should bear away a treasure that was in the monastery. And how that treasure was Columcille himself.
360. How Columcille blessed the ricks and how he prophesied of his own death.
361. How Columcille prophesied that he should die on the midnight of a Saturday.
362. Of the white nag that had foreknowledge of the death of Columcille.

XXXIII. Of the Death of Columcille and of his Burial.

363. Of the psalter that Columcille left for Baithin to finish and of Columcille's last words.
364. Of his death and of the quaking of Erin and Alba.
365. Of the signification of this miracle.
366. Of the loss that the death of Columcille was to the world and the Church.
367. How Fergna beheld the soul of Columcille being borne to Heaven.
368. How Maedog beheld the soul of Columcille being received into Heaven.
369. How Iarnan in like wise beheld a fiery pillar ascending to Heaven.
370. Of the burial of Columcille in Iona.
371. How the body of Columcille was borne to Dun da Lethglas.
372. Of the prophecies of Padraic and of Brigid that Columcille should be buried with them in Dun da Lethglas.
373. Of the prophecy of Columcille touching the same matter.
374. Of the testimony of Dallan Forgaill concerning the same.
375. Of the great storm that Columcille prophesied should be on Iona the while he lay unburied.
376. Of the honor that God showed to Columcille.

XXXIV. A Comparison of Columcille with Other Holy Men.

377. Of the reasons for the relating of the comparisons below.
378. How Columcille was like unto the patriarch Abraham.
379. How Columcille went beyond the patriarch Abraham in perfection.
380. How Columcille was like unto Moses son of Amram and how he went beyond Moses in perfection.
381. How Columcille was like unto Isaias the prophet.
382. How Columcille's prophecies excelled those of Isaias.
383. How Columcille was greater than a prophet and how he was like unto John the Baptist.
384. Of the clearness of the prophecies of Columcille.
385. How Columcille was like unto Solomon son of David.
386. How Columcille was like unto John of the Bosom.
387. How he went beyond John of the Bosom.
388. Of the virginity of Columcille.
389. How Columcille was like unto Paul the Apostle and how he went beyond Paul.
390. How Columcille was like unto Stephen the Martyr and how he went beyond Stephen.
391. Of white and of red martyrdom.
392. How Columcille was like unto Jerome the Confessor and how he went beyond Jerome.
393. Of the unworthiness of our praise of Columcille.

XXXV. *Of the Virtues of Columcille.*

394. Of the churches that Columcille built and of the books he wrote.
395. Of Columcille's Rule.
396. Of the dividing of his days.
397. Of the diligence of Columcille.
398. Of other works of Columcille.
399. Of the speech of Columcille.
400. Of his food and drink.
401. Of his standing in water and reciting the psalms.
402. Of Columcille's pillow and of his bed.
403. Of his contempt of the body.
404. Of the track of his ribs.
405. Of his prayer that his visage should not become displeasing to men
406. Of God's answering his prayer.
407. Of the beauty of his body and of his bounty to poets.
408. Wherefore Columcille would not be held by poets in disdain.
409. Of the likeness of his body to Christ's.
410. Of his washing [the feet of] his monks and of his lowliness.
411. Of his turning his back on his mother.
412. Of the two Baithins.
413. Of Baithin son of Brenainn.
414. How the brethren begged Columcille to minish the pains that he visited on his body.
415. Of the answer of Columcille to the brethren.
416. Of Columcille's answer further.
417. Of a parable that Columcille spake.
418. Of the words of Columcille touching gluttony and pride and vainglory.
419. Of the parable that Columcille spake concerning the way to Heaven.
420. More of the same parable.
421. More of the words of Columcille touching the rigor of his piety.
422. Of the softness of Columcille to others and of his hardness to himself.
423. Of the food and drink of Columcille.
424. Of a certain word of Paul the Apostle and of Columcille.
425. Of the largesse of Columcille.
426. Of Axal his good angel and of Demal his bad angel.
427. Of Padraic's good angel Victor.
428. Of the surpassing merit of Columcille.
429. Of the winter birthday and the summer deathday of Columcille.
430. Of the years of Columcille's life and of his death.
431. Of the omissions in this *Life*.

XXXVI. Of Miracles That Columcille Did After His Death.

432. Of the miracles that Columcille wrought after his death.
433. How a leaf from a book that Columcille had writ was preserved by a miracle.
434. Of one that made him shoes of the bark of Columcille's Oak and thereby was stricken with leprosy.
435. Of Mac Taidg son of Toirrdelbach of the Ui Briain that thought to make a pact with the Devil and how he was saved because he had committed to mind the *Praise of Columcille* and how he was made a leper.

The Life of Columcille

BETHA COLUIMB CHILLE.

1. (T)INNSCANTAR BEATHA AN AB[B]*AD* naemtha 7 an uas*al*-athar 7 primfaidh nimhe 7 talman andso, edhon, Colaim cilli m*i*c Fheilimidh. INtí do leig de ar son De gan cheim budh
5 airde ina abdaine manach n-dub do beith aige 'san egl*uis*, 7 cliara Erend 7 Alban 7 iarthair domain ag a togha mar ua*ch*taran orra fein. Et ni beith an dinite sin fein aige *acht* do cosnam luaigi-dhechta.¹) Oir nir b'ail leis in buaidhred *no* an tribloid bis a n-diaidh na n-dineteadh ro-ard do beith eidir se 7 a t*hr*atha *no* a
10 urnaigthe *no* molad De do bidh san do denam do gnathach. Et, fos, anti do leig rigacht Erind de mar in cedna, docum ar togadh go minic e, 7 budh dual do do beith aige o fholaidhecht.

2. IS follas gor thuig Colaim cilli an briathar ata scribtha a tegsa an t-shois*ceil,* am*ail* meabraiges G*ri*doir a n-oifiged na coin-
15 fisoired²) .i. "[ne] nos qui plus ceteris in hoc mundo accepisse a*liqui*d cernimur, ab autore mund*i* gr*avius* inde iudicemur. Cum enim augm*en*tur dona, r*ati*ones eciam crescant donorum" .i. 'Na daine gabass na tindlaicthe ro-arda cuca do taeb an t-shaegail, is trumaide breithemn*us* Dia orra e. Et as se an t-adhbor e: an
20 uair medaighter na tindluicthe, is ecen go medaighter na cundais.'

3. Do thuig se, fos, an briathar adub*air*t Sanct Augustin .i. "Spem quipe omnem seculi reliqueram, non quesiui esse quod sum 7 ab his qui diligu*n*t mundu*m* segreaui me; sed eis qui presunt p*opu*lis non me coequaui" .i. 'Do sgar me re h-ainm*í*an an t-shao-
25 ga*il,* 7 nir togh me beith mar ataim; 7 do eidirdel*aig* me adrum 7 an drong ler b'i*n*main an saog*al,* 7 nir b'ail lim dul a cosmhailes ris na h-ua*ch*taranuib do bidh os cinn na poiplech.'

4. Do gab se an tecusc-sa tug an Tigerna da deisciblíb, amail mebraig[h]es Matha suib*e*scel 'sa seisid caibidil dec .i. "Si quis
30 uult uenire post me, abneget semetips*um* et tollat crucem suam, et

¹See § 76 for its meaning.
²See Roman Breviary, *Comm. Con. Pon., Lectio* VII.

I
OF THE MAKING OF THIS LIFE AND OF THE LINEAGE OF COLUMCILLE

1. Here beginneth the life of the holy abbot and patriarch and chief prophet of Heaven and earth, even Columcille, son of Fedlimid. Albeit the clergy of Erin and Alba and the Western World chose him to be ruler over them, yet he for God's sake put from him any station in the church higher than an abbacy of black monks. And even so much of dignity had he not taken, save to gain merit; for it pleased him not that the cares and anxieties that follow after very high dignities should come between him and his hours and his prayers and his praising God, wherein it was ever his wont to be zealous. And moreover he put away from him the kingship of Erin in like manner, albeit he was oft chosen thereto; and to have it was his right by blood.

2. It is manifest that Columcille did understand the words that be written in the text of the gospel, as Gregory bringeth them to mind in the Office of the Confessors: *Nos qui,* etc.—to wit, "The folk that take unto themselves the very high offices of this world, the heavier will be the judgment of God on them therefor." And the reason thereof is this: as the portions be increased, so must the reckonings be increased also.

3. He understood also the word that St. Augustine said: *Spem,* etc.: "I did part me from the lusts of the world and did not choose to be as I am. And I distinguished between me and the multitude of them that love the world, and desired not to become in the likeness of the rulers that be over the people."

4. And he did take to himself also the teaching the Lord gave to his disciples, as the Evangelist Matthew maketh mention in the six-

sequatur me"³) .i. 'Gebe lenab ail techt am diaidh-si, diultadh se e fein 7 tocbad se a croch fen 7 lenad se mesi.'

5. Do thuig Colaim cilli an briathar adubairt Bernard IN xxii. sermone super cantica: "INcassum proinde quis laborat in aquisscione uirtutum, si alium ab alio putat quam a domino uirtutum" .i. 'As dimhainech subailche d'iarraid a m-bethaidh eli act a m-bethaid rig na subailche.' Oir do threig se beatha an t-saogail ar a smuaintighib do beith go comnaightech a m-beat[h]aidh an Tigerna, 7 ar a beith go sír aga hól ina deochaibh ro-millsi; oir do len se Crisd in a bethaid, o thoil 7 o ghnim 7 o anum glan, 7 o smeroidighib tendtighe a grada do beith in a croidhe go comnaigthech.

6. ET, fos, do thuig se an briathar eli adub(fol. 1a)airt Bernard IN lxi. sermone super cantica .i. "Tolerancia martyríí provenit quod in Christi unleribis tota deuocione uersetur, et iugi meditaconem illis demoretur" .i. 'As o smuaintighib duthrachtacha na mairtirech a crechtaib Crisd tainic a b-faidhide in a martra; 7 ar a med do batar crechta Crisd in a n-anmonnaib, nar mothaighetar na h-íaraind ga snoidhe 7 ag gerradh a corp.'

7. ET adeir Bernard nach íad na mairtirigh amhaín dorinde an foidhide-so act go n-dernatar na confesori hi. Et as follas duinn go n-derna an confisoir uasal .i. Colaim cilli, foidhide 'sa martra shuthain do cuir se ar a corp fen, do reir mar ata scribta a n-deredh an leabhair-si a tuaruscbail a crabaidh fein. Acus ni hedh amain do bidh aige foidhide in a galruib 7 in a triblóidibh, acht do bidh se go luthgairech solasach, 7 doberidh buidhechus mor do Dia ar a son. Acus as se an t-adhbhar é, nach ann fein do bi a anam acht a m-bethaidh in Tigerna, ar a med do cnedhaig sí a croide. Gonadh airi sin nach mothaigedh sé na piana ro-pendaidecha ro-ghruama do cuiredh se ar a corp fen.

8. ET bidh a fhis ag lucht legtha na bethadh-so go n-deachaidh sí a m-bathad ó cein mhair, 7 nach roibe ar fagail di acht bloidh⁴) m-big don lebar do decht Adhamnan naemtha a Laidin, 7 becan eli a n-Gaidilg, ar na dechtadh go ro-cruaid d'fhileduib na n-Gaidel; et, fos, an cuid eli in a scelaibh a fad ó cheli ar fud t-shenlebar Erind. Et as doig lemsa gorub é dob adbar do so: IN uair tancutar danair 7 allmaraidh⁵) do denam gabaltuis ar tus a n-Erinn, do milledar 7 do loiscetar aird-cella Erenn uili, 7 do milletar a scrine 7 a screbtra, 7 rugatar moran do taisib na naem leo da tirthib fen, amail mebraighid senlebair oiris Erenn,

³Matt. xvi, 24.
⁴leg. bloigh.
⁵leg. allmaruigh.

teenth chapter: *Si vult,* etc.: "Whoso would come after me, let him deny himself and take his cross and follow me."

5. Columcille did likewise understand the word that Bernard spake: *IN XXII sermone super cantica.* *"INcassum,* etc.": "It is vain to seek virtue in any life other than the life of the King of Virtues." For he did forsake the life of the world to be ever thinking on the life of the Lord, and to be ever drinking it in passing sweet draughts. For he followed Christ in his life, in will, and in deed, and in purity of soul, and in the glowing coals of love for Him that were ever in his heart.

6. And he took to himself further that other word that Bernard spake *IN lxi. sermone super cantica, "Tolerancia martyrii provenit quod in Christi unleribis tota devocione versetur, et iugi meditacionem illis demoretur"*: "From their earnest thinking on the wounds of Christ came the martyrs' patience in their martyrdom." And so strongly were those wounds in their thoughts that they felt not the irons hacking and cutting their own bodies.

7. And Bernard saith that not the martyrs only had such patience, but the confessors also. And it is manifest to us that the noble confessor, to wit, Columcille, did have patience in the continual martyrdom that he visited upon his body, as is written in the end of this book showing forth his piety. And not patient only was he in his sicknesses and troubles, but merry and glad, and right thankful for them to God. And the reason therefor was this: His soul was not in himself, but in the life of the Lord, and such sore wounds did that deal to his heart, that the passing strong and grim pains of penance that he visited upon his body he felt not at all.

8. And be it known to the folk that read it, that this *Life* was lost a long while since, and naught thereof was to be found save small parts of the book that holy Adamnan made in Latin, and another part in very hard Gaelic made by the poets of the Gael, and still another part in stories scattered wide apart each from other in the ancient books of Erin. And the cause therefor, I deem, is this: The time the Danes and the folk across the sea first came to smite Erin, they destroyed and burned the high churches of all the land; and they destroyed the shrines and the writings, and took with them to their own lands many of the relics of the saints, as the ancient books of the histories of Erin make

7 go hairithe am*ail* mebruiges an lebar dara hainm 'Cog*ad* Gall re Gaidhel*aib*'.

9. ET do loisce*tar* 7 do milletar aird-chella Colaim cilli go sundr*ad*ach; 7 as demhin lim gorab í an uair sin do milletar 7 do loiscetar a leb*air*, 7 do cuaidh a beth*a* a m-bath*ad acht* an began f*ri*th re na scrib*ad* an*d*so sis di.

10. Bidh a fhis ag lucht legtha na beth*ad*-sa gorab é Maghnas, mac Aeda, m*ic* Aeda Ruaid, m*ic* Neill Gairb, m*ic* Toirrdelbaigh an fina hi Domhnaill, do furail an cuid do bi a Laidin don beth*aid*-si do cur a n-Gaidhilc, 7 do furail an chuid do bi go cruaid a n-Gaid*ilc* di do cor a m-buga, in*nus* go m-beith si solus sothuicsena do cach uile.

11. ET do thims*aig*⁶) 7 do tin*o*il an cuid do bi spreite ar fedh shenlebor Erenn di, 7 do decht as a bel fein hí, ar f*a*g*ail* t-shaeth*air* ro-moir uaithe, 7 ar caitheam aimsiri faide ria, og a sduid*ear* cindus do cuirf*ed* se gach en-chuid in a hinad imcubhaid fen amail ata scribtha annso sis.

12. ET ar n-gabail baide 7 brath*airs*i dó rena ard-naem 7 réna combrathair genel*aig* 7 réna patrun gr*ad*hach fen, da raibe se ro-duthrachtach.

13. A caislen Puirt na t*ri* namat,⁷) u*morro*, do dechtagh⁸) in betha-so an tan b*a* shlan da bl*iadain* dec ar .xx. ar cuic .c. ar .m. bl*iadan* don Tigerna.

14. "ET sicut ex inclita pr*o*sapia 7 fulgida genirositate parentum, aliorum*que* predicessorum ei*us*, i*n*situm ei erat a natura, bellicosis armis suos hostes uisibiles in hoc mu*n*do uincere, 7 ip*s*os sup*er*asse, ita sp*irit*ualib*us* armis, uidelicet uigiliis asiduis, crebr*is* or*ati*onibus, *con*tinuis ieiunis, obediencia debita, u*ir*ginali castitate n*ec*n*on* inenarabili lacrimarum efuc*io*ne, suos in*u*ici(biles) hostes superauit 7 optatam *contra* ipsos uictoriam atq*ue* desiderata obtinuit" .i. 'Mar bud dual do*n* nech naemtha-sa dar bh'ail lind lab*air*t, o uaisli 7 o folaid*h*echt 7 o n*er*t laime, a naimte colluide do clai le harmaib cath*aige*, is mar sin do clai se escaraid a anma le harm*aib* spir*id*alta, mar ata, fuirechrus imarcoch 7 urn*ig*the gnath*ach* 7 tr*o*iscthe faide 7 uml*ach*t 7 óghacht 7 a dera do dort*ad*h go menic.'

15. "Sanctus Columba, scola uirtutum, magisterium uite, sanctitatis forma, iusticie norma, uirginitatis speculum, pudicicie titulus, castitatis exemplum, penitencie uia, peccatorum uenia,

---

⁶thims (with a dash over "s") MS.
⁷"Port of the Three Enemies", now Lifford. See Reeves' *Adam.*, p. xxxv.
⁸*leg.* dechtadh.

mention, and in especial the book called *The War of the Foreigners with the Gaels.*

9. And most specially did they burn and destroy the high churches of Columcille; and I am sure it was in that time were burned and destroyed the books concerning him, and that his *Life* was lost save the little thereof that hath been sought out to be set down here.

10. And be it known to the readers of this *Life* that it was Manus o'Donnell son of Aed son of Aed Ruadh son of Niall Garbh son of Toirdelbach of the Wine, that bade put into Gaelic the part of this *Life* that was in Latin, and bade make easy the part thereof that was hard Gaelic, to the end it might be clear and easy of understanding to all.

11. And he collected and assembled the part thereof that was scattered throughout the ancient books of Erin, and he set it forth with his own lips. And passing great labor had he therewith. And much time did he give thereto, conning how he might put each part thereof in its own fitting place as it is writ here below.

12. And having conceived the affection and the love of a brother for his high saint and kinsman by lineage and his dear patron that he was bounden to in steadfast devotion,

13. In the castle of Port Na Tri Namat in sooth this *Life* was put together in the year that twelve and a score and fifteen hundred years were fulfilled from the birth of our Lord.

14. *Et sicut,* etc., i.e.: And as it had been fitting for the holy man of the which we are to speak, by virtue of his noble breeding and blood and his strength of hand, to destroy his carnal foes with the arms of battle, so did he destroy the enemy of his soul with spiritual weapons, to wit, great vigils, continual prayer, long fasting, humility, virginity, and shedding of tears right oft.

15. *Sanctus Columba,* etc., which is to say: Holy Colum, School of Virtues, Discipline of Life, Image of Holiness, Rule of Justice, Mirror

fidei disciplina'' .i. 'Colaim naemtha, scol na subhalt*ig*e, 7 maighis-
*dre*cht na beth*adh*, 7 foirm na naemthachta, 7 riag*ail* na cora, 7
speclair na hogh (*fol.* 1b) achta, 7 tital na nairi, 7 esimlair na
ge[n]mnaidhechta, 7 slighe na haithrige, 7 loghad na pecad, 7 te-
5   cosc an credimh.'
    16. Da derbad go raibe an forbtighect-sa ag C*ol*aim c*illi*, ata
scribtha air nach tainic roime *no* 'na diaid, en-duine as mo dorinde dedail do Dia ar in cinedh *n*daenna⁹) ina e, ag silad 7 ag
senmoir breithri De doib, ga tarraing docum creidme.
10 17. Ut d*ixit* Bonauentura, ar ngabail tr*u*aige 7 compaisi do
bo*ch*t*a*ine 7 do doghraing Crisd, ar n-impod on Eigheibht do: ''O
p̣uer egregie 7 delicate, rex celi 7 terre, quantum laborasti p*ro*
nobis, 7 quam cito hoc cepisti.'' .R. 'O a m*a*caimh mín ro-uasail, 7
a ri nimhe 7 talm*an*, ca med *do* saeth*ar* dorindis ar ar so*n*-ne, 7
15 a mocha do tindscnais e.' Gonadh airi sin adub*ai*rt an faid, ag
lab*ai*rt a persain Crisd .i. ''Pauper sum ego et in laboribus a
iuuentute mea (p*ro*p*ter* genus humanum)''¹⁰) .i. 'Ataim a m'oíge
a m-bochtaine 7 a n-ilrug*ud* gacha saethair ar son an c*i*n*i*d
daenna.' Is demhin gor thuic Col*aim cilli* an briath*ar*-sa .i. 'Do
20 bi se a m-bochtaine 7 a n-imad saethair in a oige ar son De.'
    18. ET tainic an briathar adub*ai*rt Bonauentura, ag la-
b*ai*rt¹¹) do so tuas do .i. ''O d*omi*ne teips*u*m odio habuistí amore
nostro.'' 'O a Tigerna, tucabair fuath d*i*b fein ar ar ngr*a*d-ne.'
C*o*n*a*d *a*ml*aid* sin t*u*c Colaim cilli fuath dó fein ar gr*a*d De.
25 18. Cuirfidh a betha fen a ceill duinn gor tuic Colaim cilli
an focal adub*ai*rt an t-apst*al*, ag labhairt do doláss Muiri 7 na
m-b*an* ro-naemtha eli do bí faría a n-aimsir na paísi:¹²) ''Socíí
si pacionum fuerim*us*, erimus [et] solacionum'' .i. 'Da m-bem mar
compánachuib compaisi ag Muiri a n-aimsir na paisi, bíam in ar
30 companach*aib* comsholais aice a ngloir flaithesa De.'
    20. O nach dingbala mesi d'fhag*ail* m'achuinge o Dia, guidh-
im thusa, a Colaim cilli, lab*ai*rt go muindterdha ris 7 gr*a*sa d'fha-
g*ail* damh fen uadha, in*nu*s go crichnuiginn go foirfe an saethar-so
dob ail lim do dhenam duid fen, ind*us* go n-dech*ad* se a n-onoir
35 dosam, 7 a n-ardug*ad* anma duid-si, 7 a tarba dona poiplech*aib*
leghfes 7 éstfes e, 7 a tarba anma 7 cuirp dam fén, 7 a n-esonoir
7 a n-digbail imar*c*ach don diabhul.

⁹*Cf. infra* §74 *nar treicc se ar Dia acht an culaidh.*
¹⁰Psalm LXXXVII, 16.
¹¹ag′labt (with a dash over the "t") MS.
¹²II Cor. I., 7. But see *Roman Breviary, Comm. plur. Martyr., Lectio* V.

of Virginity, Title of Modesty, Ensaumple of Chastity, Way of Penance, Pardon of Sins, Lesson of Faith!

16. In proof that such perfection was in Columcille, it is writ of him that there came neither before nor after him any that did make greater renunciation to God for mankind than he made by sowing and preaching the word of God to them whereby to draw them to the Faith.

17. As Bonaventura hath said, pitying and taking compassion on the poverty and hardships of Jesu returning from Egypt: *O puer* etc., i. e.: "O gentle and right noble boy, King of Heaven and Earth, what great hardship hast thou suffered for our sakes and how early didst thou begin it!" And therefore hath the prophet said, speaking in the person of Christ: *Pauper sum,* etc., i. e.: "From my youth I am in poverty and in many hardships for the sake of the race of man." It is certain that Columcille took to himself these words, for he was in poverty and in many tribulations in his youth for God's sake.

18. And to him longeth the word that Bonaventura said, speaking of this last: *O domine,* etc., which is to say, "O Lord thou hast borne hatred to Thyself for love of us!" Even so Columcille bore hatred to himself for the love of God.

19. His Life will prove to us that Columcille took unto himself the word of the Apostle, speaking of the dolors of Mary and the other holy women that were in company with her in the time of the Passion. *Socii si,* etc.: "If we have been companions with Mary in suffering in the time of the Passion, we shall be companions with her in rejoicing in the glory of God's princedom."

20. Sith that of myself I am not worthy to obtain my request from God, I pray thee, O Columcille, in friendly wise to speak to Him and to get grace from him for me, that I may bring to perfect completness this work that I am fain to do for thee, to the end that it may be to His honor, and to the uplifting of thy name, and for the good of the folk that read and hearken thereto, and to the good of mine own soul and body, and to the Devil's dishonor and great hurt.

21. Laibeoram ar tus d'uaisle 7 d'folaidhecht Colaim cilli .i. Colam Cilli, mac Felimthe, mic Fergasa cendfada, mic Conaill Ghulban, mic Neill nai-gialluig .i. aird-ri Erind 7 Alpan 7 Saxan an Niall sin. Acus do bud eidir linde a geinelach do lenmain as sin suas go h-Adhum, mun bad fada lind a lenmain. Acus da derbad sin, ni fuil act naenmar 7 cethre .xx. uad go h-Adam, amail airmid senchaide na nGaidel, 7 amail ata ar coimed aca in a lebruib fein.

22. ET, fos, Eithne, ingen Díma mic Nae, mic Eithin, mic Cuirb filed, mic Oililla mair, mic Brecain, mic Dairi barruigh, mic Cathair moir, aird-ri Erenn, a mathair. Acus ingen righ Alpan .i. Erc ingen Loairn, a senmhathair .i. mathair a athar. Acus ni fuil fuil is anuaisli ina fuil rigruide Erenn, 7 rigruide an domain uime go h-Adamh.

23. IS follas duinn nach eadh amain do togh Dia Colam cilli a m-broind a mathar mar serbfoghantaid diles do fen, act gor tog se a fad ria techt a m-broind a mathar e. Acus da derbad sin, do batar naeimh Erenn 7 Alpan 7 iartair domain ga tairr[n]gire a bhfad ria n-a geinemain.

24.[13]) Do tairrngir sennser t-shagart Erenn he .i. Sen-mochta Lugmaid, da ced bliadan reme fen. Acus is mar so do tarrngir Mochta é .i. aimser airidhe tarla Mochta in hÍí tuc a fer fritholma .i. Macrith a ainm, cna cuige, 7 do diult Mochta na cna, 7 asedh adubairt: 'Ni limsa,' ar se, 'an feronn as a tucadh na cna sin, 7 taisidther torad an ferainn no go tí a tigerna.' 'Ca huair ticfus se?' ar an t-oclaech. 'A cind da ced bliadan,' ar Mochta. ET do gnathaiged Mochta, ar tect a n-Erinn do o hI, a agaidh bud thuaidh ag denam a urnaidhthe o sin amach. Acus do fiarfaidis a muinter fein de cred é an t-adbhar fa m-bid a aiged bud thuaid. Is ann sin adered Mochta riu: 'Geinfidh macam 'san aird tuaidh, 7 creidfid Erennaig 7 Alpanaig 7 iarthar domain uili dó, 7 is 'na onoír doberim-si m'aged budh tuaidh,' ar se, 'ag den(fol. 2a)am

---

[13]Taken literally from Old Irish Life. See *Lis. Lives*, p. 23.

21. We shall speak first of the noble lineage and blood of Columcille, son of Fedlimid son of Fergus Cennfada son of Conall Gulban son of Niall of the Nine Hostages. High King of Alba and Saxonland was that Niall. And we might trace the lineage of Columcille from Niall upward to Adam, were not the enumerating thereof too long. In proof whereof there are but nine and four score generations from him to Adam, according to the reckoning of the historians of the Gael, as they have kept it in their books.

22. His mother, moreover, was Ethne, daughter of Dima, son of Nae son of Eithin son of Corb File son of Ailill the Great son of Brecan, son of Daire Barrach, son of Cathair the Great, High King of Erin. And a daughter to the King of Alba, even Erc, daughter of Loarn, was grandmother to him, to wit, the mother of his father. And there is no blood more noble than the blood of the Kings of Erin, that embrace all kings to the days of Adam.

23. It is manifest to us that not in his mother's womb only did God choose Columcille to be a true servant to himself, but a long while ere his coming to his mother's womb. And in proof thereof the holy men of Erin and Alba and the Western world did prophesy of him a long while ere his birth.

II

OF PROPHECIES CONCERNING COLUMCILLE MADE BEFORE HIS BIRTH

24. Of him prophesied the senior of the priests of Erin, even old Mochta of Louth two hundred years before him. And thus it was that Mochta prophesied of him. On a certain time it happened that Mochta was in Iona, and one Mac Rith, his serving man, brought nuts to him.

And Mochta refused the nuts, and this is what he said: "Not to me", saith he, "belongeth the land whence these nuts came; let the fruit of that land be put by till its master come."

"When shall he come?" saith the youth.

"At the end of two hundred years," saith Mochta.

And when Mochta returned from Iona to Erin, he prayed thenceforth facing the north.

And his household inquired of him wherefore his face was to the north.

Then Mochta said to them: "There shall be born a child in the north country, and the men of Erin and Alba and all the Western World shall

m'urnaidhte; 7 bud Colam cilli a ainm.' Gonadh airi sin dorinde an rand-sa:

M*a*c*a*m gidhnither atuaid   ag turcb*ail* na mbidhtó.
toiridnid Eri an breo   acus Alpa dainech dó.

25.¹⁴) Do tairr*n*gir dno breithem bratha fer n-Eirenn .i. naem Patruic antí Colam chilli .i. an uair do bi Patruic ac bendach*ad* *Co*naill Gulp*an* 7 Fergosa cendf*ada* m*i*c Conaill ar Sith Aeda, do togaib a da laim os a cind, 7 tarla Conall ar a laim deis, 7 Fergos ar a laim cli; 7 do cuir P*a*truic a lam des t*a*r Conall ar Fergas 7 a lam cli ar Conall. Do b'ingnad le Conall sin, 7 do haithnig*ed* gr*u*aim in a aig*ed* tr*i*d, 7 do fiarfaid do P*a*truic cred fa tucc se an onoir sin d'Ferghas tairis fein. IS andsin adubairt P*a*truic: 'Biaid m*a*c mic ag Fergos,' or se, '7 bud mac ochta do ri nime 7 talman e, 7 b*u*d scathan gloine ar firinde 7 ar indrac*u*s a fiad*n*ai*s*e na n-daine e, 7 bud Colam cilli a ainm. Acus as tr*i*d gorab goire do glu*n* d'Fherghos é ina duit-si, a Conaill, do chuir mesi mo lam des ar cend Fergosa 7 mo lam cli ar do cend-sa'; go n-derna na roind-se:

Geinfid m*a*c*a*m dia fine,   b*u*d sai, b*u*d faid, bud file;
i*n*main lesbairi [glan] glé   nad eibera imargae.

Bid sai *acus* b*i*d craibtech,   *acus* budh ab la rírath,
bid buan is b*id* bithmaith,   ronbia an bithfaith dia didhnad.

26. ET, fos, do tairr*n*ger Patruic tect Colaim cilli ria n-a geinemain a n-inadh eli aml*aid* so. Fechtas do P*a*truic ag sibal Erenn da bennug*ad*, 7 tarla a n-Domnach mor Muige Híthe a Ci*n*el Conaill é, 7 do bendaig se an baile sin; 7 do b'ail leis dul ar na marach do bendug*ad* na coda eli do Cenel Conaill. Acus do cuaid in a c*a*rb*ad* go nuice an sruth re n-abarthor an Dael, 7 ar n-dul go h-or an átha do, do bris feirsde an carbaid do bi fai, 7 gach uair do daingnighthi iad 7 do teiged P*a*truic 'sa carp*ad*, do brisdis aris, 7 do ingant*a*r cach sin go mor. IS and sin adub*a*irt P*a*truic tre spir*ad* faídhedor*ach*t*a*: 'Na bid ingnad oraib fá in ní-se,' ar se, 'oir ni rigend an tal*a*m ud on tsruth-sa anund a les mesi da bendug*ad*; oir berthar m*a*c and a ceand aimsiri faide o aniug, 7 bud Colam cilli a ainm, 7 as se bendeochus an talam bud

---

¹⁴Source is O. I. L. See *Lis. Lives*, p. 23; see also *Tripartite* I, p. 151.

believe on him. And to honor him I turn my face northward," saith he, "when I make my prayer. And Columcille shall be his name."

Wherefore he made this quatrain:

> "A man-child shall be born in the north
> At the setting of ages;
> A flame shall measure high Erin
> And . . . Alba for him."

25. Of Columcille did holy Padraic prophesy, the Doomsday judge of the men of Erin. When Padraic was blessing Conall Gulban and Fergus Cennfada son of Conall on Sith Aeda, he lifted his two hands over their heads, Conall being at his right hand and Fergus at his left. And Padraic put his right hand across Conall upon Fergus and his left hand upon Conall. Conall marvelled thereat, and displeasure was seen on his face, and he asked Padraic why to Fergus thus he gave that honor rather than to him. And thus spake **Padraic**:

"A grandson shall be born to Fergus," saith he, "that shall be the darling of the King of Heaven and Earth, and he shall be the glass of purity and truth and righteousness before men, and Columcille shall be his name; and because by a generation he is nearer to Fergus than to thee, O Conall, I put my right hand on Fergus' head and my left hand on thine." And he made the quatrains:

> "A man child shall be born of his race
> He shall be a sage, a prophet, a poet,
> A loveable lamp, [pure], clear:
> He shall utter no falsehood.
>
> He shall be a sage; he shall be pious;
> He shall be an abbot of the King of Graces.
> He shall be lasting and shall be ever-good,
> The Eternal Prophet shall console him."

26. And moreover in another place also did Padraic thus foretell the coming of Columcille before his birth: On a time that Padraic was walking Erin and blessing it, he chanced to be in Domnach Mor of Mag Hithe among the clan of Conall, and he blessed that place. And on the morrow he was fain to bless the rest of the clan of Conall. And he went in his chariot as far as the stream that is called the Dael, and when he reached the border of the ford, the axles of his chariot brake. And each time they were made fast, and Padraic entered the chariot, they brake again. And all marveled greatly thereat. Then spake Padraic by the spirit of prophecy:

tuaid. Acus as demhin corab 'na onoir do toirmeisc Dia umamsa gan mo leigen do bendugad an talaim ud a ngenter é, 7 ata an talam ud fein behdaighte tre beith a n-dan dó Colam cilli do geinemain and.' Acus do firad gach ní dib sin amail adubairt
5 Patruic; 7 Ath an Carbaid ar Dail ainm an átha sin o sin alle.

27. ET, fos, do bi an oired-sa do cin ag Dia 7 ag Patruic ar Colam cilli a fad rian a geineamain, gor ordaig Patruic cís aíridhe gacha bliadna ar fer a inaid fein a n-Ard Macha fa n-a comair. Acus, fos, adubairt Patruic tre spirad faídheadórachta go raibe
10 an oired sin do cin ag Dia ar Colam cilli, nach beith cis ag ennaem da tainec reime no da tiucfa 'na diaid a n-én-baili do bailtib Colaim cilli act a m-beth ag Colam cilli fein innta, 7 go tibradh sé an oired sin d'uaisli dó tar naemaib Erenn. Acus ata Colam cilli gá dherbadh sin 'sa rand so:

15   Dorad Patruic, daingen fir,   cis ó Ard Macha 's ní gó,
        indeis, a Baeithin, aris   nocha tucas-sa cis do.

28. ET, fos, do fagaib Patruic an lebar darub ainm an soiscel a timna ag Colam cilli an uair do bí se ag dul docum bais, 7 adubairt se re Brigid naomtha do bi a n-aimsir a bais aicce, an
20 lebar sin do coimed do Colam cilli. Acus dorinde Brighid sin amail adubairt Patruic ria, ge do bi aimser fada etir sin 7 Colam cilli do geinemain. ET ataid lebair eli gá mebhrugad, nach mar so dorinde Patruic risin lebor sin acht co tucc se fadera a adhnocad leis fen 'sa tumba in ar cuired é, d'ecla go fuigedh en-duine eli é
25 go tect Colaim cilli cuice, 7 gorab aingel De fein tuc les e docum Colaim cilli, 7, fos, do fagaib Patruic a inadh fen a n-Erinn a timna ag Colam cilli an uair sin a pongc a bais.

29. ET, fos, do tairrngir Patruic amlaid so tect Colaim cilli a bhfad ria n-a genemain .i. Fechtas tainic Patruic docum na
30 h-abond ré n-abarthor an Buill, 7 as amlaid do bí an abonn sin fen: ni fhedaeis daine dul tairsi acht a luing no a n-ethar. Acus do chuir se fá umla ar an cuid soir don abainn ísliugad (fol. 2b) 7 a h-uisce do dul a tanacht, indus go m-beith sí insiubail do cois no d'ech o sin amach go brath. Acus as follas an mirbuile sin do
35 cach aniug; oir ata in cuid tíar don abainn sin mar do bí sí ó tus, 7 an cuid soir tana di. Acus do bendaig se an aband iar sin, 7 tainic torad eisc go imarcach uirri do brig an benduighthe sin Patruic.

"Marvel not at this thing;" saith he, "the land from this stream yonder hath no need of my blessing, for a lad shall be born there long hence, and Columcille shall be his name, and he it is shall bless the land northward. And truly it was in his honor that God suffered me not to bless the land wherein he shall be born. And that land is already blessed whose lot it is for Columcille to be born therein."

And all this fell out as Padraic said. And the Ford of the Chariot upon Dael hath been the name of that ford from that day.

27. Moreover, so much love had God and Padraic for Columcille, long ere his birth, that Padraic laid a certain tax each year upon his successor in Armagh for the use of Columcille. And Padraic said moreover through the spirit of foreknowledge, that God had such love for Columcille that no holy man that came before or should come after him should have tribute from a single one of Columcille's monasteries, save that only which Columcille should have from them. And thus much of honor He would give him beyond the other saints of Erin. And Columcille beareth witness thereto in this quatrain:

> "Padraic hath given—a true matter—
> Tribute from Armagh (It is no falsehood),
> Tell it, O Baithin, again.
> To him I brought no tribute."

28. Moreover, when he was nigh death, Padraic bequeathed to Columcille the book called the Gospel. And he charged Saint Brigid, that was with him at the time of his death, to keep that book for Columcille. And Brigid did as Padraic had charged her, albeit it was a long time between that and the birth of Columcille.

There be other books that say it was not thus that Padraic did with that book, but that he let bury it in the same tomb wherein he was laid himself, lest any other should get it afore the coming of Columcille. And it was an angel of God that bare it to Columcille.

And furthermore in the hour of his death Padraic left his own place in Erin in bequest to Columcille.

29. In the manner also that followeth, Padraic foretold the coming of Columcille long ere his birth.

On a time Padraic came to the river called the Boyle and in this wise was that river: men might not cross it save in a ship or fishing boat. And he bade the eastern part of the river become shoal, and the water grow shallow, that men might ford it on foot or horseback from that time till Doom. And that marvel is manifest to all today; for the part of the river in the west is as it hath been always, and the part in the east is shallow. And Padraic blessed the stream then and by the power of his blessing great abundance of fish came therein.

30.¹⁵ IS and sin do labhair P*atruic* tre spir*ad* faidedórachta 7 is edh adub*airt*: 'Ticfaid m*ac* na bethadh suthaine and so,' ol se .i. 'Colam cilli, 7 doghena ecla[i]s onórach 'san inadh so, 7 biaidh coimtinol manach uada indte, 7 is 'na onoir do bhendaig mesi an abonn-sa docum go m-beth an t-iasc-sa tainec tre mo bendachtain-si uirre do cungn*am* bidh aicce fen 7 gá manch*aib* 7 ag lucht a oibri; 7, fos, is 'na onoir do chuir me uisce na h-abonn a tanacht 7 a laghad, i*n*das go féd*fadh* lucht a oibri dul tairsi anunn 7 anall do reir a riachtanuis a les fein.' Acus do firudh gach ní dá n-dub*airt* P*atruic* ann sin; 7 Es M*ac* n-Eirc ar Buill ainm an inaidh sin a n-derna Colam cilli an eclu[i]s.

31.¹⁶ ET, fos, do tairrngeir P*atruic* aris tect Colaim cilli a bfhad rían a genem*ain* anuair tainec se co hEas Ruaid, 7 do benduigh se an taeb budh th*uaidh* de 7 do mhallaig se an taeb budh des re ulca re Cairbri mac Neill nai-*giallaig* nar gab creidim vadha. Acus adub*airt* se co ticf*ad* Colam cilli, 7 an uiresb*aidh* bennaigthe do fhagaib se fen ar an taeb sin b*ud* tuaid don Es corab fa comair Col*aim* cilli do fagaib se an uiresbaidh sin air, 7 go coimlínf*edh* Colam cilli fen hi an uair do ticf*ad* se. Acus do firudh sin am*ail* advb*airt* P*atruic*; mar bus foll*us* is in scel ata a n-inad eli sa m-beathaidh-si fein air sein.¹⁷

32. Do mheil im*orro*, an muilend ro-úasal ro-onórach-sa .i. P*atruic*, do bi ar sibhol 7 ar meilt o uisce ro-saidbir na n*gras* do bi o Dia aicce, fir Erenn 7 a mna. Gedhedh, dob ece*n* dó, o burba 7 o mísduaim na n-daine a tosach an creidimh, moran salchair 7 cogail d'fagb*ail* 'sa cruithnecht-sa do meil se *no* co tainec Colam cilli, 7 no gor glan se o gach uile ní ne*mh*-glan iad, ag síl*ad* 7 ag senmoir breit*hri* De doib, 7 go n-derna se plur ro-glan ar na pultadh 7 ar na lecen tria shaírse na n*gras* n-imarc*ach* tuc Dia do d'Erendchaib uile 7 do mor*an* d'Alp*an*chaib.

33. Do foillsig*ed* techt Col*aim* cilli a fad rian a genemain do P*atruic* aml*aid* so .i. Fechtas da raibe P*atruic* ag fag*ail* shaethair 7 anshoc*rach* ro-moiri oc tarraing fer n-Erenn 7 a m-ba*n* do*cum* creidmhe, 7 do bo truagh les gan a demhi*n* aicce cind*us* do beidis fa creideam 7 fa crabadh in a diaidh fen, no cred hi an c*rich* *do* cuirf*ed* Dia orra 7 med an t-shaethair do bi se fein d'fagail uatha. Acus do bí se ag guidhe De go duthrachtach im a fis sin do tab*airt* do. Tainec an t-aing*el* cuicce iarsin 7 do labair ris 7 ass*ed* adub*airt*, gorab do reir an taisbe*n*ta do foillseochaidhe do in a codl*ad* an oidhce sin do bi cuige do b*edh* Éri re na beo fen 7 na diaid go brath aris fa creidem. Acus is e taisenadh tuc*adh* do: Eiri uile d'fhaicsin re

---
¹⁵Abridged account in *Tripartite* I, pp. 142-3.
¹⁶See *Tripartite* I, p. 148.
¹⁷See § 133 for an account of its fulfillment.

30. And then Padraic spake by the spirit of prophecy, and this is what he said:

"Hither shall come the son of Life Eternal", saith he, "even Columcille, and he shall make in this place a noble church, and there shall be a community of his monks therein. In honor of him have I blessed the stream, that the fish therein through my blessing may be a help to him and his monks and his laborers. And it is to honor him that I have made the water in the stream grow shoal and shallow, that his labors may cross hither and thither as their need may be."

And all that Padraic then said was fulfilled, and the place where Columcille made the church was named the Waterfall of Mac n-Eirc upon Boyle.

31. And again when he came to Assaroe, a long time ere the birth of Columcille, Padraic foretold his coming; for he laid a blessing on the north side thereof.[1] And to vex Cairbre, son of Niall of the Nine Hostages that did not accept the Faith from him, he cursed the south side. And he said that Columcille should come. And as for the incompleteness of the blessing he had left on the northern side of the waterfall, it was for Columcille he had left it; for Columcille should complete it when he came. And it was fulfilled as Padraic said, as will appear from the account thereof in another place in this same *Life*.

32. The men of Erin and its women it was indeed that the right worshipful mill did grind, to wit, Padraic, that turned and ground by the right precious water of the grace he had of God. But he had to leave much filth and cockle in this wheat he milled, because of the pride and inconstancy of the folk in the beginning of the Faith, until Columcille came and cleansed them of every uncleanness, sowing and preaching the word of God to them until he made right pure flour, bolted and sifted through the sieve of the abundant graces that God gave him, for all the Irish and for many of the Scotch.

33. Long while afore his birth, the coming of Columcille was shewn to Padraic in this wise:

On a time Padraic was having labor and trouble in bringing to the Faith the men of Erin and their women; and it was a grief to him not to be sure how their faith and devotion would be after his time, or what manner of ending God would send them, inasmuch as he was having great labor with them. And he prayed God right strongly to give this knowledge to him. There came to him then an angel, and spake to him and said that Erin in his life and afterward till Judgment should be in the matter of faith as a vision that should appear to him in sleep that night. And this is the vision that was given him: All Erin he saw in flames,

[1]*Cf.* § 133-134 for the same story, in which the incompleteness of Padraic's blessing is explained.

derglasadh, 7 an lasair do ergedh di ag dul svas *con* nuice an aíer,
7 'na diaid sin doco*nn*aic se an teine sin ar na much*ad* acht cnvic
mora a bf*ad* o celi re teinigh, 7 'na diaid sin doco*nn*airc se na cnuic
fen ar na muchad, acht indshama*il* lochrai*nd no* coindle ar na lass*ad*
a n-inadh gach cnuic dib. Acus doconnairc se iad sin ar n-dul ass
aris, 7 sméroídech *no* aeibli 7 smal orra, ge do bat*ar* beo a n-inad-
haib terca a fad o ceili ar fud Erenn. Tainec an t-aing*el* cet*n*a
cuige 7 do indis dó gorab íad sin na rechta a rach*adh* Eri in a diaid
fein. Ar na cloisdin do P*atruic*, do cai go gér, 7 do lab*air* do guth
mor, 7 iss*ed* adub*airt*: 'A Dia na n-uili cumhacht, an e dob' ail let
na daeine do*cum* ar cuiris mesi do tab*air*t eoluis ort fén doib do
damn*adh* 7 do t*r*ocaire do tarraing cugad fen vatha. Gen gorab fiu
mesi tu d'éstecht rim, a Tigerna, cuir h-f*eirg* ar cul leith-riu, 7 gab
lu*cht* an oilein-si na h-Erenn at t*r*oicuiri fein'. AR crichnug*ad* na
m-briathar sin do P*atruic*, do labhair an t-aing*el* go sithcanta ris 7
assed adub*airt*: 'Fech don taeb b*ud* th*uaid* dit', ar se, '7 docífe tú
claechlodh laimhe desi De.' Dorinne P*atruic* mar adub*air*t an
t-aing*el* ris; oír do fech don taeb b*ud* thuaidh de, 7 docondaic sol*us*
ag erghe andsin nar mór ar tus, 7 é ag médug*ad* 7 ag sc*r*is an
dorchadais as a celi, ind*us* gor las Eri uile de mar in c*ed* lasair, 7
doco*nn*aic ag dol is na rec[h]taib cedna iar sin hi. ET do foill (*fol.*
3a) sigh an t-aingel ciall na taisbe*n*ta sin do P*atruic*, 7 adub*air*t go
m-beith Eri ar lasadh do creidemh 7 do crab*adh* re na lind fein, 7 go
rachadh dorchadas ar in t-soillsi sin re na bas. A*cht* ge do beidis
daeí*ni* maithe a n-inadaib t*er*ca a n-Erinn in a d*í*aid, mar do bat*ar*
na cnuic sen re lasadh a b-fhad o ceile, 7 mar do gebdaeis na daine
maithe sin bas, go ticfad daine b*ud* mesa ina íad féin in a n-inad ar
indshama*il* na lócrand 7 na coinnel dar labrumar re*m*he-so 7 'na
diaidh, 7 nach beith don chreidem ar bethug*ad* acu *acht* indshama*il*
an sméroidigh ar a raibe an smal 7 an ceo, no go tí m*a*c na soillsi
suthaine .i. Colam cilli. Acus ge m*adh* becc ar tus é ag techt ar in
saeg*al* do, go m-beith ag sila*dh* 7 ag senmoir breithr*i* De 7 ag
medug*ad* an credim no go lasadh Eri re na linn, am*ail* do las sí
re lind P*atruic*, 7 nach beith an lasadh c*ed*na go brath aris uiri,
acht ge do beidís daeine maithe c*r*abaid in a diaidh; 7, fos, go
rachadh ecl*uis* Erenn a n-egcruth a n-dereadh aimsire iarsen, in*nus*
nach beith beo don creidem *no* don c*r*abu*dh* i*n*dte act indshama*il*
an smeroidigh no na n-áibhell m-becc ar a raibe an smal 7 an
dorchadas dar labrum*ar* remhe so.

34. Do tarrngair fos Martain naemtha techt C*olaim* cilli a
fad ria na genemain a n-aimsir a bais fein, 7 ass*ed* adub*air*tt:
'Adluict*er*', ol se, 'mo leb*ar* fen .i. leb*ar* na soisc*el*, a n-enfh*eacht*

and the flames that rose therefrom going up into the air. And after that he saw the fire quenched, but great hills each far from other afire, and after that he saw even those hills extinguished, save the like of lamps or candles burning in the place of each of those hills. And he saw these fail again, leaving but dim coals or sparks in a few places only, each far from other through the length of Erin. There came to him that same angel and told him those were the shapes that Erin should come to after him. And Padraic, when he heard this, lamented sorely.

And he spake with a loud voice and said: "O God of all might, dost Thou wish to damn the folk to whom Thou didst send me to bring them knowledge of Thee? And wouldst Thou withdraw Thy pity from them? Though I be unworthy Thy heed, O Lord, put away Thy wrath from them, and take the folk of this isle of Erin under Thy compassion."

And when Padraic had ended these words, the angel spake to him in friendly wise and said:

"Look to the north of thee," saith he, "and thou shalt behold the change wrought by the right hand of God." Then Padraic did as the angel bade him; for he looked toward the north, and he saw a light rising there, not great at first, but waxing and rending asunder the darkness, so that all Erin blazed therewith, as with the first flame. And he saw it take the same shapes again after.

Then the angel showed to Padraic the meaning of this vision. And he said that all Erin should be ablaze with faith and devotion throughout his time, but darkness should fall upon that light with his death. Howbeit there should be good men in a few places in Erin after him, as there were hills ablaze a far space each from other. And when those good folk were dead, there should come folk worse than they in their stead, like the lamps and candles whereof we have spoken more than once, and that faith should not flourish thenceforth with them save in the likeness of gledes whereon lay dimness and fog, until should come the sun of Light Eternal, even Columcille. And albeit he were small at first on coming into the world, yet should he sow and preach the word of God and increase the Faith, so that Erin should be ablaze in his time as it was in the time of Padraic, and there should not be such a blazing upon her again till the Doomsday, albeit there should be good folk and religious after him. And the church of Erin should fall into decay at the end of time, so that of faith and piety there should be therein but the likeness of the gledes or sparks, dim and dull, whereof we spake a while since.

34. Saint Martin did foretell the coming of Columcille a long while ere his birth in the time of his own death. And this is what he said:

rim, 7 cuirter ar mh'ucht fein 'sa tumba é; oir geinfidhir mac
naemtha bendaighte a n-Erinn', ol se, '7 is ó nem'sa fidhair doconnaic Eoin ag luidhe ar Ihsv ag sruth Eorthanain an uair do
baisd sé é, ainmneochar leth a anma, 7 is on eclais ainmneochar
an leth eli dá ainm, 7 ticfaid se annso a cinn ced bliadan ó niugh,
7 oisceolaid sé mo tumbu-sa 7 dogeba sé mo lebar ann, 7 coimfhed-
faidh Dia fa na comhair e gan sal no dorchadus do dul ar en-litir
de, 7 béraid se go h-Erinn é, 7 bud soiscel Martain ainm an lebair
sin a n-Erinn o sin anvas'.

35. Do tairrngir Brigid naemht[h]a mar an cedna techt
Colaim cilli a fad ria na genemain, 7 assed adubairt .i. 'Fasfaidh
slat don taeb-sa bud tuaid d'Erinn, 7 biaid blatha na n-uili gras
uirri, 7 dodéna Dia crand mor di, 7 lethfaid a bharr 7 a gega tar
Erinn 7 tar Alpain 7 tar iarthor domain uile .i. beraid Eithne
taeb-fhoda, ben Feilimthe mic Fergosa cend-fhoda, mic Conaill
Gulban, mic Neill noi-giallaig, [mac], 7 bud Colam cilli a ainm, 7
rachaid a briathar 7 a senmoir 7 clu 7 esimlair a crabaid fo íarthar
an domain uile. Acus as deimin go mothaighim-si a grasa 7 a
subaltide do lathair agam, ge fada uaim an aimser a ngeinter e',
ar sí. Acus dorinne an rann so:[18]

Macam Ethne taeb-foda,   sech is bol is blathugad,
Colam cilli caidh gan on,   niruho romh a rathugad.

36. ET, fos, do tairrngir Patruic co mbadh a n-aen-tumba
ris fen 7 re Brigid a n-Dun da Lethglas do cuirfide corp Colaim
cilli tar eis a bais. Acus fos, do tairrngir Brigid fein sin mar in
cedna; 7 do firad sin amail indeosas an betha a n-inad eli; oir nír
b'ail leo gan an t-indmus ro-uasal-sa, do batar fen do tairrngire 7
do gellatar do tect do saidbriugad na poiblech 7 na h-eclaisi do
reir na n-oibrighte n-diadha do chur a n-esimlair doib ann fein,
do beith ar aen-taiscedh re a n-anmonnaib a ngloir suthain Dé, 7
a corp do beith ar aen-taisced re a corpaib a n-en-timpa [tumba]
ar an saegal-sa. Acus fos, leghtor go minec ar Colam cilli gor
tairrngir se fein re na beo gorab a n-aén-tumba riu san do beith
a corp.

37. ET fos do tairrngir Dabheoog naemtha techt Colaim cilli
a bfad ría na geinemain .i. Oidhce airide do bi se ar purcadoír

---

[18]See *Lis. Lives,* p. 23, where it is attributed to Becc mac De. Cf. *Trip.* I, p.
151 where it is ascribed to Brigid.

"Let my book, to wit, the book of the Gospel, be buried with me, and let it be put upon my bosom in the tomb, for in Erin shall be born a saintly blessed boy, and the half of his name shall be from Heaven, in the figure that John saw resting upon Jesus in the river Jordan in the hour he baptized him, and the other half of his name shall be from the Church. And he shall come hither at the end of an hundred years from to-day, and he shall open my tomb and find my book there, and God shall protect it from misuse without stain or dimness coming upon a letter thereof. And he shall bring it to Erin. And the *Gospel of St. Martin* shall be the name of that book in Erin forever."[1]

35. Saint Brigid likewise foretold the coming of Columcille a long while ere his birth, and this is what she said:

"There shall spring a sapling in this northern half of Erin and there shall be blossoms of every grace thereon, and God shall make thereof a great tree, and its top and its branches shall spread over Erin and Alba and all the Western World. That is to say, a son shall be born to Ethne Taebfhoda, wife of Fedlimid son of Fergus Cennfada son of Conall Gulban son of Niall of the Nine Hostages. And Columcille shall be his name. And his word and his preaching, and the fame and ensaumple of his piety shall reach over the whole Western World. And truly I feel his graces and his virtues here with me, though far from me is the time wherein he shall be born," saith she. And she made this quatrain:

> "The man-child of longsided Ethne,
> As a sage he is a-blossoming.
> Columcille, pure without blemish.
> It was not over soon to perceive him."

36. And Padraic foretold that it should be in one tomb with him and with Brigid in Dun da Lethglas that the body of Columcille should be put after his death. And Brigid foretold this likewise, and it was verified, as the *Life* in another place will testify. Of Columcille they had prophesied, and they had promised he should come to enrich the folk and the Church by giving them in himself an ensaumple of godly deeds. And they desired this very noble jewel to be in the same treasure house with themselves, his soul being in one keeping with their souls in the eternal glory of God and his body being in one keeping with their bodies in the same tomb in this world. And moreover we read often of Columcille that he himself foretold while living that his body should be in one tomb with them.

37. And further the holy Dabeooc foretold the coming of Columcille a long while ere his birth.

---

[1]*Cf.* §§ 101, 256.

P*atr*uic ar Loch D*er*g, 7 do*con*nairc se soillsi ro-mhor 7 delr*adh* imar*c*ach don taeb b*u*d th*uaid* de, 7 do fiarf*aig*etar na clerig do bí faris de, cred b*a* ciall don taisb*e*nadh sin tug*ad* doib. Frecrais Dabeooc iad 7 isedh adub*air*t .i. 'Lasf*aidh* Dia locrand d*on* taeb-sa
5 th*uaid* dínn, 7 dobera se sol*us* d' eclais De .i. m*a*c b*é*r*as* Eithne taeb-fhoda, ben Feidl*mthe*, m*ic* Fergosa cendfada, m*ic* *C*onaill G*u*lban, 7 b*u*d Colam cilli a ainm, 7 b*u*d gein t-schochair d'iarthair dom*ain* e, ar soillsi 7 ar ecna 7 ar oghacht 7 ar fáidhedoracht'.

38. ET, fos, do tairrng*ir* Caillin naemtha tect Colaim cilli
10 a bfad ria na genemain .i. an uair dorinne (*fol.* 3b) se faidedor*ac*t ar sli*ct* Conaill G*u*lban, m*ic* Neill nai-ghiall*aig* .i. go ngebad da righ dec dib righ*ac*t Erenn, 7 go ngebudh cethrar dib lan-righe Leithe Cui*nd*, amail asp*er*t 'sa rand-sa:

Gebtar uada fa dodhec   Eri, ni ba brec an breth,
15 is cethr*ar* do sil an Duin*n*   geb*as* go tuin*n* luim a leth.

ET do tairrng*ir* se, fos, an tan nach b*u*d leo righ*ac*t Erenn, nach beith cend*us* ag righ eli orra, am*ail* asp*er*t 'sa rann sa:

Tan nac beid os Erin*n* uill,   ní gebaid cuing *ac*t a cath,
ni beid ga*n* mal dib b*u*dei*n*,   ni *c*raidh mo ceill reim go
20   rath.

ET do tairrng*ir* se go tiucfadh Colam cilli ar sli*c*t Convill Gulp*an*, 7 nach ticf*ad* 'na diaidh go brath do clandaib na m-ban enduine as mo in a foillseochad Dia a grasa ina hé, a leith re faidedor*ac*t 7 re mirbuil*e* 7 re taisb*e*nadh aingl*ide*, 7 re cruas 7 re
25 gloine *c*rab*aid*. ET do tairrngir se go n-dingn*ad* Dia moran maithesa don cuid eli do sli*ct* *C*onaill G*u*lban ar son Colaim cilli do b*eith* ar en-sli*c*t riu, am*ail* asp*er*t 'sa rand-sa:

Ticf*aid* t*ar* mh'eis Col*am* caid   fhuícfes daib briat*ar* is
                                          buaidh,
30 is é sin ai*n*-fer is ferr   genfes tall go tí lá an luai*n*.

ET da derb*ad* sin, do fagaib Colam cilli fein mar bhuad*haibh* ar cinel Conaill, an uair nach biadh a oirbiri fein orra, go m-bvaideochdaeis re h-en-cath esbadach ar secht cathaib eli.

39. Do tairrng*ir* Brenainn é aml*aid*, so, 7 ass*ed* adub*air*t:
35 'Beraidh Ethne taebfada ben Feidl*m*the, m*ic* Fergosa cennfoda, m*ic* *C*onaill G*u*lban, m*ac*, 7 biaid gr*as*a an spir*da* naeimh go h-imar*c*ach air, 7 ata do gr*ad* againne do fein 7 da gnímharth*aib*, dar lind fen go fuil se do láth*air* againd, gen co tainec se fos.'

On a certain night he was in the Purgatory of Padraic on Loch Derg, and he saw a passing great light and mighty, blazing to the north of him, and the clerics that were with him asked him what was the meaning of the vision that was given them. Dabeooc answered them, and spake thus:

"God shall light a lamp to the north of us, and it shall give light to the Church of God, to wit, a son that Ethne Taebfhoda shall bring forth, the wife of Fedlimid son of Fergus Cennfada son of Conall Gulban. And his name shall be Columcille, and he shall be a birth fortunate to the Western World for light and wisdom, for virginity and for prophesying."

38. And holy Caillin also foretold the coming of Columcille a long while ere his birth, what time he made a promise to the race of Conall Gulban son of Niall of the Nine Hostages, that twelve kings of them should hold the kingship of Erin and four of them should have full kingship in Conn's half, as the quatrain saith:

"From him shall Erin be held twelve times;
The judgment shall not be a falsehood;
Four of the seed of the Donn
Shall hold half thereof to the bare wave."

And he prophesied also that what time the kingship in Erin should not be theirs, no other king should rule them, as he said in this quatrain:

"The time they rule not great Erin,
They take not the yoke save in battle;
They shall not be without their own chieftan,
. . . . .¹"

And he foretold that Columcille should come of the race of Conall Gulban and there should not come after him forever of the children of women one on whom God should show his grace more than on him, in respect of prophecy and marvels and angelic manifestations, and in respect of rigor and purity of devotion And he foretold that God should give many blessings to the others of the tribe of Conall Gulban, by reason of Columcille's belonging to them, as the quatrain saith:

"Holy Columcille shall come after me;
He shall leave to you blessings and fortune.
He is the one man, the best one,
That shall be born yonder till Doomsday."

And in proof thereof Columcille left it as a privilege to the tribe of Conall, that, when his displeasure was not upon them, with one scant battalion they should gain victory over seven others.

¹Rule with success troubleth me not (?)

40. Do tairrngir espoc Eogan Arda Sratha a techt ria na genemain amlaid so .i. La airidhe dochuaid Lugaid mac Sedna, mic Ferghosa Cennfada, mic Conaill Gulban 7 a mac .i. Fiachra, go h-Ard Sratha, 7 fuaratar espoc Eoghain a n-dorus a mainesdrech fein. Acus tarla imresain etar Fíachra 7 manach do manachaib espuic Eogain, cor marb se an manuch. Do fergaidh espoc Eogan trit sin, 7 do mallaig se Fíachra 7 a slicht in a diaid, 7 adubairt go fuighedh sé fein bas fa cenn nai la, 7 nach gébadh enduine da slicht righact Erenn no cinel Conaill go brath, 7 nach beith uimhir bud mo ina cuiger da sil a n-aeinfhect ann coidhce, 7 go m-beith bithainimh ar gach duine dib sin fein. Do firadh sin uile; 7 ar fagail bais d'Fiachra, mar adubairt an nech naemtha sin, do gab ecla mor a athair .i. Lugaid re faicsin na mirbol mor sin. ET tainec mar a raibhe espoc Eogan do tabairt a brethe fen do do cenn a benduighte, 7 do cend gan a escaine do luidhe air fein no ar in cuid eli dá claind. 'Gebud-sa sin,' ar espoc Eogan, '7 ni gebhaind breth ar bith uaid mona gabainn a n-onoir an mic bendaighte naemtha geinfider ar en-slict rit a cend caeca bliadan, 7 bud Colam cilli a ainm, 7 is hí Ethne taebfada, ben posda Felim[the], mic Fergasa cennfada, mic Conaill Gulban, berus an mac sin dó feín.' Gonad ann dorinde an rann-sa:[19])

Mac bearar *do* Feilimid   bud minn ar gach cleir,
Feilimid mac Ferghosa,   mic Conaill, micNeill.

'ET bud e, fos,'' ar espoc Eogan, 'bus cend 7 bus posda don eclais 7 don credem, 7 nir gein o Crisd anuas a leithéid, ar feabhus a credeim 7 a crabaid, 7 ar u mhéd naeimheochar do na cinedhaib leis, 7 rachaid a ecna os cenn cleri na crisdaigechta, 7 rachaid a cogus os cenn fer n-domain, 7 nir geinedh 7 ni genfider naem bus mo d' impidech 7 do comairlech ar an Trinoid ina é.' Acus ni fhedand tenga daenda tect ar in molad tuc espoc Eogan ar Colam cilli an uair sin. Acus do tairrngir se comadh e Gridoir beil-oir bud papa 'sa Roim re lind Colaim cilli, 7 go rachadh se ar cuairt cuige, 7 go madh é Moconna naemtha bud compánuch sligid do ag dol annsin. Acus as sí breth ruc espoc Eogan ar Lugaid: screboll gacha tres bliadna[20]) vaidh fein, 7 o gach duine dá shil in a diaidh dó fen 7 d'fhir a inaidh go brath, 7 gan he fein no duine da slict da fulang esonora a baile no a eclaisi

---

[19]Only the verse in O. I. L. See *Lis. Lives*, p. 23; *Three Middle-Irish Homilies*, p. 100.
[20]bliadna bliadna MS.

39. Brendan did promise Columcille in this wise, saying:

"Ethne Taebfhoda shall bear a son, the wife of Fedlimid son of Fergus Cennfada son of Conall Gulban. And the grace of the Holy Spirit shall be mighty upon him. And so dear is he to us and what he doth, that he seemeth already in our sight, albeit he is not yet come."

40. The bishop Eoghan of Ard Sratha did prophesy his coming ere his birth in this wise:

"On a day Lugaid, son of Sedna son of Fergus Cennfada son of Conall Gulban and his son Fiachra went to Ard Sratha, and they found the bishop Eoghan at the door of his monastery. And a quarrel arose betwixt Fiachra and one of the monks of Bishop Eoghan, and in that quarrel he killed the monk. Therewith was Bishop Eoghan angered, and he cursed Fiachra and his seed after him, and said that he should die in nine days, and that not one of his race should possess the Kingdom of Erin or of Cinel Conaill forever, and at no one time should there be living more than the number of five of his seed, and on each of these there should be a lasting blemish. And all this was fulfilled. And when Fiachra died, as the holy man had said, sore fear seized his father Lugaid, beholding this great marvel. And he came to the bishop Eoghan with intent to be adjudged by him, that he might obtain his blessing, and that his curse might not rest on him nor any of the others of his children.

"I will accept terms from thee," said the bishop Eoghan, "and I would not accept them, save in honor of a blessed holy boy that shall be born of the same seed as thine at the end of two score years and ten. And Columcille shall be his name. And it is Ethne Taebfhoda, the wedded wife of Fedlimid son of Fergus Cennfada son of Conall Gulban, that shall bring forth that boy." And thereupon he made this quatrain:

> "A son shall be born to Fedlimid
> That shall be a diadem upon every assembly,
> Fedlimid son of Fergus,
> Son of Conall, son of Niall."

"And thereto," saith the bishop Eoghan, "he shall be head and prop of the Church and of the Faith, nor hath there been born from Christ's time until now his like for excellence of faith and devotion, and for the number of the tribes that shall be blessed by him. And his wisdom shall go beyond the clergy of Christendom, and his conscience beyond the men of the world. And there hath not been, nor shall be, saint greater than he at making intercession to and counselling the Trinity."

And the tongue of man is not able to describe the praise that Bishop Eoghan gave to Columcille that time. And he foretold it should be the golden-tongued Gregory that should be Pope in Rome in Columcille's

---

[1] *Cf.* § 255.

coidhce. ET adubairt gorab ar son Colaim cilli do beith ar én-
slict ris, nar deonaigh Dia dó fein a mallugad ina a slict in a
diaid do mallugad. Acus, fos, adubairt espoc Eogan re Lugaid,
go tibrad Dia an oired sin d' onoir do ar son Colaim cilli do beith
5 ar enslict ris, anvair na bad le na shil righact, nach beidis go
brath gan an dara duine bud ferr a n-Erinn dib. ET, fos, adubairt mar an cedna an vair nac bad leo fen an righe, (fol. 4a)
nach bud rí rí da righfaide ar Eirinn muna beith an duine bud
ferr acu gá rigadh. Acus adubairt go coiméoltide sin doib da
10 coimlidis a cis 7 a onoir do fein 7 do Colaim cilli mar an cedna.
Beatha espuic Eogain 7 Moconna naemtha adeir so uili; 7 do
fagbhamar moran da n-abraid na bethada sin ar so le na fad
lind re na scribadh.

41.[21]) Do thairrngir dno Buide mac Bronaigh é a n-aimsir a
15 bais fen, 7 adubairt ria na muinntir: 'Rucad 'san oidhce anoct,'
ar se, 'mac uasal onorach a fiadnaise De 7 daine, 7 tiucfaid se
andso a cinn deich m-bliadna ficed ó nocht, 7 bud da fer dec a lín
a cosmailes an da esbol déc, 7 foillseochaid se m' adhnacul-sa 7
cuimdeochaid se mo thaisi 7 mo roilec, 7 biaid ar cumann re celi
20 a nim 7 a talmain, 7 bud Colam cilli a ainm.'

42. Ni hed amain do tairrngiretar naeim Erenn 7 a h-uasal-
aithrecha, ga raibe spirad faidhedoracta ó Dia, tect Colaim cilli,
acht do tarrngiretar na draithe 7 na daeine, ag nach raibe creidem,
go tiucfad se a fad ria na genemain. Acus da derbad sin, do
25 tairrngir Finn mac Cumaill co ticfad se an uair do lecc se Bran
.i. an cu oirderc do bi aicce, don dam allaid ag abvind t-Seng-
lenda, a crich cineoil Conuill, ris a raiter Glend Colaim cilli
aniug. Acus nir len an cu an fiadh tar abainn glinne anvnn, 7
fa h-ingnad le cach an cu nar leicc aen-bethadach uaithe riam dá
30 dénum sin. IS andsin docuaid Find a muinidhin a fesa, 7[22] ro
labair tre spirud faidedoracta, gen co raibe creidimh aice, 7 asedh
adubairt: 'Genfidher mac 'sa tir-si bud thuaid, 7 bud Colam cilli
a ainm, 7 bud é an dechmad glun o Cormac ua Cuinn e, 7 biaid
se lan do rath 7 do grasaib an dia ata 'na aén 7 'na triar, 7 itá

[21]Taken literally from O. I. L. See *Lis. Lives*, p. 24. See also Plummer's
V. S. H., I, p. 92, § 18.
[22]77 MS.

time, and that Columcille should go on a visit to him, and the holy Moconda should be his travelling companion on his going thither.¹

And the sentence that the bishop Eoghan passed on Lugaid was: "A scruple every third year from him and from every one of his seed after him, to Columcille and his successors till Doomsday; and neither he nor any of his tribe to allow dishonor to the monastery of Columcille or to his church ever. And he said it was by reason of Columcille's being of one race with Lugaid, that God suffered him not to curse Lugaid nor to curse his children after him. And moreover the bishop Eoghan told Lugaid that thus much of honor should God show him by reason of Columcille's being of his tribe: in times when his seed should not possess the kinship, it should never fail that the second mightiest man in Ireland should be of their kin. And moreover he said in like wise that in times when the kingship was not held by them, whomso men might crown King of Erin, he should be no king, save they crown the best man. He said this should be rendered to them if they rendered to him his tax and his honors, and to Columcille his in like manner.

The lives of the bishop Eoghan and of Saint Moconda relate the whole thereof. We have left out much that is written of the matter in these lives by reason of the long time it would take us for the writing thereof.

41. Moreover of him prophesied Buide mac Bronaigh in the hour of his death, and he said to his household:

"There hath been born this night," saith he, "a man-child, noble and worshipful in God's sight and in man's. And he shall come hither at the end of thirty years from this night; and there shall be twelve men with him in the manner of the twelve apostles. And he shall discover my burial place and set in order my memorials and my remains, and our fellowship shall be in Heaven and in earth. And Columcille shall be his name."

42. Not alone was it the saints of Erin and patriarchs having the spirit of prophecy of God that did foretell the coming of Columcille, but druids and such as had not the Faith foretold a long time ere his birth that he should come.

In proof whereof did Finn MacCumaill foretell that he should come, the time he loosed Bran, a famous hound he had, against the deer at the river of Senglenn in the district of the tribe of Conall that is called Glenn Columcille today. And the hound pursued not the deer across the river of the glen. And all marvelled that that hound, the which had never before let her quarry from her, should do this thing.

And then Finn betook himself to his gift of knowledge, and spake through the spirit of prophecy, albeit he had not the Faith, and he said:

"A man-child shall be born in the northern land; and Columcille shall be his name; and he shall be the tenth generation from Cormac,

ann, 7 do bi, 7 bias; 7 biaidh moran do termonnaibh 7 do cellaib
a n-Erinn 7 a n-Albain aice 7 bendeochaid se an talumh-sa on
t-sruth anonn, 7 bud termonn dá gach aen rachas ann go brath
aris é; 7 is 'na onoír tuc Bran an comairghe ud don fiadh nar
5 len si tar abhainn anonn é.' Acus Belach Damhain ainm an
inaid sin a tucc Bran an comairghe sin don fiadh o sin ille.

43. ET do tairrngired, fos, d'Fhelimid Rechtmar, d' airdrigh Erenn, tect Colaim cilli a fad ria na genemain amlaid so
.i. Tuc se ingen Righ Lochlann do mnai, 7 do bui si aimser fada
10 aicce nach tarla cland eatorra, 7 fa h-olc les an righ 7 le feruib
Erenn uile sin. La ecin dar erichc an ri go moch 'na aenar ar
faithce na Temrach iarsin, 7 tainec go Tibra an Laeich Leisc d'
indlad a lam 7 a gnuísi 7 a aidhce. Nir cian do ann go facaidh
an triar da indsaigid a n-edaighib ro-geala ro-soillsi ro-delradach.
15 Acus ba ro-ingnadh lasin rig a n-indell 7 a n-ecuse; oir ní fhaca
se a leithed do daeinibh reime sin. Tancotar do lathair, 7 do
bendaigetar a n-ainm an Athar 7 an Mic 7 an Spirda Naeimh
don righ. 'IS neamghnathaeh linde an bendugad sin donithí-si
dvinn,' ar ind rig; 'oír ní na n-ainm sen clectmaid-ne bendugad
20 dunn act a n-ainm na n-dee aeieoir da creidmíd fein.' Do fiarfaig an ri sgela dib, ca h-inadh as a tangatar, no cred iad na
gnoaighte ima tancvtar. Do frecratar san e, 7 assedh adubratar:
'Dia na n-uile cumhact .i. cruthuigeoir nimhe 7 talman 7 na n-uile
dul, 7 ata 'na aen-dia 7 'na tri persanaib do cuir cugat-sa sind,
25 da rada rit an recht rig-sa do bi agat go trasda .i. suil a suil, 7
cos a cois, 7 lam a laim, do treicen 7 recht nva do gabáil cugat
bus ferr ina sin; oir da m-benad droch-dhuine a suil no a chos
no a lam do duine maith, dobo becc an eruic andsin a shuil nó a
chos no a lamh fen; 7 da m-benadh duine maith a suil no a cos
30 no a lam do droch-duine, dobo ro-mor 7 dobo nemhimcubaid a
shuil no a chos no a lam do bvain don dvine maith ar a son sin.
ET o ata sin mar sin, ben eraic oir 7 airgid, cruid 7 cethra
amuigh and gach en-drochraed bec no mór da n-dentar fud, do
reir mar docifidher duit feín 7 do dainib eolcha ecnaidhe do
35 righacta 7 do tigernais, 7 da n-derna tú so, dobera Dia luach duit
ar a son .i. do ben ata aimrid re fada geinfider mac etrad 7 hí,
7 bud lan Eri 7 Alba 7 Saxa 7 iarthar domain uile da clu 7 da
scelaib, 7 bud Conn ced-cathach a ainm, 7 budh ar a slicht beid
righraid Erenn go brath. ET, fos, geinfider mac ar slict an
40 Chuind sin, 7 bud Colam cilli a ainm, 7 bud é an dara glun déc
uaid-se fein é, 7 bud gen t-sochair do dainib íarthair domain é,

grandson of Conn, and he shall be filled with the graces and the blessing of the God that is One and Three, and that is, and hath been, and shall be. And many shall be his sanctuaries and churches in Erin and Alba. And he shall bless this land from this stream thither, and it shall be a sanctuary to all that go there forevermore. And in his honor it was that Bran had mercy on the deer and pursued it not across the stream.''

And from that time Belach Damhain is the name of the place where Bran spared the deer.

43. And by Fedlimid Rechtmar, High King of Erin, was Columcille's coming thus foretold a long while ere his birth. He had taken the daughter of the King of Lochlann to wife, and he had had her a long time, and there had been no child between them. And it was an ill thing to the King and all the men of Erin. Early on a certain day the King of Erin arose and went along on the green of Tara to the well of Laech Lesc to wash his hands and his face and his visage. He had been there a short space only when he saw three men coming toward him in garments passing white and clear and shining, and the King marvelled at their dress and their seeming; for their like never had he seen afore. They came to him and greeted him in the name of the Father and the Son and the Holy Ghost.

"Strange to us is the salutation ye give us," saith the King, "for not in those names are we wont to be saluted, but in the name of the gods of the air we believe in".

The King asked tidings of them then, whence they came, and on what errand. They answered him and said in this wise:

"The God of All Power, Creator of Heaven and Earth and all the elements, that is one God in three persons, He it was sent us to thee to bid thee forsake the law of kings that hath been thine till now, to wit, an eye for an eye, a foot for a foot, a hand for a hand; and he chargeth thee to take a new law that is better than that. For if an evil wight pluck out the eye or the foot or the hand of a good man, his own eye or foot or hand would be small return therefor. And if a good man should pluck out the eye or the foot or hand of a bad man, excessive and unfitting would it be to take away the eye or the foot or the hand of a good man therefor. And sith it is thus, exact a fine of gold or silver, flocks and cattle, for every crime, small or great, that is done under thy sway, as seemeth right to thee and to wise and learned men in thy kingdom and thy province. And if thou do this, God will give thee reward therefor, that is, thy wife that hath long been barren shall bear thee a son, and Erin and Alba and Saxonland and the Western World shall be filled with the fame of him and with tales of him. And his name shall be Conn of the Hundred Battles, and of his kin shall be the royal line of Erin forever. And moreover there shall be born a son of the race of this Conn, and Columcille shall

7 bud dalta do righ nimhe 7 talman é, 7 doirtid Día a grasa go
h-imarcach air, 7 bíaidh se ar lassadh do gradh De, indus co m-bera
do comrad 7 d'imacallaim riss fein gacha dardaeín in a flaithemnus nemdha fein é. Acus bidh a fihis agat, a ri Erenn, gorap a
n-onoír an mic sin, 7 do cend co ticfa se ar do slicht, toilighes
Día slicht do beith ort, 7 nach ar do shon feín no at onoir dogeib
tú hé' (fol. 4b).

44. Do tairrngiretar draithe Conaill Gulban, mic Neill naigiallaig, techt Colaim cilli ria na genemain amlaid so .i. La da
raibe Conall ag seilg 7 ag fiadach a nGartan, ní headh amhain
nach dendaeis a coin no a cuan dith no digbail don fiadach, act
do bídis ac cluithe acus ag sugradh riv. Do b' ingnad le Conall an
ní sin, 7 do tuig go raibe se a n-adhaidh naduíri go mor, 7 do
fiafraigh do na draithib do bi faris cred bud ciall do sin. 'Ata
a fis sin againde,' ar na draithe .i. 'Berthor mac dot slicht-sa san
inadh-so in a bfvil tu anossa, 7 bud é an tres glun uaid-si é, 7
bud Colam cilli a ainm, 7 biaid se lan do grasaib en-día na n-uile
cumhacht 7 crutaigheora na n-dul, 7 bendeochaid se an t-inad sa,
7 bud comairghe 7 termonn da gach nech ricfas a les tect and go
brath aris é. Acus as a n-onoir an mic sin 7 na comairghe oir-
deochas se do beith ag an ferand so tucatar do coin-se, a Conaill,
comairge don fiadhach ud san inadh in a m-bertar é,' bar na
draithe.

45.[23]) Amhail do derbhatar na sen-naeimh uaisli eolcha sin
re faidedoract o Día tect Colaim cilli, 7 mar do derbotar na draithe
ag nach raibe creidemn a thecht, do derbhat (recte dh) le fisib 7 le
haislingibh a techt mar an cedna, do reir mar docondairc a mathair fein a n-aisling .i. Dar lé fen brat mor do tabairt di, 7 do

---

[23]Taken literally from O. I. L. See *Lis. Lives,* p. 24. The source of the
account in the Old Irish Life was Adamnan. See Reeves' *Adam.,* pp. 190-1.
O'D relates this same vision in § 46 which he borrowed directly from Adamnan.
Hence O'D.'s double account of the same vision.

be his name, and he shall be the twelfth generation from thyself. And fortunate shall be his birth for the Western World, and fosterling shall he be of the King of Heaven and Earth. And God shall pour out his graces richly upon him, and he shall be aflame with the love of God, in such wise that God shall bring him each Thursday to his heavenly kingdom for speech and converse with Him. And wit thou well, O King of Erin, it is in honor of that child and because he is to come of thy seed, that God doth permit thee to have offspring, and not for thy own sake nor for thine own honor is it given thee.''

III

OF VISIONS FORETELLING THE BIRTH OF COLUMCILLE AND OF MARVELS BEFORE HIS BIRTH

44. The druids of Conall Gulban, son of Niall of the Nine Hostages, did thus foretell the coming of Columcille afore his birth: On a day that Conall was hunting and chasing at Gartan, his hounds did neither hurt nor harm to the game, and not this only, but they played and gamboled with it. And this thing seemed a marvel to Conall, he understanding that it was sore against nature. And he asked his druids what was the meaning thereof.

"We wit well," say the druids. "A child shall be born of thy kin in this place where thou now art, and he shall be of the third generation from thee; and Columcille shall be his name, and filled shall he be of the graces of the one God of All Power and Creator of the Elements. And he shall bless this place and be safeguard and sanctuary to everyone that shall need to come hither till Doom. And it is to honor that child, and the sanctuary he shall ordain in this land, that thy hounds, O Conall, have granted mercy to that game in the place where he shall be born," say the druids.

45. As those wise and worshipful saints of old did avouch the coming of Columcille by the prophetic gift they had from God, and as the druids did avouch it, albeit they had not the Faith, so likewise was his coming avouched by visions and dreams. And his mother herself saw it in a dream. Her seemed a great cloak was given her, and the length and the breadth of that cloak reached from the west of Erin to the east of Alba; and of the colors of the world was not one color that was not thereon. And her seemed there came to her a youth in shining raiment, and

bi d' fhad 7 do leithne 'sa m-brat go rainec ó iarthar Ereann co
hoirther Alban, 7 nach raibe do dathaib an domain dath nach
raibe and. ET dar lé tainic oclach a n-edach taitnemhach da
indsoigid 7 ruc an brat vaithe, 7 bá dubach issi de sin. Tainec
an t-oclach cedna cuige arís 7 adubairt an comrad-sa ria: 'A
ben maith,' ar se, 'ni rige a les bron na dubachas do beith ort,
act as cora duid failte 7 subachas do denam, vair is é is fidhair
7 is esimlair don brat ut docondcais, go m-bera tusa mac 7 go
mba lan Eri 7 Alpa dá clu 7 da scelaib.'

46.[24]) Ata Adamnan naemtha ga mebrugad, gor foillsig aingel Dé é fein uair eli do mathair Colaim cilli 'na codlud 7 hi
torrach ar Colam cilli fen, 7 gur thaisben se tváille di 7 ilrad
gacha datha and, 7 baladh gach mesa 7 gacha blatha 7 gacha
neich degbholaid air. Acus do lec tamall ar lar na fiadnaise é
7 do togaib se leis vaithe arís é. Acus ar m-breith an tváille
vaithe, do gab toirrse 7 dobron mor hi, 7 audbairt risin aingel:
'Cred fá rucais adhbhar an t-sholais ro-moir do taisbenais damh
comluath 7 sin uaim.' Do frecair an t-aingel í, 7 assedh adubairt
ria: 'Comarda neich ro-moir do taisbenadh duid, 7 ni heidir a
comonorach do beith at fihiadhnaise nías faide ina sud.' Ar
crichnugad an comraid sin don aingel, do erigh a n-airde isin
aeieor 7 an tváille les. Dar le Ethne do leth an tvaille tar Eirind
7 tar Albain 7 tar iarthar domain uile. Acus docuala sí an t-aingel ga radha do guth mor iar sin: 'A ben maith,' ar se, 'bidh
luthgair ort .i. 'Berair mac dot fhir posda fen 7 biaid se mar
fáidh an Tigerna nemdha ag glaedhaig ar cach do munad na
sliged moire doib docum nimhe, 7 molfider Dia go ro-mor trid;
7 dogeba se coroin iter na faidib a flaithes De, 7 biaid se 'na
treoraigteoir ag moran do anmonnvib ga m-breith docum na cathrach nemdha.' Ar cricnugad na m-briatar sin adubairt an t-aingel re h-Eithne, do bidg si go ro-mhor, 7 do mosgail si as a codlud
iar sin. Acus do bi sí go curamach deisgridech umhal ag serbis
7 ag fritolum don toirrces sin do bi aice o sin amach, 7 do coimhed
sí an radarc sin tuc an t-aingel dí in a croide 7 in a h-inntinn go
foirfe.

47.[25]) Docondairc ben formaid 7 imthnuid[26]) d' Eithne aisi-

[24]See Reeves' *Adam.*, pp. 190-1. This vision is really the same as that related above in § 45.

[25]Source is O. I. L. See *Lis. Lives*, p. 24.

[26]O'D. misinterprets his source, i.e., the O. I. L. *Lis. Lives*, p. 24, has *atconnuic dano a ben imtha-si* (her chamber (?)—woman). *Three Homilies*, p. 100, has *itconnarc tra an ben imtha sin*.

took the cloak from her, and she was sorrowful thereat. Then came the same youth to her again and said to her these words:

"Good woman," saith he, "thee behooveth not sorrow and grief, but rather beseemeth thee to be joyous and to make merry; for the cloak thou didst see is a prefigurement and sign that thou shalt bear a son, and that Erin and Alba shall be full of his fame and renown."

46. Saint Adamnan maketh mention that an angel of God manifested himself another time to the mother of Columcille in her sleep when she was pregnant of Columcille. And he showed her a napkin, and thereon was a multitude of all colors, and the fragrance of every fruit and of every flower and of every sweet-smelling thing. And he laid it down for a space in her sight, and then he took it away from her with him again. And when the napkin was taken from her, grief and sorrow seized her, and she said to the angel:

"Wherefore hast thou thus soon taken from me the cause of such great joy that thou wast showing me?"

The angel answered her and said to her: "The prefigurement of a passing great thing hath been shown to thee, and no longer may an honor so great be in thy sight."

And when the angel had said these words he rose upward into the air, and the napkin with him. And to Ethne it seemed that the napkin spread over Erin and Alba and all the Western World.

And then she heard the angel saying with a great voice: "Good woman," saith he, "be thou joyful. Thou shalt bear thy husband a son and he shall be like one of the prophets of the Lord of Heaven, calling all men to teach them the broad way to Heaven, and God shall be praised passing well through him, and he shall receive a crown among the prophets of God's Kingdom, and he shall be a guide to many souls, conveying them to the heavenly city."

And when the words were finished that the angel spake to Ethne, she gave a great start and awoke from her sleep. And from that hour with care and watchfulness she served humbly and watched over the burden that she bare, and in her heart and mind she cherished the sight the angel had brought her.

47. A woman with ill-will and envy toward Ethne beheld a vision:

ling .i. énach 7 ethaidedha an aeieoir 7 na talman, dar le fen, do breith inathair Eithne fo crichaib 7 fo cendadachaib Erenn 7 Alpan, 7 fa luthgairech le mnai an imtnvidh a faicsin sen. Rug Etne fen breth na h-aislinge sin, 7 assed adubairt: 'Berad-sa
5 mac,' ar si, '7 rachaid a briathar 7 a senmoir fo crichaib Erenn 7 Alban, amail dorindedh a faidhedóract 7 a tairrngeri le naemaibh Erenn 7 Alpan, 7 amail doconncos a fisib 7 a n-aislingib dó.'

48.²⁷ Docondaic Finden naemtha aisling eli .i. Dar leis fein dá esca d'erghe 'san aeier .i. esga oir 7 esca airgid, 7 an t-esca
10 oir d'erghe don taeb thuaid d'Erinn, 7 gor las Eri 7 Alpa 7 iarthar domain da delrad 7 da shuillsi 7 da taitnem; 7 an t-esga airgid os cinn Cluana mic Noís, gor las medón Erenn da delrad 7 da soillsi. Rug Finden fen breth na h-aislinge sin .i. go m-berad ben Feilimthe, mic Fergosa cendfada, mac don taeb thuaid
15 d'Erinn, 7 go madh Colam cilli a ainm, 7 go rachad esimlair 7 delrad a bethad ainglidhe, 7 a gloine 7 a crabaid a ecna 7 a eolais a breithri 7 a senmora, fá iarthar domain uile, 7 go madh é Ciaran mac an t-saeir an t-esca aircid con a subaltadhaib 7 go n-deggnimhartaibh (fol. 5a).

20 49. Do labrumar don faidhedoract-sa dorindetar naeim Erenn ar thect Colaim cilli, 7 don tairrngire dorindetar na draithe, ag nach raibe creidem, ar a thect, 7 don radharc tuc Dia a fisib 7 a n-aislingib do moran do daínibh ar a tect mar in cedna. IS follus duinn asdaib so uili, nach edh amain do togh Dia Colam
25 cilli a m-broinn a mathar, acht gor togh se a fad ria tect a m-broinn a mathar mar serbfhogantaidh diles dó fein é. ET, fós, as follus duind gor b'ail le Día a molad fein do tect go ro-mor as Colam cilli nísa mó 7 nisa linmairi ina dob'ail les a thecht as en-naemh eli da tainec riamh ar a lan do ghnéthibh, amail indeo-
30 sus an betha ó so amach, tresna grasaib 7 tresna subaltaidib 7 tresna tindluictib diadha, 7 tresna mirbuilib roimarcacha romora dob'ail les do tabairt do ré na foillsivgad 'sa saeghal-sa. ET as follus dunn aris, nach eadh amhain dob'ail le Dia Colam cilli do cur a cosmuiles ris na h-uasal-aithrechaib 7 ris na naemaib
35 eli tainec reime, act cor b'ail les a cor a cosmailes ris fen ar in modh-sa; oir nir cvir cholainn daénda uime aenduine ar a n-dernad oiread faidhedoracta 7 tairrgire re Colam cilli ria na gheinemain, act an Tigerna Ihsv Crisd amain.

---

[27] Taken literally from O. I. L. See *Lis. Lives*, pp. 25-6, and p. 357; also *L. B.*, p. 131ᵇ, ll. 41-8.

her seemed the birds and winged creatures of the air and earth did bear the vitals of Ethne over the domains and tribal lands of Erin and Alba. And it was a glad sight to the envious woman to behold it. But Ethne understood the signification of that vision and said:

"I shall bear a son," saith she, "and his words and his teaching shall spread over the lands of Erin and Alba, as it hath done in the prophecies and promises of him by the saints of Erin and Alba, and as hath been manifest in visions and dreams of him."

48. Another vision did Saint Finnen behold: him thought he saw two moons arising in the air: a moon of gold and a moon of silver. And the golden moon rose up in the north of Erin; and Erin and Alba and the Western World were ablaze with its brightness and its light and its shining. And the silver moon rose up above Clonmacnoise; and the midparts of Erin were aflame with its brightness and light. Finnen himself interpreted the meaning of that vision, to wit, that the wife of Fedlimid, son of Fergus Cennfada, should bear a son in the north of Erin, and Columcille should be his name; and the ensaumple and brightness of his angelic life and of his purity and piety, and his wisdom and knowledge, his judgment and preaching should spread over all the Western World. And Ciaran son of the Wright should be the silver moon by reason of his virtue and good deeds.

49. We have rehearsed the prophesying of the coming of Columcille that the saints of Erin made, and the promises of his coming that the druids made that had not the Faith, and the sight God gave of his coming likewise to much people in visions and in dreams. And from all this it is manifest to us that God set apart Columcille as His own chosen servant, not from his mother's womb only, but long while ere his coming to his mother's womb. And moreover it is clear to us that God was fain His praise should come right largely from Columcille, and in many ways, more largely and more abundantly indeed than from any other saint that ever lived, as the *Life* from this point will tell, through graces and virtues and gifts of God, and through many and passing great marvels that it pleased Him to give to Columcille to show forth in this world. And we see moreover that it pleased God not solely to make Columcille in the likeness of the patriarchs and the other saints that went before him in this thing, but eke in the likeness of Himself. For save our Lord Jesu Christ alone, none ever did on human flesh that had made concerning him the number of prophecies and covenants that were made of Columcille tofore his birth.

50. Laibeorum anois do mirbuil*ib* Colaim Cilli a m-broinn a mathar, am*ail* mebr*aig*es an nech naemtha darob ainm Mura.²⁸)
AR m-beith do m*athai*r C.c. torrach air fein, tainec nech naemtha, darb' ainm Fergna, ar cuairt cuicce, ar na foillsivgad d'*aingel* Dé dó go raibe an toirrches bendaigthe naemtha-sin aice. ET aderaid eol*aig* gorab derbshiur dí fein m*athai*r *an* F*her*gna-sin. IS andsin do chuir an m*a*c bendaighte naemtha sin, do naemadh ria tect a m-broinn a m*atha*r .i. C. c. failte reimh F*er*ghna, 7 do cvir se a ordóg tre broinn a m*atha*r, mar com*a*rta failte 7 luthgairi remhe, amail isb*er*t Mura isna randaib-si:

Dardaein cedlabhra Col*aim*   rian a br*eith,* dal gan doghaing,
da*r* fer se failte go mbl*aidh*²⁹)   re Fergna m*a*c rig Caisil.

Mar do fer failte re Ferghna,   m*a*c rig Caisil Mvm*an* mv*a*id,
a ordain tre broin*n* a mháth*ar,*   gin cor gnáth*ach,* do sín vaid.

Et as follus ass so gor cuir Dia C. c. a coismuiles re h-Eoin baisde an uair dorinde se luthgair a m-broind Elisdabed reimh Muiri 7 í torrach ar Ihsv. Acus ni hedh amaín do cuir se a cosmailes re h-Eoin é, *act* do cuir se a ceim foirfidhechta os a chend é ar an modh-sa; oir ni derna Eoin *act* comartha luthgara a m-broinn a m*atha*r roimhe an Tigherna, 7 do cuir C. c. a ordog tre broinn a mhathar, mar comartha luthgairi reimh Ferghna, 7 gan é *act* na duine bec semplide. Acus fetar a rádha gorab tre mhaithes an Tigherna fen táin*ec* d'Eoin luthgairi do denamh reimhe an uair tainec se 'na cend; oir nirb'ingn*ad* gach uile duil dar cruthaidh se fein do denum luthgaire reimhe.

51.³⁰) Fectus d'Eithne .i. do math*ar* C. c., is an inadh ré n-abarth*ur* Gartan; 7 an oidhce ria Colam c. do br*eith,* do taisben nech óg scíam*ach* a n-edach ro-delr*ad*ach é fen d'Ethne, 7 adub*airt* ria go m-beradh sí an m*a*c do bi a tairrng*ir*e di do breith ar na márach. Acus do indis di go raibe lec lethan cloiche isin loch do bi don taeb b*ud* des don inadh sin a raibe sí dá ngoirther Loch m*i*c Ciabain aniugh. Acus adub*airt* ria a tab*airt* fodera in lec sin do breith isin inadh aírithe ris a n-abarth*ur* Raith Cno, 7 go madh uirri do toileoch*ad* Dia di an lenab do br*eith.* 'Cindus dogeb-sa an lec sin ata fai an loch,' ar sí, 'no cind*us* aitheónas me hi sech na lecaib eli.' 'Dogebair ag snam ar ua*c*tar an locha

---

²⁸He died *circ.* 650. See Reeves' *Adam.*, pp. VII, LXVIII.
²⁹*Cf.* § 159.
³⁰This account is probably derived from tradition. See Reeves' *Adam.*, LXVIII.

50. We shall tell now of the marvels of Columcille in his mother's womb, according as a certain holy man hight Mura rehearseth them. When the mother of Columcille was heavy with him, there came a holy man hight Fergna to visit her, for it had been revealed to him by an angel of God that she had that holy blessed burden. And wise men say it was her sister that was mother to that Fergna. Then the holy blessed child Columcille, that was holy ere ever he came to his mother's womb, greeted Fergna and put his thumb through the belly of his mother in token of welcome and of gladness for him, as Mura hath said in these quatrains:

> "On a Thursday the first speech of Colum,
> Ere his birth, a tryst without sadness,
> When he blithely bade welcome to Fergna,
> The son of the ruler of Cashel.
>
> When he gave welcome to Fergna,
> Prince of Cashel in Munster the lofty,
> His thumb through the womb of his mother
> He stretched,—a thing unexampled."

And clear it is therefrom that God set Columcille in the likeness of John the Baptist when he made great joy in the womb of Elizabeth before Mary, and she heavy with Jesu at that time. And in this wise he set him not only in equality with John, but surpassing him in degree of perfection. John did but make a sign of joy in the womb of his mother before the Lord, whereas Columcille put his thumb through his mother's womb as a sign of joy before Fergna, that was but a poor simple man. And we may say it was the Lord's goodness that made John rejoice when He approached him, and it were no marvel that all things He created should rejoice before Him.

51. On a time Ethne the mother of Columcille was in the place that is called Gartan, and it was the night before Columcille was born, and there appeared a fair youth in shining raiment, and he said she should bring forth on the morrow the son that was promised her to bear. And he told her there was a broad flagstone in the lake, to the south of the place where she was, and that is today called Loch mic Ciabain. And he told her to let bring that flagstone to a certain place called Raith Cno and that thereon should God will the child to be brought forth of her.

"In what manner shall I get the flagstone, seeing it is under the lake," saith she, "or whereby shall I know it from other flagstones?"

"Thou shalt find it floating on the bosom of the lake," saith he.

And Ethne found the flagstone on the morrow as it had been told her, and she let bring it from the foresaid place. And albeit it floated on

hí,' ar se. Fvair Eithne an lec ar na mairech amail adub*rad* ria,
7 do furail a breith asin inadh sin adubrum*ar* romaind; 7 ge do
bi sí ag snamh ar uachtar an locha, 7 ge rucc muinnter Ethne
gan saeth*ar* leo hi, is deimhin gorbh obair t*ric*ad fer a breith on
5 loch gusin inadh a fuil sí aniugh.

  An uair, t*ra,* tainec teinnes lenib docum Eithne, dochuaidh
sí a n-alltan uaicnech cois srotha bicc do bi a comghar di, 7 do
bi sí 'na svidhe in inadh airidhe and, 7 do fagaib si don fuil, b*ud*
dual do tect roimhe an lenabh,' san inadh sin. Acus an cre
10 dogeibther and, ni m*í*ne 7 ni gile pl*úr* ina hí; 7 ge be duine
caithes *no* imc*r*as ní don cré sin, ni loisct*er* 7 ni baither 7 ni
marbt*har* d'én-orchar an la go n-oidhce sin é, 7 ni fagand se bas
gan sagart, 7 gach ben bis re n-idhnaib caithes ní di, foiridh a
ce*do*ir hí, 7 gach nech cuires ní ar a tengaid di an ced la gab*hus*
15 fiabhrus é, ni bí blas serb in a bel ó sin amach ar fedh an fíabruis
sin, 7 as dual go foirfe si g*ach* vili esl*á*inte. ET is duine ecin do
duthcas*ach*aibh an baile sin Gart*án* is coir do tochailt na c*r*iadh-
sa, dá tab*air*t do cach; 7 da derb*ad* sin, doch*uaid* anduth-
c*as*ach da tochailt (*fol.* 5b) uair ecin 7 do teith sí reimhe, 7
20 docuaidh sí astech a medon croind no bile moir do bi dá coir,
7 n*i* f*r*ith na h-inadh fein hi no gor croithedh uisce coisrectha
air 7 gor bendaighed e. Teid Ethne ass sin gus an inad a ruc sí
C. c., an uair dob'aeis f*iche* bl*iadan.*³¹) 7 cuicc ced don Tigerna.

  52. A nGartan, u*morro*, a cenel Conaill G*ulban*, ruc*adh* C.
25 c., 7 Raith Cno ainm an inaidh airide a nGartan a ruc*adh* é, 'sa
sectmadh la do m*í* medhoin an gemrid. Acus tarla an lec so
adubram*ar* romhaind fai ga breith, 7 do leig an lenab a crois
uirri é,³²) 7 do foscail an lec remhe ind*us* cor leic sí inad do innte,
7 ata fidhair³³ na croise sin'sa leic o soin ale. Acus mairidh an
30 lec sin fos san inadh sin ag denvm fert 7 mirbuile. Acus rug a
m*atha*ir cloch c*r*uin*n* ar dath na fola a n-enf*ect* ris, 7 "an cloch
ruad" a h-ainm, 7 do fagaib se a nGartan hí ag denam f*h*ert 7
mirbhal, 7 ni gaband sí a cumdach le h-or no le h-airget; ge
minec do tairged a cumdach, 7 fuilng*ed* sí a cas airgid no o*í*r.

35   Laibeoram anois do mirbail*ib* C. c. tar eis a geineamna ar
in saeghal-sa.

---

³¹See Thurneysen's *Handbuch* § 388, p. 233.

³²"and the child rested him in (the form of) a cross on it." *Cf.* § 112, *a edan do legen uirre* "rested his forehead upon it."

³³"figure, form", not "sign". See *Lis. Lives,* p. 301.

the surface of the lake, and Ethne's folk brought it away with them without labor, certain it is that it were a task for thirty men to bring it from the lake to the place where it is to-day.

And when the sickness of childbirth came upon Ethne, she went to a lonely valley hard by a little stream. And she sat down in a certain spot there, and in that place she left some of the blood that is wont to come before the child.

And not finer and not whiter is flour than the clay that is found there. And whoso eateth or bringeth with him of that clay is never burned nor drowned, nor may he be killed by one cast that day till night. Nor shall he get a death without priest. And every woman in pangs of childbirth that eateth thereof is helped forthwith. And whoso putteth thereof on his tongue the first day that a fever seizeth him, there is no bitter taste in his mouth from that time the while the fever lasteth. And it is its nature to heal every distemper. And it must be that one of the natives of this place, to wit, Gartan, should dig this clay to bestow on all, for men say a stranger once went to dig it, and it fled from him and entered the heart of a tree or a great big trunk fast by, nor was it found again in its own place until holy water was sprinkled thereon and it was blessed.

Then went Ethne thence to the place where she brought forth Columcille, the time when the age of our Lord was five hundred and twenty years.

52. In Gartan, in sooth, in Cenel Conaill Gulban, Columcille was born. And Raith Cno is the name of the very spot in Gartan where he was brought forth, on the seventh day of December. And it befell that the foresaid flagstone was under him at his birth, and the child rested him crosswise thereon, and the flagstone opened for him in such wise that it left a place for him therein. And the figure of that cross is in that stone from that time to this day. And that flagstone remaineth in that place for working of marvels and wonders. And his mother brought forth a round stone of the color of blood along with him and it is called the Red Stone. And he left that stone in Gartan to work marvels and wonders; and it doth not take a covering of gold nor of silver, albeit men have oft endeavored to cover it, but a case of silver or of gold it suffereth.

Now speak we of the marvels of Columcille following his birth into this world.

53. Uasal igantach ag Día 7 ag daeinib an mac rug*ad* andsin .i. mac ochta rig nimhe 7 talman .i. C. c., m*a*c Felim[the]. Do baisd an t-vasal-sagart .i. Cruithnechan mac Cell*a*ch*a*in e ar na breith a cedoir, 7 tuc C*ri*mthann mar ainm air. Acus do oil 7 do coimeid é iarsin, amail adubrut*ar* aingle De ris. Acus is inand Crimtand re rada 'sa Gaidilig 7 celgach no sindach 'sa Laidin. Acus, gedheadh, do condcas do Dia cum*a*ctach nar cnesda 7 narb imcub*aid* do cailid*h*ect 7 do maithes an m*a*caim naomtha sin an t-ainm-si do beith air, 7 do cuir se a croidhedhaib 7 a m*en*main na lenab 7 na macam, do bid ag cluiche 7 ag sug*r*ad ris, Colaim do gairm de. *No* is íad a aingle fen do cuir se c*u*ca dá radha riv a gairm de, amail derb*as* M*u*ra is na rannaib-si:

Col*am* c*i*lli, a ai*n*m do ni*m*h,   mac Feilim*the*, ag aingl*i*b,
gan imroll, ga*n* dalb³⁴), gan dron,   Crimth*a*n a ai*n*m'sa
                                                        saegal.
Da*r*dai*n* nochar chainge*n* cle   ag ainglibh rig an
                                              richidhé,
dar b*en*sat*ar* C*ri*mthan de   's dar goirsead Col*am* c*i*ll*i*.

ET adubratar gan an t-ainm drochiallaidhe-se nach tiuf*ad* acht ar drochduine, do gairm de .i. Crimthann. Acus mar do bi an macaemh naemth*a-s*a ga oilem*ain* a m-baile cilli do bi a comghar doib .i. Doiri Eithne, da ngoirth*er* Cill m*i*c Nenain aniugh, do gnathaidis na leinib do bidh ag sug*r*ad ris Colam on cill do rad ris. Gonadh mar sin do an C. c. mar ainm air. Acus ata se fen ga derb*ad* sin'sa rand-so:

An*n*si*n* adubr*ad* on cill   leth m'a*n*ma, nocha ceilim,
Cell m*i*c Nenain naemhp*or*t damh,   noch*ar* aenta*idh* me a
                                                        tregea*n*.

---

³⁴*leg.* dailb.

IV

OF MARVELS FOLLOWING HIS BIRTH AND OF THE CHILDHOOD OF COLUMCILLE

53. Noble and wonderful to God and man the child that was born then, to wit, the darling of the King of Heaven and Earth, Columcille, son of Fedlimid. The noble priest Cruithnechan mac Cellechain did baptize him straightway he was brought forth, and gave him the name Crimthann. And he fostered and guarded him thereafter as the angels of God had charged him. And in Gaelic to say "Crimthann" is the same as "deceitful one" or "fox" in Latin. Howbeit, it seemed to the God of Power unmeet and unbefitting to the quality and the goodness of the holy youth for him to have that name, and He put it into the heart and mind of the children and little boys that did play and frolic with him to call him Colum. Or it was His angels He sent to them to bid them call him so, as Múra declareth in these quatrains:

> "Columcille was his name from Heaven,
> The son of Fedlimid, by angels,
> Without error or falsehood, without twisting (?).
> Crimthann his name in the world.
>
> On a Thursday, the case was no falsehood,
> He was with the angels of Heaven
> When they cut from him 'Crimthann' away,
> And Columcille did they name him."

And they declared that a name of ill-meaning, and unfitting save for evil folk, to wit, Crimthann, should not be given to him. And as the holy youth was fostered in the monastic church nigh hand, to wit, Doire Ethne, that is today called Cill mic Nenain, the children that were wont to play with him called him Colum (Dove) of the Cill (Church). Thus it was that Columcille was his name. And he himself doth bear witness thereto in this quatrain:

> "Then was called from the church
> The half of my name, I conceal not;
> Cill mic Nenain my heavenly rest,
> I was not willing to leave it."

And this is why Almighty God bade the name Colum be given him, because the dove is a figure and likeness of the Holy Spirit himself,

ET as e adbor far seol Dia cumactach Colam do tabairt mar ainm
air, gorab fidhair 7 cosamlacht don Spirud Naem fein *an* colam;
7 da derbadh sin, is a fidhair colaim docunnairc Eoin baisde an
Spirad Naem ag luidhe ar Crisd an uair do baisd se ag sruth
Eorthanain e. Acus adbar eli far seol Dia Colam do tabairt air,
oir is amlaid ata an colaim fein o naduir ronemhuirchoidech, 7 do
bi C. c. mar sin. IN tres adbar far seol Dia an t-ainm-si do tabairt
ar an macamh naemtha-sa da fuilmid ag labairt, oir tar gach uile
en don enlaith ni bi domblas aéi 'sa colam. Fétar a radha go raibe
C. c. mar sin, oir ni raibe celg no fvath no aingidecht no ní nemglan
no serb ar bith 'na croide no na indtinn don taeib astoigh, 7 ni mó
do cvir se a ngnimh don taeb amuigh en-red becc *no* mór do rachad
a n-esonoir do Dia, an fad do bvi se 'na bethaid sa saeghal-sa.

54. Tulach Dubglaisi, a cinel Conoill, ainm an inaidh in ar
baisdedh C. c. am*ail* asp*ert* an nech naemtha dana h-ainm Mura:

>   Rugad a nGartan da deoin,   do h-oiledh a Cill mac n-Eoin,
>   do baisded mac na maisi   a Tulaig De Dubglaisi.

ET an lec ar ar baisded é, do foired gach uili eslainte da m-berthai
cuice. Acus fa trom le mnai comorba an baile sin a fadhadh[35])
sí do dochur na ndaine eslan 7 na n-oilithrech tigedh d'indsoigidh
na leice, indus gor cuir an ben mallaigthe an lec bendaigthe a
n-dabaig uisce ata don taeb thuaid don baili, 7 (ni fri)th o sin
alle hi. Acus ata a tairrngire go fuig(ter hi) 7 go m-bia in baili
go maith o sin amach. Acus dorinde Crvithnechan an mac
bendvighte d'oilemain iarsin, do rer mar adubratar aingle De ris.

55. Ata indamail reilge bige 'sa m-baili-si Tulcha Dubglaisi,
da ngoirther cedimtecht C. c. .i. an aít a n-derna se a cedimtecht
7 a cedsivbal na lenabh, amail asbert Baithin naem:

>   Reilec bec don taeb atuaidh   a Tulaig Dubglaisi go m-buaidh,
>   Colam cilli coir, gan acht,   ann (?) dorinde a cedimthecht,

56. ET mebraigidh an nech naemta-sa darab ainm Baithin,
(*fol.* 6a) gebe duine dodenadh oilitre an ina[i]dh sin, na bud
dual go tibradh sé galar no esslainte ar bith les ass; amhail derbus
se fen isna randaibh-si:

---

[35]*leg.* faghadh.

and to verify this it was in the figure of a dove that John the Baptist saw the Holy Spirit resting upon Christ when he baptized Him in the river Jordan. And another reason why God bade the name Colum be given him was because the dove is guileless by nature, and so in like wise was Columcille. The third reason why God bade this name be given to the gentle holy boy whereof we speak was because, beyond every bird of birds, there is no bitterness of gall in the dove. It may be said that Columcille was in this wise, for there was neither deceit nor hatred nor wickedness nor unclean thing nor bitter, in his heart or in his mind within. Nor did he ever outward deed, small or great, to dishonor God, the while he was living in this world.

54. Tulach Dubglaisi in the domain of Conall is the name of the place where Columcille was baptized, as the holy man saith that is called Mura:

> "With his accord was he born in Gartan,
> In Cell mac n-Eoin[1] was he fostered;
> The son of beauty was baptized
> In God's Tulach Dubglaisi."

And the flagstone whereon he was baptized did succour all the sick that were borne thereto. Grievous to the warden of that place was the trouble she had of the sick folk and the pilgrims that came to the flagstone, so that the accursed creature put the blessed flag into a (flax) dam of water to the north of the village, and from that time till today it hath not been found. And there is a prophecy that it shall be found and that the place shall fare well thereafter.

Then Cruithnecan did foster the holy boy as the angels of God had charged him.

55. There is a place like a little churchyard in this townland of Tulach Dubglaisi, that is called the First Walk of Columcille, to wit, the place where he took his first steps and did his first walking as a child, as holy Baithin hath said:

> "A little churchyard to the north
> In Tulach Dubglaisi of victory,
> Columcille, righteous without doubt,
> There he did his first walking."

56. And the holy man called Baithin maketh mention that whoso goeth a pilgrimage to that place, it were against nature that he should bring malady or sickness with him therefrom, as he himself affirmeth in these verses:

[1] Cill mic Nenain.

INte timcellus, gan chair,   cedimtecht Colaim craibthig,
bud maith les a menma amuigh,   ni taed a m-berna baegan.

Cred fa m-bíadh galar no greim   a smvais no a cnaimh no a
                                    cuislind,
a cend no a cois no a n-inne,   ar slict Colaim caimchille.

57. La airdhe do C. c. 'na lenub a nGartan, 7 tucc duine brec marb chuige. Acus do glac C. c. an brec 7 do cuir a tobar do bi 'sa bhaile é. Acus tainec anam and aris, 7 mairid an brec sin fos 'sa richt a raibe an uair sin, tre mirbuilib Dé 7 Colaim cilli. Acus is minec tarla an brec sin a coiri uisce in a m-beith feoil no íasc ga bruith, ar na tabairt da daínib leo a soightig uisce gan fis doib. Acus da loiscthi a m-beith do condadh no do mónaigh sna tírthib fan coiri sin, ni bud moíde tes an coiri sin nó in uisce é, no go m-bentai an brec ass 7 go curthai 'na tobor fen arís é; 7 do derbad sen go menic.

58. Atá lec cloiche 'san oilen ata ar Loch mic Ciabain a nGartan, 7 do gnataiged C. c. dul do cluiche 7 do sugradh uirre an uair do bi sé 'na lenab. Acus na lenib eli teid uirre o sin alle, bid aimrid, 7 ni gentar vatha, a comartha oghacta 7 genmnaideachta C. c., 7 do derbudh sin go minec, 7 "lec na genmnaidechta" ainm na leice sin aniugh.

59.[36] O tainic aimser léginn do C. c., docuaidh Cruithnechna .i. oide C. c., mar a raibe nech naemtha do bí 'sa tir, da fhiarfaige de ga trath bud coir tindscna léighinn do denamh don macamh. Do labhair in nech naemtha sin tre spirad fáidhedóracta 7 assedh adubairt: 'Sgrib anois aibidil do.' Do scribad iarsin, aibidil do a m-bairghein. Acus is amlaid do bi C. c. an vair sin cois srota airidhe, 7 do caith sé cuid don bairgin don taeib tiar don t-sruth sin, 7 an cuid eli don taeib tair don t-sruth cedna. IS andsin do labhair an nech naemtha-sa tre rath ecna 7 faidhedóracta 7 assedh adubairt: 'Is amlaid bias feronn an mic sin ar gach taeibh don uisce .i. don fhairge .i. cuid a n-Erinn de 7 cvid eli a n-Albain; 7 caithfidh se fen cuid dá aimsir in gach inadh dib sin.' Acus do firadh sin, amail derbeochas an betha o so amach.

60. Oidce airidhe do Cruithnechan ag filled on eclais ag dul d'indsoigid a tighe fein, ar crichnugad seirbísi Dé dó, 7 fuair se an tech lomnan do shoillsi 7 do delrad ar a chind, 7 nell tendtidhe

---

[36]Literally from O. I. L. See *Lis. Lives*, p. 24.

"Whoso without sin maketh circuit
Of the first walk of Colum, the pious,
It shall be well with his soul there (?),
He entereth no breach of danger.

Wherefore should be sickness or pang
In marrow or bone or in artery;
In head, or in foot, or in vitals
Of those of the race of fair Colum?"

57. On a certain day that Columcille was a child at Gartan, one gave him a dead trout. And Columcille took the trout, and put it in a well that was in the village, and life came into it again, and the trout yet liveth in the same wise as it was then, through the marvels of God and Columcille. And oft hath it happed that trout to be in a kettle of water wherein were flesh or fish boiling, brought with them by folk in vessels of water unknown to themselves. And if all the firewood and peat in the lands be burned under that pot, neither the pot nor the water would be the hotter therefor until the trout were taken out and put into its own well again. And oft hath this been proved.

58. There is a flagstone in the island of Loch mic Ciabain in Gartan, and Columcille was wont to go to play and frolic thereon when he was a child. And other children that go thereon from that time to this become unfruitful, and naught is born of them, in sign of the virginity and chastity of Columcille. And oft hath this been verified. And the "Flag of Chastity" is the name of the stone to this day.

59. When the time drew nigh for Columcille to begin learning, Cruithnechan his fosterer went where lived a holy man of the land, to ask him when was the time for the gentle lad to make a beginning of studies.

Then the holy man spake through the spirit of prophecy, and said, "Write an alphabet for him forthwith."

Then was written an alphabet for him on a cake. And Columcille was at that time beside a certain stream, and one piece of the cake he ate on the western side of that stream, and the other on the eastern side. And again the holy man spake through the grace of wisdom and prophecy and said: "The land of this boy shall be on both sides of the water, to wit, the sea, one part in Erin and the other part in Alba. And he shall use a part of his time in each of those places."

And it was verified, as the *Life* will show hereafter.

60. On a certain night that Cruithnechan was returning home from the church after he had finished the service of God, he found the house filled with light and brightness, and a fiery cloud over the face of Columcille in the place where he was sleeping. And such was the

os cind aighte C. c 'san inad a raibe se na codludh. Acus do bi do
med na soillse sin, nar féd se beith ga h-amharc. Acus iar na
faicsin don t-shagart, do bidc se go mór, 7 do tuit se ar talm*ain*
tresan radharc sin do taisbenadh do. Acus ar n-eirghe do as a
nell iar sin, do tuic se gorbh'íad grasa an Spirda Naeim do doirtedh ar a dalta fen an uair sin, 7 go rabhat*ar* aingle De ga coimhéd.

61³⁷) Nir fada in a diaidh sin go n-dech*aid* C. c. 7 a oide .i.
Cruithnechan mac Cellechain, ar nodluic gosin esb*oc* naemtha go
Brugach m*a*c n-Degadh, do Raith Enaigh, a Tir Énna. Do furail
an t-espoc ar oide C. c. sargartacht do denam do ar in sollam*ain*
sin. Do bi d'ae*n*dacht 7 do naíri a Cruithnechan og radh na *tr*ath
leis in espoc gor t-saraigh an salm aíridhe si air .i. Misercordia[s]
Domini³⁸ .i. an salm is faide 7 as cruaide 'sa saltoir. Do gab,
u*morro*, an mac a raibe rath De 7 dar tidluicedh grasa an Spir*da*
Naeim .i. C. c., an salm ar son a oide; 7 is deimhin nar légh se
remhe sin riamh *act* a aibidil amhaín.

62.³⁹) Fect docuaid Colam cilli 7 a oide .i. Cruithnechan, do
torrumha duine airidhe don pop*ul* fuair bas⁴⁰; 7 ar a fill*ed* doib,
ni raibe acu acht iad fen. Acus tarla tuisled don oide-sin C. c. ar
in sligi*d*, gor tuit f*on* talm*ain*, co fuair bas fo cedoir. Acus do
chuir Colam cille ben*n* a bruit fa cend a oide, oir do shail gorab in
a codl*ad* do bi, 7 do gab se fen ag mebrvgadh a aicepta. Acus
do bi do med an mebr*uigth*e 7 d'airde an gotha, co cualat*ar*
coimtinol caill*ech* n-dub do bi mile go leith vatha foghar a ghotha;
7 fa bes dó a cluinsin an comfhad sin, amail asb*er*t in fili:⁴¹)

Son a gotha C*olaim cille,*   mór a bi*n*de os gach cler,
go cean*n* *cuic ced decc* ceimend,   aidbledh remend, eadh ba reil.

ET do bat*ar* *tr*i h-ingena do Cruithnechan fen 'sa coimtinol sin,
7 tanca*t*ar fa foghar gotha Colaim cilli ar na aithne, 7 fuarut*ar*
an clerech sin dob' ath*air* doib fen 7 dob oide dósa*m* marb aige ar

---

³⁷From O. I. L. See *Lis. Lives*, pp. 24-5.

³⁸Psalm LXXXVIII. Stokes in *Lis. Lives*, p. 303, says it is psalm c. See *LB*, 31, col. 2, l. 4; Roman Breviary, *In Nat. Domini*, III *Noct.* The longest psalm is CXVIII.

³⁹Chief source is O. I. L. See *Lis. Lives*, p. 25.

⁴⁰*do thoruma dhuine galair* Lis. Lives, p. 25, l. 4.

⁴¹See *Voyage of Bran*, I, p. 88, *Mongan cecinit do Cholum Chilli*. Also in MS. Laud 615, p. 18; *Rev. Celt.* xx, 176; *F. O²*, p. 148; *Irish Liber Hymn*, p. 165.

greatness of that light that he endured not to look thereon. And when the priest beheld it, he gave a great start and fell to the ground for the sight that was revealed him. And after that he had arisen from his swoon he understood that those were the graces of the Holy Spirit that were poured upon his fosterling in that hour, and that the angels of God were guarding him.

61. And long it was not after that Columcille and his fosterer, to wit, Cruithnechan mac Cellechain, went at the Christmas tide to the holy bishop Brugach mac n-Degadh of Raith Enaigh in the land of Enna. Then the bishop asked Cruithnechan mac Cellechain to do priestly duty for him on that festival. And Cruithnechan mac Cellechain felt such loneliness and shyness as he recited the Hours with the bishop, that he broke down in a certain psalm, to wit, *Misericordia[s] Domini*, the longest and hardest one in the psalter. Then the child, Columcille, did chant the psalm instead of his fosterer, the grace of God being on him, and the gifts of the Holy Spirit. And certain it is that never before that had he read aught save his alphabet only.

62. On a time Columcille and his fosterer, Cruithnechan, went to the wake of a certain man of the parish that was dead, and on returning there was none with them save themselves. And it befell that the fosterer of Columcille stumbled on the path and fell to the ground, so that he died forthwith. And Columcille put the skirt of his mantle under his fosterer's head, for him thought that he was sleeping, and he betook himself to conning his lesson. And with such earnestness did he con it, and so strong was his voice, that a convent of black nuns heard the sound thereof a mile and a half distant from him. For it was common to hear him thus far, as the poet hath said:

> "The sound of the voice of Columcille
> Great its sweetness, above every company
> For fifteen hundred paces (vast the distance),
> It was audible."

And there were three daughters of Cruithnechan in that convent. And when they knew it was the sound of the voice of Columcille they came toward it, and they found that cleric, that was father to them and fosterer to Columcille, dead beside him on the path. And the nuns, perceiving the holiness of the boy, asked him to waken the cleric. Then went Columcille to the cleric and wakened him. And he rose up at

an slighid. Acus mar dob' aithne doibh naemthact an macaim,
do iarratar na caillecha air an cleirech do dúscad. Do chúaid C. c.
d' indsoigid an cleirig 7 do bí gá dhúsgadh, 7 do erigh an clerech
le breithir C. c., amail do beith sé 'na codlad. Acus mar do tuic
5 C. c. gorab 'na onoir fen do aithbeoaigh Dia a oide, tuc se
bvidechas mor do Dia ar a shon sen. Acus do chuir Dia a aingel
(*fol.* 6b) fen cuige da tegasc. Acus do labair go h-ainglidhe ris,
7 do foillsig coimairledha arda an Tigerna 7 na seicréide diadha do.
Acus dochuaidh sin ar ecna 7 ar eolus 'sa scribtuir díada dósam, 7
10 dochuaid se os cinn lochta a coimleabair 7 a comaeisi go ro-mor a
n-eolus an scribtuír. Acus mar do tuic 7 mar do aithin se é fen ar
bisech 'sa tecusc ainglidhe 7 is na secreidib diadha tuc an t-aingel
do, do tarruing se é fen o truaillidhect 7 o tsalchor an t-saegail uile.

63. Ata Adhamnán ga mebrugad, ge do bi C. c. ro-ócc o aeis
15 an uair sen, go raibe croide arrsaidh eolach aice; 7 ger uasal o
folaidhect é, gur uaisle o subaltaige 7 o besaib e, 7 gerb' imlan ó
corp é, gorb imláine o creidem é. Acus fos, an gloine anma 7
cuirp fuair sé o Dia, do coimheid se an méide si hí, ge do bi se 'na
duine mailli ris na dainib a talmain, gorub betha ainglide 7
20 confersoid nemhdaidhe do bi aicce; 7 da derbad sin do bi ainglidhe
ó fhaicsin, 7 indtlechtach o ecna, 7 naemta o oibrigthib, 7 glic ó
comairli, 7 eola isna secredib díadha, 7 daingen documscaigthe a
ngrad a cruthaigtheora fen .i. Ihsu Christ os cinn gach uile gradha.

64. Fectus eli do C. c. 'na diaidh sin 7 do taisbein nech óg
25 ro-sciamach é fen dó a n-edach ro-geal, ro-delrudhach 'san oidhce,
7 adubairt ris: "Deus tecum" .i. 'Dia mailli rit, 7 bidh laidir
cobsudh[42]) daingen, 7 do cuir Dia mesi dod coimed go síraide
suthain sa saegal-so ó gach uili cair 7 pecadh.' Acus do bidg 7 do
imeclaig an macamh go mór les sin, 7 do fiarfaigh de cia he fen.
30 Adubairt an nech og: 'Mesi' ol se, 'Axal, aingel an Tigerna, 7 is
uime goirter Axal dim, gorab inand axal re radha 7 furtaigheoir,
7 is dot furtacht-sa ó gach uile guasocht 7 curum an t-saegail-se
do cuir an Tigerna me. Acus bidh go calma laidir, oir ataim-si
agad am ridiri sduamdha laidir do cathughadh 7 do comrac tar do
35 cend a n-adhaig[43]) na locht 7 ainmiana na colla, 7 na n-diabal 7
na n-droch-spirad 7 gach uile buaidridh saegalta.' Do fiarfaigh
an macamh naemtha-sa don aingel: 'In annsan aibíd gleghil sin no
isan aeis sin bfuile-si bid na huird ainglidhe a flaithes De?' Do
frecair an t-aingel e 7 assed adubairt: 'Gid aidbsech let-sa anos
40 med mo dealruid-si 7 mo sholuiss, bídh a fhis agat, gorub ro-mó

[42]or cobsaid.
[43]leg. aghaidh.

the word of Columcille, as he had been asleep. And when Columcille understood that in his honor God had raised his fosterer from the dead, he gave Him great thanks therefor. And God sent one of his angels to him to teach him, and he spake in manner of an angel to him and manifested to him high counsels of the Lord and divine secrets. And that served him in the knowledge and understanding of the holy Scriptures, and right greatly did he surpass those of his class and of his age in the understanding of Holy Writ. And when he understood and recognized that he was making progress in the angelic teaching and in the divine secrets the angel brought him, he withdrew him from the stain and defilement of the whole world.

63. As Adamnan maketh mention, albeit Columcille was passing young in years at that time, yet he had a heart old and wise; and though he was of gentle birth, yet was he more gentle in virtues and manners; and though he was perfect in body, yet was he more perfect in faith. And moreover he did so well guard the pure soul and body that he gat from God even while a man among men on earth, that his was the life of angels and the conversation of Heaven. And in proof thereof was he an angel to look upon, understanding in wisdom, holy in works, wise in counsel, learned in divine secrets, and strong and steadfast in the love of his Creator, Jesu Christ, beyond all other love.

64. Another time thereafter, a beautiful youth appeared in the night to Columcille, clothed in passing bright and shining garments. And he said to him:

" '*Deus tecum,*' " that is to say, "God be with thee; be strong and steadfast and firm, and God hath set me to guard thee ever and always in this world from all fault and sin."

And the boy was startled and sore afraid thereat, and asked him who he was.

The youth said, "I am Axal," saith he, "an angel of the Lord, and it is for this I am called Axal, because *axal* is the same as to say helper, and it is to help thee from every danger and care of this world that the Lord hath sent me. And be thou brave and strong, for thou hast in me a prudent and valiant knight to do battle and war in thy behalf against the weaknesses and lusts of the flesh, and against devils and evil spirits and every worldly disturbing else."

Then the holy boy questioned the angel: "Are the angelic orders in the realm of God of such bright habit and of such youth as thou?"

Then answered the angel and said: "Though overwhelming to thee now is the degree of my brilliance and my light, wit thou well, my splendor and my light are far greater in the realm of God than here. And I let thee wit thou mightest not look upon me in this splen-

mo dellrad 7 mo solus a flaithes De ina andso. Acus bidh a fis agad, na fedfá fechain orum 'sa dellrad-sa a fuilim anois fen muna beith grasa De go himarcuh agad, 7 da coimedair-se do genmnaidect 7 h'ogacht 'sa saeghol-sa go foirfe gan melludh do breith ort go crich do bais, beir co suthain siraidhe iter ainglib a n-aibíd gleghil taitnemhaigh nach eidir a tuaruscbail do tabairt amach, ar med a taithnemaighe 7 a maisi 7 a gloiri.' Adubairt an macamh naemtha-sa andsin: 'Massed, comarthaig 7 coisric mo corp 7 mo croide, indus go fedainn m'óghacht 7 oibrigthe na hóghachta do cothugad 7 do crichnugad uile go ponc mo bais.'Acus dorinde an t-aingel mar adubairt se ris, 7 do coisric se bruinde 7 croide 7 cliab an macaimh oig naemtha-sa; 7 on uair sin amach do sechain 7 do ingaib an macam-sa go maith é fen ar gach uile buáidred 7 fís 7 aisling, 7 ar droch-smuaintighib an t-saegail-se 7 na colla 7 an diabail. Acus do diult C. c. andsin do cúram 7 do deithide an t-saegail-se uile ó sin amach; oir do thuic se an focal adubairt Pol apstal, nach eidir le duine ar doman riderecht do denam do Dia 7 don t-shaegal a n-enfhect. Acus tuc se moid 7 gellad do Dia go coimeolad se gach ni adubairt an t-aingel ris ar fedh a bethad.

65.[44]) Fectus eli do taisbein Axal aingel e fen do C. c. 7 adubairt ris: 'Togh fen cred iad na tinnlaicthe 7 na subaltaidi dob ail let d'fhagail o Día 7 dogeba tu íad.' 'Togaim,' ar C. c. .i. 'óghacht 7 eccna.' Acus do frecair an t-aingel é 7 ised adubairt. 'Ise an Spirad Naem fen tuc ort an togha romaith sen do denamh, 7 ar son mar dorindis hí, dobera Dia tuilled tinnluicthi duit leo sin; oir dobera se spirad faidhedórachta duid, indus nach tainec romhad 7 nach tiucfa ad diaidh faid bus ferr ina thú.' Do frecair an macam bendaigthe sin don aingel 7 assed adubairt: 'Doberim gloir 7 buidechus do Día, 7 ni fhedar cred dober dó ar son na tindluiceadh 7 na tuarastal mor-sa tucc se damh, 7 gan me acht am serbfhogantaid dimain mídhingbala; 7 o na fuil agam doberaind dó ar a shon sin acht me fen, timnain 7 idbruim me fein iter corp 7 anum dó ar a shon.' (fol. 7a).

66. Ar n-imthect don aingel ó C. c. andsin, do taisbentar triar maighden roóg roalaind roscíamach rodelradach, nach faca se a n-innamail riamh, iat fen do, 7 do íadh gach bean acu a lama fa n-a braighid 7 tucatar tri poga do. Tucc fer grada na geanmnaidhechta .i. C. c., drochgnuis 7 drochagaidh dona maigdhenaib andsin, 7 do díult a poga, mar poga truaillidhe neamglana; oir do saeil se gorub docum pecaid do batar dó. Do fiarfuighetar na maigdena de an raibe aithne aice orra fein, o nach raibe se ag

[44] O. I. L. has an abridged account. See *Lis. Lives,* p. 173, l. 834 ff.

dor wherein I am even now, save for the plentiful graces thou hast of God. And if thou guard thy chastity and thy virginity in this world perfectly so that there be no falsehood on thee to the end of thy death, thou shalt wear ever and always among the angels a shining clear white garment that may not be described for its brilliance and its beauty and glory.''

Then said this holy boy: ''Bless and sain my body then and my heart, that I may be able to keep and to guard my virginity and all the works of virginity till the hour of death.''

And the angel did as he bade him, and blessed the belly and the heart and the breast of the holy gentle youth, and from that hour he did watch and guard himself well against every disturbing and vision and dream and evil thought of this world and of the flesh and of the devil.

And Columcille renounced the anxieties and cares of the world thenceforward, for he understood the word that Paul the Apostle said, ''It is not possible for any man to serve God and the world at the same time.'' And he made a vow and promise to God to be faithful throughout his life to the charge that the angel had given him.

65. Another time the angel Axal did show himself to Columcille, and said to him: ''Choose for thyself the gifts and virtues it were pleasing to thee to get from God, and thou shalt have them.''

''I choose,'' saith Columcille, ''Virginity and Wisdom.''

And the angel answered him and said: ''The Holy Ghost it was insooth that led thee to make this right good choice, and because thou hast made it, God will give thee many gifts besides. For he will give thee the spirit of Prophecy in such wise that there hath come never before thee nor shall come after thee better prophet than thou.''

Then spake that blessed youth to the angel and said: ''I render glory and thanks to God, but I know not what I can give Him in return for these gifts and passing great rewards that He hath bestowed on me, which am but an idle servant and unworthy; and since naught have I else to give Him save myself only, I do resign and offer myself to Him in return, both body and soul.''

66. And when the angel had departed from Columcille, anon there appeared to him three maidens that were passing young and beautiful and right fair and shining, such as he had never looked on before, and each maiden of them clasped her hands about his neck and they gave him three kisses. The lover of chastity, to wit, Columcille, turned a wry face and an ill visage upon these maidens, and he put from him their kisses as kisses corrupt and unclean, for he thought it was for sin they came to him. Then the maidens inquired of him if he knew who they were, since he was not taking from them their kisses nor their love. Colum-

gabail a pog no a ngrada uatha. Adubairt C. c. nach raibe, 7 adubratar-san gorub é a n-athair fen do pós re C. c. iad, 7 cor triur deirbsethar íad da celi. Do fíarfaigh C. c. cia dob athair doib, 7 adubratar san gorb é an Tigherna Íssa Crist, cruthaigeoír nimhe
5 7 talman, dob athair doib. Adubairt C. c: 'Is ro-uasal bar n-athuir 7 canuid bar n-anmonna duinn.' 'An óghacht 7 an egna 7 an fháidhedóracht ar n-anmonda', ar siad, '7 bemaid ad comhaidecht-sa a n-inadh triar ban posda cod bás, 7 biaidh do gradh ar marthain 7 ar coimhéd againn gan claechlodh go bráth.'
10   IS andsin adubairt C. c: 'Doberim gloir 7 buidechus mor do Dia cumachtach do cengail 7 do pos me fen, 7 gan me acht am serbfhogantaigh bocht anúasul, dá thríar ingen uasul fén.

67.[45]) Fecht eli tainec an taingel cedna, adubhramar romhainn, d'indsaigid C. c. 7 adubairt ris: 'Togh fein an bas as ail let d'fhag-
15 hail, 7 na hinaidh 7 na reighidhoin inar b'ail let do beatha do tabairt ass god bas.' IS andsin adubairt C. c.: 'Togaim bas d'faghail tareis dimais na hoige do dul taram, 7 sul beres misduaím na harsuidhecta gomor orum; oir is esláinte 7 as misduaim 7 as galar an arrsaidhect fein, 7 ni heidir lesin duine bis arsaidh no a n-aeis
20 moír gan beatha maith sodhamail d'fhaghail, 7 ni hail lemsa beatha maith d'fhagail dom corp fein go brath. Et toghaim an bas sin d'fhagail tré ghorta toltanaigh 7 tresan aibstinens cuirfed dom deoin fein oram, 7 gan galur no eslainte eli do beith oram a ponc mo bais acht sin fen. Et togaim fos an bas sin d'faghail a n-oilethre suthain
25 a bfhecmais mo tíri 7 mo talaimh 7 m'athardha duthcais fen maille re tuirrsi 7 re haithrighe romhoír; oir is tuirrsech duine ó beith ar deoraidhect, 7 is urasa dó gan neithe dimhainecha do beith ar a airi.' IS andsin adubairt an t-aingel re C. c.: 'Creid fen 7 na bidh amarus agad air go bfuighe tu na neithe sin uile ó do Día fen.'
30 Tucc C. c buidechas doairmidhe do Día andsin, 7 do linad ó grassaib an Spirda Naeim é, 7 do coimlinadh gach ní dar íarr C. c. andsin, amail derbhóchus an beatha ó so amach.

68[46]) Mar fuair, umorro, C. c. na haiscedha 7 na tidhluicthe móra-sa o Día, do gab se cead ga oide .i. ag Cruithnechan, dul do

---

[45]Substantially the same as in *LB*, p. 236, col. 2. See *Lis. Lives*, p. 301.
[46]Abridged in O. I. L. See *Lis. Lives*, p. 173, l. 836 ff.

cille said that he knew them not, and they said it was their own father that had given them in wedlock to Columcille, and that three sisters were they to each other. Then inquired Columcille who it was that was father to them; and they said it was the Lord Jesu Christ, Creator of Heaven and Earth, that was their father.

Said Columcille: "Right noble is your father; tell me your names."

"Virginity and Wisdom and Prophecy are our names," say they, "and we shall be three wives to cherish thee till thy death and we shall foster and keep love for thee without change for ever."

And then Columcille said: "I give glory and great thanks to Almighty God that hath joined and received me in wedlock with His own three noble daughters, and I but a poor lowly bondslave."

67. Another time came that same angel aforementioned to Columcille, and said to him: "Choose thyself the death thou wouldst liefest die, and the places and the regions where thou wouldst fain pass thy life till thou be dead."

Then said Columcille: "I choose to die after the pride of youth hath gone from me, and afore the misery of old age hath fallen too heavily upon me. For old age is itself a malady and a misery and a distemper, and it is not possible for a man that is old or well gone in years to have a life other than easy and soft. And I were loth ever to have a soft life for my body. And I choose to get my death through fasting and abstinence that I put upon me of my own will, and that there be no sickness or distemper else upon me in the hour of my death save this alone. And I choose moreover to get that death in lifelong exile from my country and my home and my fatherland in sorrow and passing great penitence. For a man is chastened by exile, and it is easier for him not to set his mind on vain things."

Then said the angel to Columcille: "Believe and have no doubt that thou shalt get all these things from thy God."

Then Columcille gave exceeding thanks to God, and he was filled with the graces of the Holy Spirit, and all that Columcille had asked was given him, as the *Life* will show from this on.

V

OF THE STUDIES OF COLUMCILLE

68. When Columcille had indeed gotten these gifts and great graces from God, he took leave of his fosterer Cruithnechan, and went

denamh leighinn docum na maighistrech b*ud* ferr ecna 7 eolas
dogebadh se a n-Erinn; 7 do fagaib a bendacht aige 7 do leic an
t-oide a bendacht lesin. Acus gé do bi C. c. linta do g*r*asaib an
Spirda N*aeim* acus ge fuair se eolus a ndiamr*ai*b an scribt*uir*
5 an ua*ir* sin, nirbh ail les a gloir dimain do beith dó fen go mbeith
eccna *no* eolas gan mebrug*a*d gan fogluim mar sen aige, *ach*t
dochuaid do denamh fogluma mar duine na fuighedh na subaltaidhe
sin ó Dia.

69.⁴⁷) Docuaid C. c., iarsin, d'fhoglaim ecna 7 legind 7 do
10 denamh eolais 'sa scribt*uir* c*us*an esp*o*c naemtha .i. go Finden
Muighe Bile. Acus aimser airithe da rabat*ar* afochair a celi, ruc
sairi uasal orra, 7 do ullm*ai*g Finden é feín do rádha an aif*r*ind.
Acus ar ngab*ail* culuidhech an aifrind uime dó, adubratar lu*ch*t
fritholma an aifrind etorra fen nach raibe fín acu; 7 do bi sin 'na
15 cas mor orra, oir nir leic ecla Findein doib an uiresbaidh sin do bi
orra d'indisin dó, 7 nir urasa leo a leicen dó an t-aif*r*end do tindscna 7 gan fin aige. Ar na cluinsin sen do C. c., do glac an cruibhed
a mbídh fin na n-aif*r*end do gnath, 7 ruc les é docum srotha
airidhe do bi laimh ris, 7 do chuir a (*fol.* 7b) lán d'uisce and, 7
20 do bendaigh 7 coisrig se an t-uisce sin, ind*us* go tainec do
brigh an bendaighte sin C. c., gor claechlodh an t-uisce a nadu*í*r
diles fen 7 co ndernadh fin de. Acus do fill t*ar*ais, iar*om*, docum
na heclaisi, 7 do cuir an cruibhéd ar an altoir, 7 do indis do lu*ch*t
fr*i*tholmha an aifrind go raibe fin and. Acus ar crichnugadh an
25 aifrind d'Fhinden les an fin sin, do fiarfaidh dá lucht fritolma
ca fuarut*ar* an fín romaith sin léa ndub*air*t se an t-aifr*e*nd. Acus
adubairt nach facuidh se a commaith d'fin riam. Et do indesit*er*
an lu*ch*t fr*i*thoilte dó mar tarla doibh, ó tus go deredh, timcell an
fina sin. Ar cloisdin na mirb*ail*e moire sin dorinde C. c. d'Finden,
30 do mhol se Dia go himarc*ach* tré med do foillsigh se a grasa 7 a
subalt*aide* fen a Columb cille, 7 tuc se buidechas 7 moladh mor do
Columb c. fen ar a son. Acus do las se fen 7 gach nech eili da
cuala na mirb*ail*e sin a ng*r*a*d* C. c. o sin amach; gor mór*a*d ainm
De 7 Coluimb c. de sin. IS follas asin sgel-so, nach eadh amhain
35 do cuir Dia C. c. a cosmailes ris na huasalaithrech*ai*b 7 ris na
faidhib 7 ris na naemhaib eli tainic reime, *ach*t cor cuir sé a
cosmhuiles ris feín e anuair dorinde se fin don uisce ar an mbanais
'sa Galile.

⁴⁷Chief source is Adamnan. Here Finden is called *Finbarrus* and *Vinnianus*.
See Reeves' *Adam.*, pp. 103-4-5. Abridged account in O. I. L. See *Lis. Lives*,
p. 173, l. 837 ff.

to study with the best masters in knowledge and learning that he could find in Erin. And he bade Cruithnechan farewell, and his fosterer gave him his blessing. And albeit Columcille was filled with the graces of the Holy Spirit, and was receiving knowledge in the mysteries of the Scripture at that time, he was loth to have vainglory by reason of having wisdom and knowledge thus without memorizing or studying; and he went to study as one that had not received those gifts from God.

69. Then went Columcille to the holy bishop Finnen of Moville to study wisdom and knowledge, and to pursue the reading of the Scriptures. And in the time that they were together, there chanced to fall a high feast day, and Finnen made him ready to say the mass. And when he had put upon him the vestments for the mass, they that served the mass said among themselves that they had no wine. And by reason of this they were sore distressed. For their fear of Finnen forbade them to tell him of the strait they were in, nor was it easier for them to suffer him to begin the mass without wine. When Columcille heard this, he took the cruet wherein the wine for the mass was wont to be, and he carried it with him to a certain stream fast by, and put its fill of water therein, and he blessed and sanctified that water. And it came to pass, by virtue of the blessing of Columcille, that the water changed its real nature, and wine was made therefrom. And he went back to the church then and put the cruet upon the altar, and told the folk that served that there was wine therein. And when Finnen had finished the mass with that wine, he asked those that had served, whence they had that passing good wine wherewith he had said the mass, declaring that never had he seen wine so good. Then those that had served related to him how it had fallen out with them from first to last. And when he had heard the great miracle that Columcille had wrought, Finnen praised God exceedingly for the measure of his graces and gifts that he had shewn to Columcille. And he gave thanks to God and great praise to Colcumille therefor. And henceforth was he enkindled, and likewise every man else that heard that miracle, with love for Columcille. So that God's name and Columcille's were magnified thereby. And it is clear from this history that God made Columcille not only like unto the patriarchs and the prophets and the other saints that had come before him; but like unto Himself when He made wine of water at the marriage feast in Galilee.

70.⁴⁸) Ceilebrais Columb c. d'Fhinden iarsin, 7 docuaid go German maigesdir do denam leighind mar an cedna. Uair airidhe dosan 7 do German fare celi, go facutar maighden og dá n-indsaiged 7 duine drochbertach do bi 'sa tir 'na ruaig uirre docum a marbtha; 7 dochuaid si ar comairce C. c. 7 Germain reimhe. Acus do bi do mhéd a hecla go ndechaid si fana n-édach a folach do teithed remhe an duine sin. Ar tect co lathair don óclaech, gan fechain do cumairce C. c. ina Germain, tuc sé sathadh slege ar an maighdin gor marbh acedoír hi. Do mallaig C. c. trid sin é, 7 do íarr ar Día bas do tabairt fa aimsir girr do. Do fhíarrfaidh German do Columb cille ca fad go ndigheoladh Dia ar an oclaech an gnimh adhuathmar sin dorinde se. Frecruis C. c. é 7 assed adubairt: 'Anuair ticfaid aingle De a coinde anma na maigdine ud da breith go flaithemnus do chaithem na gloiri suthaine, ticfaid diabuil ifrind a coinne anma an drochduine ut da breith a pianaib ifrind go síraidhe suthain. Acus ar in ponc sin fein fuair se bas ina fiadhnuise tre mallachtain C. c., amail fuair Ananias bas a bfiadhnuise Petair; gor moradh ainm De 7 C. c. de sin.

71⁴⁹) Ceiliubrais C. c. do German iarsin, 7 teid go Finden Cluana hIraird do denum legind. Acus do fhiarfaid sé d'Fhinden cait a ndingned a both. Adubairt Finden ris a denam a ndoras na heclaisi. Dorinde Columb cille a both iarom, 7 ni ag an dorus do bi ar an eclais an uair sin dorinde se hi; 7 adubairt gumadh annsan aít a nderna se a both do bíadh doras na heclaise 'na diaidh sin. Acus do firadh sin amail adubairt C. c., 7 do bi moran do naemuib Erenn ar an sgoil sin Fhinnéin. IS amlaid do ullmaighedís na clerich naemtha sin a cuid .i. gach clerech aca do mheilt a coda doib a broin gach re n-oidhce, 7 an oidhce do roichedh an meilt sin do Columb c., do tigedh aingel ó Dia do meilt ar a shon. Acus ba hí sin onoír doberedh Día dósan ar a uaisle 7 ar a shocenelaige 7 ar a saerclanndacht tar cach.

⁴⁸Taken literally from Adamnan. See Reeves' *Adam.*, pp. 137-8. Abridged in O. I. L. See *Lis. Lives,* p. 173, l. 846 ff. Stokes has pointed out that German in the *Book of Lismore* should be Gemmán. O'D. has made the same mistake. Adamnan and *L. B.* have Gemman. See *Lis. Lives,* p. 303.

⁴⁹Taken literally from O. I. L. See *Lis. Lives,* p. 173, l. 846 ff. This account is at variance with that in Plummer's *V. S. H.,* Vol. I, § 15, p. 205: *et unusquisque eorum in die suo molam propriis manibus molebat, set angeli Dei pro sancto Kiarano molebant, sicut et fecerunt in sua captivitate.* In the *Life of Columba* of Tir da Glass the account is slightly different. It says that the Lord provided for Columcille and Columb of Tir da Glass what the others had to provide *sive per laborem, sive per empcionem, sive per postulationem ab aliis.* See *A. S. H.,* p. 447, § 5, ed. Smedt and De Becker.

70. Then Columcille bade farewell to Finnen and went to Master Gemman to study in like manner. On a time that he and Gemman were together, they saw a young maiden coming toward them, and an evil man of the district pursuing her for her life. And she besought protection of Columcille and Gemman against him. And so great was her fear that she hid herself under their mantles to save her from that man. And when the man came to the spot, he heeded not the sanctuary of Columcille nor of Gemman, but he made a spear-thrust against the maid so that she died straightway. And Columcille cursed him therefor, and besought God to kill him in short space. Then inquired Gemman of Columcille how long it should be ere God avenge on the youth the shameful deed he had done.

Colcumcille made answer to him and said: "In the hour that the angels of God come to meet the soul of that maiden to bear it to Paradise, to enjoy the everlasting glory, devils of Hell shall come for the soul of this evil man to bear it to the pains of Hell for ever and ever."

And in that very moment the man died in their sight, through the curse of Columcille, even as Ananias died in the sight of Peter. So that God's name and Columcille's were magnified thereby.

71. Then departed Columcille from Gemman, and went to Finnen of Clonard to follow his studies. And he asked Finnen in what spot he should build his bothy. And Finnen said to him to build it at the church door. Columcille built his bothy then, and not at the door that the church had then did he build it. And he declared that he had built his bothy in the place where the door of the church should be afterward. And what Columcille said was fulfilled.

Many of the saints of Erin were there in that school of Finnen's, and in this wise it was that the holy clerics made ready their meal. In the evening each cleric in turn was wont to grind the portions of all in a quern. But when it was Columcille's turn for the grinding, an angel came from God to grind for him. And this honor did God show him above the others, for his gentle ways and his gentle birth and his gentle breeding.

72.⁵⁰) Fectas dorinde espoc na talman sin a raibe C. c. coindelbáthad air, ag suidhiugad pecaidh marbtha air nach derna se. Acus asse dob adbar doib cuige sin, tnuth aca ris fa méd na tindluicedh doberidh Dia dó tarrsa fen (mar do bi ag Caiin mhac Adhaim re hAibel), 7 ar med a ecna 7 a eolais, 7, fos, dimgha⁵¹) aca air fa na mince do cuired se a n-ainbfhis 7 a pecad fein na n-agaid, amail do bi ag Iubhalaib ar Isu Crist an uair do chuiretar docum bais é. Et da derbad gor breg doibh sivn a n-dubratar re C. c., andsin, ata Adhamnan naemtha ga mebhrugad, 'sa dara caibidil don tres lebar do decht se fein do beathaid C. c., nach derna C. c. énpecadh marbtha riam, 7 dá mad eidir ennech do clannaib na mban do beith gan pecadh sologha air, go mad é Columb c. é. Ar na cloisdin do C. c. go ndernadh coindelbáthad air, dochuaid mar a raibe an t-easpoc 7 a caibidil.⁵²) Et do erigh Brenainn Birra, (fol. 8a) do bí 'sa caibidil faris an easpoc, roimhe, 7 tucc pog dó, 7 dorinde raiberians 7 onoir do. Et arna faicsin sin don caibidil, docuatar do monmar ar Brenaind fa poicc do thabairt donti ar a ndernatar fein coindelbathad. Frecraís Brenaind iad 7 issed adubairt: 'Dá bfhaicedh sib na neithe docondarc-sa ag Dia ga ndenamh ar C. c., ní denad sib coindelbathad air; 7 as moide a luaighidecht 7 a coroín o Dia gac scainder da tugthai go bregach dó. Et adubratar-san narb fhír sin do reir ughdairaís an scribtuir neoch ader: "Quodcumque ligaris super terram, erit legatum 7 in celis," 7 e contra;⁵³) .i. 'Gebé ní ceingeolair ar an talmain-se, biaid sé cengailte a flaithes De,' ar Crisd fen re Peatar ag tabairt cumhacta eochracha na heclaise do, 7 a contrardha sin, 'gebé sgailfe tú ar an talmain-si, biaid se sgailte a fiadhnaisi De.' Frecrais Brenaind iad 7 issed adubairt, corub amlaid bud coir an t-ughdaras do tuicsin dona daínibh do ceingeoltai as a cairthibh fein 7 maille re cuis dlesdenaig no resunta; oir ni tuccadh cumacta cengail no sgailte don eclais acht an uair nach denadh sí sechrán on riagail airithe tugadh di. Acus adubairt go rabhotar san ag denam sechrain 7 meraighte moir .i. go rabadar ac cur pecaidh breige a n-agaid C. c. nach derna enpecadh marbtha riam; 7, fos, adubairt go faca sé fein peler tendtighe ria C. c. ag denamh tsolais ar an tsligid do, 7 aingle De gacha taebha de ga coimidecht ag tect dó docum an inaidh a rabutar-san. Acus fos

---

⁵⁰Taken literally from Adamnan. See Reeves' *Adam.*, p. 192 ff, chap. III, bk. III.
⁵¹*leg. dimdha.*
⁵²Adamnan says it was held at Teilte, now probably Teltown in Meath.
⁵³*Matt.* XVI, 19.

72. On a time the bishop of the place where Columcille was did put a ban upon him, charging him with deadly sin he had not done. And the reason therefor was their envy toward him for the many gifts that God had given him surpassing their own (like the envy of Cain, the son of Adam, toward Abel), and for the greatness of his wisdom and knowledge; and their spite against him for the many times he had cast in their faces their ignorance and sin (like the Jews' spite against Jesu Christ when they put Him to death). And in proof that all they said against Columcille at that time was a lie, Saint Adamnan saith in the second chapter of the third book he wrote of the life of Columcille, that no deadly sin did Columcille ever, and if it be possible that any one of the children of women was without even venial sin, that one was Columcille.

When Columcille heard that the ban had been laid on him, he went to the bishop and his chapter. And Brenainn of Birr, that was in the chapter with the bishop, stood up before him, and kissed him, and did reverence to him and honor. And when those of the chapter saw that, they took to grumbling against Brenainn for giving a kiss to one on whom they had laid the ban.

Brenainn answered them, and spake thus: "If ye had beheld what I have seen God do for Columcille, ye would have laid no ban upon him, and the measure of his reward from God is but the greater, and the greater is his crown, for every false charge ye bring against him."

And they said this was not true, according to the Scripture that saith: *Quodcumque ligaris super etc*, which is to say, "What thing thou shalt bind on earth shall be bound in the Kingdom of God," saith Christ Himself to Peter when he giveth him power of the keys of the church. And contrariwise, "Whatso thou shalt loose on earth, shall be loosed in the sight of God." Brenainn answered them and said that the words should be understood to be for those that were bound for their sins for cause just and in reason. For the power to bind and to loose was not given the Church except she stray not from the very rule that hath been given her. And he declared that they were indeed straying and doing great foolishness, to wit, they were falsely imputing a crime to Columcille that had never done any deadly sin. And he said moreover that he had seen a pillar of fire afore Columcille, giving him light on his way, and angels on every side guarding him as he came to the place they were in. And further he said that on one that God so loved it was not right

adubairt anti ara raibe an cin sin ag Dia air nar coir doib sivn coindelbathad do denamh air. Acus arna cloidsin sin doibh sin, ni headh amhain nach dernatar coindelbáthad ar C. c., acht do batar lán do grad 7 d'onoír air ó shoin amach. Acus nir labair C. c. moran ar a shon fen rív ar fedh an comraidh sin uili; oir dob ferr les duine eli do labairt ar a son ina se fen. Acus ge do fhédfad se a clai ó ecna 7 o eolus 7 o udarás an scribtuir, dob fherr leis a claei o fhírinde 7 ó umhla iná sin.

73.⁵⁴) Ceilebhruis Columb cille d'Fhinden Cluana hIraird iarsin, 7 docuaid go Glend ⁵⁵) Naiden uair do bi deichnemhar 7 da .xx. ag denam léigind andsin ag Mobi clairenech, 7 do bi Cainech 7 Comghall 7 Ciaran ar in scoil sin. Et don taeb tiar d'abhainn batar a mbotha 7 an eclas don taeb toir d'abuinn. Tarla uair airithe gor erigh tuile mor san abainn 7 cor benadh clog iarmerge⁵⁶) na cilli, 7 nir fhédatar na naimh dul tar in abuinn, 7 nir fech C. c. don tuili acht docuaidh tríthe. IS andsin adubairt Mobi: 'Is laidir teid ua Neill an tuile.' 'Fedaigh Dia', ar C. c., 'an saethar-sa do cosc dínde'; 7 ag techt doib tar in eclais amach san oidhce cedna, fvaratar a mbotha re taeb na heclaisi don taeb toir don abhainn le breithir Coluimb cille.

74. Fect and tarla meid ecin imresna nach roibe urchoíd mor indte iter C. c. 7 Ciaran mac an tshaeir. IS andsin tainec an t-aingel cuca 7 tuc se tuagh 7 tal 7 tarathar leis, 7 adubairt sé re Ciaran gan beith ag coimes no ag imresain re Columb cille, 7 nar treicc se ar Dia acht an culaidh tshaírse sin do bi ga athair, 7 gor treig C. c. righacht Erind air; oir fa dual do o duthcas 7 o folaidhecht hi, 7 do tairgedh dó fen go minec hi 7 do dhiult se ar son De hí. Acus is mar sin do reidigh an t-aingel etorra. Acus is follas as an sgel sa go raibhe cin mór ag Dia ar C. c. tar cleir eli Erend 7 Alban 7 iarthar domain vile.

75.⁵⁷) Fect and dorindedh eclas ag Mobí, 7 do batar na clerich ga smuainedh cred é an lan bud ferr le gach naem acu do beith aige san eclais. 'Do badh maith lem fen,' ar Ciaran, 'a lan do dainibh naemta agam do mholad De.' 'Do badh maith lemsa', ar Caindech, 'a lan do lebraib díaghachta agom do medugad sherbhisi De.' 'Do badh maith lemsa,' ar Comghall, 'a lan do

---

⁵⁴Taken literally from O. I. L. See *Lis. Lives*, p. 174, l. 858 ff.
⁵⁵*recte* Glais Naiden.
⁵⁶'nocturn'.
⁵⁷Taken literally from O. I. L. See *Lis. Lives*, p. 174, l. 866 ff. See *ibid*. pp. 303-4 for a similar story concerning Cummine Fota, Guaire and Cáimine of Inis Celtra.

for them to lay a ban. And when they had heard this they laid no ban on him, and not this only, but they were filled with love and honor for him thenceforth.

And little did Columcille say to them in his own behalf during all that talk. For him were liefer another should speak for him than himself. And albeit he could have overcome them by his skill and his knowledge, and by the authority of the Scripture, yet him were liefer to overcome them by truth and humility than by those.

73. Columcille departed then from Finnen of Clonard, and he went to Glasnevin, for there were two score and ten studying there with Mobi Clairenech. And Cainnech and Comgall and Ciaran were in that school. And their bothies were on the western side of the water and the church was on the eastern side; and it befell once that there was a great flood in the river. And when the bell was struck for matins in the church, the saints could not cross the water. Natheless Columcille heeded not the flood, but waded across therein.

Then Mobi said, "Stoutly doth the descendant of Niall breast the flood."

"God is able," saith Columcille, "to spare us this effort."

And when they were going out past the church that same evening they found their bothies there beside, on the east of the stream, according to the word of Columcille.

74. It fell on a time that there was a quarrel, wherein was no great malice, between Columcille and Ciaran, the son of the Wright. And an angel came to them and brought an ax, an adze, and an augur with him. And he told Ciaran not to liken himself to Columcille or to quarrel with him, for whereas Ciaran had given up for God naught save his father's labouring suit, Columcille had given up the kingship of Erin. For the kingship was his due by right of birth and blood, and it had been offered to him many times, and he had refused it for God's sake. And thus it was that the angel made peace between them. And from this history it is manifest that God had great love for Columcille, passing the love He had for the other holy men of Erin and Alba and all the Western World.

75. On a time Mobi had builded a church, and the holy men were wondering what each of them would liefest have the church be filled withal.

"It would please me well," saith Ciaran, "to have many holy men to fill it, praising God."

"I would fain," saith Cainnech, "have godly books enough to fill it withal, for the better service of God."

galar 7 d'eslainte do beith oram do traethad mo cuirp.' 'Do badh maith limsa', ar C. c., 'a lan d'ór 7 d'airgead agam, 7 ní do gradh indmais sin,' ar se, 'acht do chumhdach minn 7 mainesdrech 7 da tabairt dontí do rigfed do les é ar son De.' IS annsin adubairt
5 Mobi: 'Is amlaid bias,' ar se. 'Bud saidbri muinnter C. c. ina muinnter gach naimh eli a n-Erinn 7 a n-Albain.' Acus adubairt Mobi rena sgoil iarsin (fol. 8b) he fen d'fhagbail 7 sgaileadh ó celi, 7 go mbeith eslaínte granda 'sa baile-sin a rabutar fo aimsir ghirr .i. an buidech condaill a hainm .i. an buidech ar dath an
10 condlaigh. Acus adubairt sé re Columb cille gan ferand do gabhail no go tucad se fen ced dó a gabhail. Acus do sgail an sgol o celi iarsin. Acus dochuaid C. c. da thir duthaig fein .i. a tir Conaill, do teched roimh an plaidh-sin adubrumar romhainn, 7 rainec gonuice an abhainn danadh hainm Bir. IS annsin do
15 bendaigh C. c. an abhand, 7 do iarr ar Dia gan an plaid-sin da leanmhain ar in sruth sin, 7 fuair se sin o Dia; oir ní dechaid si tairis 7 tanuic si conuice é. Acus is bithbeo na mirbuili-sin; oir ni teid an plaidh no an buidhech conaill tar an abuinn-sin ó sin alle tres an mbendugad-sin tucc C. c. uirre; gor moradh ainm De
20 7 C. c. de sin.

76.⁵⁸) Fectas docuaidh C. c. do gabail graidh sagairt docum espoic naemtha⁵⁹) do bi a Cluain Foda, a Feruib Bili, a Midhe. Acus mar rainec C. c. don baile do fhiarfaidh ca raibe an t-espoc. 'Ata se ag trebad ar deredh a seisrighe fen,' ar nech do muindtir
25 an baili. Teid C. c. gusan espoc 7 fuair mar sin he. 'IS eccoir doit,' ar a muindter re Columb cille, 'techt d'iarraidh graidh ar duine mar súd; oir ni hespog é acht oireamh sesrighe.' IS andsin adubairt C. c: 'Na beridh breth don taeb amuig air go finda sib cred na subaltaide ata don taeb astig o Dia aige.' Et do labair
30 C. c. ris an espoc 7 do indeis do gorab do gabail gradha uadh tainec se. Acus ni tuc an t-espoc frecra air, 7 ni mó do coisc se don trebad. 'Benaid an t-iarand asan crand,' ar C. c. ré a muinntir, 'go mbeith an tsesrech ina tost da fis in bad moíde doberadh an t-espoc frecra oraind é. Acus ger maith le C. c.
35 fregra d'fhagail on espoc, ni dá fagail uile adubairt se sin acht tarcuisne do mothuig se gá muindtir fen ar an espoc, 7 do bi a fis aige go ndenadh an t-espoc mirbuile 'na fíadnuisi trid sin, indus nach beith amharas no tarcuisne acu air o sin amach. Acus do bi a fis aige go tiubrad Dia grasa dó ar a shon fen, 7 do guidh se Dia

---

⁵⁸This legend is also in F. O², p. 73. It differs in many points from O'D.'s narrative.

⁵⁹i. e., Bishop Etchen † 578 A. D. See Reeves' Adam., p. LXXII.

"For the chastening of my body," saith Comgall, "I would fain have upon myself sickness and distempers enough to fill it."

"I would have," saith Columcille, "gold and silver enough to fill it; and not for love of wealth," saith he, "but for stablishing reliquaries and monasteries, and to give for God's sake to any that have need."

And Mobi saith, "Thus it shall be. The convent of Columcille shall be richer than the convent of any other saint in Erin and Alba."

And Mobi charged his pupils to leave him then, and to disperse; for in short space an evil malady would fall upon the place where they were, namely the *buidech connaill* "the jaundice of the colour of stubble." And he told Columcille to take no land save he give him leave to take it. Then the school was scattered.

And Columcille went to his native place, to wit, to Tir Conaill, fleeing from the plague aforesaid, and he came to the stream that is called the Bir. And Columcille blessed the stream, and besought God that the plague might not follow him upon the stream, and this be obtained from Him. For it went not across, albeit it attained thereto. And these miracles are ever living; for through the blessing that Columcille laid thereon, cometh neither plague nor *buidech connaill* across that stream to this day. So that God's name and Columcille's are magnified thereby.

76. On a time Columcille went to receive priestly orders to a holy bishop that was in Cluain Foda in Farbill in Meath. And when Columcille reached the place, he inquired where the bishop was.

"He is at the plough behind his team," saith one of those in the place.

Columcille went then to the bishop, and so indeed he found him.

"It is wrong of thee," say his folk to Columcille, "to come seeking orders of such a man; for he is not a bishop, but a ploughman."

And thus answered Columcille, "Give no judgment upon his outward ways, ere ye learn what inward virtues he may have of God."

And Columcille spake to the bishop and told him that he had come to take orders from him. And the bishop gave him no answer, nor did he the more cease his ploughing.

"Take the coulter out of the beam," saith Columcille to his household, "that the team may stop, and we may see if thereby the bishop give us an answer the more."

And albeit Columcille would have fain got an answer from the bishop, it was not solely in order to get it that he spake thus; but he perceived the contempt that the bishop's household had for him; wherefore he knew that the bishop would work a miracle in their sight, so that they would never doubt or despise him again. And Columcille knew that for his sake God would give the bishop grace, and he prayed God

ar a shon fan tarcuisne sin do cor ar cul; oir nírb ail lé serbfo-
ghantaigh diles Dé 7 lesin te do togh sé a mbroind a mathar .i. le
Columb cille, tarcuisne do beith ag na dainib ar oclaech eli De,
oir dob ail les a mirbuile d'foillsiugad air. Acus do benadh an
t-íarann asan crand, 7 nir misde do bhi an tseisrech ag trebad é.⁶⁰)
Bentor capall as an tseisrig,' ar C. c., 7 do benad iarom, 7 do cuir
an t-espoc fa umla ar dam allaid do bi 'sa coill ren a taeb techt
cuige a n-inadh an capaill-sin. Tainec, iarom, 7 do bi ag trebad
mar gach capull eli don tshesrigh, 7 nír scuir an t-espoc don
trebad no go tainec an t-am fa sguiredh se gach lai eli. Acus do
leic a sesrech iarsin, 7 do lig an fiadh docum a coille fein, 7 ferais
failte re C. c. Acus ger maith an t-espoc and fen, is ar son guide
C. c. do foillsig Dia na mirbuiledha mora-sin dó. Acus adubairt
go tibrad se gradha arna mhárach do C. c. IS andsin adubairt
C. c.: 'Dá madh aniugh amhain dobertheá gradha damsa, do beind
im airdespoc os cind cleri Erenn 7 Alban, 7 os amarach doberi
damh iat, ni bia dínite go brath 'san eclais agam bus mo ina beith
am ab 7 am shagart crabaid. Acus gedheadh, dodena Dia an
uiret-sa do dighaltos ort-sa do cind gan gradha do tabairt aniugh
damh, oir ní ticfa énduine d'íarraid gradha ort fen re do beo no
at cill tar heis go brath ó so amach. Et as maith liumsa,' ar C. c.,
'gan cúram is mo ina sin do beith isin eclais oram fen go brath.
Acus ni biadh an curam-sin fen oram muna beith gorab mo an
luaighidecht dam beith fa umla uird ag denamh crabaid ina beith
ag denamh crabaid a modh eli. Acus do firadh an faidhedóracht-
sin C. c. aleith re gach ní da ndubhramar romaind . Acus tucad
gradha sagairt do arna marach, 7 tainec reimhe iarsin go Doiri
Calgaigh.

77.⁶¹) Dob e an baile-si Doiri dobo baile d'Aedh mac Ainmirech an uair-sin. Targaidh Aedh an baili do C. c., 7 do diult
Columb cille an baile ó nach raibe ced Mobi aige fana ghabáil. Ag

---

⁶⁰Notice the position of é.
⁶¹Taken literally from the preface to the Hymn *Noli Pater*. See *Irish Liber Hymnorum*, I, pp. 87-8. Secondary source is O. I. L. See *Lis. Lives*, p. 174, ll. 82 ff, also *ibid.*, p. 305.

to save the bishop from that reproach. For it was displeasing to the chosen servant that God had set apart from his mother's womb, to wit, Columcille, that folk should disdain another of God's servants. And he would fain show forth miracles upon him.

The coulter was taken out of the beam and the team ploughed none the worse therefor.

"Take a horse from the team," saith Columcille, and anon it was taken. Therewith the bishop humbly summoned to him in the stead of that horse a deer that was in the wood nigh hand. Straighway the deer came, and set to ploughing like any of the horses of the team. And the bishop ceased not from his ploughing, ere it came the hour that he unyoked each day. Then he loosed his team, and let the deer go to its wood, and he bade Columcille welcome. And albeit the bishop was a good man, yet it was by reason of the prayer of Columcille that God manifested those great miracles in his behalf. And the bishop said that he would give holy orders to Columcille on the morrow.

Then Columcille said: "If thou hadst but given me holy orders today, I should be archbishop over the clergy of Erin and Alba, but since it is on the morrow thou givest them to me, I shall never have higher rank in the church than to be abbot and a pious priest. Howbeit, thus much of punishment shall God lay upon thee because thou hast not given me orders this day, that none shall come to seek orders from thee in thy life, nor in thy church from this time hereafter forever. And for myself I am right glad," saith Columcille, "that I shall have no heavier burden of rank than this upon me in the church forever. And even this burden would I not have, were it not that I shall have greater merit for doing the observances of piety in obedience to rule, than for doing them in other wise."

And the prophecy of Columcille was fulfilled, touching all things whereof we have made mention above. And priestly orders were given him on the morrow, and he went his way then to Derry.

VI

OF THE LABORS OF COLUMCILLE IN DERRY AND TIRCONNELL

77. That town of Derry was the stead of Aed mac Ainmirech at that time. Aed proffereth the town to Columcille, but Columcille refuseth it, since he hath not Mobi's leave to take it. And as he came out of the mansion, two of the household of Mobi met him with Mobi's

techt do Columb cille asin dúnadh amach, tarla días do mhuinnter
Mobí do, 7 cris Mobi leo cuige tareis baís Mobí fein. Acus do
cuir se an cris 7 ced feraind do gabail leo d'indsaigid C. c. Mar
do glac C. c. an cris as and adubairt: 'Maith an fer ga raibe an
cris-so,' ar se, 'oir nir hoss—(fol. 9a) luicedh docum crais riamh
e, 7 nir híadhadh fa breic é. Conad and dorinde an rand-sa:

      Cris Mobi,
      nibdar sibne am lo,
      nir hosluigedh re saith,
      nir híadadh im go.

Gabais C. c. an baile o Aedh iarsin,[62]) 7 do loisc an baile a ndiaidh
a fagbhala do cona raibe and uili do scriss oibrech na ndaine
saegalta ass da disliugud do Dia 7 dó fein . 'As espach sin,' ar
Aedh, 'oir muna loiscthí an baile, ni biadh uiresbaid bidh no edaigh
ar duine da mbeith and go brath, 7 is baegal go mbía uiresbaid and
o so amach,' bar Aedh. IS andsin adubairt C. c: 'Dogeba gach
duine da mbía and a rigen a les o Día.' Do bi do med na teinedh
7 na lasrach gor fobair di an doiri coille do bvi 'sa baile do loscad,
co nderna C. c. an imann-sa d'anacul an doiri: *idon*

    "Noli pater indulgere tonitrua cum fulgare né frangam-
    ur formidine huis atque uridine te deum timemus ter-
    ribilem nullum credens similem te cuncta canunt carmina
    angelorum per agimina teque exultent culmina celi uagi
    per fulmina o ihsu amantisime o rex regum rectissime
    benedictus in secula recta regens regimine iohannes corum
    domino athuc matris in utero repletus dei gracia pro uino
    atque sisare Elesabet sdacarias uirum magnum genuit
    Iohannem bautistam percursorem domini mei manet
    in meo corde dei amoris flamma ut in argensio uase
    aurio ponitur gema amen."

Et adeirter inn imon-sa a n-aghaid gach tenedh 7 gach toirnighe
o sin alle, 7 gebe gabhas hi ag luide 7 ag erghe, aincid an nonbar
is ail les ar theinigh 7 ar toirnigh 7 ar teindtigh.

    78. Ar ngabail, imorro, gradha rouasail roonoraig na sa-
gartachta do C. c., 7 arna toga dá nemtoil 'na ab manuch ndub 'sa
baili-se Doiri, 7 arna bendugad do 7 ar ndenam comnuidhe dó ann,
do gab se do laim ced do dainib bochta do shasadh gach lai ar son
De. Acus do bidh duine aireidhe uaid re hadhaidh[63]) an bidh sin

[62]A. D. 546. See Reeves' *Adam.*, p. 105.
[63]*leg.* haghaidh.

girdle the which after his death they had brought away with them for Columcille. And Mobi had sent the girdle by them to Columcille with leave to accept the land.

And as Columcille took the girdle from them he said: "It was a good man that had this girdle," saith he, "for never was it opened for gluttony and never was it closed upon a lie." And then he made the quatrain:

"The girdle of Mobi
Hath not been opened before surfeit;
Hath not been shut around a lie."

Then did Columcille receive the town from Aed. And when Aed had left it, he burned it and all that was therein erasing therefrom the works of worldly men, that he might consecrate it to God and to himself.

"It is folly," saith Aed; "for had the town not been burned, none therein would lack food nor raiment forever; howbeit, I fear that there will be want there from this time forth."

And Columcille said: "Every one that is there shall have from God what he requireth."

So great was the fire and the blaze that well-nigh it burned a grove of trees in the place, so that Columcille made this hymn to protect the grove: *Noli Pater indulgere* etc. And this invocation is said against all fires and thunder from that day to this, and if a man pronounce it on lying down and on getting up, it will protect any nine persons he chooseth from fire and thunder and lightning.

78. When Columcille had indeed received the right noble and right worshipful order of priesthood, and when he had been chosen against his will to be an abbot of black monks in this place Derry, and when he had blessed it and had made his dwelling there, he took in hand to feed a hundred poor men each day for the sake of God. And he had

da tabairt dona boctaib. Acus la éicin tareis na mboct do dil, tainec duine boct eli d'iarraid deirce air, 7 adubairt óclach Coluim cille cor dil se an uimhir do gnáthuighedh se do dil gachlai, 7 adubairt se risan duine mboct tect an la ar maruch 7 go fuigedh se deirc mar gach mboct eli. Acus ni tainec se an la arna marach no gor diladh na boicht uile, 7 do iarr deirc mar an cedna, 7 ni fuair acht an frecra cedna ó oclach C. c. Acus tainec an tres la d'iarruid na dierce tareis na mbocht do dil, 7 ni fhuair acht an fregra cedna ó oclach C. c. IS annsin adubairt an duine bocht: 'Eirig mar a fuil C. c., 7 abair ris, munab uadha fen dogeib se gach ní dobeir se dona bochtaib, gan beith ag cuma re ced do sasadh gachlai. Teid an t-oglach mar a raibe C. c., 7 do indis comradh an duine boicht dó. Acus arna cloisdin sin do Columb cille, do erigh go hoband, 7 nír an rena brat no rena brogaib, acht do lean an duine bocht 7 rug acedoir air san inadh re n-abarthar "an t-impodh desivl" don taeb tiardhes do thempoll mór Doire. Acus do aithin gorb e an Tigherna do bi and, 7 do leg ar a gluinib 'na fiadhnuisi e, 7 do bi ag comrad ris o bel go bel, 7 do linadh do grasaib an Spirda Naeim e; 7 iter gach en tinnlucad da fuair se o Día andsin, fuair se eolus in gach uile ní diamrach da raibe 'sa sgribtuir, 7 fuair se spirad faidhedorachta, indus nach raibe ní sa bith dorcha air da taineg no da ticfaid. Acus ó sin amach ni raibe sé ag cuma re céd, acht na tindluicthe mora fuair se o Día gan misúr, doberidh se uadh amach gan misúr iad ar son De. Et do fhoillsiged do cach fis ruin 7 indtinde piasd na fairge 7 fis ceilebraid énlaithe an aieoír. Et da derbad sin, ata peist adhuathmar 'sa fairge darab ainm "Rocuaidh", 7 anuair sgeithes si 7 a haged for tír, is dual go mbía galar 7 gorta in gach uile talmain an bliadain sin. Acus annuair sgeithes sí 7 a haged suas, as dval go mbia doinend mor and an bliadain sin, 7 mortlaith mor ar enlaith an aieoir. Acus anuair sgeithes si 7 a haged fuithe 'sa fairge, bídh mortlaid mor ar iasgach 7 ar piasdaib na fairge an bliadain sin. Do indisedh C. c., tre spirad fáidhedórachta, naduir na píasda sin do cach, indus go mbidís ar a coimhéd uirri.

79.[64]) Fect eli do Colum cille a nDoiri, 7 do chuir cuid airithe da manchaib do buain fidhaigh, do chumdach (fol. 9b) eclaisi indte, ar coill duine airidhe don popul; 7 tugatar lan an arthruig do bi acu leo. Acus ar tect mar a raibe C. c. doib, do

---

[64]Taken literally from Adamnan. See Reeves' *Adam.*, p. 106. Abridged in O. I. L. See *Lis. Lives*, p. 175, l. 893 ff. The scene is shifted from the neighborhood of Derry to Iona in Adamnan's *Vita*. O'D. and O. I. L. place it near Derry.

a certain servant to give that food to the poor. And one day, after the poor had been satisfied, there came another poor man asking alms of him. And Columcille's almoner said that he had fed the number he was wont to feed each day, and bade the poor man come on the morrow and receive an alms like the other poor men. And on the morrow he came not ere all the poor were fed, and he asked alms then in like manner. And he gat naught from the almoner of Columcille save that answer. And he came the third day, after the poor had been fed, and asked alms, and he gat but the same answer from the almoner of Columcille.

Then said the poor man: "Go to Columcille and tell him, except it be from himself he getteth what he giveth to the poor, he should provide not to feed an hundred only each day."

Then went the almoner to Columcille and told him the poor man's words. And when Columcille heard this, he rose up swiftly, staying not for his cloak nor his shoes. And he followed the poor man and overtook him anon in the place that is called the Right Turn to the Southwest of the big church of Derry. And he perceived that it was the Lord that was there, and he fell on his knees before Him and spake with Him face to face. And he was filled with grace of the Holy Ghost and among all the gifts that he was given by God at that time, he received knowledge of every hidden thing in the Scripture, and the spirit of prophecy, so that naught was hidden from him that hath been or will be. And from that time he provided not for an hundred only, but the great gifts that he had without stint from God, these he bestowed without stint for God's sake.

And he used to manifest to all the knowledge of the mind and intent of the beasts of the sea, and of the singing of the birds of the air. And in proof hereof there is a frightful beast in the sea yclept Rochuaidh, and when it speweth to landward it is in sign that there will be sickness and disease in every land that year. And when it belcheth upward it is in sign there will be great storms that year and many deaths among the birds of the air; and when it disgorgeth downward into the sea there will be many deaths that year among the fishes and the beasts of the sea. Thus did Columcille through the spirit of prophecy set forth the nature of that beast, that all might guard them against it.

79. Another time when Columcille was in Derry he sent certain of the brethren to a grove belonging to one of his community to cut wood for the building of a church. And the cart they had they brought back full withal. And when they came where Columcille was, they

indiset*ar* dó co raibe doilghes mor ar tigerna na coill*ed* fa med
do benad di. Acus arna cloisdin sin do C. c., do f*ur*ail ar na
manchaib sé tomhais eorna do chor d'innsaig*id* an og*l*a*i*ch o tuca-
t*ar* an fidhach. Acus as hi aimser do bi and an uair sin dered
5 an tshamraid. Acus dorinnetar na manaig mar adubairt C. c.
riu, 7 docuat*ar* d'indsaig*id* an oglaich 7 rugat*ar* an eorna cuige,
7 adub*r*at*ar* ris mar adubairt C. c. ris. Acus adubairt an t-ocl*ach*
ríu-sa*n*, ná b*ud* eidir go tibr*ad* an sil do cuirf*ide* 'san ai*m*sir-sin
tor*ad* óna tes 7 ona mhéd do cuaid tairis dí. Adubairt a ben
10 risan óclach: 'Dena comairli an naoim,' ar sí, 'oir dobheir Día
dó gach ni dá n-íarrann air'. Acus adubrat*ar* na tectair*ed*a tainec
lesin tshil d'indsaig*id* an og*l*a*i*rt, co ndub*air*t C. c. ris a dóchus
do cur a nDia fan gort do tect, *acht* ge do cuirf*ide* go mall e, go
mbeith abaidh inbvana a tosach na c*ed* mís d'foghmar. Acus do-
15 rinde an t-ogl*a*ch mar adubairt C. c. ris, 7 do firadh gach ní de
sin. Acus is mar sin do cuítig C. c. digb*ail* a coilledh risan
ogl*ach.* Acus do moradh ainm De 7 C. c. de sin; 7 is e fa hainm
don oglach-sin ler leis an choill 7 ara ndernadh an mirbaile-sin .i.
Findchan.'
20   80. Fect eli tainec C. c. do buain adhmaid docum eclaisi
Doiri ar an coill darab ainm an Fidb*ad*, 7 tancut*ar* daine eladhna
cuige d'iarr*aid* spr*ei*dh*e* air. Acus adubairt sesivn ríu nach raibe
spreidh aige doib andsin, 7 da ndechdais leis don baile
go fuigedh siad spreidh. Acus adubratar-san nach rachdais, 7
25 mvna faghdaís spr*éidh* annsin fen úadh go cainfidís é. Mar
docuala C. c. an t-aes eladhna ag bagar a cai*n*te 7 gan ní aige
doberadh se doib andsin, do gab naíri imarcach é, 7 do bi do mhéd
na naire sin, go facaid a raibe do lath*air* an deth*ach* do erigh dá
chind,[65]) 7 do cuir all*us* imarc*ach* dá ag*id*, 7 do cuir a lamh fána
30 ag*idh* do bvain an allais-sin de, et dorindedh talla*nn* oir don
all*us*-sin ar a bois, 7 t*uc* sé an talla*nn* sin don aeis eladhna. Et
is mar sn do fhoír Dia naíre C. c. Acus nirb ingnadh Dia d'f*ur*-
tach*t* na haigthe-sin C. c., [oir] nir cruthaig*edh* riamh, a fecmais
daend*achta* Crisd, aghaid budh nairidhe ina [a]n agh*aid*-sin C.
35 c., 7 is mó tug amach d'ecla a cáinte 7 a imd*er*gtha, 7 nir mill sin
enní da cogús no dá tregenas *no* dá fhuirechr*us no* da urnaidthe
uime.

      81. Fect*us* do Colum cille a n-inad airithe it*er* Oilech
na righ 7 Doiri Calg*aig*, 7 tainec cliar mor do dainib eladhna 'na

---

[65]We should expect *ag eirghe da chind*. Perhaps this construction will throw
light on the peculiar construction in § 368 *infra*, "re lind anma C. C. do chuaidh
and".

told him that the owner of the wood was passing sorrowful by reason that so much of his wood has been cut down. And when Columcille heard that, he charged the monks to send six measures of barley to the churl whose timber they had taken. And the season then was the end of summer. And the monks did as Columcille had charged them. They went to the churl and brought him the barley, and told him what Columcille had said to them. And the churl said to them that it was not possible that seed sown in that season should bear fruit, by reason of the heat and of the length of the season that was gone by.

But the wife of the churl said to him: "Do the bidding of the saint," saith she, "for God giveth him whatsoever he asketh of Him."

And the messengers that had come to the churl with the seed told him that Columcille desired him to put his hope in God that the seed would grow, and albeit it had been sown late, yet should it be ripe for the sickle in the beginning of the first month of harvest. And the churl did as Columcille had charged him. And all this was fulfilled. And thus it was that Columcille gave recompense to the churl for the harm to his wood. And God's name and Columcille's were magnified thereby. And this is the name of the churl that owned the wood, and for whom the miracle was done, to wit, Findchan.

80. Another time Columcille was going to cut wood for the church of Derry in the grove that is called Fidbad, and there came to him some poets asking a gift. And he said to them that he had nothing upon him for them, but if they would return home with him they should have a gift. And they said they would not go, and except they gat a gift from him there straightway, they would make a satire upon him. When Columcille heard that the poets were threatening to make a satire on him, and he without anything to give them, exceeding shame seized him then, and so great was that shame that those that were there saw smoke rising up from his head and heavy sweat streaming from his brow. And he put his hand to his face to wipe away the sweat, and thereof was made a talent of gold in his palm. And he gave that talent to the poets. And thus it was that God saved the honor of Columcille. And it was no marvel that God should come to the succor of the honor of Columcille; for there was never, save in the person of Christ, honor that was more tender than the honor of Columcille. And much as he bestowed from fear of being mocked or reviled, in naught did that minish his strictness of life, his fasting, his vigils, or his prayers.

81. On a time that Columcille was in a certain place between Oilech of the Kings and Derry, there came to him a great company of bards, and they asked gifts and food of him.

cend, 7 do iarrat*ar* spreidh 7 biad air. 'Tig*id* lem don baile,'
ar C. c., '7 dober sin daeib.' 'Ni racham,' ol siad, '7 muna fagham
gach ní dib sud andso fein, aorfam 7 cainfem tú.' 'As urasa le
Día mesi do saeradh oraib,' ol C. c., 'masa toil les fen,' 7 do gab
5 naire mor he; oir nir gened 7 ni genfidher, a fegmais daendachta
Crist, neoch bud fheli 7 bud nairidhe ina sé. Acus do guidh Día
go duthrachtach fana fhurtacht on cas-sin a raibe se. Et ass*ed*
adubairt: 'A Tigerna, 7 a Ih*s*u Crisd,' ar se, 'os ar fhighair fein
do crutuighis mesi, na leic naire d'fhag*ail* don fidhair-sin anois;
10 7 ata a fhis agad fein, da mbeith a furto*cht* agam-sa, *go* fuirteo-
chaind ar do son-sa hi, 7 ni fiu mesi himd*er*g*a*dh tr*i*m fen.' Teid
C. c. go dochusach iarsin d'indsaighid tobair fhíruisce do bi 'san
inadh sin, 7 do bendaig 7 do coisric a n-ainm Íssu Crist e, 7 dorinde Dia m*aith* m*or* air andsin, uair do claechlodh sé an t-uisce
15 a fin do ré fedh uaire do lo; conadh "Maith" ainm an tobair-sin.
Acus do bo nair le C. c. gan soithighe aige asa tibr*ad* se an fin
sin don cler 7 do cach arcena. Acus do foills*ig* an t-aingel dó go rabhatar cuirn, do folchatar sendaine aim*ser* fada roimhe-sin, a cladh
na ratha romoíre bui laím ris; 7 fuair sé na cuirn san inadh adu-
20 bairt an t-aingel a mb*eith*. Acus do bi raith eli do coír an inaidh
sin, 7 ruc se an cliar 7 gach duine eli do bi faris les indte, 7 tug
se fl*edh* mor don fin-sin doib; gor mor*adh* ainm De 7 C. c. de sin.
Gonad "Raith na Fleidhe" ainm na ratha-sin ó sin alle.

82. Fectas doch*uaid* C. c. ina aenar ó Doire go Carraic
25 Eolairce os ur locha firalaind Febhail, 7 ba gnath leis dul don
inadh-sin do denamh duthrachta do Día, oir ba halaind uaignech
é, 7 ba rominec do tigdís na haingeil do comr*adh* ris and. Acus
ar crichnugad urn*aidh*e faide dó, docond- (*fol.* 10a) airc se manach
da manchaib fen cuige, 7 do bendaighet*ar* dá celi, 7 do fiarf*aig*
30 C. c. sgela de. 'Ata drochsgel agam,' ol an manach, '.i. do brá-
thair-se 7 do dalta spiridalta d'fhag*ail* bais .i. Maelcabha mac
Aedha, mic Ainmirech, mac airdrigh Erenn. 'Truagh sin,' ol
C. c. 'Fir ón,' ol in manach. Do hia*cht*adh 7 do hacainedh an
sgel-sin go mór le firu Erenn uile. Acus docuaid C. c. os cind
35 cuirp an maca*im* iarsin, 7 do leig ar a gluinibh é, 7 adubairt nach
eireochadh dona gluínibh sin coidhce nó go fagadh se aiseg anma
a dalta fen o Día. Acus do gab teora saltoir and sin, 7 do bi ag
guidhe De go roduthractach mailli re caí 7 re toirsi moir, 7 do
ben cros dia bachaill ar ucht an m*a*caim maille re dochas laid*ir*,
40 7 adubairt do guth mór ris erghe a n-ainm Ih*s*v Crist o marb*aib*.
Ro erigh an macam a cedoír le breithir C. c. amail do ereoch*ad*
as a codladh. Acus an dolás 7 an tuirrsi do bi ar rig Erenn 7

"Come home with me," saith Columcille, "and I will give them to you."

"We will not go," say they, "and save we get all these things straightway, we will mock and revile thee."

"It is easy for God to save me from you," saith Columcille, "if it be His will."

And sore shame seized him. For there hath not been nor will be born, save in the person of Christ, one that hath excelled him in largesse or hath been more tender in his honor than he.

And he besought God earnestly for help out of the hard case he was in, and he said: "O Lord, Jesu Christ," saith he, "since in Thine own likeness Thou hast created me, let not shame be put upon that likeness now. For Thou knowest that if I could, I would save it for Thy sake. And I merit not that reproach should fall thereon through me."

Then went Columcille in expectation to a well of spring water that was near by, and he blessed it, and sanctified it in the name of Jesu Christ. Then did God show him great favor, for he did change for him that water into wine during one hour of the day, so that *Maith*, which is to say Good, is the name of that well. And shame fell on Columcille that he had no vessels wherewith to give that wine to the poets and the rest. And an angel revealed to him that there were goblets that the folk of old had hidden a long while since in the wall of a great barrow that was fast by. And he found the goblets in the place where the angel told him. And there was another barrow in front of that place, and thither he led the bards and the others that were with him, and he gave them a great feast of that wine, so that God's name and Columcille's were magnified thereby. And the Barrow of the Banquet is the name of that barrow from that day till now.

82. On a time Columcille went alone from Derry to Carraic Eolairc above the brink of truly fair Loch Foyle, for it was his wont to go thither to make orisons to God, because it was beautiful and solitary, and angels came right oft for converse with him there. And when he had prayed a long while, he beheld one of the brethren coming toward him. And either gave greeting to other, and Columcille asked tidings of the brother.

"I have ill news," saith the monk, "to wit, the death of thy kinsman and spiritual fosterling, even Maelcabha mac Aeda mic Ainmirech, son of the high King of Erin."

"Alas for that," saith Columcille.

"It is true," saith the monk, "and for those tidings hath great sorrow been made, and lamenting by all the men of Erin."

Then Columcille went to the body of the youth and fell on his knees there, and he declared he would not rise up from his knees forever until

ar Erendchaib uile reimhe-sin fa bas Mailcabha, do línadh ni budh
romhó ina sin iad do luthgair 7 do sholas fana hatbeougad doib,
7 do molatar Día 7 C. c. go himarcach tresan mirbail-sin. Et
tuccad tricha bo 7 tricha brat 7 tricha da gach uile crodh do
Día 7 do C. c. ar a shon-sin. Acus tuc Maelcoba fen an cís-sin
d'fhir inaidh C. c. ar a slicht fen ina dhíaig go brath uair gacha
bliadna. Acus do fhagaib se coimerghe ag mindaib 7 ag muintir
C. c. ar a slicht fen gach menci vair do rachdais a cenn duine
dib coidhce. Acus do bi Mailcobha deich mbliadna ina righ Erenn
iarsin,[66]) 7 do lec an righe de 7 dochuaid a crabud; gor naemadh
fa deoigh é. As follus dunn as an sgel-sa, corab mogenair ga
mbí C. c. 'na chara, oir nir lór les an cara-sa do bi aige d'ath-
béougad gan maithes saegalta do tabairt dó 7 flaithes De fa deoigh.

83. Ni hurusa a bfaisneis a tug Dia d'fhertaib 7 do mirbuilib
do C. c. rena ndenamh a n-Doire 7 in a lan d'inadaib eli gacha
taebha do Loch Feabail. An uair, tra, tigedh aeidhedha no aes
eladna a cenn C. c. 7 gan biadh aige daib, do cuiredh fa umla ar
iasc Locha Febail techt cuige go ríaradh leis iad, 7 do cuired brig
fina 7 blas lemnochta a n-uisce an locha cedna daib, amail atbert
Baithin mac Cúanach ga derbad so is na rannaibh-se sis:[67])

An uair bui a Carraic Eolairc   Columb cille gan mebuil,
dogeibhedh iasc gan doinnmhe   dá choindmhib a Loch Febuil.

IS é Dia rodelbhusdair,   raidim-si rib go tuicse,
doberthai blas lemnochta   is brigh fhína 'na uisce.

---

[66] See Reeves' *Adam.*, p. 37. According to *Annals of Ulster* he was slain in
A. D. 614 (*recte* 615) by Suibhne Menn at the battle of Sliabh Belgadain, after
a reign of three years. In *F. M.* his death occurs under A. D. 610.
[67] See *Z. C. P.*, VII, p. 303 for the whole poem.

he should obtain from God that the life of his fosterling be restored. And thrice did he recite the psalter, and he besought God right urgently with tears, and with great sorrow.

And in strong hope he sained the boy's breast with his staff and bade him in a loud voice in the name of Jesu Christ to rise up from the dead.

And straightway at the words of Columcille, the youth rose up as he might rise up from sleep. And as for the sorrow and heaviness that had lain on the King of Erin and all the men of Erin before, by reason of the death of Maelcabha, they were the more filled with joy and solace because he was restored to them. And they praised God and Columcille exceedingly for that marvel. And in return therefor, thirty kine and thirty cloaks and thirty of each breed of cattle were given to God and Columcille. And Maelcabha it was that laid that tax for the successor of Columcille upon his seed after him once each year forever. And for the treasures and the household of Columcille he enjoined safeguard for them so oft as they had recourse to his seed till Doom. And Maelcabha was king in Erin for ten years thereafter, and then he gave up the kingship and took him to pious works so that he became a saint thereafter. It is clear to us from this history that it was a good fortune to be the friend of Columcille, for it sufficed him not to restore his friend to life except he give him also earthly blessings, and the Kingdom of God in the end.

83. Not easy were it to relate all the marvels and wonders that God gave Columcille to do in Derry and in many other places on both sides of Loch Foyle. When indeed guests or bards came to Columcille, and he had no food for them, he used to bid the fish of Loch Foyle to come to him to satisfy his guests therewith, and he put the taste of wine and the taste of new milk on the water of the same lake for them, as saith Baithin mac Cuanach in proof thereof in these quatrains:

> "The while he was in Carraic Eolairc,
> Columcille (without falsehood)
> Used to catch fish without labor,
> Repast for his guests from Loch Foyle.
>
> God it was that so shaped it,
> I tell thee with understanding.
> There was put the taste of new milk
> And the taste of wine on the water."

84. Fectas eli do C. c. a nDoire 7 céd do daínib naemtha maille ris, 7 tainec Brenainn ced⁶⁸) eli do daínib naemtha 'na cend. Acus ní tarla do bíadh ag C. c. ar a ceann an uaír-sin *acht* nai mbairghena 7 nai n-oirdne eisg. Acus do gabh naire mor C. c. uime sin. Acus do bendaig se an meid bidh sin, 7 taínec do brigh an bendaighte sin C. c., go rainec bairgen 7 orda eísc a laim gach enduine da raibe do lathair andsin. Et ni hed amain, act dá tigedh a raibe na comhghar isna tírthaib cuca, doghebdaeis a ndil araín 7 eisc an oidhce-si; 7 do batar na *nai* mbairgena 7 na nai n-oirdne ésc imlan arna mhárach. As follus assin scel sa, nar lór le Día C. c. do chur a cosmailes risna huasalaithrech*aib* 7 ris na naemhaib eli tainecc reime, *acht* gor cuir se a cosmailes ris fén é an uair do shás se na cuíg mile ar an bhfásach lesna *cuig* aránaib 7 lesan dá íasg.

85. Fect eli do C. c. a nDoire, 7 tainec cerrbhach 7 duine bocht dá indsoig*id*. Acus tuc se bon*n* don cerrbhach 7 pinginn don duine bocht. Acus doba roingnadh le cach gorab mo tug se don cerrb*ach* ina don duine bocht. Acus do foillsig Dia do C. c. cach dá chur sin a n-ingn*ad* air, 7 adubairt se re dainib airithe, da raibe do lath*air* andsin, an cerrbach 7 an dvine bocht do lenmhain da fech*ain* cred doghendaís risan airged-sin tuc sé doib. Acus fuaratar an cerrbach a taibeirne ag ól luacha an buind 7 se ga tab*air*t dá gach duine rainec a les é da tainec cuige. Acus as amlaid fuaratar an duine bocht marb ar an slig*id* 7 an pingind sin tucc C. c. do 7 *cuig* marg eli fuaighte 'na édach. Acus tangatar lesna sgel*aib*-sin d'indsaig*id* C. c. IS andsin adubairt C. c.: 'Do foillsigh Día damh-sa nach roibe do shaeghal ag an duine bocht ud ní dob faide ina sin, 7 dá m*ad*h fada a saegal, nach cuirfedh sé a tarba dó fein nó do duine eli enní dá mbeith aige *acht* a taisg*id* mar dorinde ris na cuig marg, 7 gerbh olc an cerrbach and fein, ní hé taisgid a bfuair se dorinde *acht* do tshás sé e fein 7 daine eli ara raibe riachtanas a les re luach a buinn; 7 ar an adhbhar-sa tucas-sa ní b*ud* mó dó ina tuc*as* don duine bocht' (fol. 10b).

86.⁶⁹) Fectas eli do C. c. a nDoire, 7 tug*ad* lenabh becc dá baisded cuige, 7 ni raibe uisge a ngar do an uair-sin. Acus tuc C. c. comarta na croiche ar in carraig cloiche do bi 'na fhiadhn*aise*

---

⁶⁸One should expect *le* before *ced*. But see § 120 for a somewhat similar construction *cuirfider Munda mac Tulchain an cethramhadh fer lind*.

⁶⁹Partly taken from O. I. L. See *Lis. Lives*, p. 175, l. 900 ff. In § 269 O'Donnell relates a similar story which he borrowed from Adamnan. See Reeves' *Adam.*, p. 118. The story in O. I. L. is evidently based on Adamnan's. Hence O'D., borrowing from each separately, makes two stories out of one.

84. Another time, when Columcille was in Derry, and a hundred holy folk with him, Brenainn came to him with another hundred holy people. And it befell that Columcille had spread before them at that time but nine loaves and nine morsels of fish. And great shame fell on him. Then he blessed what food he had, and it came to pass by reason of that blessing that there came a loaf and a morsel of fish in the hand of each one that was there present. And not this only, but if there had come all that were in districts neighboring to them, they too would have had their fill of bread and of fish that night. And the nine loaves and the nine morsels of fish were whole on the morrow. It is clear from this history that it sufficed not God to make Columcille like to the patriarchs and the other saints that came before him, but He made him like to Himself when He satisfied the five thousand in the wilderness with the five loaves and the two fishes.

85. Another time when Columcille was in Derry, there came to him a gambler and a poor man. And he gave a groat to the gambler and a penny to the poor man. And it seemed passing strange to all that he gave more to the gambler than to the poor man. God revealed to Columcille that all were amazed thereat. And Columcille bade certain that were present to follow the gambler and the poor man to see what they would do with the money he had given them. And they found the gambler in a tavern drinking the worth of the groat and sharing it with every needy man that came to him. And it is thus they found the poor man: dead upon the road, and the penny Columcille had given him sewed in his garments, and five marks thereto. And they came with these tidings to Columcille.

And Columcille said: "God did manifest to me that the poor man had but thus long to live, and even had his life been long, he would have put to no use either for himself or for any other what he might have; but he would hoard it up, as he hath done the five marks. And albeit the gambler was an evil man in himself, yet did he not hoard what he gat, but with the worth of the groat he sustained himself and other poor men that were in need, and for this I gave him more than I gave the poor man."

86. Another time that Columcille was in Derry, a little child was brought to him to be baptized, and there was no water near him at that time. And Columcille made a sign of the cross upon the rock that

gor leig srut firuisce eisde, 7 do baisdedh an lenab ass. Conudh
tobar C. c. ainm an tobair-sin ó sin alle. IS mor 7 as ingantach
a tuc Dia d'fertaib 7 do mírbhuilib do C. c. rena ndenamh a
nDoire. Acus do fhágaib C. c. clerech maith⁷⁰) bud combrathair
geinelaig do fein a comhorbacht Doire .i. clerech do cenel Conaill,
7 do fhagaib uaisle 7 onoir 7 tigernus tuaithe an baile-sin 7 na
tuath 'na timchell ag cenel Conaill go brath.

87.⁷¹) Fectus da tainecc C. c. 'na aenar o Doire go Carraicc
Eolairg os ur locha forlethain Feabhuil d'iarraid uaignis do
guide De 7 do radh a trath 7 a urnaidhe. Acus nir cian do and
an uair docondairc se an t-aenoglach alainn ingantach trid an
loch dá indsoigid amail nobeith se ag siubal tíri no talman, 7 ass
oir fana chois, 7 an coss do benad re⁷²) lar aige, is uimpe nobidh
an t-ass. Acus ar tect go lathair dó, assed adubairt: 'Gor ben-
naighe na dee adhartha duit, a Coluimb cille,' ar sé. 'Cía thusa
fen doní an bendugad-sin,' ar Columb cille, 'no ca tír no talam
asa tanec tu, no cia is ri no as tigerna duid, no ca dia da creidend
tu?' 'Me fein as tigerna damh,' ar se, '7 is dona deeib adartha
chreidim.' 'IS ingnad lem, dá madh ri no mac righ tu, do beith
at aenar mar sin,' ar C. c. 'Ataei-si fen at aenur, a clerigh,' ar
in t-oclach, '7 bid a fhiss agat-sa, dá mad áil lium-sa go mbeidís fiche
ced oclach am coimhidecht annso,' ol se, '7 indisim duit-si gorab
me fen Mongan mac Fiachna .i. mac righ Ulad, 7 corab do coimes
fhesa 7 eolais rit-sa tánag.' 'INnis duinn ní don fhis 7 don eolass
mor sin ata agat, a Mongain,' ol C. c. 'INdeosat,' ar se, 'oir ni
fhuil, on corrmiltoig co rige an mil mór, bethadach nach teigim-si
'na richt, 7 as eola me ar moran do tirthib 7 d'indsib agas d'oile-
naib díamhracha in domain, 7 go hairithe as eola me ar tri coicait
oilen ata do taeb tiar d'Erinn 'sa fairge, 7 ata tri uired Erenn
in gach oilén dib.' 'Cia aitrebhus na tirtha 7 na talmana-sin
nach cualamar cus aniugh?' ar Columb cille. 'Aitrebaid innta,'
ar Mongain, 'daine onóracha is maith delb 7 denamh iter fhir 7
mnai, 7 ataid ba finda eoderga indta go laegaib a comhdatha
maille riu, 7 ataid cairig finna go himarcuch indta, 7 is siad sin
is spred 7 is airnes doib.' 'As mor an fis 7 an t-eolus enduine sin,
a Mongain,' ar C. c., '7 gidh mór é, as bec é ag fechain an eolais
7 an fesa ata agam-sa, oir is eolach mé a nimh 7 a talmain 7 an

---

⁷⁰i. e. Da-cuilen. See *Lis. Lives*, p. 308.
⁷¹See poem (twenty-two stanzas) called
    Coinne Mongáin is Coluim cháim   mic Feidlimthe an ardnaoim.
This is found in the Bodleian MS. *Laud* 615, p. 21. See also *Eriu* V, part I-II, p. 9;
Z. C. P., II, pp. 314-16; *Voyage of Bran*, I, p. 88.
⁷²*Cf.* § 277, *na benaid rem urraidh* "do not touch my freeman".

was before him, so that it spouted forth a stream of spring water, and therewith the child was baptized. Hence Columcille's Well is the name of the well from that day to this.

Many and passing strange the marvels and wonders that God gave to Columcille to work in Derry. And Columcille left a good cleric that was kinsman by blood to him to be his successor in Derry, to wit, a cleric of the clan of Conall. And he left the headship and honor and lordship of the folk of that town and of the folk thereabout to the clan of Conall forever.

87. On a time Columcille came alone from Derry to Carraic Eolairc above the brink of broad Loch Foyle to seek a solitary place to pray to God and say his hours and his prayers. And he had not been there long when he beheld a passing beautiful youth coming toward him across the lake, as if he were treading on the earth or ground. And there was a golden sandal on his foot, and whichever foot he set upon the ground, it was thereon the sandal was. And when he came nigh him he spake to him.

"May the gods of worship bless thee, Columcille," he saith.

"Who art thou that givest me such greeting," saith Columcille, "or from what land or country hast thou come, or who is thy king or lord, or on what God dost thou believe?"

"Myself am mine own Lord," saith he, "and in the gods of worship put I my faith."

"It is strange to me," saith Columcille, "if thou art a king or the son of a king, that thou art thus alone."

"Thou art thyself alone, O cleric," saith the youth. "And wit thou well, there would be twenty hundreds of followers with me here if it were but my pleasure," saith he. "And I tell thee I am Mongan mac Fiachna, the son of the King of Ulster, and it was to match skill and knowledge with thee that I came."

"Tell me some of that knowledge and great skill of thine, O Mongan mac Fiachna," saith Columcille.

"I will," saith he, "there is not a creature from the gnat to the whale that I can not take on its shape. And I have knowledge of many of the countries and islands and the hidden isles of the world. In especial know I the thrice fifty islands that are westward from Erin in the sea. And thrice the measure of Erin is each of these islands."

"And who is it dwelleth in those lands and districts whereby until today we have had no tidings?" saith Columcille.

"There dwell therein," saith Mongan mac Fiachna, "worshipful folk of fair shape and form, both men and women, and there be white cows with red ears there that have with them calves of like hue. And

ife*rn*n.' 'As maith an t-eol*ach* ar talm*ain* me,' ar Mongan, '7
docuala me ife*rn*n 7 ni fhed*ar* cred é flaithes De, 7 cia is ri *no* is
tigerna ar in nemh-sin adeiri, a clerigh,' ar se. 'Día na n-uili
chumh*acht* .i. cruth*aigt*heoir nimhe 7 talm*an* 7 if*ri*nd 7 na n-uile
creatuír is rí and,' ar C. c., '7 go saera se tusa, a Mongain ar
an merugad 7 ar an sechran creidmhe ata ort. Acus as tr*u*agh
liumsa fer hfesa 7 t-eol*ui*s-si do beith coimh ainbfhesach 7 sin
and.' 'IS mor test 7 tuaruscb*ail* an ocl*aig*-sin as aendía and
agat-sa,' ar Mongan, 'et a n-onoir do daendachta 7 ar gr*ad* an
aendía-sin, beir mesi d'fech*ain* flaithesa De 7 if*ir*nn, 7 gab*aim* do
comuirce-si fam rogh*ain* do tab*air*t damh dibh ar mbreith eolais
orra.' 'Tarr-sa cugam-sv andso amárach ar maidin 7 dober fhrec-
cr*a* ort im gach ní da fhuile d'iarr*aid* orm,' ar C. c.

Do gabatar ced ga cheli an oidhce-sin, 7 teid Mongan remhe
dá sithbrog*aib* fein; oir ba himarcach a cumhachta a nd*r*uighect
7 a ndiabhuldán*acht*. Et teid C. c. remhe go Doire, 7 do gabh
se ag guidhe De go duthrachtach an oidhche-sin fa Mongan do
leig*en* les d'fech*ain* gloire flaithesa De 7 peíne if*ir*nd. Acus ticc
an t-aingel cuige 7 ass*ed* adubairt ris: 'Gach ní as ced leat-sa a
talm*ain* as ced le Día ar nimh é, 7 is ced les tussa do breith Mongain dá fechain sin.' Teid C. c. iarsin ar maidin go Carraic
Eolairg, 7 ger moch dochu*aid* and, fuair se Mongan ar a cind 7
do benduighetar dá celi. IS andsin adubairt Mongan: 'In cum-
hain let-sa an gell*ad* tucais damh-sa ané, a C. c.'? ar sé. 'As
cum*ain*,' ar Columb cille,' 7 tab*air* do cenn fa bein*n* mo bruit 7
docífe tú gach ní dá bfhuile d'íarraidh.' Cuiris Mongan a cend
fa brat C. c., 7 do foillsig*ed* if*r*enn co*na* ilpianaib do. Acus do
eigh g*o* hard arna fhaicsin sin, 7 ass*ed* adubhairt (*fol.* 11a): 'O
a Choluimb cille, guidhim tu, a hu*ch*t an día da creidinn tú, an
taispenadh tugais damh do ceilt orm, oir is lor lim a bfhaca de.'
Do tog C. c. a brat do cend Mong*áin*, 7 do fíarfaidh de cred hi
an aitreb-sin do*co*nnaic sé. 'Ni hurassa dam a tuarascb*ail* do
tabairt uaim,' ar Mongan, 'oir da mbeith mile teanga am cenn
7 saeg*al* go la na breithe agam, ni fhedfaind uile dh*uad* uilc[73])
an tighe ud 7 na haitrebhe d'indisin, acht amhaín da bfechdaís
sil Ádhaimh ar an endiab*ul* is lugha gr*ain* indte, dogebdaeis bas
fo cedoír; 7 is deimhin co bfhuigind-se bas co hobann muna beith
do coimhet-sa orum. Et beir d'fech*áin* flaithesa Dé anos me.'
'Cuir do cenn fam coim,' ar C. c. Cuiris Mongan a cenn fa coim
C. c., 7 do foillsighedh flaithes De dó co*na* gloir 7 co*na* aibnes 7
co*na* ilceol*aib*. Acus do tuit a codl*ad* air les na ceol*aib*-sin; 7 mar

[73]*dh* (with a dash over "h") *uilc* MS.

there be white sheep exceeding many. These be the cattle and gear they have."

"That is great skill and knowledge for man to have, O Mongan mac Fiachna," saith Columcille, "but great though it be, it is small beside the skill and wisdom that is mine; for I have knowledge of Heaven and of Earth and of Hell."

"I am right learned as to Earth," saith Mongan mac Fiachna, "and I have heard of Hell; but I know not what may be the Kingdom of God, or who is the king or the lord of that Heaven thou speakest of, O cleric," saith he.

"The Almighty God, creator of Heaven and Earth and Hell, and of all created things, He it is that is king there," saith Columcille, "and may He save thee, O Mongan, from thy errors and delusions of belief; for it is a grief to me that a man of knowledge and learning should be thus ignorant of Him."

"Many are the witnesses and the tidings thou hast of that one God," saith Mongan. "For the honor of thine own kindness and for love of the one God, take me to see the Kingdom of God and Hell, and I crave thee mercy to give me my choice, when I have learned of them."

"Come to me here on the morrow morn, and I will give answer to thee in all thou dost ask of me," saith Columcille.

Then either took leave of other for that night, and Mongan went to his fairy mansions. For exceeding great were his powers in magic and infernal art. And Columcille went to Derry, and he betook him to earnest prayer to God that night to let Mongan see the glory of the Kingdom of God and the pains of Hell.

And an angel came to him and said to him: "Whatsoever thou dost suffer on earth, that doth God suffer in Heaven, and he suffereth thee to bring Mongan to behold it."

On the morrow then went Columcille to Carraic Eolaire and albeit it was early when he went thither, yet found he there Mongan before him, and either greeted other.

Then Mongan said: "Dost remember the promise thou didst give me yestreen, O Columcille?" saith he.

"I am mindful thereof," saith Columcille, "and put thy head beneath the hem of my mantle, and thou shalt see all thou desirest."

Then put Mongan his head under the mantle of Columcille, and there was revealed to him Hell with its many torments.

And on seeing them he cried out and said: "O Columcille, for the sake of the God thou believest in, hide now from me the sight thou hast shewn me, for what I have beheld sufficeth me."

Then Columcille lifted his mantel from the head of Mongan and inquired of him what manner of place he had seen.

dob fhada le C. c. do bi Mongan 'na chodlud, tocbais a brat da
cinn, 7 do moscail Mongan íarsin, 7 do fíarfaigh C. c. de cred
hí a bhreth ar an taisbenadh-sin tuccad dó. 'Ni heidir limsa
breth do breith air,' ar Mongan, 'oir da mbeith mile cenn orum
7 mile tenga in gach cenn dibh, ni thicfed dim an gloir is lugha
a bflaithes De d'indisin duit; 7 gabaim do comairce-si, a Coluimb
cille, fam cuid don gloír-sin do tabairt go suthain damh iar mbas.'
'Dober-sa sin duit,' ar C. c., '7 dena fein maith 7 bud tú an tres
mac ochta bess am ucht-sa la na breithe got anacul ar tenidh
in bratha .i. tú fen 7 Maelumha mac Baódain 7 Suidemhain mac
Samhain. Ceiliubruis cach da cele dib, 7 do bi Mongán 'na oclach
maith do Día 7 do Columb cille ó sin amach gó a bás 7 iar mbás.

88. Fectus do C. c. ag techt timchell reilge an Duibregleis a
nDoire .i. an duirrthech a mbidh ag radh a trath, 7 do leic se ar
a gluinibh é 7 tuc a aighidh soir gach ndírech,[74]) 7 do thogaib a
lama suas amail do beith ag esteacht aifrind. Acus ar n-erge dó
dá gluínib, do fhíarfaigh manach airidhe día mhanchaib fen do
bi maille ris de cred fá nderna an umla-sin 7 cred é an taisbenadh
tucad dó an uair-sin. Frecrais C. c. é 7 assed do raid: 'An
papa,' ol se, '.i. Gridhoir beil-oir do bí ag rádh aifrind ar altoir
moir tempaill Petair 'sa Roím anos,' ar se, '7 an uair docon-
narc-sa an corp naemtha ga thogbail aige, do leces ar mo gluinib
me, 7 as dó tucas an umla ud.' Acus do mórad ainm De 7 Coluimb
cille de sin.

89. Do bi an oired-sin do gradh ag Columb cille ar Doire 7
do doilgess aige fan doire choilledh do baí and do buain no do
gerradh, mar nach fuair se inadh don duirrtech ra n-abarthar an

---

[74]See § 274 for similar phrase.

"Not easy were it for me to give thee tidings thereof," saith Mongan, "for if there were a thousand tongues in my head, and if I should have life till Doomsday, I could not tell thee all the hardship of evil in that house and dwelling. Howbeit, could the sons of Adam see but a single one of the least horrible demons that are there, they would die straightway. And I had surely been dead forthwith, had it not been for thy safeguard. Take me now to behold the Kingdom of God."

"Put thy head under my mantle," saith Columcille.

Then put Mongan his head under the mantle of Columcille, and he revealed to him the Kingdom of God with its glory and its delight and its many melodies. And on hearing these melodies he fell asleep. And when it seemed to Columcille that Mongan had been long asleep, he lifted his cloak from his head and therewith did Mongan awake. And Columcille inquired of him what he thought of that vision that had been shewn him.

"Not easy were it for me to give tidings thereof," saith Mongan, "for were there a thousand heads upon me, and a thousand tongues in every head, I could not describe to thee the least of the glories of the Kingdom of God. And I crave thy mercy, O Columcille, to give me some of that glory forever at my death."

"I give it thee," saith Columcille. "Do good for thy part, and thou shalt be the third of my dear sons on my breast on the Doomsday for thy protection, and be safe from the fire of doom, thou and Maelumha mac Baodain and Suidemhain mac Samhain."

Then either bade other farewell, and Mongan was a faithful servant to God and to Columcille from that time till his death and after.[1]

88. On a time that Columcille was making the rounds of the churchyard of the Black Church in Derry, to wit, the oratory wherein he was wont to say his hours, he cast him down upon his knees, and turned his face full to the east, and lifted his hands upward as he were hearing the mass. And when he had risen from his knees, there inquired of him one of the monks that was with him, wherefore he had bowed himself and what vision had been given him in that hour.

Columcille answered him and said: "The Pope," saith he, "to wit, Gregory of the Golden Lips, was but now saying the mass at the high altar in the church of Saint Peter in Rome," saith he, "and when I beheld him raising the sacred body, I fell on my knees; and for that it was I bowed myself." And God's name and Columcille's were magnified thereby.

89. Herein is seen how greatly Columcille loved Derry, and how

[1] *Cf.* Colloquy of Columcille and the youth at Carn Eolairg in *Z. C. P.* II 313-320.

Duibreigles aniugh an uair do bi sé ga denamh ar cor go mbeith edon na haltora de san aird soir le dlus na coilledh, 7 narb ail lei[s]-si*n* an coill do gerradh, gorab é a thaeb do fhurail sé do tabairt san aird soir. Acus dá dearbudh sin, is ana thaeb ata an altoír ara n-abra*d* se fein an t-aifr*en*d, 7 is follass do cach gorab é sin suidhiug*ad* an duirrtige sin anuigh. Acus an crann do tuitf*ed* uad fen *no* do legfadh an gaeth sa baile-sin, do fhagaib se mar aithne ag lucht a inaidh 'na diaig, gan a gerr*ad* co cend nomhaidhe 7 a roinn andsen ar dainibh maithe 7 saithe an baile, 7 an tres cuid de do chur a tigh na n-áidhedh fa comhair na n-áid*ed* fen 7 a dechm*ad* do roind a*r* na bochtaibh. Acus ata an rann dorinde se fen tareis a dul ar deoraidhect a n-Albain do, ga derbadh nach raibe 'sa mbith ní ris[75]) nar chomholc les coill Doire do gerradh:

Act gidh ecail lem, gan fhell, an t-écc 7 an t-if*ern*n,
as ecclaidhe lem, gan cleith, fuaim tvaidhe tíar a nDoire.

90. Fectus do C. c. 'san inadh re n-abarta*r* Cluaine, a p*or*t Doire Calgaidh don taeb toir do Loch Feaba*il*, 7 do bendaig se san inadh-sin[76]) 7 dorinde temp*ul* and. Acus do labair tre spirvid faidhedorachta 7 ass*ed* adubairt: 'Ticf*a* esp*o*c gallda a cenn aimsire faide am diaid-se 'san inadh-sa, 7 scailf*id* an tempul-sa dorinde mesi do denamh oibre eli da cloch*aib* san inadh re n-abart*ar* Bun Sentuin*n*e sa baile-si fen. C*on*adh and dorinde an rann-sa:

Mo t*hru*aidhe![77]) ticfaid goill go Clúaine,
7 beraid mo te*m*poll go Bun Sentuinde fuaire.

Acus do firadh sin uile, amail is follas do cach aniugh .i. Tain (*fol.* 11b) ig espog gallda go Doire darb ainm Nicól Bastún, 7 isse do scaeil an tempul-sin do denamh cuírte de. Acus nir crichnaig*ed* an cuirt-sin fós; 7 is demin leamsa corub do mirbuil*ibh* C. c. tainec gan crich do chur uirre les na clochaib-sin a temp*uil* fen.

91.[78]) Do bendaig 7 do cumhd*aig* C. c. Rath mBoth iarsin, 7 do baith*ed* an saer do bi ag denamh mhuilind 'sa baile-sin a lind an muilinn fein. Acus arna indesin sin do C. c., docuaidh os cind a cuirp arna togbail asin lind 7 do leig ar a gluínib é, 7 do cuir

---

[75]See § 223 for similar construction.

[76]"and he made a holy habitation in that place." *Cf.* §§ 141, 156, *infra*, for the same expression.

[77]*leg.* thruaighe.

[78]Abridged in O. I. L. See *Lis. Lives*, p. 175, l. 912 ff.

loth he was to cut or fell the grove of trees there. When he was building the oratory that men call today Dubhreigles, because of the nearness of that grove, he could not find a place to build the oratory in such wise that the front of the altar should be toward the east. And so loth was he to cut down the grove, that he bade the side of the oratory be toward the east. In proof hereof the altar where he was wont to say the mass is on the side thereof, and it is manifest to all today that thus is the site of the oratory. And he charged his successors to chop no tree that fell of itself or that was blown down by the wind, till the end of nine days, and then to divide it among all the folk of the place, good and bad; a third part of it to be put in the guest-house for the guests, and a tenth part as a share for the poor. And this is the quatrain he made after going into exile in Alba, and it proveth that naught was so grievous to him as to cut the grove of Derry.

> "Though I am affrighted, truly,
> By death and by Hell;
> I am more affrighted, frankly,
> By the sound of an ax in Derry in the West."

90. On a time that Columcille was in the place that is called Cluaine, in the port of Derry on the west side of Loch Foyle, he blessed it, and built a church there.

And he spake by the spirit of prophecy and said: "There shall come a Lowland bishop to this place a long while after me, and he shall put down this church that I have made, to build another work of its stones in the place that is called Bun Sentuinde in this same town-land." And he made this quatrain:

> "Woe is me!
> Strangers shall come to Cluaine,
> And they shall bear away my church
> To Bun Sentuinde the cold."

And all this was fulfilled, as is manifest to all today; for there came a Lowland bishop hight Nicholas Bastien, and he destroyed the church to make a palace thereof. And never hath that palace been all builded entire. And I am certain it was by reason of some miracle of Columcille that they might not build it to the end with the stones of his church.

91. Columcille blessed and built Raphoe thereafter; and the wright that was making a mill in that stead was drowned in the mill pond. And when this was told to Columcille, he went to the body that had been drawn out of the stream, and he fell on his knees and prayed earnestly

urnaigthe duthractach docum Dia fana athbeougad dó. Acus ar
crichnugad na hurnaidhe-sin do C. c., do érich na shesamh go
dóchusach 7 do bean crois da bachaill ar ucht an tshaeir, 7 adubairt
ris erghe beo ar a chossaib fen a n-ainm Ihsv Crisd. Do eirigh
an saer acedoir le breithir C. c., amail do éireochad se as a chodlud;
gor mórad ainm Dé 7 Coluimb cille de sin.

92.⁷⁹) Fectas eli do C. c. a Rath mBoth, 7 docuaidh iarand
na sesrighe amugha o na hoireamhnaib, 7 dobendaigh C. c. lam
macaimh oig do bi 'na fhochair nach derna goibhnecht riam
roimhe sin .i. Fergna a ainm. Acus do iarr air íarann do denamh
a n-inadh an íarainn-sin dochuaid amugha. Dorinde Fergna sin
go maith amail do beith re goibhnecht ríam connuice sin. Acus
ba saei gabonn ó sin amach e do brigh an bendaighte-sin C. c.
Acus ní he sin an Fergna rer cuir se an failte a-mbroind a
máthar.

93. Gabuis Feidlimid mac Fergassa cendfoda, mic Conaill
Gulpan .i. athair Coluimb cille, rigacht Ulad, 7 ar mbeith do
athaidh fada 'sa rige-sin 7 ar tect a aísi 7 a arsaidhecta go mor,
légiss an righe de 7 roindis ar a braithrib í. Acus assiad so
anmonda na mbraithrech-sin .i. Brenaind 7 Nindigh, Fiachaidh
7 Fidruidhe, Cathrand 7 Loarn, 7 Sedna an mac fa hoige dib.
Acus dorindedh flegh⁸⁰ mór iarsin le macuib Ferghossa san inadh
re n-abartar Both Brain, a tir Fergna aniugh, a termonn Cille
mic Nenain. Acus do bi Columb cille an uair-sin a cuigedh Laigen
ag bendugad cell 7 eclus. Et ro foillsig aingel Dé do cor léic
Feidlimid .i. a athair, an rige de 7 gor roindetar na braithre
adubramar romainn a ferand etorra fen.

IS andsin teid Columb cille remhe bud thuaidh gussin inadh
a raibe a athair .i. go Cill mic Nenaín, 7 nir cían dó and an uair
tancatar techta a braithrech ar cend an tsenóruch .i. Feidlimthe,
dá breith do comórad na fleidhe. Assed adubairt Feidlimid nach
rachad se andsin 7 go raibe se arsaidh egcruaidh, 7 adubairt riu
C. c. do breith leo do bendugad na fleidhe. Teid C. c. les na
techtaib-sin go Boith mBrain, 7 ar ndul don baile dó, tarla Sedna
mac Fergassa cendfoda do ceddainib dó, 7 ba rofhailid remhe he.
Et do fhíarfaigh C. c. de nar roindetar a braithri 7 se fen ferand
re cele. 'Do roinnemar,' ar Sedna. 'Nar gabadh dechmad an
ferainn-sin lib'? ar Columb cille. 'Nir gabad,' ar Sedna. 'IS
ced limsa, masa ched le Dia he,' ar C. c., 'gan an roinn sin do

---

⁷⁹Taken literally from O. I. L. See *Lis. Lives,* p. 175, l. 914 ff.
⁸⁰*leg.* fledh.

to God to restore the wright for him. And when he had finished his prayer, he rose up trustfully and made a cross with his staff upon the breast of the wright, and he bade him rise up to his feet alive, in the name of Jesu Christ. At the word of Columcille the wright rose up straightway as he might rise up from sleep, so that God's name and Columcille's were magnified thereby .

92. Another time when Columcille was in Raphoe, the iron of the plough was lost by the ploughmen. And Columcille blessed the hand of a young lad that was with him, that ere that had never done smith work, to wit, one called Fergna, and he asked him to make an iron in place of the iron that was lost. And Fergna did it as well as if he had been at smith work always till that time. And he was a master smith thenceforth by virtue of the blessing of Columcille.

This was not the Fergna that he welcomed from his mother's womb.

93. Fedlimid, the father of Columcille, took the kingship of Ulidia, and when he had been long in the kingship, and old age and great feebleness were come upon him, he gave up the kingdom and divided it among his brothers. And these were the names of those brothers: Brenaind and Nindigh, Fiachaidh and Fidruidhe, Cathrand and Loarn. And Sedna was the youngest of them. And a great feast was made by the sons of Fergus in the place that is called Both Brain in the land of Fergna to-day at the boundary of Cill mic Nenain. And at that time Columcille was in the province of Leinster, blessing chapels and churches. And the angel revealed to him that his father Fedlimid had given up the kingdom, and that the kinsmen whereof we have made mention had portioned the land among themselves.

Then Columcille fared northward to the place where his father was, to Cill mic Nenain, and not long had he been there when there came messengers from his kinsmen to bring the old man Fedlimid to celebrate the feast. And Fedlimid said he would not go thither, for he was old and feeble, and he bade them take Columcille with them to bless the feast. Then went Columcille with the messengers to Both Brain. And on the way thither Sedna son of Fergus Cennfada met him among the first, and made great joy of him. And Columcille asked him if he and his brothers had not divided the land among themselves.

"We have divided it," saith Sedna.

"Have tithes of the land been set apart by you?" saith Columcille.

"They have not," saith Sedna.

"It is my will, if it be God's will," saith Columcille, "that this division be unblessed and prosper you not, until tithes thereof be set apart by you."

"Thy wish is granted thee, O cleric," saith Sedna, "for a share of the division that fell to me shall be given thee as tithes."

beith ar bail *no* do dul a soirbes etraibh *no* go ngabt*ar* dechm*ad* an
feraind lib.' 'Do riar deit, a clericc,' ar Sedna, '.i. an cuid ronda
rainec mesi don ferann doit ar son na dechm*ai*de.' Gonadh é sin
Termonn cille m*i*c Nenain aniugh. 'Dober-sa luach ar a shon-sin
5 duid-si,' ar Columb cille, 'oir dobér cendus 7 tigernas deit ar do
braithribh is sine na tú fen. Et is ar dot slicht beid rigraidh 7
tigern*a*da slecta Conaill G*ulban* go brath aris.' IS andsin tanc*atar*
an cuid eli do macaib Ferghosa a coinde C. c. 7 do fersad failte
fris. Fiarfuighis C. c. dib, ó do fuair se dechm*ad* an feraind o
10 Sedna, an bfuigedh se dechm*ad* na fle*di*⁸¹) 7 gach neich eli as ar
imcub*aid* dechm*ad* do gab*ail* o sin amach uatha san. Do éstet*ar*
uile fris. 'Frecr*aid* C. c.,' *ar* Sedna, '7 na hesdigh ris am énní
dá n-íarrand oraib, oir is dó is coir bur ndechmaidh-se .i. do mac
bur nderbhráth*ar* .i. an clerech as ferr a n-Erind.' 'Tabr*aid* bur
15 ndechm*ai*d do C. c.,' ar Loarn mac Fergasa .i. an dara mac rob
oige do cloind Fergussa cennfhoda. 'Fada gor labrais,' ar C. c.
'7 dá (*fol*. 12a) n-abartha mo ríar ní b*ud* luaithe ina sin, a Loairn,
do beid*ís* righti 7 tigernadha a n-Erinn fen ar do tslicht, 7 o nach
dubruis mo ríar *acht* co mall,' ar se,'ni beid righti a n-Erinn ar
20 do sli*cht* 7 beid righti a n-Albain dot slicht. Conadh ar slicht an
Loairn-sin m*i*c Fergosa do batar cland Maeil Colaim, m*i*c Dondchada, a rigacht Alpan aimser fhoda. Acus do fíradh gach ní
da ndubairt Columb cille an uair-sin.

94. Fectus d'Aedh mac Ainmirech 'san inadh ré n-abartar
25 Druim Cliab a Cairp*ri* C*on*nucht aniug, 7 do baíthed ing*en* d'Aed
ar abainn Droma Cl*íab* .i. ar in Meth*en*aigh, c*on*udh Lind ing*ine*
Aeda ainm na lindedh inar baith*ed* í ó sin alle. Do bi C. c. a
comghar doib an uair-sin 7 cuiris Aodh techta ar a cend. Tic C. c.
les na techaibh-sin 7 íarrais Aedh air a i*ngen* d'aithbeougad do.
30 Benais C. c. crois da bachaill ar ucht na hing*ine* 7 tathbéouigheis
hí; gor móradh ainm De 7 Coluimb cille de sin. Et marbai*s* Aedh
an ferond-sin do Dia 7 do C. c. . Bendaighis Columb cille an
baile-sin iarsin cor cumhd*aig* ecluss and, 7 do fhágaib clerech da
mui*nn*t*ir* a comarbacht an baile-sin .i. Motharen D*roma* Cliab a
35 ainm. Acus do labair Columb cille tré spir*ud* faidhetórachta 7
adubairt, com*ad* lé cenel Conaill uaisle 7 onoír an baile-sin 7 na
tuath 'na timchell go brath. IS andsin do fhiafr*aich* Aed mac
Ainmir*ech* do C. c. ga med do righaib Erenn *no* dá tigern*aib* do

---

⁸¹na fl*edh*i in smaller handwriting, but apparently by the same hand, written
in the margin of MS.

Hence is Termonn Cille mic Nenain [the name of that place] today.

"I will give thee a reward therefor," saith Columcille, "for I will make thee head and give thee lordship over thy kinsmen that are older than thou. And of thy seed shall be the kings and lords of the race of Conall Gulban forever."

Then the rest of the sons of Fergus came to meet Columcille, and they bade him welcome. Columcille asked them, inasmuch as he had been given tithes of the land of Sedna, if he should be given by them also tithes of the feast and of all things else whereof it were fitting to set apart tithes forever. And they were all silent thereat.

"Make answer to Columcille," saith Sedna, "and be not silent touching aught he asketh of you, for to him are your tithes owing, to wit, to your brother's son and the best cleric in Erin."

"Give your tithes to Columcille," saith Loarn mac Fergasa, the second youngest son of the children of Fergus.

"Long was it ere thou didst speak," saith Columcille. "Hadst thou yielded sooner to my will, O Loarn, there should be kings and lords of thy seed in Erin itself, but since thou hast not agreed thereto save tardily, there shall be no kings of thy seed in Erin. But in Alba the kings of thy seed shall be."

Hence it was of the seed of Loarn son of Fergus, that the sons of Maol Colm, son of Donnchadh sprang, that were kings in Alba a long time. And all that Columcille said then was fulfilled.

94. On a time Aed son of Ainmire was in the place that is called Druim Cliab in Cairpre Connacht today. And a daughter of Aed was drowned in the river of Druim Cliab, to wit, in the Methenach, so that the Pool of the Daughter of Aed is the name from then till now of the water wherein she was drowned. Columcille was not far distant from them at the time, and Aed sent messengers for him. Columcille came with the messengers, and Aed asked him to restore his daughter to him. Columcille traced the cross with his staff upon the maiden's breast, and restored her to life, so that God's name and Columcille's were magnified thereby.

And Aed gave that land forever in mortmain to God and Columcille. And Columcille blessed the place then and built a church there. And he left a cleric of his household to succeed him in that place. His name is Motharen of Druim Cliab. And Columcille spake by the spirit of prophecy, and declared that the lordship and honor of that place and of the regions thereabout should belong to the clan of Conall forever. Then Aed son of Ainmire, inquired of Columcille how many of the kings of Erin or its lords God had saved during their time ere that.

"Three only have been saved without long while in Purgatory,"

slanaigh Día rian a lind fein.⁸² 'Ni derna g*an* purgadoir romoir ach*t* tri*ú*r amhain,' ar Columb cille .i. Daimhín daimh-airgid,⁸³) rí Oirgiall, 7 Oil*ill* in ban*n*a, ri C*o*n*n*acht, 7 Feradh*a*ch m*a*c Duach, rí Osruidhe, ar feabhas a ngni*m* leth re Día 'sa saegul-sa.' Is
5 andsin do fiaf*r*aidh Aedh do C. c. an slaineoch*a*d Dia é fen fa deóidh. 'Ni dingna,' ar Columb cille, 'mu*n*a derna tu aithrighe romhor at pecadh 7 deghoibri*g*the o so amach.' Iarais Aed iarsin mar athcuinghe ar Columb cille buaid do breith ar Laighn*ib* do bí ag cogadh fris 7 gan e fen do toitim leo. 'Ni heidir lem,' ar
10 Columb cille, 'oir is do Laighn*ib* mo m*athair*, 7 tancot*ar* cugam go Durmhuig, etir shen 7 og, 7 do íarrat*ar* athcuinge m*i*c tshethar oram .i. gan righ eli do breith buaidhe orra, 7 do ghell*as*-a sin doib *acht* co mbeith an coir acu. Gidhedh, dob*er* mo cochall doid-si, 7 ní muirfidher tu an cein bías umad.' Acus do bi an briathar sin
15 Coluimb cille ar comhall no go ndechaidh Aedh aimser iarsin ar sluaig*ed* a lLaighn*ib*, 7 cor derm*aid* a cochall, 7 go marb*ad* a cath Bel*aig* Duín Bolg le Laignecha é.⁸⁴)

95⁸⁵) Fectus tucatar a oidedha Domnal mac Aedha mic Ainmirech ar cuairt mar a raibe C. c., 7 se 'na macamh og an
20 uairsin, 7 do íarrat*ar* air a bendugad. 'Ni aniugh ata a ndan damh a bennugad,' ar Columb cille, '*acht* a cend aimsire faide ó aniugh⁸⁶) bendachus me é san inadh re ráit*er* Druim Cet a Ciana*ch*ta Glinde Gemhin, airm a mbeid fir Erenn 7 Alpan, idir laech 7 clerech, a n-aini*n*adh am Aed mac Ainmirech .i. am righ Erenn, athair an
25 lenib-sin fen. Acus adeirim ribse a coimet co maith, 7 biaid se 'na rig roclumar a n-Erind iarsin aimser fada, 7 biaid se os cend a braithrech fen uile, 7 ni beraid a naimhde *no* a escharaid buaid go brath air, 7 dogebha se bas maith 'na tigh feín a fiadhnaise a carad 7 a muindt*ir*e fein, 7 rach*aid* a anam do caithem na gloiri suth*aine*.'
30 Do firadh sin mar adubairt C. c., amail indeós*as* an leab*ur*-sa a n-inadh eli a mordail Droma Cet.

---

⁸²A fuller version is in *L. L.*, p. 303ᵇ ff. (cited by Stokes in *Lis. Lives*, p. 306 ff.) See also *Silva Gadelica*, p. 378 *seq*.

⁸³He died 565 A. D.

⁸⁴*F. M.* under year A. D. 594; *Annals of Ulster* under year 597 (*recte* 598).

⁸⁵Taken literally from Adamnan. See Reeves' *Adam.*, p. 36 ff.

⁸⁶Domnall was only a child when the convention of Druim Ceat was held in 574 (*recte* 575) according to *A. U.*, and it was to Druim Ceat his tutors first brought him according to Adamnan.

saith Columcille, "to wit, Daimhin Damh-airgid, King of Oirgiall, and Oilill the Womanish, a king of Connacht, and Feradach son of Dua, King of Ossory, for the goodness of their deeds the while they were in this life."

Then inquired Aed of Columcille if God would give him Heaven at the last.

"He will not," saith Columcille, "except thou do for thy sins passing great penance and good works henceforth."

Then did Aed ask from Columcille as a boon, that he should be victorious over the Leinstermen that were fighting against him, and that he should not fall by their hands.

"That I can not give," saith Columcille, "for my mother is of the Leinster folk; and young and old have come to me to Durrow, and have asked of me as the boon of a sister's son, that no other king should have victory over them. And I promised it them, if so be their cause is just. But I will give thee my cowl, and so long as it is upon thee thou shalt not be slain."

And that promise of Columcille was fulfilled until a time afterward when Aed went warring among the Leinsterfolk, and forgat his cowl, and was killed in the battle of Belach Duinbolg.

95. On a time his fosterers brought Domnall son of Aed son of Ainmire, to visit Columcille. And Domnall was a small lad at that time, and they asked Columcille to bless him.

"It is not today I shall bless him," saith Columcille, "but a long while from today in the place that is called Druim Ceat in the Cianachta of Glenn Gemhin where the men of Erin and Alba, both lay and cleric, shall be together round Aed son of Ainmire, King of Erin and father of this same child. And I say to you, keep him well and he shall be a king right famous in Erin for a long time hereafter, and he shall be above all his own brothers. And his enemies and foes shall have no victory over him forever, and he shall have a good death in his own house with his friends and his household around him; and his soul shall go to the glory everlasting."

It came to pass as Columcille had said, and as this book will relate in another place touching the Assembly of Druim Ceat.[1]

---

[1] *Cf.* § 327.

96.⁸⁷) Docuaid C. c. 'na diaid-sin a crich Tefa, 7 tuc rí an tire sin ferond do .i. an t-inadh a bfuil Durmach aniug, gor cumdaiged eclus les ann. A n-Durmaigh, imorro, do bi C. c. an uair do bendaigh sé an cloidem do Colman mór mac Diarmada, 7
5 do bí buaidh an cloidhim tresan mbendugad-sin gan bás ar bith d'fhagail don tí aga mbeith se. Do iarr duine airidhe do baí a n-eslainti iasacht an cloidhim-sin, 7 do cuir Colman an cloidhem cuige, 7 do bi se bliadain aige 7 ni fuair bás risan ré sin. Acus docuaid se a n-égcruth romhor, 7 arna thuicsin da cairdib narb ail
10 le Dia aisec a slainti do tabairt dó 7 corab é an cloidhem do bi ga congbail 'na beathaid, rucad an cloidem uadh 7 fuair bas fo cedoir; gor morad ainm De 7 Coluimb cille de sin.

97⁸⁸) Fectas eli do Columb cille a nDurmaigh, 7 tuccad ubla cvige. Acus tarla uball searb drochblasta amescc na n-uball air
15 7 do fhiafraigh C. c. cait a bfrith an t-uball-sin. Adubratar cach ris corab abhall airithe do bí san aballgort 7 corb e sin (fol. 12b) bud blas da hublaib do gnath. Arna cloisdin sin do Columb cille, teid san abullgort 7 bendaighis an aball-sin 7 assed adubairt: 'Bendaigim tu 7 cuirim ort a hucht en Día uilecumhachtaig, a
20 aball ud, an naduír serb miblasda do bi agat gotrasda, do chlaech- hlod 7 naduir milis degblasda do gabail cugad anoiss.' Acus dorinde an duil balb amail adubairt C. c. ria an uair-sin fen, indus gorub íad a hubla ubla budh millsi 7 dob fherr blas 7 baludh dá facutar cach riam reime sin. Acus as follus as sin nach edh amhaín
25 tuc Dia cumachta ar duil an uisce do C. c. leth re fín do denamh de, acht tuc sé cumachta dó ar duilib na talman, mar ataid croind 7 clocha 7 luibenda 7 gach duil talmaide ó sin amach.

98⁸⁹) Dochuaid C. c. 'na díaid-sin gusan inadh re n-abarthar Cenannus aniug .i. baile righ Erenn an uair-sin é .i. baili Díarmada

⁸⁷Taken literally from O. I. L. See *Lis. Lives,* p. 175, l. 917 ff.
⁸⁸Taken literally from Adamnan. See Reeves' *Adam.,* p. 105. Abridged in O. I. L. See *Lis. Lives,* p. 175, l. 918 ff.
⁸⁹O'D. follows rather closely the O. I. L. See Stokes' *Lis. Lives,* p. 176, l. 927 f. In a note, *ibid.* p. 306, Stokes writes: "Aed Slane, otherwise called Aed mac Ainmerech". They were two distinct persons. Aed Slane was the son of Diarmaid mac Cerbhaill.

VII

OF THE LABORS OF COLUMCILLE IN MEATH

96. Then went Columcille afterward to the country of Teffia. And a king of that country gave him land, to wit, the region where Durrow is today. And a church was built by him there.

It was in Durrow, indeed, that Columcille blessed the sword of Colman Mor, son of Diarmaid, and such was the virtue of the sword through that blessing, that he that had it could not die. And a certain man that was sick asked for the loan of that sword; and Colman sent it to him, and he had it a year. And for that length he did not die. And he fell into passing great weakness; and when his friends understood that it was not the will of God that he should be restored to health, and that it was the sword that was keeping him alive, they took the sword from him and he died straightway, so that God's name and Columcille's were magnified thereby.

97. Another time that Columcille was in Durrow, apples were brought to him, and he chanced upon a bitter apple of evil taste. And he inquired whence that apple was got. They all told him it was from a certain apple-tree in his orchard and that such was the taste of its apples always. When Columcille had heard this, he went into the orchard, and blessed that apple-tree.

And he said: "I bless thee and I charge thee by the bosom of the one God Almighty, O apple-tree, to change that bitter ill-tasting nature to sweet and savory."

And forthwith the dumb thing did as Columcille had commanded, so that these were the sweetest apples and of the best savour and taste that any had seen ere that time. And it is clear to us from this that God gave Columcille power not solely over the element of water, to the end that he might make wine thereof, but he gave also to him power over the elements of the earth, such as trees and stones and herbs and every element of earth, from that time forth.

98. After that Columcille went to the place that is called Kells today, that was the stead of the King of Erin in that time, to wit,

mic Cerbaill. Acus do congbad C. c. amuigh a ndorus an baile sin.
IS andsin docuaidh C. c. do denamh faidedorachta don baile 7
adubairt na bud buan an baili ag an muinntir-sin do bi and. Et
tarla Bec mac De do .i. drai Diarmada mic Cerbaill 7 dob faidh
5 maith é. Adubairt C. c. ris: 'A Big mac De, dena faistine don
baile-si cindus bias se, an rigthi no an clerig bías and.' 'Clerigh
co deimin bias and,' ar Becc, 'ó so amach 7 bud tusa cend na
clerech-sin 7 ní bud baili rig co brach arís é;' oir ni raibhe an ri
and an uair-sin, 7 tainic se don baili [í]arsin 7 tuc se an baili uile
10 do C. c. a n-eraic a congbála amuigh ann 7 tuc Aedh Slaíne mac
Diarmada a ced cuige sin. Do bendaigh C. c. an baile ina diaidh
sin, 7 dorinde se faidhedóracht d'Aed Slaíne 7 adubairt, go mbeith
se 'na righ Erenn 7 go mad maith a crich muna dernad se fingail no
fell 7 da ndernadh, na bud fada a shaeghal na diaid. Acus do
15 bendaigh C. c. cochall d'Aedh Slaíne mac Diarmada⁹⁰) 7 adubairt
ris, nach dergfad arm air an fad do beith an cochall sin uime.
Doroíne Aedh Slaine fingail tar comairli C. c. ar Shuibne mac
Colmain moir .i. mac a derbhbrathar fen. Docuaid Aed Slaine
ar sluaiged a cinn cethre mblíadan ón uair-sin 7 do dermaid se a
20 cochall, mar dob ail le Día 7 le C. c., 7 do marbadh isin ló-sin he.⁹¹)
Et ac denum na faidhedorachta sin do C. c., tuc a adhaigh siardes
7 do gab gengairi 7 subaltaige mor é. Do fhiarfaig Baithin adbhar
a subaltaige. Do frecair C. c. é 7 issed adubairt: 'Bertar,' ar se,
'deichenbar 7 da fichid san enbaile-si thiar anocht 7 bud muindter
25 dileas do Dia iad;' 7 budh iad sin an macraid Cille Sciri. Acus
gach fáidhedoracht da nderna C. c. andsin, do comhaill Dia go
fírindech íad.

⁹⁰Cf. § 94. L. L., p. 303ᵇ ff (cited by Stokes in Lis. Lives, p. 306) and the Book
of Lecan, fol. 308ᵇ (cited by Reeves in Reeves' Adam., p. 39) make Aedh mac Ainmirech the recipient of the cowl. The only authority for giving it to Aed Slane is
the O. I. L. (See Lis. Lives, p. 176, ll. 945 f.) O'Donnell incorporated both these
legends into his Life of Columcille. The account in the O. I. L. concerning Aed
Slaine is based on Adamnan. (See Reeves' Adam., p. 42.) But Adamnan makes no
mention of the cowl incident. The O. I. L. has probably confused Aed Slaine with
Aed mac Ainmirech, who was the recipient of the cowl according to the oldest
source, namely, L. L.

⁹¹He reigned from 598-604 A. D.

Diarmaid mac Cerbaill. And Columcille was kept without the door of the palace in front of that place. Then did Columcille betake him to making prophecies touching that stead, and he said it would not be for long that the household therewithin should hold it. And there chanced to come upon him Bec mac De, the which was druid to Diarmaid mac Cerbaill, and a good prophet.

Columcille said to him:

"Bec mac De, make a prophecy touching this place. How shall it be? Shall it be kings or clerics that shall dwell therein?"

"Of a sooth it shall be clerics," saith Bec, "henceforward; and thou shalt be head of those clerics, and never again shall it be the place of a king."

The King was not there at that time. He came thither after, and he gave the whole place to Columcille as compensation, because he had been kept outside, and Aed Slaine son of Diarmaid consented thereto.

After that Columcille blessed the place, and he prophesied touching Aed Slaine, and he said he should be King of Erin, and good should be his ending, except he slay a kinsman or do treachery; but if he do that, his life should not be long thereafter. And Columcille blessed a cowl for Aed Slaine, son of Diarmaid, and told him that weapon should not redden on him so long as that cowl was around him.

But Aed Slaine slew a kinsman in spite of the counsel of Columcille, to wit, Suibhne son of Colman Mor, his brother's son. Aed Slaine went a-hosting at the end of four years from that time, and by the will of God and Columcille he forgat his cowl, and was killed that day.

And when he had made that prophecy, Columcille turned his face to the southwest, and smiled and was exceeding merry. And Baithin asked the cause of his mirth.

Columcille answered and said:

"There shall be born ten and two score," saith he, "in this one place in the west tonight, and they shall be loyal folk to God." And they were the youths of Cill Scire.

And all the prophecies that Columcille made in that time, God fulfilled truly afterward.

99.⁹²) Do cumd*ai*g C. c. moran cell ar fud criche Br*egh* 7 Midhe 7 do fhagaib comarb*ada* 7 min*n*a uadha fen innta .i. do fág*ai*b se Oissi*n* mac Cell*ai*g a Cluain moir bfher n-arda. Docuaid C. c. iarsin go Mhain*istir* Buide m*ic* Bronaig. IS andsin do ben bachall C. c. risan soithech⁹³) ngloine do bi a laimh Buide a n-aimsir a bais 7 do clos a foghar fo*n* cill uile, 7 do foillsigh C. c. annsin an t-inadh inar hadluic*ed* Baíde. Acus do coisric a cell 7 do cumdaigh a taisi mar do ghell Buide fen a n-aimsir a bais ag tairrng*ire* C. c.

Do chumd*ai*g Columb cille ecl*uis* a Rachraind oirthir Bregh 7 do fág*ai*b Colman deochain indte.

100.⁹⁴) Fectus eli doch*uai*d C. c. ar cuairt mara raibe a maigest*ir* fen .i. Finden. Acus arna fhaicsin d'Finnen chuige, adubairt re raibe do latair: 'An é nach faicí-si C. c. cugaind 7 aingli De maill*e* ris ga coimid*echt?*' Acus arna cloisdin sin da raibe do lathair, do lasatar a ngrad C. c. . Acus is na laithib-sin fen docuaidh Columb cille go Bretain⁹⁵) 7 dá manach déc mailli ris, do sil*ad* an creidim, 7 tucc móran docum creidme 7 crab*uid* isna tírib-sin.

101⁹⁶) Gabais C. c. iarsin dá oilit*hri* go Toirinis Mart*ain*, 7 docuaidh se ar in lec fá ar hadluic*ed* Martain 7 do tócaib se an lec don tumba, 7 fvair sé leab*ar* na soiscel ar muin Mart*ain* 'sa tumba, 7 do bi Mart*ain* 7 an leab*ar* sin c*ed* bliad*vin* remhe sin a talm*ain*,⁹⁷) 7 do coimh*éd* Dia an leabar an fad sin fa comhair C. c. ind*us* narb fherr an c*ed* lá é ina in uair-sin. Acus tuc C. c. do toil De 7 Mhartai*n* an leabar sin les go Doiri, amail do tairrngir Martain fen a n-aimsir a bais go tibr*ad* sé les hé.

---

⁹²Taken literally from O. I. L. See *Lis. Lives*, p. 176, ll. 951 ff.

⁹³*Cf.* O. I. L., *ibid.*, p. 28, ll. 953 ff. *Is ann sin roben a bachall-som risin*n*a arradh nglainidhi fris rofreasghabh Bóiti docum nime*, which O'D. intentionally or unintentionally misinterprets.

⁹⁴Taken literally from Adamnan. See Reeves' *Adam.*, pp. 195-6.

⁹⁵Hence C. C. went to Britain before his compulsory exile mentioned in § 198. Is the story of his enforced exile a fabrication?

⁹⁶Based on O. I. L. See *Lis. Lives*, p. 175, ll. 904 ff.

⁹⁷St. Martin died *circ.* 397 and C. C. was born *circ.* 518, thus making the discovery of the Gospel take place 21 years before the birth of Columcille. O'D. tells the story of the discovery of St. Martin's Gospel more fully in § 256 where it is evidently borrowed from the *Acts of St. Eugenius* of Ardstraw and *St. Mochonna or Machar*, the patron saint of Aberdeen. (See Reeves' *Adam.*, pp. 324-5.)

VIII

OF THE JOURNEYS OF COLUMCILLE IN SUNDRY PLACES TO SOW THE FAITH AND IN ESPECIAL OF HIS LABORS IN LEINSTER

99. Columcille built many churches throughout the country of Bregha and Midhe, and he left successors of his therein, and memorials sent by himself. He left Oissin mac Cellaig in Cluain Mor of the Tall Men.

And after that he went to the monastery of Buide mac Bronaig. There it was that the crozier of Columcille touched the glass vessel that had been in the hand of Buide when he was dying, and the sound thereof was heard throughout the whole church. And then Columcille revealed the place where Buide was buried.[1] And he blessed his church and enshrined his relics as Buide had promised when he was dying, prophesying of Columcille.

Columcille built a church in Lambay in the east of Bregia, and he left Colman the Deacon therein.

100. Another time Columcille went to visit his teacher, to wit, Finnen.

And when Finnen saw him coming, he said to those that were with him: "See ye not Columcille coming toward us, and angels of God in his company?"

And when those that were there heard that, they were consumed with love for Columcille.

In those days also it was that Columcille went to Britain with twelve monks to sow the Faith. And many of those lands did he bring to the Faith and to pious works.

101. Then Columcille went on a pilgrimage to Tours of Martin. And he went to the flagstone whereunder Martin was buried. And he lifted the stone from the tomb, and he found the book of the gospels upon the neck of Martin in the tomb. And Martin and that book had been a hundred years in the earth, and God had kept the book that while for the use of Columcille, so that it had been no better its first day than in that hour. And by the will of God and of Martin, Columcille took that book with him to Derry, as Martin himself at the time of his death had prophesied that Columcille should bring it.

[1] *Cf.* 101, 256.

102. Fectus and do bí C. c. 7 Comghall 7 Cainnech maille ris 'san inadh darub ainm Sord⁹⁸ aniugh. Adubairt Comghall re C. c. an t-aifre*nd* do radh. Tinn- (*fol.* 13a) scnais Columb cille an t-aifrend. IS andsin doconnaic Caindech colamhan tend*tige* os cinn C. c., 7 do indis Caindech sin do Comghall 7 doconncat*ar* re céle sin. Acus do cumdaig*ed* eclu*is* andsin le C. c. . Gonadh é Sord C. c. sin aniugh, 7 do fagaib C. c. fer m*aith* da mui*n*dt*ir* 'na comarba and .i. Fína*n* lob*ar,* 7 do fagaib an leb*ar* aifrind do scrib sé fen ann.

103. Do bendaigh C. c. Sord 7 do bendaigh tobar Suird .i. Glan a ainm, 7 do fhágaib cross and; oír fa bes do Columb cille crosa 7 leb*air* 7 gach uile chul*aid* eclaisi do cumhdach 7 d'fhagbail in gach baile da mbendaig*ed* sé.

104⁹⁹) Fechtus eli do Columb cilli 7 do Caindech re taebh fhairge 7 do bi anf*ad* mor ar in fairge. 'A Coluimb cille,' ar Caindec*h*, 'an bfuil a fhis agat cred adei*r* an tonn'? 'Ata a fis sin agam-sa,' ar C. c., 'adeir sí go fuil do mui*nd*te*r*-si a nguasacht mór ar an bfhairge 7 go bfu*air* duine dib bás, 7 dobera Dia cugainde 'sa p*ort*-sa íad sul ti maidin amáruch.' Acus do firadh an faidhedóracht sin C. c. amail fa minic les.

105. Fecht eli do C. c. 7 do nech naemtha eli, darb ainm Baithin, ag siub*al* re taeb fairge a n-inadh airthe, 7 doconncatar long aga báthad. Acus do fhiarf*aigh* Baithin do Columb cilli cred far fulaing Dia an long do bath*ad*. 'Enpecach do bi indi,' ar C. c. '7 do ceadaigh Día lucht na luingi do bathadh cuige.' 'Dar lind,' ar Baithin, 'dorinne Dia ecoir ar lucht na luingi.' Acus do leic C. c. sin tairis, 7 ni tuc se frecra an uair-sin ar Baithin. Acus do tinoil se lan a lamha*in*de do bech*aib* 7 tuc da coimed do Baithin hí. Acus tainec bech asan lamhain*n* 7 do cailg sí Baithin go ger indas gor gort*aig* sí go mor é, 7 tainic do brig an gortaige sin tuc an bech air, go marb se a raibe do beach*aib* sa lamaind uile. 'Cred far marbais na beich?' ar Columb cilli. 'Bech dib do gort*aig* go ger me,' ar Baithin. 'Bidh a fis agad, a Baithín,' ar C. c., 'amail do cailg an bech tusa, gorab aml*aid* sin cailges an duine Dia ina pecadh, 7 amail do marb tusa lan na lama*in*de do beach*aib* as gortugad na henbeiche, gorab amlaidh sin fuilnges Dia bas morain do dainibh ar son pecaidh enduine, amail as foll*us* mar do fulaing se lucht na luinge do báth*ad*| ó chianaib ar son an

---

⁹⁸O. I. L. has *Rechra* (Lambay).
⁹⁹§§ 102-4 follow closely O. I. L. See *Lis. Lives,* p. 177, ll. 960 ff.

102. On a time Columcille, and with him Comgall and Cainnech, were in the place that is called Swords today. Comgall told Columcille to say the mass. When Columcille began the mass, Cainnech beheld a column of fire above his head. And he told this thing to Comgall. And both of them beheld it. And a church was builded there by Columcille. And that is Swords-of-Columcille today. And Columcille left a good man of his household to succeed him there, even Finan the Leper. And there he left the missal that himself had copied.

103. Then Columcille blessed Swords, and he blessed the well of Swords that is called Glan, and he left a cross there. For it was his wont to make crosses and books and all manner of church gear and to leave them in each place that he had blessed.

104. Another time Columcille and Cainnech were by the shore of the sea, and there was a great storm thereon.

"Columcille," saith Cainnech, "knowest thou what the wave saith?"

"I wot well," saith Columcille, "it saith that thy household are in great peril upon the sea, and one of them is dead. But God will bring them to us to this port ere the morrow morn."

And Columcille's prophecy was fulfilled, as oft had happed to him before.

105. Another time Columcille and another holy man hight Baithin were walking by the shore of the sea in a certain place, and they saw a ship that was sinking. And Baithin inquired of Columcille why God suffered the ship to sink.

"By reason of a sinner that was aboard her," saith Columcille. "On account of him it was that God hath suffered the folk in the boat to drown."

"Meseemeth," saith Baithin, "that God hath served the folk in the boat unjustly."

Columcille let that pass. And he gave no answer at that time to Baithin. But he assembled his glove full of bees and gave it to Baithin to keep. And there came a bee out of the glove, and stung Baithin sharply, so that it wounded him sore. And by reason of the sting he gat from that bee, it befell that he killed all the bees in his glove.

"Wherefore hast thou killed the bees?" saith Columcille.

"A bee of them hath stung me sharply," saith Baithin.

"Wit thou well, O Baithin," saith Columcille, "as the bee stung thee, so doth man sting God by sin. And as thou hast killed the full of the glove of bees for the stinging of one bee, so doth God suffer the death of many for the sin of one only, as is manifest since he suffered the folk in the ship to drown a while since, by reason of the one sinner that was therein."

enpecaid do bi indti.' 'Tuigim-si, a athair naemtha,' ar Baithin, 'gorab maith do cuiredh sin a n-esimláir dam, 7 ni cuirfe mesi oibrigthe De a n-ingnad ó so amach, 7 ni rach do disporacht orra fedh mo bethad nísa mó.'

5   106¹⁰⁰) Fecht eli do C. c. a Cluain mic Nois, 7 tainec mac bec dá indsaigid. Acus do tarraing roínde becc as a brut gan mothugad dó fen. Acus do foillsig Dia sin do Columb cille, 7 do fhech ar an mac bec 7 do labair ris 7 dorinde faidedóracht dó, 7 adubairt gomad eacnaidh 7 comad saí clerigh 'na díaid-sin e. Do fíradh an faidetóracht-sin C. c., uair dob é sin Iarnán Cluana Deochrach.

107. Fechtus do Brigid ag imtecht Muighe Lifi, 7 mar doconnairc an naemogh an uair-sin an magh alaind 'na fiadhnaise, adubairt dá madh le comus an magha co tibrad si do Dia cumachtach e. Acus do foillsiged an smuainedh bendaigthe-sin Brigde do C. c. 7 é 'na regles fein a Sord, 7 adubairt sé ó guth mór: 'As inand don banoígh an smuainedh-sin 7 an magh do tabairt uaithe,' ol sé.

108. Docuaidh C. c. iarsin a coicidh Laigen 7 do cumdaigh moran do cellaib and. Acus do gab iaram go Cluain mic Noís 7 imann dorinde se do Dia leis da taisbenadh do Cíaran Cluana; oir fa gnath les Dia do mholad go menic a Laidin 7 a Gaidilg 7 as gach tengaid, oir tucad cuma 7 tuicse dó in gach tenga.

Docuaid Columb cille iarsin tar Es Ruaidh, 7 do bendaig 7 do cumdaigh se moran do cellaib 7 d'eclasaib a tir Conaill. Acus do gabh go Gartan iarsin 7 dorinde comhnaidhe and.

109. Fechtus dó-san san inadh airithe re n-abartar Gort na leci a nGartán don taeibh tiar don inadh a rucad é fen .i. do Raith Cnó, 7 tainic duine airithe don popul 'na cend andsin óna bfhuair moran da cairdib 7 dá dainib muindtiri bas 7 do bi tuirsi 7 dobrón mór air in a ndiaid. Acus do bi do med a cumadh corb ferr les bas d'fhagail ina beith beo in a ndíaidh. Et arna fhaicsin

---

¹⁰⁰§§ 106, 107, 108 follow O. I. L. See *Lis. Lives*, p. 177. The O. I. L. borrowed the story in § 106 from Adamnan. See Reeves' *Adam.*, pp. 23-6.

"I understand, holy father," saith Baithin, "that well hath this been given me for an ensaumple, and I shall marvel no more at the works of God, nor be again disputing concerning them throughout my life."

106. Another time that Columcille was in Clonmacnoise, a little lad came to him and pulled a little hair out of his coat without his perceiving it. And God revealed this to Columcille. And he looked at the little lad, and he spake to him and made a prophecy concerning him, saying that he should be a wise man and learned cleric thereafter.

The prophecy of Columcille was fulfilled, for he was Iarnán of Cluain Deochrach.

107. On a time Brigid was going over the plain of Liffey. And as the holy virgin then beheld the fair plain before her, she said that if hers were the power over that plain, she would give it to God Almighty.

And that blessed thought of Brigid's was made known to Columcille in his abbey church at Swords, and he cried with a loud voice, "It is as much for the virgin to have that thought as to bestow the plain," said he.

108. Then went Columcille to Leinster, and he builded there many churches, and thereafter went he to Clonmacnoise, and with him he took a hymn he had made to God; for he would fain show it to Ciaran Cluana. For it was his wont to be ever making hymns of praise to God, both in Latin and Irish and every tongue; for the gift and understanding of all tongues was given him.

After that Columcille departed into Assaroe. And he built many chapels and churches in Tir Conaill. Then went he to Gartan and made there his dwelling.

IX

OF THE LABORS OF COLUMCILLE IN TIRCONNELL AND IN TORY ISLAND

109. On a time he was in a certain place that is called Gort na Leici in Gartan, westward from the place where he was born, to wit, Raith Cno. And there came to him there a certain man of the folk. And many of that man's friends and kinsmen had died, and he was heavy and sorrowful after them. And so great was his sorrow that he would liefer die than live after them. And when Columcille saw him,

do Columb cille, do gab truaighe mor uime é, 7 do bendaigh sé
lec cloiche do bi laim ris (*fol.* 13b) 7 tuc se ar an duine-sin uisce
d'ól dí co ndechaid a cumha ar cul; gor morad ainm De 7 Coluimb
cille de sin. Acus do fhaccaib C. c. mar buadhaib ar an lec-sin,
5 gebe nech ar a mbeith cumha do íbhadh uisce di ó sin alle, a
cumha do dul de. Acus ata sin ga fírad ó sin, 7 "Lec na Cumadh" ainm na leice aniugh a cuimhniugad na mirbal mor-sin.

110. Fechtus do C. c. ag techt o Gartan ag gabail laimh
risan cend oirtheruch do Loch Bethach, go facuidh duine airithe
10 darb ainm Crimthann ó Coinneannta 'na rith tairis. 'Ag sin an
t-oglach 'na rith docum fhoíd a bais,' ar Columb cille, '7 gabthar
lib he 7 na léiccidh d'indsaigid an foid-sin é.' Do gabhatar
muindter C. c. an t-oclach an uair-sin, 7 mar nar leigedh siubal
dó, docondcatar an fod cuca 'na rith, 7 tainec se fa cosaib an
15 oclaig, 7 ní luaithe raínic se faí ina fuair an t-oclach bas. IS andsin
adubairt C. c.: 'Bidh a fis agaib, a daeine, corab mar esimláir
tuc Dia an taisbenadh ud dá cur a ceill nach eídir le henduine,
dar gab corp daénda uime, fod an bhais do sechna. Acus bid a
fhis agaib,' ar C. c., 'go bfuilid tri foide and nach edir do aennech
20 a sechna .i. fód a gheine 7 fod a bais 7 fód a adhnacail. Acus
adubairt an rann-sa:

Tri fodain nach sechantar,   mar aderid a mor-fhocuil:
fód a gene, fód a bais,   7 fod a adhnacail.[101])

Et ina diaigh-sin do guid C. c. Día fan oclach d'aithbeougad
25 indus go ndernadh sé aithrige 'na pecadh 7 go mbeith sé 'na
oglach maith do Día 7 do fein ó sin amach. Acus fuair se sin
amail do íarr. Acus ata ula san inadh a ndernadh sin mar co-
mardha mirbaile do Día 7 do Columb cille. Acus do athbeoaigh
sé duine eli san inadh cedna-sin .i. Beglaech o Beclaidhe a ainm.

30 111. Teid C. c. remhe íarsin a Tuathaib Toraidhe, 7 tainic
an t-aingel cuige 7 adubairt ris dul san oilen darb ainm Torach
7 a bendugad 7 ecluis onorach do denamh ann. Acus teid ar cnoc
ard da bfhaca se Toruch uadha re n-abartar Belach an Adhraidh
aniug. Acus do batar na naeim eli do bi faris ga radha comadh
35 íad fein do bendeochadh Torach 7 go madh acu fen ba ail leo a

[[101] This quatrain reads thus in the Royal Irish Academy MS——$\frac{23}{P.\ 3}$——fo. 18 a 2:
Trí fódáin nach sechaindter   cia toiscet na habrochtair
fót in ghene fót in bháis   ocus bhót in adhnacuil.
K. M.]

great pity seized him, and he blessed a flagstone that was beside him, and caused the man to drink water therefrom, so that his sorrow went from him, and God's name and Columcille's were magnified thereby. And Columcille left as its virtue upon that flag that whoso in sorrow should drink water therefrom from that day, his sorrow should go from him. And from that time hath this been verified. And the Flagstone of the Sorrows is the name of that flagstone today in memory of that great miracle.

110. On a time that Columcille was coming from Gartan, past the eastern end of Loch Bethach, he saw a certain man hight Crimthan o Coinneannta running past him.

"Lo, the youth runneth toward the sod of his death," saith Columcille, "and do ye seize him, and suffer him not to reach that sod."

Forthwith the household of Columcille laid hold on the youth, and suffered him not to proceed. Anon they beheld the sod running toward them; and it came under the feet of the youth; and no sooner came it thereunder than he died.

Then said Columcille, "Wit ye well, O folk," saith he, "God hath shewn this sight as an ensaumple to signify that it is not possible for him that hath taken on him the body of man to avoid the sod of death. "And wit ye well," saith Columcille, "there be three sods that none may escape, the sod of his birth and the sod of his death and the sod of his burying." And he spake this quatrain:

> "Three little sods that cannot be shunned,
> As they say in the proverb;
> The sod of his birth and the sod of his death,
> And the sod of his burying."

And thereafter did Columcille pray God to restore the youth to life, that he might do penance for his sins and be a good servant to God and to himself from that time. And what he asked was given him. And in the place where he did that, there is a stone set to God and to Columcille in sign of the miracle.

And he restored to life in that same place another man, Beglaech o Bechlaidhe his name.

111. Then Columcille set out toward the tribes of Tory. And there came to him an angel and bade him go to the island yclept Tory and bless it and build a noble church in that place. And he went to an high hill that is called Belach an Adhraid today, and thence he beheld Tory in the distance. And the other saints that were with him said that it was they that should bless Tory, and that they were to have it for themselves.

beith. 'Maith mar dodenam-ne sin,' ar C. c., 'teilgem ar trosdaín ria, 7 geb é againn da toileocha Dia a trostan do chur indti, bidh an t-oilen aige 7 ainmnighter uadha é.' Doronsad amlaid, 7 teil-
5 gis C. c. a trosdan 7 dorindedh ga no fogha ar siubal anairde de, 7 rainec se 'san oilen; conadh Lacc an Fogha ainm an inaidh inar ben se aniug. Acus as deimin go raibe Torach feadh radairc uadha as an inadh inar chaith sé an trosdán-sin, 7 ní rainic trostain na naemh ele sech na hoilenaib ata iter Toraigh 7 tir mor. Teid C. c. reimhe iarsin a Toraig, 7 fuair a trostan na 'fogha isin inad-sin
10 adubramar romainn. Tocbais 'na laimh he iarsin, 7 dorindedh trostán de amail do bí ó tús comluath 7 do glac sé é. Et ni raibe an tigerna ler les an t-oilen an uair-sin .i. Oilill mac Báedain ag légen do C. c. a bendugad no aítiugad do dénamh and. IArrais C. c. air lethed a bruit don oilen do tabairt dó o nach fuair sé ní
15 bud mo ina sin uadha. 'Dober,' or Oilill, ' oir ni digbail lim sin do tabairt duid.' Cuiris C. c. a brat de 7 do sín ar lar é, 7 do leath an brat tar an oilen uile. Arna fhaicsin sin d'Oilill, do lin ferg adbulmor e, 7 tuc cu neime do bi aige cuige, 7 ni ticcedh duine no beathadhach uaithe gan marbad re ligthí hí, 7 gresaighis re Columb
20 cille hí. Arna fhaicsin sin do C. c., cuiris sighnum na croiche iter se 7 sí, 7 cuiris fa umla ar in coin fuirech 'na sesamh ar a comair 7 gan techt ni bud ghoire iná sin dó, 7 bas d'fhagail ar an pongc-sin fen. Fuair an cu neimhe-sin bás fo cedoír le breithir C. c., 7 do fhagaib mar aithne gan choin no madraig do tabairt 'san oilen
25 sin go brach[102]) aris, ag cuimniugad na mirbhailedh mor-sin. Ar faicsin na mirbailedh-sin d'Oilill, do leicc ar a gluínib é 7 do creid do Día 7 do Columb cille, 7 tucc sé an t-oilen uile do. Bendaighis C. c. an t-oilen iarsin, 7 dorinde se eclais onórach and, 7 do fhagaib se clerech maith dá mvinntir fen a comarbacht an baile-sin .i.
30 Ernan [103]) Toraidhe.

112. Atá, umorro, cloch a Toraidh dána hainm "an glacach," 7 assí fa cerchaill do C. c. an fad do bí sé 'sa mbaile-sin. Acus as amlaid do bidh sí aigi 7 a dhá glaic ina timchell 7 sí ar a glun 7 é na shuidhe 7 a edan do legen uirre, 7 ni dingnadh sé do chodlud
35 acht an meíd donídh sé [fol. 14a] amlaid sin. Acus ata slicht a meor indti osin alle. Acus doní si moran d'fertaib 7 do mirbuilib 7 foridh an t-uisce cuirther 'na timcell mna re n-idhnaib acédoir da laghad do ibhdaeis de.

[102]Phonetic spelling for *brath*.
[103]O. I. L. has "Ernine" See *Lis. Lives*, p. 30, 1. 999. See also Reeves' *Adam.*, pp. 237-8.

" 'Tis well for us to do that," saith Columcille, "but let us cast our staves toward it, and whoso of us it be that God willeth his staff should reach it, the island shall be his, and it shall be named after him."

Thus did they, and Columcille cast his staff. And it was made a spear or dart, speeding from him through the air till it reached the island, so that the Hollow of the Dart is the name this day of the place where it struck. And certain it is that Tory was as far as the eye could see from the place where he cast the staff. And the staves of the other saints reached but to the islands between Tory and the mainland.

Then Columcille fared forth to Tory, and gat his staff that was become a dart in the place forementioned. Then took he it in his hand and straightway he put his hand thereto, it was made a staff, as it had been before.

And the lord that held the island in those days would not suffer Columcille to bless it, nor to make his dwelling therein. Columcille asked him to give him of that island the width of his cloak, since no more than that might he obtain from him.

"I will give it," saith Oilill, "for I think it no harm to give thee thus much."

Then Columcille did off his mantle, and stretched it on the ground, and the mantle spread over the whole island.

And when Oilill beheld this, anger passing great filled him, and he set upon Columcille a venomous hound he had. Neither man nor beast that she was set on might escape her without death. And Oilill urged her against Columcille. And when Columcille saw this he made the sign of the cross betwixt him and her, and he made the hound to stand before him, and to come no nearer to him, and to die on the spot. Upon the word of Columcille, that venomous hound straightway gat his death. And in token of that great miracle Columcille gave command that no hound or dog should be brought to that island again forever.

And when he had seen that marvel, Oilill fell on his knees, and believed in God and in Columcille. And he gave him the whole island. Then Columcille blessed the island, and built a noble church there, and left a good cleric of his household to succeed him in that place, to wit, Ernan of Tory.

112. There is indeed a stone in Tory hight the Hand-stone. And it was a pillow for Columcille the while he was in that place. And thus it was he held it: his two hands around it and it upon his knee, and he sitting and resting his brow thereon. And no sleep had he save he gat it thus. And the mark of his fingers is therein to this day. And it doth work many miracles and marvels, and water wherein it is steeped doth succour women in labour forthwith, how little soever they may drink thereof.

113. Fectus eli do Columb cille 'san oilen cédna-sin darub ainm Toruch, 7 docuaidh clu a ecna 7 a eolais, a creidme 7 a crabuid, fan uili doman, 7 tucatar cland naemtha do bi ag righ na hIndía gradh ecmaisi dó fana tuarascbail .i. seisiur mac 7 enderbshiur do bui acu. Acus do tindscanatar tect ar cuairt chuige do gabáil riagla 7 degesimlára uadh 7 do beith tamall ina fochair ag certugad a mbeathad. Dochuatar ina luing iarsin, 7 ni haithrestar a scela no gur gabutar tir 'sa chend tíar do Toraid 'san inadh ren abartar port an moirsheser aniugh. Acus ar techt a tir doib, fuarutar bas le scís na mara 7 na fairge. Do foillsiged sin do C. c., 7 docuaidh os a cind 7 do bi ag cai 7 ag toirrsi go himarcach 'na timcell, 7 do indis do cach gorb íad cland righ na hIndía do bi andsin. Do leicc ar a gluinib é iarsin, 7 do togaib a ruisc 7 do cuir urnaidhe milis duthrachtach dochum Ihsu Crisd imá a taithbeougad do. Ar crichnugad na hurnaidhe-sin do Columb cille, do ergheatar clann righ na hIndia 'na sesumh a fiadhnaise caich uile mar daínib do beith na codlud no mar dainib nach fuigbed bas remhe-sin. Acus do indisiter gorb íad fein do bi ann 7 gach ní dar imdigh orra 7 na tosca ma tancvtar. Et do indis C. c. iarsin doib fen 7 do cách nach raibe d'fhuirech orra gan bas d'fhagbáil arís acht go tucad se fein esbaloid doib 7 go lesaiged se iad do molad na hecluisi. Do firadh sin amail adubairt C. c.; oír tucc esbaloíd doib ar an pongc-sin fein, 7 fuaratar bas focédoír. Acus do furail a n-idlacudh go roonóruch 7 sepel bec tempuil do denam os a cinn; conad tempul an moirshesir a ainm o sin alle. Acus gach uair dá n-idlaicí an ingen-sin righ na hIndía maille rena braithrib, dogeibthi a corp os cinn talman arís. Ar na faicsin sin do C. c., do bendaigh 7 do coisric inadh ar leith di fen leath amuigh don tempoll, gairid bec uadha don taeb tiar de, 7 do hadhlaicedh andsin í 7 nir eirigh a corp os cinn talman ó sin suas. Acus as mor d'fertaib 7 do mirbuilib doní uír an adluicthe-sin inar cuiredh hi ó shin alle. Et do foillsig C. c. do cach gorb é adbhar nár fulaing corp na bannaeimhe-sin a n-entumba re corpaib a braithrech an meid go raibe graín aice ar caidrib na fer rena beo narb ail lé a corp do beith a n-éninad rena braithrib 'na eisimlair sin. 'IS urussa duind a tuicsin,' ar Columb cille, 'an uair do bi an grain-sin ag an bannaeimh-sin ar a corp do beith a n-entumba risna braithribh naemtha-sin do bi aice fen, gorab maith bud inshechanta dona mnaib nó dona feruib, le budh ail a n-óghacht do coimhed, caidriub a céli 'sa saeghal-sa.

113. Another time that Columcille was in that same island hight Tory, the fame of his wisdom and knowledge and of his faith and his piety went through all the world, and for the tidings they heard of him the holy children of the King of India conceived love for him though absent. Six sons and the one sister were they. And they made ready to go seeking him, to receive rule and good ensaumple from him, and to be a while in his fellowship for the bettering of their lives. Anon they took ship. There are no tidings told of them until they reached land at the western end of Tory in the place that is called the Port of the Seven today. And when they came ashore they died of weariness of the sea and ocean. This was shown to Columcille, and he went to them, making for them exceeding great sorrow and lament. And he related to all how it was the children of the King of India that were there. Then fell he on his knees and raised his eyes, and made a sweet and fervent prayer to Jesu Christ to restore them. And when he had finished that prayer, the children of the King of India rose up in the sight of all, as folk that had been asleep or had never died. And they related how it was they that were there, and all that had befallen them, and the reason of their coming. And Columcille then told them and told all, that there was no respite for them from a second death, save the while he should give them shrift and strengthen them with the blessing of the Church. Then all fell out as Columcille said, for he gave them shrift straightway, and they died forthwith. And he charged that they be buried right worshipfully and that a little chapel of a temple be built over them. And the Temple of the Seven is its name to this day.

And each time they laid that daughter of the King of India in the grave beside her brothers, they found her body above the earth again. And when Columcille saw this, he blessed and hallowed a place apart for her without the temple, to the west thereof a short space distant, and they buried her there. And her body rose above the ground no more from that time. And many are the marvels and wonders wrought by the clay of that grave wherein she was laid from that day till now. And Columcille revealed to all that the reason wherefor the body of that holy woman did not endure to be in one tomb together with the bodies of her brothers was that as she had hated the conversation of men whilst she lived, in like manner was it displeasing to her as an ensaumple for her body to be in one place with her brothers.

"And well may we understand," saith Columcille, "when that holy woman had such great displeasure that her body should be in one tomb with those holy brothers of hers, how good it were for men and women that would fain be virgin, to shun the conversation of each other in this world."

114. Fectus do C. c. ag radh a tráth 7 a urnaidhe re cois na fairge a Port Toraidhe a thuaidh a crich ceneoil Conaill, 7 do gab tart 7 íta imarcach clerech óg budh dalta dó fen do bí faris an uair-sin .i. Fíonán ratha, 7 ni raibe uisce a comghar doib an uair-sin. Acus arna thuicsin do Columb cille go raibe Fíanan a n-guasacht bais le méd an tarta do bí air, tucc trí buille dá bachaill a n-édan cairge cloiche do bi 'na fhíadhnaise, gor ling trí srebha uisce esde innas cor coisc Finan a thart 7 a íta lesin uisce-sin. Acus ataít na srebha-sin ag techt as an carraicc-sin aniug amail do batar an céd lá, 7 doní an t-uisce-sin moran d'fhertaib 7 do mhirbuilib gach lai o sin alle; gor moradh ainm De 7 C. c. de sin. Acus tuc C. c. mar onoír d'Fhinán an t-inadh-sin d'ainmniugad uadha. Conadh ess Finan a ainm aniugh.

115. Fechtas do Columb cille 'san inadh airithi ré n-abartar Bvn Lindedh a crich cineoil Conaill Gulban, 7 do bhatar íascuiredha ag iascuirecht ar an inbher-sin, 7 do fhíarfaig C. c. dibh an raibe íasc acu. 'Ni fuil,' ar síad; 7 nir b'fhir doib-sen sin vair do baí iasc gerrtha 'na oirnech acv 7 nir admhadair do Columb cille e. 'Mvna fuil go rabh, 7 má tá corab clocha,' ar C. c. . Ar ndenamh cloch don iasc lesan mbreithir-sin, tucatar na híascuiredha scandail comraidh do C. c. . Do mhallaigh 7 do escain C. c. na híascairedha, muindter Gualan íadsen, 7 adubairt nach beidís dá thenidh a n-enbaile da slicht go bráth. Acus ata in briathar-sin ga fíradh ó sin, 7 do mhallaigh C. c. an t-inbher-sin indus nar gabhadh íasc air [fol. 14b] ó sin alle, 7 ataid na clocha dorindedh don íasc-sin ar ulaidh airithe a cill do cellaib C. c. fen do bi do choir an inaidh sin da ngoirter Cill mic Nenain aniug. Acus is ar cuma an oirnigh doníther don bradan ataíd na clocha-sin, innus con n-aithnigter sech clochaib eli na hulaidhe iad.

116. Fectus and tarla oglach do cinel Énna mic Neill nai giallaig a mbraighdenus ag Ronán mac Luig[d]ech, mic Shetna, mic Fergosa cendfada, mic Conaill Gulban, mic Neill .ix. giallaig, 7 dob ail le Ronan an t-oclach do cur docum bais. Acus docuaid C. c. cuige d'iarraid an oclaig air. Oir docondcus dó nar tuill se a chor docum bais fan adhbar fá rabhadus do anuaír-sin. Adubairt Ronan, ger lesc les an t-oclach-sin do lecen uadh gan milledh, go tibrad se dó-san é, 7 nach edh amhaín acht go tibradh se do gach dail da mbeith etorra coidhche. 'Dobeirim-se rath saeghalta

114. On a time that Columcille was saying his hours and his orisons beside the sea at the port of Tory in the north in the land of the clan of Conall, thirst and exceeding craving seized a young cleric with him that was his fosterling, to wit, Fianan of Grace. And there was no water near them at that time. And when Columcille perceived that Fianan was nigh death with the great thirst that was on him, he gave three blows with his staff upon the brow of a rock that was before him, and three streams of water sprang forth therefrom, so that Fianan satisfied his thirst and his craving with that water. And those streams come forth from the rock today as they came that first day, and the water worketh many marvels and wonders all days since, so that God's name and Columcille's are magnified thereby. And Columcille granted as an honor to Fianan that the place should be named for him, so that its name today is the Waterfall of Fianan.

115. On a time that Columcille was in a certain place that is called Bun Linded, in the region of the clan of Conall Gulban, there were fishers fishing in that estuary; and Columcille asked them if they had fish.

"We have none," say they. And they spake not truth, for they had fish cut in fragments, and they told this not to Columcille.

"If ye have none, may ye have them, and if ye have, may they be stones," saith Columcille. The fish became stone with that word, and the fishers took to reviling Columcille. Then Columcille cursed and banned the fishers. They were Gualan folk. And he declared that there should not be two fires belonging to their seed in the same townland forever. And that word of his was fulfilled thereafter. And Columcille cursed that bay, so that no fish have been taken therefrom from that day till now. And the stones that were made of the fish are upon a certain stone station in one of the chapels of Columcille fast there beside, that is called Cill mic Nenain today. And the stones are in the form of the fragments that a salmon is cut into, so that they may be known from the other stones of the heap.

116. On a time a youth of the clan of Enna son of Niall of the Nine Hostages fell captive to Ronan mac Luig[d]ech, son of Sedna son of Fergus Cennfada son of Conall Gulban son of Niall of the Nine Hostages. And Ronan desired to put the youth to death. And Columcille went to him to ask the youth of him, for him seemed the youth had not merited death for the charge that they were making against him at that time. Ronan said that albeit he was loth to let the youth go from him without destroying him, natheless he would give him to him. And not that only, but he would yield to him whatever moot matter should be between them forever.

7 flaithes De fa deredh dhuid-se,' ar Columb cille. Acus fos adubairt C. c. tre spir*ud* faidedorachta: 'O doleic tusa, a Ronain, an dail-sin lium-sa, genfid*er* mac ar do shlicht-sa 7 bud Daluch a ainm 7 is ar [a] shli*cht* beid riga 7 tig*er*nadha sleachta Conaill Gulp*an* go brath. Acus an uair b*us* mesa a slicht coidhce biaidh siad mar chach, 7 an uair nach bia di*m*gha¹⁰⁴) Día orra i*n*a mo dimgha-sa budh ferr iad iná cach. Acus b*ud* é an Daluch sin an sectmadh glun vaid-si fen.' Acus do fírad an faidhedóracht-sin C. c. Gonad ar slicht an Dal*uig*-sin ataid clann Dál*uig* ó sin ille. Acus asse an Daluch-sin mac dob oíge don cuiger m*a*c do bi gá athair fen, 7 nír slan dó acht a .uíí. mbliadhna ag ég dá athair uadh, 7 tucatar na brait*ri* ba sine ina sé fein tigernas dó orra fen tré mirbhuili*b* de 7 C. c.; oir nír fédadh faidhedóracht C. c. do brécnugad.

117. A n-Doiri Eithne, im*orro*, da n-goirter Cill m*i*c Nenaín aniugh, do hoiledh C. c., 7 ata tobar sa baile-sin da n-goirt*er* tobar Eithne 7 o mathair C. c. ainmnigt*er* é. Acus do bi C. c. lá airide ag an tobar-sin 7 do labhair se tre spir*ad* faidetórachta 7 assed adubairt .i. '*G*einfid*er* m*a*c sa tir-se 7 bud Dál*uch* a ainm 7 budh é an t-aenmad glun dec ó Chonall gulb*an* e, 7 budh ar a slicht beid righr*ad* cineoil Conaill Gulb*an* co brath. Acus atá an oired-sa do chin 7 do gradh agam-sa do fen 7 dá slicht ina diaidh, gach uair muirfid*er* duine da slicht le harm, go mbía an tobar-sa 'na chru 7 'na fhuil a comartha bais tamall remhe a marb*adh*.' Acus ata sin ga derbad ó shin alle.

118.¹⁰⁵) Do batar tri peta ag C. c. .i. cat 7 dreollan 7 cuil. Acus do thuig*ed* se urlap*ra* gach beath*a*daigh d*ib*, 7 do chuiredh an tigherna techtair*ech*t lev cuige 7 do tuigedh seisin gach enní uatha amail do thuicf*ed* ó aingel no o duine do cuirf*ide* a tectairect cuigi. *ET* t*a*rla doib g*ur* ith an dreollan an chuil 7 gor ith an cat an dreollan. Acus do labhair C. c. tre spirad faidhedoracta 7 adubairt se gorab am*laid* sin dogendais daíne deridh aimsiri .i.

---

¹⁰⁴*leg.* dimdha.
¹⁰⁵See Dinneen's *Keating*, III, p. 73, for a similar story.

"And to thee I give worldly riches and the Kingdom of God in the end," saith Columcille. "And further," said Columcille by the spirit of prophecy, "since thou hast yielded in this matter to me, there shall be born a son of thy seed, and Daluch shall be his name, and of his blood shall be the kings and lords of the race of Conall Gulban forever. And when his tribe are at their worst they shall be as others; and when the displeasure of God shall not be upon them, or my displeasure, they shall be better than any. And that Daluch shall be the seventh in descent from thee."

And that prophecy of Columcille was verified. So that of the seed of that Daluch are the clan of Daluch from that day to this. And that Daluch was the youngest of five sons that his father had. And he had completed but seven years at the death of his father. And his elder brothers gave him lordship over them through the miracles of God and Columcille. For it was not possible to belie the prophecy of Columcille.

117. In Doire Eithne, that is called Cill mic Nenain today, was Columcille fostered. There is a well in that place hight Tobar Eithne, and from the mother of Columcille it hath its name. And on a certain day Columcille was at the well, and by the spirit of prophecy he spake and said:

"There shall be born in this land a boy that shall be called Daluch; and he shall be the eleventh in descent from Conall Gulban; and of his seed shall be the kings of the clan of Conall Gulban forever. And so great affection and love have I for him and for his seed after him, that each time one of his blood shall be about to die by weapons, this well shall be blood and gore a short space ere his death in sign of his dying."

And this is verified from that day to this.

X

OF SUNDRY MIRACLES AND PROPHECIES OF COLUMCILLE AND OF CERTAIN VISIONS

118. There were three pets that Columcille had; a cat, and a wren, and a fly. And he understood the speech of each of those creatures. And the Lord sent messages to him by them, and he understood all from them as he would understand an angel or human folk that might be sent with a message to him. And it happed that the wren ate the fly, and the cat ate the wren. And Columcille spake by the spirit of prophecy, and he said that it was thus men should do in a later time: the

go n-isadh in duine bud tresi acu an duine b*ud* anfhainde .i.
go mbenfad se a spreidh 7 a airneis de 7 nach denadh se coir
nó cert ris. Acus adubairt C. c. an uair do beidis Gaid*il* Ere*nn*
mar sin, go mbeith tren allmharuch orra, 7 gebe huair do b*eith*
coir 7 cert ar congbail acu, go mbeith a tren fein aris acu. Acus do
bi do cin ag C. c. ar na beath*adach*ai*b* becca sin do bi aicce gor
íarr sé ar Día a n-aithbeougad dó .i. aissec na cuile d'fhag*ail* on
dreollán 7 aisseg an dreoll*ain* do faghail on chat. Acus fuair se sin
o Día, 7 do bhatar mailli ris ó shin amach, amail do batar ó thus
nó gor caithet*ar* an saegal nadurdha do bi acu. *Con*[ad] and
sin dorinde an rann-sa:

IN gnimh-sin doronsat*ar*,   masached le Dia romclui*n*;
taibhghedh om chat mo dreollán   taibg*ed* óm dreollán mo chuil.

119[106]) F*echt* and do Columb cille a n-eclais moir Arda Macha,
7 do bí clerech eclaisi 'sa mbaile an uaír-sin ga raibe dut*racht*
do fresd*al* na tráth 7 na n-aifr*end*. Acus do bi scolairi aírithe
sa mbaile-sin ag tathaig*e* ar mnai an clerich-sin an f*ed* do bídh
an cleirech ag na haifrendaib. Acus tainec an scolaíri an la-sin
docum na n-aifrend 7 ni raibhe a fhis aicce an clereach do techt
cuca. IS andsin taínic an t-aibirseoír a n-deilb an duine aírithe
do bidh ag tectairecht do gnath it*er* an scolaíri 7 ben an clerich
a ndorass na heclaisi, 7 do smeid sé [*fol.* 15a] amach ar an
scolaire dá indisin do go fuighedh sé faill ar mnai an clerig.
Mar dochondairc C. c. sin, ruc se ar in scolaire 7 do indes gorb'e
an t-aibirseoir do bi and ag smeideadh air, 7 adubairt ris dá
bfhaicedh se 'na cruth fen é nach freiceor*adh* sé é. Acus leis sin do
chuir fa umhla ar an aibirseoir a taisbenadh 'na cruth fein don
scolaidhe. *ET* mar docondairc an scoluidhe sin, do ghab g*r*ain
7, adhuathmairecht mór e 7 doberadh an taisbenadh-sin bas dó
muna beith coimhed Dia 7 C. c. air. Acus dochuaidh ar cumairce
C. c. annsin, 7 do gell do nach denadh an pecadh-sin no pecadh eile
coidhce, 7 do bi 'na ogl*ach* maith do Dia 7 do C. c. o sin amach.
Acus fos an fad docluindis na drochspiraid foghar gotha C. c., do
chengl*ad* se íad amail do ceingeoltai én a painter *nó* a ngaisde,
indus nach bidh ar breith doib aibirseoracht do denam air fen
ina ar duine eli go brath. Acus an uair do cuiredh fá umla orra
scela d'innisin do dob eicen doib gach ni dá fiarf*aig*edh se dib
d'innisin do.

[106]Abridged in *Amra Choluimb Chille*. See R. C. xx, p. 176.

strong of them should eat the weak, that is to say, should take his wealth and his gear from him, and should show him neither right nor justice. And Columcille said that the while the Gael of Erin were thus, the power of foreigners should be over them, and whenever right and justice were kept by them, they should themselves have power again. And such love had Columcille for those little creatures of his, that he asked God to revive them for him, to get back the fly from the wren, and the wren from the cat. And he obtained that from God. And they were with him thenceforth as they were before, till they had lived out their lives according to nature. Wherefore he made this quatrain:

> "The deed they have done.
> If God wills it, may He hear me:
> May he get from my cat my wren;
> May he get from my wren my fly."

119. On a time that Columcille was in the great church in Armagh, there was a cleric of the church in the place that time that liked well to serve at the offices and the masses. And there was a certain scholar of that place that was wont to go to the wife of the cleric the while the cleric was at the mass. And on that day the scholar came to the mass not knowing that the cleric had come thither. Then came the Adversary in front of the church in the likeness of a certain man that was wont to act as messenger between the scholar and the wife of the cleric; and he nodded to the scholar, to let him wit that he should take the occasion with the wife of the cleric. When Columcille saw this, he laid hold of the scholar, and told him it was the Adversary that was there nodding to him and he said that if he might see him in his own form he would not answer him. And forthwith he put bonds upon the Adversary to show himself to the scholar in his own likeness. And when the scholar beheld him, horror seized him and exceeding dread, and the sight had brought him to death, had not the safeguard of God and Columcille been upon him. And then he sought the protection of Columcille, and he promised that he would not do that sin nor any other ever, and he was a good servant to God and to Columcille from that time. And moreover when the evil spirits heard the sound of the voice of Columcille, it bound them as birds are bound in a gin or snare, so that it was not in their power to tempt him nor any other forever. And when he put bonds upon them to tell tidings, they must needs tell him whatsoever he asked of them.

120. Fectas do C. c. a n-Ard Macha, 7 docuaid do radh trath 7 urnaidhe timcell cros 7 uladh 7 reilic Patruic, go facutar na mairb lomnochta act a mbruit roíndigh impo. Gabais ecla mor Baithin naemtha do bi afochair C. c. fan ní-sin, 7 docuaid do denamh mhonmair 7 athimraidh ar Padruic fana lethéd-sin do taidbhsi d'fhaicsin 'na baili. Feargaighter C. c. re Baithin 7 assed adubairt: 'A Baithin,' ol se, dá mbeith a fhis agat-sa amail ata agma-sa, a teinde rachus Patruic ar son fer nErinn a lo an bratha, nocha biadh fodhord agat air.' INnis dam a C. c.,' ar Baithin, 'o atái gum cairiugad cred é an taisbenadh ud tucad duind.' 'INnisim,' ar Columb cille, 'ag sud muinnter diles Padruic aga congbail gan truailled a corp ona cumhachtaib fein, 7 ni faicid na daine saegalta iad le ceo an pecaid do beith etorra 7 íat.' 'INniss dam anos, ar Baithin, 'cindus rachas Patruic ar son fer nErenn a llo an brátha.' 'INneosad ni eicin de,' ar Columb cille, 'amail toilighes Dia damh .i. ticfaidh Patruic go Cluain mac Nois a coinde bfher nErenn. IS andsin fulairfess se an cloc do buain a Cruachan aigle .i. an bernán Padruic a ainm do bris se fein remhe ar na deamhnaib ga n-indarbad don Cruaich. Acus ticfaid fir 7 mna Erenn fa guth an cluic-sin, 7 as mór an onoir do Ciaran gorab ina baili fen cruindigther na sluaig-sin. Acus budh mor mo sochraide-si fen sa lo-sin, a Baithin,' ar Columb cille, 'oir biaid tossach mo sluaigh-se a Cluain mac Nois 7 a deredh a nDun Cuillinn a nAlpain. Mogenar bias do réir Padruic 7 naem eli Erenn isin ló-sa, 7 as mairg bíass dá n-aimhréir, 7 is madhngenair gá mbeith re maidhem ar Padruic an uair-si serbhis do denamh dó leith re na fheil do denamh go honórach 7 re hurnaigthe 7 re déirc 7 re troscad do denamh 'na onoír, oir is é bus aighne 7 bus breithemh d'Erindchaib uile a llo an bratha. ET rachum uile am Patruic go Crosa Cail a Mide 7 anfam re deridh ar sluaigh annsin 7 rachum ass sin go Martain 7 rachaid Martain 7 Padruic romaind go Petor 7 go Pól 7 racham uile am Petor 7 am Pol go Sliab Oiliféd. Acus adera Padruic andsin re Petar 7 re Pol 7 re Martain dol remhe fein co Sliab Sioín do bendugad don Coimdhedh. Acus suidhfid Padruic a cathaír oír ós feruib Érind ar in slíaph-sin. ET cuirfid se Ailbhe Imlech iubair go .uíí. n-espocaib imme mar

120. On a time that Columcille was in Armagh he went round the crosses and the cairns and the burying ground of Padraic to say his office and his orisons. And the dead were seen stark-naked save for their sarks. And St. Baithin, that was with Columcille, was seized with great fear at that thing, and he fell to murmuring and reviling Padraic that such a sight should be seen in his place.

Then waxed Columcille wroth with Baithin and said, "O Baithin," saith he, "didst thou know as I know how hard it will go with Padraic for the sake of the men of Erin on Doomsday thou wouldst not be murmuring against him."

"Tell me, O Columcille," saith Baithin, "since thou art rebuking me; what signifieth that sight that hath been shown us?"

"Those are the chosen household of Padraic that have their bodies kept through his power without corruption, but worldly folk see them not, by reason of the mist of sin that cometh atween such and them."

"Tell me now," saith Baithin, "how will it go hard with Padraic for the sake of the men of Erin on the day of Doom?"

"Some part thereof I will tell thee," saith Columcille, "as God suffereth me to do. Padraic shall come to Clonmacnois to meet the men of Erin. Then shall he let strike the bell in Cruachan Aigle, that is called the Bernan of Padraic, that he did break upon the demons when he banished them from the Rick. And the men and women of Erin shall come at the sound of that bell, and great is the honor to Ciaran that in his place those multitudes shall assemble. Great also shall be my following in that day, Baithin," saith Columcille, "for the forefront of my host shall be in Clonmacnois and its rear in Dun Cuillin in Alba. Lucky is he that shall be a follower of Padraic on that day, and woe to him that shall not. And well for him which in that time may boast to Padraic of service done him touching the keeping of his feast day solemnly and with prayer, and with almsdeeds and fasting to do him honor; for Padraic shall be the advocate and the judge of all the men of Erin in the Day of Doom. And we shall all go with Padraic to Crosa Cail in Meath; and we shall tarry there for the last of our host. And thence we shall go to Martin. And Martin and Padraic shall go before us to Peter and Paul. And all of us shall go with Peter and Paul to Mount Olivet, and there Padraic shall tell Peter and Paul and Martin to go before him to Mount Sion to salute the Lord. And Padraic shall sit in a chair of gold above the men of Erin on that mountain. And he shall send Ailbe of Emly of the Yew Tree with seven bishops to Christ on Mount Sion, to learn what He hath to say to Padraic and his hosts. And the Lord shall bid Ailbe welcome and shall ask him where is the Lightning Flash of the Western World, and shall say he is long in coming to Him.

" 'He will come to Thee,' saith Ailbe.

a mbia Crísd a Sliabh Sioín da fhis créd aderadh sé ris fein (nó)
re na sluaga. Acus ferfaidh an Coimdhe failte re hAilbe 7 fiar-
fóchaid de caít a fuil sraibtine íarthair domhain 7 adéra as fada go
ticc dochum na dala.' "Ticfa cugaib," or Ailbhe. "IS mor do
5 pecachaib 7 do drochdaínibh ata maille ris," ar Crísd. "Sailid
sesivn," or Ailbhe, "gorab aés martra 7 aithrighe tuc les iar mbeith
doibh secht mbliadhna fo tondaib mara, amail fuair se fen uaib-si
fairge do tabairt ar Eirinn sect mbliadhna [fol. 15b] re mbrath,
indus co madh lucht pene 7 martra poiplecha na hErind uile 'sa
10 coimhéd do cuireabhair-se air fen." "Abair ris an meid is olc da
sluagh d'fhagbail," ar Crísd. "IS doigh lim na ding(n)a se sin,"
ar Ailbhe, "oír is lond 7 as feargach an fer ata and sud, 7 ni do
tectairect uad tanuc-sa act do bendachadh duid-se 7 do breith
scel uaid, 7 sailim co ticfaid techta co hullamh cugad uaidh."
15 'Ticfa Ailbhe docum Padruic iarom 7 bendóchaid dó.' "Nar aicillis
an Coimdhe," ol Pátruic. "Do aiccilles," ar Ailbe, "7 adubairt se
rit-sa an méid bud olc dot sluagh d'fhagbhail." "Ni tossach failte
an ní-sin," ol Padruic, "7 ni ba hamlaid bías,' ar se. 'Cuirfidh
Patraic,' ar C. c., 'mesi 7 Cíaran mac an tshaeir 7 Caindech mocua
20 Daland a techtairecht docum Crist 7 ferfaidh sé failte rind, 7 ferfaidh fó tri re Caindech, 7 cuirfidh lind a rad re Patraic a pe-
caid¹⁰⁷) uili do fhagbail. Racham-ne co Patraic lesin uirighell-sin 7
indeósam dó é 7 assed adera rinn:' "Ni fuigeabh-sa," ar se, "aenduine dá tainic lim andso go ma follas d'fheruib Erenn m'fhogh-
25 namh doib isan laithe-si aníu." 'ET adera se rind dol arís co Crísd
7 a breith mar comhartha cuige an la do chuir se é fen do shiladh
creidmhe a n-Erind, cor gheall se dó go madh é bud brethemh
d'feraib Erind isan ló-sin 7 gor gell an t-aingel dó an uair dorinde
se an troscad fada ar Cruachan aighle, ar aithris an troiscthi
30 dorinde an tigerna fen 7 Maíse, go madh é bud breithemh doib
mar an cedna, 7 cuirfider Munda mac Tulchain an cethramhadh
fer lind. Racham-ne iarom an cethrar-sin go Críst 7 doghenam
techtairecht Padruic ris 7 aigeóram in gach gellad dibh-sin é.'
"Ni dichell daeib-se," ag cuimhniugad dó, ol Crisd. "Cred hí an
35 anbfhailte-sin agat ría Padruic," ol Munda mac Tulchain. "Do
badhais at drai an uair do bí tu og," ar Crisd. "Dar mo draidhecht," or Munda, "ni thicfa Padruic as an sleibh ina bfhuil cumá
ríaruch uaib-se é." "Massed ticced Padruic cugainn cona sluagaib

---

¹⁰⁷ *leg.* pecaigh.

" 'There be many sinners and evil men with him,' saith Christ.

" 'He weeneth,' saith Ailbe, 'that they be martyrs and penitents he leadeth with him, that have been seven years under the waters of the sea, seeing that he had prevailed on Thee to send forth the ocean over Erin seven years before Doomsday, so that all the folk of Erin might be penitents and martyrs in the protection of Erin Thou didst grant Him.' "

" 'Bid him leave behind those that be evil,' saith Christ.

" 'Methinketh he will scarce do that,' saith Ailbe, 'for a wrathful and choleric man is he yonder, and for no errand have I come from him save to salute Thee and to bring tidings of him. Messengers will come to Thee from him, I ween, anon.'

"Ailbe shall go to Padraic then and shall greet him.

" 'Hast thou not had converse with the Lord?' saith Padraic.

" 'I have had converse with Him,' saith Ailbe, and He bade thee leave behind those of thy host that be evil.'

" 'That is not a beginning of welcome,' saith Padraic, 'and thus it shall not be.'

"Me shall Padraic then send," saith Columcille, "and Ciaran son of the Wright and Cainnech descendant of Dala, on an embassy to Jesu Christ. And He shall bid us welcome, and He shall thrice greet Cainnech, and send with us his command to Padraic to leave behind all his sinners. We shall go to Padraic with that decree and tell him.

"This is what he shall say to us: 'I will not leave behind a single one of those that came with me here; for I would show the men of Erin how I have succored them this day.'

"And he shall bid us go again to Christ and bear to Him as testimony that the day He sent Padraic to Erin He promised him that he should be the judge of the men of Erin in this Day [of Doom].[1] And when he made the long fast on Cruachan Aigle in likeness of the fast that the Lord Himself and Moses made, the angel promised him in like wise that he should be their judge.[2] And Munda son of Tulchan shall be sent as the fourth man with us. Then the four of us shall go to Christ, and give Him the message of Padraic, and plead with Him touching each of those promises.

" 'Ye are not negligent [in reminding me],' saith Christ, upon remembering.

" 'Why this want of welcome of Thine touching Padraic?' saith Munda son of Tulchan.

" 'Thou wert a druid when thou wert young,' saith Christ.

" 'By my druidhood,' saith Munda, 'Padraic will not come from the mountain where he is until Thou agree to his terms.'

" 'Well then, let Padraic come to us with all his hosts,' saith Christ,

[1] *Cf. Tripartite Life*, I, p. 31.
[2] *loc. cit.*, I, p. 117.

uili,'' ol Cr*ist*, "go n-aigillium naí n*gra*dha nimhe dá *f*his cred is indenta dund ris fén 7 rena muindt*ir*.'' Do be*n*adh cloc an medho*í*n-lai a nArd Macha andsin. 'Frec*r*um an cloc,' ar C. c., 'oir is dá toirmesc umam-sa na sgelu-sa d'indisin nías mó do thoil*ig* Dia an cloc do buain com luath 7 súd, 7 ni cead damh nías mó dona sceluibh-se d'indesin.' Acus nir *cri*chnaig*ed* an taisbenadh-sin acht mar sin. Finit.

121.[108]) Fechtus docuaidh C. c. ar cuairt mar a raibhe Mochuda Rath*ai*n, 7 dorinde faidhetoracht do 7 adubairt nach a Rathain do beith a eseirghe 7 *go* foigeor*adh* rí Erenn 7 a cland a nderidh a aisi aisde é mailli re comhairle morain do naemaiph Lethe Cuinn og a mbeith imthnud riss. IS andsin do fhíarf*aig* Mochuda do Columb cille ga hinadh a mb*eith* a eseirghe. 'Andsan inadh a faca tú cruindiugad na n-aingiul do mhulluch slebhe Cúa, ar brúach abhann Nime, ag tocbhail eclaisi airgidhe o talmhain go *h*aeier 7 imhaigh oír indti, bías heserghe,' ar C. c. Acus adubairt co madh í an ecl*uis* dodenadh Mochuda fen an eclas-sin 7 go m*adh* é fen an imháigh oir nobeith indti. Acus do firadh an faidhedóracht-sin C. c., oir do fógair Blathm*ac*, m*ac* Aedha Slaíne, Mochuda as Rathain ar comairle na clerech tnúthach dar labhrum*ar* a tossach an sceoil, amail derbhas beatha Mochuda feín. Acus is a Cluain Iraird doronadh an comhairli ler cuiredh Mocuda a rRathain.

122.[109]) Fectas da t*ar*la C. c. le toisc ecin a cenn Molaisi Daimh indse, 7 do bídh imthnuth ag Molaissi re C. c. do gnath. Acus do cuir se C. c. do tigh leptha an oidche-sin, 7 dob aimsir catairech and, 7 as é bíadh do cuir se cuigi .i. saill muice 7 da n-eitig*edh* C. c. an fheoil-sin d'ithe, dob'ail les a cur ina aghaidh go tuc se mímogh 7 scandail mor dó fen trena beith gan biadh ina tigh. Acus dá n-ith*ed* se hí, dob'ail les a chur 'na aghaidh gor bris se an catair. Acus arna thuicsin do C. c. gorab tre imthnúdh do cuiredh an feoil-sin cuigi, do ith se beagán di. Acus fós issé biadh do buí ag Molaisi fein an oidhci-sin .i. uidhe [109a]) cerc 7 aran. Acus do foillsigh an t-aingivl sin do Columb cille, 7 rvgatar ass an oidhce-sin. Acus teidh C. c. 7 Molaisi don eclais ar na maruch do radh na tr*á*th [*fol*. 17a] 7 na n-aifrend, 7 do fiarfaidh Molaisi do Columb cille cred far ith se feoil sa catair. 'Ni budh maith a*n* mogh[109b]) damh', ar C. c., 'gebe biadh do cuirfea-sa cugam gan a ithe d'ecla naire do beith ort-

---

[108]Source: *Life of St. Mochuda* expressly mentioned. See Plummer's *V. S. H.*, I, p. 186, § 42; p. 190, § 53.
[109]*Cf.* § 182 *infra* for similar story.
[109a]*leg.* uibhe.
[109b]*leg.* mòdh.

'until we consult the nine hierarchies of Heaven to know what we shall do with him and his folk.' "

Anon forthwith the noon-day bell was struck in Armagh.

"Let us answer the bell," saith Columcille, "for to forbid me to tell this tale further God hath willed the bell to be struck thus soon; and I am not suffered to relate more of these tidings."

And no ending was made of the vision save that.

121. On a time Columcille went to visit Mochuda of Rathan, and he made a prophecy to him. And he said that his resurrection should not be in Rathan, for the King of Erin and his children should banish him therefrom in his latter end by the counsel of the many saints of Leth Cuinn that bare him hatred. Then inquired Mochuda of Columcille in what place his resurrection should be.

"In the place where from the summit of Sliabh Cua thou didst see a company of angels on the brink of the river Neim, raising up a church of silver from earth to the upper air, and an image of God therein, there shall thy resurrection be," saith Columcille.

And he said that church should be one Mochuda should himself build, and that he should himself be the golden image therein. And that prophecy of Columcille's was fulfilled, for Blathmac son of Aed Slaine banished Mochuda out of Rathan by the counsel of the envious clerics aforementioned in the history, as the *Life of Mochuda* showeth. And in Clonard was the council held by the which Mochuda was banished from Rathan.

122. On a time Columcille chanced for some cause to be with Molaise of Devenish. Now Molaise ever had ill will toward Columcille. He sent him to the guest-house that night, and it was in the ember days, and this is the food he sent him, to wit, salt pork. And if Columcille should refuse to eat the meat, then would he cast it in his face that Columcille had brought dishonor and great disgrace upon him by reason that in his house he was without food. And if Columcille ate it, he would cast it in his face that he had broken the ember abstinence.

And when Columcille understood that it was out of ill-will he had sent him the meat, he ate a small part thereof.

And the fare Molaise had that night was hens' eggs and bread. And the angel revealed this to Columcille, and the night passed. And on the morrow Columcille went with Molaise to the church to say the hours and the masses. And Molaise asked Columcille why he had eaten meat in the time of the ember abstinence.

"It beseemed me not to refuse the food thou didst send me, lest shame fall on thee if I should be in thy house without food, and I not

sa dá mbeind gan bíadh ad tigh 7 gan a fis agam an raibhe aitherruch na feola ud do biadh agat-sa damh. Gidedh,' ar Columb cille, 'cuirter uidhe cerc 7 leithéid na feola do bi agam-sa aréir ar in altoír, 7 guidfet-sa Día ima fhoillsivgad do cach cia againd do bris an cataír.' Doronadh amlaid, 7 ar crichnugad a guide do C. c., do erigh coilech as uidh dona huidibh 7 do bi se ag gairm ar in altoir a fhiadhnuise caich, 7 dorindedh dercain daruch don tsaill. Gurub mar-sin ruc Día breth le Columb cille a n-agaid Molaissi Daimindsi 7 do saer se ar a imtnudh é.

123.¹¹⁰) Aissling docondairc Baithin naemtha do bid afochair C. c. do gnath .i. mar do taisbenfuidhe flaithes De do, 7 iter gach taisbenadh da tuccad and, docondairc se tri cathairedha folmha a fíadnuise an Tigherna .i. cathair oir 7 cathair airgid 7 cathair gloine, 7 fa hí an cathair gloine fa goire don Tigerna fén acu. Acus ar musclad as a chodlad do Baithin, do indiss se an aisling-sin do C. c. IS andsin adubairt C. c : 'Indeósat-sa ciall t-aislinge doid, a Baithin,' ar C. c. 'An cathair oir sin docondairc tu, as hí sin inad Ciaraín mic an tshaeir a flaithes De ar uaisle 7 ar daingne a crábaidh. IN cathaír airgid docondaic tú, hinadh fen a flaithes De sin, a Baithin,' ar C. c., 'ar daingne 7 ar taitnemhaidhe 7 ar cruas do crabaid. An cathair gloine-sin doconnairc tú, m'inadh-sa fen sin a flaithes De,' ar Columb cille, 'ar delraidthi 7 ar gloine 7 ar aibrisce mo crábaidh.' Oir isé as naduir don gloine a beith roglan rodelraduch indti fen indus co faicedh cach gac enni innte 7 trithe, 7 corab éidir ilradh gacha datha examail do cur uirri, 7 ata si sobrisde édaingen o naduír. ET as mar so, imorro, do bi C. c. acht nach raibe se edaingean mar atá an gloine.

Do bi sé roglan rosholus rodelraduch and fein indus gorb e fa scathan do naemhaib iarthair domain 7 corab and 7 trid docidís mar bud coír doib crábad do denam. Acus gidhedh, do bi in oiread-sain do daendaighecht 7 do grádh aige da braithrib 7 da cairdib colluidhe uili gu mbidh se aibrisc do tabairt aighti doib 7 do bidh se sochraidh subaltuch riu, 7 do bi se aibrisc dochum aighte do tabairt d'aes eladhna 7 d'filedhaib Erenn mar in cedna ar son a n-eladhna 7 na molta donídis do. Oir do bi da uaisli 7 da onoraidhe 7 da socinelaidhe sech cach nach gabhdaeis uadha gan aghaid do tabairt doib nach tucdaeis

---

¹¹⁰See *F. O.*², p. 146. This story was evidently borrowed from the *Notes* to *F. O. L. B.*, p. 236 col. 2 (cited by Stokes in *Lis. Lives*, p. 302) substitutes Molaisse for Baithin. The *Life of Laisrianus* also has Laisrianus for Baithin. See Plummer's *V. S. H.*, II, p. 139, § 32.

knowing if thou didst have for me food other than that. Howbeit,'' saith Columcille, ''let there be put upon the altar hens' eggs and the like of the meat I had last night, and I will pray God to reveal to all which of us hath broken the ember abstinence.''

Thus it was done. And when the prayer of Columcille was ended, a cock rose up from one of the eggs and fell to crowing upon the altar in the sight of all. And of the salt pork was made an acorn of an oak. Thus was it that God gave judgment for Columcille against Molaise of Devenish, and saved him from his malice.

123. Saint Baithin, the which was ever in the fellowship of Columcille, did behold avisions, as it were the revealing of the Kingdom of God to him. And in each one of these avisions he saw three empty chairs afore the Lord, a chair of gold, and a chair of silver, and a chair of crystal. And it was the chair of crystal that was nighest to the Lord. And when he awoke out of his sleep, Baithin related that dream to Columcille. Then Columcille spake.

''I will tell thee the meaning of thy vision, O Baithin,'' saith Columcille. ''The golden chair thou didst see is the place of Ciaran son of the Wright in the Kingdom of God, for the loftiness and the strength of his piety. The silver chair thou didst see is thine own place in the Kingdom of God, O Baithin,'' saith Columcille, ''for the strength and the brightness and the rigors of thy piety. The crystal chair thou didst see is mine own place in the Kingdom of God,'' saith Columcille, ''for the brightness and the purity and the fragility of my piety. For it is the nature of crystal to be very pure and very bright, so that all men may see all things therein and through it. But it is possible to chequer it with every kind of color, and it is lightly broken and not strong by nature.''

And thus in sooth was Columcille, save that he was not fragile like the crystal. He was passing pure and bright and shining in himself, so that he was a mirror for the saints of the Western World; for in him and through him they perceived how they should do holy works. And yet so much of human kindness and of love had he for his brethren and all his kinsmen by blood, that he was weak in favoring them; and he was kind and forbearing with them. And he was weak in indulging bards and poets on account of their art and because of the praises that they made for him. For so noble was he, so worshipful, and of such gentle blood passing all others, that they would not leave him till he had

naeimh eli Erenn doib. Acus ge doberidh sesen an agaid-sin do
cach, donídh se aithrighe romor indte, 7 gach gne a ndenadh se
gloir dimhaín lé cach nó a tuccudh se aghaid doib do gortaiged a
cogús, donídh se aithridhe ar leith 'sa gné-sin fen indus co mbidh
gloir 7 taithnemh 7 soillse na n-uile grás ag Dia 7 ag daínibh ar
a cocus 7 ar a crábadh. ET fetar a samlugad ris an gloine in
gach gné dib so acht amaín esiun—rodhaingen a ngrádh Dé 7 'sa
creideamh, ge do bi sé aibrisc aleith re daendaighehct do beith aige
ris na daínibh.

124.[111]) Fectus and tainic combráthir genelaig do C. c. .i.
Annadh mac Duibh indse, mic Caibhdenaigh, mic Enna, mic Neill
nái-ghiallaidh, ar cuairt chuige 7 do fhiarfaig de cá fad a saeghal.
Do frecair C. c. e 7 assed adubairt ris: 'Na híarr sin, a Andaidh,'
ar sé, 'oir ní hail le Día a fhis sin do beith ag en duine 'sa saeghal-sa ar tri hadbhuraibh. An céd adhbar dib, da faghadh duine
a fhis co madh gairid a saegal, ní dingnadh se deghoibrighte nó
ecna no eolas 'sa saeghal-sa ar ecla an bais. ET an dara hadhbar,
umorro, da fagad sé a fhis co madh fhada a shaogal, do biadh se
ag denamh peccadh 7 drochgnimhartha go dereadh a aimsire a
ndóchas go mberud se ar leoarghnímh do denamh indta fa deoigh.
IN tres adbhar nach ail lé Día énduine do cur a cosmailes eolais
fris fén isna neichib benus re díamhair a sheicréde féin. ET
bidh afhis agad, a Andaigh, go mbím-si gacha dardaín ag comhradh
rem Tigherna 7 go mbíd aingle De ag comradh rim-sa gachlaí, 7
an fis nach iarraim-si ar Día, ní hoirches doid-si beith gá iarraidh.
Acht bidh a fhis agad, a Andaigh, co ndubairt Día re cach uile
beith ullam gach aen la ar fedh a mbeathad a n-oircill an baís, 7
tuicc fen, a Andaigh, dá fagtha saegal o tossach an domain gó
a dheredh, comadh écin duid bas d'fhagail fá dheredh, 7 fós nach
badh [fol. 17b] aidbsighe let sin uili ina enmoimint d'fhechain na
haimsire ata romhad ar fagbail an tsaegail-se duit, 7 dena fen
deghoibrighte ó so amach 7 dogeb-sa flaithes De doid.'

125. IN uaír, tra, thicdís daine ga mbidh betha maith 7 da
mbidh Dia buidhech da ngnimhartaib docum C. c. d'fhagbail fhesa
a saeghail uad nó d'faghail a fhesa an sláineochad Dia iad, ní
tuccad sé a fhis sin doib d'ecla go rachdais a ndimus ass no co
ndéndais claechlodh na bethad maithe do bhídh acu, 7 do gabadh
se lesscél resunta ríu amail do gab se re hAndaidh mac duib indse
'sa scel-sa tuas. Oir nirb ail les a gloir saegalta fen do mhédu-
gad d'foillsiugad na seicreide diadha do cách acht an uair do
aithniged se fen a riachtanas a leas orra.

[111]Based on a poem attributed to C.C., published in *Z. C. P.*, VII, p. 301.

bestowed on them such favors as no other saints of Erin else would give them. And albeit he was thus indulging to all, yet did he very great penance therefor. And for such times as he bare him orgulously afore any, or showed to any such countenance as did hurt to his own conscience, he did penance in especial therefor, so that afore God and men, his conscience and his piety wore the beauty and light and brightness of all graces. And he may be likened to crystal in all these ways save in this alone that he was passing steadfast in the love of God and in the Faith, albeit weak in respect of the indulgence he showed to men.

124. On a time there came a kinsman of Columcille to visit him, to wit Annadh mac Duibh Innse son of Caibdenach son of Enne son of Niall of the Nine Hostages. And he inquired of him how long his life should be.

Then answered Columcille and said to him: "Ask not that, O Annadh," saith he, "for God willeth not that any man in this world should have knowledge thereof, and for three causes. The first of these causes in this: if a man learned his life days to be short, for fear of death he would do no good works nor seek wisdom or knowledge in this life. And the second moreover is this: if he learned his life days to be long, then would he be sinning and doing evil deeds till the end of his time, in hope to get occasion to repent of them in the end. And the third cause is this: it were displeasing to God to make any man like unto Himself in the things that be hid in His secrets. And wit thou well, Annadh, I am each Thursday in converse with my Lord, and angels speak with me each day. And the knowledge that I ask not of God, it beseemeth not thee to inquire. But wit thou well, Annadh, that God hath charged all men to be ready each day throughout their lives for to meet with death. And wit thou, Annadh, that hadst thou had life from the beginning of the world to the end, thou must get death at the last. Nor would all that space seem to thee longer than a moment, seeing the time before thee when thou wilt have quit this world. Do thou good deeds henceforth, and I will get Heaven for thee."

125. When there came to Columcille folk of good life and pleasing to God for their works, and sought of him knowledge of the length of their life-days, or to get tidings of their salvation from God, to them gave he naught thereof, lest they be puffed up thereby with pride, or change the good life they led. And he excused him in such wise prudently to them as he did excuse him to Annadh mac Duibh Innse in the history above. For him were loth to increase his worldly glory by the revealing of a divine secret to any, save only he saw need thereof.

ET anuair ticdis daíne cuigi ga mbidh drochbetha acu no dha mbidh Dia dimghach da ngnimharthaib, do indesedh se doib co mbidh indechadh Dia os a cind, 7 do indised se fis a saeghail doib, 7 do indised se doib an uair do bidh damnadh ina cinn do chur gráine 7 ecla orra docum gu treicfidis an drochbetha do bidh acu. Acus ger leasc les a gloír saegalta fen do medugad leth re fis scel na neichedh do bid cuca do tabairt dona dainib-se, dob ussa les sin ina iad san do tuitim go suthain ina pecadh.

126. Fectus do Columb cille a Temhraig na rig, 7 do labhair tre spirud faidhedórachta 7 assed adubairt, ger línmhar sloigh 7 sochraide na Temrach, 7 gerb' imdha a fleagha[112]) 7 a fesda, 7 gerb aibind a háenaide 7 a hoirectais in uair-sin, co mbiadh sí a ndeiredh aimsiri fas folumh 7 nach beidís rigthi inaíd tigernada indte. ET dorinde an fáidhedóracht cédna-sin do Cruachain 7 d'Aillind 7 d'Emain Macha, 7 do fíradh ar can C. c. andsin, oír nir brecnaig Día enní da ndubairt a serbfhoghantaid diles fen riamh.

127. Fectus do C. c. ag denamh urnaidhe a n-inadh aíride 7 began da manchaib fen mailli ris; 7 do tuicetar na manaigh dobrón 7 athtoirrsi mor air, 7 do fíarfaidhetar na manaigh de créd dob adbhar da tuirrsi. IS andsin adubairt C. c. tre spirud faidhedoracta: 'As truagh lim a ndingnaid Gaidil Erenn a ndeired aimsiri d'fheill 7 dfhinghail ar a celi 7 a ndingnaid a righthe 7 a tigernada d'eccoir 7 d'aindlighedh ar na dainib bus loige ina iat fein 7 a tibhraid do micadhus do cellaib 7 d'ecclusaib Erenn. IS truaighe lim iná sin gach ní tiucfus doib as sin .i. ferg Dé do techt ríu ar fulairem naem na n-eclus ara ndingnaid eccoir 7 ar son a ndrochgnimartha fen, indus go scrisfuither as a ndutchus 7 as a n-athardha fen iad fa glentaib 7 fa sleibtib 7 fo aimhreghib[112a]) Erind le nert 7 le tren echtrand 7 allmurach. Gidhedh chena is luthghairech lim anuair dogenaid Gaidil coir 7 cert etorra fen 7 doberaid onoír 7 cadhus do celluib 7 d'eglusaib Erind 7 go hairithe do celluib Padraic 7 dom celluib-si fen 7 do cellaib Brighde. Acus anuair éreóchas cogad 7 esaenta iter gallaib fen 7 dodenaid aithris ar Gaidhelaib leith re feill 7 re fingail do denum ar a celi 7 re heccoir 7 re haindliged do denum ar cellaib 7 ar eclusaib Erenn,' co n-aiseóga Día a nert 7 a trén fen do Gaedhelaib aris 7 go scrisfaid siad goill 7 allmaruidh a hErind, 'trem guide-si 7 tre guide na naemh archena.'

[112]leg. fleadha.
[112a]leg. aimhredhib.

And when there came to him folk of evil life or whom God would fain punish for their deeds, to them he reported that the vengeance of God was on their heads, and to them he gave to know of their life. And when damnation was hanging over them, that would he report to them, with intent to fill them with horror and fear, that they should turn them from their evil life. And albeit he was full loth to exalt his own glory in the world by knowing tidings of that which was to befall those folk, yet this were easier to him than that they should fall into lasting sin.

126. On a time that Columcille was in Tara of the Kings, he prophesied and said that many as were her hosts and her legions, and many her feasts and her banquetings, and delightful as were her assemblies and her gatherings, yet in the end of time she should be waste and desolate, and there should be in her nor lords nor rulers. And he made that same prophecy of Cruachu and of Aillend and of Emain Macha. And so it came to pass, for that which His chosen servant did say, thereof did God never aught gainsay.

127. On a time that Columcille was praying in a certain place, and a few of the brethren with him, they perceived that heaviness and great grief lay on him. And the monks inquired of him what was the reason of his sorrow.

And Columcille said, prophesying: "It grieveth me for the treachery and the slaying of kinsmen that the Gael of Erin shall do hereafter, each upon other, and for the wrong and injustice that their kings and lords shall do against them that be weaker than they; and for the dishonor they shall do to the chapels and the churches of Erin. And it grieveth me yet more for all that shall come upon them therefor, to wit, the anger of God coming upon them at the supplication of the saints against whose churches they do wrong, and for their evil deeds, so that they shall be driven from the land of their fathers to the glens and mountains and the rough places of Erin by the might and strength of strangers and foreigners. But when the Gaels do justice and right among themselves, I make great joy, and when they do honor and worship to the chapels and churches of Erin, and in especial to the churches of Padraic, and mine own churches and the churches of Brigid. And when there shall arise strife and division among the foreigners themselves, and they shall do after the Gael in respect of treachery and in respect of kinsmen slaying each other, and in respect of wrongdoing and injustice against the chapels and churches of Erin, then shall God give back again to the Gaels their strength and their might. And they shall drive out the strangers and the foreigners from Erin through my supplication and through the supplication of the other saints besides."

128.¹¹³) Fectus do C. c. 'san inadh ren aburtar Termonn Cumaínigh aniug a tir Eogain, 7 do bendaig sé an t-inad-sin 7 do fagaib se termonn aice ó sin amach go brath. Acus do buail se tri builli da bachaill 'sa talmain, 7 do erich tobar as lorc gach buille dib sin. Acus do labhair tre spirud faidedoracta 7 assed adubairt: 'Ticfa Domnall mac Aedha, mic Ainmirech, rí Erenn, 7 cineol Conaill maraen ris don termond-sa,' 7 go ndenaid an sluagh moran domblais and 7 combeith sé fen an uair-sin a n-Alpain, 7 cor truag do cinel Conaill domblas do denamh 'na termonn 7 se fen ar deóraigecht shuthain afecmais Erenn. Acus adubairt go bfhuighedh se fen o Día ri Erenn 7 i shluagh do linadh do galur 7 d'eslaínti, 7 nach beith nert mna re n-idhna a n-enduine dib ar in pongc-sin fen no go bfhaghadh comarba an baile a breth fen on rig a milledh a thermaind. Acus anuair dogebudh se an breth-sin, uisce na toibrech tainec as lorc na bachla do crothadh [ar] an rig 7 ar a sluagh 7 go mbeidís slan fochédoír. Acus co madh Tobair na Conalluch ainm na toibrech-sin ó sin amach a cuim- [fol. 18a] niugad na mirbuiledh mor-sin. Acus do fíradh an fhaidedóract-sin dorinde C. c. a leith re gach ní dib sin.

129.¹¹⁴) Lá airithi da ndechaid C. c. do Temraig na righ 7 tarla Beg mac De dó .i. drui Diarmada mic Cerbaill ri Erenn, 7 do bi spirud faidedoracta ó Día aicce, ge do bi 'na draidh, 7 ni derna se faidhedoruct brege riamh. Gidedh, do tairrngir C. c. go ndenadh Bec faidhedóract breice fá dó sul do gebadh se bas. Acus do bendaig C. c. dó 7 docuaidh a caeines comraidh ris 7 assed adubairt: 'As mór an fis-so 7 an t-eolus-sa agat, a Bic mac De, a leith re fis a mbais do tabairt dona dainib eli 7 an bfhuil a fhis agad ca huair dogebha tu fen bas.' 'Ata a fhis sin agam gu deimhin,' ar Bec., 'oir ataid .úíí. mbliadna dom tshaegal agam.' 'Dogenadh duine deghoibrighti re haimsir bad girra ina sin,' ar C. c., '7 an demhin let fen go bfhuil an oired-sin do shaegal agad?' Do bi Becc tamall 'na tost 7 do labair ris 7 assed adubairt: 'Ni demhin,' ar se, 'oir ní fhuil do saegal agam acht .úíi. mí.' 'As maith sin fen,' ar C. c., '7 an deimhin lat an oired-sin fen do beith dot shaeghal gan techt?' 'Ni deimhin,' ar Beg, 'et ag so an comairce a Coluim cille,' ar se, 'oir ní fetar techt a n-adhaid na faidhetoruchta dorinne tussa, oir do geallais co ndingnaind-se

---

¹¹³Cf. § 142.
¹¹⁴Literally in LB, [260], col. 2, 1. 57 seq.

128. On a time that Columcille was in the place that is now called Termon Cumainig in Tir Eogain, he hallowed that place and left thereon the right of sanctuary thenceforth. And he struck three strokes with his staff upon the ground, and a well sprang from each stroke thereof.

And he spake, prophesying, and said, "To this sanctuary shall come one Domnall mac Aeda son of Ainmire, King of Erin, and the tribe of Conall together with him."

And [he prophesied] that they should do sore ill there. And he himself should be in Alba in that time. And it was an ill thing for the tribe of Conall to do evil in that sanctuary, and he in exile forever far from Erin. And he said he would prevail on God to fill the King of Erin and his host with sickness and disease, and there should not be in one of them in that hour the strength of a woman in childbirth, until his successor should be given his own terms from the King for the destroying of his sanctuary. And when the compensation had been received [he bade] him shake water upon the King and his host from the wells that had sprung at the touch of his crozier. And they should be whole straightway. And the Well of the Conalls should be the name of that well from that time in remembrance of that great miracle. And the prophecy that Columcille made touching all of these things did come to pass.

129. On a certain day Columcille was going to Tara of the Kings, and by adventure he met Bec mac De, the druid of Diarmaid mac Cerbaill, King of Erin. And Bec had the gift of prophecy from God, albeit he was a druid, and he had made no false prophecy ever. But Columcille had foretold that Bec should twice prophesy falsely ere his death. And Colcumcille saluted him, and entered into friendly converse with him.

And he said: "Great is thy wisdom and knowledge, Bec mac De, in the tidings thou givest to other folk touching their deaths. Hast thou knowledge also of when thou shalt thyself die?"

"Thereof have I knowledge in sooth," saith Bec. "There be yet for me seven years of life."

"A man might do good works in shorter space than that," saith Columcille. "And knowest thou for a surety that thou hast so much of life still?"

Then was Bec silent for a space, and thereafter spake he to Columcille and said, "I have not. It is but seven months of life I have."

"That is well," saith Columcille, "and art certain thou hast still so much of life to come?"

"I am not," saith Bec, "and this is a token, O Columcille. I cannot withstand the prophecy thou hast made. For thou didst foretell that I should make two false prophecies ere I should die. There is left me but

breg fá dhó im fhaidhetoracht sul dogebaind bas[115]) 7 ni fhuil
do saeghal agam acht .uíí. n-uairi don la aniug amhain,' ar se,
'7 tabair-se faiside 7 sacramaint damh.' 'IS dá tabairt sin duit
tanuc-sa so aniugh,' ar C. c., 'oir do foillsigh Dia damh co bfhuigh-
tea-sa bas aniug.' Acus as andsin do lesaidh C. c. Becc do molad
na heclaisi 7 tuc cumhaínech as a laimh fen do. Acus fuáir bás
iarsin, 7 docuaidh a anam docum nime tre maithes De 7 tre guidhe
C. c.

130. Uair airithe da raibe C. c. ag scribneoract leabair na
soiscel, 7 do iarr se ar Ciaran mac an tshaeir a cuidiugad les an
leabar-sin do scribad. 'Cuideóchad-sa let,' ar Ciaran, 'oir scribeóbha me leth do liubair doit.' 'Dobér-sa luach duit-si ar a shon-
sin,' ar Columb cille, 'oir gellaim duid-se go n-ainmneochar leth
cell Erind uaid.' Acus is mar sin nach derna énduine riam maith
bec nó mór do C. c. nach cuiteochad se tall nó abhus ris hí.

131.[116]) Fectus do Columb cille ag suibhal re cois na hab-
hond re n-abartar an Boinn, 7 do cuired cloicenn duine cuicce 7
ba hingantach le C. c. cona naemhaib med na cloicne-sin, oir fa
mó co mór í inaid cloicne luchta na haimseri-sin. IS andsin adubratar a muindter re C. c.: 'As truagh duinn,' ar síad, 'gan a
fhiss againd cia hí an cloicenn-sa nó cait afuil an t-anum do baí
'sa chorp ar a raibhe sí.' Frecrais C. c. iat 7 assedh adubairt:
'Ni fhúigebh-sa an t-inad-sa no go faghar afhis sin o Día daib.'
Teid C. c. do guide De co duthrachtach fa an ní-sin d'fhoillsiu-
gad dó, 7 do eíst Día an guide-sin C. c. indus cor labhair an
cloicenn fen ris 7 adubairt si, corbh í fen cloicenn Cormaic mic
Airt, mic Cuind ced-cathaigh, righ Erenn, a sendser san feín.
Oir dob e an dechmad glun o Cormac e, 7 do indis do, gin corbh
imlán a creideamh, co raibe an oiret-sa do creidem aige 7 do coimhet ar in firinde, 'agus fos mar do bi afhis ag Día coticfa-sa ar a
slicht 7 co nguidhfea ar a anmuin, nar damhain se dáririb é, ge
do bí se a pianuib roghera ag feitheam ar do guidhe-si.' IS
andsin do tocaib C. c. an cloicend 7 do nidh se hí co honorach 7
do baisd 7 do bendaich í, 7 do adlaic as a haitli hí. Acus nir
fagaib C. c. an t-inadh-sin co ndubairt se .x. n-aifrend .xx. ar
anmuin Cormaic. Acus ar an aifrend ndeigenuch dib, do foill-
sicced do C. c. aingli Dé ac breith a anma leo docum nime do
caithemh na gloiri suthaine tré guidhe C. c.

[115]See Plummer's *V. S. H.*, II p. 138, § 28. Here he is also said to have made a false statement.

[116]Abridged account in Keating. See Dinneen's *Keating*, II, pp. 346-8.

seven hours of this same day," saith he. "Do thou assoil me and give me the sacrament."

"It was to give thee this that I came hither today," saith Columcille, "for God revealed to me that thou shouldst die today."

Then did Columcille succor Bec with the consolation of Holy Church, and gave him the sacrament from his own hand. And Bec died then. And his soul went to Heaven through the goodness of God and the intercession of Columcille.

130. On a time that Columcille was copying a book of gospels, he asked Ciaran son of the Wright to aid him in writing that book.

"I will aid thee," saith Ciaran. "I will copy the half of thy book for thee."

"I will requite thee therefor," saith Columcille, "for I promise thee that the half of the churches of Erin shall be named from thee."

And thus it is that no man hath done aught of good, small or great, for Columcille, that he hath not rewarded it in the next life or in this.

131. On a time that Columcille was walking by the side of the river that is called the Boyne, the skull of a man was sent to him. And Columcille and the saints marvelled at the size of that skull, for it was far greater than the skulls of the folk of that time. Then said his household to Columcille:

"It is a poor thing for us," say they, "to be without knowledge of whose this skull may be, or where is the soul that was in the body wherein it dwelled."

Columcille answered them and said: "I will not quit this place save I get knowledge thereof for you from God."

Then gan Columcille to pray God earnestly to reveal to him this thing. And God heard that prayer of Columcille, so that the skull spake to him. And it said how it was the skull of Cormac mac Airt son of Conn of the Hundred Battles, King of Erin and ancestor to himself. For Columcille was the tenth degree from Cormac. And the skull related that albeit his faith had not been perfect, yet such had been the measure thereof, and his keeping of the truth, that, inasmuch as God knew that Columcille would be of his seed, and would pray for his soul, He had not dammed him in very truth, albeit it was in sharp pains that he awaited the prayer of Columcille.

Then Columcille lifted up the skull and cleansed it right worshipfully. And he baptized it and blessed and buried it thereafter. And he left not the place ere he had said thirty masses for the soul of Cormac. And at the last of those masses the angels of God appeared to Columcille, bearing with them the soul of Cormac to Heaven to enjoy glory everlasting through the intercession of Columcille.

132.¹¹⁷) Anuair, tra, do scris 7 do indarb Patraic na drochspirda do Cruchan oighli re ráiter Cruach Patraic aniugh, docuaid drong dib 'san inadh re n-abartar Senglend C. c. a crich cineoil Conaill Guilban, bud tuaid anuigh, 7 rouhátar and ó aimsir Patraic co haimsir C. c. Acus do cuiretar ceo na timcell and indus nach bfaicedh énduine an méd do bi fan ceo-sin don talumh. Acus an abhann as coiccrich don termonn-sin ris an tuaidh aniug, dorindetar sruth tendtide dí ar cor nach fédadh enduine ar bith dul tairis. Acus gibe ré mbenadh becan no morán don tsruth-sin dogebad bás focédoír. ET do foillsigetar aingle Dé an ní-sin do C. c., 7 docuaid mailli re morán do naemhaib eli do díchar 7 d'indarbud na ndiabal as an inadh-sin, et dorindetar comhnaide re hucht an tsrotha tendtide adubramar romh[fol. 17b]aind. Acus nír cian doib and anuair tuc an t-aibirseoír urchor do bir cuilind asin ceo tarin sruth, cormarb an Cerc .i. gilla C. c. don urchor-sin. Conad "Srath na circe" ainm an tsratha o sin ille. Fergaigther C. c. go mor fá an ní-sin, 7 glacais an bir cedna 7 tuc urchor tar an sruth de, cor lecidh an talum ris anfad docuaidh an bir sa ceó 7 cor teich an ceo fen tresin urchar-sin C. c. Acus do fas an bir 'san inad-sin inar ben sé a talmain an uair-sin, cobfhuil 'na crand úrcuilind aniugh gan crinadh ó sin alle 7 co mbia go bráth. Bendachais C. c. an sruth iar sin, 7 docuaidh a neimh 7 a draidhecht de 7 teid tairis anonn. ET tuc an t-aingel cloch cruind glass dó 7 adubairt ris a teilgen ris na demhnaib 7 co teithfedis fen 7 an ceo rempe. Acus fos adubairt an t-aingeal ris a cloc fen do caitheamh riv mar an cedna .i. an dub duaibsech a ainm. Acus dorinde C. c. amail do seol an t-aingel dó, indus cor leicedh an talam uili ris on ceo 7 cor theithetar na diabail remhe ar carraic cloiche do bi 'sa bfhairge moir amuigh ar comair an cind tiar don talumh-sin. Acus do caith C. c. an cloch-sin tuc an t-aingel do 7 a cloc .i. an dub duaibsec ríu, 7 do chuir fa umla orra dul trid an carraic cloiche-sin ar a rabatar 'sa bfhairge 7 beith a rectaib ésc indti go brath 7 gan aiberseóracht do denamh ar enduine ó sin amach. Acus dob écen doib sin do denam tre breithir C. c. Acus do rachudh fer fána éidedh tres an poll dorindetar 'sa cloich ag dul trithe doib 'sa bfhairce. Acus do fhágaib C. c. comartha orra sech gach íasc eli d'egla co n-ísdais daine iad .i. a mbeith leth-caech ruadh. Acus gabaid iascuiredha go minec íad aniugh, 7 ni denaid riu arna n-aithne doib, acht a teilgiun 'sa bfhairce arís. IS andsin ro íarr C. c. ar Día a cloc

¹¹⁷Evidently most of this account is based on tradition. See Reeves' *Adam.*, p. 206; also *Three Middle-Irish Homilies*, pp. 36-8.

132. When Padraic had banished and driven away the evil spirits from Cruachan Aigle that is today called Cruach Padraic, there went a throng of them to the place that is now called Senglenn Colaimcille in the region of the clan of Conall Gulban to the north. And they were in that place from the time of Padraic to the time of Columcille. And they raised a fog about them there, so that none might see the part of the land that lay beneath that fog. And of the river that formeth a boundary to the north they made a fiery stream so that none of all might go across it. And whoso should touch of that stream little or much, he should die straightway.

And angels of God revealed this thing to Columcille. And he went with many others of the saints to drive away the demons and banish them out of that place. And they made a stay beside the fiery stream we have aforementioned. And they had not been long there when the Devil hurled a holly rod out of the fog across the stream. And it killed An Cerc, Columcille's varlet, with that cast, so that Srath na Circe is the name of that stream thenceforth.

Thereat Columcille waxed exceeding wroth and he seized that same javelin, and hurled it across the stream. And the land was yielded to him for the space the javelin went into the fog, for the fog fled before that cast of Columcille's.

And that javelin grew in the place whereas it struck the ground that time, so that today it is a fresh holly-tree, and it hath not withered from that time till now, and thus it shall be till Doomsday.

Then Columcille blessed that stream, and its venom and enchantment departed therefrom. And he crossed it. And an angel brought him a round green stone, and bade him cast it at the demons, and they should flee before it, and the fog also. And the angel bade him throw his bell Dub Duaibsech at them in like wise. And Columcille did as the angel commanded him, so that the whole land was yielded to him from the fog. And the demons fled before him to a rock out in the great sea opposite the western headland of that region. And Columcille cast at them that stone that the angel had given him, and his bell Dub Duaibsech. And he bade the demons go into the sea through the rock whereas they were, and to be in the form of fish forever, and to do no deviltry against any thenceforth. And by reason of the word of Columcille they must needs do that. And a man having on his armour might go through the hole they made in the stone, when they went through it into the sea. And lest folk should eat them, Columcille left a mark on them passing every other fish, to wit, that they should be blind of an eye and red. And fishers oft take them today, and they do naught to them when they perceive them, save to cast them again into the sea.

7 a cloch do aisec asin fairce dó. Acus les sin docondaic se 'na
*n*dáchair tenedh cuicce íad 7 do benatar ar lár laim ris. Acus
do beandaigh se an tal*am*-sin as ar chuir se na hainspir*da* 7 do
fhag*aib* se term*onn* aige o shoin alle. Acus do fagaib se an cloch-
sin mar airdmhinn ann ag denum fert 7 mirbuil*edh*. *ET* an aít
inar bean an cloc, docuaid se go domain a talumh and gor fagaib
se a tenga and. Acus adubairt C. c. nar misde an cloc a beith
gan tengaidh; 7 gebe duine do denadh esonoír an termaind-sin
an cloc do chur 'sa pholl inar fhacaib se a tenga mar comartha
escaine air 7 nach coimheol*ad* sé a bliad*ain*.¹¹⁸) Acus do derbadh sin co minic, 7 do íarratar a muindt*er* ar C. c. an sruth
tendt*idi*-sin adubram*ar* romhaind do bendaig se, do beith a com-
domhain sin, indus nach rachad 7 nach tiucf*ai*dis daine co brath
air *acht* a luing *nó* a n-ethar, ar cor co m*ad* lughaide do tiucf*ad*
an tuath do milled an termaind a beith mar sin. Do raidh C. c.
corub do na! fandaib 7 dá gach duine do beith 'na feidhm do
ord*aig* se an termonn 7 nach cuirf*ed* se toirmesc etorra 7 é; 7
nach eadh amhaín acht co bfuicf*ed* se mar buadhaib ar an abh-
ainn-sin nach b*eith* sí enla coidhce do mhed a tuile nach soichfidís daine a n-inadh écin tairsi. Acus ata an briat*har*-sin C. c.
gá comhall ó shin alle; oir nir brecnaidh Dia enní da ndubhairt se
ríamh.

133. AR scris 7 ar n-innarbudh na ndeman do C. c. a Senglend, 7 ar ndenamh ésc 'sa bfhairge dib amail adubramar romhaind, tainec reimhe do benduch*ad* 7 do reidhech*ad* Essa Ruaidh.
Oir is amlaid do bi an t-Es an uair-sin—ní shoichedh an t-íasc tairis
súas ar an abhaind—7 do mallaigh Patraic abfhad reme-sin an
taeb bud des de ré ulca re Cairp*ri* mac Neill nai ghiall*aig* nar
gab creidemh uadha, (oir ba lé Cairbri an talam don taeb-sin
de ó Drobaís go hEss Ruaidh, arna tabairt do Chonull Gulb*an*

---

¹¹⁸See § 353 for a similar phrase.

Then required Columcille of God to give back to him his bell and stone from the sea. And lo, he beheld them coming toward him in the likeness of a glow of fire, and they fell to the ground fast by him.

And Columcille blessed that land whence he had banished the evil spirits. And he bestowed thereon the right of sanctuary from that time. And he left the stone as a chief treasure to do marvels and miracles. And in the place where the bell fell, it sank deep in the earth, and it left its clapper there. And Columcille said the bell was none the worse without the clapper. And he charged them, if any man should do dishonor to the sanctuary, to put the bell in the hole where it had left its clapper, as a token of a curse upon him, and that man should not live out his year. And this hath oft been proved.

Then the folk besought Columcille that the fiery stream aforementioned that he had blessed, should be so deep that there might not go nor come any thereon forever save in a ship or a boat, to the intent that if it were thus, there should less folk come and abuse the sanctuary. Columcille said that he had ordained that sanctuary for the weak and for all those in need, and he would put no hindrance between them and it. And not this only, but he would obtain as a virtue for that stream that it should never be even for a day so much in flood that a man might not attain at some place to cross it. And that word of Colcumcille's hath been fulfilled from that time till now, for naught that he ever said hath God gainsaid.

XI

OF THE VIRTUE OF COLUMCILLE'S BLESSING AND OF HIS CURSE

133. When Columcille had driven out and expelled the demons from Senglenn and when he had made of them fishes in the sea, as we have said toforehand, he went forward and blessed Assaroe and levelled it. And it is thus Assaroe was at that time: the fish could not cross over it up the river. And Padraic had cursed the south side thereof long while afore, by reason of a grudge against Cairbre son of Niall of the Nine Hostages that would not take the Faith from him, and because Cairbre did not suffer Padraic to make churches or dwellings thereabouts. (For from Drobais to Assaroe the land to that side thereof belonged to Cairbre, having been given him by Conall Gulban as largesse, along with his allotted portion.) But he blessed the north side

a nduthracht re cois a choda ronna dó), 7 nar leic Cairbri do
Patraic eclusa no aítiugad do denamh 'na timchell. Acus do
bendaig se an taeb bud tuaidh de. *ET*, fos, ní gabthai íasc a n-
aít ar bith air acht an méid do ghabthai don taeb budh thuaid
5 de tre bendachtain Patraic, 7 ni línmhar do gabthai andsin é. *ET*
do labhair Patraic tre spirud faidhetorachta an uair-sin 7 assed
adubairt, corub a n-onoír C. c. do bendaigh se an cuid-sin dhe, 7
co tiucfad C. c. fen dá bendachad ina díaigh-sin 7 nach beith a
n-Erind aít as mó a ngebthai d'íasc iná sé ó shin amach. Teid
10 Columb cille reime do coir Essa Ruaidh, 7 doní comnaidhe ag
bun na habann bicce atá don taeb [*fol.* 19a] bud thuaidh de mar
a teid sí 'sa bfhairge da ngoirther an Fuindsendach. Acus do
labhuir re naem airithe do budh combrathair genelaig dó fen do
bi faris .i. Barrann mac Muiredhaigh, mic Echach, mic Conaill
15 Gulban, 7 do fiarfaig de cait a raibe a bachull. Frecrais Barrand
é 7 assed adubairt: 'Do theilges ris na demnaib ag dul doibh isan
bfhairge í anuair do bhámar ga n-indarbudh a Senglend,' ar se,
'7 ni tarla sí rim ó sin.' 'IS ced lim massa ced le Día e,' ar
C. c., 'do bachull do tect cugat conuige so.' Les sin docondcatar
20 an bachall ag ergi cuca as carruicc cloiche do bi 'na fiadnaise, 7
do ling sreb uisce as a lorc go bfhuil 'na thobar fhíruisce 'san
inadh-sin aniugh, 7 adubairt C. c. co tiubrad se d'onoír do Barrand an tobar-sin d'ainmniugad uadha. Conad ballán Barruinde
a ainm o sin alle.
25 134. IS andsin do gluais C. c. reme co hEss Ruaidh, 7 docondcus dó gur digbalach do cach uile a comhcoitchinde, 7 go
hairithi da bhraithrib fen, fa raibe se rográdhuch 7 dá raibi
daendaigecht romhor aige .i. cinel Conuill Gulban, gan toradh
imarcach do beith ar in Ess 7 ar in Erne uili. Acus doconncus do
30 fos nach beith an torudh-sin air mvna beith ced dul 7 techt ag an
íasc tar an Ess ó an abaind gusan fairge moir. *ET* as ar na had-
baraib-sin uili do bendaigh Columb cille an t-Ess, 7 do cuir se
fa umla ar clochaib agus ar cairrgib an taeibhe bud thuaidh de
isliugad indus go fédadh an t-iasc dul tairis amhail adubramar.
35 Dorindetar na duile balbha-sin umla do C. c. 7 do isligetar amail
adubairt ríu, mar as follas do lucht fechana an Essa aniugh .i.
an cuid bu[d] des ard anshocair de 7 an cuid bud thuaidh ísel
de. Conadhe inber eisc as ferr a n-Erinn aniugh e tres an
mbendugad-sin C. c. Acus is le comarba C. c. iascairecht Essa Ruaid
40 gach enla feili C. c. o sin alle ag cuimniugad na mirbuile mor-sin.
135. Fectus do C. c. a n-inadh arithe 7 do tindscain se
aifrend do radha, 7 ni raibe uisce a comghar do, 7 do bendaigh

thereof. And by reason of Padraic's blessing there had been caught no fish in that place save on the north side only, and there not many. And Padraic had prophesied at that time, and had said that it was to honor Columcille that he had blessed that side, and that Columcille himself should come to bless it after him, and from that time there should not be a place in Erin where more fish should be caught than there.[1]

Columcille went then towards Assaroe. And he made a stay at the mouth of a little river called the Fuindsennach that issueth into the sea to the north thereof. And he spake to a certain holy man that was in his fellowship, one Barrann mac Muiredhaigh son of Echaidh son of Conall Gulban, that was a kinsman to him by blood, and he inquired of him where his staff was.

Barrann made answer and said to him, "I cast it at the demons as they went into the sea when we were driving them from Senglenn," said he, "and I have not chanced upon it since that time."

"It is my will if it be God's will," saith Columcille, "for thy staff to come to thee to this place."

With that they saw the staff coming up to them from a rock before them. And a stream of water gushed forth in the track thereof, so that there is a well of fresh water in that place to this day. And Columcille said that he would give as an honor to Barrann that the well should be named from him. So that the Stone Trough of Barrann hath been its name from that day till now.

134. Then Columcille fared onward to Assaroe. And him seemed it great damage to all in general and to his own dear kinsman in especial to the which he bare great love, to wit, the clan of Conall Gulban, that there should not be abundance [of fish] in the waterfall [of Assaroe] and the whole Erne. And he saw there could be none such abundance except the fish be free to go and come across the waterfall from the river to the great sea. And it was by reason of all this that Columcille blessed the waterfall. And he bound the stones and the rocks of the northern side to abase them that the fish might pass, as we have said afore. And these dumb things did obeissance to Columcille and did abase them, as is manifest to those that visit the waterfall [of Assaroe] today, for the south side is high and rugged, and the north side thereof is low. And by reason of that blessing of Columcille's it is the best river for fish in Erin today. And every feast day of Columcille from then till now, his successor hath the fishing of Assaroe in remembrance of that great miracle.

135. On a time that Columcille was in a certain place, he began to say the mass, and there was no water near him. And he blessed a

[1] *Cf.* § 31.

se carraic cloiche do bí 'na fiadhnaise, 7 do ling sreb fhíruisce
esde indus gonderna se a riachta*nus* a less fein leis. *ET* as follus
ass so gor cuir Día C. c. a cosm*ail*es re Maisi anuair do bhatar
m*i*c Israel a ríachta*nus* a les an uisce ar an bfhásach 7 do buail
se an tshlat Maeisi ar an carraic co, taínic uisce esde ler shás
sé a popul uli it*er* dhuine 7 ainmide. Acus ni hedh a[119]) amhaín do
chuir se a cosmailes re Maíssi é, acht do cuir se a cem foirbtechta os
a ceand é, oir do bí congnamh an pop*uil* uile ag Maísi dochum
an visce d'faghail ó Dia, 7 do troisc se fen 7 a popul da iarraid
7 ni fuair se lena c*éd* íarraidh e, 7 ni raibe congn*am* endhuine
ag C. c. docum an uisce do fhuair se fen ó Dia 7 nir chuir Dia
cairde air, *acht* comluath 7 do bendaig se an charruic cloiche,, do
bí 'na fiadnaise, uisce do t*echt* este amhail adubramar.

136. Ni hedh amhain dogheibedh gach nech do bendaig*ed*
C. c. flaithes De, acht dogeibed sé maithes saegalta uadh. Acus
da derbhad-sin is tresan mbeandugad dorinde se ar Domn*all*
mac Aedha, mic Ainmirech, a mordhail Droma Cet, do ghab se
rigacht Erenn, amail asp*ert* se fen 'sa rand-sa:

Domnall dori*nde* oirn*e* maith,   fa deoigh coma fer raith;
sochaidhe ag dail a dighe,   a airemh 'sa rem righraidhe.

ET fos is tresan mbendugad dorinde se ar Fínd*ach*t*a* mac Duna-
dh*a*, mic Aeda Slaine, do gab se righacht Erenn, 7 is tresan
mbendugad dorinde se ar Guairi mac Colmain do bi se fíal
deghen*igh* 7 do gab se righe C*on*nocht.

137.[120]) Fectus do C. c. ag bendugad cell 7 ecl*us* a crich Br*egh*
7 Mhidhe, 7 do batar naeimh eli maille ris .i. Baithin 7 Caindech
7 Comghall 7 Ternóc 7 Brughach. Acus la aíridhe da rabutar ag
siubal, ruc an oidhce orra, 7 do bi snechta 7 doinenn ainmesardha and 7 ni raibe afhis acu gá rachdaís *nó* cá mbeidís an oidhce-
sin. Acus do bi dvine bocht uasal 'sa tir-sin dar dual righacht

---

[119]Omit.

[120]This beautiful story is based on the poem *maith ar n-áighidhecht anocht.
a tig Finnachta co becht.* See *Eriu*, V, Part I-II, p. 12. See O'Donovan's *Three
Fragments* for a different version of the story, pp. 70-2.

rock that he saw, and a stream of spring water gushed forth, so that he served his need therewith. And it is manifest from this that God made Columcille like unto Moses the time that the children of Israel were in need of water in the desert. And he struck the rod of Moses upon the rock so that water came forth therefrom. And therewith did he satisfy all the folk, man and beast both. And not only did he make him like unto Moses, but he put him in a degree of perfection above him; for Moses had help of all the folk to obtain the water from God, and he fasted, and his folk also, to require it. And he gat it not from God with the first asking. And Columcille had help of none to get the water from God. And God made no delay, but so soon as he blessed the rock that was afore him, the water came forth as we have said toforehand.

136. Not only did each of those that Columcille blessed get the Kingdom of God, but he gat also from him the goods of the world. And in proof thereof it was by virtue of the blessing that he laid on Domnall mac Aeda mic Ainmirech in the Assembly of Druim Ceat that Domnall gat the sovereignty of Erin, as Columcille hath himself said in this quatrain:

> "Domnall hath done us a favor.
> May he be a man of bounty hereafter!
> May many be serving his drink!
> May he be numbered with kings!"

And it was by virtue of the blessing that he laid upon Finnachta son of Donnchadh son of Aed Slaine, that Finnachta gat the sovereignty of Erin. And it was by virtue of the blessing that he laid upon Guaire mac Colmain that he was bounteous and hospitable, and that he gat the sovereignty of Connacht.

137. On a time Columcille was blessing chapels and churches in the region of Breagha and Mide, and other holy men were in his fellowship, to wit, Baithin and Cainnech and Comgall and Ternóc and Brugach. And one day, as they were walking, night fell on them, and there was snow and exceeding bad weather. And they knew not whither they might go, nor where they might be that night. And there was a poor nobleman in that region that should have had the kingship of Erin, to wit, Finnachta son of Donnchadh son of Aed Slaine. And albeit he was poor and needy, yet was he hospitable and stainless of his honor as beseemed his blood. And it befell that Columcille with his saints came to his house that night. And Finnachta bade them welcome and gave to them his best of food and drink and tending. And on the morn Columcille blessed him and said to him:

Erind .i. Fíndachta¹²¹ mac Dunadha mic Aeda Slaíne; 7 ge do bí sé bocht daidhbir, do bi sé fial naírech mar bú cubaid ris do reir fholaidechta. Acus tarla C. c. cona naemhaib docum a tighe an oidhce-sin 7 do fer Finnachta failti rív 7 tuc a díchell bídh 7 dighe 7 frithoilte doib. Acus do benduigh C. c. arna máruch e 7 adubairt ris: 'Ó do fhoir tussa sinde arér on riachtanus a les imarcach do bi oraind,' ar se, 'foirfed-sa do bochtaine-si 7 do daidhbres 7 do ríachtanus [fol. 19b] a les 7 dobera righe nErinn duit 7 flaithes De fa deoigh.' Acus do firadh sin uile ut dixit C. c. ga derbad so:

Sesiur duind do muinnter De   atigh Findacta gongne,
Baithin, Brugach, Comgall, Caindech,   Ternoc, Columb cille ó Neill.
Findachta go condailbe,   bendaigim é go gléthend;
fuicfed-sa ar a comairli   coig coicedhaig na hEreand.

138. Fectas do C. c. ag bendugad cell 7 eclus a cúicced Condacht, 7 do bi duine og uasul a cúiged Conacht an uair-sin darbo comainm Guaire mac Colmain 7 ni raibe a n-Erind duine ba doichlighi 7 bú drochenigh iná in Guairi-sin. Ó'tclos do C. c. sin, teid mar a raibe Guairi 7 do bendhaig 7 do tecaisc do briathraib rográdacha romhillse é 7 assed adubairt ris: 'As lor duit, a Ghúaire, a ndernais d'ulc fa duillebar brégach dimbuan an tsaeghail-si, 7 as imdha adhbhor agat fá nach denta duit olcus uime, oír ni tuc tu enní let ar an saegal-sa ag techt duid air, 7 ní mo berus tu enní let de ogá fagbail duit. ET bid afhis agat, gebe nech dá tabair Dia moran do spreidh 7 d'airnés an tsaeghail-se, co bfhuill d'fiachaib air a roind arna daínib docífed se 'na riachtanus a les; 7 fós bidh afhis agat, corub rodimgach Dia do lucht na mítrocaire 7 dona dainib nach denadh maith ar a bochtaib fen. Acus bidh a fis agat arís, dá léghtha an scribtuir diadha uile nach fuigthea scribtha co madh comartha slanaighthe do duine gan a beith fial dércech daendachtach. Acus da derbad sin, nir ér an tigerna .i. Isv Crist fen enduine riamh an fedh do bí se a colaind daenda 7 ni mó roératar a espoil nó a deiscipail; 7 fós nír ér Padraic no Brigid, 7 nír ér mesi fen aenduine riamh,' ar C. c: Gonadh and dorinde an laidh .i.¹²²).

Dena, a Guairi, maith imni,   na seoid adchí as dorn amceó,
at aenar tainic tú a clí,   dogebhair ní céin ber beo. 7rl.

---

¹²¹According to *A. U.*, he reigned from 675-95.

¹²²The whole poem is in Bodleian MS. Laud 615, p. 23. It is printed and translated in *King and Hermit*, p. 28.

"Since thou didst save us yesternight from the exceeding need we were in," saith he, "I will save thee from thy poverty and misery and from thy need, and I will give thee the sovereignty of Erin and the Kingdom of God at the last."

And all this came to pass. As Columcille hath said in proof thereof:

> "Six of us of the household of God,
> In the house of Finnachta the kindly,
> Baithin, Brugach, Comgall, Cainnech,
> Ternoc, and Columcille o Neill.
>
> Finnachta of friendship,
> I bless him right heartily;
> I shall leave to his ruling
> The five pentarchs of Erin."

138. On a time that Columcille was blessing chapels and churches in the province of Connacht, there was a young nobleman of the province at that time hight Guaire mac Colmain. And there was not in Erin a man more churlish and inhospitable than that Guaire. And when Columcille heard this he went to Guaire, and blessed him, and gave him counsel with sweet and loving words.

And he said to him: "Thou hast done enough of evil, O Guaire, touching the vain and deluding leafage of this world. And thou hadst many reasons not to do ill in this wise, for naught didst thou bring with thee into the world when thou didst come hither, and naught wilt thou bring with thee therefrom on leaving it. And wit thou well, he to whom God giveth much of goods and cattle in this world is bound to share them with folk that he seeth in want thereof. And I let thee wit that God is wroth with them that are without pity and that give no alms to his poor. And wit thou also that wert thou to read in holy Scripture, thou shouldst find it written that it is not a token of salvation for any to be without bounty or charity or largesse. And in proof thereof the Lord Jesu Christ did never refuse any the while He was in this human body. Nor did His apostles nor His disciples, nor yet Padraic nor Brigid. Nor have I refused any ever," saith Columcille.

And then it was he made the lay:

> "Give somewhat of alms, O Guaire,
> The goods thou seest are as a fist around mist.
> Sole didst thou come in the body;
> Thou shalt have enough the while thou dost live."

Do gab Guairi an te*cusc*-sin go maith cuice, indus n*ach* taínic a n-Erind riamh an tres duine dob fheili 7 do*ba* naíridhe ina é, amail as*pert* an nech naemtha .i. Baithin mac Cúanuch 'sa rann-sa:

    Guairi m*ac* Colm*ain* aníar,   Cucul*ainn*, Colu*mb* na clíar;
5   isíat sin t*riar*, gan deibech,   as fherr enech taínec riamh.

ET fós tainec do brigh an bendaigthe-sin tuc C. c. air 7 an tecusc *tuc* se dó, gor gab se righe *Co*nnacht iar sin. Oír nir bendaig C. c. enduine riamh nach tiucf*ad* do brigh an bendaigh-the-sin righacht a duthaidhe¹²³) fen do gabail do 7 a cuid do rigacht
10 flaithesa De fa deoigh.

    139. *ET* fos is tresan mallach*tain*-sin tuc C. c. ar Diarmaid mac Cerbaill, anuair ruc se breth 'na ad*haid*¹²³ª) le Finden fan leabar, 7 anuair do marb se mac righ Cond*acht* a Temraigh ar a comairce, tuc cath Cula Dremne do brisedh air 7 tuc rath 7 righe
15 do buain de iarsin 7 tuc a saegal do gearrugad, indus co fuair se o Día bas do tabairt do, amail derb*us* Diarmaid fen isna randaibh-si:

    T*ri* ní do ben dím mo rath,   's tuc me gan righe Temr*ach*:
    mallocht C. c. caidh,   7 escaine Ruadhaín.
    Breth leab*air* C. c.   7 Finden gombinde,
20   dár chan*us* tre mebhul radh,   "re gach leb*ar* a lebhr*án*."

ET as follus duinn asna scelaib-so tuas gorab mogenar ga mbeith bendocht C. c. 7 g*orab* mairg ga mbeth a mallacht.

    140.¹²⁴) Do bi duine airide a n-aimsir C. c. darb ainm an Ser-senach 7 nir maith a gnimartha a tossach a beath*ad*, 7 bá daidbir
25 é a*muil* mebr*aige*s Comgall naemtha air. Acus do bí se la airide ag siub*al* a cuidechta C. c. 7 tuc se a leab*ar* da imchar ina laimh. Acus tainecc do brigh leab*air* C. c. do glacudh do, go bfhuair se grasa ó Dia, indus gor linadh do saidbres saeg*alta* o sin amach é 7 go nderna se aithrige romhór an a pecaib. Acus do bidh
30 a chom*mor*-sin do comartha aicce co ndech*aid* se dá oilithre docum

---

¹²³*leg.* duthaighe.
¹²³ª*leg.* aghaidh.
¹²⁴Based on poem called *Sersenach Coluim Cille*. See *Eriu,* V, Part I-II, p. 14.

And well did Guaire take that counsel, so that there hath never been in Erin a third man of more largesse and more pure of reproach than he, as holy Baithin mac Cuanach hath said in this quatrain:

> "Guaire mac Colmain from the west,
> Cuchulainn, and Colum of the companies.
> These be the three without dispute
> The best of largesse that ever have lived."

And it came to pass by virtue of that blessing that Columcille gave him, and of the counsel that he gave him, that he gat the kingship of Connacht thereafter. For never did Columcille bless any man that he gat not the sovereignty of his land by virtue of that blessing, and his portion also of the Kingdom of God in the end.

139. And it was by virtue of the curse that Columcille laid upon Diarmaid mac Cerbaill the time he gave the judgment in favor of Finnen touching the book, and put to death the son of the King of Connacht at Tara, notwithstanding he was under the safeguard of Columcille, that it befell that he was routed in the battle of Cuil Dremne and his fortune and his sovereignty were taken from him afterward, and his life was shortened, so that he prevailed on God to grant him death, as Diarmaid himself hath said in these quatrains:

> "Three things that took from me my luck,
> And brought me from the kingship of Tara;
> The curse of chaste Columcille
> And the curse of Ruadhan.
>
> The judgment of Columcille's book
> And of excellent Finnen,
> When I spake the false words:
> 'To every book is its transcript.'"

And it is clear to us from the histories above that it was well for him that had the blessing of Columcille, and ill for him that had his curse.

140. There was a certain man in the time of Columcille that was called An Sersenach. And not good had been his deeds at the beginning of his life. And he was a poor man, as holy Comgall telleth of him. And one day he was walking in the fellowship of Columcille, and Columcille gave him his book to bear in hand. And it came to pass by virtue of holding the book of Columcille, that he was given grace of God, so that he was filled with the riches of the world from that time. And he did passing great penance for his sins. And in sign that it was very great he went on a pilgrimage to Rome. And he gave the costs of going to two score

na Romha 7 cotucc se cosdus do .x. enbar 7 do dá .xx. do daeinibh
bochta do bi ag dul dá n-oilethre mar an cedna docum na Roma
7 gan cosdus acu fen. Acus atá Comgall ga mebrugad air nach
raibe a nErinn duine ba saidbhre iná sé tre mirbuilib De 7 C. c.
a fecmais an Mic medha orrderc ga raibe an saidbres mór.

141. Ri do gabustar righi dá cóicedh Muman .i. Aonghas
mac Nadfraich, 7 docondairc a ben aissling ingnath aen do oidhce
.i. dar lé a beith fen taebtrom torruch 7 cuilen ferchon do breith
di 7 a fothracad a lemhnocht, 7 gach inadh a n-Erind a tég-
headh an cuilen ó sin amach do bidh lan do lemhnocht acédoir.
INnisis an righan a haisling don righ 7 rucc an rí fen breth na
haislinge 7 assed adubairt .i. 'Bérair-si mac,' ar se, 7 baistfither
a ngras [fol. 20a] aib Dé hé, 7 biaid sé 'na nech naemtha ag sílad
7 ag senmoír breithre Dé in gach inadh a racha sé ar fud Erenn.
Oir do gell Patraic damh, anuair tucus mo baili fen do .i. Caissel
Mumhan, co mberthá-ssa mac damhsa 7 combeith se 'na nech ro-
naemtha.' Beris an ben-sin righ Muman mac iarsin 7 adubairt
aingel Dé risan sagart do bi ga baisted Náail do tabairt mar
ainm air. Acus ar ndenum ecna 7 leighind don mac-sin an righ,
tainecc an t-aingel cuige 7 adubairt ris·tect mar a raibe uachtaran
7 cend creidme 7 crábaid cleri íarthair domain uili .i. C. c. mac
Feidhlim 7 a comairli do gabáil góa bas 7 fearunn do gabail
uadha a n-inadh a ndingnad sé áitiugad 7 ecluis ina mbeith se ag
molad De.[125])

Gluaísis Naail iarsin 7 cuidechta clerech maille ris do
techt a cend C. c. Acus do bi C. c. anuair-sin 'san inad re n-abartar
Inber Naaili aniugh a crich cineoil Conaill Gulban 7 naim Lethe
Cuind mailli ris, 7 do labair tre spirud faidedórachta 7 assed
adubairt .i. 'Ticfa nech naemtha cucaind aniugh,' ar se, '.i. Naail

---

[125]See Dinneen's *Keating*, III, pp. 25-6, for a beautiful story concerning this Aonghus.

and ten poor folk that were fain to go likewise on a pilgrimage to Rome, but had not the costs. And Comgall saith of him that through the miracles of God and Columcille there was not in Erin a man of greater riches than he, save that Mac Meda of great fame that had great possessions.

XII

OF THE MIRACLES AND PROPHECIES OF COLUMCILLE AND OF HIS REVEALING OF SECRET THINGS

141. There was a king hight Aongus mac Nadfraich that had the sovereignty of Munster. And one night his wife had an avision. Her seemed that she was heavy and great with child, and that she brought forth a whelp and bathed him in new milk. And in what place soever in Erin that whelp went from that time, the place was straightway filled with new milk. The Queen told her avision to the King and the King himself did rede the avision and he said:

"Thou shalt bear a son," saith he, "and he shall be baptized in the graces of God, and he shall become a saint, sowing the word of God and preaching it in every place whereas he goeth throughout Erin. For Padraic ensured me when I did give him my stead, Cashel of Munster, that thou shouldst bear me a son, and that he should be a very holy man."

And thereafter the wife of the King of Munster did bear a son. And an angel of God bade the priest that baptized him give him the name Naail. And when that royal boy was grounded in knowledge and learning, an angel came to him and told him to go to the Master Cleric of all the Western World and the Lord of Faith and Piety, to wit, Columcille son of Fedlimid. And he bade him follow the counsel of Columcille till death, and obtain land from him whereon to build a dwelling and a church wherein to praise God. Then went Naail with a company of clerics in his fellowship to seek Columcille. And Columcille was at that time in the place that is now called Inber Naaile, in the territory of the clan of Conall Gulban, and the saints of Leth Cuinn in his fellowship. And he prophesied and said:

"There shall come to us this day," saith he, "a holy man, to wit, Naail son of the King of Munster, and angels of God in his fellowship. And I shall give him this land, and we two shall bless it and from him it shall have its name forever."

mac righ Mumhan 7 aingle De 'na coimhidecht, 7 dober-sa an
ferond-sa dó 7 bendeochad-sa 7 é fen and 7 bad uadh-san
ainmneochar go brath aris é.' Do fírad, umorro, an faidhedórachtsin C. c. .i. tainic Naail an lá-sin fen 'na cend, 7 dob follus do
5 C. c. 7 dá naemhaib aingli De a coimhidecht an macaímh naemtasin ag techt do láthair dó. Acus failtighis C. c. reme 7 tuc pocc dó.
Acus do leicc Naaile ar a gluínib a fíadnaise C. c. é 7 do fiarfaig
de cait a bfuighedh se ferund a ndingnad se aitiugad 7 eclus
a mbeith se ag moladh De, amail adubramar romaind. 'San inadh-
10 sa fen,' ar C. c. Beanduigis C. c. 7 Naail an t-inadh-sin iar sin,
7 toiligis do Naail comnaide do denamh and. Gonadh Inber
Naaile a ainm ó sin ille.

Ba nair umorro le Naail C. c. 7 a naeim do beith gan
biadh aige tar eis baili do gabail uadhu, 7 ba nair le C. c. esiun
15 do beith gan biadh an céd oidhce tainic sé 'na chend, 7 do cuiretar fa umhla ar in fhairge a ndil ésc do chur a tír cuca cor lín
sí an tráigh do bí a comghar doibh d'iasc, 7 do cruindighetar
an méid ba lór leo do gainemh na trágha íarom, 7 do benduighetar é co ndernadh plúr de, go raibe a ndil pluír 7 eisc ag
20 C. c. 7 ag Naail con a naemhaibh an oidhce-sin, 7 cor moradh ainm
Dé 7 Coluimb cille 7 Naail de soin.

142.[126]) Fechtus eli da ndechaid C. c. 7 Comghall naemtha a n-aimsir samraidh do radh a trath isna dumhachaib ata re coiss
na fairge a Ciandachta Glinde gemhin do choir Droma cet, 7
25 tuccadh uisce dá n-innsaigid as tobar aírithe do bi laim ríu d'indladh a lamh ass. Acus do labair C. c. tre spirud faidhedorachta
7 assed adubairt: 'An tobar asa tainic an t-uisce ud,' ar se, 'ticfa
aimser and 7 bad graineamail lesna dainib a ól nó indladh ass
mar uisce nglan.' Do fhíarfaig Comghall cret é an t-adbhur
30 fa mbeith se mar sin. Adubairt C. c. go tibradís a braitri fén 7
braitri Comgaill cath dá celi timcell an tobair-sin 7 co muirfidhe
nech airithe re mbeith a pairt fen isan tobur-sa 7 co truaillfed fuil
an fhir-sin 7 fuil a muirfide do dainib eli gacha taebha de a
uisce, 7 adubairt co madh le Domnall mac Aedha mic Ainmirech
35 doberthai an cath-sin. Acus ata Finden naemtha do bí 'na ancaire
aimser foda a mainestir Muighe Coscaín[127]) ga mebrugad coraibe se
fen a fiadhnaisi an catha-sin ogá cur 7 go faca sé an corp-sin
isan tobur, amail adubairt C. c. Acus nír léir uisci and o imarcaigh
na fola, 7 fós atá se ga mebrugad co ndechaid sé fén d'indesin scel

---

[126]Taken literally from Adamnan. See Reeves' *Adam.*, pp. 91-7.
[127]Adamnan has *Finanus . . . iuxta Roboreti monasterium Campi* (which Reeves identifies as Durrow, *ibid.*, p. 96).

And that prophecy of Columcille's was fulfilled, which is to say, Naail came to him that day. And it was clear to Columcille and to his holy companions that angels of God were with the holy youth as he approached him. And Columcille bade him welcome and kissed him. And Naail fell on his knees before Columcille and asked him where he should get land whereon to make a dwelling and a church wherein he might praise God as we have said toforehand.

"In this very place," saith Columcille.

Then Columcille and Naail blessed that place. And Columcille suffered Naail to make a dwelling there. And Inber Naaile is its name from that day.

It was shame to Naail that Columcille and his saints should be without food when he had been given a stead by them, and it was shame to Columcille that Naail should be without food the first night he had come to him. And they put the sea under bonds to send to land enough fish to satisfy them, so that the sea filled the strand beside them with fish. And they assembled then as much of the sand of the beach as seemed sufficient to them, and blessed it, and it was made flour. So that Columcille and Naail and their saints had enough of flour and fish that night, so that the God's name and Columcille's and Naail's were magnified thereby.

142. Another time that Columcille and holy Comgall went in the summer season to say their office on the sand dunes by the sea in the Ciannachta of Glenn Gemin, fast beside Druim Ceat, there was brought them water from a certain well hard by for to wash their hands. And Columcille prophesied and said in this wise:

"The well from whence this water came," saith he, "there shall come a time when folk shall be loth to drink it or to wash therein as in clean water."

Then Comgall asked wherefore it should be so. And Columcille said that his kinsmen and Comgall's should do battle with each other around the well, and there should be slain at that well a certain man that was dear to him. And the blood of that man should defile the water, and the blood of others that should be killed on every side of him. And he said that by Domnall mac Aeda son of Ainmire that battle should be made. And holy Finnen that was long time an hermit in the monastery of Mag Coscáin saith that he was in sight of the battle, and he saw the body in the well as Columcille had said. And for the exceeding quantity of blood the water was not visible. And he saith moreover that he went to tell the tidings of that battle to the holy and

an catha sin do manch*aib* naemtha roaesda do bi 'san eclais re n-
abur*tar* Camass Comghaill 7 cor-indesi*ter* dó co ndubairt C. c. re
Comghall 'na fiadhnaisi fen co tiub*ar*tai an cath sin mar sin; cor
mora*tar* le celi ainm De 7 C. c. de sin.

143. Fecht eli da raibe C. c. a n-Druim Cet ag síl*ad* 7 ag
senmoír breit*hri* De do cách, 7 dorinne se moran do mirbuil*ib*
and .i. doberedh sé a suili do dainib dalla 7 a cossa do dainib
bacacha 7 esdecht do bodhruib; 7 fos doberedh se a slainte da
gach duine da ticeadh cuicce o gach uile eslainte da mbidh orra
ona laimh do tocbail os a cinn nó ó uisce coisrectha do crathad
orra nó on arán 7 ón tsaland do beanduig*ed* se do caitemh doib
nó ó imel a edaigh do glacadh, 7 do lab*air* sé tre spir*ud* fáid-
etorachta andsin 7 assed adubairt, gerb aidbsech le cách a nderna
se do mirbuil*ib* an lá-sin, co ticf*ad* aimser eli a ndenadh sé mirbuil*edha* b*ad* mo *ná* a nderna se an uair-sin 'san inadh-sin fen. Acus
do firadh sin, amail indeosus mordail Droma Cet 'sa leabhur-sa
feín [*fol.* 20b].

144.¹²⁸) Fechtas eili do ullmaigh esp*oc* naemtha, dárbh ainm
Conall, flegh fa comair C. c., 7 tainic C. c. do caith*em* na fleighe-
sin 7 moran do dainib naemtha eli maille ris. Acus ar techt dó ar
faithce an baili-sin a raibe Conall, ruc les do bendugad na flege
é, 7 mar dob ail les a bendugad, do fech se ar cuid airithe di 7
do fiarf*aig* cia he an nech trocairech dorinde trocairi arna bochtaib
ag tabairt choda don bíadh 7 don digh-sin doib ler tarraing
se trocairi De air fen. ET do fech sé arin cuid eli don fhl*eid*
7 adubairt ná b*ud* eídir les fen a bendugad. Oir gor duine
ecnaidhe sandt*ach* tuc do Conall í 7 *nó* go nder*nadh* aitrighi a
pecadh na sainte nach bendeob*ad* 7 nach caithf*ed* sé enní da
tuc se uadha. Acus ar ndul na mbriathar-sin fa cach, do léicc
an duine sin ar a gluínib hé a fiadhnaise C. c., 7 dob é sin
Colm*án* mac Aedha, 7 do bendaigh C. c. e, 7 tainic do brigh an
bendaighte-sin nar tagaill se an pecadh-sin na sainte o sin amach.
ET fos ar cluinsin na mbriathar c*ed*na-sin don duine eile adubrumar romaind tuc an bíadh dona bochtaib, do leic ar a gluínib
a fiadnaise C. c. e 7 do cuir C. c. pecadh airide 'na aghaidh do
bi go folaigh*tech* aige nach raibhi afhis ag duine 'sa bith air 7
adubairt ris aithrighe do denam and. Acus do gell sesin go
nding*nad* se sin 7 do benduigh C. c. e, 7 tainic do brigh an
benduighte-sin nach tarla 'sa pecadh cedna ó sin suas é. Corub mar
sin do shaer C. c. an días-sin ona pecuib folaightecha do bi orra;
gor mórudh ainm De 7 Coluimb cille de sin.

¹²⁸Literally in Adamnan. See Reeves' *Adam.*, pp. 97-9.

passing ancient monks that were in the church that is called Camas Comgaill. And they told him that Columcille had told Comgall when they were with him that the battle should be fought in that wise. And they magnified together God's name and Columcille's therefor.

143. Another time Columcille was in Druim Ceat, sowing the word of God and preaching it to all. And he did many miracles there. He gave their eyes to blind folk and their feet to the lame and their hearing to the deaf. And he gave health moreover to all that came to him, from every sickness that lay on them, by raising his hand above their heads or by shaking holy water upon them. Or he healed them in this wise that they ate the bread and salt he blessed for them, or by this that they touched the hem of his garment. And he spake prophesying, and said that albeit exceeding great seemed to them the miracles he had done that day, there should come another time that he should do miracles in that place greater than those he had done at that time. And this came to pass, as the Assembly of Druim Ceat will set forth in this same book.

144. Another time a holy bishop that was called Conall prepared a feast for Columcille. And Columcille came to partake of the feast. And much holy folk were with him besides. And when he had come to the green in that place, Conall brought him to bless the feast, for it was his desire that Columcille should bless it. Then looked he on a part thereof, and asked who was the man of bounty that had shown mercy to the poor, giving them of food and of drink and thereby drawing the mercy of God upon himself.

And he looked upon the other part of the feast, and said that it was not possible for him to bless it. It was a man of learning that was a miser that had given it to Conall. And until he should do penance for his sin of covetousness, Columcille would not bless or partake of aught that he had given. And on those words going about, the man fell on his knees before Columcille. And he was Colman mac Aeda. And Columcille blessed him and it came to pass by virtue of that blessing that he did never more that sin of covetousness. And also that other man of the which we have made mention toforehand that he gave food to the poor, fell on his knees before Columcille. And Columcille cast up to him a certain sin that he had hidden and whereof no man at all had knowledge. And he bade him do penance therefor. And the man promised that he would do it. And Columcille blessed him. And it came to pass by virtue of that benediction that he fell not into that same sin from that time. And in this wise did Columcille save those twain from their hidden sins, and God's name and Columcille's were magnified thereby.

145.¹²⁹) Fechtus do Columb cille a n-inadh airide, 7 ruc saíri an domnaigh air 7 docuaidh d'estect aifrind a máinestir do bí dá chóir re n-abarthar Trefhoíd aniugh. Acus ar ndul astech dó, docondarc se sagart ag rádha an aifrind, 7 do bi an sagart fen cráibthech do reir barumhla caich. Acus iar na fhaicsin sin do C. c., adubairt do guth mór: 'Ata ni glan 7 ní nemglan fáré a celi anos, oir dochím an tsacramaint naemtha ga glacudh 7 ga caithemh ag an tsherbfhogantaid ga fuil cogus nemglan ara fuil pecadh folaightech nach derna se aithrighe and fos.' Acus ar cloisdin na m-briathar-sin da raibe astigh, do bidhgatar co mór. Acus ar crichnugad an aifrind don tsagart, do leic ar a gluinib a fiadnaise C. c. e, 7 do doirt a dera 7 dorinde aithrighe rogher, 7 do cintaigh é fein do Dia 7 do C. c. 'sa pecadh-sin 7 do adaimh co nderna se é. Acus ar faicsin umla 7 aithrighe an tsagairt do C. c., do bendaigh sé é. Acus tainic do brig an bendaighte-sin gor maith Día a pechad dó 7 go raibe se 'na óglach maith do Dia 7 do Columb cille ó sin amach.¹³⁰).

146. Fechtus do Padraic 'san inadh ren abartar an Aird a Ciannachta Glinde gemhin, 7 do bendaig se 'san inadh airithe ren abartar Dun cruin 7 dorinde duirrthech and. Acus do fhurail se ar cerd Connla cás onórach do tindscna dó a mbeidís na soisceil 7 moran do taisib na naemh a coiméd aige. Acus sul do cuir se crich ar an obair sin, testa se feín 7 do bí sin 'na doilghes mor ar Patraic. Oir ni raibhe 'sa mbith cerd ba commaith ris. Tainic an t-aingel cuige 7 adubairt ris gan dobron do beith air 7 nach dó do toilig Día crich do cur ar in obair sin acht do mac na bethad suthaine .i. do C. c. A cenn morain do blíadnaib iarsin, tainic C. c. 'san inadh cédna 7 fuair se an obair-sin anullam and, 7 ni fuair se cerd a n-Erind do críchnóbadh í mar bud mían les. Acus dochuaidh ar in tumba inar cuiredh Condla cerd 7 do fhurail a fhosclad, 7 do cruindigh a cnamha fare celi 7 do bendaigh 7 do coisric iad 7 adubairt: 'A n-ainm Ihsv Críst, ericch o marbhaib, a Connla cerd'. Acus do eric acédoir le breithir C. c. a fiadnaise caich uili amail do eireochad se as a codladh, 7 do bi sé beo deich' mbliadna .xx. iarsin 7 ruccad cland dó. Conadh ar a slicht ataid cland cnaimhsighe trena beith fen ina cnamhaibh aimsir foda

---

[129] Literally in Adamnan. *Ibid.*, pp. 76-7.
[130] See *V. S. H.*, (ed. by Plummer) II, p. 102, § 14, for a similar story.

145. On a time that Columcille was in a certain place and it came the feast of Sunday, he went to hear the mass in the monastery nigh hand, that is now called Trefhóid. And on entering in he beheld the priest saying the mass. And in the belief of all that priest was a holy man. And when Columcille beheld, he said with a great voice,

"Now is a thing pure with a thing unpure together, each with other in fellowship, for I see the Holy Sacrament touched and partaken of by a servant that hath a conscience unclean, and on him hidden sin for the which he hath not yet done penance."

And on hearing these words those that were within were adrad passing sore. And when the priest had finished the mass, he fell on his knees afore Columcille, and he wept and repented bitterly. And he accused him of his sin to God and Columcille, and he confessed that he had done it. And when Columcille perceived the humility and contrition of the priest, he blessed him. And it came to pass by reason of that blessing that God forgave him his sin, and he became a good servant to God and to Columcille from that time.

146. On a time that Padraic was in a place called the Height in the Ciannachta of Glenngemin, he blessed a certain spot that is called Dun Cruin. And there he built an oratory. And he caused Connla the Craftsman to make a precious casket for him, where he might hold in safeguard the gospels and many relics of the saints. And ere he had made an end of that work he died. And this was a great grief to Padraic, for there was not in the world his like of a smith. And there came to him an angel and bade him be not sorrowful, for it was not for him that God had willed that work should be completed, but for the son of Eternal Life, to wit, for Columcille.

And many years thereafter Columcille came to that same place. And he found that work unfinished there. And he gat not in Erin a smith to finish it as he would fain have had it. And he went to the tomb wherein Connla the Craftsman was laid, and he let open the tomb. And he assembled the bones of Connla together and blessed and hallowed them.

And he said, "In the name of Jesu Christ, arise from the dead, Connla the Smith."

And at the word of Columcille straightway he rose up in the presence of all, as he might rise up from sleep. And he lived twenty years after that, and he begat children. And of his seed is the clan Cnaimhsige, by reason that he had been a long time in bones (*cnamaib*) ere he was brought back to life. And Columcille gave the work that Padraic had begun to Connla the Craftsman that he might finish it for him. And it is the Shrine of Columcille to-day. And Columcille laid therein many

riana aithbeougad, 7 tucc C. c. ar cerd Condla an obair-sin do
tindscain Patraic do crichnugad dó feín. Gonadh í scrin C. c.
aniugh hí. Acus do cuir C. c. morán do taisib naemh Erenn indti.
Acus aderth*ar* cor cuir se lethfolt Muiri innti. Acus do bí nech
naemhtha 'san inadh ren abartar Ath Lunga 'sa tir-sin fen darb
ainm Tice, 7 docuaid C. c. d'iarraidh choda dá taisibh air dá cur 'sa
scrin 7 adubairt Tige nach tibr*ad*. Adubairt C. c. tre fherg co
tiubr*ad* dá m*adh* olc maith les é. Do imtig C. c. asin mbaili íarsin,
[*fol*. 21a] 7 teid Tige d'indl*ad* a lamh a sruth do bí a comgar
dá ecluis fen. Acus ag buaín a lamh*ainde* de do indladh a lamh,
do thuit ordóc a laimhe desi de isin lamhain*n*. Gonadh Ath
na hordoige ainm an átha ósin ille. Do aithin Tige gorub tre
mirbuil*ibh* C. c. do imth*ig* sin air 7 do len é 7 tuc an ordóg
dó 7 do cuir C. c. 'sa scrín í 7 do marb Aedh mac Ainmirech .i.
rí Erind an duth*aig*-sin na harda do Dia 7 do C. c. tresna mirbuil*ibh* mora-sin dorinde se indti. Gonadh e sin termond Arda meg
Gillagai*n* aniugh, 7 isí an scrín is airdmhind do C. c. and osin
ille ag denum fert 7 mirbhol.

147.¹³¹) Fechtus do C. c. a n-oilen áiridhe ar loch Cé a Con-
dachta tan*ic* file 7 duine el*adh*n*a* dá indsuig*idh* 7 do
bi tamall ag comr*ádh* ris 7 do imd*ig* uad íarsin. Acus dob ingnadh
lesna manchaib nár íar*r* C. c. ní dá eladhai*n* fen ar an file-sin mar
do íarrad se ar gach nduine eludna eli da tic*ced* cuice 7 do
fhiarf*aig*etar de cred fa nderna se sin. Frecrais C. c. iad 7 assed
adubairt, nar cnesta 7 nar imchub*aid* dó fen neithin*na* solásacha
d'iarr*aid* ar duine ga raibe dolás a ngar do. Acus adubairt nach
fada go faicfidís duine ag techt dá indesin doib co muirf*ide* an file-
sin. Nir mór gur dhel*aig* deredh an comráidh-sin ríu anuair
docualatar glaedh a p*urt* na hindse-sin 7 adubairt C. c. corub lé
scel*a* marbtha an file tain*ic* an duine dorinde an glaedh-sin. Acus
do fíradh sin uile amail adubairt C. c.; gor morad ainm De 7
Coluimb cille de sin.

148.¹³²) Fectus tainic esp*oc* airithe as an Mum*ain* aníar ar cuairt
mar a raibe C. c., 7 tucc an umla air a ceilt ar cách corb espoc
é 7 do indis gor shagart é. Gerb edh, nirb éidir enní do ceilt
ar C. c., 7 do furail se ar in espoc dul do rádha an aifr*ind*. Acus
do tindscain an t-espoc an t-aifrend iarsin, 7 ar naemadh na
sacramainti do 7 anuair dob ail les a roind, do ghoir se ar
C. c. cuice. Acus do erich C. c. go hum*al* docum na haltóra 7 do
fech sé 'na agaidh ar an espoc 7 do labair ris 7 assed adubairt:

---

¹³¹Literally in Adamnan. See Reeves' *Adam.*, pp. 79-80.
¹³²Literally in *Adamnan, ibid.*, pp. 85-6.

relics of the saints of Erin, and it is said that he put therein the side hair of the Virgin Mary.

And there was a holy man in a place in that land hight Ath Lunga, and his name was Tice. And Columcille went to require of him some of his relics to put in the shrine. And Tice said he would not give them. Columcille said that he should give them whether him were lief or loth. And Columcille left the place. Anon went Tice to wash his hands in the stream fast by the church, and when he took off his gloves to wash his hands, his thumb fell from his right hand into the glove. And hence Ath na Hordoige (Ford of the Thumb) is the name of that ford from that time to this. Then Tice saw that this had happened him through a miracle of Columcille. And he followed him and gave him the thumb. And Columcille put it in the shrine.

And Aed mac Ainmirech granted that land of the Height to God and to Columcille for the great miracle he had done there. And that is the sanctuary of Mac Gilligan's Height today. And this shrine is the chief relic of Columcille in the place from that time to this, doing wonders and miracles.

147. On a time Columcille was in a certain island in Loch Ce in Connacht, and there came to him a poet and man of learning that remained for a while in converse with him, and then went away. And the monks marvelled that Columcille had not asked him to show forth his poetic art, for he had been wont to ask this of all the men of learning that came to him. And they asked him wherefore he had done in this wise. Columcille answered them and said that it beseemed him not and was not fitting for him to ask solace of one that was nigh sorrow. And he said it would not be long ere they should see one coming to tell them that the poet had been slain. Scarce had they understood the last of these words when they heard a shout in the port of the island. And Columcille said that the man that gave that shout was come with tidings of the death of the poet. And it was proved true as Columcille had said, so that God's name and Columcille's were magnified thereby.

148. On a time there came a certain bishop from the west of Munster to visit Columcille. And his lowliness caused him to conceal from all that he was a bishop. And he said that he was a priest. Howbeit it was not possible to hide aught from Columcille. And he asked the bishop to say the mass. Thereupon the bishop began the mass. And when he had consecrated the Sacrament and was in point to divide it, he called Columcille to him. And Columcille went up humbly to the altar and looked into the visage of the bishop, and spake to him and said:

'Go mbendaighi Críst tú, a brathair grádhaigh,' ar se, '7 roind an tsacramaint ó ata cumhachta a ronda agad. *ET* aithnim-se anos corab espoc tú, 7 cred far ceiles tú fen orainne custrást 7 co tiubhramaís honóir feín duid da n-aithnidhmís corub espoc tú'. Acus ar crichnugad an aifrind, do adaimh an t-espoc a fiadnaise caich uile co raibe an fhirinde ag C. c. 7 corb espoc é fen. Ar cloisdin na mbriathar-sin don popul 7 da raibe do lathair an uair-sin, do molatar Dia 7 C. c. ina oibrighthibh.

149. Fectus do C. c. ag siubal re cois na habonn re n-abartar an Boind, 7 tarla a cenn rig Érenn é dochuaid re tesbaigh na haimsire do snamh 7 d'onfaisi ar an abaind sin. Acus aderaid aroili co mbad é Conghalach mac Maeilmithidh ba ri Erenn an uair sein. Acus másse ní fhaghaim-si corub lucht enaimsire da celi C. c. 7 Congalach.¹³³) Gidhedh, gebé ri do bi and, nir maith a betha 7 do bo mitrócairech e, 7 doconncus do C. c. co roibe bas anma 7 cuirp afoccus dó 7 do bí se ga smuainedh cinnus do shaerfad se anam an righ ar pianaib ifrinn. Acus as amlaid docondcus dó .i. nech naemtha do bi faris darbh ainm Baithín do cur d'íarraid dérce air, indus co mbad tslighe les fen dá fhaghail o Dia trocaire do denamh ar anam an righ dá tuccad se an dérc-sin uadha. Téid Baithín d'iarraid dérce arin righ, 7 ni hé amhain nach bfhuair sé sin uadha, acht do bhagair se a marbadh 7 a cur docum bais. Tainic Baithín ar a ais mar a raibhe C. c. 7 do indes sé sin dó. Acus ba truagh le C. c. an ní-sin 7 docuaid mar a raibhe an rí 7 do íarr déirc air. Acus do gab ferg mor an ri ris 7 dob ail les bás d'imirt air. Acus mar nach raibe arm eli aige re ndenadh urchóid do, do cuaidh se fai an abhainn d'íarraid cloiche do telgfad se ris 7 nir eirich se no gor baithed e. Acus do teich C. c. reme ar na fhaicsin sin dó, 7 tarla a cos a luib na srainge sida do bí 'san édach becc purpair do cuir an ri de reme-sin ag dol aran snamh dó. 'Cred fá mbereann tu an t-edach beg-sin let,' ar Baithín, 'anuair do bi an rí ag bagar ar marbtha gan adbhur. IS demhin go muirbfad se sind da faicedh sé lind é.' 'Biaidh sé a ndéirc agam-sa uadh,' ar C. c. 'Dar linde ni cosmail sin do dul a tarba dó,' ar Baithín, 'oir ní da thoil fen dober se duid e.' 'Na habair,' ar C. c., 'gebe deirc dober duine da deoin fen uadha, dober Dia a luach dó, 7 ni furail lemsa go fhuighe me ó Día, gingora fíu me a faghail uadha, an deirc-si do benus [fol. 21b] dá aindeoín don righ a dul a tarbha mhoír dó amail doberadh sé da thoil fén uadha hi.' Do féch C. c. 'na diaidh íarsin, 7 do condaic se cruindiugad romor

---

[133]O'D. is correct. Conghalach was slain at Ard Macha A. D. 954 (F. M.).

"May Christ bless thee, dear brother," saith he, "and do thou divide the sacrament, for it is thou that shouldst divide it. And I see now that thou art a bishop. Why hast thou hid thee from us till now? We had given thee honor befitting thee, had we known thou wert a bishop."

And when he had finished the mass, the bishop confessed afore all that Columcille had spoken truth, and that he was a bishop. When the folk that were then in that place heard those words, they praised God and Columcille for his works.

149. On a time Columcille was walking beside a stream that was called the Boyne, and by adventure he met the King of Erin that for the heat of the weather had gone to swim and dive in the river. Some say it was Conghlach mac Maeilmithidh that was King of Erin in that time, but though it may be so, I have not found that Columcille and Conghlach were of the same age with each other. Howbeit, whatever king it was, he was of evil life, and hard of heart. And Columcille saw that the King was nigh death, body and soul. And he considered how he might save his soul from the pains of hell. And he resolved to send an holy man hight Baithin that was in his fellowship to ask alms of him, that it might be a means for him to prevail on God to have mercy on the King's soul if he gave alms. Anon went Baithin to ask alms of the King. And he gat naught of him. Thereat did the King make threat to slay him and put him to death. Baithin repaired to Columcille and told this to him. And Columcille was grieved at this thing and he went himself to the King and asked alms of him. And the King waxed exceeding wroth and would have killed him. And since he had no weapon wherewith to do him harm, he went down under the water to find a stone to cast at him. And he rose not again until he was drowned. And when Columcille saw that, he fled. And by adventure his foot caught in the loop of a silken cord that was on the little purple garment the King had done off afore he had gone swimming.

"Why dost thou take with thee the little garment?" saith Baithin. "The King did make threat to kill us without cause, and he would surely kill us if he saw that with us."

"I shall keep it as an alms from him," saith Columcille.

"I deem it will scarce profit him" saith Baithin, "for not of his own will did he give it to us."

"Say not so," saith Columcille, "Whatever alms a man giveth of his own will, God giveth him reward therefor. But I shall not be content, save God grant me, albeit unworthy, that this alms that I took from the king malgre his head, shall profit him as much as if of his own choice he had given it."

Then Columcille looked behind him, and he saw a great assembling of devils above the stream and on both sides thereof. And he told Baith-

ag na díablaib os cind na haband 7 gacha taebha dí, 7 do inniss
se do Baithín cor baithedh an rí 7 go rabatar na diabail ag píanadh
a anma. 'Faicem anois,' ar Baithin, 'cindus rachass an deirc ud
do benadh dá ainneoín don ríogh a tarbha dó.' Docuaid C. c.
fana corp fen 'san aiér anairde do cathugad ris na diablaibh fa
an anam-sin amail aingel nó anum glan ag nach beith a corp
uime. Acus do bí ag cathugad go laídir ríu 7 do fiarfaigher (sic)
na diabail de cred í an coír do bí aige cuca fen do buain an anma-
sin dib 7 nach derna se maith ar bith an fad do bi sé 'sa saeghal
do rachad a tarbha dá anum. 'Atá deirc agamsa uadha,' ar C. c.
'Ni dlighend se luáighidecht ar son na dérce nach dá thoil fen
tuc se uadha í,' ar na díabail. 'Bidh afhiss agaibh-se,' ar Colum
cille, 'gebe ar bith cor ara fhuighe óclach Día ní o duine corub
fiu maithes Dia luaigidecht do tabairt dó ar a shon sin.'
Do claídh C. c. na díabla 'sa cathugadh-sin indus co bfhuair
sé o Día, do brigh na dérce-sin do ben sé dá aindeoin don righ,
anam an rígh do chor ina curp fen arís innus co ndernadh se
aithrige 7 leoarghnimh ina pecadh 7 co mbeith se 'na oclach maith
do Día 7 do C. c. ó sin súas. Gonadh e an righ-sin enduine do
slánaiged d'aindeoin an duine fen riam. As follas duinn ass so
corb imarcach an cin 7 an grádh do bí ag Día ar C. c. anuair tuc
se cumhachta dó ar in ní-si do denamh, 7 co bfuil scribtha nach
slánaighend Dia fen duine ar bith gan congnamh on duine fen
ina slánugad.

150. Fectus do C. c. ag radh a tráth 7 a urnaidhe 'san inadh
airide re n-abartar Tulach na salm don taeb toir do Cill mic
Nenain, 7 do léicc sé ar a gluínibh e 7 do bí ag guide De co
duthrachtach, 7 do íarr tri hathcuingheadha ar Día .i. gan duine
ar bith do breith a enich go bráth, 7 grádh De do beith go
coimhnaitach gan claechlód ina chroidhe, 7 sith suthain do bheith
iter a braithribh fen .i. cineol Conaill Gulban, 7 an burba 7 an
merdhacht do bí indta do chur ar cul 7 cundlucht 7 cendsacht
do tabairt doib na n-inadh-sin an cein do beith sé fen buidhech
dib, 7 anuair do tuillfidís a dimdha, galur 7 gorta do beith acu.

in that the King was drowned and the devils were in point to torment his soul.

"Let us see now," saith Baithin, "how these alms we gat from the king malgre his head will avail him."

Then in his own body did Columcille rise up into the upper air to do battle with the demons for that soul, as he were an angel or a pure soul that dwelt not in a body. And he fought strongly with them. And the demons asked him what right had he to take from them that soul that had never done aught good for its profit the while it was in life.

"I have an alms of his," saith Columcille.

"No reward doth he merit for an alms that he gave malgre his head," say the devils.

"Wit ye well," saith Columcille, "in what way soever God's servant may get aught from a man, the goodness of God doth grant him reward therefor."

Then did Columcille vanquish the devils in that fight and thus he prevailed on God that by virtue of the alms that he had from the King malgre his head, the King's soul was returned again into his body, that he might take him to penance and good works for his sin, and be a good servant to God and Columcille forever. And in this wise that King was the only man that was saved ever malgre his head. It is clear to us from this that Columcille was to God exceeding lief and dear, since He gave him power to do this thing, albeit it is written that God never saved any without help from him that would be saved.

XIII

OF THE LABORS OF COLUMCILLE IN THE WEST OF ERIN AND OF SUNDRY MATTERS

150. On a time that Columcille was saying his hours and his prayers in a place that is called Tulach na Salm to the east of Cill mic Nenain, having fallen on his knees he was beseeching God fervently. And he was asking of Him three gifts: that to none should he ever forfeit his hospitality; that the love of God should be forever unchanging in his heart; and that there should be peace forever among his kinsmen the clan of Conall Gulban, and that He should put away the folly and madness that were in them and give them prudence and mildness in their stead, so long as they should be in his favor. But when they should do him displeasure they should be sick and anhungered.

151. IS andsin do fhíarfaigetar na naimh do bi afochair C. c. .i. Baithin 7 Brughach 7 Ternóg scela derigh an domain de. Do caí C. c. go gér 7 do laphair ris na naemaibh-sin 7 assed adubairt: 'Do combuaidhred mo chíall 7 mo chroide co romhór,' ar se, 'tresin taisbenadh tuccad damh ar na scela-sin do fiarfaigebhair dím, oir dochiter damh go ndingnaid lucht deirich aimsiri foslongport im chellaib 7 co muirbfither mo manaigh 7 co mbrisfid mo comairce 7 co sladfuid 7 co saíreochaid mo reilge 7 co n-airgfid mh'árais.' 'Truagh sin,' ar Baithín. 'Fír ón,' ar cach.

'Acht ge truag lemsa sud,' ar C. c., 'is truaide lem na dighailtais doghena Día indta ina íad .i. dobera sé plaidh 7 gorta 7 galair imdha eli ar dainib 7 ar cethra tríthu, 7 tiucfa ferg Dé co himarcach re lucht na haimsiri-sin, indus co muirbfid na mic a n-aithri 7 co muirbfid na braithri aroili 7 nach bia urraim agan ingin don mathair no ag an tshóssar don tshendsir.

152.¹³⁴) Teid C. c. íarsin a crich Brethfne 7 do bendaigh sé inis mór Locha gamhna. Téid iarsin tarsin amainn síar 7 do bendaigh Ess mac nEirc ar Buill, amail do tarrngair Patraic co mbendóchad se ann 7 do fagaib nech naemtha dá mhuindtir and .i. Daconna a ainm.

153. Téid C. c. iarsin o Ess mac nEirc tar Corrslíabh budh thuaid cor cumdaigh ecluis a n-Imlech foda a Corann don taeb thíarthuaid do Tulaig seghsa, 7 do fágaib nech naemtha da muindtir indte .i. Enna mac Nuadain 7 fagbhus buaidh n-aénaigh ar fer a inaidh do grés.

154. Téid C. c. iarsin co Druim na macraidhe a tír Oililla ris a ráiter Druim C. c. aniugh, 7 dorinde senmoír da braithribh and .i. do clainn maicne Oililla mic Echach muighmhedhóin 7 tuc moran docum creidimh 7 docum crabhaidh dibh [fol. 22a].

Do idhbratar an t-inadh-sin dó 7 do cumdaigedh ecluis les and 7 adubairt co mbeith sonus 7 onoir uirri co brath. Acus do fhagaib an glassan .i. a chloc fen indte 7 ro fagaib nech naemtha da muindtir indte .i. Findbharr a ainm, 7 do cuir sé cros 'na sesamh ris an eclais anoirdhes 7 adubairt an fad do mairfed an cros-sin 7 an glassán, co mbíadh sonas indte; ut dixit C. c.:

Mo cros a n-Druim mocroide,   imgha aingel nosadrann;
mochen bís na haice-si.   's anaice glassain Findbharr.

---

¹³⁴See O. I. L. in *Lis. Lives*, p. 178, 1. 996.

151. Then the saints that were in his fellowship, to wit, Baithin and Brugach and Ternog, inquired of him tidings of the end of the world. Then did Columcille weep right bitterly, and he spake to those holy men and said:

"My mind and heart have been sore troubled," saith he, "by an advision that hath been given me of these tidings ye have inquired of me, for me seemeth at the end of time men will besiege my churches, and they will kill my monks and violate my sanctuary, and ravage and desecrate my churchyards and dismantle my dwelling places."

"Alas for that," saith Baithin.

"Alas in sooth for that," say all.

"But though these things be grievous to me," said Columcille, "yet more grievous to me is the punishment that God shall visit on them therefor. For famine and hunger and many distempers shall He bring upon men, and upon cattle by reason of men. And the wrath of God shall fall exceedingly upon men in that time, so that sons shall slay fathers, and one kinsman shall slay another, and daughters shall not be obedient to mothers nor young men to ancient."

152. Then went Columcille into the region of Brefny. And he blessed Inis Mor of Loch Gamhna. Then went he across the river westward. And he blessed Ess mac nEirc on the Boyle, as Padraic had foretold he should bless it. And he left there a holy man of his household, hight Daconna.

153. Then goeth Columcille from Ess mac nEirc over Corrslíab to the north, and he builded a church in Imlech Foda in Corann to the northwest of Tulach Segsa. And he left there a holy man of his household, Enna mac Nuadain. And he left the supremacy in assembly to his successors forever.

154. Then goeth Columcille to Druim na Macraidhe in the land of Ailill, which is called Druim Colaimcille today. And he preached to his kinsmen in that place, to wit, to the seed of Ailill mac Echach Muigmedóin. And he brought many of them to the Faith and to good works. And they bestowed on him that place, and there was builded by them a church, and he said there should be joy and honor therein forever. And therein he left the Glassan, his stone, and a holy man of his household hight Findbharr. And he raised a cross to the southeast of the church. And as he said that so long as that cross and the Glassan were there, there should be happiness in that church. And Columcille said:

> "My cross in Druim of my heart,
> A host of angels worshiping it.
> My welcome to them that be nigh it,
> And nigh the Glassan of Findbarr."

155. Fectus da ndechaid C. c. ar cuairt go hÁraind na naemh mar a raibhe Énde Arand 7 mar a raibe morán do naemaib eli do bi innti, 7 tarla dó co raibhe sé fen 7 na naeimh-se eli adubrumar ac rádh a tráth 7 a n-urnaighte ag techt timchell reilge Árand 7 co facatar an tumba roarsaidh 7 lia romhor dochumhscanta ar a mhuin 7 do machtnaighetar na naeimh co romhór arrsaidecht an tumba 7 méd na cloiche bai fair. ET do fiarfaig Baeithin naemh, do bi faré C. c., do naemaib an baili fen cia ro adhnacht 'sa tumba-sin. 'Ni fhedamar-ne sin,' ar síad, '7 ni mó ro cualamar cía ro adhnocht and.' Do frecair antí ar nach raibe ainbfhis am enní da taínic remhe no dá tiucfaid 'na díaigh é .i. C. c. 7 assed adubairt: 'Dofedar-sa cía ro adhnacht and,' ar sé, '.i. fectas and tánic ab Irusalém remhe-so ar cuairt faré naemhaib Erenn fa túaruscbhail a creidmhe 7 a crábaid 7 ar cruas a riagla 7 a mbethad, 7 tarla do co tainic sé don oilen-sa 7 go fuair se bas and, 7 assé ro adnacht fan leic úd. ET da derbadh corb fhir do C. c. an ní-sin, táinic aingel De do denamh fhíadhnaise les a fíadnaisi Énne 7 na naemh archena an uaír-sin. Gonadh andsin adubairt C. c. an rand-sa:—

A Baithin anum coleic fadás antal gaeth sailmglic,
is anum co maidin and ag abaidh Irusalem.

156. Do bi C. c. ag iarraid pairte don oilen-sin Arand ar Enne an uair-sin 7 ni tucc Enne sin dó; oir dob ecail les, da tucadh se pairt don oilen do, gorub uadha da hainmneochaide uili é, ar med a creidmhe 7 ar crúas a crábaid 7 ar a uaisli 7 ar a onóraighe 7 ar a shocenelaighe sech naemhaib eli Erenn, 7 ar linmhuire 7 ar tresi a braithrech 7 a comghail .i. cenel Conaill 7 Eogain 7 ar med a tuaruscbala fán uile doman. 'Atá do grádh 7 do toil agamsa don oilen-sa,' ar C. c., 'indus go mbenduighinn 7 co n-ainmnighter cuid ecin de uaím, gorb ail lim cuid bec nó mór d'fagail uaib-si de.' 'Ní fhuighbe,' ar Énne. 'Tabair letheat mo cochaill dam de,' ar C. c. 'Ní mesti leam an uiret-sin do tabairt duid de,' ar Enne. Do cuir C. c. de íarsin 7 do shín ar talumh e, 7 do bí se ag lethad ar fedh an oilen assa celi indus

155. On a time Columcille went to visit Ara of the Saints where dwelt Enne of Ara and many other holy men. And it happed that he and the other saints aforementioned were saying their hours and their prayers as they made the round of the churchyard of Ara. And they saw a very ancient tomb, and a passing great and unmovable stone thereon. And the saints marvelled greatly at the age of the tomb and the size of the stone. And Saint Baithin that was with Columcille asked the saints of the place who it was that was buried in that tomb.

"That know we not," say they, "nor have we heard who is buried therein."

But he to whom naught was concealed that had befallen or should befall, to wit, Columcille, did make answer to them and say:

"I know who is buried here," saith he. "On a time there came an abbot of Jerusalem to sojourn with the saints of Erin, by reason of the renown of their faith and their good works, and by reason of the rigor of their rule and of their lives. And he came by adventure to this island and he died here. And he it is that is buried under that flagstone."

And to prove that Columcille spake truth, there came an angel of God to bear witness for him before Enne and the other saints. And then Columcille uttered this quatrain:

> "Let us tarry now, O Baithin,
> Beneath . . . . . wise, versed in psalms.
> Let us tarry there till morn,
> With the abbot of Jerusalem."

156. At that time did Columcille ask of Enne a portion of that island of Ara, and Enne gave it not to him because he was afeared, if he gave Columcille a part of the island, that the whole thereof would be called after him for the greatness of his faith and for the rigor of his piety, and for his honor and worship and for his gentle blood passing the other holy men of Erin, and for the multitude and the power of his kinsfolk and his family, to wit, the clan of Conall and of Eogan, and for the greatness of his fame through the whole world.

"So lief and dear to me is this island," saith Columcille, "that I would bless it. And that some portion thereof might be called after me, I would fain get from you a portion, small or great thereof."

"Thou shalt not get it," saith Enne.

"Give me the width of mine hood thereof," saith Columcille.

"I should be none the worse for giving thee so much," saith Enne.

Then Columcille did off [his hood], and stretched it on the ground, and it began to spread out the length of the island so that it covered a great field of ground. And the Field of the Hood is its name

cor leth sé tar gort mor feraind. Conid "gort an cochaill" a
ainm ó sin alle. Ar ná fhaicsin sin d'Énne, do gabh ferg mór é, 7
ruc ar an cochall 7 do thógaib é, 7 muna beith a luas do tocaibh
sé é, do lethfad tar an oilen uili, 7 adubairt se nach fuighedh
5 C. c. an gort-sin no cuid eli don oilén-sin co bráth. 'Bud mesde
an t-oilen sin,' ar C. c., 'oir da lecthí damsa bendugad and, ní
tiucfad en long coidhce ann acht long do thiucfad le hoilethre-
chaibh and, 7 ni beith port a tiucfad long and acht énport amhaín do comhair an inaidh re raíter Acaill, 7 do choiseónadh
10 énduine é ar loinges bfer ndomain. Acus ní dendais goill ináid
allmaraigh gabáltus and, 7 an duine dogenadh domblas nó anaoibh
and, do lenfad a dhá bonn d'uír an oiléin innass nach beith ar
breith dó encoiscém do tabairt nó co n-ícadh se an domblas-sin,
7 ise bud roimh adhlaicthe do sloghaib iarthair domhain. Acus
15 fós do beidís drong d'enlaith parthais ag celiubrad gachlai and,
7 ni biadh galur nó esslaínte ar dhuine and acht galur a baís, 7
do beith sásadh 'na uisce amail nó beith se cumuscte do mhil, 7
do tiucfad a guirt 7 a arbhunda gan cur gan trebad 7 gan d'fhaghail do shaethar uatha acht a mbuaín 'sa bfhogmhar, 7 ní ric-
20 faidís lucht an oilen-se a less re buaibh do beith acu acht bó gacha
tighe, 7 dogebdaeís a frestal fen 7 frestal a n-aidhedh do bainde
uaithe. Acus do benfaidís na cluicc uatha fen a n-aimser an
aifrind 7 na tráth, 7 do lasfuidís na coindli uatha fen san aifrend
7 'sa medhón-oidche ag rádh a tráth dona naemuib. Acus ni beith
25 esbuidh mona dá ndentaí tene co bráth arís and. Acus as baegh-
lach combía cach uir [fol. 22b] easbaidh da ndubhramar-ne air
ó nar lécedh damhsa bendugad and,' ar se. Acus do fíradh sin
uile amail adubairt C. c.; 7 go haírithe do fírudh e leth re tenidh,
óir ní fuil moin no condadh ag lucht an oilén-si ó shin alle da
30 ndingantaí tene acht bualtuighe na mbó do tirmugad re gréin;
conad de sin doní siad tene.

157. Fechtus do cuaid Senchan senfhile, ardollumh Erend,
cona tromdhaimh co baili Guaire mic Colmain, ri Connacht. Agus
ba he so a lín .i. naenbhar re gach encheird, agus tri *caecait* eces,
35 agus tri *caecait* ecsín, agus dá mhnaí, agus gilla agus cu ag gach
fer dib, amail assbert an file:

Tri caéca eces nach mín,   acus tri caeca ecsín,
da mhnai as gilla is cú gach fhir,   do bhiathaidh Guaire
a n-entigh.[135])

[135]See *Oss. Soc.*, vol. V, p. 108.

from that day to this. And when Enne saw this he waxed exceeding wroth, and he seized the hood and lifted it up. And had he not raised it swiftly, it would have spread over the whole island. And he said that Columcille should not get that field nor any part of that island forever.

"The isle shall be the worse therefor," saith Columcille, "for if thou hadst suffered me to bless it, there had come thereto no ship save a ship that came with pilgrims, and there had been no port where a ship might come to, save one port only, in that place that is called Acaill. And one man might have defended it against ships of the men of the world. And no stranger nor foreigner had come there ever. And he that had done shame or evil there, his two soles should have stuck to the soil of the island, so that he might not have taken one step until he made good that shame. And it had been a burying ground for the hosts of the Western World. And there had been a throng of birds of paradise singing there each day. And there had been no sickness nor distemper upon the folk there save the sickness of death. And the taste of its water had been mixed with honey, and its fields and its harvests without sowing or plowing and labor from them save the labor of harvest. And the folk of this island had had no need of kine save one cow for each house. And they had had from her their fill of milk and the fill of their guests. And the bells had been struck of themselves at the hour of the masses and of the hours, and the candles been enlumined of themselves at the mass and in the midst of night when the saints were saying their hours. And there had been no lack of turf for laying a fire again forever in that place. And since I have not left my blessing, belike there shall be every want thereon whereof we have made mention," saith he.

And all that came to pass as Columcille had said. And in especial it came to pass touching the laying of the fires, for the folk on that island have nor turf nor fire-wood from that time till this, but they do make fire of cow-dung only, dried in the sun.

157. On a time Senchan, the old poet and High Bard of Erin, with his importunate company repaired to the stead of Guaire son of Colman, King of Connacht. And this was the reckoning of them: nine men of each craft, and three fifties of the masters of bardic art, and three fifties of bardic prentices, and each man of them with two women and a servant and a dog; as the poet hath said:

> "Three fifties of bards not meek,
> And three fifties of bardic probationers,
> Each with two women, a servant, and hound
> Did Guaire feed in one house."

Do rónad ríthech¹³⁶) romhor ag Guairi fana comhair a nDurlus.¹³⁷) Agus do batar ceithri mhí agus bliad*ain* ga fresdul agus ga fritholumh 'sa tigh sin aice, amail aspert Senchán fen ag imthecht ó Ghuaire:

Triallaim¹³⁸) uaíd, a Ghuaire gloin,   fagmaid agud ben-
[dachtain;
bliadhuin *acus* raithe is mi,   bám*ur* acut, a airdri.

Et ni ticedh mían¹³⁹) do nech acu ris an ré sin narb ecen do Guaire a fag*ail* do *no* an tromdamh uile da glámadh agus da aerudh; agus ger dhoil*ig* dofhaghala na miana sin, amail leght*har* 'sa lebur re n-abart*har* Tromdhamh Guaíre, dogeibthi le Guaire uile íad tre grasaib De agus tre fertaib na féli. La n-ann tain*ec* Marban, mucuidhe Guairi, agus fa brathair do Guairi fen é, agus ba nech ronaemtha é, do tigh na tromdaimhe do chor a n-uilc agus a n-eccóra agus a n-ainbfhis ina n-adhaidh;¹⁴⁰) oir ba truagh les med a n-ainbreth ar Guaire agus ar Connachtuib agus ar shaerclannuib Erend ar chena. Agus do mallaigh agus do escaín a huct De na n-uile cumh*acht* iad, da mbeidís da oidhce a n-entigh agus da mbeirdís ainbreth ar aennech a nErind nó co n-indsidís scela Tána Bo Cuailgne dó fen. Agus fuair Marbhán ó Día an uair sin a ndán do ceilt orra, ind*us* nach raibe ar breith doib aoír *no* moladh do denamh, nó co n-indsidís Taín dó.¹⁴¹) Agus ba doil*ig* lesin tromdhaimh sin, agus do bhat*ur* blíadhain ag iarr*aidh* Erenn agus Alban do scel*a* Tána. Agus ní fhuarat*ur* enfhoc*al* di. Agus is hí comairli tuc Caillín naemtha do Senchan, do bi 'na m*ac* máth*ar* dó, dul mar a raibe Colum Cille¹⁴²) d'fag*ail* scela Tána uadha; os air nach raibe enní 'na ainbfhis dá tainic reme *no* da tiucfadh 'na dhíaidh a nimh nó a talmain. Teid Senchan andsin, agus do íarr a huc[h]t Día agus a hucht na hécsi agus na heludhan ar Colum Cille seol*adh* ecin do denumh dó assa fuighedh se scela Tana. Nirbh urassa le C. C.

---

¹³⁶*leg.* ríghthech.
¹³⁷ *l. c.*, p. 36 and p. 108.
¹³⁸*leg.* triallam.
¹³⁹*l. c.*, p. 40 ff.
¹⁴⁰*leg.* aghaidh.
¹⁴¹*l. c.*, p. 102. According to this account they were allowed to compose one poem.
¹⁴²*l. c.*, p. 122 has *Marbhan*. C. C. was not a contemporary of Guaire (d. 662) or of Seanchan (d. about 650).

Guaire made a right mighty royal house for them in Durlus, and for four months and a year they were served and waited upon in that house, as Senchan said on departing therefrom:

"We depart from thee, O spotless Guaire,
We leave thee a blessing;
A year and a quarter and a month
Have we been with thee, O High King!"

And not a whim that took one of them throughout that time but Guaire must needs gratify it for him, else must he endure the abuse and satire of the whole importunate band. And albeit irksome and arduous were it to gratify those whims, as is related in the book hight *The Importunate Company of Guaire*, yet Guaire satisfied them all, through the grace of God, and by virtue of his acts of largesse. On a day came thither Marban, Guaire's swineherd and own brother, a passing holy man, to the house of the importunate company, with intent to charge them with their wickedness and injustice and ignorance, for he grieved for the multitude of their unjust demands upon Guaire and the Connacht men and all the free tribes of Erin. And he called down curses and malisons upon them from the breast of Almighty God if they should be two nights in one house or if they should make unjust demands on any in Erin until they should relate to him the tale of the *Cattle Raid of Cualnge*. And then Marban prevailed on God to take away from them their gift of poesy, so that it was not in their power to make satire or enconium save they first relate the *Cattle Raid* to him. And this was hard for the bardic company, and they were a year searching Erin and Alba for the tale of the *Cattle Raid*. And they gat not a word thereof. And this is the counsel that the holy Caillin gave Seanchan, that was his mother's son: to go to Columcille and get the story of the *Cattle Raid* from him; for to him was naught unknown that ever was or will be in Heaven or on earth. Then departed Senchan, and he begged Columcille for the sake of God and learning and poesy, to give him the counsel he needed how to get the tales of the *Cattle Raid*. It was in no wise easy for Columcille to refuse aught that was asked of him for God's sake. And moreover it was in no wise easy for him to

duine ar bith d'eitech fá enni da n-íarfaide ar son Dé air. Agus
fos nír urusa leis duine eladhna 'sa bith d'eitech; oir ni tainicc
riam duine ba deghenich ina sé. Agus do bí C. C. ga smuaínedh
aice fen cindus do gebadh na scela sin. Agus ass í comairli
5 dorinde sé, dul ar fhert Ferghussa mic Róich agus a fhaghail
ó Dia a aithbeoughadh d'indisin scela Tana dó; oir do bí a
fhis aicce nach raibe 'sa domhan duine as ferr ga raibhe na
scela sin iná hé, an uaír do bí se 'na bethaidh. Oir dobo tríd
fen tainic an cocudh asa rucadh tain a hUlltaib a Connachtaib,
10 agus do bí se ar sluaigedh tana o thús co deredh. Teid Colum
Cille go naemhaib Erenn uime ar fert Ferg[h]usa mic Roich,
agus do troisc re Día¹⁴³) fana cur ina bethaigh dó. Do erich
Ferghus assan fert a fiadhnaise fer nErend iter laech agus clerech.
Agus iss e fad do bí sé marb 'sa bhfert remhe sin .i. o aimsir
15 Criost do beith a coluind daenna gusan aimsir sin Coluim Cille
agus Grighóra beil-oír do beith 'na Papa 'sa Roim. Agus leghthor
'sa leabhur re n-abart[h]ar Tromdamh Guaire, co raibe do med
Fergusa, nach clos a bec da comradh an ceín do bi sé 'na
sesumh no cor leícc se ar a lethuillind é, agus do indes Taín
20 Bo Cuailgne uile an uair sin. Agus do scrib Cíarán
Clúana a seichidh na hUidhri Ciaraín uadh hí. Agus do cuaidh
Ferghas ina fert fen iar sin, agus do claídhedh air e. Agus do
cuired techta on tromdaim ar cend Marbhain mucuide go Glend
an Scail d'indesin scela Tána dó. Agus adubhairt Marbhan nach
25 tiucfadh se cuca no co faghadh se a breth fen uatha
fa shlánaib Coluim Cille agus naemh Erenn. Agus ar ngelladh a brethe fen dó amlaidh sin, tainic cuca, agus do hinnesedh
Tain dó. Agus iss í breth ruc orra, gach ollam acu do dul na tír
duthaigh fen, agus gan an tromdhamh do beith faré celi co brath
30 aris ag lot no ag milledh Erenn, agus gan beith ni ba lía doibh ina
buidhen a farrudh gach ollamhan.¹⁴⁴) Agus nir coimhletar na
filedha an gelludh sin tucutar do Marbhan acht do buailetar
fán a n-ainbretaibh fen aris no gur reidhich C. C. etorra 7
fir Erenn a mordhail Droma Cét, amail léghthor a lebhur na
35 mordhála fein (fol. 23a).

158.¹⁴⁵) Fechtus do cuiadh nech naemtha re n-abarthaí
Cairnech Tuilen ar chuairt mara raibhe nech naemtha eli re

---

¹⁴³See Joyce's *Social History of Ancient Ireland*, I, 204 ff., for an explanation
of this practice.

¹⁴⁴See *R. C.*, XX, p. 42.

¹⁴⁵Taken almost literally from some copy of the notes to *Félire Óengusso*.
See Stokes' edition (H. Bradshaw Society), p. 244. There the cutting of Cianan's
hair etc. is continued to Adamnan's time, while O'D. limits it to C. C.'s time.

refuse a man of learning, for never was one that surpassed him in largesse. And he pondered in himself how he might get those tales. And the counsel he took was this, to go to the tomb of Fergus mac Roich and to prevail on God to raise him up to tell him the stories of the *Cattle Raid*, for he knew there was not in the world a better at those tales than he in his life time. For it was because of him, the foray whereby the cattle were raided from the Ulstermen by the men of Connacht. And he was with the hosts in that cattle raid from first to last. Then goeth Columcille with the saints of Erin round about him to the tomb of Fergus, and he fasteth on God to raise him to life for him. Then rose Fergus out of the tomb in the sight of the men of Erin, lay and clergy.

And this space had he been dead in his tomb ere then, to wit, from the time Christ was in human flesh, till the time of Columcille, when Gregory the Golden Tongued was Pope in Rome. And as it may be read in the book the which is called the *Importunate Company of Guaire* so tall was Fergus that naught could be heard of his words so long as he was standing, until he let himself down on his elbow. And then he related the whole of the *Cattle Raid*. And Ciaran of Cluain took it down upon the hide of the dun cow of Ciaran. Then Fergus went back to his tomb and was enclosed therein. Anon were sent messengers from the bardic company to fetch Marban the Swineherd at Glenn An Scail, that they might relate to him the stories of the *Cattle Raid*. And Marban said he would not come to them until he had his own terms from them under the sureties of Columcille and the saints of Erin. And when they had promised him his own terms thus, he came to them, and they related the *Cattle Raid* to him. And these are the terms he made with them: that each of the bards should go to his own land, and the bardic company should never be together again to raven and consume the land of Erin, and that they should be no longer in a company in the following of a High Bard.

But the poets kept not this promise they gave to Marban, but rather they took again to their unjust demands, until the time that Columcille made a pact between them and the men of Erin at the Assembly of Druim Ceat, as we read in the Book of that Assembly.

158. On a time a certain holy man hight Cairnech of Tuilen went to sojourn with another holy man hight Cianan of Duleek. And they

n-abarthai Cíanán Daimhliac, 7 triallaid fothrucadh do denamh.
Agus ni frith dabhuch a raib[h]e édon docum an fothruicthi.
'Is aindis duinn sin,' ar Cianan. 'Ni hedh,' ol Cairnech. 'Cuirther
an t-uisce 'sa dabaigh 7 fédaigh Día gan uiresbaidh a hedain do
5 techt ría.' Do cuiredh iaramh 7 ní dechaidh enbraen este.
'Eirich 'sa dabaigh anois, a Chairnigh,' ol Cianan. 'Tiagam araen,'
ar Cairnech. Tiaghaid a n-enfhecht indti íarsin. 'As alaind
an corp sin agat, a Cianain,' ol Cairnech, '7 guidhim-se corub
amlaidh sin bías sé gan leghadh gan claechlodh tareis do baís
10 go ticid fir domhain do ghabhail a corp impo a llo an bratha.'
Do fíradh sin amail adubairt Cairnech, oír nir legh corp Cianaín
'sa tumba inar cuiredh é; 7 do berrthaí a aghaidh 7 do
gerrthaí a ingne gacha dardaín mandail 'sa bliad[h]ain,[146])
7 do bí se amlaidh sin ó re Pátraig co haimsir C. C.
15 Agus as é Pádraig do scrib ríagail an Cianain sin 7 is é Cíanan
do scrib riagail Padraig. Fec[h]tas dia ndechaidh C. C.
co Damhlíacc Cianaín, 7 ar ndul os cind tumba Cianain
dó, do shín Cianán a lamh tre thaeb an tumba amach
mar luthghair 7 mar raiberíans ría C. C. Agus do cuir C. C.
20 a lamh mar an cedna tríd an tumba astech ar corp Cianain mar
gradh 7 mar onoír dó. Gonadh desin ata a cadach 7 a cumann re
celi a nimh 7 a talmain o shin ille. Et nir fulaing
Cíanán d'énduine a glacudh no lam[h] do chur ar a corp ó
sin alle, mar onoír 7 mar médughadh anma do C. C. Agus dá
25 derbhadh sin, do chuaidh nech ronaemtha re n-abarthaí Adamhnán
co tumba Cianain 7 do fhoscuil é, 7 mar dob ail les a glacadh no a
fhechain, do dalladh a cedoír é, cor throisc re Día 7 re Cíanan, co
bfhuair aissec a amhairc arís, 7 nír leic an ecla d'énduine an tumba
sin Cianaín d'fhoslucadh no a corp d'fhechain ó shin ille.
30 Agus is follus duinn asan scel-sa, nach edh amhaín dob ail
le Día na naeimh 7 na daíne eli do bi beo re lind C. C. dá
onórughadh, acht corb ail les na mairb dá onórughadh.

159. Iss iad so na hadbhuir fana coír onoír 7 oirmhidin
mór do denumh a n-onoír C. C. dardaín sech gach lá eli, amail
35 mebhruighes an nech naemtha dana hainm Mura[147]) .i. dardaín do

---

[146]leg. a ingne dardaín mandail gacha bliadhna. See F. O.², p. 244, ll. 31-32:
No tescad dano uasalepscop a fholt 7 a ingne dardain caplaiti cacha bliadna co
haimsir Adamnain.

[147]Moru of Fothain, now Fahan, Co. Donegal. He died about 650. See
Voyage of Bran, I, p. 87.

went to take a bath. And no vat was found that had a bottom† therein for bathing.

"It is distressful for us," saith Cianan.

"Not so," saith Cairnech, "Let water be put in the vat, and God can make the default of bottom to be no imperfection therein."

It was put in then, and not one drop leaked out.

"Get thou into the vat now, Cairnech," saith Cianan.

"Let us go in together," saith Cairnech.

Then they went in both at the same time.

"Beautiful is thy body, O Cianan," saith Cairnech, "and I pray it may continue thus without mouldering or decay after thy death till the men of the world come to seek their bodies at the Day of Doom."

And this was fulfilled as Cairnech had said; for the body of Cianan decayed not in the tomb wherein it was placed; and every Maundy Thursday of each year his face was shaved and his nails cut and it was thus from the time of Padraic to the time of Columcille.

And Padraic it was that transcribed the rule of Cianan, and Cianan that transcribed the rule of Padraic.

On a time that Columcille went to Duleek, and stood over the tomb of Cianan, Cianan stretched his hand out through the side of the tomb in joy and in worship toward Columcille, and Columcille likewise stretched out his hand through the tomb upon the body of Cianan in love and worship toward him. Hence their friendship and affection each for other, in Heaven and earth, from then till now. And with intent to honor and exalt the name of Columcille, Cianan hath suffered none to touch him nor to lay hand on his body from that time.

159. These be the reasons it beseemeth to honor and venerate Columcille on a Thursday passing every other day, as maketh mention the holy man hight Mura:

On a Thursday did he speak in his mother's womb the time he bade welcome to the holy man called Fergna. And on a Thursday was he brought forth. And on a Thursday was he baptized. And on a Thursday

labhair se a mbroinn a mháthar an tan do fher se failte ris an
nech naemtha darbh ainm Ferghna. Et dardaín ruccadh é. Et
dardaín do baisdedh é. Et dardain dorinde se a chéd-
shiubhal 'na leanumh. Et dardain adubhratar na haingli C. C.
do tabhairt mar ainm air, 7 gan an t-ainm baisde tuccadh ar tús air
do gairm de .i. Crimthan. Et dardaín tainec Mongan chuice co
Carraic Eolairc,[148]) an uair do taisbén se ifren 7 flaithes Dé dó,
7 do creid se do Día 7 do C. C. íarsin. Et dardaín do cuaidh
sé do rádh a trath 7 urnaighte ar mulluch an cnuic ata soirdhes
os cind Tolcha Dubhglaisi .i. an t-inadh inar baisdedh é 7 do
shuidh air. Conidh Cnoc an tShuid[h]e a ainm ó sin
ille. Agus do tuit nell bec codulta air, 7 do bí an
talamh ag fás faí, 7 do gab ecla mór na clerich naemtha eli do bí fáris fán ní sin, 7 do mosclatar é, 7 adubratar
fen gor doigh leó muna beith a luás do mosclatar é, co n-éreóchadh
an talam suas conuice an aieór faei. Et díadardaín do brisedh cath
Cula Dremh[n]e les. Et gacha dardaín do berthí ar nemh é
d'imagallaimh re hainglibh, ut dixit [Mura] ga derbhadh so isna
randuibh-se:

Dardaín cedlabra Coluim   riana breith, dail gan dodhaing,[149])

dár fer sé faílte co mbloidh   re Fergna mac rig Caissil.

Dardaín breith Coluim Cille   a nGartan uasal ainglidhe,
dár indis Pádraig na fledh   do Brighid re ndul ar nem.

Dardain baisded Colum caimh   a Tulaigh Dubglaisi co n-áibh,

dá tuccadh Crimthan glan gle   d'ainm air ria Colum Cille.

Dardaín cedimthecht Coluim,   raidhim rib, dail gan dod-
                                haing;[150])

fa maith a aisde ar gach taeib,   mar ar baisdedh a ndardaín.

Dardain, nochar caingen cle,   ag ainglib righ an ri[g]thoighé,

darbensatar Crimthan de   's dargoirset Colum Cille.

Díadardaín tainic gan meirg,[151])   Mongan co Carraic Eolairg,

d'agallaim Coluim Cille,   a tir tredaig tairrngire.[152])

[148]See Z. C. P., VII, p. 303.
[149]doghaing MS.
[150]doghaing MS.
[151]leg. mairg.
[152]tarringire MS.

he took his first steps as a child. And on a Thursday the angels bade give him the name Columcille and not call him the baptismal name Crimthann that was laid upon him in the beginning. And on Thursday came Mongan to him at Carraic Eolairc, the time Columcille showed him Hell and the Kingdom of God. And Mongan believed on God and on Columcille thenceforth. And on a Thursday he went to say his hours and his orisons on the top of a hill to the south east above Tulach Dubhglaisi, the place whereas he had been baptized. And there he sat him down. Hence its name, the Hill of the Sitting, from that day to this. And a little cloud of sleep fell on him. And the earth began to rise beneath him. Therewith great fear seized the other holy clerics in his company. Then roused they him. And they said that had they not done so right swiftly, them seemed the earth beneath him had risen to the heavens. And on a Thursday was he victorious in the battle of Cuil Dremne. And on every Thursday was he borne to Heaven for converse with angels, *ut dixit* [Mura], bearing witness in these quatrains:

"On Thursday the first speech of Colum,
Ere his birth, a thing without trouble,
When famous welcome he bade
To Fergna, the King's son of Cashel.

On Thursday was born Columcille
In lofty Gartan of Angels,
As Padraic of Feasts had foretold
To Brigid ere going to Heaven.

On Thursday fair Colum was christened,
In Tulach Dubhglaisi the lovely;
They gave him then pure bright "Crimthann,"
For a name before Columcille.

On a Thursday Colum's first walking
I tell you, a thing without sadness.
Good was his nature in all ways
When he was baptized on a Thursday.

On a Thursday, no sinister contract,
He was with the King's angels of Heaven.
They shore him of Crimthann at that time,
And the name Columcille did they give him.

Dardaín do cuaid isan cnoc Colum caeimfhertach gan locht,
cusan Tulaig cuanna caimh, mar a fuil suidhe an ardnaeimh.

Dardain doradadh an cath Cula Dremne, dail go rath,

mar do toiligh Dia duilech dar gabudh an Sciathluirech.[153])

Ut dixit an file .i. Dallan Forcaill:—
Teighe[dh] Colum gach dardain co tech airdrigh nimhe naimh;

glac toindghel ar tocht anonn mac ochta on Choimdedh
[Colum.[154])

Dixit C. C. fen ga derbhadh so 'sa rann-sa:—

Is mesi Colum Cille, gan mire 7 gan borbglor;
bím gach dardain ar nemh nar as me abhus am cli
[comlan. (fol. 23b).

160.[155]) Fectus dia raibe Findtan mac Gaibrein fare senoir rob oide foircetail dó, 7 do labhair go faidhemhail rena oide 7 assed adubhairt ris oircill do beith aicce ar na hainglib[156]) uaisli onóracha do beith aige an oidhce sin. Ro gab ferg an senoír re Findtan, 7 tucc aicept mor dó 7 do fiarfaigh de cindus do beith afhis sin aice sech cách. 'Mo Tigherna .i. Isa Criost do fhoillsigh damh co mbeith an t-ardnaem 7 an t-uasulathair .i. C. C. gon a compánchaibh fárinn fein anocht.' A hait[h]li na mbriat[h]ar sin, tainic C. C. do choír an inaidh sin, 7 adubhairt rena muindtir gur coír doib gabail ar cuairt mar a raib[h]e na naeimh uaisle do bi a comghar doib. Ro gabhsatar andsin iaromh, 7 do labhair C. C. re hoide Findtain 7 assed adubhairt ris, nar coir dó ferg do denamh ré Findtan ar son a indisin co tiucfadh se fen cuca; 7 do indes dó co cuala se fen gach ní dá ndubhairt se ris acht ger fada uadha e; 7 adubairt corub d'Findtan do beith se fen 7 a chill ag foghnamh 7 ag serbhís co brath. Agus do firadh an faidhetóracht sin C. C. amhail derbus betha Finntain fén.

---

[153]This refers to the poem called *Sciathluirech of C. C.* See *Martyrol. of Donegal*, p. 12 and Stokes' *Mart. of Gorman*, p. VII; *LB*, 262, col. 2, l. 15.
[154]The same stanza is found in the Bodleian *Amra C. C., R. C.* XX, p. 164:
Teged Colomb cundail cáin.   i teg a Ríg cech dardain,
glacc tonngel ic tescad mong.   mac ochta in Choimded Colomb.
Evidently this was not the copy O'D. used.
[155]See Plummer's *V. S. H.*, II, pp. 96-97.
[156]Here the Franciscan copy rightly has *aoighedhaibh*.

> On a Thursday came without danger,
> Mongan to Carraic Eolairc
> For converse with Columcille,
> From the land flock-abounding, the promised.
>
> On a Thursday went to the Hillock
> Guileless Colum, the gentle of action,
> To the Tulach, fair and full lovely,
> Where the seat of the High Saint is stationed.
>
> On a Thursday was fought the battle,
> Of Cuil Dremne, a meeting with grace,
> For God the Creator consented.
> When the *Lorica* then was recited."

Ut dixit the poet, even Dallan Forgaill:
> "On every Thursday went Colum,
> To the house of the High King of Holy Heaven
> A clear skinned palm going thither,
> Colum, the darling of God."

Dixit Columcille himself, confirming this, in the quatrain that followeth:
> "I, Columcille, am accustomed,
> Without levity and without boasting,
> Each Thursday to be in happy Heaven,
> Though here in my body entirely."

160. On a time Fintan mac Gaibrein was with an old man that was his teacher, and he spake in prophecy to the old man, and told him to expect noble and worshipful guests that would be with him that night. Then anger seized the old man against Fintan, and he chid him right sharply, and asked him how it was he rather than any other that knew this.

"My Lord, even Jesu Christ, hath revealed to me that the high saint and patriarch Columcille, along with his companions, is to be with us this night."

"And as these words were spoken, Columcille was drawing nigh that place, and he said to his companions that it would be right to visit the noble saints that dwelt so nigh them. Then went they in, and Columcille spake to the fosterer of Fintan, and this is what he said to him: that he should not be angry with Fintan for declaring that he would come to him. And he told him he had heard every word that he had spoken to him, albeit he was far away. And he said that he and his church would serve and obey Fintan forever. And that prophecy was fulfilled, as the *Life of Fintan* witnesseth.

161.¹⁵⁷) Fechtas do cuaidh C. C. do choir an inaid a raibhe Munda mac Tulchain, 7 adub*hai*rt réna muindtir an lenub[h] sciam*ach* sochr*aidh* dogebhdaís san inadh sin do thabhairt cuice fen. Agus ar na tabhairt 'na fiadh*naise*, do linadh do gradh an macai*m* é, 7 adubhairt com*adh* mór ainm a athar 'sa seaghal ar son an m*i*c sin do beith aicce; 7 adubhairt go raibe an mac sen fen lán do grasaibh an Spir*ta* N*aim*[h], 7 co n-aibeorthaí it*ir* naemaib uaisli onóracha na hErenn é, 7 do bendaigh C. C. an m*acam* go roduthr*ach*tach an tan sin. An uair tr*a* tainec am legind do denamh do Mhunda, do cuaidh ar scoil Comgaill naemtha, 7 do cuaidh ass sin ar an scoil do bi ag C. C. a cill moír Dithruimhe. Et do bi C. C. ag dénamh ecna 7 legind 7 eolais an scribt*úra* gu duthrachtuch dó. Lá aíridhe dá raibhe C. C. ag leghthór*acht* don scoil, do línadh do grasuib an Spir*ta* N*aei*mh é mar ba gnáth les, 7 do fiafr*aidh* do Baithín naemtha cia don scoil b*a* goire dó an uair do bí se ag léghtoracht. Adubhairt Baithin gorb é Munda mac Tulcaín b*a* goire dó ar a laim deis. 'Aderim-se rib-se,' ar C. C., 'co mbía Munda lan do grássaib an Spir*ta* Naeimh 7 co rach*aidh* se ar ecna 7 ar e*olus* os cinn na scoile-si uili.' A cinn aimsiri faide iarsin, ar ndul C. C. a nAlbain, do tri*all* Munda dul mar a raib[h]e C. C. go hÍ, indus go ngabadh se aibid manaigh uadha. Do bi C. C. a nderedh a beth*adh* an uair sin, 7 do labhair go faidhem*hail* re Baithin naemt[h]a 7 ren a mhanch*aibh* fen do bi 'na fochair, 7 adubhairt riu co tiucfadh clerech naemtha o Erind dá indsoig[h]e tareís a bais fen, 7 co mbeith n*aemh*ta ó oibright*ibh* 7 solus ó indtind 7 sciam*ach* ó corp, 7 co mbeith gr*ua*g cas air, 7 co mbeidís gr*ua*id[h]e derga aicce, 7 com*adh* Munda a ainm. Agus adubhairt g*er* minec do condaic se 'sa saegal é, gurub meince iná sin do condairc se fáré Criost é itir ainglib, 7 adubhairt gurb é dob adhb*har* dó do dhul andsin docum co ndern*adh* se fén manuch dhe. Agus adubhairt go mberadh Día é fen do caithemh na gloire suth*aine* sul do tiucf*adh* se, 7 do athain do Baithín 7 dá mhanchaib, gan íad fen do dénamh manaigh dhe 7 a indesin dó co ndubhairt se fei*n* ris filledh tar a ais a nEri*nn* san inadh aírithe re n-abart[h]*ar* Hí Cennsel*aig* don taeb b*od*es do cuicedh Laighen, 7 co mbeith sé 'n-a chend ar poiblech*aibh* imdha and, 7 comadh an*d* nobeith a eserghe 7 a

---

¹⁵⁷Here the source is Munda's *Life*, which O'D. follows almost literally. See Plummer's *V. S. H.,* II, § II, p. 226; § IV, p. 227; § V, p. 228; § VII, pp. 228-229. See Reeves' *Adamnan*, pp. 18-22, where he is called *Fintenus*. See also § 225 *infra* where O'D. evidently did not know he was treating of Munda mac Tulcháin.

161. On a time Columcille came in sight of the place where Munda mac Tulcain was. And he bade his companions bring him the fair and comely child they should find in that place. And when it was brought before him, he was filled with love for the gentle lad. And he said that his father's name should be great in the world by reason of that son of his, and that the son himself should be full of the graces of the Holy Spirit; and that he should be reckoned among the noble and worshipful saints of Erin. And Columcille blessed the little lad right fervently. When the time came to put Munda to reading, he went to the school of Saint Comgall. Thence went he to the school that Columcille had in Cell Mor Dithruimhe. And Columcille taught him right diligently wisdom and learning and knowledge of the Scriptures.

On a day that Columcille was reading to the school, he became filled with the graces of the Holy Spirit as was his wont, and he asked holy Baithin what pupil it was had been next him the while he had been reading. Baithin said it was Munda son of Tulcan that had been next on his right hand.

"I let thee wit," saith Columcille, "that Munda shall be full of the graces of the Holy Spirit, and he shall surpass the whole school in learning and knowledge."

At the end of a long while after, when Columcille had gone to Alba, Munda journeyed to Iona to Columcille, that he might take from him the habit of monk. And Columcille was in the end of his life days then, and to Saint Baithin and the other monks that were with him he spake prophesying, and told them there should come to them after his death a holy cleric from Erin. And holy should he be in works, and enlumined of intelligence, and comely of body. And there should be curly locks upon him and ruddy cheeks. And Munda should be his name. And he said, albeit oft had he seen him in this world, more often had he seen him with Christ amid angels, and the reason of his coming to him was to be made a monk by him. And Columcille said God would have borne him away to everlasting glory ere the youth arrived. And he charged the brethren not to make a monk of him, but to tell him that Columcille had bidden him return again to Erin to a certain place called Hi Cinnselaigh, to the south of the province of Leinster, and that he should be the leader of much people in that place, and there should his resurrection be and his fame. And all that prophecy of Columcille was verified, as the *Life of Munda* testifieth.

onoír; 7 do fíradh an fhaidetoracht sin C. C. co himlan, am*ail* dhearb*hus* beatha Munda fén.

162.¹⁵⁸) Do chuir Col*um* C*ille* cuairt timchell Er*enn* uili an tan sin do siladh agas do medug*adh* a creidme 7 a crab*aidh*. Do baisd moran da sluag*aibh* 7 dá sochr*aid*ibh, 7 do cumhd*aigh* moran da cellaib 7 da heclusaib, 7 do fagaib moran da eolchaib 7 da dainibh naemtha a comarbacht cell Er*enn* do denamh lesa cilli 7 tuaithe re celi.

163. Fe*chtus* do C. C. a bFánaid 'san inadh re n-aburt[h]*ar* Glend Fanad aniugh, 7 do dermaid se a leab*uir* ar druim airide re raiter Druim na lebur. Ac*us* nir cian do ag siubal anuair do cond*aic* se fiadh ba*rr*¹⁵⁹) cuice, 7 a leb*uir* leiss ar a mhuin, 7 do lec ar a gluinib do C. C. e, 7 do lec na leabuir ar lar 'na fíadhnaise, 7 do muigh¹⁶⁰) tobur and san inadh i*n* ar lic*c* an fíad a gluine fai dá ngoirther Tobar C. C. aniugh, 7 ata ula mor cloch aice a c*om*art[h]a na mirbal sin (*fol.* 24a).

164. Fechtus eli do C. C. san inadh airidhe re n-aburthar Tobur an Deilg aniugh, a port Cairthe [Sh]namha¹⁶¹) don taeb toir do Loch Febuil, 7 tainic duine cuige ga raibe delg ina cois, 7 nir fedadh leges dó. Do bendaigh C. C. an tobur sin. Do reir droinge eli, as i an uair sin fen do muigh¹⁶²) an tobur; 7 geb' é aca é, tuc C. C. ar in ocl*aoch* a coss do cur and, 7 tan*ic* a delg ass, 7 do bi se slan ar i*n* pongc sin fen; cor morad ainm De 7 C. C. desin. Agus as bithbeo an mirb*huil* sin; oir gach duine a mbi delg teid cuice, bid slan ga fagbail.

165. Bó do bi ag C. C. re hadhaig [aghaidh] bainde do thabhairt da chataib. Dub na cat a hainm-si dheín, 7 do goideadh í, 7 tainic do mirbuilibh De 7 C. C. ga faghtaí a lorc isna clochaibh com[h] maith 7 do-geibthí sa tal*umh*. Agus da derbadh sin, atal lec cloiche aga fuil cros 7 ula docoir an tobuir sin an deilg dar labram*ar* sa scel-sa túas, ina bhfuil lorg na bó sin aniug; 7 do lenadh ar a lorg í co frith cengailte ar coillidh do coir na haband re n-aburt*har* an Fochain í, 7 do muigh tobur 'san inadh sin. Conad Tobur na Duibhe a ainm aniugh; cor moradh ainm De 7 C. C. desin.

---

¹⁵⁸See *Lis. Lives*, p. 176, ll. 956 ff; pp. 177-178, ll. 944 ff.
¹⁵⁹See § 297 for same word.
¹⁶⁰*leg.* muidh.
¹⁶¹See *R. C.*, XX, p. 48, where it is called *Coirthi Snáma*.
¹⁶²*leg.* muidh.

162. In that time Columcille made a circuit round all Erin to sow and to increase her faith and devotion. Then baptized he many of her hosts and multitudes and founded many chapels and churches. And he left many men of learning and holiness to succeed him in the churches of Erin for the profit of the Church and the people both.

163. On a time Columcille was in Fána, in the place called Glenn Fánad to-day, and through forgetfulness he left his books on a certain ridge called Druim na Lebur (Ridge of the Books). And not far had he gone when he saw a stag coming toward him, and his books on his back. He fell on his knees before Columcille, and cast down the books before him. And a spring burst forth in that place where the deer fell on his knees, and it is called the Well of Columcille today. And it hath a great stone station in sign of those marvels.

164. Another time Columcille was in a certain place that is today called Tobur an Deilg (Well of the Thorn), at the port of Cairthe Snamha, east of Loch Foyle. And there came to him one that had a thorn in his foot. And thereof could he get no healing. Columcille blessed that well. Other folk say it was in that hour the well burst forth. And which so of these it be, Columcille did cause the youth to put his foot therein, and the thorn issued forth and he was whole from that hour, whereby God's name and Columcille's were magnified. And ever-living is this marvel; for all folk that have thorns, if they go thither, are whole on coming away.

165. A cow Columcille had for to furnish milk to cats, Dubh na Cat her name. And she was stolen. And it came to pass, by the marvels of God and Columcille, that her track was got in the stones, as well as found in the earth. And in front of that Tobur an Deilg forementioned in the history is a flagstone with a cross therein and a calvary in witness thereof. And therein is the footprint of that cow to this day. Folk followed in her track till she was found fast bound in a wood, in front of the river that is called Fochain. And a well burst forth in that place, and its name is Tobur na Duibhe to this day, whereby God's name and Columcille's were magnified.

166.¹⁶³) Batar dno cuid do mindaibh Patraicc a n-inadh airithe a bfholach fo thalmhui*n* f*r*ia re tri fichit bliadhan tar eis a bhais fen; clog an udacht[a] 7 an cuach 7 soiscel an aingil a n-anmonda. Ro fhoillsigh an t-aingeal in ní sin do Colui*m* Cille, 7 r*u*stogaib iad. Et assi so roind ro orduigh an t-aingeal fen do tabhairt orra .i. clog an uda*ch*ta do Ard Macha, 7 an cuach do Dun da Lethglass, 7 soiscel an aingil do C. C. Is uime adeirt[h]ar soiscel an aingel fris .i. is assa laim fein tucc an t-aingeal do C. C. he. (*fol.* 24b).

167. T*i*ndscantar andso cur C. C. a nAlbain 7 na hadbuir far cuiredh a nAlbain é, do rér mar fhoillseoch*us* an beatha óaso amach.

168. Fecht n-aén do cuaidh C. C. a cend Findeín Droma Find, 7 do íarr iasucht lebhair air, 7 fuair se sin ó Fhindén. Agus do anadh sé a ndiaidh caich tareis na trath 7 na n-aifr*en*d sa temp*ull* do bi sa baile sin fen, 7 do bi se ag scribhudh an lebuir and gan fhis d'Findén.¹⁶⁴) Agus anuair ticedh an oidhce cuice assíad budh coinnle dó ag denamh na scribneó*rach*ta sin .i. cuig meoir a laimhe desi do lassadh am*hail* cuíc lochranda rolasumhna, indus co cuirdís delradh 7 solus fan tempull uile.¹⁶⁵) Et an oidhce deighenuch do C. C. ag scibadh derich an leb*air* sin, do cuir Finden duine d'iarr*aidh* a lebhair air. Agus ar ndul co dorus an tempuill a raibhe C. C. dó, dob ingantach leis med na soillse do conda*i*c se astig, 7 do gab ecla mor é, 7 do fech sé go faitech tre pholl do bí ar coml*a*idh doraiss an tempuill, 7 ar faicsin C. C. do ar an indell sin, amail adubramar romaind, nír leig an ecla do labhairt ris no an leabur d'iarr*aidh* air. Do foillsigedh, imorro, do C. C. an t-oclach do beith ga feithemh aml*aidh* sin, 7 do gab ferg mór é fá an ní sin, 7 do labhair se re peata cuirre do bi aicce, 7 assed adubhairt ría. 'Is ced lim-sa, massa ced le Dia, tu-sa do buaín a shul as an ochl*ach* ud tainec dom fhechain gan fhis dam fein.' Do erich an chorr acedoír le breithir C. C. 7 tuc buille da gob tre pholl na comla*dh* a suil an ocl*aig*, cor ben a shuil asa cinn, cor fhacuib ar a gr*u*aid amuigh hí. Do imd*igh* an t-ocl*ach*

---

¹⁶³The same anecdote is found in *A. U.*, A. D. 552.

¹⁶⁴Keating took over the same story from *Black Book of Molaga* (now lost). See Dinneen's *Keating*, III, p. 88. Perhaps O'D. used the same source.

¹⁶⁵A similar story is told of S. Columba of Tir da Glass. See Smedt and De Becker's *A. S. H.*, p. 447, § 6.

166. Some of the holy jewels of Saint Padraic were in a certain place hidden beneath the ground for three score years after his death. The names thereof be the Bell of the Testament, the Goblet, and the Angel's Gospel. This thing the angel revealed to Columcille, and he let lift them out. And this is the charge that angel gave, touching the distributing thereof, to wit: the Bell of the Testament to be given to Armagh and the Goblet to Dun da Lethglas, and the Angel's Gospel to Columcille. And for this it is called the Gospel of the Angel, because it is from the hand of the angel himself that Columcille received it.

XIV

OF THE EXILE OF COLUMCILLE FROM ERIN

167. Here beginneth the sending of Columcille to Alba and the causes of his exile to Alba, as his *Life* anon will show.

168. On a time Columcille went to stay with Finnen of Druim Finn, and he asked of him the loan of a book, and it was given him. After the hours and the mass, he was wont to tarry behind the others in the church, there transcribing the book, unknown to Finnen. And when evening came there would be candles for him the while he copied, to wit, the five fingers of his right hand blazing like five passing bright lights, so that they lit up and enlumined the whole temple. And on the last night that Columcille was copying the end of that book, Finnen sent one to ask it of him. And when that one had come to the door of the church where Columcille was, he marvelled at the greatness of the light he saw within. And passing great dread seized him, and he peered timorously through the hole in the leaf of the church door. And when he was ware of Columcille in the manner we have set forth, fear suffered him not to speak nor to require the book of him.

Howbeit it was revealed to Columcille that the youth was thus watching him, and he waxed passing wroth at this thing, and he spake to a pet crane he had there, and said: "Thou hast leave of me, if thou hast leave of God, to pluck out the eye of that youth that cometh to spy upon me without my knowledge."

Anon withal arose the crane at the words of Columcille, and he gave a peck with his beak through the hole of the door into the eye of the youth, so that he plucked out his eye from his head, and left it upon his cheek. Then went the youth to Finnen, and related to him how it had gone with him from beginning to end. Illpleasing to Finnen was this

iarsin mar a raibe Finden 7 do indis dó mar do imd*igh* air ó
tús co deredh. Nir maith le Finden an ní sin, 7 do benduigh 7
do coisricc sé suil an ocl*aigh*, 7 do chuir ina hinadh fein aris í,
gan digbail, gan uiresbuidh do b*eith* uirre am*hail* do bi sí o tús.
Agus mar do cuala Finden a lebur do scribadh gan cead do fen,
do ch*uaidh* se d'accra C. C. and, 7 adubhairt nar coir a lebhor
do scribh*adh* gan ced dó. 'Do-ber-sa breth rig Erenn dind,' ol
C. C. .i. breth Diarmada mic Cerbuill. 'Gebut-sa sin,' ar Finden.
Do chúatar re celi 'na diaidh sin co Temr*aigh* na Righ, mar a
roibe Díarmaid mac Cerbuill, 7 do inneis Finden a scela ar tus
don righ, 7 ass ed adubhairt ris: 'Do scrib C. C. mo leabhur gan
fhis damh fen,' ar se, '7 aderim corub lim fen m*ac* mo leabh*uir*'.
'Aderim-se,' ar C. C., 'nach mesde leb*hur* Findeín ar scrib me ass,
7 nach coír na neiche diadha do bi sa leb*hur* ud do much*adh* no
a bacudh dim fein *no* do duine eli a scribh*adh* no a léghadh *no*
a siludh fa na cinedach*aib*; 7 fos adeirim ma do bí tarba dam-sa
ina scribh*adh*, 7 corb ail lium a chur a tarba do na poiplech*aibh*,
7 gan dighbail Fhindein *no* a lebhair do techt ass, cor cedaigthe
dam a scribudh.' Is andsin ruc Diarm*aid* an breth oirrd*earc* .i.
'le gach boin a boinin' .i. a laogh 7 'le gach lebhur a leabrán,'
'7 da reír sin, is le Finden an leabur do scrib tusa, a C. C.', ar
Diarmaid.[166]) 'Olc an breth sin,' ar C. C., '7 digheolt*ar* ort-sa í.'

Et do bi Curnan mac Aedha[167]) mic Ech*ach* Tir in Carna
.i. mac righ Connocht a ngiallaidh*eacht* ona athair ag righ Eirenn
an uair cedna sin, 7 tarla imresain iter se 7 mac rechtaire na
Temra fa líathroid 7 síad ag imain *no* cor buail se mac an
rectaire do camán ina cend, cor marb a cedoír e, 7 do cuaidh fen
a comairce C. C. íarsin, 7 do furail an rí mac righ Condacht do
tarraing ass ucht C. C. 7 a ch*ur* docum baís triasan gnimh sin
dorinne se.

169. Is andsin adubhairt C. C.: 'Rachud-sa a cend mo
braithrech .i. Ci*n*el Conaill 7 Eog*ain*, 7 dober cath duit-se a
ndighail na drochbrethe rucais orm fan lebur 7 a ndigail m*ic*
righ Connacht do marbh*adh* ar mo comairce; oir ní lór lem Día
do dénamh indighthe ort and gan me fen do denamh digailtais
ort do taeb an tshaegh*ail*-se.'

---

[166]*Eg.* 13 b 1 has *ro briss cathu na tri Cúl* .i. *cath Cuili Dreim*n*i i Connachtaib
for Molaisi i cintaib a chlaeinbrethi euangeli,* [7] *for Díarmait mac Cerbaill.* See
R. C., XX, p. 434.

[167]Keating (*l. c.,* p. 86) has an abridged version and expressly states that
his source was the *Uidhir Chiarain.*

thing, and he blessed and sained the youth's eye and put it again in its place as it had been afore, without hurt or harm thereon. And when Finnen heard that his book had been copied without leave from him, he accused Columcille and said it was not lawful for him to copy his book without his leave.

"I shall require the judgment of the King of Erin between us," saith Columcille, "to wit, the judgment of Diarmaid, son of Cerball."

"I shall accept that," saith Finnen.

Anon withal they went together to Tara of the Kings, to Diarmaid son of Cerball. And Finnen first told the King his story, and he said:

"Columcille hath copied my book without my knowing," saith he, "and I contend that the son of my book is mine."

"I contend," saith Columcille, "that the book of Finnen is none the worse for my copying it, and it is not right that the divine words in that book should perish, or that I or any other should be hindered from writing them or reading them or spreading them among the tribes. And further I declare that it was right for me to copy it, seeing there was profit to me from doing in this wise, and seeing it was my desire to give the profit thereof to all peoples, with no harm therefrom to Finnen or his book."

Then it was that Diarmaid gave the famous judgment: "To every cow her young cow, that is, her calf, and to every book its transcript. "And therefore to Finnen belongeth the book thou hast written, O Columcille."

"It is an unjust judgment," saith Columcille, "and punishment shall fall on thee therefor."

At this time Curnan, son of Aed, son of Echaid of Tir in Charna, that is, the son of the King of Connacht, was with the King of Erin as hostage from his father. And there befell a quarrel between him and the son of the seneschal of Tara as they were playing, touching a hurling ball. And in the quarrel the boy struck the son of the seneschal upon the head with his playing-club. And he died straightway. And the son of the King of Connacht betook him to the safeguard of Columcille. And King Diarmaid bade him be dragged from the bosom of Columcille and put to death for the deed he had done.

169. And then Columcille said: "I will go to my kinsmen, the clan of Conall and of Eogan, and I will make war against thee to avenge the unjust judgment thou hast given against me touching the book, and to avenge the killing of the son of the King of Connacht that was under my safeguard, for it sufficeth me not that God take vengeance on thee hereafter, save myself take vengeance on thee in this world."

170. Is andsin adubhairt ri Erenn nach lémhadh nech d'feruib Erenn C. C. d'indlucadh asin mbaile sin, 7 nach lémhadh enduine acu dul a cath leis 'na aghaidh fen. Do gluais C. C. remhe (fol. 25a) asin mbaile gan ched do righ Eirenn, 7 do bi coiméd Dia air an mede-si, indus nar leir do cach ag imtecht as a fiadnaise fen é; 7 do cuaid go Mainester Baide an oidhce sin, 7 adubhairt cach fris beith ar a coimhed a sleib Breg an la ar na mháruch, 7 co raibe ri Erenn 7 a muindtir a bhfoirirechaibh remhe 'sa sligidh d'ecla co tiucfadh a cenn a braithrech dá cur 'na agaidh fen.

171. Is andsin do eirich C. C. co moch arna mhárach, 7 do cuir a mhuindtir a sligidh ar leith 'sa sliab, 7 do gabh fen eolus eli 'na enur. Conadh and dorinde an laidh:[168]) .i.

'Am aenurán damh 'sa sliab,   a Rí grian, rob soreidh sét!
nocha n-eclaighe damh ní   no da mbeind trí fichtib céd.'
Et reliqua.

Et ruc Día C. C. gan fhis do rig Erenn 7 da mhuindtir trid an sliabh.

172. Is andsin tainic a cend Conullach 7 Eoganach, 7 do cosaid se riu gach ainbreth da ruc ri Erenn air, 7 do gabutar san an cossaid sin uadh, 7 do cuatar les do tabhairt catha cusan inadh re n-aburtar Cuil Dremhne a Connachtuib aniugh iter Sligech 7 Druimcliab.

173. Is íad so na rígha batar ar Cinel Conaill 7 ar Cinel nEogain anuair sin .i. Ainmiri mac Setna, mic Fergusa cendfada, mic Conaill Gulban, mic Neill Naighiallaig, ar Cinel Conaill, 7 Ferghus 7 Domnall dá righ Cineoil nEogain, .i. dá mac Muirchertaigh, mic Muirethaich, mic Eogain, mic Neill Naigiallaig. Et tainec dno Aedh mac Echach Tir an Charna ri Connacht 7 Ua Mhaine Condacht cusan inadh sin do cungnumh le C. C. Do troisc C. C. re Día an oidhce remhe an cath fa buaidh catha do breith ar rig Erind 7 fa gan digbhail do denumh da braithribh fen no da sluagh.

174. Tainec Michel arcaingel cuice dá indesin do nar maith le Día an athcuinge sin do iarr se air; 7 gen cor maith, nar fhed se a eitech am enni da n-íarfadh se air 7 co bhfuighedh se o Día í, 7 nach beith Día reidh ris fana comshaeghulta sin d'athchuinge d'iarruidh no co ndeachadh se a n-oilithre tar muir 7 gan filledh tar aiss a nErinn co brath aris, 7 gan biadh no deoch na hErend

[168]See Z. C. P., VII, p. 302; Miscell. of Arch. Society, p. 3.

170. Then said King Diarmaid that none of the men of Erin should be suffered to accompany Columcille from that place, nor a man of them to go into battle with him against himself. Then Columcille went his way from the place without leave of the King of Erin. And the safeguard of God was upon him in such wise that he was invisible to all as he departed from their sight. And he went to Monasterboice that night. And all men warned him to be on his guard in Sliabh Breg on the morrow morn, for Diarmaid and his folk were in ambush for him on the way, lest he reach his kinsmen to set them against the King.

171. And so on the morn Columcille rose early and set his following on one side of the mountain, whilst he took another way alone. And there he made the lay:

> "Alone I am on the mountain
> O King of Suns, may the way be smooth.
> No more am I affrighted
> Than if I were three score of hundreds."

And unknown to the King of Erin God bare Columcille and his folk through the midst of the mountain.

172. And then he came to the clans of Conall and of Eogan, and to them all he made complaint of the evil judgment that the King of Erin had pronounced upon him. And they upheld his cause, and went with him to give battle in the place that is now called Cuil Dremne in Connacht, between Sligo and Druim Cliab.

173. And these are the kings that were of the clan of Conall and Eogan in that time, to wit, Ainmire son of Sedna son of Fergus Cennfada son of Conall Gulban son of Niall of the Nine Hostages, King of the clan of Conall and Ferghus and Domnall, kings of the clan of Eogan, that is to say, the two sons of Muirchertach the son of Muiredach the son of Eogan son of Niall of the Nine Hostages. And to aid Columcille there came to that place moreover Aed son of Echaid of Tir in Charna, King of Connacht and of the Ui Maine of Connacht. Then did Columcille fast on God the night before the battle, to give him victory over the King of Erin, and to cause no hurt to his kinsmen or their host.

174. Then came to him Michael the Archangel, and told him that illpleasing to God was the boon he had asked of him. Natheless naught that he required could He refuse him. And therefore he should obtain it. But because he had asked so worldly a thing, God would not be reconciled with him until he should go into exile beyond the sea. And he should not come back to Erin again forever, nor partake of her food nor

do caithemh acht an fad do beith sé ar slig*idh*, 7 gan a fir *no*
a mna d'fhaicsin coidhce. Et do indis an t-aingel do iarsin, nach
tuitfedh dá muinntir sin and acht enduine. Agus adubhairt an
t-aingel re C. C. gan enduine da muindtir do lecen t*ar* an sruth
do beith idir in dá sluagh ac cur an catha 7 gebe do rach*adh* co
muirf*idh*e¹⁶⁹) é.

175. Is aml*aidh* im*orro* do bi C. C. a croisfighill ar cul an
catha ag guidhe De an fad do bi an cath ga chur. Agus Suidhe
C. C. ainm an inuidh a raibhe se anuair sin o shin ille. Agus
do condcus Michel aircaingel a ndeilb curudh romhoír, 7 a sciath
ar a gualuinn, 7 a cloid*eamh* nocht*uigh*te 'na laimh, 7 se a tossuch
mhuindt*ire* C. C. ag brisedh an catha ar righ Erenn. Do ghuidh
C. C. Dia gan righ Erenn do marb*hadh* sa chath; 7 do muirbf*adh*
Garb mac Ronain do Cinel Conaill Gulb*an* e muna beith guidhe
C. C. ga coimet.

176. Et fos do bi Finden, mar an cedna, a croisfigill ar cul
righ Erenn 7 a muindtire, 7 do chuir C. C. techta cuige da rádha
ris gan a beith a croisfighill aml*aid* sin, 7 corbe an t-adbhur é
nach brisf*ide* ar in righ an cein do beith sesiun a croisfighill ar
a chul, 7 co muirbfidhe a muindtir uili *acht* muna lecedh san da
guidhe 7 da croisfighill, indus co ngebdaíss maidhm cuca 7 nach
andaeís rena marb*adh*. Ar 'na thuicsin d'Fhinden cor fihir sin
7 nach dubairt C. C. brécc riamh 7 go raibe Dia ar a comairli
go mór, do léic se a lamha ass a croisfighill 7 do fácuib an t-inadh
a raibhe se. *Agus* do brisidh an cath sin Cula Dremhne ar righ
Erenn 7 do marbudh *deich ced* ar xx. c. dá mhuinntir and, 7
nír marbad do m*uinntir* C. C. and acht en duine amhain do cuaidh
tar an sruth do bi it*er* in dá sluag t*ar* aithne an aingil 7 Col*uim* C.

177. Ar mbrisedh an catha sin Cula Dremne ar righ Erenn,
dorinde C. C. sith ris, 7 do aisic se a righacht do, oir nir bec les
a ainbreth do digail air; 7 do fhedf*adh* se rigacht Erenn do beith
aige fen an uair in, muna lecedh se de ar son Dia í. Oir dob
fherr les an righact ba mo aige .i. rigacht flaithessa De.

178.¹⁷⁰) An Cathuch, im*orro*, ainm an leab*huir* sin triasa
tug(*fol.* 25b)adh an cath, as é is airdmhind do C. C. a¹⁷¹) crich
Cineoil Conaill Gulban. Agus ata sé cumhdaigthe d'airged fa
ór, 7 ni dleghur a fhoscludh. Agus da cuirther tri huaire desiul
a timchell sluaigh Cineoil Conaill é, ag dul docum cat[h]a doib,
is dual co ticf*adh* slan fa buaidh; 7 is a n-ucht comhorba no

---

¹⁶⁹*leg.* muirbfidhe.
¹⁷⁰See Joyce's *Social History,* I, p. 501 ff.
¹⁷¹a a MS.

her drink save the time he was on the journey, nor should he look upon her men nor her women forever. And then the angel told him there should not fall of his folk there save one man. And the angel charged Columcille that no man of his following should cross the stream that was betwixt the two armies that were doing battle, and if one went he should be slain.

175. It was in this wise Columcille was: at the back of the host the while the battle lasted, in cross vigil praying to God. And the seat of Columcille is the name from that time to this of the place where he was in that hour. And Michael the Archangel was seen in the form of a passing great warrior,—on his shoulder a shield, and a naked sword in his hand, in the vanguard of the folk of Columcille, routing the King of Erin in the fray. Columcille besought God not to kill the King of Erin in the battle. And Garb son of Ronan of the clan of Conall Gulban would have slain him, had not Columcille prayed for his protection.

176. And Finnen was likewise in cross vigil in the rear of the King of Erin and his men. And Columcille sent his messengers to him to forbid him to pray thus. And the reason he gave was that the King would not yield the while the saint was thus in cross-vigil in his rear, so that all his folk would be slain save he leave his praying and his cross vigil to the end they should accept defeat and not wait to be slain. And Finnen knowing that this was true, and that Columcille had never spoken lie, and that God was right firmly in league with him, dropped his arms from his cross vigil, and left the place where he was. And in that battle of Cuil Dremne, the King of Erin was routed, and there were slain ten and a score hundred of his men. And of the folk of Columcille were none slain, save one man only that went across the stream betwixt the two hosts against the command of the angel and Columcille.

177. When the King of Erin had been routed in the battle of Cuil Dremne, Columcille made peace with him and gave back to him his kingdom, for he thought it enough to punish him for his unjust judgment.

And Columcille might have had the Kingdom of Erin for his own that time, had he not renounced it for God's sake; for him were liefer to have the greater kingdom, to wit, the Kingdom of the Realm of God.

178. The *Cathach* for a sooth is the name of that book by reason whereof the battle was fought. And it is covered with silver under gold. And to open it is not lawful. And if it is borne thrice sunwise round the host of the clan of Conall when they go into battle, they come back safe in triumph. And it is in the bosom of a successor or a cleric

clerich can pecadh marbtha air, mar is ferr is eídir leis, as coir an Cathach do beith ag techt timchell an tshluaigh sin.

179. Is andsin adubhairt C. C. rena braithr*ib* 7 rena muindtir: 'As ecen dam-sa dul dom oilithre 7 Ere d'fagbail 7 gan techt indti gu brath, arís, am*hail* adubhairt an t-aingel rium ar a mhed do dainib do cuirebuir-se docum bais trím sa cath-sa Cula Dremhne, 7 a cath Cula Fedha do brisebhair-si ar Colman mór mac Diarmuda,¹⁷²) a ndigail mar do marb a m*a*c .i. Cumaine mac Colmain, Baedan m*a*c Nindedha ri Erenn, ag Leím an Eich ar mo slanuib-si, 7 a cath Cula Ratha*in* do brisebuir ar righ Ul*adh* .i. ar Fiachna m*a*c Baedain, 7 ar clanduib R*u*g*ra*ide trím ag cosnum Ruis Torathair¹⁷³) .i. an ferond fa tharla imresuin adrum-sa 7 Comghall. Agus da derbudh co tucutar a braithre na cathu-sa trid, adb*er*t an file .i. Dallan Forgaill:

Cath Cula Dremne na ndrend   atcualut*ur* fir Erend,

cath Cula Fedha, fath mbil,   ac*us* cath Cula Ratha*in*.¹⁷⁴)

180. Et fos do cuatar naeimh Erenn a monmar ar C. C., 7 adubrutar ris nar coir dó ar cuiredh da dhainib docum bais andsna cathuib sein tria na comhairli. Is andsin do cuaidh C. C. do comairli naem Erenn, do tab*hair*t a culpa do Molaissi Daim indse¹⁷⁵) ar a shon sin. Agus assi breth ruc Molaisi air .i. an br*eth* ruc an t-aingel air reme sin .i. Éri d'facbail 7 gan a faicsin co brath, 7 gan a bíadh no a deoch d'ithe no d'ibhe 7 gan a fir nó a mna d'faicsin 7 gan saltairt ar uír Erenn go br*áth*.

181. Do gab toirrsi mór C. C. andsin, 7 adubhairt se: 'As mesde Eri mesi do cur esde, 7 muna curthai esde me, do gebaind o Día gan galur no esslainte do beith ar Erendcha*ibh* gu brath¹⁷⁶) acht galur a mbais;, amhail asp*er*t se fen 'sa rand-sa:

Mona beith briathra, Molaisi   gun crois os Ath Imlaise,¹⁷⁷)

nochon fhuicfind-se re mo lind   saeth no galur a nEir*ind*.

---

¹⁷²See Reeves' *Adam.*, p. 249; *R. C.*, XX, p. 254; *ibid.*, p. 434; Dinneen's *Keating*, III, p. 87.

¹⁷³See Reeves' *Adam.*, p. 253, where Ross Torathair is called a church. See also *R. C.*, XX, p. 254; *ibid.*, p. 434.

¹⁷⁴See Reeves' *Adam.*, p. 249.

¹⁷⁵See Plummer's *V. S. H.*, II, § 31, p. 139.

¹⁷⁶*leg.* re mo lind.

¹⁷⁷Ath Imlaise is situated at the extreme north of Co. Sligo. It belongs to Innishmurry and we naturally conclude that Molaise of Innishmurry is meant here. But § 180 says it was Molaise of Devenish who passed the sentence.

that is so far as may be without mortal sin, that the Cathach should be borne around the host.

179. And Columcille said to his kinsmen and his people: "It behooveth me now to go on my pilgrimage and to leave Erin, and to return hither no more forever, as the angel told me, by reason of the numbers ye have slain for my sake in the battle of Cuil Dremne and in the battle of Cuil Fedha when ye overcame Colman Mor son of Diarmaid for vengeance because his son Cumaine son of Colman killed Baedan mac Nindedha, King of Erin, at Leim an Eich, in despite of my sureties, and in the battle of Coleraine where you routed the King of Ulster, to wit, Fiachna son of Baedan and Clan Rugraide, by reason of my contending for Ross Torothair, to wit, the land touching which there was a quarrel between me and Comgall. And to prove that his kinsmen fought these battles for his sake, the poet said, to wit Dallan Forgaill:

"The battle of Cuil Dremne of strife
The men of Erin have heard thereof;
The battle of Cuil Fedha, a good cause;
And the battle of Cuil Rathain."

180. And the saints of Erin fell to murmuring against Columcille, and they condemned him for all the folk that were slain in those battles of his making. And by the counsel of the saints of Erin, Columcille went then to Molaise of Devenish to accuse himself thereof. And this was the sentence Molaise laid upon him, even the sentence of the angel had lain on him afore, to wit, to leave Erin and to behold her no more, her food and her drink to eat not or to drink, nor to see her men nor her women, nor to tread on the soil of Erin forever.

181. And great sadness fell on Columcille therewith, and he said: "It shall be the worse for Erin to cast me out from her, and were I not cast out from her I would obtain from God that no sickness or distemper should be on the men of Erin forever, save the sickness of death." And he hath said it in this quatrain:

"Were it not for the words of Molaise,
At the cross above Ath Imlaise
I would not leave in my life-time
Distemper or sickness in Erin."

182. Do cuaidh C. C. iar cath Cula Dremhne ar cuairt mar a raibe an nech naemtha darb ainm Cruimtheir Fraech. Da fher déc a lín. Agus tarla dó beith oidhce a Cill Mudaín.[178] Is andsin fuair se an anbfhailte mor o Mhudán .i. áith shaluch deroil do tabhairt mar tech leptha do, 7 muc guna finda do cur díahaíne mar biadh cuice, 7 coiri brisde do chur lé, 7 becán do chraibech úr ferna do cur docum teinedh cuige. 'Ni ré maith rinn do cuiredh so cugaind,' ar C. C., 'gidhedh tairgidh an fheoil do bruith 7 caithidh ní di, 7 cuirfidh ar nDia fen sin a n-onoír duinn do nemthoil Múdain.' Ar cur uisce 'sa coire docum na feola do bruith, ni narb ingnadh, do bí an coire brisde ac lecen an uisce trid. 'Cuiridh sop fón cuire,' ar C. C., 'a n-ainm an Coimdegh 7 Cruimt[h]ir Fraech.' Doronudh amlaidh sin 7 do gab fris fo chedoir, 7 gabaid fria gach coire o shin ille. Et ní he nach fédfadh C. C. fen sin do cosc acht corbh ail les a dul a n-ardugadh anma do Chruimter Fraech. Do caithset muindtir C. C. med ecin don feoil sin ar fulairemh C. C. fen. Agus ass e do bo biadh do Mudán 7 da muintir .i. arán 7 imm 7 íasc. Ruc fer fritholma Mudaín fuidlech muinntire C. C. les da coimét don tigh a raibe Mudán fen. Et ro taisich fuidlech Múdain 7 a muindtire mar an cedna. Et is amluidh fuair sé ar na máruch na míassa ar a raibe fuiglech muindtiri C. C. lan d'arán 7 d'iasc 7 na miassa ar a raibe fuiglech Mudain lan do cru 7 d'fhuil. Ro escain C. C. an baili íar[179]) sin, 7 adubairt co mbeith fás folum tré bitha sir, 7 co mbad coin allta a clerich 7 a scola gacha nóna gu brath. Ro imthigh C. C. asin mbaili iar sin, 7 do dermaid leabur na soiscel 'san aíth ina raibe sé an oidche reme sin; 7 do lass an aíth uaithe fen cor loiscedh uili í co nar fédadh anucal dí, 7 tainic an lebhur uadha fen cusan ard do bi os cind an baile re n-aburthar Escert na Trath; co bfuair an clerech do fhill C. C. dia íarraidh andsin é, cor (fol. 26a) moradh ainm De 7 C. C. desin. Do bi C. C. ag siubul iarsin nó cu raibe deredh an lai ag drud ris, 7 co cuala se guth cluig espartan na cilli a raibe Cruimther Fraech, 7 dorinde comhnaidhe andsin, 7 do srethadh a pubull tairis; oir nir gnathach le C. C. tairimthecht ó espart dia Sathairn co maidin Luain. Do foillsigedh do Cruimther Fraech C. C. do beith a comfhocus do. Tainec mar a raibe se 7 do fer failte fris, 7 do bi Cruimthir ag tabhairt aicepta do C. C. trias an cath sin do cuiredh trid. 'Nocho mesi as cintach ris sin,' ar C. C., 'acht

---

[178] See above, § 122, for a similar story.
[179] ár MS.

182. After the battle of Cuil Dremne, Columcille went on a journey to where there was a holy man called Cruimtheir Fraech. Twelve men were in his company and it chanced that he was one night at Cill Mudain. And there he gat a poor welcome from Mudan, to wit, a dirty wretched kiln was given him as a sleeping place and a hairy pig on a Friday as food for him, and therewith was sent a cracked cauldron, and some damp branch-wood of the alder-tree to make a fire thereunder.

"It was with no good will toward us that this was sent us, but let us boil the meat and eat thereof," saith Columcille, "and our God will account it to our honor in Mudan's despite."

When the water was put in the pot to boil the meat, the cracked pot (it was no wonder) let the water through.

"Let us put a wisp under the cauldron," saith Columcille, "in the name of the Lord and Cruimtheir Fraech."

It was done thus, and forthwith the wisp clung thereto, and it clingeth to every cauldron from that time till now. And it is not that Columcille was not able to calk the cauldron himself, but he rejoiced in exalting the name of Cruimtheir Fraech. And at the command of Columcille his followers ate some of that meat.

And this was the food of Mudan and his folk: bread and butter and fish. And one of the varlets of Mudan took the leavings of Columcille's followers with him to set them by in the house where Mudan was. And he set by the leavings of Mudan and his folk in like wise. And this is how he found on the morn the dishes wherein were the leavings of Columcille's followers: full of bread and fish. And the dishes wherein were the leavings of Mudan: full of gore and blood. Columcille cursed that place, and said it should be barren and desolate for all time and that its clerics and scholars should be wolves at nones each day forever.

Then departed Columcille from that place, and he forgat the book of the gospels in the place it had been the night before. And the kiln took fire of itself, so that it was wholly burned and might not be saved. And the book departed of itself to the height that was above the place called Escert na Trath, so that it was found by the cleric that Columcille sent to seek it. And God's name and Columcille's were magnified thereby.

Then went Columcille on his way walking, till the end of day was closing upon him, and he heard the sound of the vesper bell of the church where Cruimtheir Fraech was. And there he made a stay, and his tent was spread, for it was not his wont to be journeying between the vespers of Saturday and Monday morn.

It was revealed to Cruimtheir Fraech that Columcille was not far from him. He came forth to meet him, and bade him welcome. And

ainbretha Diarmada mic Cerbaill oram.' 'Do budh usa do
cleriuch ainbretha d'fulang iná dul dá sesumh,' ar Cruimther
Fraech. 'Anuair lasass an ferg 'sa duine bis fa masla moir, ni
heidir les sin d'fulang,' ar C. C. 'Múchadh na ferge bud coír,'
ar Cruimther Fraech, 'd'ecla ní bud aithrech do denamh lé.' 'Gé
mor d'ulc doní duine le feirg,' ar C. C., 'maithfidh Dia dó é acht
go nderna*dh* se aithr*ighe*. 'Dob ferr an t-olc do sechna ina
beith ag íarraid a maithmhe,' ar Cruimther Fraech. 'An é nach
fuil a fhis agat-sa, a Cruimther,' ar C. C., 'gurub luthghairdhe Dia
7 muindtir nimhe reme an pecach fhilles cuca fein le haithrige
na reme an tí nach denand pecadh, 7 anus do gnath a ndegs-
daid. Et narub ingnadh leat-sa sin, a Cruimther,' ar se, 'oir is
bés duinne fein na daíne, gurub forbfhailtighe sind risan duine
bud inmain lind 7 do beith a fad ina fecmhais iná risna dainib
do beith do gnath inar fochair. Agus bidh a demhin agad,' ar
C. C., 'na fuil ar bith duine is luaithe soiches nemh iná an pecuch
doní aithrige. Et ní dernadh 7 ní dingant*ar* gnimh budh mó
iná a nderna Loingínus,'[180]) ar sé, '7 do maithed dó é ar son a
aithrighe.' 'Massed,' ar Cruimther, 'co nderna Día daine maithe
dínn araén.' 'Go ma fír,' ar C. C. Gonadh andsin doronsad[181])
araón an duan dianadh ainm imagall*am* C. C. 7 Cruimthir
Fraech .i. moch*en* a Coluim na clog 7 rl. Doronsad iar sin a
cadach 7 a cumand re cheli 7 do ceilebrutar dá celi.

183. Tainec C. C. go Doire íarsin 7 dob inmain les an
baile sin 7 fa lesc leis a fhacbail, 7 do bí gá moludh co mór co
ndébert an rand:

Is uim*me*[182]) caraim Doire ar a reidhe, ar a gloine,
'sar imad na n-aingel fin*d* ón ci*nd* go soich aroile.

Et adubairt nar lía duilleabar ar crandaibh no fér ar faithche
inaíd aingli os cind an baile sin. C*on*adh and aspert an rand-sa:

Nochon fhuil duilleog ar lár[183]) a nDoire cuan*na* comlán
gan da aingel go n-oige a n-aghaidh gach duilleoíge.[184])

---

[180]See Atkinson's *Passions and Homilies,* p. 60.
[181]This poem is found in *Laud* 615, p. 40. See *Ériu,* V, p. 13.
[182]leg. *aire.* See Reeves' *Adam.,* p. 288.
[183]See § 219 for a similar phrase.
[184]See Reeves' *Adam.,* p. 288:
    fa lomlán d'ainglibh uile cech duille im dairbribh Doire.

then Cruimtheir fell to rebuking him for the battle that had been fought because of him.

"It is not I that am to blame therefor," saith Columcille, "but the wrong judgment of Diarmaid son of Cerball against me."

"It were more easy for a cleric to submit to a wrong judgment than to set about defending himself," saith Cruimtheir Fraech.

"When a man's wrath is up and he is sore tried, he can not submit," saith Columcille.

"It is right to stifle wrath," saith Cruimtheir Fraech, "lest it make matter for regret."

"Though a man do much ill through anger," saith Columcille, "yet will God pardon him therefor if he do penance."

"It were better to shun evil than to seek forgiveness therefor."

"Knowest thou not, O Cruimtheir Fraech," saith Columcille, "that God and the folk of Heaven have more joy for a sinner that returneth to them with repentance, than for one that doeth no sin and remaineth continually in a state of virtue? For it is the wont of us mortals to have more welcome for those that are dear to us and that have long been absent, than for those that are ever with us. And wit thou well," saith Columcille, "that in the world is none that shall sooner reach Heaven than the sinner that repenteth. And there hath never been nor ever will be done a worse deed than did Longinus," saith he, "and it was forgiven him by reason of his repentance."

"If it be so," saith Cruimtheir, "may God make us good men both together."

"Amen," saith Columcille.

So then they made together the poem that is called the *Colloquy of Columcille and Cruimtheir Fraech*: 'Welcome, O Colum of the Bells' *et reliqua*.

Anon they sealed friendship and fellowship, and each bade other farewell.

183. Then went Columcille to Derry. And the place was dear to him and he was loth to leave it. And right greatly did he praise it, as the quatrain saith:

> "This is why I love Derry:
> For its level fields, for its brightness,
> For the hosts of its white angels,
> From one end to the other."

And he said that not more numerous were the leaves on the trees, or the grass on the meadows, than the angels that hovered over that place. So that he uttered this quatrain there:

184. Et adubhairt nach edh amhaín do bidís ar tír os a cend acht do bidís fedh naí tond ar muir ina timchell, ⁊ adbert an rand-sa:

Ní faghaid inudh ar tir   d'imad na n-aingel maith mín,

ar nai ton[n]aib amach dhe   ass *edh* gabhaid ó Dhoire.

185. Et co hairidhe an t-iubhor agan a*bradh* C. C. ⁊ na naimh a tratha do coir an duibreicleís,[185]) do bidh deich *ced* aingel os a cind isin iubhar sin ga coimhidecht, amhail derbus se fen isna randuib-se:

Asse sin iub[h]*ar* na naemh   goa ticind-se is íad araén,

do bidh *deich ced* aingel find   os ar cind taeb ré taeb.
Is i*n*main lium-sa an t-iub*ar*   me fen do chur 'na inadh,
dom laimh cli bud suairc an grés   ag dol damh 'sa duibreicles.

186. Et gerb inmhain les an baile sin, do tindscain se a fagbail ⁊ dul da oilithre a nAlbain do comairli an aingil ⁊ naemh Erenn. Agus do bí an oiret sin do gradh aige ar an mbaile sin gur cuir sé a long thairis súas a Loch Febail cusan inadh re n-aburt[h]ar Glais an Indl*uidh* aniugh, ⁊ do cuaidh se fein do tír 'na coinde andsin, ⁊ do indail a lamha asin sruth sin. Conudh Glais an Indluidh a ainm ó sin ille, ⁊ do bendaigh se cloch do bhi re taeb an tsrotha sin, ⁊ do impó se desiul uirre, ⁊ asdí do cuaidh se 'na luing, ⁊ adubairt se, gebé do impobudh desiul uirre ó sin amach ag dul ar sed nó ar siubhal, go madh dual co tiucf*ad* se slan. *Agus* ass é adbhor fa rucc se a long tar an mbaile sin suas 'sa loch, mar adubramar remhainn, indus co madh fhaidide do beith amhorc an baile aicce dul taireis suas ⁊ beith a[g] gabail ría na taebh sís arís. (*fol.* 26b).

187. Et ar ndul do C. C. ⁊ da naemhaib 'na luing, do bí duine airidhe 'sa p*or*t ⁊ lorg bengánuch 'na laimh, [186] ⁊ do chuir an lorg ris an luing dá cur amach o thir. Mar do condairc C. C. sin adub*airt*: 'Fagbuim buaid ndeoraigechta dot[187]) aindeoin ort

---

[185]C. C. spent three years there. See *R. C.,* XX, p. 168, § 24.
[186]*lorg benglanach aige 'na laimh*. Franciscan copy (Dublin).
[187]*doth* MS.

> "There is not a leaf on the ground,
> In Derry lovely and faultless,
> That hath not two virgin angels,
> Overthwart every leaf there."

184. And he said that not only were they hovering over the land, but they reached for nine waves on the sea around it, and he spake his quatrain:

> "They find no room on the land,
> For the number of good gentle angels,
> Nine waves distant therefrom,
> It is thus they reach out from Derry."

185. And in especial above in the yew tree in front of the Black Church, where Columcille and his saints were wont to chant the hours, were there ten hundred angels keeping guard, as Columcille hath said in these quatrains:

> "This is the Yew of the Saints
> Where they used to come with me together.
> Ten hundred angels were there,
> Above our heads, side close to side.
>
> Dear to me is that yew tree;
> Would that I were set in its place there!
> On my left it was pleasant adornment
> When I entered into the Black Church."

186. And though dear to him was that place, yet he made him ready to leave it and to go into exile to Alba at the counsel of the angel and of the saints of Erin. And so great was his love for that place that he let send his ship to Loch Foyle to a stead that is called Glais an Indluidh today. And he went himself by land to meet it then, and he washed his hands in that stream. Wherefore is its name Glais an Indluidh to this day. And he blessed a stone fast there beside, and made a circuit around it sunwise, and from that stone it was he went into his boat. And he said that whoso should make a circuit around it from that time, going on a journey or a pilgrimage, it would be likely that he would come safe. And for this he let send the boat beyond that place in the loch, as we have said above: that he might the longer have sight of that stead on his way up beyond it, and coming down again by its side.

187. And when Columcille and his saints were entering into the boat, there was a certain man in the port with a forked club in his hand. And he set the club against the boat to push it off from land.

fan oired sin do congnum do tabairt damh d'fhagbail Erind ar
deoraigecht, 7 fagbhuim na buadha cedna sin ar fer hinaidh aga
mbía lorg benganach co brath,'

188. Do leicetar an long ar siubul andsin, 7 do bhátar a
braithre fen .i. Conullaig 7 Eoganaig 7 a tirtha uile gacha taeb
do Loch Febuil an uair sin, 7 mar do condcatar C. C. ar crichnugadh imtecta uatha dárírib, do lecetar enghair guil 7 com-
harc[188]) ina díaidh.

189. 'Is truag lium-sa na gárthu-sa atcluinim,' ar C. C. .i.
'gair Conullach 7 Eoghanuch, mo braithri gradhucha fen, ag eolchuire 7 ag tuirrsi am diaidh, 7 do buaidhretar m'indtind go
mór, 7 ni fhedaim a n-estecht nó a fulang'; 7 do bi C. C. ag
dortadh a dér go himarcach andsin 7 adubhairt gor cumain da
braithribh tuirrse do denumh 'na diaidh, 7 co mbeith an oiret
sin do thuirse air fein ina ndiaidh sin nach beith sé enlá ar fedh
a bethadh gan a dera do dortadh dá cumhaidh. Gonadh andsin
dorinde se na roind-se:

  Truag lem-sa na gaírthe guil dá gach taeb do Loch Febhuil,
  gair Conaill, gaír Eogain tra, ag eolcuire am deaghaidh-sá.

  O fhuícfed mo braithri fen, indeos-[s]a mé fis mo ruín,
  ni bet énagaig, ní chel, nach tiucfa dér ar mo shuil.

  Mo delughadh re Gaidhealaibh indta tarla mo sbés-[s]i;
  cuma leamh gidh aenagaidh[189]) mo shaeghal tar a n-éssi.

190. Is andsin adubhairt Odhrán naem do bi 'sa luing maille
re C. C.: 'Est-si ríu 7 na tabhair h'aire doib 7 cuir h'airi sa tí
ar ar tréic tú íad .i. Día na n-uile chumhacht.' 'Is maith ader
tu-sa sin, a Odhrain,' ar C. C. '7 gidedh, as sgarudh cuirp re
hanmuin do duine scaradh rena braithrib 7 rena tír duthaig 7
dul uathuibh a tírib ciana comhaighecha ar deoraidhect 7 ar
oilithre tshuthain.' Agus adbert an rand-sa:

  Gé maith adeir tussa sin, a Odhrain uassail idhain,
  as scarudh cuirp re cride, damh deghail[190]) rem dherbhfine.

---

[188]*comhaircim,* 'I bewail'.
[189]*leg.* aenadhaigh.
[190]*leg.* dedhail.

When Columcille saw this he said: "I leave upon thee the gift of unwilling exile by reason of the help thou hast given me in leaving Erin for exile, and to those after thee that have a forked club I leave the same gift forever."

188. The ship departed then. And his kinsfolk, to wit, the Conalls and the Eogans and all that dwelt in that place were there on both sides of Loch Foyle. And when they saw that Columcille was in truth departing from them, they gave one cry of sorrow and lamentation for him.

189. "Woe is me for the cries I hear," saith Columcille, "the cry of the clan of Conall and of Eogan, my own beloved kinsmen, sorrowing and mourning my departure. Sorely have they troubled my spirit. I cannot listen to them nor endure them."

Then did Columcille shed tears passing many, and he said that it was right for his kinsmen to make dole for him, and so sorely would he grieve for them that there would not be a day of his life without his shedding tears lamenting them. And so he made these quatrains:

"Sad to me the lamenting
On this side and that of Loch Foyle;
The cry of Conall and Eogan,
In truth, bewailing my going.

Since I am to leave mine own kinsmen,
I shall give them to know of my secret:
A night shall not pass, I conceal not,
That tears shall not come to mine eye.

Since my leaving the folk of the Gael,
On whom I have set my affection,
It is naught to me though but one night
Were the length of my life days thereafter."

190. Then said holy Odhran that was in the boat with Columcille, "Be silent, and heed them not, and set thy mind on Him for whose sake thou hast given them up, to wit, Almighty God.

"Thou hast well said, Odhran," saith Columcille, "Howbeit it is a parting of the body from the soul for a man to part from his kinsfolk, and his native land, and to go from them to distant foreign places in pilgrimage and lasting exile." And he spake this quatrain:

Though well it is that thou speakest,
O Odhran, noble and spotless,
Yet the parting of body from soul
Is the parting to me from my kinsfolk."

191. Do gluaisetar rompo *no* cor fhagbhutar Doire ina ndiaidh, ⁊ do cuala C. C. gair ad*bal*-mór ag muindtir Doire. Is andsin adubhairt se: 'Gé truagh lem gach gair da cluinim, is truaighe ⁊ as tuirside lem an gair mhor-sa m*uindtir*e Doire iná íad, ⁊ dorinde sí ceith*ri* cuid dom cride am cliab, ⁊ ni racha a foghar as mo cluasaib com bás.' Conudh andsin dorinde se na roinn-si:

Ona gaírthib-se adcluini*m* créd fa bfhuilim am beath*aidh?*
gair mor muin*ntir*e Doiri do bris mo c[h]roide a cethair.

Fagbuidh duínd Doire dairgech dub*ach* deruch domenmnach,
scarudh ris is c*r*adh c*r*ide, is dul uadh go hainfi*n*e.

Inmain fidh asar cuireadh me gan ci*n,*
dainim d'aindr*ib* cloi*n*de Néill mo chur a céin 's dá gach fir.

Is anba luas mo curaidh[191] *acus* a d*r*uim re Doire;
saeth lim mo toisc a*r* ardmhuir, ag t*ri*all go hAlbai*n*
[mbroinigh[192]).

192. Is andsin do chuiretar an long ar siubal ar fedh Locha Febuil cusan inadh a teid an loch isan bfhairge moír re n-abortar na Tonda Cenanda aniugh; ⁊ ni hedh amhain do bi cumha *no* tuirsi ar daínibh a tire fen a ndiaidh C. C. acht do bi cumha ar énuch ⁊ ar ainmindt*e* eccíall*aidh*e 'na diaidh. *Acus* do derbad an sceoil sin, do batar failenda ⁊ énach Locha Febuil dá *gach* taeb da luing ag imthecht dó ⁊ iad ag scredaigh ⁊ ag screch*adh* ar a olcuss leo C. C. d'fhagail Erind.[193]) *Agus* do tuigedh se-siun a n-urlabhra| ag denam na tuirsi sin, ama*il* do tuicf*edh* se ó dainibh hí; ⁊ do bi an oiret sin do daendaigecht ⁊ do gradh ag C. C. ar a tír ⁊ ar a athardha duthch*u*sa fen nach mor gur mo an tuirse do bi air ag delugadh rena dainib ina in tuirse do bí air ag delugad re failendaib ⁊ re hénlaith*ib* locha [Febuil]. Gon*adh* andsin dorinde se an rand-sa:

Failenda Locha Febhail, romham *acus* am degh*aid,*
ni tegaid leam am curuch, uch is dubach ar ndegail![194])

---

[191]*leg.* curaigh.
[192]See Reeves' *Adam.,* p. 285.
[193]*leg.* Érenn.
[194]*leg.* dedail.

191. Then sailed they onward till they left Derry behind them. And Columcille heard a passing great lamentation of the Derry folk; and he said, "Though sad to me is every cry that I hear, yet sadder and heavier to me than any is this great weeping of the folk of Derry. And in my breast it hath made of my heart four fragments, and the sound will not go from my ears till death."

So it was then that he made these quatrains:

"Since I have heard this lamenting
Why do I still live my life days?
The loud wail of the people of Derry,
It hath broken my heart in four fragments.

Derry of Oaks, let us leave it
With gloom and with tears, heavy hearted;
Anguish of heart to depart thence,
And to go away unto strangers.

Forest beloved,
Whence they have banished me guiltless!
On the women of Niall's clan a blemish,
And on each man of them, is my exile.

Great is the speed of my coracle,
And its stern turned upon Derry;
Woe to me that I must on the main,
On the path to beetling-browed Alba."

192. Then steered they the boat through Loch Foyle to the place where the lake entereth into the great sea, that is called the Tonna Cenanna today. And it was not the folk only of his land that were heavy and sorrowful after Columcille, but the birds and the senseless creatures were sorrowful after him. And in token of this thing, the seagulls and the birds of Loch Foyle were pursuing on both sides of the boat, screaming and screeching for grief that Columcille was leaving Erin. And he understood that they were uttering speech of sorrow as he would understand it from human folk; and so great was his gentleness and his love for his land and the place of his birth that no greater was his sorrow in parting from her human folk than his sorrow in parting from the seagulls and the birds of Loch Foyle. So that he made this quatrain:

"The seagulls of Loch Foyle,
They are before me and in my wake;
In my coracle with me they come not;
Alas, it is sad, our parting."

Et do derb*adh* an sceoil sin, do cuaídh corr ar cuairt docum C. C. ó Erinn a nAlpain go hI, amail mebhruighes Adhamhnan naem air.¹⁹⁵)

193. Is andsin do co*nn*catar peist adhúathmar ag eirghe asin bfhairge, ⁊ nir aibsidhe¹⁹⁶) leo cnoc mor sleibhe iná sí, ⁊ do chui*r* si anfadh ⁊ (*fol.* 27a) combuaidredh mor ar in bfhairge 'na timchell, indus co raibe an long a cuntabairt a baite uaithe; ⁊ do gab ecla mór muindtir C. C. ⁊ do íarratar ar Colum Cille fen Día do guidhe ar a son da mbreith on guasacht mor sin a rabutar.

194. Is andsin adubairt C. C.: 'As ecen daibh duine eiccin da bur muindtir do tabairt do comhaidh don peísd ud ar bhur son fen uile, ⁊ as ferr sin na bur mbeith uili a nguasacht uaithe, ⁊ gebe duine do rach*ad* ar ar son cuice, doberuind-se flaithes Dé dó.'

195. Is andsin adubairt óclac*h* do mhuindtir C. C.: 'Racad feín ar bur son a mbeol na piasda úd. ⁊ geb*ad* flaithes De ar a shon sin.' *Agus* les sin tuc se leim assan luing, co tarla a mbeol na píasda é; ⁊ do imigh an peisd uatha less sin fan muir, ⁊ fuarutar ciúnus on muir íar sin.

196. Is andsin adubhratar a mhuindt*ir* re C. C.: 'Is truagh duinn an bas út fuair an t-oclac*h* do bí ag techt lind ar ar ngradh ón a tir duthaig fen a tírthaib cíana comhaighthecha.' Do guidh C. C. Día andsin ar son an óclaig, ⁊ nir fhada iar sin co facutar an pesd cuca ⁊ do aisic sí a oclac*h* co himlán do C. C., ⁊ ni derna an pesd digb*ail* dó, ⁊ ní mó dorinde don luing o shin amach.

197. Do gluais C. C. cona naemhuib iar sin a Loch Feabuil tar Banda, ⁊ nír anutar *co* ndechatar a tír a nDál Ríata a n-Ullt*aib*, ⁊ do chuaidh do tigh duine aíridhe and, ⁊ Coimghellan ainm fir an tighe; ⁊ ní fhuair se do daínib astigh acht tríar ban ⁊ lenub becc faríu, ⁊ tic an lenab d'innsoige C. C. ⁊ tuc póc dó, ⁊ do gab C. C. 'na ucht é ⁊ tuc pocc don lenubh¹⁹⁷). Conadh andsin dorinde an rand oirrd*erc*:

    A chubh*us* con,   a anam glan,
    ag so poíg doid,   teli pog damh.

Et dorinde C. C. faidhetóracht dó, ⁊ adubhairt co mb*adh* ecnaidh eol*ach* é ⁊ co mb*adh* oglac*h* diles do Dia é ⁊ co madh mór a

---

[195] See Reeves' *Adam.*, pp. 90-1.

[196] aibsidhe MS. (with *d* by a later hand over the first "i").

[197] *Amra* C. C. has the same story. See *R. C.*, XX, p. 132. It was probably the **source of** § 197.

And in witness of this story a crane went to seek Columcille from Erin to Iona in Alba, as Saint Adamnan maketh mention.[1]

193. And then they saw a monstrous beast rising out of the sea; and not more vast to them seemed a mountain peak than seemed she; and she raised a storm and a great tempest on the sea round about them, so that the boat was in peril of sinking therefrom. And great fear fell on Columcille's folk, and they besought him to pray God for them to bring them out of the great danger they were in.

194. And anon Columcille said: "For the sake of all of you, it is needful that ye give one of your folk to propitiate that beast. And better were that, than for all of you to be in danger from her, and whoso goeth unto her for the sake of all of us, to him will I give the Kingdom of God."

195. Then spake a lad of the household of Columcille, "I will go for your sakes into the jaws of that beast, and I shall be given the Kingdom of God in reward therefor."

And therewith he made a bound out of the vessel, and by hap he fell into the jaws of the beast. And the monster made off with him then over the sea. And they gat peace from the sea thereafter.

196. Anon said those of his household to Columcille: "It grieveth us for the death of the lad that was coming with us from his own land to distant foreign shores for love of us."

Then prayed Columcille to God in behalf of the youth and it was not long thereafter that they beheld the beast coming toward them, and she gave back the youth to Columcille entire. And no hurt had the beast done him nor any more did she do harm to the boat thereafter.

197. Anon went Columcille with his holy men from Loch Foyle beyond the Bann, and they halted not till they came to land in Dal Riada; and he went to the house of a certain man there, and Coimgellan was the name of the man of that house. And there was none in the house save three women and a little child with them. And the child came toward Columcille and kissed him. And Columcille took him to his bosom and gave him a kiss. It was then he made the famous quatrain:

> "O conscience clear,
> O soul unsullied,
> Here is a kiss for thee;
> Give a kiss to me."

And Columcille made a prophecy about him, and said he would be a wise and learned man and a faithful vassal to God, and he would be

---

[1] *Cf.* § 265.

eolus 'sa scribt*uir* 7 co madh e doberadh an breth oirr*derc* itir feruib Erenn 7 Alpan am Dail Ríada a mordail Droma cet.¹⁹⁸) Agus dob e sin Colman mac Coimgellá[i]n, 7 do fírudh gach ní dá ndubhairt C. C. ris.

198. Do gluais C. C. 7 a mhuindtir d'fhagbhail Erenn, 7 is é lín do batar .i. ficha esp*og*, 7 da xx sagart 7 deich ndeoch*ain* xx 7 deichenbur 7 da xx do macuib leghind nar gab gradha sagairt no deochain, amail aspert an fili .i. Dallan Forgail 'sa rand-sa:

Ceathracha sagart a lín,   fiche esp*og*, uassul brígh;
frisan sailmchet*al* gan a*cht*   tr*i*cha deochain, *coeca* m*ac*¹⁹⁹).

199.²⁰⁰) Et do bi an muindtir sin C. C. lan d'ecna 7 d'eoluss 7 do grassaib an Spir*ta* naeimh. Et dob i aeis C. C. an uair sin .i. da bliadhain 7 dá xx. Agus do caith se cethri bliadna decc ar fichit eli da saeghul ar deoraighecht 7 ar oilithre a n-Alpain.

200. Is andsin do cuaidh C. C. 7 a mhuindtir ina luing. Conadh and dorinde an rand-sa:

Mo choss am churchan ceoluch,   mo c[h]roidhe truagh
  [taigeoruch;
fand duine mar nach treór*uch*,   dall uile gach aineol*uch*.²⁰¹)

201. Et do celebratar d'Erinn íarsin 7 do lecetar do siubhul mara 7 fhairge íad, 7 do bí C. C. ag feithemh na hErend no cor folaidh an fairge air í, 7 ba dub*hach* dobronuch do bi C. C. an uair sin. Gonadh and dorinde na roinn-si sís:

Mo radharc t*ar* sal sínim   do clár na nda*r*ach ndighain*n*;

mor dér mo ruisc glais glemhoill   mar feghaim tar mh'ais
  [Erind.
Fuil suil nglais,   fech*us* Er*inn* t*ar* a hais;
is ní faicfe sí ré a lá   fir Erend naid a m*ná*.²⁰²)

¹⁹⁸*chet* MS.
¹⁹⁹The *Amra* is expressly mentioned as the source. But the *Amra* applies this verse to C. C.'s retinue at the convention of Druim Ceat. See *R. C.*, XX, p. 38. This copy of the *Amra* has *coica deochain, tricha mac*, so that it cannot be the source used by O'Donnell.
²⁰⁰The sources of this paragraph are Adamnan and the O. I. Life. See *Reeves' Adam.*, p. 9 and *Lis. Lives*, p. 178.
²⁰¹See Reeves' *Adam.*, p. 285. Franciscan copy has *munba treoruch*.
²⁰²See *R. C.*, XX, p. 38, which has: *nocon fhaiccbe iarmothá firu Hérenn nach a mná*.

great in the knowledge of the Scriptures, and it would be he would give the illustrious judgment between the men of Erin and Alba touching Dal Riada at the Assembly of Druim Ceat. And it was Colman son of Comgellan.[1]) And every word that Columcille said was verified.

198. Then Columcille and his household departed from Erin, and this is the number they were: twenty bishops, two score priests, thirty deacons, and two score sons of learning that had not yet the rank of priest or deacon, as the poet, even Dallan Forgaill, hath said in this quatrain:

> "Forty priests their number,
> Twenty bishops, lofty their virtue,
> For psalmody, without doubting,
> Thirty deacons, fifty boys."

199. And these folk were full of wisdom and knowledge and the graces of the Holy Ghost. And the years of Columcille at that time were two and two score. And other fourteen and twenty years of his life he spent in Alba in pilgrimage and exile.

200. Then went Columcille and his household into their ship. And there he made his quatrain:

> "My foot in my tuneful coracle;
> My sad heart tearful;
> A man without guidance is weak;
> Blind all those without knowledge."

201. And he bade farewell to Erin then, and they put out into the ocean and the great deep. And Columcille kept gazing backward on Erin till the sea hid it from him. And heavy and sorrowful was he in that hour. And it was thus he made this quatrain below:

> "I stretch my eye across the brine,
> From the firm oaken planks;
> Many the tears of my soft grey eye
> As I look back upon Erin.
>
> There is a grey eye
> That will look back upon Erin;
> Never again will it see
> The men of Erin or women.

---

[1] *Cf. below,* §§ 343-4.

Moch trath is am noín caínim, uchán an turass teighim;
ass e m'ainm-se, run atraídhim: cul re hErind,

202. Et ni haithrestar a scela osin amach noco rancutar an t-oilen darub ainm hÍ Colaim Cilli aniugh, 7 ann aspert an rand-sa:

Dochím hÍ, bendacht ar gach suil docí,
anté doní les a cheli, ass e a les fene doní.

203. A De is imgha inadh inar len C. C. a Tigherna fen .i. Issu Crist ina beathaidh; 7 as follass duinn anos go fuil se gá lenmhain ina indarbud 7 ina deoraigheacht 'san Eibgheit.

204.²⁰³ Oidhc[h]e cingcísi do cuatar a tír 'san oilen sin, 7 do batar draithe 'san oilen sin 7 tancutar a rectaibh espog d'indsoighe C. C. Acus adubratar²⁰⁴) ris nar coír do tect do'n oilen sin 7 go (fol. 27b) rabutar fen and remhe ag siladh creidmhe 7 crabaidh 7 nach rainic se a les daine naemtha eli da bennughadh. 'Ni fír daib-si sin,' ar C. C., 'oir ni hespoig iar fir sib act draithe diablaide ata a n-agaidh creidimh, 7 fagbuidh an t-oilen-sa, 7 ní daeib do deonaigh Dia é.' Agus do fagbhatar na draithe an t-oilen le breithir C. C.

205. Is ansin adubairt C. C. ren a muindtir: 'As maith duind ar fremha do dul fon talmain-si a tancamar, 7 gebe nech naemtha dar muindtir do aeinteochudh bas d'faghail 7 a cur fa huír na hindse-si doberaind-se flaithes De dó.'

206.²⁰⁵) Is andsin adubairt Odhran naemh do bui maille re C. C.: 'Aentaighim-si bas d'faghail ar an cunnradh sin.' 'Doberim-si flaithes Dé duid-se,' ar C. C., '7 fos doberim duit gach nech iarfas atchuinghe ag mo tumba no ag mo luidhe orm-sa, gan a fag-

---

²⁰³From § 204 to § 213, O'D. closely follows the *O. I. Life*. See *Lis. Lives*, pp. 30, 31.
²⁰⁴adubrathar MS.
²⁰⁵See Reeves' *Adam.*, p. 417.

At dawn and at eve I lament;
Alas for the journey I go!
This is my name—I tell a secret—
'Back to Erin'."

XV

OF THE LABORS OF COLUMCILLE IN IONA

202. And the history telleth no more of him until he came to the isle called Iona of Columcille to this day. And there he made this quatrain:

"I behold Iona.
A blessing on each eye that seeth [it].
He that doth good to his fellow
'Tis he that doth good to himself."

203. O God, many were the ways wherein Columcille did during his life follow his Lord Jesu Christ. And it is clear to us now that he doth follow him in His banishment and exile into Egypt.

204. On the eve of Pentecost they cast anchor on that island; and there were druids there, and they came in the guise of bishops toward Columcille. And they said to him that it was not right for him to come on that island and that themselves had been there afore him sowing the Faith and piety, and it had no need of other holy men to bless it.

"It is not true what ye say," saith Columcille, "for ye be not bishops in truth, but druids of Hell that are against the Faith. Leave this island. Not to you hath God granted it."

And at the word of Columcille the druids left the island.

205. Then said Columcille to his household, "It were good for us that our roots should go beneath this earth where we have come, and whatever holy man of our household is minded to get death and be put beneath the clay of this island, I will give him the Kingdom of God."

206. Then spake holy Odhran that was with Columcille: "I would fain die under that covenant."

"I will give thee the Kingdom of God," saith Columcille, "and moreover I grant thee this, that whoso maketh request at my tomb or at my resting place shall not get it until he first make prayer to thee."

hail dó *no* go nguidhe se thussa ar tús;' 7 fuair Odhran bas andsin do toil De 7 C. C., 7 do haidluicedh fa uír na hindsi sin é. Gonadh Reilec Odhrain a n-Í ainm an inaid sin aniug.

207.²⁰⁶) Do bendaigh C. C. an t-oilen sin, 7 do cumhd*aigh* eclu[i]s onoruch and, 7 do tócuib reilge 7 uladha ann 7 crossa imga fa mbidh se fen 7 a naeimh ag radh a trath 7 a n-urn*aidh*e; 7 dorinde se faidhetóracht don baile sin, 7 adub*er*t co m*adh* mor do righib Erend 7 Alban do hadhnaicf*idh*e ann, 7 co m*adh* mor do cinedhuibh an domain do ticf*edh* da n-oilithre don baile sin. Do fíradh an briatar sin Coluim Cille.

208. Et ar ndenamh comnaidhe an baile sin dó, do ordaigh sé ord manuch and, 7 do bi sé fein 'na ab orra. Is mor d'fhertaibh 7 do mirbuilibh dorinde C. C. and ar Er*enn*chaib 7 ar Alb*an*chaibh 7 ar Bretnachaibh 7 ar Shacsanchuibh 7 ar tirth*ibh* an domain o sin amach.

209.²⁰⁷) Lá da raibe C. C. ag radh senmóra re taebh aband airidhe 'sa tír sin 7 sluaigh mora 'na timchell, do fagaib duine airide an tsenmoir 7 do cuaidh se tar an sruth anonn do teichem breithri De d'estecht ó C. C. Tainic nathair nemhe cuige, 7 do marb sí é co hobann a fiadhnaisi na sluagh, 7 tucudh an corp a fiadhn*ai*se C. C., 7 do ben se crois lena bachaill ar ucht an duine mairb, cor aithbeoaigh sé é, 7 cor érich 'na shesamh a fíadn*ai*se na sluagh sin, 7 co tuc buidhechus do Día 7 do C. C. tresan mirb*huil* sin dorindedh air; 7 do chreid moran dona sluagaibh do Día 7 do C. C. trid sin.

210. La eli tuc Sacsanach builli ga a manuch do muindtir C. C., 7 do shaeil cor marb é; 7 ger gér an ga, ni derna do digb*hail acht* a *cri*os do gerradh; 7 do mallaigh C. C. an Sacsanuch 7 fuair bás foch*e*doír.

211.²⁰⁸) Fechtus do C. C. a nhÍ ag scribneoracht, 7 do cuala se glaedh a p*or*t na hindse, 7 adub*hai*rt re cach an duine dorinde an glaedh do tab*hai*rt tairis, 7 do indes do cach co ticf*adh* an duine sin do tabhairt pács da cossaib fen, 7 co ndoirtf*edh* an adharc duibh asa raibe se ag scribneoracht. Gonadh and dorinde na roind-se:

    Bachlach isan p*ur*t,   co mbachaill 'na crub;
    taidlidhf*e* m'adhaircín,   is doirtf*e* mo dubh.

    Toir*n*idhf*idh* sís   d'indsoig*e* mo pacs,
    nod*us*doirtfe m'adhaircín,   con*us*fuícfi fás.

---

²⁰⁶*l. c.*, pp. 410, 418.
²⁰⁷Taken literally from the *O. I. Life*. See *Lis. Lives*, p. 31.
²⁰⁸Taken literally from the *O. I. Life*. See *Lis. Lives*, p. 31, and Reeves' *Adam.*, p. 54.

And Odhran received death then by the will of God and Columcille. And he was laid beneath the clay of that island. Hence the Grave of Odhran in Iona is the name of that place today.

207. Then Columcille blessed that island and built a noble church therein, and put up sacred memorials and stations there, and many crosses whereunder he and his holy men were wont to recite their hours and prayers. And he made a prophecy touching that stead, and he said that many of the kings of Erin and Alba should be buried there, and that many of the nations of the world should come on pilgrimage to that place. And that word of Columcille was verified.

208. And he builded a dwelling in that place, and founded an order of monks there, and himself was abbot over them. And from that time forth many were the marvels and the wonders that Columcille wrought in that place upon the men of Erin and Alba and upon the Britons and Saxons and the men of the regions of the world.

209. On a day that Columcille was teaching by the side of a certain river in that region, and much people around him, a man left the sermon and made off across the stream, fleeing from the sound of the word of God from Columcille. To him came a venomous serpent, and forthwith in the sight of the multitude she killed him. The body was brought before Columcille, and he made the cross with his staff upon the breast of the dead corpse, so that he restored it to life. And the man rose up and stood before the multitude, and gave thanks to God and Columcille for the marvel that had been wrought upon him. And many of the multitude believed on God and Columcille thereby.

210. On another day a Saxon dealt a monk of Columcille's household a blow with a javelin, and he thought that he killed him. And albeit the spear was sharp, yet it did him no harm, save to cut his girdle. And Columcille cursed the Saxon and he fell dead straightway.

211. On a time that Columcille was in Iona writing, he heard a shout in the harbor of the island. And he gave command to all to bring to him the man that had given the shout. And he told them all that the man would come and kiss his feet and would spill the inkhorn wherefrom he was writing. Thereupon he made the quatrains:

> "A pilgrim is in the port,
> A staff in his fist.
> He shall come near my little horn,
> And shall spill my ink.
>
> He shall stoop down
> To give me a kiss;
> He shall upset my little horn,
> And leave it empty."

Et do firadh an faidetoracht sin C. C. mar fa gnath leis gach ní adérud se d'fhírudh.

212. Fechtas eli do C. C. a nhÍ, 7 do chuir se meithel do buain arbha do bi ag an coimthinol, 7 do cuir se Baithín 7 na manaich leo, 7 do an fen re haghaidh coda na meithli d'ullmhughadh; 7 do furail mart do cur da bruith fá a comhair. Agus do bi senlaech mor d'feraib Erenn fare C. C. an uair sin, 7 fa brathair do fen é. i. Maelumha mac Baedaín do Cineol Eogain mic Neill. Agus do mothaigh C. C. ocarus ar an senlaech, 7 do gab truaidhe mor 'na timchell é, 7 do fiarfaig de cred í an tshaith ass mo do ithedh se anuair do bi se óg. Adubairt an senlaech con n-ithed se mart do shaith. 'Fech do sáith anoss ar an mart-sa na meithle,' ar C. C. Do fech Maelumha sin, 7 do ith se an mart uile. Tainec Baithin cuca iar sin, 7 do fiarfaigh do Colum Cille narb ullamh cuid na meithli. Do indeis C. C. dó gach ní da nderna sé re cuid na meithli, 7 do cuaidh Baithin do monmar go mor ar C. C. trid sin. 'A Bhaithín,' ar se, 'do b'urussa le Día ar n-anacal ort;' 7 do furail C. C. cnamha an mairt do cruindiugad 'na fiadhnaise, 7 do thocuib a lamha (fol. 28a) os a cind 7 do bendaigh iad, 7 tainic a feoil fen orra, 7 tuc a saith do na manchaib 7 don meithil dhe; 7 ni hedh amhain acht da ticdis lucht na hindse uile cuice, dogebdais a ndil don mhart sin tre bendachtain Coluim Cille.

213.[209]) Fectus eli do cuaidh Caindech ar cuairt a cend C. C. go hÍ; 7 ag tect anoir do, do fhagaib a bachull a ndermad toir; 7 iarna faicsin sein do C. C., do cuir aingel De lesin mbachaill, 7 do chuir se a lene fen les co Caindech, mar comartha gradha 7 duthrachta, indus go fuair Caindech abus remhe íad.

214. Fechtus do cuaidh C. C. do siladh breitre De o hI cusan oilen re n-abartar Muili; 7 tarla da lobur decc dó, 7 do iarratar derc air. 'Ni fhuil deirc oir no airgeid agam daeib,' ar Colum Cille. Do iarrutar tre dochus daingen air a slanuccadh on lubra o nach raibe derc eli aige doib. Ar na thuicsin do C. C. co raibe aithrige acu ina pecuib 7 co raibe dochus mor acu as fen, do benduig 7 do coisric se tobur do bi san inad sin, 7 tuc ar na lobraibh a bfhothrucadh ass, cor slanaigedh a cedoir iad amail do slanaiged Naman .i. prindsa ridiredh righ na Sirie do bi 'sa lubra lena fotruccadh secht n-uaire a sruth Eorthanain re tecusc hEliseus faidh, amail mebraiges ebisdil an tres luain don corghus mor idón.

---

[209]Taken literally from *O. I. L.* See *Three Middle-Irish Homilies,* ed. Stokes, pp. 118-20.

And that prophecy of Columcille's was verified, for it was always so, and every prophecy he uttered was verified.

212. Another time when Columcille was in Iona, he sent a band of reapers to cut the corn that belonged to his household. And he sent Baithin and the brethren with them. And himself remained behind to make ready a meal for the reapers. And he bade put on to boil for them a ox. And there was a mighty old warrior of the men of Erin with Columcille that time, and he was kinsman to himself, to wit, Maelumha son of Baedan of Clan Eogain mic Neill. And Columcille perceived that the old warrior was hungry, and great ruth seized him therefor. And he asked him what was the biggest portion he used to eat when he was young. The old man said he used to eat an ox as his share.

"Behold thy portion now in the reapers' ox," saith Columcille.

Maelumha beheld, and ate the whole ox. Then entered to them Baithin, and asked Columcille if the meal was not ready for the reapers. Then Columcille told him what he had done with the reapers' meal. And Baithin murmured loudly against Columcille therefor.

"O Baithin," saith Columcille, "it were easy for God to save us from thee."

And Columcille bade gather together before him the bones of the ox, and he lifted his hands above them and blessed them.

And their flesh came upon them. And thereof he gave to the brethren and to the reapers their fill. And not that only, but had there come to him the folk of the whole island, they would have got their fill from that ox through the blessing of Columcille.

213. Another time Cainnech went to visit Columcille in Iona, and when he returned westward, he forgat his staff and left it in the east. And when Columcille saw it, he sent an angel of God with the staff. And he sent his own sark therewith in sign of love and goodwill, so that Cainnech found them there afore him.

214. On a time Columcille went from Iona to the island called Mull to sow the word of God. And twelve lepers met him. And they asked alms of him.

"I have no alms of gold or silver for you," saith Columcille.

Then with strong hope besought they him to heal them of their leprosy, since he had no other alms for them. And when Columcille understood that they had true sorrow for their sins and great hope in him, he blessed and hallowed the well that was in the place and bade the lepers bathe therein. And they were healed forthwith, as was healed Naaman, the leader of the host of the king of Syria, that had been a leper, when he bathed seven times in the Jordan at the command of Elisha the prophet, as maketh mention the epistle on the

In diebus illis Naman prindceps milisie regis Sirie. Et amail mebruighter a lebur na Rigraide 'sa Pipla.²¹⁰)

215. Fechtus do Gridhoir beil-oir .i. Papa na Romha ag estect aifrinn in a eclais fen 'sa Roimh, go facaid se aingli De 7 cross croind acu ga lecen ar an altoir 'na fiadnaise; 7 do brethnaighetar na carthanail do bí faris an Papa an cros do togbail, 7 nir fed enduine acu a tocbail. Agus dob ingnadh le cach sin. Agus mar do condaic an Papa sin, teid fen da hindsaige, 7 do glac sé í, 7 do erich sí les co humhal. Is andsin adubhairt an Papa: 'Ni cuccam-sa no docum enduine eli do Romhanchaibh do cuir Día an cros-sa acht docum C. C. mic Feidlim .i. an nech naemta as mo ina bfoillsigend Dia a grasa fen do clanduib na mban.' Et do cuir an Papa clerich dá muindtir fen lé a cend C. C. go hÍ.²¹¹) Agus do fhoillsig aingel De do C. C. go raibe techta an Papa cuice 7 an cros sin leo. De raid C. C. le Baithin 7 risna manchuib: 'Ata coindemh uassal onoruch cugaib anocht,' ar se, .i. 'muindtir Gridoir Papa 7 ullmhuighidh biad 7 deoch 'na n-oirchill.' Is andsin adubhairt Baithin: 'Ní fuil do biad no do digh againd doib,' ar se, 'acht enbairghen 7 enpota fina do bi re haghaidh na n-aifrend.' Tainic muindtir an Papa don baili fai sin, 7 do gab naire mor C. C. uime sin, 7 do furail se an becan fhina 7 arain sin do tabhairt na fiadnaise cuige 7 do bendaig e, indus co raibhe a saith araín 7 fína acu fen 7 ag muindtir an Papa. Agus ni headh amain acht da tigdís a raibe isna tirthaib cuca an uair sin, dogebdais a saith araín 7 fina mar an cedna. Et tucc an Papa an cross sin do C. C. Conadh di goirther an cross mor C. C. aniugh. Agus conadh í ass airdmhind do C. C. a Toraig tuaiscert Erend ag denumh feart 7 mirbhol ó sin alle, ar n-a cur anoir do Colum Cille o hI go Toraidh.

216. Tuc C. C. buidechus romhór do Día 7 don Pápa isna tidluicibh romhóra fuair se uatha mar adubramar romainn 'sa scel-sa tuas, 7 do tinnscain moludh do denumh do Día andsin .i. an t-Altus²¹²) C. C. ainm an molta sin; 7 leighend rochruaidh

---

²¹⁰See *IV. Reg., 5.*

²¹¹See *Leabhar Breac,* p. 109a, and Reeves' *Adam.,* pp. 318, 319.

²¹²i. e. the hymn *Altus Prosator.* According to the preface to this hymn, the immediate cause of its composition was, 'to beg God's pardon for the three battles he had caused in Erin.' See Reeves' *Adam.,* p. 253.

third Monday of Lent.' *In diebus illis Naman prindceps milisie regis Sirie,* and as it is recorded in the Book of Kings in the Bible.

XVI

OF COLUMCILLE AND POPE GREGORY OF ROME

215. On a time that Gregory of the Golden Tongue, to wit, the Pope of Rome, was hearing the mass in his church in Rome, he beheld angels of God letting down a wooden cross upon the altar afore him. And the cardinals that were with the Pope thought to lift away the cross. But none could do it. And it seemed a marvel to all. And when the Pope saw this, he went himself thither and laid hold thereon, and it rose up for him obediently.

Then said the Pope: "Not to me more to any other of the Romans hath God sent this cross, but to Columcille the son of Fedlimid, the holy man in whom God hath, more than in any of the sons of woman, revealed His graces. And the Pope sent clerics of his own household therewith to Columcille in Iona. And an angel made known to Columcille that messengers were coming to him from the Pope, and that cross with them. Anon said Columcille to Baithin and his brethren:

"A noble worshipful company will be coming to us this night," saith he, "to wit, the household of Gregory the Pope, and let us make ready food and drink to provide for them."

Then said Baithin: "We have for them nor food nor drink," saith he, "save one loaf and one jar of wine that were set apart for the mass."

Anon withal entered the household of the Pope, and great shame seized Columcille thereat and he bade bring to him the little wine and bread. And he blessed it in such wise that they had their fill, both they and the household of the Pope, of bread and of wine both.

And not that only, but if there had come to them in that hour all the folk of the land, they should have had their fill in like wise of bread and wine. And the Pope gave that cross to Columcille. And to this day it is called the Great Cross of Columcille. And it is the chief treasure of Columcille in Tory, working wonders and marvels from that day to this in the north of Erin, whither Columcille sent it westward from Iona.

216. Columcille gave great thanks to God and to the Pope for the passing great gifts he gat from them, as we have told afore in the

ro-onorach ro-uassal an moladh sin ina tucc sé eolus uadh a seicreidib na diagachta, 7 go hairidhe inar labhair sé co mor do
thuicsin na Trinoide; 7 do foillsigh se moran d'eolusaib diamhra-
cha and leth risna duilib talmanda; 7 itir gach eolus da nderna
se and, adubairt se go fuil daine fai an talumh-sa 7 a cossa anís,
7 gu fuil siad ag aitreb a tíre 7 a talmhan fen mar atámaid-ne
ag aitreb ar tire fen, 7 gorub inand Dia da creidend siad 7 sinde.
Et do cuir se triur cleriuch da mhuindtir fen lesan moludh mben-
duighte naemtha sin dorinde se do Día da taisbenadh do Grighoir
Phapa docum go moladh se é; 7 do bi an Papa sin ronaemtha ann
fein. Et do cuiretar na clerich sin C. C. tri caibhdil uatha fen
ar lár an molta-ssa, 7 do benatar tri caibdil da nderna C. C. ass,
da fechain an aitheonadh an Papa a legend fen tar an legend dorinde C. C. no an inand moladh doberadh se orra. Acus docuatar
(fol. 28b) ar sin dochum na Romha. Mar do cuala an Papa
muindtir C. C. don baile, do furail se a llecen ina cend fen, 7 do
indesitar na clerich gorub lesan moladh sin do cuir C. C. iad da
taisbenad do san. 'Gabthur dund é,' ar Grighóir. Et mar do
tindscain siad an moludh do gabail, do erich an Papa 'n-a sesamh,
7 mar do tindscain síad na tri caibdil dorindetar fen do gabail,
do shuid an Papa; 7 mar do tindscanatar an cuid eli dorinde
C. C. don moladh do gabail, do eirich an Papa 'n-a shesamh, 7
do bi se 'n-a shesamh no gor gabudh an moladh uile. Acus do
bud ro-ingantach le a raibe do lathair mar dorinde an Papa sin,
7 do fhíar[f]uigetar de cred fa nderna se sin. 'Dorindes,' ol se,
'an uair do tindscnatar na clerig tossach an molta ud do gabhail,
do [c]ondarc-sa aingliu De maille riu 7 síad [g]o ro-onoruch 'n-a
timchell, 7 mar do tindscnatar na tri caibdil airidhe ud don
mo[l]adh do gabail, do imghetar na haingli úatha, 7 do suidhes-a
mar do condarc na haingil ag imtect. Et mar do tindscnatar an
cuid eli don moladh do gabail, do impodur na haingeil cuca aris.
Mar do condarc-sa na haingil ar n-impodh, do erghess 7 do badhus
am sesumh no gor gabadh an mo[l]adh uile. 'Is fir sin, a athair
naemtha,' ar na clerich. 'As maith an t-adbhur do bi agad 7 as
orainde fen do bí an scel-sin ag na hainglib ler fagaib siad sind.'
Et do indisitar na clerich o tus go deredh gach ní dá ndernutar

history. And anon he set to making a hymn of praise to God. And the *Altus [Prosator] of Columcille* is the name of that hymn of praise. And it is a composition passing lofty and passing noble, but passing hard of understanding; for therein he giveth from him knowledge of the secrets he had from God. And in especial he speaketh much of the meaning of the Trinity, and he revealeth much secret knowledge therein, touching the earthly elements, and among other knowledge that he revealeth there, he saith there be folk beneath this earth with their feet upward, and that they dwell in their land and on earth as we dwell in our land, and that it is the same God they believe in as do we. And he sent three clerics of his household with the blessed holy work of praise he had made for God, to show it to Pope Gregory, that he might adjudge it.

And that Pope was indeed very holy. And those clerics of Columcille put three chapters of their own in midst of that work of praise, and they cut out therefrom three passages that Columcille had made, to see if the Pope would know their composition athwart the composition that Columcille had made, or if he would give the same praise to them. And forthwithal went they to Rome. When the Pope heard that the household of Columcille were in the place, he bade admit them to him, and the clerics related that Columcille had sent them with that hymn of praise to show it to him.

"Recite it to us," saith Gregory."

And when they began to recite the hymn of praise, the Pope arose. But when they began to recite the three chapters they had composed themselves, the Pope sat down. And when they began to recite the rest of the hymn, that Columcille had made, the Pope rose up and continued standing until they had recited all the hymn. And it was passing strange to those present that the Pope did this. And they asked him why he had done it.

"I did this," saith the Pope. "When the clerics began to recite the opening of the hymn of praise, I beheld angels of God, and they right worshipful, around them, and when they began to recite those three chapters of the hymn in especial, the angels departed from them. And I sat down when I saw the angels depart. And when they began to recite the rest of the hymn, the angels returned to them again, and when I beheld the angels returning, I rose up and continued standing until the whole hymn was recited."

"It is true, O holy Father," say the clerics, "Thou hadst good cause. And it is by reason of us the angels had the portent whereby they left us."

And then the clerics related from beginning to end everything they had done, and they asked pardon of the Pope; and the Pope said

fen, 7 do iarratar a maithemh ar an Papa; 7 adubairt an Papa, gerb olc a ndernatar, co maithf*edh* sé doib é a n-onoír C. C. Acus do mol se C. C. go romhór and sin, 7 adub*airt* se nach tainic 7 nach ticfa, a fecmais daendachta Crist, duine bud ferr ina é in gach uile subalt*aigh*e 7 do mol se an t-Altus go romhor mar an cedna, 7 do fhagaib se do buaduib air, gebe dogebhadh uair gach lai é, nac daimeóntai coidhce hé.

217. Et fos da derbudh sin do bi clerech airithe ag a raibe duthracht do Dia 7 do C. C. Acus do gnathaig*edh* se an t-Altus do radh uair gach lai. Tesda enmac muirnech do bí aige, 7 adubairt sé ó do leg C. C. bas docum a mic, nach gebud sé an t-Altus co brath arís; 7 do bi companuch aíridhe ag an clerech 7 do gellatar da cheli gebe acu duine dogebudh bas ar tús, a techt d'indisin scel don fir eli. Tesda companuch an cleirich ar tus, 7 tainec se d'indisin scel don clerech. 'Cindus ataí?' ol in clerech. 'Do slanaidh Dia me,' ol sé, '7 ata droch-scel agam duid-se.' 'Cred sin?' ol an clerech. 'T*u*-sa do damnadh,' ol se, 'trid mar do treicis an t-Altus do rádh.' 'In bfuil furtacht ar bith air sin?' or an clerech. 'Ata,' ar se, '.i. an t-Altus do radh fo tri gach lai an fedh beir at beth*aidh* a n-eraic ar licis tort de gan radh'; 7 do gabudh an t-Altus fo tri gach lai ó sin amach gó a bás. Acus do slanaigh Día 7 C. C. an clerech sin docum na glóire suthaine iar sin.

218. Is andsin adub*airt* an Pápa re muindtir C. C.: 'Muna beith méd mo churaim-se,' ar se, 'do taeb na nduine eli, do rachuind ar cuairt docum C. C., 7 ós air sen nach fuil a leitheid sin do curam, ticedh se chucam-sa.' Do imghetar muindtir C. C. t*ar* a n-ais, 7 do indsetar do C. C. go raibhe an Pápa ga íarraidh ar cuairt cuice. Gluaisis C. C. andsin, 7 ar techt fa cuig mile decc don Roimh dó, do benatar cluicc na Romha uile uatha fen; 7 nir fedadh cosc doib 7 do bidhgatar lucht na Romha uili uime sin. Et do gab ingnadh mór íad. 'Na bidh ingnadh oruib fan ní úd,' bar an Papa, 'Colum Cille an naem erlumh ata ag techt am cend-sa, 7 as dó doberid na cluic an onoír úd; 7 ni fedf*aid*er cosc doib no co ti se fén don baile.' Is andsin do erich an Papa amach 7 moran do mhaithibh na Romha farís, maille re honoír 7 re reueria*ns* mór a coinde C. C.; 7 ar rochtain a celi doibh, do pogsad a celi 7 doronsad luthgair*ed* 7 gairdechus imarcuch re roile; 7 do filleatar don baili ar sin; 7 ar ndenamh slectana do C. C. a tempull mor na Romha, do coiscetar na cluic uatha fen. Acus ar mbeith aimser do C. C. fa onoír moír faris an Papa, do gab sé ced aige fa techt da tir fen, 7 do lig an Papa a bendacht

that albeit they had done ill, he would forgive them in honor of Columcille.

And therewith praised he Columcille exceedingly. And he said that there had not come, nor should come, save the person of Christ, one better than he in every virtue. And he praised the *Altus* right highly likewise, and he left as a virtue thereon that whoso should recite it once each day should not be damned forever.

217. And moreover in witness of this, there was a certain cleric that was devoted to God and to Columcille. And he was wont to say the *Altus* once each day. And his one dear son died. And he said that since Columcille had let his son die, he would never say the *Altus* again.

And the cleric had a certain comrade, and each promised other that whoso of them should first die would come and bring tidings to the other. The comrade of the cleric was first to die. And he came to bring tidings to him.

"How is it with thee?" saith the cleric.

"God hath saved me," saith he, "but for thee I have ill tidings."

"What are they?" saith the cleric.

"Thou art damned," saith he, "for that thou hast left saying the *Altus*."

"Is there any help thereof?" saith the cleric.

"There is," saith he, "to wit, to say the *Altus* thrice daily the length thy life lasteth in amends for what thou hast neglected thereof."

And from that time till his death he recited the *Altus* thrice daily. And therefore God and Columcille did save that cleric for the glory everlasting.

218. Then said the Pope to the household of Columcille: "Were it not for the greatness of the cares I have for others," saith he, "I should go to visit Columcille. And since there is not the like care on him, I would that he come to me."

Then departed the household of Columcille. And they told Columcille that the Pope had asked him to visit him.

Columcille set out then. And when he had come within fifteen miles of Rome, all the bells of Rome rang of themselves. And none might silence them. And all the folk of Rome were startled thereat, and great wonder seized them.

"Be not amazed at this thing," saith the Pope, "the holy patron Columcille cometh to see me, and it is to him that the bells do honor, nor can they be silenced until he hath entered the place."

"Then the Pope went out, and many of the nobles of Rome with him, with honor and great worship, to fetch Columcille; and when they had met and kissed each other, and had made great mirth and joy either of other; and when Columcille had bowed down in the great temple

les 7 do fhagaib C. C. a bendacht aige sen; 7 tuc an Papa tidluic-
the mora do C. C. andsin .i. gebé baile da bailtibh fen a n-oir-
deochadh C. C. do cach oilithri do denamh, luaigidhecht sdasioín
na Romha do beith ag an duine dodenadh an oilithre sin. Acus
as é ba(*fol.* 29a)ile dá tucc C. C. an onoír sin .i. do Doire 7 ssé
fen a nAlbain; acus asse inadh inar ordaigh se an oilithre sin do
denamh .i. ó an ul*aidh* ata ag p*or*t na long 'sa cend toir don baili,
c*on*uige an t-impódh dessiul ata 'sa cend tíar de.

219. An uair *tra* do cuaidh C. C. a n-Albain, tancutar
maithe Lethe Cuind 7 go haírithe a phráithre fen .i. clanda Conaill 7 Eoghain 7 cl*and*u Cuind uile ar cuairt chuice rian imtecht
a hErind dó, 7 do fiarf*aigh*etar de cía he an naem *no* an clerech
do fhuicf*edh* sé 'n-a inadh fen acu *no* dá creidfidis mar athair
spirudálta. T*ar* a eís sen do labuir C. C. riu 7 assedh adubairt:
'Fuicfeat-sa triúr naemh agaib diteónus ar gach n-olc sib acht
go creide sib doib 7 co nderna sibh a comairli .i. Colman Ela 7
Colman Lainde mac Luacha*in*[213]) 7 Mocaemhóg[214]) Comruire a
Midhe 7 bed fen ga bur ndíden oss a cend sin ge dech uaib a
n-Albain, 7 do gébh o Día gach duine dobera esonoir do na naem-
bib sin fháguim agaibh, báss do tabairt acedoir do.' Tarla cocadh
mór ina diaidh sin edir Brandumh[215]) mac Ech*ach* rí Laig*h*en
7 Leth Cuind, co tainic Brandamh f*or* sluaiged a Leith Cuind, cor
gabud longport les a termond Cluana hIraird.

Do cuiretar Leth Cuind an triur naem-sa do fhagaib C. C.
acu d'iarraidh sithe ar righ Laighen 7 do taircs*in* córa dó, 7 ni
derna an rí sith nó coir ar a comhairli. 'Dogebaim-ne ó Día bass
do tabairt duid-se 7 gan do tren do dul nías faide ina in t-inadh-sa
ina bfuil tú a Leith Cuind, o nach gabond tu ar comairli,' ar na
naeimh. 'Ni ferr sib nó an nech naemtha do gell damh-sa nach
fuighinn bás no co caithind sacramaint as a laimh fen,' ar Bran-
dum .i. Maedóg Ferna. Dorindetar na naeim escaine ar Brandumh an uair sin, o nar gabh sé a comhairli ar sith do denumh.
Acus tainic do bridh na hescaine sin 7 an gelltanais tuc C. C.
doib, gebe dogenadh a n-esonoír, go ngerreoch*adh* se fen a saeghal,
nach tainic se tairis sin a Leith Cuind 7 gor marbudh ar an
sluaighed sin fen é. Et rucatar na diabuil a anum 'san aeier a
n-airde leo 7 do bátur ga píanudh and. Do bi Maedhóg an uair
sin re hagaidh meithli a búi ag buaín arba dó, 7 do cuala sé sian

[213]See Meyer's *Betha Colmáin Maic Lúacháin*, p. 28.

[214]*leg. Mocholmóc.* Mocaemhóg is probably Kevin of Glendalough.

[215]The story about Brandubh is taken literally from the *Book of Lecan, fol.*
183a. See also Reeves' *Adam.*, p. 205; *Silva Gadelica*, p. 374 *seq.*

of Rome, the bells ceased of themselves. And when Columcille had been for a time with the Pope in great honor, he took leave of him to go to his own land. And the Pope gave Columcille his blessing. And Columcille left his blessing with the Pope. And the Pope bestowed great gifts upon Columcille then, to wit, whatever place of his domains Columcille should appoint for making pilgrimage, the folk that should make the pilgrimage should have the same indulgence as for the station of Rome. And it is to this place that Columcille gave this honor, to wit, from the calvary that is in the harbor of the ships east of the town, to the turn sunwise that is west thereof.

219. When Columcille was on his way to Alba, the nobles of Leth Cuinn came to see him before his departing from Erin, and in especial his kinsfolk, the clan of Conall and Eogan and the whole clan of Conn. And they inquired of him what holy man or cleric he would leave with them in his place, the which they should trust as their spiritual father.

Then spake Columcille, and said in this wise: "I shall leave with you three holy men, that shall protect you against every evil if ye but trust them and follow their counsels, to wit, Colman Ela, and Colman son of Luachan of Lann, and Mochaemhog of Comruire in Meath. And I shall be your protection above them albeit far from you in Alba. And I shall obtain from God that every one that faileth in honor toward those holy men that I shall leave with you, shall die forthwith."

Thereafter it befell that there was a great war between Brandubh mac Echach King of Leinster and Leth Cuinn, so that Brandubh made a hosting into Leth Cuinn and pitched his tents in the sanctuary of Clonard.

Then Leth Cuinn sent the three holy men that Columcille had left with them to make peace with the King of Leinster and to offer him just terms. But the King would not make peace nor terms at their counsel.

"We shall prevail upon God to kill thee and suffer not thy forces to advance further than the spot where thou art in Leth Cuinn since thou wilt not heed our counsel," say the saints.

"Thou art no better than Saint Maedog Ferna that promised me I should not die until I should take the sacrament from his own hand," saith Brandubh.

Then the holy men laid curses on Brandubh, since he took not their counsel to make peace.

By reason of that curse and of the promise that Columcille had made them that whoever misprized them, he would cut off his life, it befell that Brandubh came not further into Leth Cuinn, and in that same hosting was slain, and devils bare his soul up into the air with them, and they were tormenting it there.

na hanma ga pianudh, 7 do cuaidh se tre cumhachta Dé 'san aeieór a n-airde a ndiaidh na ndíabal, 7 do bi ag cathugad riu fa'n anam sin Branduibh. Acus do cuadur iarsin os ceand hI C. C. a n-Albain. Acus do bi C. C. ag scribneoracht an uair sin, 7 do foillsigh aingel De an ní sin dó. Acus ba truag les an t-anum ga pianadh, *acht* gerb é fen fuair o Día saegal Branduibh do gerrugadh tríd gan comairli na naemh-sa dá mhuindtir fen adubrumar romhainn do gabail ar sith do denumh re Leith Cuind; 7 do cuir a delg in a phrut,[216]) 7 do ling a n-airde 'san aier do cuidiugadh le Maedhóg anam Branduib do buain do na demnaib. Acus do batur ar an cathugad sin no cu ndechutar ós cind na Romha. Tuitiss a delg as brat C. C., gor ben ar lár a fiadhnuisi Grigoir Papa. Tocbais Grighoir an delg 7 aithnigheis é. Do cuatar na diabuil íarsin co ro-ard is an aiér do teithemh remhe C. C. Lenais C. C. iad, 7 do cuaidh os a cind san aiér co cuala sé ceiliubr*adh* muindtire nimhe; 7 ba hiad so tossaighe na salm aderdís ag moludh an Tigerna .i. Te decet .u.;[217]) 7 Benedic .a. m.;[218]) 7 Laudate pueri;[219]) 7 dobeiredh C. C. ar a naemhuib 7 ar a manchuib fen a radha a tossach a trath 7 a ceilebradh ó sin amach. Et fuair C. C. o Día an t-anum sin Branduib do bí ga píanadh ag na demhnaib ris in ré sin, do cur in a corp féu aris indus co nder*nadh* sé aithrighe in a pe*cadh* 7 co mbeith se 'n-a óclách maith do Día 7 do C. C. ó sin amach, 7 co ngabudh se sacramaint ass laímh Maedhoig Ferna a pongc a bais, amail do gell se dó. Do impo C. C. mar a raibe Grighoír íar sin a ndiaidh a deilg, 7 do fasdó an Papa delg C. C. aige fen 7 do leícc se a delg fen le C. C. as a haithli. Acus do bo ro-ingantach le Grighoir ai*r*de na didhluicthe[220]) 7 imad na ngras 7 méd na mirbuil*ed* tuc Día do C. C. ré a ndenamh an uair sin. Tic C. C. remhe iar sin co hÍ, 7 do fhagaib se an dealg sin Grighoír Papa ag fer a inaidh fen a nhI a comartha 7 a cuimhniugadh na mirbuil*ed* mor sin.

---

[216] Read *bhrut*.
[217] Psalm 64.
[218] Psalms 102, 103.
[219] *punto* MS.
[220] Phonetic spelling for *dtidhluicthe*.

And in that time Maedhog was with the reapers that were cutting corn for him. And he heard the cry of the soul in torment, and by the power of God he went up into the air after the demons. And he was battling with them for the soul of Brandubh.

And they came above Iona of Columcille in Alba. Columcille was writing at that time, and an angel of God revealed the thing to him. And he grieved for the soul in torment, albeit he it was himself that had obtained from God that the life of Brandubh should be cut off because he had not taken the counsel of the holy men of his household forementioned touching the making of peace with Leth Cuinn. And he fastened his cloak with his brooch, and leaped into the air to aid Maedhog to save the soul of Brandubh from the demons. And they were struggling thus until they came above Rome. The brooch of Columcille fell out of his mantle, and dropped to the ground before Pope Gregory. Gregory lifted it and recognized it. Soon the devils rose passing high into the air, fleeing before Columcille. Columcille followed them, and went higher above into the ether, so that he heard the singing of the heavenly household. And these were the first words of the psalms they were singing in praise of the Lord: "*Te decet u.,*" and "*Benedic a. m.,*" and "*Laudate pueri.*"

And Columcille caused his holy men and monks to recite them at the beginning of their office and singing from that time on. And Columcille obtained from God that the soul of Brandubh, that was all that time in torment from the demons, should be restored to his body again, and that he should repent of his crime, and be a good servant to God and to Columcille thenceforth, and should receive the sacrament from the hands of Maedhog Ferna in the hour of his death as he had promised him.

Columcille went to Gregory for his brooch. But the Pope kept it for himself and left his own brooch to Columcille afterward. And right marvelous were to Gregory the height of gifts, and the wealth of graces, and the multitude of miracles that God granted Columcille to do in that time. And afterward Columcille went back to Iona, and there he left that brooch of Pope Gregory's to his successor in Iona in witness and in sign of these great miracles.

220. Fectus eli do C. C. 7 da coimthinol a nhí, 7 ar tect aimseri na nóna cuca dob ail les an sacrista cloc na nóna do buain, (fol. 29b) 7 do cuaidh se d'iarruidh C. C. 'sa duirrth*ig* a ngathuigedh se a duthracht do denamh do Día, da chedugadh de cloc na nóna do buain; 7 ní fhuair se and sin hé, 7 do iarr se gach inadh eli inar shaeil se a beith, 7 ni fuair se é; 7 tainic se mar a raibe an coimthinol 7 do indis se sin doib. 'Ben-sa an clocc,' ar síad, '7 gebé hinadh a bfhuil C. C., tiucf*a* se fa guth an cluic.' Do ben an sacrisda in cloc iar sin, 7 do conncatar C. C. cuca 7 delrudh ro-mor in a agaidh 7 lasrucha tendt*idh*e in a timchell. Acus arna faicsin don coimthinol amlaidh²²¹) sin do shailetar co raibe ferg air, 7 do lecetar ar a ngluinib uile iad, 7 do iarrutar ma dorindetar misduaím fan a luas do benatar an cloc, a maithemh doib. Ar faicsin umla 7 ecla in coimthinoil do C. C., adubairt se riu gan ecla do beith orra 7 nach raibe ferg air riu; 7 do fiarf*aigh*etar san scela de ca raibe se an fad do bi sé in a fecmais fen. Frecruis C. C. íad 7 assed adubairt: 'Do bádh*us* fen 7 Caindech naemhta,' ar se, 'ag cathugadh re demhnuib san aiér a n-airde ag cuidech*adh* le hespog Eogan Arda Srath anamcarat do fen, do bi ga pianadh acu re haims*er* fhada, do buain dibh, 7 nír ail lem-sa gan techt do fhressdal na nona an uair docuala in clog ga buain; 7 is fan a luas do benadh é do bi ferg oram rib-si, gan a leicin dam fuirech ris an anam do buain do na diabluib; 7 gidedh rucc aingel De oram ag techt in huar bfhiadnaise damh d'ecla co mb*eith* ferg orum rib, 7 dá indisin damh cor shaér Día an t-anam sin adubramar romhaind am onoír fen, o nar féd me fuirech ren a buain amuigh gan techt fa guth an cluic do fresdul na trath; cor moradh ainm Deí 7 Colaim Cille de sin.

221.²²²) Do bi duine airidhe a nDisert Garuidh a tuaiscert Osruidhe a nErind .i. Longarad a ainm, 7 fa sai in gach n-elaidhuin é 7 do scribud se morán de lebr*aib*; 7 do chuaidh C. C. dá indsuige d'*i*arruidh coda do na leabruib sin air, 7 do foluid se na lebhair ar C. C. 'Is ced lium-sa,' ar Colam Cille, 'masa

---

²²¹*amlaidh* amlaidh MS.
²²²See *Fél.*², p. 198.

220. Another time, when Columcille and his household were in Iona, and evening was falling upon them, the sacristan desired to strike the bell of nones. And he went to seek Columcille in the oratory where he was wont to do his observances to God, to get leave of him to strike the bell of nones. And he found him not there, and he sought him in every place else where he thought he would be, and he found him not. And he came to where the brethren were and he told them this.

"Strike the bell," say they, "and wheresoever Columcille is, he will come at the sound thereof."

Then the sacristan struck the bell, and they beheld Columcille coming toward them, and a passing great radiance upon his face, and flashes of lightning around him. And at the sight of him in this wise, the brethren thought that he was wroth, and all fell on their knees. And they besought his forgiveness if they had done wrong by the haste wherewith they had struck the bell. When Columcille saw the brethren humble and fearful, he bade them be not afraid, and said he was not wroth with them. They asked him where he had been the while he had been absent from them.

Columcille answered and spake thus: "We were struggling, Saint Cainnech and I, with the demons aloft in the air, helping to save Bishop Eoghan of Ard Sratha, his confessor, that was for a long time in torment from them. And I was loth to come not to nones when I heard the bell striking, and I was wroth that it was struck so soon, not suffering me to wait to seize the soul from the demons. Howbeit, lest I should be wroth with you, there overtook me an angel of God as I came toward you, and told me that in my honor God had saved that soul forementioned, since I could not tarry there to save it, without coming at the sound of the bell to attend the hours. And God's name and Columcille's were magnified thereby.

XVII

MORE OF THE LABORS OF COLUMCILLE IN IONA

221. There was a certain man that dwelt in Disert Garad to the north of Ossory in Erin. Longarad was his name. And he was wise in every kind of learning, and wrote many books. And Columcille went to him, and asked him for some of those books. And he hid the books from Columcille.

ched le Día e gan do leabuir do dul a foghnamh do nech eili tar
heís fen go brath.' 'Dober-sa na leabhuir duid-se,' ar Longarudh,
'7 na hescain me fein na na lebuir nías mó.' 'Ni dingen escaine
ort-[s]a,' ar Colam Cille, '7 gidedh an escaine dorindes ar na
lebruib ni heidir a cur ar ais.' Beris C. C. na leabuir les iar
sin, 7 ar dul a nAlbuin do, ruc na lebair les, 7 do bi do chin ar
na leabruib sin aicce, nach taebudh sé a coimhéd re duine ar bith
acht ris fen. Acus an uair nach bidh sé ag leghoirecht indta,
do cuired sé a n-airde 'n-a sella fen íad os cind na leptha a
ndenadh se an meid codulta donídh se. Et uair aíridhe do bí
se 'sa sella sin ag radh a trath 7 ag denam a duthrachta do Día
7 nech airidhe dá mhanchuib fen darub ainm Baithín mailli ris,
do tuitear na leabhuir adubhrumar romhaind don ealchuing ar
a rabhutur 7 doronat*ur* torand romhór ag tuitim doib. 'Truagh
sin,' ar C. C., 'oir fuaír an tí oc á rabutar na lebhair úd bas san
uair-si fen .i. Longarudh 7 aga cained 7 a comartha a bais do
tuitetar na lebhuir anos 7 doronutar an torand ainmesardha úd';
7 dorinde na roind-se:

    Is marb Lon   do chill Gharudh, mor and on!
    d'Erind co n-ilur a trebh   as dith leghind 7 scol.

    Atbath Lon   do cill Garudh, ro gab don,
    is díth leighind 7 scol   d'inis Eirind dar a hor.

Et ó an uair sin a fuair Longarudh fen bas, ní fhedadh enduine
'sa bith enfhocul do legadh isna lebruibh sin ó sin amach tresan
escuine adubramar rómaind dorinde C. C. orra, an uair do folaigh
Longarudh air íad; 7 ni dechaid claechlódh no sal no dorchudas
ar bith ar a litrib, 7 do mhairetar na leabhair sin aimser fhoda
a nhí a ndiaidh C. C. ar an cor sin. *C*onadh amlaidh sin do
fhíradh Día gach ní dá n-abradh C. C.

    222. F*echtus* dochuatar ceithri m*ic* Luig[d]ech Laimdheirc
do sheilg 7 d'fhiadhuch .i. Crimthand 7 Cairbre 7 Cael 7 Ferudhuch, co tuc Cairbre urchur sleighe docum an fhíadha, co tarla
tre Chael, gur marb acedoír é. Agus do bi Crimthand ag íarruidh
érca ar Cairbre 'san gnímh sin, 7 tarla imresain etorra fá an
éruic sin 7 fa oighr*echt* Chaeil; 7 nir fhéd Ri Erend no naim
Erend a sídhugadh (*fol*. 30a) *no* cor cuiredar d'fhiachuib orra dul
c*us*an uasulathair 7 co primfhaidh nimhe 7 talman .i. co Colum
C., do bi an uair sin 'san inadh airithe re n-abarthur hí a rigacht
Albun, ó asse dogeb*adh* a fhis o Dia gach ni budh ferr indenta
etorra. Do gluaisetar cland Luighdech Laimdherg do dul a nAl-

"It is my will, if God suffer it," saith Columcille, "that thy books be of no avail to any other after thy death forever."

"I will give the books to thee," saith Longarad, "curse me and my books no more."

"I shall lay no curse on thee," saith Columcille, "but the curse I did put on the books, I may not revoke it."

Then did Columcille bear the books away with him, and when he went to Alba he took them with him. And so lief were those books to him that he would not give them into the keeping of any at all save himself. And the time he was not reading in them, he would keep them in his cell above the bed wherein he took the little sleep he suffered himself.

And on a time that he was in this cell saying his office and making his devotions to God, a certain one of the brethren being with him, hight Baithin, the books forementioned fell from the shelf where they were, and they made a passing great noise in falling.

"Alas," saith Columcille: "for Longarad, the man that had those books, hath got his death in this hour, and to keen and to signfy his death the books have fallen now, and they have made that exceeding great noise. And he composed these quatrains:

"Dead is Lon
Of Kilgarrow. O great hurt!
To Erin with its many tribes
It is ruin of study and of schools.

Dead is Lon
Of Kilgarrow. Great the woe!
It is ruin of study and of schools
To the isle of Erin and beyond her border."

And from the time Longarad died there was none in the world that could read a word in those books forever for the curse forementioned that Columcille had put on them the time Lon hid them from him. And there hath not come any change or defilement or dimness upon those letters; and thus those books remained a long time in Iona after the death of Columcille. Thus did God verify all the saying of Columcille.

222. On a time the four sons of Lughaidh Red Hand went to hunt and to chase, to wit, Crimthann and Cairbre and Cael and Feradhach. Cairbre made a cast of the spear at the deer, and by hap it pierced through Cael, so that he died straightway. And Crimthann sought compensation from Cairbre for that deed, and a quarrel arose, touching the compensation and touching the inheritance of Cael. Nor could the King of Erin nor the saints of Erin make peace until those two were

buin; 7 assedh ba lín doib .i. cethrar ar xx re gaisced 7 cethrur
ban .i. mna na desi sin c*laind*i Luighdech Laimd*eir*c, 7 a dá cum*al*
coimdechta, 7 ochtar amh*us* do bidh ag bruith a selga 7 a fíad*a*,
et fós do bidh ag iascairecht doib an fad do beidis ar muir ag
5 dul 7 ag techt. Do foillsiged an ní sin do C. C., 7 do labair re
nech naemtha do bi fáris an uair sin darbh ainm Baithin 7 assed
adub*air*t ris: 'Ataíd aidhedha uaisli d'feruib Erend cugaind
anocht,' ar se, .i. 'c*lann* Luigdech Laimhdeirg, 7 dent*ar* tene fá
n-a comhair a tigh na n-aidhedh. *Conadh* and asp*er*t an
10 rand-sa:²²³)

   Mith*igh* tene a tech n-aidhedh,   do gab teimhel treb taidhen,
   is na trégim na damha   ar roimhéd g*ra*dha Gaidhel.

Oir ni thigedh aídhedha dá indsaighe nach indesidh sesean dá
mhanchaib go mbidis cuca sul do ticdís don baile, 7 do bi an
15 uiret sin do coimhed ag Día ar feli 7 ar nairi C. C. nach lecedh
sé aídhedha na cend gan fhis dó fen, d'ecla co mbeith naire air
da mbeith se aindis ar a cind. Do cuiredh se a aingel fen le
sceluib cuice remhe na haídhedhaib. Do firudh an faidetór*ucht*
sin C. C. leith re c*loind* Luigdhech Laimhdeirg; oir rancatar
20 cuige an oidce sin, 7 do bí se go roluthgairech rompa, 7 do
reidigh se etorra, 7 tuc righe do Cairbri *acht* ger b'oíge é ina
Crimthann, 7 gidh é dorinde an marbadh, ó nach da deoin
dorinde se é, 7 ar méd a aith*righ*e and 7 ar febhus a beth*adh* 7
a gnimhart*hadh* sech Crimthand c*on*uice sin, 7 tuc tanuistecht
25 do Crimthan; 7 do leic reidh da tigh iad aml*aid* sin. Gonadh
and aspert an rand-sa .i.:

   Righe duid, a Cairp*ri* cain,   7 dot shil ad deg*aidh;*
   gan toigecht adrud 's do rath,   a Cairp*ri* moír m*ic*
                                Luigdech.²²⁴)

30 Et fos c*onadh* and aspert-samh an rand-sa eli:

   Feith*ig*, a C[h]*ris*t, an muir mall   do Cairbre 7 do C*ri*mtha*nd;*
   go roissidh slánceill ga*n* meirg   dia tir m*a*c Luigdech
                                          [Láimhdheirg.²²⁵)

---

²²³See *R. C.,* XX, p. 140.
²²⁴*l. c.,* p. 142:
    Cen tudecht etrut rorath   duit, a Choirpre meic Lugdach.
Stokes translates 'without quarrelling, great grace (?), to thee O Coirbre son of
Lugaid'.
²²⁵*l. c.,* p. 143. Stokes translates 'that they may come sane, without ill-will,
from the land of Lugaid Redhand's sons'.

made to go to the Patriarch and Prophet of Heaven and Earth, to wit, Columcille, that was at that time in a certain place called Iona, in the Kingdom of Alba; for he it was that had knowledge from God of what would best to be done between them.

The children of Lughaid Red Hand set out for Alba, and this is the number thereof: four and twenty warriors and four women, to wit, the wives of the two sons of Lughaid Red Hand and their two waiting maids and eight servants that cooked their game and deer and fished for them the while they were on the sea, going and coming.

This thing was revealed to Columcille, and he spake to a certain holy man hight Baithin that was with him at that time, and this is what he said: "There are noble guests of the folk of Erin on their way to us tonight," saith he, "to wit, the children of Lughaidh Red Hand. Let a fire be made for them in the guest house." And he made this quatrain then:

> "It is time for a fire in the guest-house;
> Darkness hath fallen upon the dwelling of companies.
> Let us fail not the company
> For the greatness of our love of the Gael."

For there came no guests to him that he did not tell the brethren that they were coming, ere they reached the place. And so much was Columcille in the keeping of God in respect of hospitality and shamefastness that God suffered no guests to come upon him without his knowing, for fear there should be shame upon him if he were unready before them. So he sent his angel with tidings to him before the guests. Then was fulfilled the prophecy of Columcille touching the sons of Lughaidh Red Hand; for they came to him that night, and very joyous welcome did he give them, and he made peace betwixt them. And to Cairbre he awarded the kingship (albeit he was younger than Crimthann, and albeit he had done the slaying; for not wilfully had he done it), by reason of his penance there, and of the goodness of his life, and by reason of his doughty deeds, passing those of Crimthann. And he gave the tanistry to Crimthann. And thus he sent them home in peace. Then he made this quatrain:

> "The kingship to thee, fair Cairbre;
> And to thy seed the kingship after thee!
> That thy luck may not go against thee,
> O Cairbre, great son of Lughaidh!"

And moreover he made then this other quatrain:

Et as demhin an ní nach fédadh Rí Erend no naemh Erind do reítech, corub docum C. C. do chuirdís a reítech go hí, amhail derbhus an scel-sa 7 moran do sceluib eli mar fhoillseochus an betha a n-inadh eli remaind sísana.

223. F*echtus* do cuir an nech naemtha .i. Findía m*a*c Ua Fhíathruch manach da coimthinol fen re gnoaighib 'n-a aenar gan compánuch les, 7 tarla ben dó ar in sligidh, 7 do cuaidh sí da guidhe, 7 ni raibe sesiun ga gabhail sin uaithe, 7 do chuir sí lamh and fa deredh *no* gorb ecen dó a comhairli do denamh. Acus do lín tuirrse 7 aithrech*us* é iarsin fa'n pecadh sin do denumh. Acus ar filledh t*ar* a aiss dó mar a raibe Findía, tuc se a culpa do 7 tuc Findía esp*o*lo*í*d dó--san 7 adubairt nach raibhe pudh*ar* and sin 7 corub mór do daínibh maithe do mell an t-aidhberseoír remhe sin 7 gor gab Día aithrighe uatha 7 go ngebudh uadha-san mar an cedna. Acus ar n-erghe don manuch ó Fhindía, tainec an t-aibirseoír a ndeilb duine cuice 7 do fhadoígh se teine pecaidh an midóchais and 7 adubairt se ris narb ferrde dó an esp*o*lo*í*d sin tucc Findía dó, 7 g*ur* bec an breth aithr*igh*e do cuir se air, 7 adub*air*t ris dul mar a raibe Comhghall Bendchair 7 a culpa do tabairt 7 breath aithrighi do gabail uadha. Teíd an manuch iar*omh* mar a raibe Comgall 7 tuc a culpa dó; 7 assí breth aithrighe do cuir Comgall air .i. an breth do chuir Findia reme sin air, 7 adubairt ris mar in cedna aithrighe do denamh in a pech*adh* 7 co mb*eith* Dia reidh rís. Et ar fagbail Comgaill don manach, tarla an t-aibirseoir 'sa deilb cedna dó, 7 do labuir ris 7 asedh adubairt gan creidemh do enní da ndubairt Comghall ris 7 gur ro-mho a pecudh ina in breth aithrighe do cuir sé air, 7 adubairt se ris dul mar a raibe C. C. 7 breth aithrighi do gabhail uadha. Teid an manuch mar a raibe C. C., 7 mar dob'ail les a culpa do tabairt dó, do foillsigh C. C. fen dosan gach ní dar imthigh air ó thus co deredh, 7 do adaimh an manuch corb fhír do C. C. sin. 'Go mbendaighe Dia thú,' ar Colam Cille, 'as mór an buaidr*edh* 7 an merughadh sin do cuir an diabul fúd. Nar tuicc tu gur lor duit méd na mbreth aithrighe do chuir (*fol. 30b*) Findia 7 Comgall ort, 7 bídh a fhis agad,' ar se, 'da ndernta pec*uidh* fer ndomhain nach fuil breth aithr*igh*i da laghad do cuirf*edh* an sagart, da tiubartha do culpa, ort 7 a híc, nac fuil tu reidh re Día at pecadh *acht* co raibhe aithrighe agad. Agus is dod chur ar secrán 7 ar merughadh do cuir an t-aiberseoír a mídochas tu 7 do cuir se a ceill duid cor becc na bretha

"Calm, O Christ, the slow sea,
For Cairbre and for Crimthann,
That Lughaidh Red Hand's son, without ill-will,
May reach home safe and whole."

And certain it is that the matters the King of Erin could not set straight, nor the saints of Erin, those matters they sent to Columcille at Iona to set straight, as this tale beareth witness, and many other tales, as the *Life* showeth us in other passages below.

223. A certain holy man, to wit, Findía, descendant of Fiathrach, once sent a monk of his household on an errand alone and without a companion; and a woman met him on the way and besought him of love; and he denied her. And she laid hand on him at last, so that perforce he did her bidding. And grief and repentance filled him then for the sin he had done. And he went back to Findía, and told him his sin. And Findía assoiled him and told him there was no wrong therein, and that the Adversary had deceived many good men ere that, and God had accepted their repentance, and his likewise would He accept. And when the monk left Findía, the Adversary came to him in shape of a man, and enkindled in him the fire of the sin of despair, and told him that the shrift that Findía had given him would not avail him, and too light were the terms of the penance he had put upon him. And he told him to go to Comgall of Bangor, and to tell his sin, and from him to receive the sentence of penance.

The monk went therefore to Comgall, and confessed his sin to him. And this was the sentence of penance that Comgall laid upon him, to wit, the same sentence that Findía had laid on him afore. And he likewise told him to repent of his sin, and God would be reconciled with him. And when the monk had left Comgall, the Adversary met him in the same form. And he spake to him and told him to believe naught that Comgall had said to him, and that his sin was far greater than the penance Comgall had laid on him. And he told him to go to Columcille and to receive sentence of penance from him.

Then went the monk to Columcille, and as he was about to confess his sin to him, Columcille revealed to him all that had befallen him from first to last. And the monk confessed to Columcille that this was true.

"May God bless thee," saith Columcille; "much anxiousness and much uneasiness of spirit hath the Adversary brought upon thee. Dost thou not understand that sufficient was the measure of penance that Findía and Comgall laid upon thee? And wit thou well," saith he, "if thou wast to commit the sins of all the men in the world, there is no penance, however small, that the priest thou dost confess to should put upon thee, if thou perform it, that would not set thee right with

aithrighi do cuir Findía 7 Comghall ort, indus dá faghad sé ar
an sechran creidimh sin thu, go tiubradh se bas duid 7 go mberudh
sé hanum a pianuib síraidhe suth*aine* ifr*ind;* 7 bidh a fis agad
nach fuil pecadh ris nach co mór an midóch*us*²²⁶); 7 dá d*er*bhudh
5 sin as mó do pecaidh Íudas in a mídochas iná a mbrath an
Tigerna; 7 ó do chuaid tu-ssa a midochus 7 ó do creid tú on
diabul nar maithedh do pecudh duid ar son laghad na mbreth
aithrighi do cuiretar na naímh sin ort, cuirim-se *cúig* bliadhna
dec ar aran 7 ar uisce ort, indus corub moíde creidfes tú co
10 maithfe Día do pecadh duit, an breth aithrighi mor sin do chur
fort.' Do bendaigh 7 do coisric C. C. an manuch iarsin; 7 ni
raibe ar breith don diabul an pecadh sin an midóchais do cur
faí o sin amach tres an mbendughadh sin C. C. Et is follas duinn
as so nac edh amhain do claídhedh C. C. na diabuil a leith
15 ris fen *acht* co claídedh se a leith ris na dainib eli íad. Et fos
as follus duind ass na neithe nach fedaeis naeim íarthair domhain
do shoirbhiughadh corub cuice do cuiredh Día a soirbiughadh 7
a reítech.

224. Fechtus do C. C. a nhI, 7 do chuir an t-aidbirseoir fa
20 mnai airidhe 'sa popul sin grad ro-mor do tabairt do, da fechain
an ticf*edh* trithe a tarraing docum pecaidh do denamh ría; o nar
fhed se fen a clai *no* a mhelladh *no* buaidh do breith air léa
cuirf*edh* se docum pecaidh bicc no moir do denamh riamh é do
taeb a co*ir*p fen; 7 do cuaidh an gradh tuc an ben sin do tar
25 modh aice, indus gorb ferr lé bas d'fhagail iná gan techt d'foillsiughadh an gradha sin do C. C. da fhis an fuigedh sí uadha a
toil do coimlinadh leith re pecadh do denamh ría. Agus do
gluais sí mar a raibhe se do chur a hindtinde a ceill dó. Ar
n-a fhaicsin sin d'fhir graduighte na ge*n*mnaidechta, 7 d'fhir claite
30 na n-aibirseoradh, 7 d'fhir congbala aithnidhedh De co laidir n-a
sesamh, 7 d'fhir scisda na n-uile locht ass fen 7 as cach, do aithin
se an t-adbhur fa ndechaidh an ben sin 'n-a fiadnaise sul do indes
sí fén scela dó. Agus do labuir C. C. ria 7 assedh adubhairt: 'A
ben,' ar sé, 'smuaintigh ar breithemhn*us* bratha 7 smuaint*igh*
35 gorub o marbuib tainic tú 7 co mbía tu ar na marbuib.' Acus do
benduigh 7 do coisric se uadha í iarsin, indus co taínic do bridh
an bendaighthe sin C. C. gachuile ainmían dá raibe timchell a
gradha aice do dul ar cul uaithe, 7 a gradh d'fuirech 'n-a inadh
fen aice air d'estecht breithre De 7 senmóra uadha 7 do gabail
40 creidmhe 7 c*ra*buidh uadh, indus co raibe an ben sin 'n-a mnaí
naemtha fa deoigh; cor morudh ainm Dé 7 C. C. de sin.

²²⁶See § 89, § 386 for a similar construction.

God, if so it be that thou repent. And it is to lead thee astray and adrift that the Adversary hath brought thee to distrust and hath put in thee the thought that the penance that Findía and Comgall laid on thee was too small, so that if he might find thee in that heresy he might bring thee to death and bear thy soul to the everlasting pains of Hell. And wit thou well, there is no sin greater than despair, in proof whereof did Judas sin more in his despair than in his betraying of the Lord. And because thou hast fallen into despair, and because thou hast believed the Devil that by reason of the slightness of the penance that those saints laid upon thee thy sin was not forgiven thee, I lay upon thee fifteen years of bread and water, that by reason of this great penance that I put upon thee thou mayest the more believe that God will pardon thee thy sin. Then Columcille blessed and sained the monk, and through the blessing of Columcille the Devil had no power to put that sin of despair in him thenceforward. And it is clear to us from this that Columcille did rout the fiends not only in matters touching himself, but in matters touching others. And moreover it is clear to us from this that the troubles that the saints of the Western World could not calm, these God sent to him to calm and to allay.

224. On a time that Columcille was in Iona, the Adversary set on a certain woman of his congregation to bestow on him passing great love, to see if it might come to pass through her that he should entice him to sin with her; for of himself could he not overcome or tempt him, or bring him ever to do sin, small or great, in things pertaining to his body. And the love the woman had for him passed all bounds, so that she would liefer die than not come to reveal her love to Columcille, to try if she could get him to fulfill her desire touching the matter of having ado with her fleshly.

And she went to him to declare her purpose to him. And when this was perceived by that man that loved chastity, that subdued demons, that did strongly maintain the commands of God, that did tear out every flaw from himself and from every other, he knew the reason of her coming to him afore she told it him.

And he spake to her and said: "Woman," saith he, "think on the judgment of Doom, and consider that it is from the dead thou hast come, and to the dead thou shalt return."

And he did bless and consecrate her then from where he stood, and it came to pass by virtue of the blessing of Columcille, that when she heard from him the words of God, and his exhortation, all the evil desires that surrounded her love withdrew from her and her pure love remained within her, and she received from him faith and piety. So that woman became holy in the end, whereby the names of God and Columcille were magnified.

225. Do bi nech naemtha aírithe a n-Erind darbh ainm Finde*n*,²²⁷) 7 do bi clu crabuidh 7 genmnaidhechta air, 7 do coimhéd se gloine 7 óghacht a c*uir*p gan melludh do breith don diabal air, 7 do fhoglaim sé ecna 7 eolas as a oíge; 7 do smuaín se in a menmain fen C. C. do lenmain a nAlpain, 7 do batar a braithri 7 a cairde colluidhe ga toirmesc sin uime. Et teid co nech glic ars*aid* dobo brathair dó fen do bí 'n-a clerech ro-maith darb ainm Colman 7²²⁸) do denamh comairli ris, 7 do foills*igh* se dó an tríall do bi fai. Is andsin adubairt Colman ris: 'Bidh a fhis agad, a Findein, ma's ferrde le C. C. fen tu da lenmhain, nach eidir a toirmesc umad; 7 aderim-si red braithr*ib* gan a bachudh dít a lenmhuin, oir nir cuir a dóchus ann riamh 7 ni raibe gradh dariribh ag en duine air nach tiubr*adh* Dia grasa dón duine ar a shon.' Acus ar an pongc sin fen do gair Findén ainm C. C. mailli ré duthracht mór 7 re gradh, 7 do íarr se air grasa d'fha*gail* o Día dó in a onoír fen; 7 nir mor cor deal*aigh* deiredh an anma sin ren a bel anuair fuair se spirad fháidhetorachta o Dia. Et ar cluinsin gach comraidh da nd*earna* Col (*fol. 31a*) man 7 Finden do macamh óg do bí do láthair andsin darb ainm Irial, do gair se ainm C. C. 7 do íarr air grassa d'fhaghail dó fen o Día mar an cedna. Is andsin do labhuir Findén tre spirad faidhetórachta 7 assedh adubairt: 'An tenga sin, a Iriail, ler goiris an t-ainm benduighthe naemtha sin .i. C. C. biaidh sí fen bendaighte naemtha ó so amach, 7 biaidh blas 7 grasa ag cach ar gach enní da laibeora si coidhce aris; 7 gen co fuil cin ag cach anoiss ort, biaidh cin mór aris acu ort 'sa coimhtinol-sa in a bfuil tu fen anoss ac siludh 7 ag senmoir breithre De doibh.' Et do indis Irial gach ní da ndubramar andso d'ab naemtha airithe darb ainm Segenus, 7 do indis an t-ab sin d'Adhamhnan íad. Et ata Adhamnan naemtha ga mebrughadh cor foillsigh Día moran eli tre spirad faidhetorachta ar furailemh C. C. don Finden-sa adubramar romhaind, 7 go hairidhe cor foillsigh se dó mar do reidhechadh se an imresain do bi itir na naemaib fa fhésda na casc[a] a fiadhnaise Ciarain.²²⁹) Et as follus duínd ass so gebé lenab ail gradh do bheith aige ar C. C. no cengal do beith aige ris, go tiubra Dia grassa dó amail tucc sé do na naemaib-se adubramar romhaind .i. do Fhinden 7 do Írial.

---

²²⁷*recte* Fintan, more commonly known as Munda mac Tulcháin. See § 161 *supra*. See Reeves' *Adam.*, p. 18 ff, where he is called *Fintenus*.
²²⁸*sic* MS. Omit.
²²⁹O'D. completely misinterprets Adamnan throughout this paragraph. See Reeves' *Adam.*, p. 23 ff.

225. There was a certain holy man in Erin, Finnen by name, and his piety and chastity were famous. And he kept his purity and the virginity of his body without being deceived by the Devil, and from youth upward he took him to wisdom and knowledge; and he resolved in his heart that he would follow Columcille to Alba. And some kinsmen and wicked friends were opposing him touching this matter. He went then to a certain wise old man hight Colman, that was a kinsman of his and a right good cleric, and asking him to give him counsel, he discovered to him the purpose that was in him.

And thus spake Colman to him: "Wit thou well, O Finnen, if it pleaseth Columcille that thou follow him, it will not be possible for them to hinder thee. And I charge thy kinsmen not to detain thee from following him, for none hath put his faith in Columcille ever, and none hath truly loved him, to whom God hath failed to give grace for his sake."

And therewith Finnen cried out the name of Columcille with great good will and love, and besought of him to obtain grace for him from God in his own honor. And the end of that name had scarce passed his lips when he received the spirit of prophecy from God.

And there was a gentle youth called Irial that was with them there listening to all that Colman and Finnen were saying to each other. And he called upon the name of Columcille and asked him to obtain grace for him from God in like wise.

And therewith Finnen spake by the spirit of prophecy and said, "That tongue of thine, O Irial, wherewith thou hast called upon that blessed holy name, to wit, Columcille, shall be itself blessed and holy henceforward, and all shall have delight and grace from all it speaketh from this day forth, and albeit not all have affection for thee now, yet they that be in this communtity whereas thou now art shall have great affection for thee, when thou shalt be sowing and preaching to them the word of God.

And Irial related to a certain holy abbot called Segenus all that we have here told, and that abbot told it to Adamnan. And holy Adamnan maketh mention that God did reveal much else through the spirit of prophecy to the foresaid Finnen through the prayer of Columcille. And in especial he revealed to him how in the sight of Ciaran he would settle the dispute between the holy men touching the feast of Easter. And it is clear to us herefrom that whoso would fain love Columcille, or be bound to him, God will give him grace, as he gave it to the holy men we have told of above, to wit, Finnen and Irial.

226.²³⁰) Fechtus eli do Colum Cille a nhÍ, 7 do togaib a rusca suas docum nimhe 7 adubairt na briathru-sa: 'As bendaighthe conaích an ben 'sa hanam ataid aingli De do breith leo docum na cathrach nemdha anois.' Agus do bi duine craibtech airithe do lathair andsin ag estecht ris an comhradh sin C. C. darb ainm Generifebus²³¹), 7 ass e do bidh os cind bacuís ag na manchaibh, 7 tuc a aire gu ger don comhradh sin 7 do coimheid go descreidech in a menmain e. Et do leícetar sin tarrsa go cend mbliadna ón lá sin. Is andsin adubairt C. C. ris an nech cedna sin do raidhsemar romhaind: 'Ag siud anum na mna dar labrus at fhiadhnuisi bliadain cus an la aniugh,' ar se, 'ag tabairt aircissi ar anam a fir posda fen, 7 ata sí ag tabairt cobrach dó a n-agaid na ndrochspirad ata ga pianadh 7 ag cuidiughadh le hainglib De a anum do breith do caitemh na gloire suthaine.' Agus ní mor gor delaigh deredh an comraidh sin riú an uair do condcatar na haingle ag breith na n-anmond sin leo a flaithes De; 7 do bi an t-anum sin na mna go luthghairec[h] frithoiltech fá anum a fir posda fen. Agus as folus duínd as so gur lec Día moran do ruinibh a shecreíde diadha fen re C. C.

227. Fechtus eli do Colum Cille a nhÍ, 7 do gair se a descibul fen cuige .i. Diarmaid; 7 ba he an Diarmaid sin do bidh do gnath in a seicreidib sech cach, 7 adubairt ris: 'Erigh co luath,' ar se, '7 desigh na haltóra 7 cuir a culaidhecha orra; oir is aniugh as coir sollamain bais Brenaind naemtha do denamh'²³²). Frecru[i]s Diarmaid é 7 assedh adubairt ris: 'Cred fa cuirthai an tshollamain sin da denam 7 nach facubair tectadha cindte a h-Erind doberudh deimhin bais Brenaind dib'? 'Dena mar adubart-sa rit,' ar C. C., 'oir do condac-sa,' ar se, 'flaithes De foscailte aniugh 7 aingli De ag techt a coinde anma Brenaind, 7 tucutar delradh 7 solus don tshaegul uile an uair sin.'

228.²³³) Fechtus eli do Colam Cille a nhÍ, 7 adubairt ren a mhanchaibh iad féin d'ullmhughadh co luath docum na n-aifrend 7 sollamain an lai sin do mhedughadh a n-onoir an te 'sa hanam do cuaidh d'indsaighe flaithesa De an lá soin. Et adubairt C. C., gen co raibe sé fen dingbala cuice, go n-aibeoradh se an t-aifrend; 7 ar crichnughadh na hoifige doib conuice an inadh a fuil cuimhne ar ainm Martain 'sa prefaid, adubairt C. C. ris na manchuib: 'Aniug as coir daeb cuimhne bais Colmain Espoig do beith agaib

---

²³⁰Literally in Adamnan, *ibid.*, pp. 208-9.
²³¹*Genereus* in Reeves' *Adam.*
²³²See Plummer's *V. S. H.*, I, p. 151, and Reeves' *Adam.*, pp. 209-10.
²³³Taken literally from Adamnan See Reeves' edition, page 210 ff.

226. Another time that Columcille was in Iona, he turned his eyes upward to Heaven and spake these words: "Blessed and fortunate the woman whose soul the angels of God are bearing with them to the heavenly city now."

And there was a certain pious man beside him there, listening to the words of Columcille, hight Generifebus, that was charged with the bake-house of the monks, and he gave thought attentively to those words, and guarded them prudently in his mind. And he let them pass till the end of a year from that day.

Then said Columcille to that same man we have spoken of afore: "Yonder is the soul of the woman whereof I spake in thy presence a year and a day ere this," saith he, "making great dole for the soul of her husband. And she is helping him against the evil spirits that are torturing him, and lending aid, with the angels of God, to bear his soul to partake of the everlasting glory. And scarce had he made an end of speaking, when they saw the angels bearing the souls with them to the Kingdom of God. And the soul of the woman was merry and attending upon the soul of her husband. And it is clear to us from this that God discovered many of His divine secrets to Columcille.

227. Another time when Columcille was in Iona, he called to him his disciple Diarmaid, and it was this Diarmaid that was wont beyond every other to be in his secrets.

And he said to him: "Arise quickly," saith he, "and make ready the altars and put the linen coverings thereon, for this day it behoveth us to solemnize the death of holy Brenainn."

Diarmaid answered him and spake thus: "Wherefore dost thou purpose to hold this festival, when we have not seen trustworthy messengers from Erin bringing us certain tidings of Brenainn's death?"

"Do as I have told thee," saith Columcille, "for today I have seen," saith he, "the Kingdom of God opened, and angels of God coming to meet the soul of Brenainn, and splendor and light brought to the whole world in that hour."

228. Another time when Columcille was in Iona, he told his monks to make ready with speed for the mass, and to hallow that day for increase of glory to him whose soul was going to the Kingdom of God on that day. And Columcille said that he would celebrate the mass, albeit he was unworthy to do so.

And when they had completed the office to the point where there is mention of the name of Martin in the preface, Columcille said to the brethren: "Today it behoveth you to be mindful of the death of Col-

fuair bás a cuígedh Laighen a nErind, 7 do condac-sa aingli De
ag breith a anma leo do caithemh na gloire suthaine.' Agus do bí
an comhradh sin ar cuimne ag na manchaib no gu facatar daine
naemtha eli a hErind tucc a demhin doib corub é an la sin fen
adubairt C. C. bas d'fhagbhail dó fuair Colman Espog bás; cor
móradh ainm De 7 C. C. de sin.

229.²³⁴) Fechtus eli do Colam Cille a nhÍ, 7 do cruindigh na
manaigh cuice san inadh a raibe se fen, 7 do labuir riu 7 assedh
adubairt: 'Rachud-sa ani (fol. 31b) ugh,' ar se, 'sa cuid siar don
oilen-sa le gnoaighibh airithe 7 na lenudh nech ar bith me;' 7
do toilighetar na manaigh sin dó. Agus teid remhe san inadh
in ar ghell dul, 7 do lean manuch airithe é gan fhis dó fen, ler
b'ail a fhis do beith aige créd é an t-adbhur fa ndeachaidh se
'san uaignes sin, 7 do folaidh é fen a cnocan tshleibe do bi os cind
an inaidh a raibe C. C. as a facu se amharc air. Agus as amluidh
do condairc sé é a croisfighill 7 a agaidh suás ar nemh 7 é a
guide De co duthrachtuch 7 leighión d'ainglib gacha taebha de;
oir ba bés do na hainglib techt do tabairt sholais do C. C. an
uair do bidh se go dólásach on a beith ag denamh crabuidh a
n-inaduib fuara anshochra, no ó beith 'n-a shesamh a n-uisce gó a
smeig ag radh urnaidhte rofhaide a n-aimseruib geimhreta no
shneachtamla, nó on aibsdinians romór do cuiredh se ar a corp
fen do dith bidh 7 dighe. Et ass e adhur fá tuc Día an taispénad-
sa na n-aingel don manach, do médughadh anma C. C., o nar b'ail
le C. C. fen a medughadh leth ris na taisbentadha dobertaí do
d'foillsiughadh do cach. Oir ni foillsighedh sé coidhce iad d'ecla
gloir dimhain do beith dó fen and, muna thuicedh se riachtanas
a les a foillsighe do beith ar daínibh eli leath amuig de feín;
mar tá guidhe do cur ar anum duine dogebudh bas no le guidhe
do chur ar dhainib do beith a nguasacht mara no tire, no muna
beith médughadh anma no onóra do nech naemtha eli and é da
foillsiugadh. Et ar crichnughadh a urnaidhe do Colam Cille, do
imgheatar na haingle uadha 7 do fhill fén tara ais docum na
mainistrech, 7 tuc na manaigh cuige 7 do fiarfaigh dib cia acu
do len é a n-agaidh na haithne do chuir se orra; 7 adubratar
na manaigh do bi saer iarsin nach raibe a fis sin acu fen. Ar
na cloisdin sin don manuch do lean é, do lec ar a gluinibh a
fiadnaise C. C. é 7 adubairt gur pecaigh se fen co mór 7 do íar
se a maithem dó; 7 do maith C. C. sin dó ar tuicsin a umla 7
a aithrechais. Et in a diaidh sin ruc C. C. an manuch sin les
a n-inadh ar leith, 7 do íarr air gan an radhurc ainglidhe sin

---

²³⁴ Taken literally from Adamnan. See Reeves' edition, page 217 ff.

man that hath died in Leinster in Erin, and I have seen angels of God bearing his soul with them to enjoy glory everlasting."

And these words were held in mind by the brethren till they saw other folk from Erin that bare witness to them that on the very day that Columcille had said he had died, Bishop Colman had for a sooth perished, so that God's name and Columcille's were magnified thereby.

229. Another time that Columcille was in Iona, he gathered the monks to him in the place where he was, and he spake to them and said:

"Today I am going," saith he, "to the western part of this island on a certain errand, and let no man at all follow me."

And the monks consented. And he went forth then to the place whither he had declared he would go. Howbeit there followed him, without his knowing, a certain monk that would fain learn the reason of his going into that solitary place. And he concealed himself in a hillock overlooking the place where Columcille was. And from thence he had sight of him. And thus it was he beheld him, in cross vigil, and his face turned upward toward Heaven, and praying God fervently, and legions of angels round about him on every side. For it was a custom of the angels to come to bring solace to Columcille when he was worn out with pious exercise in places chill and comfortless, or with standing in water to his chin, saying very long prayers in wintry weather or snowy, or from passing strong constraint that he put upon his body for lack of food and drink.

And this is the cause why God gave the monk the sight of the angels: to magnify the name of Columcille. And Columcille would not magnify it himself by letting men wit the visions that were given him. For in fear of feeling empty vanity he never made them known save he understood that to others beside himself there was need of disclosing them—as to pray for the soul of one that had died, or for those that were in peril on sea or land, or when to reveal them would increase the name or honor of some other holy man.

And when Columcille had finished his prayers, the angels left him; and he returned again to the monastery. And he gathered the brethren to him, and asked them which of them had followed him against the command he had laid upon them. And the monks that were innocent said that they knew naught thereof. When the monk that had followed him heard this, he fell on his knees before Columcille, and said that he had done a great sin, and begged forgiveness of Columcille therefor. And Columcille forgave him this when he saw his humility and contrition. And after this Columcille took that monk

do condairc se d'indesin do énduine an cein do beith se fen n-a beathuigh. Et ar faghail bais do Colam Cille, do foillsigh an manach cedna an radhurc sin do condairc se do na manchuib; gor morudh ainm De 7 C. C. de sin. Et da derbudh sin, goirther cnocan na n-aingel aniugh don cnocan sin in a bfhaca in manuch na haingle timcell C. C.

230. Fechtus do Colam Cille a n-oilen aírithe a nAlbain, 7 do bi doinend ainmesardha and an uair sin, indus cor erich sdoirm adbal-mhór ar in fairge, 7 do bi C. C. 7 a manaigh a tigh airidhe 'san oilen an tan sin. Et do cuir fa aithne ar a manchaibh biadh 7 deoch 7 uisce innalta do beith co des acu, 7 tene d'fhadógh ar cend na n-aídhedh do bi ag techt cuca an la sin. 'Cindus bud eídir le nech 'sa doman an fairce do siubal aniugh re med na sdóirme ata uirre?' ar na manuig. Is andsin adubairt C. C. 'As deimhin co tiucfa oclaoch Dia .i. Caindech naemtha[235]), san uair reme espartain aniugh cucaib, 7 dobera ante gá fuil na huile chumacht a nimh 7 a n-ifren, ar muir 7 ar tir, ciunus dó'; 7 ar cur an lai tarrsa doib conuice an uair airithe-si adubairt C. C., docondcatar an long a raibe Caindech cuca, 7 do- cuatar 'na coinde, 7 tainic se a tir 'sa port a rabutar-san ar a cind; 7 do bi lutghair mór ar C. C. 7 ar na manchaibh remhe 7 do fiarfaigh manuch do manchuibh C. C. do Caindech cred far thairc se an fairce do siubal ina commor sin do sdoirm 7 do doinind, 7 adubairt Caindech co bfuair se ciunus ó Dia 'san uair airithe adubramar romaind don ló; 7 do molutar na manuigh Dia 7 C. C. go himarcuch trid sin, 7 adubratar cor follus do cach nach raibhi ní sa doman 'na dorchadus ar C. C.

231. Fechtus eli do C. C. a nhí 7 dorinde gaire,[236]) 7 do fiafraigh manuch airidhe de créd é an t-adbur fa nderna sé an gaire sin. Adubairt C. C. gorab nech naemtha airite darbh ainm Colman[237]) do bi ag techt ar cuairt cuige fen an la sin, 7 gur erich anfadh 7 sdoirm ar an fairce, indus co raibe sé fen 7 a raibe 'na luing a ngúasacht a mbaíte (fol. 32a), 7 go raibe Colman fen ar a gluinibh a tosach an arthraigh ag bendugadh na fairce reimhe 7 gacha taeba de, 7 co raibe ecla mór air, 7 co raibe se ag guidhe De co duthrachtach fa furtacht d'faghail dó on guasacht mor sin a raibe se; 7 adubairt C. C. nach baithfide é 7 co n- éstfedh Dia a guidhe 7 co tiubradh se ciunus dó, 7 corb e dob adbur do Día ag leíccen an michiúnuis sin cuice, do mhedughadh

---

[235] See Plummer's *V. S. H.*, I, p. 161, and Reeves' *Adam.*, p. 27 ff.
[236] *subridens* Adamnan.
[237] See Reeves' *Adam.*, p. 29.

with him to a place apart, and required him so long as he should live not to relate to any one the angelic vision he had seen. And when Columcille died, the monk disclosed to the brethren the vision he had seen, so that the names of God and Columcille were magnified thereby. And in proof thereof, the Hillock of the Angels is to this day the name of the hillock where the monk saw the angels around Columcille.

230. On a time Columcille was on a certain island in Alba and the weather was evil passing bounds, so that a right terrible storm arose upon the sea. And Columcille and his monks were in a certain house on the island at that time. And he charged his monks to make ready neatly food and drink and bath-water and to kindle a fire for the guests that were coming to them that day.

"How were it possible for any in the world to travel the sea today with the greatness of the storm that is on her?" say the monks.

And Columcille said, "Certain it is that the servant of God, holy Cainnech, shall come to you today in the hour before vespers, and He that hath all power in Heaven and Hell, on sea and land, will give calm to him."

And when the day had gone by to the very hour that Columcille had said, they saw coming toward them the boat wherein Cainnech was. And they went to meet him, and he landed in the harbor where they were awaiting him, and Columcille and his monks made great joy of them, and one of Columcille's monks asked Cainnech wherefore did he seek to travel the sea in such a passing great storm and tempest. And Cainnech said that he had had calm weather from God in the very hour of the day that we mentioned afore. And the monks praised God and Columcille mightily therefore, and they said it was clear to all that there was naught in the world that was hidden from Columcille.

231. Another time when Columcille was in Iona, he laughed. And a certain monk asked him the reason wherefore he had thus laughed. Columcille said that a certain holy person named Colman was coming to visit him on that day, and a tempest and storm had arisen on the sea, so that he and those in the boat were in peril of drowning. And he said that Colman was on his knees in the bow of the vessel, blessing the sea afore him and on every side, and great fear was upon him, and he was praying God fervently to get help from Him from the great danger he was in. And Columcille said that he should not be drowned, and that God would hear his prayer and would give him fair weather, and that this was the reason that God sent that storm to him, to increase his vigilance

a fuirechruis 7 a duthrachta acus da chur a ceill dó co raibe a
cumhachta fen ar muir ac*us* ar tír; 7 adubairt C. C. co tiucfadh
Colman san uair sin fen do ló da n-indsaighe. Agus do firadh
an faidhedoracht sin uile; 7 do indis Colman fen gur imdigh gach
5 enní dib-sin air amail adubairt C. C., gur moradh ainm De 7
C. C. de sin.

232.[238]) Fechtus eli do Colum Cille a nhí, 7 tancatar dias
airidhe don popal da indsaighe 7 a ndís m*a*c fariu, 7 do fhiarf*aigh*
nech acu de cred hí an cailidecht a rachadh a mac fen no cindass
10 do teicemhadh dó 'sa saeghal. Frecrais C. C. é 7 assedh adubairt:
'Cia he an lá aniugh?' ar se. 'An satharn,' ar an t-oclach. 'Mass
e,' ar C. C., 'dogebha do mac-sa bas dia haíne-si cugad 7 andluic-
fidher sectm*ain* ó aniug sa mainestir-se fen é.' Do fiarf*aigh* an
dara nech scela a mic fen de mar an cedna. Frecrais C. C. é 7
15 assedh adubairt: 'Docife do mac-sa cland a c*l*ainde,' ar se, '7
dogeba se bás a n-aeís fhoirbthe 7 adlaicfi*dh*er 'san oilen-sa e.'
Agus tainic gach ní dib-sin amhail adubhairt C. C.

233.[239]) La airidhe da raibe C. C. a ní, 7 tainic*c* manuch
airidhe darbh ainm Bera dá indsoig*h*e do bi ag dul a n-oilen eli
20 darbh ainm Etica le gnoaighth*ibh* na manuch. Acus do íarr ar
C. C. a bendacht do lece*n* les. Acus frecruis C. C. é 7 assedh
adub*h*airt: 'Lécfet-sa bend*ach*t let,' ar se, '7 ar a shon sin,
sechain an t-eolass comcoitchenn gabus cach docum an oilen sin
7 gab timchell na n-oilen mbec eli ata romhad d'ecla go faicféa
25 ní do chuirf*edh* aduathmhairecht ort.' Do imd*i*gh an manach
iarsin ina luing, 7 do gab se an t-eolas do toirmisc C. C. uime, oir
ni raibhe ecla air o do fhuair se bendacht C. C. Acus nír cían
dó ac síubul na fairce an uair do condairc se péisd adhuathmar
ag tocb*ail* a cind as in muir, 7 nar mó cnoc sleibhe ina hí. Acus
30 do foscail a bel 7 dob ail lé an long c*on* a foirind do shlucadh ina
braghaid. Acus ar na fhaics*in* sin doib, do lecadur a seol 7 do
imret*ar* an long t*ar* a n-ais, 7 do cuir an peisd an uired sin
d'anf*adh* 7 do combuaidhredh ar an fairce, muna beith coimhéd
Día orra 7 an bend*ach*t do lecc C. C. léo, nach rachdaís a tir gan
35 báth*adh*. Acus do aithnet*ar* corub ar ecla na pesde sin
adubhairt C. C. ríu gan an t-eol*us* sin do gabhail. Et do
gabhadur an t-eolus adubhairt C. C. ríu iarsin, 7 rancat*ar* slan
gan guas*acht*. Acus as follas assin scel-sa nach ar tír amain tuc
Dia radarc a sheicréde fen do C. C., *acht* co tuc se radurc 7
40 eolass ar piasda*ibh* na mara 7 na fairce dó.

[238] See Reeves' *Adam.*, p. 45.
[239] Literally in Adamnan, *l. c.*, p.p. 48-9.

and zeal, and to bring to his mind that God's power was on the sea and on the land. And Columcille had said that Colman should come to them in that very hour of the day. And all this prophecy was fulfilled, and Colman himself told them that every thing had come to pass as Columcille had said, so that God's name and Columcille's were magnified thereby.

232. Another time when Columcille was in Iona, there came to him two men of the community, and their two sons with them. And one of them asked him what rank his son would come to, or what manner of lot would be his in the world.

Columcille answered him and said: "What day is it today?" saith he.

"Saturday," saith the youth.

"If so," saith Columcille, "thy son shall die next Friday, and shall be buried a week from today in this very monastery."

Then the other man asked him tidings of his son in like wise. And Columcille replied to him and said,

"Thy son shall see the children of his children," saith he, "and he shall die at a great age, and be buried in this island."

And all these things came to pass as Columcille had said.

233. On a certain day that Columcille was in Iona there came to him a certain monk hight Bera, the which was setting out to another isle named Etica on business of the brethren. He asked Columcille to give him his blessing, and Columcille answered,

"I will give thee my blessing," saith he, "Natheless do thou shun the highway that all take to that isle, and go thou around the other small isles afore thee lest thou behold aught that should affright thee."

Then entered the monk into his vessel, and took the way that Columcille had forbidden him; for he feared naught, having received his blessing. He had not been long travelling the sea when he saw a terrible beast heaving her head above the sea. And a mountain peak was not larger than she. And she opened her mouth and would fain have swallowed ship and crew into her gullet. And beholding this, they lowered their sails and rowed the vessel back. Such great turmoil and tempest did the beast make on the sea, that save only for God's protection of them and the blessing that Columcille had left them, they had not come to land save drowned. They understood then that it was for fear of that beast that Columcille had forbidden them to pass that way. Then they went the path Columcille had charged them, and they arrived safe without danger. It is clear from this history that it was not on land alone that God did manifest his secret things to Columcille, but He gave him vision and knowledge of the beasts of the sea and its waters.

234.²⁴⁰) Fechtus eli do Colum Cille a nhÍ, 7 do bi Baithín naemtha ag dul docum an oilein sin do raidsimar romhaind. Acus adubhairt C. C. ris co tainic peisd adhuathmur a medhon-oidhce remhe sin 'sa chuan itir hÍ 7 an t-oilen inar b'ail les dul, 7 co mbeith gach duine do iméochadh an cuan sin a nguasacht romhór uaithe. Frecrais Baithín é 7 assedh adubhairt: 'Ataim-si 7 an péisd sin fa cumhachta De,' ar se. 'Imidh,' ar C. C., 'maille re bendacht De 7 re mo bendachtain-si, 7 saerfaidh an creidemh daingen ata agat ar an peisd ud tú.' Teid Baithin 'n-a luing iarsin, 7 nir cian dó ag siubhal na fairce, anuair do erigh an pest doib. Acus do gab ecla 7 adhuathmairecht a raibe 'sa luing uile acht Baithín amain, 7 do tocaib a lamha 7 a rusca súas docum nimhe 7 do bi ag guidhe De go duthrachtach im a shaeradh ar an ghuasacht sin a raibe sé. Acus ar crichnughadh na hurnaidhe sin do Baithin, do bhendaigh se an mhuir 7 an fhairce, 7 do theich an pésd rempe. Acus ni facus san inadh sin hí ó shin suas.

235.²⁴¹) Fechtus eli do C. C. a nhÍ, 7 do duísich se na manaigh 'sa medhón-oidche 7 ruc les don eclais íad, 7 do labhuir ríu 7 assedh adubhairt: 'Guidem an Tigherna go dúthrachtach; oír (fol. 32b) dorindedh pecadh ro-adhuathmhur 'sa saeghal so anois, 7 as baeglach co tiucfa díghaltus Dé ar cach uile tríd. Agus as Erendach dorinde é'. Agus do fhoillsigh C. C. an pecadh sin do cuid airide do na manchuib do bi fáris an uair sin, 7 adubhairt co tiucfadh an nech dorinde an pecadh sin faris an manach darb ainm Lughaidh²⁴²) fa aimser girr san oilen sin a raibe se fen, 7 nac raibe a fhis ag Lugaidh an pecadh sin do beith air. Acus do firadh sin uile amail adubhairt C. C.; gor moradh ainm De 7 C. C. de sin.

236. Fa aimsir ghirr iarsin, adubhairt C. C. ren a desscibul fen .i. Diarmaid: 'Erigh co luath,' ar se, 'a coinde an manaigh dar labhrus custrásda .i. Lughaidh, 7 abair ris na tucudh sé an drochduine ata fáris 'sa luing cugaind d'ecla co saileochadh se fonn an oileín sin ina fuilmíd da ticedh se and, 7 cuiredh se uadha e cus an oilen dán hainm Muili.' Do imdigh Diarmaid 7 dorinde a techtairecht re Lughaidh amhail adubhairt C. C. ris. Acus ar na cloisdin sin don drochduine sin do bí faré Lughaidh, adubhairt nac caithfedh se biadh no deoch 7 nach fillfedh se tar ais no co bfhaghadh se bas no co faicedh se fen C. C. 7 go labradh se riss ó bél go bél. Tainec Diarmaid mar a raibe C. C. 7 do indis sé

---

²⁴⁰Literally in Adamnan, *l. c.,* p. 49.
²⁴¹§§235, 236 taken literally from Adamnan, *l. c.,* pp. 51-2.
²⁴²*Lugaidus* Adamnan.

234. Another time when Columcille was in Iona, holy Baithin set out for that foresaid isle. Columcille warned him that in the middle of the night tofore a terrible beast had come into the harbor betwixt Iona and the isle that he was bound for; and that all that should go past that harbor should be in sore peril from her.

Baithin replied, "I and the monster are in God's hand," saith he.

"Go," saith Columcille, "with God's blessing and mine. Thy stout faith shall save thee from that beast."

Then went Baithin into his ship. And he had not been long travelling on the sea when they met the beast. Then were they all affrighted and adrad that were in the boat, save only Baithin. And he lifted his hands and eyes to Heaven and prayed God fervently to save him from the danger whereas he was. When Baithin had ended that prayer, he blessed the sea and its waters, and the beast fled before him. And she hath not been seen in that place from that time.

235. Another time that Columcille was in Iona, he awakened the monks in midst of the night, and brought them to the church.

He spake to them and said: "Let us pray the Lord fervently, for there hath been done but now in the world a passing great sin, and it is to be feared that the vengeance of God therefor will fall on all. And it is a man of Erin that hath done it.

Then Columcille revealed that sin to certain of the brethren that were with him, and he said that in a short while he that had done it would come to that isle where Columcille was, in the fellowship of the monk hight Lughaidh. And [he said] that Lughaidh knew not of the sin that lay on the man. And all this came to pass as Columcille had said, so that God's name and Columcille's were magnified thereby.

236. A short while after this, Columcille said to his disciple, to wit, Diarmaid:

"Go quickly," saith he, "to meet the monk whereof I but now spake, to wit, Lughaidh, and charge him not to bring to us the wicked man that is with him in his ship, lest, coming hither, he sully the earth of this our isle. And let him send him away to the isle called Mull."

Then went Diarmaid and bare tidings to Lughaidh, as Columcille had charged him. When that wicked man that was in company with Lughaidh heard that, he said that he would take nor food nor drink, nor would he return again till his death, save he behold Columcille and

sin dó, 7 do mhol nech naemtha darbh ainm Baithín do bi faré
C. C. 7 do mhol an coimhthinol uile dó techt do comradh ris an
drochdhuine sin dá fhis an raibe aithrighe fhírindech ina pecadh
aige. Acus adubratar cor choír aithrechus do gabail ón pecach do
5 reir mar adubhairt an Slánaigtheoir: In cacuimque ora ingemuerit pecátur omnium inicetatem eius non rexordabor .i. 'gebe uaír
docífed-sa aithridhe fhírindech ag an pecach, ni cuimhneochad
en-pecadh dá nderna sé riamh do.' Et adubhairt C. C. re Baithin
co nderna se coimhríachtain ren a mháthair. Teid C. C. remhe
10 cus an port a raibhe an long, 7 tainec an drochduine sin ina
fhiadhnaise 7 do léc ar a gluínibh é, 7 do adaimh se a fiadhnaise
caic co nderna sé na pechaidh sin amhail adubhairt C. C. a
ndenamh dó. Et do ghell gebe breth aithrighe do cuirfedh C. C.
air, co n-ícfedh se hí. Do labuir C. C. ris 7 assedh adubhairt,
15 da mbeith se da bliadhain decc a mBretain[243]) ag caí 7 ag tuirrsi
7 ag denamh aithrighe 'n-a pechadh 7 gan dul air ais go brath a
n-Erinn arís, go mad doigh les go maithfedh Dia a pechadh do.
Tainic C. C. tar a ais docum na mainestrech iarsin, 7 adubhairt
ris na manchuib cor duine mallaigthe an duine sin re raibe se ag
20 comhrádh, 7 nach ícfadh se an breth airthrighi do chuir se air,
7 co fillfedh se co luath tar a ais a n-Erinn 7 co muirbfidhe len a
escairdib iarsin é. Acus do fíradh sin uile amhail adubhairt C. C.
237.[244]) Fechtus do C. C. a n-inadh uaícnech a nhí ag
denamh urnaidhe, tainic an Lughaidh[244a])-se adubramar remhainn
25 dá indsoighe, 7 nir eídir les fechain air re méd na soillse 7 an
delraidh do bi 'n-a agaidh. Acus do gab ecla Lughaidh 7 do
teich sé úadha iarsin. Acus ar crichnughadh a urnaidhe do C. C.,
do gair sé Lughaidh cuice 7 do fhíarfaigh de cred far teich se
uadha anuair sin. 'Egla do bí oram,' ar Lughaidh, 're méd an
30 delraidh do condac at aghaid[h]-se, 7 guidhim tu-sa mádha taisbenadh radarc ar bith duid an uair úd, a indisin damh fen.'
'Indeósad,' ar C. C.; 'oir dorindedh ní adhuathmhar 'sa domhan
toir o chíanaib; oir tainic lasair tenedh ar cathraigh airidhe da
cathrachaibh na Romha 'san Edaill,[245]) 7 do chuir sí tri mile fer
35 docum bais leth amuigh do mnaib nó do lenbuib, 7 ni racha an
bliadhain se a bfhuil tú tort anuair thicfidh cendaighte ón Frainc
don talumh-sa derbeochus na scelu-sa duid.' Acus tancatar na

---

[243]inter Brittones Adamnan.
[244]Literally in Adamnan, l. c., pp. 56-7.
[244a]Reeves' Adam. has Lugbeus. Codex D has Lugidus.
[245]super Romani juris civitatem, intra Italiae terminos sitam Adamnan. It is the modern Citta Nuova, on the north of the river Quieto, in Istria.

speak with him mouth to mouth. Then came Diarmaid again to Columcille and related this thing to him. And the holy man, hight Baithin, that was with Columcille, counselled him, and all his household counselled him in like wise, that he should enter into conversation with that sinner, to learn if he had true contrition for his sin. And they said it is was right to accept repentance from a sinner, according as the Saviour said, *"In quacumque hora ingemuerit peccator omnium iniquitatum ejus non recordabor,"* to wit, "When I shall see the sinner truly repentant, I shall no longer remember any sin he hath ever done." And Columcille told Baithin that the man had had ado fleshly with his mother. Then went Columcille to the port where the ship was, and the wicked man came to him and fell on his knees, and confessed afore all that he had sinned as Columcille had said he had done. And he promised that he would do what penance soever Columcille should put upon him. Columcille spake to him and said that if he would stay twelve years in Britain lamenting and sorrowing and doing penance for his sin, and if he would never go again to Erin, he believed that God would forgive him his sin. Then Columcille went back to the monastery, and he told the monks that the man he had been in converse withal was a wicked man, and that he should not do the penance he had laid on him, and that he should return right soon to Erin, and that he should be slain then by his enemies. All that came to pass as Columcille had said.

237. On a time that Columcille was praying in a lonely place in Iona, there came to him the Lughaidh we have afore mentioned. And by reason of the greatness of the light and shining that was in the face of Columcille, it was not possible to look upon him. And fear seized Lughaidh and he fled from him. When Columcille had ended his prayers, he summoned Lughaidh to him and asked him why he had fled from him at that time.

"I was adrad," saith Lughaidh, "by reason of the greatness of the shining I saw in thy face. And if thou didst get any vision at that time, I pray thee tell it me."

"I will tell thee," saith Columcille, "for a terrible thing hath late befallen in the Eastern World. A flame of fire did come on a certain city of the cities of Rome in Italy and it hath destroyed three thousand men without women and children. And this present year shall not pass ere merchants shall arrive in this land from France, the which shall confirm these tidings for thee."

cendaighte sin san uair airidhe a ndubhairt C. C. a techt, 7 do indesetar na scelu-sa amhail adubhairt C. C.; cor moradh ainm De 7 C. C. de sin.

238.²⁴⁶) Fechtus do C. C. a nhÍ, 7 é ag legthoírecht, do gabh tuirse mor é. Acus ar na fhaicsin sin don Lughaidh cednu-sa do bi maille ris an uair sin, do fiarfaigh cred dob adbhar da tuirrse. Frecrais C. C. é 7 assedh adubhairt, gurub dís do daínibh uaisli na hErenn do tuit le celi a comrac san uair sin fen do ló .i. Colman liath²⁴⁷) 7 Rónan a n-anmonda, 7 adubhairt gorub é inadh a ndernadh an comrac sin laimh re Cill Rois 'sa Mumuin.²⁴⁸) 'Acus fa cend ocht la ó aniugh, do cluinfir-se glaedh (fol. 33a) duine ticfus a hErind an uair sin a port na hindse-si ag iarraidh imlochta,²⁴⁹) 7 indeosaidh sé na scela-sa duid,' ar C. C. Acus ar cur na haimsire sin tarrsa doib conuice an lá sin, do cualatar an glaed 'sa port. Is andsin adubhairt C. C. re Lughaidh: 'As si so glaedh an duine dar labrus at fhiadhnaise is na laithibh se do cuaidh tort, 7 eirigh 'n-a coinde 7 tabuir let e.' Tucc Lughaidh an t-oclaoch a fíadnaise C. C., 7 do indeis na scela-ssa adubramar romaind amail adubhairt C. C.; gor morad ainm De 7 C. C. de sin. Ruc Lughaidh iarsin C. C. les a n-inadh uaicnech, 7 do guidh se e imá a indesin dó cindus dogeibhedh se na scela seicreidecha sin, an é a cluinsin no a faicsin donídh, no cred é an modh ele ar a bfoillsighte dó íad. 'As mór an ni íarras tu,' ar C. C., '7 gell damh, fa ainm Dé, co ndingnair run ar gach ní indeósus me duit an fad bías me fen am bethaidh.' Ar na gealladh sin do Lughaidh, do labuir C. C. ris 7 assedh adubhairt, co rabatar daine airithe and ga raibhe an meid se do grasaib o Día, indus corub comsolus doib a bfiadnaise a n-indtinde, flaithess Dé 7 ifrenn 7 an talumh 7 an fairce 7 a fuil indta 7 etorra a n-en moimint. 'Acus as tearc duine da tucthar na grasa sin,' ar se. Acus ata Adhamnan naemtha ga mebrughadh gorub ag C. C. fen do batar na grása sin co sbeselta, acht ge adubhairt se a mbeith ag dainibh airithe do shechna gloire dímhaine d'faghail dó fen, indus co lenadh sé Pól apstal do bi 'n-a soightech toghta ag Crist, nech

---

²⁴⁶Literally in Adamnan, l. c., pp. 80-5.

²⁴⁷Colman canis Adamnan. O'Donnell incorrectly translates canis 'dog' (cú), confounding it with canus 'gray', 'liath'.

²⁴⁸Adamnan has Cellrois in provincia Maugdornorum, which O'D. incorrectly translates as 'sa Mumuin. Cellrois, now called Magheross, is a parish in the county of Monaghan. The Maugdorni were coextensive with the modern baronies of Cremorne and Farney, forming the southern portion of the county of Monaghan. l. c., p. 82.

²⁴⁹imlochtaidh Franciscan copy, Dublin.

And those merchants came at the very time that Columcille had foretold their coming; and they related those tidings as Columcille had said, so that God's name and Columcille's were magnified thereby.

238. On a time that Columcille was in Iona reading, a great sadness fell upon him. And when that same Lughaidh that was with him beheld that, he asked what was the cause of his sorrow.

Columcille replied and said that two of the nobles of Erin were falling either by other in a combat in that very hour of the day, to wit, Colman Liath and Ronan. And he said that the stead where that combat was taking place was near Cill Roiss in Munster.

"And at eight days end thou shalt hear the shout of a man that cometh from Erin to the Port of the Isle of the King in quest of shelter, and he shall tell thee these tidings," saith Columcille.

And when the time had passed to the very day, they heard the shout in the port.

Then said Columcille to Lughaidh: "This is the shout of the man whereof I spake to thee in days past. And go thou to meet him and bring him hither."

Lughaidh fetched the man to Columcille's presence, and he related those tidings we have rehearsed above, as Columcille had told them, so that God's name and Columcille's were magnified thereby.

Thereafter Lughaidh brought Columcille to a lonely place and prayed him to tell him how he had those secret tidings, if it were from hearing or from seeing that he had them, or in what manner else they were revealed to him.

"It is a great thing thou askest," saith Columcille, "and promise me, under God's name, that so long as I live thou wilt keep secret all that I shall tell thee."

When Lughaidh had promised this, Columcille spake to him and said that there were certain folk, the which had so many graces from God, that alike clear to their minds were in the same moment Heaven and Hell, land and sea, and all in them and among them. And few be they to whom such grace is given," saith he.

Holy Adamnan maketh mention that it was Columcille that had those graces in especial, but to shun vainglory he had said that certain persons had them, following Paul the Apostle that was a chosen vessel of Christ, that touching the vision he had from God said these words, "I know one that was lifted up to the third Heaven." And he did not say that he was the man, albeit he it was in truth that was carried thither. And moreover Columcille followed the noble apostle in the revealing of divine secrets to his companions. And these things did Lughaidh relate to other holy folk and they related them truly to Adamnan. And it doth appear from this history that God revealed

adubhairt na braith*ru-sa* fan radurc fuair se ó Día: 'Is aith*ne* dam duine ruc*adh* cus an tres nemh'.²⁵⁰) Acus ní dubhairt gurb é fen an duine sin, *acht* gerb é go firindech rucc*adh* and. Acus fós is mar sin do len Colum Cille lorg an apst*ail* im fhoillsiughadh
5 na seicréde diadha da companchuib. Acus do indis Lughaidh na neiche-si do dainib naemt[h]a eli, 7 do indesit*ar* na daine sin d'Adhamnan íad co firindech. Acus is follas as an scel-sa gor foills*igh* Día a secreide fen co himarcach do Colum Cille 7 go tuc se grasa na humhla 7 na gloíre dimhaine do sechna dó, amail tuc
10 se do Phol apstal.

239.²⁵¹) Fechtus eli do C. C. a nhÍ, 7 do gair día*s* manuch da manchaibh fen cuice .i. Lughaidh 7 Sillan. Acus do cuir fa aithne orra dul is in oilen dara hainm Muile, 7 do indes doib go ndech*aidh* gadaighe airithe darbh ainm Er*cus* a n-art*h*ra*ch* 'san
15 oidhce gan fhis ó an oilen dana hainm Colunsa go Muile, 7 go raibe se a n-uamhaigh 'san oilen sin, 7 gurb é bud triall dó dul a n-oilen aíridhe a mbidh ronach ag na má(nc)ha*ibh*²⁵²) 7 lu*cht* a arthraig do breith les a ngaduige*cht* dib. Do imghetar na manaigh iarsin, 7 fuarut*ar* an gaduidhe 'san uamhaid a ndubhairt C. C.
20 a beith, 7 tucatar leo é mar a raibe C. C. Acus do fiarf*aigh* de cred fa mbidh se ag goid an réda nar leis fen a n-aghaidh aithne De, 7 adubhairt dá n-iarradh se ní air fen anuair do biadh ricen a les *no* boch*tacht* air, co tiubr*adh* sé dó é. Acus do furail C. C. an t-oclaoch do lece*dh* amach 7 meid airidhe do caerchuib do
25 marbh*adh* do 7 a cur les dá tigh mar do mothaig se ria*cht*anas a les air. Acus nir fada 'n-a diaidh sin anuair adubhairt re Baithin co raibe deredh beth*adh* ag an gaduidhe sin. Acus do fhurail feoil 7 arán do cur cuice, 7 do indeis do Baithin corb e sin lon degeanach an gadaidhe. Acus fuarutar na daine do cuaidh les
30 in mbiadh an gaduidhe marb ar a cind. Acus is é an biadh sin rucatar leo, ba biad do na dainibh do bí ar a sochr*aide* (an oidhce sin).²⁵³) Acus is follas ass sin co tuc Dia mórán d'fhis a seicreíde fein do Colum Cille.

240. Fechtus do Colum Cille a n-inadh aíridhe a n-Albain,
35 7 tuc Aedhán mac Gabhrain .i. m*ac* righ Alpan moirsheser ar xx do d*r*aith*ibh* diabluide les do denam aibsireora*cht*a air, 7 da fhis an bfhedfuidis a clai o a cumachtaib fen. Acus do bui an oired sa do cumha*cht*a on díab*ul* aca .i. gebé duine ar a tucdaís

---

²⁵⁰2 *Cor.* xii, 2.
²⁵¹Literally in Adamnan. See Reeves' *Adam.*, pp. 77-9.
²⁵²*insulam ubi marini nostri juris vituli generantur et generant* Adamnan.
²⁵³*in exequiis ejus* Adamnan. *an oidhce sin* is omitted in *Franciscan copy*.

His many secrets to Columcille, and that He gave him the graces of lowliness and to shun vainglory, even as He gave them to Paul the Apostle.

239. On a time that Columcille was in Iona, he called to him twain of his monks, to wit, Lughaidh and Sillan. And he bade them go to the isle hight Mull. And he told them that a certain reaver, by name Ercus, had gone to Mull that night in a vessel secretly from the isle of Colunnsa and that he was in a cave in that isle, with intent to proceed to a certain island wherein were seals belonging to the brethren. Then the monks set out. And they found the reaver in the cave whereas Columcille had told them he was. And they brought him with them. And Columcille asked him wherefore, against the command of God, he was taking things that were not his own. And he told him that if he should ask aught of him, when he was in need or distress, he would give it him. Then Columcille bade the brethren let the reaver go.

And thereafter he was wont to let slaughter for the reaver a certain portion of meat and send it to his house when he had need thereof. And not long thereafter he said to Baithin that then was the end of that reaver's life. And he bade send to him meat and bread. And he told Baithin that was the reaver's last provender. And those that went with the food found the reaver dead. And the provision they bare with them was the provision of the folk that were at the wake that night. And it is manifest from this history that God gave much knowledge of His secrets to Columcille.

240. On a time that Columcille was in a certain place in Alba, Aedan son of Gabhran, to wit, the son of the King of Alba, brought two score and seven fiendish druids to practice deviltry upon him and to see if they might overcome him by their powers. And so great power

a mbendacht, go ndenadh sin maith mór dó, 7 gebe duine ar a
tucdaís a mallacht, go ndenadh sí urchoid mór dó.²⁵⁴) Acus mar
do fosclatar a mbeoil do mallughadh C. C., tainic do mirbuilibh
Dé 7 C. C. corub é a bendughadh doronsad 7 nar fhédatar a
mallughadh. Acus ni headh amaín nac derna a mallacht digbail
do C. C., acht ni derna sí digbail do nech eli ó sin súas.

241.²⁵⁵) Fechtus eli do C. C. a n-Alpain, 7 do chuir se Baithín
naemtha le gnoaightibh aíridhe a cenn Aedhain mic Gabhrain.
Et do fhíarfaigh Aedhan de cred é in duine sin ar a raibe an
tuaruscbhail mor ag lucht iarthair domhain .i. C. C. 'As maith
é,' ar Baithin, 'oir nir bris se a oghacht 7 nir oibrigh se go bec
no co mór'sa dimhaínes 7 ni derna se brecc riam. Do brethnaigh
Aedhan 'n-a inntind feín cindus do brecnóchadh se sin 7 tuc
(fol. 33b) se C. C. 'n-a chend iarsin, 7 do chuir se a inghen fen .i.
Coinchend inghen Aedaín 'n-a suidhe a cathaír a bfiadhnaise C. C.
go n-édach righnaide impe. 'Is alaind an n-inghen úd,' ar Aedan.
'Assedh ón,' ar Colum Cille. 'In budh ferr let-sa co mbeitheá
ag luidhe lé?' ar Aedhan. 'Do budh ferr,' ar C. C. 'An cluintí
an té-si re n-abarthur nar bris sé a oghacht riam ga rádha co madh
fherr les co mbeith sé ag luidhe les in ingen,' ar Aedhan. 'Nirb
ail lium-sa brecc do denamh,' ar C. C., '7 bidh a fhis agat-sa, a
Aedhaín, nach fuil duine ar bith na budh mían les pecad do
denamh. Gideadh, as se an duine leces an mían sin de, ar son Dé,
coróntar a flaithes De. Acus fos bidh a fis acud ar tighernus an
betha nach luidhfind-se les an inghein, ge madh mían lium luidhe
lé o ainmían an coirp daenna-sa ata umam.' Dá n-abradh C. C.,
umorro, an uair sin na budh mían les luidhe les in inghin, do
cuirfedh Aedhan sin mar bhréic 'n-a aghaidh, do rér an ughdairaís
sin adubhairt se fen .i. nar chuir corp daenda uime a fecmais
daendachta Crist, duine na budh mian leis pecadh do denamh.

242. Tuc Aedhan demhes allaimh C. C. iarsin, 7 da cuiredh
se an deimhes ar a celi, dob ail lé hAedhan a cur 'n-a aghaidh co
nderna se dimhaínes, 7 do íarr air a cur ar a cele. 'Ni cuirebh,'
ar C. C., 'oir do budh dimaínes dam a cur ar a cheli gan adbhur.'
Is mar sin do clai C. C. Aedhan san indtind celgach sin do bi
aicce dó.

---

²⁵⁴Referred to in *Amra C. C.* See *Irish Liber Hym.*, I, p. 179; *ibid.*, p. 298.
²⁵⁵§§ 241, 242 are taken from *Amra C. C.* See *R. C.*, XX, p. 284. See also
Y. B. L, 164ᵃ.

had they from the Devil that to whomsoever they gave blessing, he had great good thereof, and to whomso they gave a curse, he had great harm. But when they opened their mouths to curse Columcille, it befell by the miracles of God and Columcille that they blessed him and might not curse him. And not only to Columcille did their curse do none harm, but to none did it work injury thenceforth.

241. On a time that Columcille was in Alba, he sent holy Baithin on certain errands to Aedan son of Gabhran. Aedan inquired of him who that man was, to wit, Columcille, of the which the folk of the Western World gave such great report.

"He is a good man," saith Baithin, "for he hath not broken his virginity, and he hath done naught, small or great, in vain-glory, and never hath he spoken falsehood. Then Aedan bethought him how he might confute that. And he brought Columcille to him. And he let seat his own daughter Coinchenn in a chair in the presence of Columcille, and she with royal robes upon her.

"Beautiful is the maiden," saith Aedan.

"She is in sooth," saith Columcille.

"Were it pleasing to thee to lie with her?" saith Aedan.

"It were pleasing," saith Columcille.

"Hearest thou him of whom it hath been said that never hath he broken his virginity, and he saying he were fain to be lying with a maiden!" saith Aedan.

"I would not speak falsehood," saith Columcille. "And know thou, O Aedan, there is none in the world that is without the desire to sin. Natheless he that leaveth that desire, for God's sake, shall be crowned in the Kingdom of God. And wit thou well, I would not lie with the damsel for the lordship of the world, albeit for the lust of the fleshly body that is about me, it is indeed my desire."

If now Columcille had said at that time that he had no wish to lie with the damsel, Aedan had laid that against him as a lie, according to the word he had himself spoken, to wit, that save the human body of Jesu Christ, there hath none put on flesh that doth not have desire toward sin.

242. Then Aedan put a pair of shears into the hand of Columcille. And if he should put the shears together, Aedan would cast in his face that he was guilty of vanity. And he required of him to put them together.

"I will not," saith Columcille, "for it were vanity for me to put them together without cause."

Thus did Columcille overcome Aedan in the deceitful intent he had toward him.

243.²⁵⁶) Fechtus eli do Colum Cille a n-Alpain san oilen re n-abarthar Imba, 7 tainic aingel De cuice 'san oidhce 7 é a cíunus indtinde 7 leab*har* gloine²⁵⁷) in a laimh, 7 ordughadh denta righth*acht* na hAlban and 7 tuc do C. C. é. Acus itir gach ní
5 da raibhe scrib[h]tha and, adubhairt se cor chuir Dia fá aithne ar C. C. rí Alpan do denamh d'Aedhan mac Gabhraín. Do léc C. C. sin tairis an oidhce sin 7 nir fhoscail se an leabur; oir nírb ail les ri do denamh d'Aedhán, oir nir chara do é an uair sin. Acus do bí mac dob oícce ina hé ga athair ar a raibe gradh
10 mor ag C. C. air ass a deghgnimarthuib, 7 do brethn*aigh* sé rí do denam de ar beluib Aedhain. Et tainec an t-aingel an dara hoidhce chuice 7 an leabhar cedna les da rad[h] ris rí do dhenamh d'Aedhan, 7 do lecc C. C. sin tairis an oidhche sin mar an cedna. Et tainec an t-aingel an tres oidhce cuice 7 an leabhur
15 les, 7 do fhoscail 'n-a fiadnaise é 7 do taisben sé do an t-inadh a raibe scribtha and ri do denamh d'Aedhan mac Gabhraín. Et ar na thuicsin don aingel narb í sin toil C. C., do buail se buille do sciursa fan a taeb des air 7 do gortaigh sé co rogher é. Acus do bi slicht an sgiursa sin ina taeb an cein do bi se 'n-a beath*aidh*,
20 7 adubhairt an t-aingel arís ris, mu*na* dherna*dh* se an ni do bi scribtha 'sa lebhur, co ngoirteochadh Día ni budh mó ina sin é. Ar ngabail aithrechais do C. C. fa gan beith umal don ced aithne do cuir Día cuice, do cuir techta ar cend Aedhain 7 tuc cuice co hí é, 7 do beandaigh e 7 do gair sé rí de. Et do labhuir an
25 t-aingel do guth ard os a cend san aiér an uair sin 7 assedh adubhairt: 'Ó, a Aedhain m*ic* Gabhrain, na dena fen *no* do slicht ad diaidh en-ní b*us* mesde re C. C. a n-Erinn no a n-Alpain, 7 dá nderntaí, cuimhneocha Dia sciursa C. C. daib.' Et atá n*ech* naemtha .i. Cumaín fada m*ac* Fíachna ga mebrughadh 'sa lebur
30 do scrib se fen ar subhált*aidh*ibh C. C., co nderna C. C. faidhedoracht d'Aedhán 7 da slicht in a diaidh an uair sin, 7 co ndubhairt se riu nac berdais a naimhde buaidh orra an ceín do coimheoldaís dó fen 7 do lu*cht* a inaidh 'n-a diaidh. Acus adubhairt riu gan an rigacht do chur as a laimh leth ren a nem-
35 comhmairle (*sic*) do denamh; 7 gebe uair dogendaís enní bud mesde les fen leth re digbail do denamh da braithr*ibh* no dá cairdibh no do lu*cht* a inaidh a n-Erinn no a n-Albain, go cuimhneochadh Dia doib an scíursadh tuc an t-aingel dó fen timcell Aedhain, 7 go ngoirteoch*adh* sé go mor íad leth ren a tren 7 ren a tresi do
40 cur ar cúl, 7 le tren do tabha*irt* dá naimdibh 7 da n-escairdib

---

²⁵⁶Literally in Adamnan. See Reeves' *Adam.*, pp. 197-8.
²⁵⁷*Vitreus liber* Adamnan.

243. Another time, when Columcille was in Alba in the island hight Imba, there came to him in the night an angel of God, when he was at rest. He had in his hand a crystal book wherein were commands touching the matter of who should have the Kingdom of Alba. And he gave the book to Columcille. And among the things that were written therein, he said God had put there the command upon Columcille to make Aedan mac Gabhrain king of Alba.

And Columcille let pass that night, and opened not the book; for it was not pleasing to him to make Aedan king, for at that time he was not a friend to him. And his father had a younger son for whom Columcille had great love by reason of his good deeds. And he thought to make him king over the head of Aedan.

And the angel came to him the second night, and with him the same book bidding him crown Aedan. And Columcille let that night pass in the same manner. And the angel came to him the third night, and the book with him. And he opened it afore Columcille. And he showed him where it was written therein to crown Aedan son of Gabhran.

And when the angel saw that he would not, he dealt him a stroke along his right side with a scourge. And it did him passing sore hurt. And the track of that scourge was in his side the while he was alive. And the angel spake to him again, and said except he do the thing that was writ in the book, God would do him more hurt than that.

And Columcille repented that he had been disobedient to the first command that God had laid upon him. And he sent messengers to Aedan and brought him to Iona and blessed him and proclaimed him King.

And in that hour the angel spake above him in the air and said: "O Aedan son of Gabhran, do thou naught in Erin nor in Alba displeasing to Columcille, and let not thy seed after thee displease him; for if ye do, God will remember the scourging of Columcille for your sakes."

And a holy man hight Cumain Fada mac Fiachna doth make mention in the book that he wrote upon the virtues of Columcille that Columcille made a prophecy at that time concerning Aedan and his seed after him. And he said their foes should have no victory over them the while they were obedient to him and his successors. And he bade them not let the kingdom from their grasp by heeding not his counsel. And when they should do aught displeasing to him, as injury to his kinsmen or his friends or his successors in Erin or Alba, God would remember the scourging that the angel gave him for the sake of Aedan, and He would do them great hurt, making their might to wane, and giving power over them to their foes and their enemies. And it is holy Adamnan that

orra. Et ata Adamhnan naemta ga mebrughadh cor fíradh an fhaidhetoracht sin C. C. an tan tancatar cland Echach buide m*i*c Aedhain m*i*c Gabrain a nErinn re *Co*ngal claen m*a*c Scandlain sciathlethain .i. rí Uladh a n-agaidh brathur C. C. .i. Domhnaill m*i*c Aedha mic Ainmirech rí Erenn, anuair do bris Domnall cath Muighe Rath orra. Acus do marbh*adh* cland Ech*ach* buidhe and uile. Acus fos, ata Adhamhnan ga mebrughadh corub ren a lind fein tucadh an cath sin Muighe Rath.

244.[258]) Fechtas eli do C. C. a nhÍ, 7 do cuaidh don ecl*ais* 7 do gair a serbfhoghant*aidh* fen cuice .i. Diarmaid, 7 adubhairt ris an cloc do bua*in* docum go tiucfaidís na manaigh cuca. Acus dorinde (*fol.* 34a) Diarmaid sin, 7 tancatar na manaigh fa guth an cluic. Labrais C. C. ríu 7 assedh adubhairt: 'Lecem ar ar ngluinib sind 7 guidem ar Aedhan mac Gabhrain rí Alpan 7 ar a bfhuil fáris ata ac tabhairt catha dá escairdib anos.' Acus doronsad amlaidh sin. Acus ar crichnughadh a urnaidhe do C. C., do erich da gluínibh 7 tucc buidechus do Día in a tindlaicibh, 7 do innis da manchuib co brisiudh an cath sin le hAedhán; 7 ge tucadh buaid cathaige dó, gor marbud tríur 7 t*ri* ced da muindt*ir* fen and. Acus do firadh an faidhetóracht sin uile amail adubhairt C. C.; mar do derbhatar daine aíridhe tainic as in cath sin fen do na manchaibh iarsin. Acus as follus do cach as an scel-sa corab imarcach tuc Dia fis a sheicreide fen do C. C.

245.[259]) Fechtus eli do C. C. a fochair a celi 7 d'Aedhan mac Gabra*í*n, 7 do fiarf*aigh*[260] Aedhan de cia dá cloind do beith a rigacht Alban in a diaid fen. Frecrais C. C. e 7 assedh adubhairt, nach beith én-duine don triur m*a*c bud si*n*e aice 'n-a rígh go brath, 7 co muirbf*edh* a n-escaraid íad. Acus adubhairt se ris an cl*ann* ócc do bi aice do tabhairt 'n-a fiadhnaise fen, 7 gebe aca do ticfadh in a ucht gan íarraidh 7 doberadh póg dó, co madh e do beith 'n-a rig Alban a ndiaidh a athar. Tuc*adh* iar*omh*, m*a*caímh óga do b*adh* cland don righ a fiadnaise C. C. iarsin, 7 tainec nech airidhe dib darb ainm Eochaidh a n-ucht C. C. can íarr*aidh* 7 tuc pócc dó. Do bendaigh C. C. é, 7 adubhairt ris co mbeith se 'n-a righ a ndiaidh a ath*ar* fa aimser girr. Acus do firadh gach ní dib sin uile amhail adubhairt C. C.

246.[261]) Fechtus do C. C. 7 dá descibul fen .i. do Dhíarmaid ag radh a trath 7 a n-urnaidhe ar cnocán ard sleibe ata a nhÍ;

---

[258]Source is Adamnan. See Reeves' *Adam.*, pp. 33-4.
[259]Literally in Adamnan. See Reeves' *Adam.*, pp. 35-6.
[260]*leg.* fiafraigh.
[261]*Ibid.*, pp. 58-9.

maketh mention of the verifying of this prophecy of Columcille the time the children of Echaidh Buide son of Aedan son of Gabhran came to Erin with Congal Claen son of Scannlan Sciathlethan, to wit, the King of Ulster, against the kinsman of Columcille, to wit, Domnall son of Aed son of Ainmire, King of Erin, when Domnall won the battle of Magh Rath against them. And in that place were slain all the clan of Echaidh Buide. And Adamnan maketh mention that it was in his time the battle of Magh Rath was fought.

244. Another time that Columcille was in Iona, he went to the church. And calling to him his servant Diarmaid, he bade him strike the bell so that the monks should come to them. And Diarmaid did that, and the monks came at the sound of the bell.

Then spake Columcille to them and said: "Fall we on our knees and pray we for Aedan son of Gabhran, King of Alba, and for all that are with him giving battle to his foes in this hour."

And this they did. And when Columcille had ended his prayer he rose from his knees and gave thanks to God for His gifts. And he told the brethren that the fight had been won by Aedan, and albeit the victory in the battle had been given him, yet had there been slain three and three hundred of his folk. And all this thing he prophesied did come to pass as he had said, according as certain folk that came from that battle confirmed it afterward to the brethren. And it is manifest to all from this history that God gave Columcille to know exceeding many of His secrets.

245. Another time Columcille and Aedan were together, and Aedan asked him which of his sons should be king in Alba after him. And Columcille answered him and said that of his three oldest sons, not one of them should be in the kingship till Doomsday, but their enemies should kill them. And he bade bring to him the young sons that he had, and the one of them that should come to his arms without asking, and should give him a kiss, should be king in Alba after his father. Then were brought to Columcille the young lads that were sons to the King. And there came one of them that hight Echaidh to the arms of Columcille. And Columcille declared that in short space he should be king after his father. And all of these things came to pass as Columcille had said.

246. On a time that Columcille and his disciple Diarmaid had been saying their hours and their orisons on the summit of a high mountain

7 ar crichnughadh a urnaidhe do C. C., do labuir re Díarmaid
7 assedh adubhairt: 'As ingnadh lium,' ar se, 'a fhad co ticc
an long ata ag techt o Erind cugaind in a bfuil nech airidhe do
thuit a pecadh marbtha 7 ga bfuil tuirsi 7 aithrechas ina pecadh
anois, 7 ata ag techt da íarraidh orm-sa maitemh a pechaidh
d'faghail o Día dó.' Nirb fada iar sin an uair do condaic Diarmaid an long ac lecadh a seoil 'sa port laim ris 7 do indis sin do
C. C., 7 tainic an duine sin do raídhsimar romhaind a tír a cend
C. C., 7 do léic ar a glúinib 'n-a fhíadnaise é 7 do cai go gér.
Acus ar na thuicsin do C. C. go raibe aithride fírindech aige,
do cai se fen leis 7 do guidh se Dia co duthrachtach fan a pecaib
do maithemh dó. Acus do labuir ris iarsin 7 assedh adubhairt:
'A mic graduig,' ar se, 'bid luthgaír 7 solas ort, oir do maith
Dia do pechadh duid ar med do tuirrsi 7 t'aithrechais do reir
an fhocail ata scribtha 'sa Scribtuir .i. Cor contritum et umiliatum, deus [non] despicies .i. ni cuirend Dia an croide umal tuirsech a tarcuisne. Ar na cloisdin sin don duine sin, do eric da
gluinibh maille re luthgair 7 tuc buidechus mór do Día 7 do
C. C. ar a shon, 7 do cuir C. C. fare Baithin da coimhed é d'ecla
a tuitim sa 'pecadh sin nó a pecudh eli. Acus fuair se bas fa
deiredh, 7 as é dob ainm don oclaoch sin fen .i. Fiachna.²⁶²)

247.²⁶³) Fechtus eli do C. C. a ní, 7 do cuir dias manuch do
bi faris ar cend manuich eli darb ainm Cailtean do bi a sella
airidhe 'sa mainistir ag radh a duthrachta, 7 do indsetar dó co
raibe C. C. ga iarraid[h] cuice. Ar na cloisdin sin do Cailtean,
do cuaidh mailli re deithfir moír 7 re humlacht mar a raibe C. C.
Do labuir C. C. go humhal failidhe ris 7 assedh adubhairt: 'As
maith dorindis, a Cailtein,' ar se, 'gan cairde do chor ar an
umhlacht acht tect mar adubart-sa rit, oir is ar do grad fen do
iarrus-a tú, indass co cuirteá crich ar do beathuich 'san umlacht.
Acus bid a fhis acud co bfuighe tú bás a nderedh na sechtmhaine-
si fen 7 rachaidh hanum faré Día do caithemh na gloire suthaine.'
Ar cloisdin na mbriathar sin don manach, do gab luthgair imarcuch é, 7 do bendaig C. C. é, 7 fuair bas iarsin amail adubhairt²⁶⁴)
[C. C.] ris; gor moradh ainm Dé 7 C. C. de sin.

248.²⁶⁵) Do bi espog ronaemtha a n-Erinn .i. Aedh mac Bric
esidhein, 7 do bi manuch airidhe dá mhanchaibh fen oc a guidhe
co gnathach, gebe uair ba mithigh le Día a breith do caithemh

---

²⁶²Feachnaus Adamnan.
²⁶³Literally in Adamnan. See Reeves' *Adam.*, pp. 60-1.
²⁶⁴adubt (with a dash over t) MS.
²⁶⁵Literally in Aed mac Bric's *Life*. See Plummer's *V. S. H.*, I, p. 45, § 36.

in Iona, and Columcille had ended his prayers, he spake to Diarmaid and said.

"It is strange to me," saith he, "how long it is till the boat cometh from Erin to us wherein is a certain lad that hath fallen into a deadly sin, and that is sorrowful and repentant for his sin now. And he cometh to require of me to get him pardon from God for his sin."

Not long thereafter Diarmaid saw the boat dropping its sails in the port fast beside. And he told this to Columcille. And the lad aforementioned came to land before Columcille. And he fell on his knees before him and wept sore. And when Columcille perceived that he was truly sorry for his sins, he wept with him, and prayed God earnestly for pardon for them. And he spake to him then and said.

"Beloved son," saith he, "be thou merry and glad, for God hath forgiven thee thy sin by reason of thy heaviness and thy repentance, according to the word that is written in the Scripture, *Cor contritim et umiliatum, deus [non] despicies*,[1]) which is to say, 'A humble and sorrowful heart God will not hold in contempt.'"

When the lad heard this, he rose up from his knees with joy, and he gave great thanks to God and to Columcille therefor. And Columcille sent him to Baithin, to watch him lest he fall into that or another sin. And he died in the end. And the name of this lad was Fiachaidh.

247. Another time that Columcille was in Iona, he sent two of the brethren that were with him to fetch another monk hight Cailtean, that was in a certain cell in the monastery making his orisons. And they told him that Columcille was asking for him. When Cailtean heard that, he went swiftly in obedience to Columcille. Then Columcille bade him welcome in right humble and joyous wise and said:

"Thou hast done well, O Cailtean," saith he, "to make no delay in thy obedience, but to come straightway as I did charge thee, for it is for thy love I sent for thee that thou shouldst end thy life in obedience. And wit thou well thou shalt die at the end of this very week, and thy soul shall go to God to enjoy everlasting glory."

And when the monk heard these words, he was exceeding glad. And Columcille blessed him. And he died then as Columcille had foretold him, so that God's name and Columcille's were magnified thereby.

248. There was a right holy bishop in Erin, hight Aed mac Bric. And a certain one of his monks begged him not to leave him behind in the noise of the world when God thought it time to take him to have joy

---

[1] Psalm 50, 19.

na gloire suth*aine*, gan é fen d'facbail a míciu*n*ass an tshaeghail
se *acht* a breith les a n-aínf*echt* ris fen a ciun*us* flaithessa De.
'Berad madh ail let fen,' ar an t-espog. Ar mbeith daib aimser
airidhe iar sin ag ridirecht do Dia, adubh*air*t an t-espog naemh-
5 (*fol.* 34b)tha ris an manach a ullmhug*hadh* 7 cor mithigh le Dia
é fen do breith les as an prisun sin a*n* cuirp daenna a raibe se
d'estecht re hilceoluib na n-aingel tre bitha sír. Dorinde an manuch drochcomairli an uair sin, ar n-a dalladh do seoltuib an
aiberseora, 7 adub*hairt* nar mith*igh* les an saeghal d'fhacbail a
10 comluath sin. Acus do bi bodach airidhe don phopal do lathair
an uair sin 7 adubhairt, cor tr*u*agh nach ris fen adubhairt an
t-espog an t-ullmugadh sin do denamh. 'Dena-ssa an t-ullmhu-
g*hadh*,' ar an t-espog, '7 luidh ar enlebaidh rim-sa ano*cht*, 7 berad lium a n-inadh an manuich tú.' Doronsad aml*aidh* sin, 7
15 frith marb ar na marach íad, 7 do cuaid a n-anmonda docum
nimhe. Et do bi C. C. an uair sin 'san oilen dánadh hainm hÍ
a rigacht na hAlpan, 7 do foillsig*edh* sein dó ar an pongc sin
fen. Acus do labair go faidhemail re na manchuib 7 do indes
doib gach ní dar imd*igh* ar Aedh m*a*c Bric 7 ar in manuch 7 ar
20 in mbodach. Acus adubhairt cor laídir 7 gorb imarcach na grasa
tuc Día d'Aedh mac Bric léa ruc sé an pecuch, nar cossain
flaithes Dé coruice sín, les do caithemh na gloiri d'aindeoín na
ndiab*al* 7 narb eídir leo toirmesc do chur air, 7 corab ar aithris
Cr*iost* 7 gaduidhe na laimhe [deise] ruc sé lés é. Acus do molu-
25 t*ar* na manaigh C. C. co mor trías na subalt*aidh*ibh sin tuc Dia
dó nach raibe en-ní a nimh *no* a talm*hain* 'n-a dorchad*us* air.

249. Do ch*uaidh* m*anuch* naemtha iarsin, darbh ainm Colma*n*
Eala,[266]) on talumh dana[dh] hainm Laighes a Laighn*ibh* da
oilithre 7 ar cuairt crabuid[h] mar a raibe C. C. go hÍ a righocht
30 na hAlpan, 7 do bi faris *co n*derna se esp*og*[267]) de. Acus an uair
do b*a* mithidh les imp*ódh* tar a aiss co hEirinn, do fiarf*aigh* do
C. C. cind*us* do-berudh sé a betha ass *no* cia he an naem Er*enn*uch
as mó re mbeith a cumann nó a paírt *no* do beith 'n-a oide
faisidnech aige. 'Bidh an nech naemhtha docim-se fen gach
35 oidche Do*mh*nuigh a fiadnaise Criost it*ir* ainglib nimhe 'n-a oide
faisidnech agat,' ar Colum Cille. 'Cia hé sin *no* cind*us* as duine

---

[266]*recte* Colman macua Laoighse, also called Colman Espog. See § *228 supra*.
Dele Eala throughout this paragraph. See *V. S. H.*, II, pp. 105-6, ed. Plummer.
Columbanus . . . . . de plebe que dicitur Laighys natus est. According to Adamnan, Colman Eala was a descendant of Ui Sailni. See Reeves, *ibid., p. 29*.

[267]Colman Eala was not a bishop when Columcille died. See Reeves, *ibid.*,
p. 125.

of the everlasting glory, but to bear him with him into the peace of the Kingdom of God.

"I will take thee, if thou wilt," saith the bishop.

And when they had been for some time after in the service of God, the holy bishop bade the monk make ready, for that God thought it time to bear him away from the prison of the body whereas he was, to listen to the music of the angels for evermore. Then the monk followed evil counsel, for he was blinded by the snares of the Adversary, and he said he would fain not leave the world so soon. And there was a certain old rustic there at that time, and he said it was a pity it was not he the bishop had told to make ready.

"Make ready then," saith the bishop, "Be with me in one bed this night and I will bear thee with me in the monk's stead."

Thus it was done, and on the morrow they were found dead, and their souls gone to Heaven.

Columcille was at that time in the isle hight Iona, and this thing was revealed to him in that same hour. And he spake in manner of prophecy to the brethren, and he told them all that had befallen Aed mac Bric and the monk and the rustic. And he declared that mighty and exceeding were the graces God had given Aed mac Bric, whereby he had taken that sinner the which till then had not striven for the Kingdom of God, to enjoy glory in the Devil's despite. And it was not possible for them to hinder him, for after the manner of Christ with the thief at His right hand he took him. And the monks praised Columcille greatly on account of the powers bestowed on him by God, whereby naught in Heaven or on earth was hid from him.

249. Then a holy monk hight Colman Eala went from the place called Laighes in Leinster on a pilgrimage and visit of piety to Columcille in Iona in the Kingdom of Alba. And he was in his fellowship until Columcille let make him bishop. And when him seemed time to return to Erin he asked Columcille how he should spend his life and with what saint of Erin he should bind him in fellowship withal, or who should be his confessor.

"Let that holy man be thy confessor the which I behold each Sunday night in Christ's presence amid angels," saith Columcille.

"Who is he and what semblance hath he?" saith Colman Eala.

"A holy man and kindly is he, and of thine own kin," saith Columcille, "and he is ruddy of visage, with eyes vair, and the locks upon him do be a little gray."

é?' ar Colman Eala. 'Nech naemtha sochraidh dod cinedh-sa
fen é,' ar Colum Cille, 'ag a fuil agaidh dearg 7 suile glasa 7 becán
do gruaig leith fair.' 'Ni haithne dam-sa,' an Colman Eala,
'a leitheíd sin do duine a n-Erinn acht madh Findtan mac Gabrein
5 namá.' 'As é sin aderim-se do beith 'n-a companuch acud,' ar
C. C., '7 bidh a demhin agad,' ar se, 'corub maith an buachail
tréda do Christ é, 7 co mbera sé moran d'anmonnaib docum nimhe
tren a naemthacht 7 trian a crabhudh 7 tren a esimlaír.' Tainicc
Colman Ela a n-Erinn iarsin, 7 do indeis d'Fhindtan gach ní da
10 ndubhairt C. C. ris, 7 do aithin Findtan do Colman Ela gan sin
d'indisin ren a beo fen. Do coimhed Colman Ela an aithne sin;
oir is tar eís baís Findtain do indis se an scel-sa ar naemthacht
C. C. 7 Findtain amail derbus beatha Fhindtain fén.²⁶⁸)

250.²⁶⁹) Do bi nech ronaemtha a n-Erind, Mochonna a ainm
15 7 Macarius ainm eli do. Acus Fiachna rí Erenn a athair, 7
Findcaemh ainm a mathar. Acus do bí ga oilemain ag righ
Connacht co cend a seacht mbliadhan. Acus do tairngir Espog
Eoghan Arda Sratha, a fad rian a genemain, go ngenfidhe in mac
sin 7 go mad[h] é bud companuch slighedh do C. C. ag dul do
20 Roimh, 7 go tibradh Grigoir Pápa an tres ainm air .i. Mauricius.
Acus do tindscnadh lécend do denamh dó, 7 mar do cuala imrádh
C. C. do bi 'n-a brathair fogas do, do cuaidh mar a raibe se do
sheoladh na n-aingel do bidh 'n-a coimhideacht 7 do grasaib an
Spirita Naeimh do bi 'n-a croide. Acus taínec do mirbuilibh C. C.
25 gor mebraigh se legend na hecluissi re tri mí uadha, 7 gur gab se
aibid uadha. Acus do len sé sdaid C. C. .i. a maighisdir fen mar
us fherr gor fhed se a lenmain; gin gor fhéd nech da taínic riamh
a lenmhuin gu huilidhe. Acus ag dul do Colum Cille ar deoraidhecht a nAlbain, adubhairt an lenub naemthu-sa dá bfhuilmíd
30 ag labhairt .i. Moconda, go rachadh se les. 'Na heirich,' ar C. C.,
'acht an faré hat[h]air 7 réd mathair ad duthaigh fen.' 'Tu-ssa
mh'athair,' ar Moconda, '7 an eclus mo mathuir 7 assí an aít as
mó ina fédfainn serbís do denamh do Día is duthaigh damh,' ar se;
'7 ós tu-ssa, a Colaim Cille, do cengail re Crisd me, lenfad tú
35 go mberi tú mar a bfhuil se me;' 7 tuc moid na hoilithre andsin.

²⁶⁸See Reeves' *Adam.*, p. 213.
²⁶⁹See Reeves' *Adam.*, p. 325.

"I know not," saith Colman Eala, "such a man in Erin, save it be Findtan son of Gabhran only."

"He it is," saith Columcille, "that I tell thee is to be thy companion. And wit thou well," saith he, "that he is a good shepherd to Christ, and shall bear many souls to Heaven through his holiness and good works and ensaumple."

Thereafter Colman Eala came to Erin, and he told to Findtan all that Columcille had said to him. Findtan charged Colman Eala to hold that close while his life lasted. And Colman Eala kept his commandment, for it was after Findtan's death that he told this history touching the sanctity of Columcille and Findtan, as the *Life of Findtan* rehearseth.

XVIII

OF COLUMCILLE AND MOCHONDA

250. There was a right holy man in Erin hight Mochonda. And Macarius was his other name. Fiachna, King of Erin was his father, and Findcaemh was his mother's name. He was in fosterage with the King of Connacht till he was of seven years of age. And Bishop Eoghan of Ard Sratha prophesied a long time afore his birth that he should be born, and that he should go in Columcille's fellowship to Rome, and that Pope Gregory should give him his third name, to wit, Mauricius. And he began his studies. And when he heard tell of Columcille, the which was his near kinsman, he went to him, being guided by the angels that were wont to be with him, and by the graces of the Holy Spirit that were in his heart. And it came to pass by the miracles of Columcille that he mastered the learning of the Church in the space of three months with him. And he took the habit from him. And as best he might he followed Columcille his master, albeit wholly might none ever follow him. And when Columcille went into exile into Alba, Moconda, the holy child we have aforementioned, said he would go in his fellowship.

"Go not," saith Columcille, "but abide with thy father and mother in thine own country."

"Thou art my father," saith Moconda, "and the Church is my mother, and that place is my country where I can best do service for God. And sith it is thou, O Columcille, that hast bound me to Christ, I will follow thee till thou take me where He is."

Ar tuicsin fhoirbfhidhechta an leinb oícc sin do C. C. 7 an las (*fol.* 35a) aidh gra*dha* do bi aige air he fen do lenmhai*n* ina oilithre, do toilidh do tect les.

251. Fechtus do Colum Cille a nhI, 7 do fhurail ar Moconda a beith ag scribneora*cht,* 7 ruc an oidhce air 7 ni raibe coindli aige, 7 tainic do naemhacht a maigheistrech .i. C. C. 7 da naemh*acht* fen, gor comsholus la 7 oidhce do. Do condairc manach airidhe do na manchuib an ní sin, 7 do indiss don coimthinól e, 7 do gab imtnudh mór re Moconda íad. Acus do comairligeta*r* bas do tab*hair*t dó, 7 do cuireta*r* neimh a ndigh cuicce. Do foillsigedh sen do C. C. 7 é 'n-a duirrtech fen 7 Macairius 'sa proindtigh, 7 do thógaib a lamh 7 do coisric an deoch uadha. Acus tainic do mirbuil*ibh* De 7 C. C. co ndechuidh a neimh tr*í*d an tshoithech a raibe an deoch 7 gur an an deoch glan and. Acus ar na hibhe do Moconda, ni derna si digbail ar bith do tre mirbuil*ibh* Dé 7 C. C. Acus as mar sin do coimheid C. C. a dalta fen ar a neimh sin.

252. O'dconduirc C. C. aingidecht an coimhtinoil do Macairius (7 do Mochonda), tuc cuice he 7 do coisric 'n-a hespog é, 7 tuc faínde 7 bachall dó, 7 tuc gach indstraimint eli do foigeonadh d'espog do frecur ecluisi Dé dó. Acus tuc se da fher dec dó do dainib duth*r*achtacha do bi foirbthe a frecur ecluisi Dé, 7 adubhairt se ris dul a proibhindse Pictora 7 comhnuidhe do denamh san inadh ina bfuidhedh se abund ar cuma bachla 'sa talamh sin, 7 adubhairt gurub andsin do toil*igh.* Día dó comnaidhe do denamh athaidh dá aimsir.

253. Do gluais Macairius 7 a muindt*ir* rompa, 7 do ceilebrata*r* do Colum Cille, 7 do cuaidh go p*r*oibindse Pictora, 7 do condaic se abond uadha ar cuma bachla amail adubhairt C. C. ris. Acus do cumdaighedh eclus a n-inadh airidhe re taeb na haband sin les. Acus do bi pest neimhe san inadh sin, 7 do lecedh si lasracha tend*tidh*e as a braghaid lea marba*dh* si moran do na cinedhacha*ibh*. Acus ar na faicsin do Macairius amluidh sin an uair dob'ail lé urchoid do denumh dó, do malluigh hí 7 dorinde cairthe cloiche di do cumhachtaib De 7 do mirbuil*ibh* C. C.; oir is do scris na piasda sin do sheol C. C. Macairius docum an inaidh sin sech gach inadh eli a proi*b*indse Pictora, ar na foillsiug*hadh* dó ina spir*aid* an pesd sin do beith ac scr*i*s na poiblech.

254. Is mor, t*r*a, do mirbuil*ibh* dorinde Macairius 'sa p*r*oibindse sin, 7 as mór da sluag*haibh* 7 da sochruidib tuc se docum creidimh , 7 as mor d'eaclusaib do cumhd*aigh* se indte. Acus do chuir sé a n-idhbarta demhnuidhe ar cul 7 do scris se ímhaidhe na ndeiedh ndiabluidhe da creidís.

And then he took the vow of exile. And when Columcille saw the perfection of that young lad and the ardent love he had for him, he granted him to follow him in his exile.

251. On a time that Columcille was in Iona, he charged Moconda to make a transcript. And night came on him and he had no candles. And it befell through the sanctity of his master, to wit, Columcille, and through his own sanctity, that the night was as bright for him as the day. A certain one of the monks perceived this thing, and told it to the household. Whereat they had great jealousy of Moconda. And they took counsel to kill him. And they put poison in his drink. Then was this revealed to Columcille in his oratory what time Macarius was in the refectory. And from where he stood he heaved his hand and blessed the drink. And so it came to pass by the miracles of God and Columcille that the poison went away through the vessel wherein the drink was, and the drink remained unpolluted therein. And when Moconda drank it, it did him no hurt, through the miracles of God and Columcille. Thus it was that Columcille saved his fosterling from that poison.

252. When Columcille perceived the illwill of the household toward Macarius [Moconda] he summoned him to him and let make him bishop. And he gave him a ring and a staff and every other gear whereof a bishop hath need in the service of the church of God. And moreover he gave him twelve men of good will that were diligent in the service of the Church of God. And he bade him go into the province of Pictora and make his abode in a place where he should find a river shaped like a staff, for there had God willed him to pass a share of his time.

253. Then Macarius and his followers set out. And they bade farewell to Columcille and they repaired to the province of Pictora. And in the distance he saw a river shaped like a staff, as Columcille had told him. And on a certain spot near the river he built a church. And there was a poisonous beast in that place, and she belched forth sparks of fire whereby she killed much folk of the place. And right as Macarius saw the beast in point to do him hurt in that wise, he cursed her. And by the power of God and the miracles of Columcille he made of her a pillar of stone. For it was to destroy that beast that Columcille had sent Macarius to that place passing every other place in the province of Pictora, for it had been revealed to him in spirit that she was destroying the folk there.

254. Many in sooth were the miracles that Macarius wrought in that province, and great the hosts that he brought to the Faith. And many were the churches that he builded there. And he did do away the diabolical sacrifices, and did break the images of the infernal deities they believed in.

255. Fechtus dá ndechaidh C. C. dá oilethri don Roimh, 7 do chuir se gairm ar Macairius .i. a descibul fen, 7 do togh se mar companuch sligedh é tar gach uili manuch da naemthacht da raibhe aige. Acus ar ndul docum na Romha doib, do cuatar a cend Grigoir Papa, 7 ar mbeith ag comradh daib re celi, do fiarfaigh Grigoir do C. C. ga hainm do bí ar a companuch. 'Moconda no Macairius a ainm,' ar C. C. Acur mar nar thuic Grigoir na hanmonda sin, tuc se fen ainm eli air .i. Maurisius .i. Manus recta .i. lamh direch, ar son gor direch ina oibrighthibh é. Gonad annsin tainec tairrngire espoig Eoghain docum criche leth re Grighoir do tabairt an tres anma ar Macairius. Mar do fhuair Grighoir afhis ó Colum Cille gurub espog Macairius 7 gur nech ronaemtha romirbuilech é, do aithin do maile ré honoír romoir beith ag frecor ecluisi Torón do bi an uair sin gan espog .i. an ecluis inar handluicedh Martain naemtha.

256. Ar crichnughadh a ngoaighedh re Grighoir doib, 7 ar ndenumh oilithri na Roma co himlan, do gabutar a ced aice, 7 do léc a bendacht leo 7 do fácbhatar a mbendacht aice. Acus do gabhutar gu Torón. Acus ní raibe a fhis ac lucht na cathruch sin ga hinadh airidhe inar hadluicedh Martain. Acus ar na cluinsin doib nach raibe enní a nimh no a talmhuin a n-ainbhfis do C. C., 7 go raibe se 'n-a faidh ag an Tigherna nemdha, do taircetar morán oir 7 airgid 7 aiscedh eli do do cind a foillsiughadh doib ca raibe an t-andluicedh sin. 'Ni geb-sa aiscedha oír no aircid uaib,' (fol. 35b) ar C. C. '7 foillseochad andlacudh Martain daib da faghar an ní eli ata san andlacadh faris an corp.' Tucatar lucht na cathrach cuir 7 minda dó air sin. Acus do foillsig[h] C. C. an t-andlucadh iarsin. Acus ar na foscladh doib, fuaratar leabur aifrind and, 7 adubhairt C. C. gorb'e an lebur sin do bi se fen d'íarraidh, 7 gurab uime dorinde se cuir re lucht na cathrach. Do brethnaighetar lucht na cathruch brisedh air 7 gan an lebur do tabhairt dó, 7 adubratar muna fhagbudh se nech naemtha ecin da raibe faris go suthain acu, nach fuig[h]edh se an lebhur. Do fagaib sesen Macairius naemtha aca do reir furailmhe an Papa do frecar oifice espoig doib, mar do batar an uair sin gan espog, 7 tucadh an lebhor do C. C. Agus is mar sin adeir betha espoig Eoghain 7 betha Macairius an lebur sin d'faghail. Acus do foillsigh Martain é fen do moran do lucht na cathrach an oidhce sin 7 iad ina codladh 7 assedh adeiredh riu: 'Onoraigh Macairius

255. On a time Columcille was going on a pilgrimage to Rome. And he sent for Macarius his disciple. And passing every other monk he chose him to travel in his fellowship by reason of his holiness.[1] And when they came to Rome they sought out Pope Gregory. And whilst they were in converse together Gregory asked Columcille what was the name of his companion.

"Moconda or Macarius is his name," saith Columcille.

And Gregory, understanding not these names, gave him another name, to wit, Mauricius, to wit *Manus recta*, which is as much to say, Straight-handed, by reason that he was straight in his works. Thus was fulfilled the prophecy of Bishop Eoghan that Gregory should give a third name to Macarius. When Gregory was told by Columcille that Macarius was a bishop, and that he was a passing holy man and of wondrous works, he gave him the see of Tours that was at that time without a bishop. And that was the church wherein Saint Martin was buried.

256. When they had ended their business with Gregory and had made a pilgrimage throughout Rome, they took leave of him. And he gave them his blessing and they gave him theirs. And they departed to Tours. And the folk of the city knew not the very spot whereas Martin was buried. And having heard there was naught in Heaven or on earth hidden from Columcille, and that he was a prophet of the heavenly Lord, they offered him much gold and silver and other gifts to discover to them where that burying place was.

"I will not take from you gifts of gold or silver," saith Columcille, "but I will discover to you the grave of Martin if I get another thing that is in the tomb with the body."

The folk of the city gave him then sureties and oaths, and Columcille discovered to them the burying place. And when they had opened it they found a missal therein. And Columcille said it was that book he had required of them, and it was touching that book he had the covenant with the folk of the city. But the folk of the city would have broken faith with him and would have denied him the book. And they said he might not have the book save he leave there some holy man of his fellowship. So he left holy Macarius with them according to the commandment of the Pope, to be a bishop to them, since they were without a bishop. And the book was given to Columcille. And in this wise it was that the *Life of Bishop Eoghan* and the *Life of Macarius* declare that the book was got. And that night Martin himself appeared to much folk of the city whilst they slept.[2]

And he said: "Honor Macarius as myself, for he is mine own be-

---

[1] *Cf.* § 40.
[2] *Cf.* §§ 34, 101.

mar mesi fen, oír is é mo mac gradach fen é, 7 as air tainic toil
Gridhoir Papa 7 C. C. dá chur do fhrecor na heclaisse Torón.'

257. Ar frecur na hecluisse do Macairius tri bliadhna go
leith, do ghoir a coimthinol uili chuige 7 adubhairt riu, gor fhocus
dó fen an aimsir ar a raibe se ag feichemh on a naídhendacht
conuice sin .i. aimser a bais, 7 adubhairt go fuighedh bas fa cend
tri la. Do ba rodobrónach an coimtinol 7 lucht na cathrach uile
de sin. Acus adubhairt Macairius ríu gan tuirrse do beith orra
7 corb'í toil Dé gach nech do gebudh betha d'fagail bais.
Do facbutar lucht na cathrach uile Macairius a pongc a bais acht
espoig 7 manaigh. Do labhair Macairius riu 7 assedh adubhairt:
'Coisrigidh bar suile 7 bhar croidhedha, indus go bfaicedh sib
gach ní atchim-se 7 go cluinedh sib gach ni adcluinim.' Doronsad
amlaidh, 7 do condcatar Issu Christ gon a espulaibh 7 an cuirt
ainglidhe 7 Martain naemtha 7 C. C. ina corp daenna 'n-a coraid
timchell Macairius. Acus fa gnathach do C. C. beith ina corp
daenna faris na hainglib 7 gnimhartha ainglidhe do dhenamh
amail leghtar go minic air. Acus dob ainglide dó dul ina corp
daenna a luas aingeil mar gach aingel eli o hÍ C. C. a rigacht na
hAlpan go Toirinis Martain. Acus assedh aderdis uile: 'Tarr
cugaind, a Macairius, 7 dena comhnuidhe farind a flaithes t'athar
fen.' Do cualatar a raibe do dainib naemtha do lathair an uair
sin Pedur espol da fiarfaighe d'Ísa Christ: 'Cred hi an maith
dorinde an duine si ar a fuair se an onoir mor se uaib.' Do
frecair Issu e 7 assedh adubhairt: 'Do coimeid se gac[h] uile
ait[h]ne da fuil 'sa tsenrecht 7 annsa rec[h]t nua gan oired en-
litre do brisedh dib, 7 do coimeid se é fen o gach uili salchur ó'n
a gein go a báss tre grasaib De 7 tre coimed C. C. do bi air dar
dalta 7 dar deiscibul é.'

258.²⁷⁰) Domnach airidhe do C. C. a nhI, 7 do cuala se glaedh
a port na hindse sin, 7 adubhairt se re na manchaib imthec[h]t
go luath 7 na hoilithrigh tainic a fad do tabhairt leo. Do imgedur

---

²⁷⁰Literally in Adamnan. See Reeves' *Adam.*, pp. 61-2.

loved son, and on him hath come the choice of Gregory and Columcille, sending him to rule over the church of Tours."

257. When Macarius had been for three and a half years over the church of Tours, he called his whole household to him and told them that the time was nigh that he had been awaiting from childhood till that hour, that is to say, the time of his death. And he added that he should die in three days. Then were his household and all the folk of the city sorrowful, and Macarius bade them be not sad, and he told them it was the will of God that each one that gat life should get death. Then the folk of the city left the dying Macarius, all departing save the bishops and the monks.

And Macarius spake to them and said in this wise: "Bless ye your eyes and your hearts that ye may see what I see and hear what I hear."

Thus they did. And they beheld Jesu Christ with His apostles and the angelic court, and the holy Martin and Columcille in the flesh in pairs round about Macarius.

And oft was Columcille in the flesh in the fellowship of angels, and he was wont to do angelic deeds as it is read of him right oft. And it was in the manner of an angel that he went, albeit in the flesh, with the swiftness of an angel like the rest of the angels, from Iona-Colaimcille in the Kingdom of Alba to Tours of Martin.

And they all cried, "Come to us, O Macarius, and dwell with us in the kingdom of thy Father."

Then the holy folk that were there heard the apostle Peter inquiring of Jesu Christ what good that man had done wherefor he gat such great honor from them.

Then answered Jesu Christ and said in this wise: "He hath kept every command of the Old Law and of the New Law. And he hath not transgressed a single letter of them. And he hath kept him from all uncleanness from his birth till his death, through the grace of God and the care that Columcille hath had for him, his fosterling and disciple."

XIX

MORE OF THE MIRACLES AND PROPHECIES OF COLUMCILLE IN IONA

258. On a certain Sunday that Columcille was in Iona, he heard a shout in the port of the isle and he bade the brethren go quickly and bring with them the pilgrims that were come from afar. Then went

na manaig 7 tucatar dís oilithrech leo. Acus ar na faicsin do C. C.,
do pocc iad 7 do fiarfuidh dib cred dob'adhbor da turus. Adubratar san gorb'ail .leo beith go cend mbliadhna fare C. C.
Adubhairt C. C. nach beidís faris fen muna tréicdis an saeghal 7
techt is na manchuib. Adubhairt an nech fa sine dib nach raibe
an triall sin aca remesin, 7 go ndendaís a comairli sen ar gach
uile ní da n-íarfadh se orra. Acus ruc C. C. les don mainesdir
iad íar sin, 7 do leccatar ar a ngluínib a bfhiadnaise na haltóra
íad, 7 tuc gach nech dib moíd manaigh andsin, 7 do bendaigh
C. C. íad. Et adubhairt co ndernatar an dís uasal sin idbairt beo
dib fen do Crist, 7 adubhairt co ngebadh galur an manuch fa sine
dibh, 7 go bfhuigedh se bas fa cend sectmhuine on lá sin inar gab
an aibíd, 7 adubhairt se co fuighedh an dara manach dib bas fa
cend cet[h]re la ndécc on la cedna sin. Acus do firadh sin uile
amail adubhairt C. C.; gor moradh ainm Dé 7 C. C. de sin.

259.[271]) Fechtus do Colum Cille a nhÍ,[272]) 7 do cuaidh fen 7
cuid da manchuib do radh a trath 7 a n-urnaidhe re cois na fairge.
Acus ar crichnughadh a n-urnaidhe doib, do buail C. C. an lorg
no an baitín do bí 'n-a laimh a n-inadh airidhe ar talamh, 7 do
labuir ris na manchuib 7 assedh adubhairt: 'A cland gradach,'
ar se, 'docife sib ingnadh mor aniugh .i. tiucfaidh nech arsaidh
airidhe do na cinedhachuib ata a n-agaidh creidim[h] cugaind andso, 7 gebaidh se baisde uaim-se, 7 do— (fol. 36a) géba se bas com
lúath 7 baistfidher é, 7 adhlaicfidher 'san inadh-sa inar buail mesi
mo lorg ar talmain é. Acus asse adbhur fa tucand Dia na grasa-sa
do .i. co raibe an maith nadurdha ar coimhed aige go mór an
méidi-si, indus nach nderna se en-ní bud mesde les do denamh air
fen ar ennech eli riam.' Ar crichnughadh an comraidh sin doib,
do condcatar an long cuca 'sa cuan. Acus ar techt a tír dí, do
tocbatar a muindtir fen an duine arsaidh sin etorra ass in luing
7 tucatar leo a bfhiadnaise C. C. e. Acus do senmoir C. C. an
creidemh do, 7 as fer tengha eile do chuiredh a ceill dó gach ní
da n-abradh C. C. ris, oir ní tuicedh se Laiden no Gaidelc uadha.
Acus do bendaigh C. C. e; 7 tainic do brigh an bendaighthe sin
gor gab se baisde na heccluisi cuige. Acus fuair se bas iarsin,
7 do handluicedh 'san inadh inar buail C. C. a lorg ar talmain é;
cor moradh ainm De 7 C. C. de sin. Acus dorindetar na manaich
do bi fare C. C. an uair sin ula 'san inadh sin a cuimhniughadh
an sceoil sin, 7 mairidh sí and ó sin ille.

[271]In Adamnan, ibid., pp. 62-3.
[272]Scia Adamnan.

the monks and brought back two pilgrims. When Columcille saw them he kissed them, and asked them the cause of their journey. They said they would fain pass a year with Columcille. Columcille said that they might not be in his fellowship, save they forsake the world and become monks.

Then said the elder of them that they had not had that purpose afore that time, but they would follow his counsel in all he should ask of them. Then Columcille took them to the monastery, and they fell on their knees afore the altar. And they took the vow to be monks both. And Columcille blessed them and said those two nobles had made of themselves a living sacrifice to Christ. And he said a sickness should overtake the older monk and he should die at the end of a week from the day that he took the habit. And he said the other monk should die at the end of fourteen days from the same day. All that fell out as Columcille had said, so that God's name and Columcille's were magnified thereby.

259. On a time that Columcille was in Iona he went with some of his monks to say his hours and his prayers at the edge of the sea. And when they had finished their prayers, Columcille struck the earth in a certain place with the club or staff he had in his hand. And he spake to the brethren and said,

"Beloved children," saith he, "ye shall see a great marvel this day. There shall come to us here an ancient man of the tribe that is against the Faith, and he shall be baptized by me, and shall die straightway. And he shall be buried in this spot of ground that I have struck with my staff. And this is the reason that God hath given him these graces, that by nature he hath been thus far good that he hath never done aught to others that he were loth men should do to him."

And when they had ended that conversation they saw a ship coming up the harbor toward them. And when it reached land the folk thereon lifted an old man from among them upon the boat, and brought him into the presence of Columcille. And Columcille instructed him in the Faith. And a man of tongues made clear to him what Columcille said to him, for he understood not Latin nor Irish. And Columcille blessed him. And it came to pass from that blessing that he received the baptism of the church. And then he died. And he was buried in the spot where Columcille had struck the ground with his staff. And so God's name and Columcille's were magnified thereby. And the monks that were with Columcille at that time made a mound in that place in memory of this history, and it remaineth there to this day.

260.²⁷³) Fechtus do C. C. a nhí 7 se ag scribneoracht, 7 taínec manach airidhe da manch*aibh* fen chuige dar oific beith os cind na cisde*n*aidhe ag an coimhti*n*ol 7 daigér 'n-a laimh. Acus do íarr ar C. C. a bendug*hadh* do. Do tócaib C. C. an lam a raibe an pend 7 tuc a chul ris an lebh*ur* 7 do bennaigh an daigér. Acus ar n-imtecht don manach amach uada, do fiafr*aigh* da descib*ul* fen .i. do Diarmaid cred é an t-íarand sin tuc an manach da coisregadh cuige. Adub*hairt* Diarmaid gorab daigér le marbthai mairt 7 cairigh tuc se les. 'Ata dochus as Dia agam-sa,' ar C. C., 'nach dena an t-íarand úd do bendaigh mé fen digbail do duine *no* d'ai*n*mhidhe ó aso amach go brath.' Acus do fíradh sin amail adub*hairt* C. C.; oír do cuaid an manach an uair sin fen do marbadh doimh docum na cisdenaidhe, 7 do comail se an daiger do braighid an doimh. Acus nir fhed se dergadh air, 7 ní hedh amaín acht ní fédtai d*er*gadh ar¹ beathadhach ar bith les. Acus ar na thuicsin sin do na manchaib nach¡ raibe fognamh mar sin a*ir*, do furailet*ar* gabhaind do bí 'sa mbaile a leaghadh aris, ind*us* co ndentaí as a núa é 7 co mbeith faebur maith air. Acus ar na leag[h]adh don gabhaind adub*hairt* corb íarand cinealta rocruaidh é, 7 gurb ferrde na hairm eli do bi ag na manchaib le marbhthai mairt 7 cairigh doib, ar a raibe esbuidh c*ru*adach, cuid de do chur ar gach arm dib. Acus doronadh aml*aidh* sin, 7 ní fedtaí dergadh le hén-arm ar ar cuiredh cuid don daiger sin ar duine *no* ainmhidhe o sin suas; cor mor*adh* ainm De 7 Col. C. de sin.

261.²⁷⁴) Aroile aimser do bí C. C. a nhI, 7 do gab tendess ger a descip*ul* fen .i. Diarmaid, indus go raibhe se a nguas*acht* baís. Acus do cuaidh C. C. ar chuairt chuige; 7 ar na fhaicsin 'san guas*acht* mor sin dó, do gair ainm Crist 7 do guidh se co duthr*acht*ach é, 7 do íarr air gan bas do lecen docum a serbfhogant*aidh*e fen an ceín do beith se fen 'n-a beth*aidh*. Acus ar crichnug*hadh* na hurnaidhe sin do Col*um* C*ille*, do bí se tamall 'n-a tosd 7 do labuir arís 7 ass*edh* adubhairt: 'Ni hedh amaín nach fuighe Diarmaid bas don tendes-sa ata air anois *acht* biaid sé beo meid airidhe do bliadhn*aibh* tar eís mo baís-i.' Acus do fíradh sin uile amail adubhairt C. C. Acus as follus as in scel-sa go bfaghadh C. C. o Día gach ní do iarrad[h] se air.

262.²⁷⁵) Fechtus do cuir C. C. derbrathair mathar dó fen 'n-a ua*cht*arán²⁷⁶) a mainistir airidhe do bi san oilen dana comainm

---

[273] In Adamnan's, *ibid.*, p. 143.
[274] In Adamnan's, *ibid.*, p. 144.
[275] Literally from Adamnan. See Reeves' *Adam.*, pp. 86-88.
[276] uas*acht*arán MS.

260. On a time that Columcille was in Iona writing, there came to him one of the brethren that had the task of being over the kitchen of the household. And he had a knife in his hand, and he asked Columcille to bless it for him. Then Columcille raised the hand where the pen was, and he turned his back upon his book and blessed the knife. And when the monk had departed, Columcille asked his disciple Diarmaid what was the iron gear that the monk had brought to be blessed by him. Then said Diarmaid that it was a knife for the killing of oxen and sheep.

"I trust in God," saith Columcille, "that the iron I have blessed will do no hurt to man or beast from this time till Judgment."

And it fell out as Columcille had said, for the monk went straightway to the kitchen, and he laid the knife to the throat of an ox. And it might not redden thereon. And not only that, but of no other beast in the world might blood be drawn with that knife forever. When the monks saw that it was in vain, they bade a smith of the place melt it again, that it might be made anew, and have a good edge. And when the smith had melted it, he said it was iron very hard of kind, and it would be well for the other tools that the monks had for killing oxen and sheep that had need of hardness, to have a portion thereof put in each tool. And thus it was done. But no tool wherein was put aught of that knife hath reddened on man or beast from that time. So God's name and Columcille's were magnified thereby.

261. Another time Columcille was in Iona and sharp sickness seized his disciple Diarmaid, so that he was in danger of death. And Columcille went to visit him. And when he beheld the peril whereas he was, he called on the name of Christ and prayed fervently to Him. And he asked Him the while he should live to spare his servant's life. And when he had ended these prayers, he was a while silent.

And then he spake and said: "Diarmaid shall not die of this sickness, and not this only, but he shall live for a space of years after my death."

And that fell out as Columcille said. And it is clear to us from this history that Columcille did get from God all things that he required of Him.

262. On a time Columcille set his mother's brother over a certain monastery that was in the island called Imba. And when he departed

Imba, 7 ag imt[h]echt dó uadha, tuc pócc do, 7 do bendaigh é, 7 do labair C. C. ris na manchuib do bi faris an uair sin, 7 assedh adubairt, nach faicfedh se an manach naemtha sin budh brat[h]air do fen ina beathaidh go brath arís. Acus nirb fada 'n-a diaidh
5 sin an uair do gab galur trom an manach sin, 7 iar na thuicsin dó co raibe sé fen a nguasacht bais, do triall se filliudh tar ais día fis an fedfadh se tect mar a raibe C. C. sul degebadh se bas, 7 tainic se a port na hindse a raibe C. C. Acus ar na cloisdin sein do C. C., do cuaidh 'n-a aircis maille re luthgaír 7 re reuerens
10 mor, 7 tainic an manuch a tir; 7 gerb anfand egcruaidh ó corp é, do bi do med a miana ar C. C. d'fhaicsin cor tindscain se dul ina aircis gan cungnamh en-duine eli aice. Acus do cuatar a n-aircis a chele mar sin indas náċh raibe etorra acht ceithri coisceím XX do cnocán becc nach facutar a celi tairis, 7 fuair an manach bas ar
15 an (fol. 36b) pongc sin fen. Acus as mar sin do coimlinadh briathur C. C. an uair adubairt se, ag imthecht uadha don manuch sen do bo brathair dó fen, nach faicfedh se n-a bethaigh co brath aris e. Acus do saithedh cros onoruch san inadh araibe C. C. 'n-a sesamh an uair sin, 7 cros eli san inadh a bfhuair an manach
20 bas a ciumhais na fairge, a cuimhniughadh an sceoil sin.

263.[277]) Fechtus do C. C. a n-inadh airidhe a n-Alpain, 7 tainec duine nach faca se riamh remhe sin ina fiadhnuisi, 7 do fiarfaigh se de cá talamh do. Do frecair an t-oclaoch é 7 assedh adubairt, gurab a reidighón eli do bidh se 7 nach don talum sin
25 fen do. 'Ata in proibindse bec ina mbínn tu ar na milledh 7 ar na scris oc a naimdib ó do fagbuis fen í,' ar C. C. Ba dubach dobronach an t-oclaoch de sin tre gan a fhiss do beith aicce cred do imdigh ar a mnai no ar a cloind no ar a airnes ina diaidh. Ar na tuicsin do C. C., do labuir ris 7 assedh adubairt: 'Imigh
30 romad ad duthaig fen,' ar se, '7 do teich do ben 7 do cland fa sleibtibh 7 fa daingnightibh an tire indus nach rucatar a naimhde orra. Acus gidedh rucatar ar do spreidh 7 ar airnes do tighe uile,' ar se. Do imthigh an t-oclaoch iar sin da tir fen 7 fuair se gach én ní dib sin ar na denamh amhuil adubairt C. C., 7 ar
35 techt ar ais do arís mar a raibe C. C. do derb se fen gach en-ní dib sin amail adubramar romhainn; cor moradh ainm De 7 C. C. de sin.

264.[278]) Fectus eli iar sin do C. C. a n-Albain, 7 tainic nech uasal cumhachtach darbh ainm Guaire ina cend, 7 do fiarfaigh se
40 de créd é an bas dogebudh se fen. Frecruis C. C. é 7 assedh

[277]Literally from Adamnan, ibid., pp. 88-9.
[278]In Adamnan, ibid., pp. 89-90.

from Columcille, the saint kissed him and blessed him. And Columcille spake to the brethren that were with him, and said that never again should he see alive that holy monk, his kinsman. A short while thereafter a sore sickness seized that monk, and when he knew himself nigh death he sought if he might come again to Columcille ere he died. And he arrived in the harbor of the island where Columcille was. And when the saint heard that, he went towards him with joy and with great worship. Then the monk came ashore, and albeit he was heavy and sore in body, yet had he so strong a desire to see Columcille that he set out towards him with no help from any. Thus they went each towards other till there was betwixt them but a small hillock of four and twenty paces that hindered them so that one saw not the other. And at that same moment the monk died. Thus it befell as Columcille had said when he left that monk his kinsman, that never again should he see him alive. And to keep in remembrance this history there was set a high cross on the spot where Columcille stood that time, and another cross on the brink of the sea on the place where the monk died.

263. On a time that Columcille was in a certain place in Alba, there came to him one that he had never tofore seen. And Columcille asked him what country he came from. And the man answered that he belonged to another region and not to that land.

"The little place where thou didst dwell hath been destroyed and laid waste by foes, since the time thou didst leave it," saith Columcille.

Thereat was the man heavy and sorrowful, not knowing the fate of his wife and children or the goods that he had left behind him. When Columcille saw this, he spake to him and said:

"Go to thy country," saith he, "for thy wife and children have fled to the mountains and strongholds of the land, so that their enemies have not taken them. But they have seized thy goods and all thy household gear," saith he.

Then the man went back to his land and found that all had happed as Columcille had said. When he came again to Columcille, he bare witness to all that we have said above, so that God's name and Columcille's were magnified thereby.

264. Another time afterward, when Columcille was in Alba, a mighty noble hight Guaire came to visit him. And he asked Columcille what manner of death he should die. Columcille made answer that

adubairt, nach fuighedh se bas a cath *no* ar fairge 7 gorub 'n-a coimidecht fen do bí an ní doberad[h] bas do. Ar na cluinsin sin do Guaire, do shaeil se corub nech ecin da cairdib fen do bi ar tí baís do tabairt do, no corab í a ben posda do bí ar tí
5 a cur dochum bais mar an cedna, le mailís *no* le piseógaibh docum co mbeith fer bud oíce ina é fen aice. Acus adubairt C. C. nach cechtar dib sin doberud bas do. 'Indes-i dam-sa,' ar Guaire, 'cia heli dobera bas damh.' 'Ni indeosad,' ar C. C., 'oir ní ced le Dia me da indesin duid.' Fa aimser ghirr iar sin,[279]) do bi
10 Guaire ac snoidhe croind a sleighe, 7 do leic a scían ar lar laimh ris, 7 do cuala se daine ag bruighnechus re celi a comghar do; 7 ag erghe do ag dul dá n-anacul ar a ceile, tarla a glun fan scín acus tucc cnedh guasachtach air; 7 do aithin sé an uair sin gorub don scín do labuir C. C. an uair adubairt se, corub 'n-a coimhidecht
15 fen do bí an ní doberadh bas dó. *Acus* fuair Guaire bás a cedoír iar sin don cneidh sin tuc an scian air; cor moradh ainm De 7 C. C. de sin.

265.[280]) F*echtus* do C. C. a n-Í, ar crichnug*hadh* oifice De do díasathairn do sundr*ách,* do gair se manuch airidhe da manchaibh
20 fen cuicce, 7 do labuir go faídhem*hail* ris 7 assedh adubairt: 'Erichc a mic gr*a*duigh,' ar se, 'a ndiaidh nóna do ló dialuain-se cucad cois na fairge san oilen-sa fen, 7 docífe tu aídhigh uasal ag techt chucad .i. corr Erennuch ata ac tect ar cuairt cucam-sa ó Erinn, 7 biaidh sí cuirthe tuirsech, 7 rach*aidh* a n*e*rt ar cul go
25 mor tre mhéd a siubuil 7 a haisdir 7 t*re* fhad na heiteoícce berus sí; 7 rachaidh a luth ac*us* a luaighill as a sciathanaibh indus co tuitfe sí a comrac na tuinde 7 na tragha, 7 biaid an tond ga buala*dh* amach 7 astech, 7 ni bía n*e*rt aice fen air sin d'fhagail, 7 taphair-se furtacht di,' ar se, '7 tabhuir let don cisdenaigh
30 í, 7 tabuir biadh 7 frit[h]olamh co cend t*ri* la 7 teora n-oidhche di; 7 ni anfa si nías faide ina *sin* againn, 7 rach*aidh* sí ar a hais co hErinn arís. Acus as uime cuirim sin d'fhiach*aibh* ort-sa t*ar* manach eli, corub d'én duth*aigh* 7 d'en talm*hain* duid fen 7 d*on* chuirr sin, indus co mbeith combaidh 7 comtruaige agad di, 7 co
35 ticedh do trocaire uirre, 7 comadh ferrde dode*n*thá fritholamh di é.' Ar cur na haimsire tairis don manach co*n*uice an uaír sin (*fol.* 37a) adub*a*irt C. C. ris, do cuaid se cois fairce 7 do *con*nairc se an corr cuige, 7 do imd*igh* gach ní da ndub*airt* C. C. uirre; 7 do tóccuib se les don chisdenaigh í, 7 do bi ga fritholum mar is ferr
40 cor fhéd, 7 do tairc se biadh di 7 nir ith sise sin uadha. Acus do

---

[279]*Post aliquot annorum excursus* Adamnan.
[280]In Adamnan, *ibid.,* pp. 90-91.

he should not die in battle nor at sea; but what should cause his death was in his own company. When Guaire heard that, he weened it were one of his friends that was purposed to kill him, or else his wife, that should do it through malice or by witchcraft, that she might have a younger man than he. Columcille said nor one nor other of those should cause his death.

"Tell me," saith Guaire, "who then else should kill me?"

"I will not tell thee," said Columcille, "for that doth God not permit."

Short while thereafter Guaire was trimming the haft of his spear, and let fall his knife close by him. He heard men quarrelling one with another nigh hand, and as he gat him up to go to make peace betwixt them, his knee chanced on the knife, and he was hurt to the death. Then he understood that it was of the knife Columcille had spoken when he said that what would cause his death was in his own company. And he died straightway of the hurt done by the knife, so that God's name and Columcille's were magnified.

265. On a time that Columcille was in Iona, when he had read his office on a certain Saturday, he called one of the brethren to him, and speaking in a manner of prophecy, he said:

"Go, beloved son," saith he, "after the hour of nones on Monday next coming, to the shore of this island, and thou shalt see a noble guest coming toward thee, to wit, an Irish crane that cometh from Erin to sojourn with me. She shall be weary and fordone, and her strength shall fail her sore by reason of the length of the journey and the voyage, and of the space she shall have flown. And life and fulness shall fail her wings, and she shall fall in the encounter of the wave and strand. The wave shall drive her in and out, and she shall have no strength to take the shore. "Do thou aid her," saith he, "and bring her to the kitchen. Give her food and care for three days and three nights. No longer than that shall she remain with us. And she shall return again to Erin. And why I am putting this task upon thee rather than upon any other monk is because thou and that crane are from the same country and the same land; so that thou shouldst have compassion and ruth upon her, and show her kindness, and the better serve her."

And time passed till the hour came that Columcille had told him. And the monk went to the shore and espied the crane coming towards him. All fell out with her as Columcille had said. And he brought her with him to the kitchen, and served her as best he could. And he offered her food, but she ate it not from him; and the monk went then to Columcille to tell him that. Columcille asked of him no tidings; for of naught was he without knowledge. And he spake to the monk and said:

"May God bless thee, for well hast thou done service for the little

cuaidh in manach mar a raibe C. C. dá indisin sin dó, 7 nír
fhiarfaidh C. C. scela de; oír ní raibe ainbfhis air fen fá en-ní; 7 do
labair ris an manach 7 assedh adubairt: 'Co mbendaighi Dia tu,
a meic gradhuig,' ar se, 'oir is maith dorindis serbis don cuirr
bicc Erendaig tainic da hoilithre cugaind, 7 tabuir let cucam-sa
í; oir ní caithfe sí bíadh no deoch go faice sí mesi fen.' Tuc an
manuch an corr les iar sin mar a raibe C. C., 7 ar techt do láthair
di, do fhill a glún 7 do crom a cend a comartha umhla dó, 7 do
rinde luthghair imarcach 'n-a fiadnaise, 7 do caith si biad as a
laimh fen fo cedoir, 7 nir delaigh si ris o sin amach an fad do
bí sí sa mbaile; 7 do bidh sí faris ina shella, 7 do teigheadh si
leis don eclais 7 in gach inadh eli a tégedh se fen. Acus a cend an
tress lai iar sin, tainicc an corr a fiadnuisi C. C., 7 do bí sí ag
screduigh 7 ac screchaigh 7 ag bualad a sciathán fa ceile; 7 do
fiarfuidheatar na manaigh de cred fa nderna sí sin. Frecrais
C. C. iad 7 assedh adubairt: 'Ag gabail cheda agam-sa ata sí,' ar
sé, '7 rachaid sí ar a haiss dá duthaigh fen anoss, 7 ata sí lán do
tuirse 7 do dobrón tre na olcus le beith ag delughadh rim-sa di, 7
mar ata adhail aice nach faicfe sí misi go brath arís. Et is cumaín
disi sin,' ar C. C., 'oir ata tuirse 7 dobrón mor orum-sa ina diaidh-
se.' Acus do cai sé go ger iar sin 7 assedh adubairt sé, corb
aibhne don cuirr bicc sin ina dó fen trian a ced do beith aice dul
ar a hais co hErinn arís. Ceiliubruis an corr iar sin do C. C.
7 do lécc sen a bendacht le; 7 do eirich sí as fíadnaise caich uile
an uair sin, 7 tuc a haghaidh docum na hErenn; 7 do batar san
gá feithemh co ndechaidh sí as a n-amharc. Gor moradh ainm De
7 C. C. de sin. Acus as folluss as an scel sa cor fhoillsigh Dia
diamhair a seicreide fen go himarcach do C. C. Acus fós as follus
ass, nach edh amain do bi grad ag C. C. ar dainibh a thíre
duthaighe fen, acht co raibe gradh aicce ar a henach 7 ar a
heitheídibh 7 ar a bethadhachaibh bruídemla uile. Acus as follus
ass, gradh do beith ag na beathadhachaibh air sin mar an cedna.

266.[281]) Fechtus do C. C. a nhí, 7 do cuaidh se ar cnoc airidhe
san oilen sin dana hainm an Daingen Mór, 7 do condaic se nell
dorcha san aeiér don taeb bud thuaidh de, 7 adubairt se ré manach
airide do bi faris darb ainm Sillan, co rachad an nell sin os cend
coda airide do righacht na hErenn, 7 co lecfedh se ar ferthain
moír ass sin co hespart e, 7 gach duine no ainmhidhe re mbenfadh
an ferthain sin, co linfidhe do ghalur 7 d'eslainte rotroim íad,
indus co mbeidís a nguasacht bais. Acus adubairt cor truagh les
fen sin, 7 co raibe do daendaigecht don talumh sin aicce, cor coir

[281]Taken literally from Adamnan, *ibid.*, pp. 107-11.

Irish crane that hath come to us on a pilgrimage. And bring her to me, for she will take neither food nor drink ere she hath seen me."

And when she had come into his presence, she bent her knee and bowed her head in sign of obeissance to him, and she made exceeding joy of him, and straightway she ate food from his hand, and would not be parted from him from that time so long as she was in the place. And she was ever in his company and went with him to the church and to every other place that he went. And at the end of the third day thereafter, the crane came afore Columcille and gan to scream and flap her wings. And the brethren inquired of him wherefore she did this.

Columcille answered, and said to them: "She taketh leave of me," saith he, "and returneth now again to her own land, and she is full of heaviness and sorrow for the grief she hath in her departing from me; for she hath a fear that she may not see me again till Doom. And well may she be sorrowful," saith Columcille, "for I shall be heavy and sad for her also."

And he wept right bitterly therewith, and he said that better was the fate of that little crane than his; for she had leave to go back again to Erin. The crane bade farewell then to Columcille, and he blessed her. Then rose she up afore all, and turned her face toward Erin. And they watched her till she went out of their sight, so that God's name and Columcille's were magnified thereby. And it is clear from this history that God revealed his secrets abundantly to Columcille. And it doth appear further therefrom that not only did Columcille love the human folk of his native land, but that he loved also the feathered things and winged creatures, and all her dumb living things. And it appeareth that the dumb things loved him in like manner.

266. On a time that Columcille was in Iona, he went up a certain hill in that isle, hight the Daingen Mor. And he espied a cloud in the heavens to the north of him. And he told one of the brethren that was with him, hight Sillan, that the cloud would rise above a certain part of the Kingdom of Erin, and that it would rain heavily from that hour until vespers, and that each man or beast whereon that rain should fall, should be filled with sickness and passing sore distemper, so that they should be nigh death. And he said that it was a sore grief to him, and that he had so much love for that land that it behooved him to come to its succor with the help of God as best he might. And straightway he blessed bread and charged the monk that was with him to go to Erin and to bear with him that blessed bread and to put it in water, and every man or beast whereon he sprinkled the water should get healing straightway from the exceeding sore sickness that lay on him.

The monk entered then into his boat, and went back to Erin. And in the first house he entered when he landed were six lying there, and

dó sin d'fhurtacht faré cungnamh Día mar us ferr bud eidir les.
Acus do coisric se aran an uair sin, 7 adubairt ris in manach sin
do bi faris, dul a n-Erinn 7 an t-arán coisrictha sin do breith les, 7
uisce do chur 'n-a timchell, 7 gach duine no ainmhide ar a
craithfedh se an t-uisce sin, co fuighedh slainte a cédoir ó an
eslainte romhoir sin a rabatar. Teíd an manach 'n-a luing iar sin,
7 do cuaidh a n-Erinn; 7 an ced tech a ndechaidh se ar ndul a
tír dó, fuair se sesiur 'n-a luidhe ann, 7 siad a nguasacht bais; 7
dorinde a manach mar adubairt C. C. ris, 7 do craith se an t-uisce
adubramair romainn orra, cu fuaratar slainte ar in pongc sin fen.
Acus ar na cluinsin sin dona poiplechaib uile, gerbh anfand eslan
galruigthe íad, do cruindighetar itir duine 7 ainm[h]idhe cuice,
7 dorinde sen mar an cedna ríu, co fuaratar slaínte a cedoír; 7
tainec an manach tar a ais mar a raibe C. C., 7 do indiss an scel
sin ó thus co deredh don coimhthinol; cor moradh ainm De 7 C. C.
de sin. Acus as follass (*fol.* 37b) *ass* in scel sa, nach edh amhain
do chuir Día C. C. a cosmhuiles ris na faidhib naemtha tainic
remhe a leith ren a seicreíd fen d'fhoillsiughadh do, *acht* cor cuir
se a cosmailes ren a espoluib naemtha fen é, a leith re gach teindes
7 re gach eslaínte do scris as gach inadh as arb'ail les a scris.

267.[282]) Fechtus do C. C. a nhÍ, ar crichnughadh serbíse Dé
do, 7 do gair se manach airidhe da manchaib fen cuice darb ainm
Lugaidh, 7 do labuir go faídhemail ris 7 assedh adubairt: 'Desigh
long go luath do dul a n-Erinn,' ar sé, '7 ass e is adbhur domh
dot chur indte .i. bannaemh darub ainm Mor[283]) ata san inadh
airidhe re n-abartar Clochur 7 ag filledh ó an aifrenn aniugh di
docum a tighe fen, do ben legadh di, 7 do briseadh cnaimh a
lesi,[284]) 7 do cuimhnigh si orm-sa, 7 do gair sí m'ainm maille re
duthracht romhor, 7 do cuir sí a dochus co daingen indam d'faghail tslaínte o Día di. Et do cuir C. C. a bendacht scribtha a
comhraidh bicc croinn les an manuch an uair sin, 7 adubairt ris
uisce do cur timchell na litrech a raibe an bendacht sin scribta,
7 an t-uisce do crathadh a n-ainm an Tigherna ar in cnaimh do
brissedh ag an bannaeimh-se adubramar romaind, 7 go ceingeóladh
sé re celi comh daingen re gach cnamh eli da cnamhaib, 7 go
rachadh a tendes ar cul, 7 go fuighedh se slaínte a cedoír amlaidh
sin. Acus do labuir ris an manach aris 7 assedh adubairt: 'Bidh
a fhis agad,' ar se, 'go fuil scribtha a clar na comradh bice sin let,
nach edh amhaín bías an bannaemh sin slan ón cnáimh sin do

[282]Taken from Adamnan *ibid.*, pp. 111-13.
[283]*Maugina* Adamnan. Hence read *Moghain*.
[284]*coxaque ejus in duas confracta est partes* Adamnan.

all nigh death. And the monk did as Columcille had charged him, and sprinkled them with that same water aforementioned, so that they were healed forthwith. And when all the folk heard that, albeit they were weak and sick and stricken with the malady, they flocked to him all together, both man and beast. And in like manner did he for them, so that they gat healing straightway. And the monk went back to Columcille, and he related this history to the congregation from first to last, so that the name of God and Columcille were magnified thereby. And it doth appear from this history that not only did God make Columcille like unto the holy prophets that had come before him, in that he revealed to him his secrets, but he made him like unto the holy apostles, for that he banished every sickness and distemper from every place wherefrom he willed to banish it.

267. On a time that Columcille was in Iona, after doing the service of God, he called to him a certain one of the brethren by name Lugaidh, and he spake to him by the spirit of prophecy and said:

"Make ready a ship swiftly," saith he, "to go to Erin. And the reason I send thee thither is this: there is a holy woman hight Mor in a certain place that is called Clochur. And returning from the mass today to her house, she fell and brake her hip-bone, and she bethought her of me, and called out my name with exceeding great fervour. And she put firm trust in me to get healing from God for her."

And Columcille sent with the monk at that time a written blessing in a little wooden casket, and he charged him to put into water the letter whereon the blessing was written, and to sprinkle the water in the name of the Lord upon the broken bone of the woman aforesaid, and it should be joined together as strongly as any of her bones else, and the pain should withdraw therefrom and thus it should be healed straightway. And he spake further to the monk and said:

"Wit thou well," saith he, "that it is written on the front of the little casket that thou hast, not only that the holy woman shall be healed of the bone that was broken in her, but that she shall live four and twenty years hereafter."

brissedh aice, acht co mairfidh si ceithri bliadhna xx ina diaid
sin.' Do imthigh an manach reme, 7 dorinde amail adubradh ris,
7 do fíradh gach ní da ndubairt C. C. and a leith re slainte an
cnamha sin do brissedh ag an bannaímh, 7 leth ris an saeghul do
gell se dí do comhall; cor moradh ainm De 7 C. C. de sin. Acus
do bi an bhannaemh sin ag serbís do Dia 7 do C. C. ar fedh an
tshaeg[h]ail sin tuccadh di ó sin amach. As follus duinn as an
scel sa, corub mor as tarbuch do duine a dóchus do cur a C. C. a
n-aimsir a ansochrach 7 a docamla.

268.[285]) Fechtus do C. C. a n-Alpain, 7 tainic nech airidhe
don popul cuice da égaine ris a suile do beith ag dul ón
a mathair 7 on a derbshiair. Do coisric C. C. saland don oclaoch
7 adubairt ris uisce [do chur] n-a timchell, 7 an t-uisce sin do chur
fa shuilibh na mban sa adubramair romaind, 7 go fuighdís furt-
hacht fo cedoir. Dorinne an t-oclaoch a ndubradh ris, 7 nir
mothaighetar na mná sin tendes súl ó sin suás, 7 do cuiretar an
soightech a raibe an saland a n-airde os cind a lepta, 7 do batar co
ro-onórach uime. A cind beccaín do laithib iar sin, do loiscedh
an tshraid don baile a rabatar na mna sin, 7 do loiscedh an tech
a rabutar fen acht an chuid a raibhe an saland sin do bendaigh
C. C. don toigh, 7 do an an tene ren a ucht, 7 ní derna sí dith
no digbail don tshoightech a raibe in saland no don cuid a raibe
se don tech; gur moradh ainm De 7 C. C. de sin. Et is follus
duind as an scel sa, nach edh amhaín de cuir Día na duile fá
umhla do C. C. fen, acht co cuiredh se fa umhla do na neichib
do bendaigedh se íad.

269.[286]) Fechtus do C. C. a n-inadh aíridhe a n-Albain, 7
tuccadh lenabh becc da baistedh cuice. Acus ni raibe uisce a
comgar doib an uair sin, 7 do lecc C. C. ar a gluínib é, 7 do cuir
urnaidhe duthrachtach docum Isa Crist; oir fa gnáth les a uiresbuidh d'egaíne ris; 7 ar crichnughadh na hurnaighte sin do, do
erich se 7 doben se comhartha na croiche naeimh a n-edan cairrce
cloiche do bí 'n-a fhiadnaise, indus cor leiccedh sruth uisce esti,
7 gor baisd sé an lenab as an uisce sin, 7 do labuir re hathair
an lenibh co faidhemhail 7 assedh adubairt ris: .i. 'Biaidh saegal
fada ag an lenabh sa, 7 lenfaidh se ainmhían a coirp fen a tossach
a aísi, 7 dobera Dia grasa do do cind mesi da baistedh, indus co
caithfe sé deredh a aeíse re haithrighi 7 re leoargnímh do denamh
ina pecuíbh, 7 co mbía se ag ridirecht do Crísd co haimsir a bais
7 co ra (fol. 38a) chad a anam do caithedh na gloire suthaine iar

---

[285]In Adamnan, ibid., p. 114.
[286]Taken literally from Adamnan. See Reeves' Adam., p. 118.

Then departed the monk and did as he was commanded. And all came to pass as Columcille had said here, touching the healing of the bone that was broken in the woman, and touching the fulfilling of the life-days he had promised her. And thus God's name and Columcille's were magnified, and the holy woman served God and Columcille throughout the life-days that were given her from that time. It appeareth to us from this history that it is great gain to put one's trust in Columcille in time of mishap and distress.

268. On a time that Columcille was in Alba there came to him one of the folk, complaining that the eyes of his mother and his sister were going from them. Then Columcille blessed salt for the man and charged him to put it in water and to put the water upon the eyes of the women aforementioned, and they should get help straightway. The man did as he was commanded and those women had no more suffering of their eyes form that time. And they put the vessel wherein the salt had been above their bed, and it was held in great honor by them. A few days thereafter the street of the town where the woman lived was burned, and the house where they were was burned save the spot wherein the salt had been that Columcille had blessed. And the fire stopped at the edge thereof, and to the vessel where the salt had been it did no hurt nor harm, nor to the part of the house where it was. And thus God's name and Columcille's were magnified. And it is clear to us from this history that God did put the elements under obeissance not only to Columcille himself, but also to the things that he had blessed.

269. On a time Columcille was in a certain place in Alba, and a little child was brought to him to be baptized. And there was no water near them at that time. And Columcille fell on his knees and made a fervent prayer to Jesu Christ, for it was his wont to make known his needs to Him. Then rose he up and made the sign of the holy cross upon the face of a rock that was beside him, so that it sent forth a stream of water. And he baptized the child with the water, and he spake to the father of the child by the spirit of prophecy, and he said to him:

"This child shall have long life, and he shall follow after the lusts of his flesh in the beginning of his age, but God shall give him grace by reason that it was I that baptized him, so that he shall spend the last of his life doing penance and making atonement for his sins, so that he shall be doing knightly service for Christ at the time of his death, so that afterward his soul shall go to enjoy the glory everlasting.

sin. Acus do firadh gach ní dib sin amail adubairt C. C., mar mebruighes Adamnan naemh air; 7 fos an t-uisce sin tuc C. C. as an charraicc ler baisd se an lenabh, ata se ag techt aniugh esde tre maithes De 7 C. C., 7 doni se moran d'fhertaib 7 do mirbuilibh gach laí.

270.²⁸⁷) Fechtus do C. C. 'sa proibindse darb' ainm Pictoria, 7 do bi tobur 'sa tir sin, 7 gebe nech do ibeadh ní dá uisce no do indledh a cossa no a lamha ass, do bidh se dall no bodhur no do gabudh lubra no pairilís no esláinte granda eli é. Acus do batar lucht na talmhan sin gá onorughadh co himarcach 7 ag creidemh mar Dia dó, tres na cumachtaib diablaidhe sin do bi aicce, tre fulang De 7 tre aiberseoracht na ndiabul 7 tre diabluidecht na ndráithedh do bi sa proibhindse sin an uair sin. Ar na cloisdin sen do C. C., do cuaidh d'indsaighe an tobair sin co nemheclach; 7 do batar draithe ag coimhed an tobuir da tucc C. C. scandail mór remhe sin fan a ndrochcreidemh, 7 do gab luthgair iad; oir do shailetar co ndénadh uisce an tobuir sin digbail do C. C. mar donidh da gach nech eli. Do tóc C. C. a lamh os cind an tobair 7 do bendaigh 7 do coisricc a n-ainm Íssu Crist é, 7 do teicheatar na diabuil do bi ag dénamh aiberseorachta ar cach eli reme ass; 7 do indail a cossa 7 a lamha ass, 7 do ibh fen 7 a mhanaigh ní dá uisce, 7 ni derna urchoíd 'sa mbith doib. Acus ní hedh amhaín nach denadh uisce an tobuir sen urchoid do cach ó sin amach, acht do slánaighedh se gach uile galur 7 eslainte da ticedh cuice ó sin suás, tre maithess De 7 tre mirbuilib C. C.

271.²⁸⁸) Fechtus dár len nech naemtha do bídh a nDurmaigh²⁸⁹) a Midhe, .i. Cormac ua Liathain, C. C. a n-Albain, 7 do tindscain se iar sin a dul ar fasach no a n-inadh rouaicnech a mbeith se ac denamh crabuidh gó a bás, 7 do bi fairce mor guasachtach itir se 7 an t-inadh sin. Acus gach uair do tindscnadh se dul and, do eirgedh stoir[m] mór ar an bfairce sin; indus corb' ecen dó filledh tar a ais mar a mbídh C. C. Acus dob' ingnadh le manchuibh C. C. an ní sen, 7 do fiarfaighetar de créd fa cuiredh Dia an toirmesc sein ar Cormac. Frecruis C. C. íad 7

---

²⁸⁷In Adamnan, *ibid.*, p. 119.
²⁸⁸See Reeves' *Adam.*, p. 30.
²⁸⁹*enavigare incipit ab illa regione quae, ultra Modam fluvium sita, Eirros Domno dicitur* Adamnan. *Eirros Domno* is now the barony of Erris, Co. Mayo.
There was a *Dairmagh* 'Durrow' near Rath Croghan in Roscommon. See *ibid.*, p. 58. Was Cormac abbot of this Durrow and not of Durrow in Meath?

And all came to pass as Columcille had said, according as holy Adamnan maketh mention. And moreover as for the water that Columcille brought forth from the rock and baptized the child withal, it cometh forth therefrom today through the goodness of God and Columcille. And each day it doeth many miracles and wonders.

270. On a time Columcille was in the region hight Pictora. And there was a well in that land, and whoso drank aught of its water or laved his feet or his hands therein, he was made blind and deaf or he was seized with leprosy or paralysis or other foul distemper. And the folk of the land honored it exceedingly and believed thereon as it were a God, by reason of the infernal powers it had through God's sufferance and the cursedness of the devils, and the deviltry of the druids that were in the region in that time. And when Columcille heard that, he went to the well without fear. And there were druids that kept guard at the well, and Columcille had ere that given great offence to them touching their evil creed. And they made great joy, for they weened that the water of that well would work evil to Columcille as it had done to all men else. Then Columcille heaved his hand over the well, and blessed and sanctified it in the name of Jesu Christ. And straightway those devils fled that had ere that wrought evil against all men else. And he laved his feet and hands in the water, and he drank thereof and his monks. And it did them no harm at all. And not only hath the water of that well done no harm to any from that time, but it hath healed every malady and distemper that hath drawn nigh it from that time, through the goodness of God and the miracles of Columcille.

XX

OF COLUMCILLE AND CORMAC

271. There followed Columcille to Alba a certain holy man of Durrow in Meath, to wit, Cormac O Liathain, and afterward he purposed to go into a wilderness or solitary place where he might live in piety till his death. And there was a vast and perilous sea betwixt him and that place, and each time he sought to go thither a great storm arose upon the sea, so that he must needs return to Columcille. And the monks of Columcille marvelled at this thing, and they asked why God laid this hindrance upon Cormac. Columcille answered them and said there was a certain monk in Cormac's company without the leave of his superior

assedh adubairt, co raibe manach airidhe a n-agaidh na humla
7 gan ched da uachturan fare Cormac, 7 an fad do beith an
manuch sin faris, nach crichnóchadh se an ní do triall se. Acus
fos adubairt se tre spirid faidetórachta, da mince uaír do
tindscónadh Cormac dul ar an bfhasach, nach ereochadh se les, 7
comadh a n-Erinn fen do beith a eseirghe. Acus do firadh sin
amail indeósus an betha 'n-a diaidh so; 7 ar na cloisdin sen don
mhanach-sa adubrumair romhaind do bi faré Cormac, do leicc' ar
a gluínib a fíadhnaise C. C. é, 7 do caí co gér 7 do adaimh a
fíadhnaise caích, co raibe se fen mar adubairt C. C. ris; 7 adubairt
Cormac da mbeith a fhis sin aice fen nach beith sesen faris.
Beandaighis C. C. an manach iar sin, 7 adubairt ris dul có a
uachtarán fen, 7 corab dó budh coír breth aithrighe do cur air
ar son a anumla dó. Acus dorinde an manach sin amail adubairt
C. C. ris, go raibe 'n-a oclaech maith do Día 7 do C. C. o sin suás.

272.²⁹⁰) Uair eli iar sin do cuaidh an Cormac-sa, do raidhsemar
romaind, d'íarraidh oilein uaicnich 'sa bfairce síar a mbeith se
ag denamh crabaidh 7 ac ridirecht do Crist. Acus do bi C. C.
an uair sin a mBretain faré rí an tire sin .i. Bruidhe a ainm,
7 adubairt ris co cuirfedh sechrán fairce an Cormac sin san oilen
darb' ainm Orca, 7 go rabatar lucht na talmhan sen fen 'n-a
ndrochdaínib 7 siad a n-agaidh creidimh, 7 ó do batar umhal dó
san 7 a mbraighe aice, a cur fa aithne orra gan Cormac do chur
docum bais 7 beith co maith ris. Acus do ronadh sin uile, amail
adubairt C. C., gur moradh ainm De 7 C. C. de sin.

273. Fechtus eli do chuaidh an Cormac cedna sa d'íarraid
an oilein darb'ainm Oilen na Naémh (fol. 38b) do denamh
crabaidh and, 7 do bi C. C. a ní an uair sin, 7 do cuala se daine
airidhe ga radh cor doicch leo nach tiucfadh Cormac tar a aiss
co brath. Acus ar na cloisdin sin do C. C., adubairt co tiucfadh
se san uair sin fen do ló, 7 nach fuair se an t-oilen do bi sé
d'iarraidh. Acus ar crichnughadh an comraidh sin doib, do condcatar Cormac cuca, amail adubairt C. C. riu; cor moradh ainm
De 7 C. C. de sin.

274. Fechtus eli do cuaidh an Cormac-sa, da fuilmíd ag
labairt, d'iarraidh an oileín cednu sa re n-abarthar Oilen na
Naemh; 7 ar ndul dó 'n-a luing, fuair se gaeth an a diaidh gac
ndirech,²⁹¹) indus nar lecc se a seolta co cend cheithri la ndécc;
7 as minic do bí se a nguasacht a baíte ris an ré sin. Et ar an

---

²⁹⁰§§ 272, 273, 274 in Adamnan, ibid., pp. 166-171.
²⁹¹"Straight behind him". See § 88 for similar phrase. See also § 295. plenis velis, austro flante vento Adamnan.

and in violation of obedience. And so long as that monk was with him he should not accomplish the thing he sought.

And moreover he said through the spirit of prophecy that how oft soever Cormac might set out upon the sea, it should profit him naught; in Erin itself should be his resurrection. And thus indeed it came to pass, as the *Life* shall relate hereafter.

And on hearing this, the monk aforesaid that was in the company of Cormac fell on his knees before Columcille and made great dole. And he confessed before all that it was with him as Columcille had said. And Cormac said that had he known that, the monk had not been in his fellowship. Then Columcille blessed the monk and bade him go to his superior that he should put a penance upon him for his disobedience to him. And the monk did as Columcille had charged him, so that he was a good servant to God and to Columcille thenceforward.

272. Once afterward that same Cormac aforementioned set out to seek a lonely island in the western sea with intent to do works of piety and knightly service to Christ. And at that time Columcille was in Britain with the king of that country, that was called Bruide. And Columcille told the king that Cormac's wanderings upon the sea should bring him to an island called Orca where the folk of the land were passing evil folk and against the Faith. And since they were vassals to the King of Britain and he had their hostage, Columcille told him to forbid them to put Cormac to death and to make him good cheer. All fell out as Columcille had said, so that the God's name and Columcille's were magnified thereby.

273. Another time that same Cormac set out to seek an island that was called the Island of the Saints, with intent to practise devotion there.

And at that time Columcille was in Iona, and he heard certain saying they weened that Cormac would never return. And when Columcille heard that, he declared that Cormac should return that very day in that very hour, and that he had not found the isle he sought. And when he had spoken to them these words, they saw Cormac coming toward them as Columcille had said, so that God's name and Columcille's were magnified.

274. Another time this Cormac aforementioned went in quest of that island that was called the Island of the Saints. And entering his coracle he gat a breeze in his wake so that he slacked not sail for the space of fourteen days, and oft was he in sore peril of drowning in that time. And in the tenth hour of the fourteenth day he came by chance

dechmhadh uaír den cethramadh la décc sin, tarla a fairce
aduathmair é, 7 hí lomnán do piasdaibh ro-uathmhara nach faca
se fen no duine eli a leithéid riamh, 7 síad ag erghe gacha taeba
don luing, 7 fos síad ga gerrudh len a bfíaclaibh 7 len a n-ingnibh;
mar do derb Cormac fen 7 araibe fárís ar techt tar a n-ais doib,
7 siad a meid rana *no* lasán;[292]) 7 ni raibe eiteóga mar énach
orra, 7 ní mo do batar ag snamh mar íasc no mar bethadhachaibh
écsamhla na fairce fen, acht iad ac lemhnigh os cind na fairce 7
na luinge, 7 ag erghe les na maidedhuibh ramha as an bfairce
anís, 7 a n-ingne 7 a fiacla saite inntadh. Ar ná fhaicsin do
Cormac 7 da muindtir, do gab ecla adhuathmhar íad, 7 do bidhgatar
go himarcuch, 7 do guidhetar Dia 7 C. C. fa furtacht d'fhaghail
doib. Acus gerb fada C. C. uatha ó corp an uair sin, do bi sé
faríu ó spiraid; 7 da derbudh sin do gair se a manaigh fen les
don eclais, 7 do labuir go faidhemail ríu 7 assedh adubairt, co
raibe Cormac 7 a muindtir san guasacht mor sin, 7 co rabadar ar a
ngluinib 'sa luing ac dortad a nder, 7 siad ac guidhe De co
duthrachtach fá fhurtacht d'fhagail doib as an guasacht mor sin
a rabhatar, 7 fa ngaíth athuaidh d'fhagail doib le tiucfidís tar
a n-ais: 'Acus guidhmíd-ne Día leo co duthrachtach,' ar se, 'fá
fhurtacht d'faghail doib, oir is coir duinn comtruaighe do beith
againd dar comballaibh fein, oir is boill do Crist sind ré celi.'
Acus ar crichnughadh an comraidh sin do C. C., do leíce ar a
gluinibh a fiadnaise na haltora, 7 do doirt a dera, 7 do guidh se
Dia co duthrachtach fá gach ní da ndubramair romainn d'fagail
do Cormac. Et ar crichnughadh na hurnaidhe sin do C. C; do
eirich da gluinibh 7 tuc buidechus do Día in a tindluicib, 7 do
indis do na manchaib go fuaratar gach ní dár íarratar an uair
sin ar Dia; 7 do indis doibh co tiucfadh Cormac a cind n-uimhrech
airidhe do laithib íar sin; 7 dob follus do cach gurb fhír sin; oir
tainic an gaeth athuaidh ar in poncg sin fen, 7 do bi an comradh
sin ar coimed ag na manchaibh no co tainic Cormac slan cuca
san uair cindte a ndubairt C. C. a techt; 7 do indeis se gach ní
dar imthigh air o tús co deredh amail do indis C. C. da manchaib
ria Cormac do techt; cor moradh ainm Dé 7 C. C. de sin. Acus
as follus ass so nach eadh amhain tuc Dia spirid faidheteorachta
do C. C., acht do shaéradh se gach nech ar a nguidedh sé on
ghuasacht a mbidh ar muir no ar tír.

275. Ceileabruis Cormac do C. C. íar sin 7 teíd reinhe a
n-Erinn, 7 do bi athaigh dá aimsir a nDurmhag C. C. a Midhe

---

[292] *prope magnitudinem ranarum* Adamnan. *Ibid.*, p. 170. leg. *losgán* 'frog'.
(O'Reilly.)

into a terrible sea, and it full of monsters passing dreadful, whereof nor he nor any other had ever seen the like, and they rising up on every side of the vessel, and cleaving it with their teeth and with their claws, as Cormac and all that were with him bare witness when they came back. And they were as big as a *rana*. And there were no wings upon them like to birds, nor swam they as fish or the creatures of the sea; but they leaped above the water and the boat, and rose up from the sea with the oars; and their claws and their teeth stuck fast therein.

And exceeding great fear seized Cormac and his household when they saw this and they were sore adrad, and they prayed God and Columcille to get help for them. And albeit Columcille was far from them in the flesh at that time, natheless he was with them in spirit. In proof thereof he called his monks to him in the church, and he spake to them in a manner of prophecy. And he told them that Cormac and his household were in that sore peril, and that they were on their knees in the boat, shedding tears and praying God fervently to get them help from that sore peril wherein they were, and a wind from the north that they might return.

"And let us pray God fervently to get help for them," saith he, "for it behooveth us to have compassion on our fellow-members, for we are all members of Christ."

And when Columcille had ceased speaking, he fell on his knees afore the altar, and he wept and besought God fervently, touching obtaining for Cormac all things as we have related afore. And when he had ended his prayer he gat him up from his knees and gave thanks to God for His gifts. And he told the brethren that they had obtained from God all that they had asked in that hour, and he declared to them that Cormac should come at the end of a certain number of days after. And it was clear to all that that was true; for there came a wind from the north straightway. And those words [of Columcille] were kept by the brethren until Cormac came to them safe, at the very time that Columcille had foretold his coming. And he related all that had befallen him from first to last, as Columcille had related it to the brethren afore his coming. And thus God's name and Columcille's were magnified. Hence it is manifest not only that God gave the spirit of prophecy to Columcille, but that he saved from peril all those for the which he prayed, both by sea and land.

275. Then departed Cormac from Columcille, and went on to Erin, and for a space he was in Durrow-of-Columcille in Meath, serving Christ, till grief and longing for Columcille seized him, so that he must needs go again seeking him to Alba. And when he had come to Iona where Columcille was, Columcille welcomed him and asked him, albeit

ag ridirecht do Crist no gur linadh do cum*h*aidh 7 do tuirse C. C.
é; indus corb ecen dó dul aris in a diaidh a n-Albain. Acus ar
ndul go hÍ dó mar a raibe C. C. do fer C. C. failte ris 7 do
fhiarf*aigh* de, gin go raibe ainbfhis air fen fa enní, cred iad na
tosca ima taínec se on a tigh. Frecruis Cormac é 7 asse*dh* do raidh:
'Do gradh-sa tucc oram tect ad diaidh, oir nir fheduss beith at
fhecmhais, 7 dob ail lium beith farit gó am bas 7 gan dul ar mh'ais
a n-Erinn go brath arís.' 'Truag sin a Cormaic,' ar C. C; 'oir
dob'aibne doid-se a n-Erinn ina damh-sa a n-Alpain, 7 dá fédaind-
se fen beith indte, ní fhúicfind co brath hí, 7 dob ferr lium bas
d'fhaghb*ail* a n-Erinn ina sirbeatha d'faghail a n-Albain;' 7
dorinde an rand sa:[293])

    Is sí mo cubus gan col,   is ní fétar mh'eiliug*hadh*,
      ferr écc a n-Erinn gan oil (*fol.* 39a)   ina sírbeatha a n-Albain.

'Et a Cormaic,' ol se, 'as mairg do fhúicf*edh* Eri do neoch do
fhedf*adh* beith indte; oír is bind gotha a hén 7 nuall a sroth, 7
as mín a muighe 7 as cluchar a coillte, 7 as imgha naem 7 naemhógh
oc á fuil betha roglan ronaemtha indte. Et as maith a righte
7 a rodhaíne.' Acus tuc se tres mor admolta ar Gaideluib uile
iar sin, 7 do bí ag dimol*adh* fer n-Alpan; conad and dorinde na
roind se:[294])

    Gaeth a clerigh, bind a heoín   aille a mna, mi*n* a senoír,
      fial a fir fa c*r*od gan airc,   maith a righ ga rothab*air*t.

    Áille a mberrtha, buidhe a fuilt,   maith a trebhtaigh, troma
                                                                                 [a tuirc.
    ní fhaca dib tíar *no* toir   nech nach fial re file*dh*aib.

    Gaid*h*el Gaid*h*el, i*n*main ainm!   is se mencomharc a ghairm,
      i*n*mhain Cuimín is cain ba*rr,*   i*n*mhuin Cainnech as Comghall.

    As tíar ata Brenaind bind,   acus Colaim m*ac* Crimt*hain*
      astíar ata Baithín bán,   *acus* tíar bías Adamhnán.

---

[293]See Reeves' *Adam.*, p. 266.
[294]See *ibid.*, p. 286.

of naught was he without knowledge, what errand it was that he had come on.

Cormac answered him and said: "The love of thee it was that led me to come in quest of thee, for it was not possible for me to be away from thee, and I would fain be with thee till death and go never again to Erin."

"Alas for that, O Cormac," saith Columcille, "for it is more joy to thee to be in Erin than to me to be in Alba, and if I might be in Erin I would never leave her, and I would liefer die in Erin than to have life forever in Alba." And he made this quatrain:

"It is my soul telleth me without sin,
No blame can be to me:
Better death in Erin without stain,
Than life forever in Alba."

"And, O Cormac," saith he, "woe to him that quitteth Erin when he might be still there; for sweet are the voices of her birds and the rippling of her rills. Smooth are her plains and sheltered her woods, and therein is many a saint and holy virgin of passing pure and holy life. Good are her kings and gentle-folk."

And for a long space then he was praising all the Gaels and dispraising the folk of Alba, and so he made these verses:

"Wise are her clerics, melodious her birds,
Beautiful her women, gentle her elders,
Generous her folk, rich without greed;
Good her king for abundance of gifts.

Comely her tonsured ones, golden their locks,
Good her husbandmen, heavy her hogs;
West or east have I not seen among them
One that was not bounteous to poets.

Gael! Gael! Beloved name!
It gladdeth the heart to invoke it.
Beloved is Cummin of the beauteous locks;
Beloved are Cainnech and Comgall.

In the west is sweet Brendan,
And Colum the son of Crimthann,
In the west is pale Baithin,
In the west Adamnan shall be."

It is easy for us to understand from this quatrain that Columcille prophesied the coming of Adamnan when he said, "In the west Adamnan shall be."

Et as urussa duínd a tuicsin as an rand sa, cor tairrger C. C.
co ticfadh Adamnan an uair adubairt se: 'As tiar bías Adhamnán.'

Uchan! a Crist, a mhic De!   a mic Muire inghene!
gan abhus, ni radh breíce,   do aes cumtha a leitheíde.

5   Imdha tiar toradh abhla,   imdha righ as righdamhna,
imdha airne gan cessa,   imdha dairghe dairmhesa.

Is imdha abhus laech leabhair,   imdha saeth and is galur,
imdha file ar becc n-édaigh,   imda cridhe cruaidédaigh.

'Et fos co hairidhe a Cormaic,' ar C. C; 'is mairg nech do
10 fhuícfedh cinel Conaill 7 Eoghain da deoín .i. mo braithre gradacha
fén; oír is fial re filed[h]aib 7 as cruaidh a cathaibh 7 as ciuin
cendais re a cairdib 7 as borb re naimhdibh iad;' 7 ar tabairt an
tesmolta moir sin do C. C. ar cinel Conaill 7 Eoghain, caíis co
gér da cumhaig, 7 adubairt o nár fhéd se fein beith ó corp faríu,
15 co mbeith se o croidhe 7 o spiraid faríu ar fedh a beathadh; 7
adubairt co raibe 'na doilges 7 'na ecla air, nach ticfidís naeimh
no cleirigh eile Erend re cinel Conaill mar tainic se feín leo; 7
dorinde na roind-si sís:

Daghar leam gan a n-aithne   do clerchib eli as m'aithle;
20 reír naídhen dogeibdís uaim   cland firglan Conaill crandruaidh.

Inmain oirect bias gan ord,   inmain cinedh bádhuch borb;
mairg dana dual an righe   gébhus íad tre ainmíne.

Me as ferr ina n-altrom feín   cland Conaill on Gulpain géir,
dul a tlas re feirg na fer   maith a n-aís, olc a n-écen.

"Alas, O Christ, O Son of God!
O Son of Mary the Virgin!
That there are not here (My words are not false!)
Companions that are like them.

Plentiful in the west the fruit of the apple tree,
Many kings and makings of kings,
Plentiful the luxurious sloes,
Many oaks of noble mast.

Many here the lanky chiels,
Many diseases there be and distempers,
Many those with scanty clouts,
Many the hard and jealous hearts."

"And moreover, O Cormac," saith Columcille, "it is in especial a misfortune for any of his own will to leave the race of Conall and Eogan, mine own loved kinsfolk, for they are generous to poets, and hardy in battle, mild and gentle to friends, and fierce to enemies."

And giving that great praise to the clan of Conall and of Eogan, Columcille wept sore in his grief. And he said that seeing he might not be with them in the body, he would be with them in heart and in spirit the length of his life. And he said that he was sore troubled and afeard, lest the saints and the other clerics of Erin might not avail the clan of Conall as he had availed them. And he made these quatrains:

"My grief that they shall be unknown,
To other clerics after me.
The obedience of a child they had from me,
The right stainless clan of Conall of lordly lot.

Beloved the clan that shall not decay!
Beloved race, warlike and noble!
Woe to him that hath the lot of a king
That useth them ungently!

I am better than their own foster-father,
O clan of Conall from sharp Gulba!
To yield before the anger of the men.
Good their compliance, evil their compulsion!"[1]

[1] The text of the stanza that follows is evidently corrupt. The literal translation of it is:

> Compared to ever following Connla
> Not sweeter the true fragrance,
> A storm of anger, the wrath of men
> Against tribute or compulsion.

Re sirlenmhain co Condla nocha millse an fircubhra;
anfadh ferge,fich na fer re cís nó re coimhécen.

Do fhácbus ag cloind Conaill mo cathach, mo cochall gleri;
acus uatha ge tancus, aca d'fhacbus me féne.

276. Et ar mbeith aimser fhada do C. C. amlaidh sin ac tuirrse 7 ac eolchaire a ndiaidh a braithrech, do labuir re Cormac 7 assedh adubairt ris: 'Ni hail lium-sa gan tu-sa d'impodh tar hais a n-Erind, 7 a fhurail ar Laisrén. .i. ar ab Durmhaigh, an baile do corughadh 7 do cumdach co maith.' 'Ni impodhbhad, uar Cormac, '7 muna b'ail lat-sa farit me, rachad d'íarraidh oiléin uaicnigh ecin sa bfairge a mbed ag denamh crabaid có am bás.' 'Dimhaín duid-se an saethar sin,' ar C. C; 'oir da sirthea an doman uile itir mhuir 7 tír, is a nDurmuigh bías heseirghe fa deredh.' Conadh and dorinde an rand:[295])

Ge tshire an doman uile, toir tíar tes tuaidh, traig tuile,
a degmic Díma! miadh ngle, bidh a nDurmhaigh heseirghe.

Dixit Cormac:

Truagh mo saethur-sa, a mic De, a athair na trocaire,
a ndenaim tar saile slán, ma's a n-Erind mo tiughdhál.

Gan fechain do breithír C. C., imdighis Cormac remhe 'n-a curach do siubal na fairce; 7 gér b'fhada dó ga siubhal, ni tarla oilen nó inadh uaicnech air a ndenadh se comhnuidhe, 7 fuair sé mórán cundtabarta 7 guasachta baite ar an fairce; 7 ger mór naemh 7 bannaemh do guidh se, ni fuair se furtacht on guasacht sin nó cor guidh se C. C.;7 ar na guidhe dó, fuair se cíunus on anfadh do bí (fol. 39b) ar an fairce a cedoír, 7 fuair se gaéth gu cert ina díaidh ler fill se a cend C. C. arís co hí. Acus rob failidh C. C.

[295]See Reeves' *Adam.*, p. 266.

> I did leave to the clan of Conall
> My *cathach*, my cowl of purity,
> And albeit 'tis they I have sprung from;
> To them I bequeathed me."

276. And when Columcille had been for a long space thus, making great dole and lamenting his kinsmen, he spake to Cormac and said:

"It will be displeasing to me if thou go not again to Erin. And do thou charge Laisren, the abbot of Durrow, to set in order the monastery and enclose it well."

"I will not go," saith Cormac, "and if thou wilt not have me with thee, I will go seek some solitary island in the sea where I may take me to holy works till my death."

"That is labor in vain," saith Columcille, "for though thou seek the whole world, both sea and land, yet it is in Durrow thy resurrection shall be at the last." And there he made the quatrain:

> "Though thou seek the whole world
> East, west, south, north, track of flood,
> O good son of Dima, bright honor!
> In Durrow shall be thy uprising."

Dixit Cormac:

> "Alas for the labor, O Son of God,
> O Father of Mercy,
> That is mine beyond the full sea-brine,
> If my end be in Erin at last!"

And heeding not the word of Columcille, Cormac went away in his coracle, sailing the sea. And albeit he was a long time roving about, yet he reached no isle or solitary place where he might make his abode. And he was in danger and in sore peril of drowning in the sea. And he cried to many a saint and holy woman, yet he gat no help till he cried to Columcille. And when he had besought Columcille, straightway he gat quiet from the storm that was on the sea, and the wind came full at his back. And therewith he returned again to Columcille in Iona.

And Columcille made great joy of Cormac, and said to him: "Since thou didst not heed my counsel at first touching the return to Erin, go now thither and do good works henceforth and I will give thee the Kingdom of God."

"I will not go," saith Cormac, "except I bring some relic of thee with me."

"Thou shalt have such," saith Columcille.

roimhe Cormac 7 assedh adubairt ris:²⁹⁶) 'O nar gabhuis mo comairli ar tús ar dul a n-Erind, eirigh anois indte 7 dena degoibrighte óso amach, 7 do ber-sa flaithes De duid.' 'Ni rach,' ar Cormac, 'gan ní do[t] taisibh-se lim.' 'Dogeba tú ní dib,' ar C. C.
5 'Cindus sin,' ol Cormac, '7 tu-sa ad beath*aidh*, 7 nach ail leat mesi d'fhuirech réd bás.' Síneis C. C. a lamh cuice 7 benais Cormac cend a lúdacaín de. 'Is ger do gortaighis me, a Cormaic,' ar se, '7 as se bas dobera Dia duid a ndighail mo gortaighe .i. coin allta d'ithe do cuirp.' 'Ata dot gradh sa agam-sa,' ar Cormac,
10 'corab ferr lim coin dom ithe iná gan ní dod taisib-se do breith lium, 7 fagh-sa o Día gan díghaltus as mó ina sen do denamh damh.' 'Dogheb,' ar C. C., '7 as olc lium gere an dighailtaiss úd fen dogent*ar* ort.' Ticc Cormac a n-Erinn iar sin ,7 do fíradh gach ní da ndub*airt* C. C a lleith riss.
15   277. A De! as mor 7 as imarcach an gradh sa do bí ag C. C. ar Eirendach*aibh* uile, 7 go hairidhe ar cinel Conaill; oir nir gair se dib ríamh o do cuaidh se a n-Alpain acht cinel Conaill croide, 7 nir gair se d'enduine aca dar lean a hErinn co hAlpain é, ge mór dib do lean he, *acht* mar an cedna; mar ata se fen gá dherbadh
20 'sa rand:

Rí na n-uile, ri na naemh,   deghm*a*c Muire na m*a*c[c]aemh,
dá bhur saeradh ar olc De,   a cinel Conaill croidhe!

Ó a Día na n-uile cumh*acht!* mássedh cá mhed bud coir doibh sen C. C. do gradhughadh 7 d'onórughadh ar son an gradha moir
25 sin do cuaidh t*ar* modh do bui aice doib; 7 ger mór a gradh ren a beo orra, as romhó a gradh anois a flaithes De orra ina sin, 7 as romho fhédus se anois maith do denamh doib ina ren a beo; 7 ar na hadhbhuraib sin as coir d'Erindchuib uile, 7 go hairide do cinel Conaill esiun do gradhugadh a n-ag*aidh* a gradha, 7 gan ní
30 ar bith budh mesde les do denamh ar a cellaib no ar a termondaib in a diaidh as a mbeith a fh*er*g ríu. Do guidh se fen cinel Conaill

---

²⁹⁶The rest of this narrative is taken from the notes to *Félire Oengusso*. See *F. O.*², p. 157. See Reeves' *Adam.*, p. 272, for the poem on which these notes are based.

"How so," saith Cormac, "when thou art living, and wilt not that I tarry with thee till thy death?"

Then did Columcille stretch forth his hand, and Cormac cut therefrom the tip of his little finger.

"Thou hast hurt me sore, O Cormac," saith he, "and the death God will give thee to chastise thee for my hurt shall be this, that thy body shall be devoured by wolves."

"Such love have I for thee," saith Cormac, "that sooner would I be devoured by wolves than have no relic of thee to carry with me. And do thou obtain from God to give me no greater punishment than this."

"I will obtain it," saith Columcille, "and it grieveth me sore that so sharp a punishment shall be put upon thee."

Cormac went to Erin then, and all came to pass as Columcille had said concerning him.

XXI

OF COLUMCILLE'S LOVE FOR ERIN AND OF THE MIRACLES HE DID FOR THE FOLK THERE

277. Great and bounteous, O God, was the love Columcille bare to all the folk of Erin, and in especial to the clan of Conall, for never called he them aught from the time he went to Alba save "beloved clan of Conall;" nor did he call a man of them that followed him from Erin to Alba aught else but the same, though many there were that followed him, as he himself testifieth in the quatrain:

> "The King of All, King of the Saints,
> Gentle Son of Mary of the Virgins,
> May He save you from the anger of God,
> O clan beloved of Conall."

O Almighty God, how dearly they should love and honor Columcille for the sake of the great love passing all bounds he had for them. And albeit during his lifetime his love for them was passing great, yet hath he still greater love for them now in the Kingdom of God. And greater is the good he can do them now than in his life. And for these causes it is right for all the folk of Erin, and in especial for the clan of Conall to return him love for love; and to do naught that would be displeasing to him against the churches or church lands which sur-

7 cinel Eoghain gan en-ní do denamh air asa mbeith a ferg ríu,
amail adubairt sé 'sna randaibh se:

 Mo bendacht-sa ar in cloind   ar cinel calma Conaill;
 na denaid ní, mór an modh,   ar bith acht mo ríarughadh.

5 Mo bendacht-sa leo da tigh   sluag Conaill as sluagh Eogain;
 na benaid amuig nó a tigh   rém[297]) urraidh na rém deoraidh.

 Mo bendacht ar cloind Eogain   itir urraidh is deoraidh,
 's ar cinel Conaill croidhe,   's gabuid ac lucht mo cille.

Et fos do tairrger se nach beidis cinel Eoghain a mbun pairte
10 dó a ndereadh aimsire, amail aspert sé fen 'sa rand sa:

 Mo bendacht sa ar cloind Eoghain   itir urruidh is deoraid;
 ge trom lem croidhe romfes   mar[298]) beidíd[299]) síad fam
                    [cairdes.

  278. Fechtus do C. C. a nhÍ, 7 do bi sé ac cur Baithín
15 naemtha a nErinn le comhairlechaibh airidhe a cend a braithrech
feín .i. cinel Conaill 7 cinel n-Éogain, 7 itir gach comhairli dar
cuir se cuca, do aithin se dib maith do denamh ar gach ndeoraidh
a cuimhnighadh na deoraidhechta ar araibe se fen a n-Alpain,
7 do lín tuirse 7 maeích menman e trian a beith a fecmhais Erend
20 7 a braithrech, co nderna na roind-se sís.

 Eirigh a Baithin uaim síar   cus an tír as tocha am ghren,
 go cinel Conaill saeir slaín   's co cinel Eoghain mic Neill

 Tu-ssa siar is mesi abhus,   corub soraidh an turuss:
 acht ge fada lem-sa sin   a Baithin uasail idhain!

25 Cinel Conaill comhromhaigh   7 cinel n-aird n-Eoghain,
 beir cuca mo bendachtain   's denaid maith ar gach ndeóruidh.

 Fir Erend nach dual d'athól   menic bíd ar cuairt crechól,
 maith gne a mbuird is a muchól   nirsat methol a n-athól.

 A fir teid a n-Erind síar   as brisde mo croidhe am clíab:
30 dá ro go hécc ndala damh,   is ar mhéd gradha Gaidhel.

---

[297]Cf. § 87.
[298]leg. nach.
[299]Cf. Adventures of Suibhne Geilt, p. 20, for similar form beittid.

vive him, that would kindle his wrath against them. And he himself besought the clan of Conall and the clan of Eogan to do naught against him that would kindle his wrath, as he hath said in these quatrains:

> "My blessing on the children
> On the valiant clan of Conall
> Let them do naught (Great the honor!)
> In the world, except my will.
>
> My blessing home with them
> The host of Conall and the host of Eogan!
> Meddle not, abroad or at home,
> With my high ones, or my lowly!
>
> My blessing on the children of Eogan,
> Both the high and the lowly!
> And on the beloved clan of Conall,
> If they aid the folk of my church!"

Moreover the saint prophesied that the race of Eogan would break with his friendship at the last, as he hath said in the quatrain:

> "My blessing on the children of Eogan,
> Both the home ones and the exiles,
> I know, though it grieve my heart,
> That they will [not] be under my gossipred."

278. On a time that Columcille was in Iona, he sent holy Baithin to Erin with certain counsels to his kinsmen, the clan of Conall and the clan of Eogan, and in every counsel that he sent them he charged them to show kindness to every exile, remembering his exile in Alba. And he was filled with sorrow and heaviness to be away from Erin and his kinsfolk. And so he made these quatrains:

> "Go westward, Baithin, from me
> To the fairest land under the sun,
> To the high and hearty race of Conall
> And the race of Eogan mac Neill.
>
> Thou in the west and I here,
> May the journey be safe!
> But long to me doth it seem,
> O Baithin noble and pure!

Do Gaidhealuib mé fene³⁰⁰) 's do Gaidel*aibh* mo naíre
do Gaidhel*uibh* mo leighend 's d'fheruib Erend mh'aille.

Ro-m-lín maích a nfhécmhu*is* (*fol.* 40a) damh ní coimsech,
[Erend,
5 a tir ainíuil co*n*umtarla taidhiuír toirrsech.

Is amluidh roindim-se si*n* mo biaid is mo bend*ach*tain,
a leth ar Erind fo sheacht, a leth ar Albain ainfhecht.

Mo bend*acht* ort indis tiar, do at mo croidhe am cliab,
do cumhaigh sil Eog*hain* uill, 's do cumhaidh cineoil Conaill.

10 279. Tucc C. C. tres mor adhmolta ar a ardbailtib fen a n-Erind iar sin, 7 gu hairidhe ar Doire Calgaidh 7 ar Cenand*us* 7 ar a airdchealluib eili ar chena, 7 dorinde eolchuire mor in a ndiaidh;

Dogén eolchuire truagbi*n*d, truagh m'eolchuire fa Er*ind!*
Doire tiar, inmhain baile, ata ar m'aire, ci*n* go teighim

15 Treidhe as dile leam ro facbus ar bith buidnech:
Durmagh, Doire, dind ard ainglech, as Tír Luighdech.

Inmhain Durmagh as Doire, inmhuin Ráthboth go ngloine,
inmhain Druim Túama as mín mess, inmhain Sord as
[Cen*an*ddus.

20 Inmhain Druim Cliab mo cr*oidh*e, 's beith tíar ac traigh
[Eothaile,
fechain Locha Febhuil find co*n* a ealuib as aibhind.

---

³⁰⁰See *R. C.*, XXVI. p. 138. *Do feraib Erind dam* = of the men of Erin am I.

O race of triumphant Conall
And high race of Eogan!
Bear them my benediction,
And be they good to every exile!

Men of Erin, not needful to them twice drinking,
Oft make they a foray, of plunder a-drinking;
Good the sight of their board and their early drink;
Their second drink never was failing.

O man that goeth westward to Erin,
My heart in my side is broken;
If sudden death overtake me,
It is for greatness of love for the Gael.

To the Gaels myself,
To the Gaels my honor,
To the Gaels my learning,
To the men of Erin my glory.

Sadness hath filled me,
Distant from Erin I am not content,
In a foreign land I happened
Sad, heavy-hearted.

Thus it is I distribute
My blessing and my benediction,
One half upon Erin sevenfold,
One half upon Alba in like wise.

My blessing on thee, western island,
My heart in my bosom is swollen,
Lamenting the seed of great Eogan,
Lamenting the children of Conall.''

279. Then did Columcille give exceeding great praise to his chief monasteries in Erin, and in especial to Derry and Kells, and his other high churches in like wise; and he was right homesick away from them, and it was then he made these quatrains:

"I shall make sad sweet lamenting,
Alas, my longing for Erin!
Derry in the West, beloved place,
Is on my heart though I return not.

As aibhind sin 's as aibind   fairce ruad adhruid failind,
ar ndol damh o Doire a ceín   as reidh sin as as aibind.

Dá madh uile [*leg.* lium] Alba uile   o ata a broine go a bile,
do budh fherr lium aít tighe   agam ar lár caemh-Doire.

280.³⁰¹) La ecin do C. C. a nhÍ, 7 do éirigh sdoirm mor 7 fúa*ch*t ainmesardha and, 7 do gab dobron mor 7 tuirrse imarcuch C. C. gor chai se go gér, 7 do fhiarfuidh a serbfoghant*aidh*e fen de .i. Diarmaid cred dob adbor don caí 7 don tuirrse do bi air. 'Ni gan adb*ur* ata sin oram,' ar C. C., 'oir doc*ím* ab Durmaigh .i. Laisren, ag coimhécniug*hadh* na manach docum oibre 7 docum saethair ro-moír sa drochaimsir-se, indus co fuilid lan d'anshocair 7 do dolás tre mhed a bfhuachta 7 a saethair; 7 as truagh lem-sa mo manaigh fen do beith mar sin,' ar C. C. *Acus* ar in pongc sin fen tainec do mirbuilib Dé 7 C. C., gor lass indtind Laisrein an meide sin indus corb'ecen dó cosc do chur ar na manchuib fan obuir ecnesta docum ar coimecnich se íad; 7 ni hedh amain do coisc se da n-obuir no dá saethur an lá sin íad, acht tucc se biadh 7 deoch maille re honoír 7 re solás 7 re raibirians doib, 7 ní iarr*adh* se obair no saethar orra a ndoinind no a ndrochaimsir ó sin suás. *Acus* ar'n-a faicsin sin do C. C. in a spiraid fen co fuarut*ar* na manuigh an furtacht sin, do rinde sé solás mor a fiadhnuisi caích uile, 7 do inniss an ni sen doib. Acus do derb Laisren fen cor imd*igh* gach ní dib sin air amhuil adubairt C. C., mar meabruigess Adamhnan naemtha air 'sa naemadh caibidil déc don c*ed* leabhur do decht se fen do beath*aidh* C. C.

281.³⁰²) Fechtus do C. C. ag siubul na fairge a n-oireruib Albun, 7 do eirich sdoirm ainmesardha uirre indus co raibe an long a raibe se a nguasacht a baíte; 7 tuc an umhla ar C. C. beith ac taemadh na luinge,³⁰³) oir dá faghadh se obuir budh deroile

---

³⁰¹In Adamnan, *ibid.*, pp. 57-8, chap. 29, book I.
³⁰²In Adamnan, *ibid.*, pp. 119-120.
³⁰³*Nautae tum forte Sancto, sentinam cum illis exhaurire conanti, aiunt* Adamnan.

Three things have I left behind, the dearest to me
On the spacious earth:
Durrow, Derry, high Hillock of Angels,
And Tir Luighdech.

Beloved are Durrow and Derry,
Beloved is Raphoe the stainless,
Beloved Drumhome with sweet acorns,
Beloved are Swords and Kells.

Delightful Drumcliff of my heart,
And to be in the west at Traigh Eothuile,
To gaze upon Loch Foyle
With its swans is delightful.

Delightful that is; and delightful,
The dark-red sea which the gulls haunt,
As I come from Derry afar,
Peaceful it is and delightful.

If mine were all of Alba,
From its center to its border,
I would liefer have space for a hut
In the middle of fair Derry.''

280. On a certain day that Columcille was in Iona, a mighty storm came up, and passing cold, and a great sadness and exceeding heaviness seized Columcille, so that he wept sore. And his servant Diarmaid asked him what was the cause of the sorrow and heaviness that lay on him.

"Not without reason it lieth on me," saith Columcille, "because I see the abbot of Durrow, even Laisren, driving on the brethren to toil and sore labor in this evil weather, so that they be full of discomfort and woe for the extremity of the cold and their toil. And it is grievous to me that my monks be in this case," saith Columcille.

And lo—in that same moment it happed by miracle of God and Columcille, that the mind of Laisren was enlumined in so much that he must needs release the brethren from the unseemly toil whereto he had forced them, and not only did he release them from toil and labor, but he gave them food and drink with great honor and solace and worship on that day. Nor did he require of them toil or labor in rain or in ill weather thereafter. And it being revealed to Columcille in spirit that the monks gat that succor, he made great joy afore all, and he told them that hap. And Laisren himself witnessed that all had befallen him as Columcille had said; for holy Adamnan maketh men-

ina sin ren a denamh, as í doghénadh se trian a mhéd do bi an
umhla cengailte de. Acus tancatar foirend na luinge cuige da
iarruidh air scur don obuir sin 7 Dia do guide co duthrachtach
ar a son d'faghail furtachta doib on guasacht mor sin a rabutar.
Et adubratur nach raibe nert acu fen mesnech ar bith do denamh
le méd na sdoirme 7 an anfaidh do bi ar an bfhairge an
uair sin. Do leic C. C. ar a gluínibh maille re humla and sin
é, 7 do cuir urnaidhe mileis duthrachtach docum a Dia fen; 7 ar
crichnughadh a urnaighte dó, do benduigh 7 do coisricc an fairge,
7 do cuir se fa umla uirre, a hucht Íssu Crist, a sdoirm 7 a hanfadh
do lécen uáithe 7 cendsacht 7 cíunus do ghabail cuice. Acus ar an
pongc sin fen, do umlaigh an fhairge le breithir C. C. indus cor
imthigh gach uile sdoirm 7 anshocair da raibe uirre uaithe, 7 co
bfuair se aimser ciúin sithcánta co ndechaidh se a tír; cor moradh
ainm De 7 C. C. de sin. Acus as se adbur far lécc Dia an buaidredh
sa docum na luinge sin araibe C. C., do medughadh fhuirechruis
arai (fol. 40b) be fáris, 7 do médughhadh a anma 7 do medughadh
na tindluicedh do C. C.

282.[304]) Fechtus eli do C. C. ag siubal na fairge cedna, 7 do
eirigh an oired sin do sdoirm 7 d'anfadh uirre indus co ndeachuidh
a ciall 7 a resún fen on a raibhe fáris 'sa luing re hecla, 7 do
glaedhatar co roard ac iarruidh air furtacht d'fhaghbail o Día
doib on guasacht sin a rabhutar. Do frecuir C. C. go cendsa iad
7 assedh adubairt: 'Ni horum-sa ticc guide ar bur son aniugh,'
ar se, 'acht ar in ab naemta .i. ar Caindech ata 'n-a mainistir fen
a n-Achudh Bó a ríghacht na hErend;' 7 do cuala Caindech an
comradh sin C. C., gerb fada uadha é, ar na fhoillsiughadh a
cluasuib a croidhe don Spiraid Naem. Acus as amluid do bi
Caindech an uaír sin a ndíaidh serbíse De do crichnughadh san
ecluis dó, 7 se ac suide docum an buird ac tindscna an proind do bí
n-a fiádnuise do roind ar cach, 7 a lethbrócc ime 7 a lethbrog eli
n-a fecmais; 7 do erich go ro-deithnesach, 7 nír an ris an mbroicc
sin do bi n-a fhecmais do cur uime no ris an mbiadh do bi 'n-a
fiadnaise do roind ar cach, acht do cuir 'n-a rith d'indsaighe na
hecluisi é, 7 do len a coimthinol e 7 do indeis doib co raibhe C. C.
ag siubul na fairge, 7 co raibe an long araibe se a nguasacht a
baíte o mhéd na doininde 7 na sdoirme do bi uirre, 7 cor cuimhnich
se air fen, 7 corub ag tabairt taeba ris, do lecc sé de Dia do guidhe
d'faghail furtachta dó on guasacht mor sin araibe se. Les sin do

[304] In Adamnan, ibid., pp. 120-22.

tion thereof in the nineteenth chapter of the first book he made on the life of Columcille.

281. On a time that Columcille was travelling the sea by the coasts of Alba, a great wind arose so that his ship was in great danger of sinking. And through humility Columcille was bailing the bilge-water out of the boat. And if he could have got a task more lowly than that to do, it is that he would have been doing, for the great humility that was fastened in him. Then came the ship's crew to him and said he should cease that labor and pray God fervently for their sakes to get them succour from the great danger whereas they were. For they said there was no force in them to show any hardihood then by reason of the greatness of the storm and by reason of the tempest on the sea. Columcille went on his knees right meekly and he made sweet fervent orisons to his God. And having finished his prayer, he blessed and hallowed the sea. And he put her under bonds by the power of Jesu Christ, to do off her the storm and the tempest, and to do on gentleness and quiet. And straightway the sea obeyed the word of Columcille, so that all the tempest and unrest that had been on her left her, and he gat quiet tranquil weather to take harbor. And thus God's name and Columcille's were magnified. And this was the reason that God suffered that distress to be upon the ship where Columcille was; to increase the vigilance of those that were with him, and to magnify his name and increase his merit.

282. Another time that Columcille was travelling the same sea, such grievous storm and tempest arose on her that sense and reason went from all that were with him in the vessel for fear. And they cried loudly on Columcille, and did beseech him to get help from God for them in their peril. Columcille answered them meekly and said:

"It is not on me it falleth to pray for you today," saith he, "but on the holy abbot Cainnech that is in his monastery in Achudh Bo, in the realm of Erin."

And Cainnech heard those words of Columcille, albeit he was far from him; for they were revealed to the ears of his heart by the Holy Spirit.

And in this wise was Cainnech then: having ended the service of God in the church, he sat at table in point to deal the meat that was afore him to every man. And half his shoes were on him, and the other half wanting. And he rose with great haste, and he did not tarry to put on him the boot that was lacking, or to deal to every man the meat that was afore him. But he bent his running toward the church, and the household followed him and he told them that Columcille was travelling the sea, and that the ship he was in was in peril

leic Caindech ar a gluínib é, 7 do guid se Dia co duthrachtach fa
furtacht d'fhag*ail* do C. C. Acus ar crichnughadh a urnaidhe dó,
fuair C. C. cíunus 7 aimser maith sithcánta, 7 do indiss d'fhoirind
na luinge corub é Caindech naemh fuair sin ó Día doib. Et tainec
5 C. C. fen ó spir*aid* an uair sin mar araibe Caindech san ecluis sin,
acht gerb fhada uadha ó corp 7 o inadh é, 7 do labuir ris 7 assedh
adub*hairt*: 'A Caindigh,' ar se, 'as urussa duínd a tuicsin co
n-estend Día red guidhe 7 ret urnuide, 7 as maith do cuir an rith
dorindeis docum na hecluise aniugh rinde, 7 gan umat acht leth-
10 brocc, oir fuaru[i]s o Dia ar saerudh on guasacht ro-mhor arabum*ar*
ar an fairge.' Do imt*high* C. C. remhe iar sin tar eís na cuarta
ainglidhe sin do denamh ac Caindech; cor moradh ainm De 7 C. C.
7 Caindigh de sin.

283.³⁰⁵) Fechtus do C. C. a n-oilen airidhe a n-Alpain, 7 do bi
15 se ac cur coda da manchuib naemtha fen gacha taeba de le gnoaigib
an *com*thinoil, 7 do iarrutar air soirbes aimsire 7 gaeth cert
d'fág*ail* ó Día doib. Do fhrecuir C. C. iad 7 adubairt co bfhuigdis
sin. Do cuaidh nech naemtha darbh'ainm Baithín in a luing iar
sin, 7 nir lecc sé a seolta *co n*dechaidh se a tir a machuire Luighne,
20 sa talumh re n-abarthur Etica. Et do cuaidh nech naemtha eli
darb ainm Colm*an* 'n-a luing, 7 fuair se iar sin gaeth *c*ert in a
diaidh indus nar lecc se a sheolta *co n*dech*aidh* se a tir a rigacht
na hEirend. Et as follus duínd as an scel-sa co tuc Dia cumhachta
do C. C. ar na duil*ibh* os cind cúrsa na naduíri .i. an dís tuc a
25 dhá cul re celi, co tuc se gaeth cert dá gach nech acu a n-en-ló co
ndechatar lé a ngoaighib is na hinaduib se adubram*air* romhaind.
Do labhair C. C. tre spir*aid* faidhetorachta íar sin 7 assedh
adubairt: 'An nech naemtha sa,' ar sé, 'do chuaid uainn a n-
Erind .i. Colman, ní faicfe mh'agaidh se co brath arís ar in
30 saeghul sa.' Acus do firadh sen amail adubairt C. C; oir fa
aimsir girr iar sin, fuair Colman³⁰⁶ bas 7 do cuaidh a anam a
flaithes De do caithemh na gloire suthaine faré na crut[h]aigheoir
fen; corub amlaidh sin do fhíradh Día gach ní adeiredh C. C.

---

³⁰⁵In Adamnan, *ibid.*, pp. 124-5.
³⁰⁶*recte* Colam Cilli. O'D. misinterpreted Adamnan.

to sink for the passing evil weather and for the tempest that was on the sea. And he had thought on Cainnech. And it was to yield place to him that Columcille had ceased to pray to God for help from the sore peril he was in. With that Cainnech went on his knees and prayed fervently to get help for Columcille. And right as Cainnech finished his prayer for Columcille he gat calm and quiet peaceful weather. And he told the crew that it was holy Cainnech that had got that from God for them.

Columcille came in spirit in that hour to Cainnech in that church, albeit he was far away from him in body and in place. And he spake to him and said:

"O Cainnech," saith he, "it is easy for us to understand that God hearkeneth to thy prayer, and to thy intercession. And well hath served us today the run thou didst make to the church, and on thee but half thy boots; for thou didst get from God our safety from the sore peril we were in on the sea."

And Columcille departed then, after that angelic visit to Cainnech, and thus God's name and Columcille's and Cainnech's were magnified.

283. On a time that Columcille was in a certain island in Alba, he sent certain of his holy monks from him in contrary directions on errands of the brotherhood. And they asked him to get for them from God calm weather and the right wind. Columcille answered them and said they should get their wish. Then went the one holy man, named Baithin, into his ship, nor did he lower his sails till he landed in Magh Lunge in the land called Etica. And the other holy man, hight Colman, entered into his ship, and he too gat the right wind behind him, so that he did not furl his sails till he landed in the Kingdom of Erin. And it is clear to us from this history that God gave power to Columcille over the elements, passing the course of nature, to wit, of the two that turned their two backs either to other, he gave the right wind to each of them, on the same day when they went on their errands to those parts aforesaid.

Columcille spake in manner of prophecy thereafter, and said: "That holy person," saith he, "that went from us to Erin, to wit, Colman, shall not see my face again in this life."

And it befell as Columcille had said; for short while thereafter Colman died, and his soul went into the Kingdom of God to enjoy the everlasting glory with his Creator. Thus did God verify all that Columcille said.

284.³⁰⁷) Fechtus do C. C. in a duirrthech fen a nhÍ, 7 tainicc duine aíridhe darb ainm Colman 'sa dorus amuig cuice 7 soightech lan do ba (*fol.* 41a) inde ar a muin, 7 do íarr air é fen do bendug*hadh*. Acus do thócuib C. C. a lamh os a cend fen 7 os cend an tshoig*tigh* do bi ar a muin 7 do benduig iad; oir do bi a fis aice gurb e an soightech as mo rainic a les a beandughadh; 7 ar an pongc sin fein do eírigh combuaidhirt ainmesardha sa soightech astigh, indus cor bris sé an ted nó an indstraimint le n-imcarthaí e, 7 do ling se do muin an oclaigh ar talmuin, 7 do cuaid an clar no an cibhir do bi air de, indus cor doirted an bainde uile. Ar na fhaicsin sin don oclaoch, do lécc ar a gluínïb a fiadnuise C. C. e 7 do caí co ger tuirrsech, 7 adubairt co fuighedh se aicept ger díghaltach on a tigerna 7 ón a baindtigherna tres an bainde do dortadh. 'Bidh a fhiss acud-sa,' ar C. C; 'corub tú fen as cintach ris sin, oir nir coisricc tú an soightech reme an mbainde do cur and, 7 do bi an díabul a foluch in a ichtar docum go ndenadh se urchoíd no digbhail do na daínibh do ibhadh an bainde, 7 mar do thocbus-sa mo lamh os cind an tshoig*thigh* da bendughadh, do teich an diabhul romham, oír nir fhéd se sesamh do denadh³⁰⁸) re bratuib Ihsu Crist .i. re comartha na croiche do benus-sa oss a cind, 7 as les an crithnug*hadh* dorinde se 'sa soightech ac teichedh roman-sa dó, do bris na cengail do bi air an uaír do doirtedh an bainde.' Do benduigh 7 do coisricc C. C. an soightech iar sin, indus cor línadh do bainde arís é amail do bi se o tús; 7 as mar sin doshaér se an duine si ar aiberseóracht an diabuil, 7 ar an ecla do bí air remhe a tig*her*na 7 reme a baintigherna; cor móradh ainm De 7 C. C. de sin.

285³⁰⁹) Fechtus do C. C. in a diaid sin a tigh duine airidhe don popul, 7 do cuala se dís a coindtind fá an ní tarla don bainde dar labrum*ar* sa scel sa tuas .i. duine aca ag buain ceille maithe ass, 7 duine eli acu ga thairraing docum droch-chelle. Ar na cloissdin sin do C. C., dob'ail les a foillsiughadh do chach corub on a Día fen do bi cumachta aice. Acus do batar draithe diabluide sa tir an uair sin, 7 do bui damh acu, 7 do bendaís bainde uadha len a ndraigecht fen a n-ag*aidh* naduíre, 7 do fhurail C. C. orra bainde do buaín uadh in a fiadnaise fen. Et do labuir do guth mór a fiadnaise caich 7 assedh adubairt: 'Deirbeochad-sa anois,' ar se, 'corub o cum*ach*taib maithe dorindess fen mirbuile ar an mbainde ud as a raibe an duine úd o cianuib ag buain droch-ceilli, 7 der-

---

³⁰⁷In Adamnan, *ibid.,* pp. 125-6.
³⁰⁸*leg.* denamh.
³⁰⁹In Adamnan, *ibid.,* pp. 126-7.

XXII

MORE OF THE MIRACLES OF COLUMCILLE IN IONA

284. On a time that Columcille was in his oratory in Iona, a certain Colman came to the door and a vessel full of milk on his back. And he asked Columcille to bless it. And Columcille heaved his hand over him and over the vessel on his back, and blessed them; for he knew that it was the vessel had most need of a benison. And forthwith arose a mighty commotion in the vessel within, so that it brake the rope or the gear whereby it was carried. And it jumped from the back of the youth to the ground and the top or the cover that was thereon sprang off, so that all the milk was spilled. When the lad saw that, he fell on his knees afore Columcille and made sharp dole and sore, and said he would get harsh reproof and chastisement from his lord and lady for spilling the milk.

"Know," saith Columcille, "thou thyself only art to blame therefor; thou didst not bless the vessel ere thou didst put the milk therein. And the Devil was in hiding in its bottom, to do mischief to the folk that should drink the milk. And as I did heave my hand above the vessel to hallow it, the Devil fled afore me; for he could not make a stand against the ensign of Jesu Christ, to wit, the sign of the cross, that I made thereon. And it is with the shivering he made in the vessel as he fled afore me that the knot that was thereon brake, when the milk was spilled."

Columcille hallowed the vessel then, so that it was filled with milk again as it had been at the first. And thus it was he saved that lad from the deviltry of the evil one and the terror he had of his lord and lady. And thus God's name and Columcille's were magnified.

285. On a time after that, Columcille was in the house of a certain one of the congregation, and he heard two persons contending concerning the hap that had befallen the milk whereof we have related in the history above, and one of them was plucking well the purport therefrom, and the other was twisting it to evil signifying. When Columcille heard that, he desired to show to all that it was from God he had his powers. There were diabolical druids in the land in that time. And they had an ox from which, against nature, they used to get milk by their magic powers. And Columcille ordered them to get milk from the ox in his sight. And he spake with a loud voice afore all, and said:

bochad corub ó droch-cumachtuib benaid na draithe an bainde úd ón
damh, 7 nach bainne firindech é acht fuil ar cur datha bainde don
diabul uirre do melludh na poiplech, 7 docum co creid*fidí*s do
fen. Acus do benduig C. C. an bainne iar sin, 7 tainic a dath diles
5 fein air .i. dath na fola, 7 an damh sin ó a ticedh an bainde, do
cuaidh se a tr*ua*s 7 a n-écruth ro-mór, ar tarruing a fola a ngne
bainde ass do na draithib diabluide sin amail adubramar romaind
indus co raibe se a ri*cht* bais d'faghail. Ar na fhaicsin sen do
C. C., do coisric se uisce 7 do *cr*aith ar an damh é, 7 do eirigh se
10 slan imlán a fiadnaise caich amail do bí o thús. Acus ar na
fhaicsin sin do na poiplech*aibh*, do creidetur do Dia 7 do C. C.,
7 do molatar Dia in a gnimarthaib, 7 tucatar buidhechus
mór do C. C. tre mar do shaer se ar ilcelg*aibh* an diabuil 7 ar
draig[h]echt na ndraith*edh* ndiabluide sin íad.
15 286.³¹⁰) Fechtus do C. C. a tigh duine airidhe don popul darb
ainm Colman, 7 do bi an duine si feín daigbir, 7 do bi se ag denamh
a díchill onóra 7 frithoilte do C. C. an oidche sin; 7 ag imtecht
do C. C. ar na marach, do fiarf*aigh* do Colman cred é an saidbris
do bi aice. 'Ni fhuil acht cuíc ba amaín, 7 ata do doigh a Día 7
20 asad-sa agam, da mbeandaighta-sa íad, co mbeidís ar buil 7 ar
bissech.' Acus do fulaír C. C. na ba do thabairt n-a fhíadhnaise,
7 do bendaigh iad, 7 adubairt co mbeith *fiche* bo do bisech ar gach
mboin dibh, 7 co mbeith a cuic ba fen aicce ren a cois sin, 7 nach
beith ní budh mo ina sin aicce do buaib. Acus do fíradh sin uil*e*
25 .i. an uair ticcedh barr *no* bisseach tairis sin orra, do ge (*fol.* 41b)
ibeadh se bás a cedoir, indus nach bídh do ghnath aige acht an
uimhir airidhe do gell C. C. dó .i. cuic ba 7 ced bó. Acus do
bendaig C. C. an t-ocla*ech* fen íar sin, indus co raibe se fen 7 a ben
7 a cland 7 gach airnés talmu*nd*a eli da raibe aice ar bissech, 7 do
30 bui 'n-a oclaech maith do Día 7 do C. C. ó sin suás, 7 corub mar
sin do cuítigh C. C. a aídhidhecht 7 a onoír re Colman. Acus as
follus duínd as an scel-sa corub mor as maith 7 as tarbuch do
duine a pairt do beith re C. C. *no* onoír no seirbis do denamh dó.
 287.³¹¹) Do bi droch-duine d'fhuil na righachta³¹²) 'sa tal-
35 *muin* sin, 7 do bidh sé ac sladuighecht 7 ag crechuire*cht* ar na
dainibh nemcintacha, 7 co hairidhe do bi se ag denumh moraín
egcóra 7 aindlig*hedh* ar an duine si tuc C. C. ó daidhb*res* dar
labram*ar* sa scel sa tuas. Et la ecin da raibe a crech
7 airnéis a tighe les docum a luinge, tarla C. C. do, 7 do íarr

---

[310] In Adamnan, *ibid.*, pp. 131-2.
[311] In Adamnan, *ibid.*, pp. 132-4.
[312] *de regio Gabrani ortus genere* Adamnan.

"I will now show forth," saith he, "that it is through good powers that I did do a miracle on that milk from which, a while since, a certain one was plucking evil pith. And I will show that it is through evil powers that the druids get milk from the ox, and that it is not true milk, but blood, whereon the Devil putteth color of milk to beguile folk to put trust in him."

Then did Columcille bless the milk. And the true hue thereof appeared, to wit, the hue of blood. And that ox the milk had come from, had fallen in a swoon and passing great disfigurement with the drawing of his blood in semblance of milk by those hellish druids whereof we have spoken. And he was nigh death. And when Columcille saw that, he blessed water and sprinkled it on the ox. And in sight of all, the beast gat up whole and sound as he had been at the first. And when the folk saw that they believed in God and Columcille. And they praised God in His works, and gave great thanks to Columcille that he had saved them from the many wiles of the Devil and the magic of those hellish druids.

286. On a time Columcille was in the house of a certain one of the congregation, hight Colman, that was a poor man. And he gave honor and service to Columcille that night. And when Columcille was leaving on the morrow, he asked Colman what wealth he had.

"I have five cows only, but I have hope in God and in thee, if thou bless them, that they may flourish and multiply."

Columcille bade bring the cows to him. And he blessed them and said that for each there should be increase of a score, and that Colman should have his own five cows thereto at their flanks. But more cows than this he might not have. All that came to pass, to wit, whatever issue they had passing or exceeding that number used to die, so that Colman had always but the very number that Columcille had promised him, to wit, five cows and a hundred. Thereafter Columcille blessed Colman, so that he prospered, and his wife also, and their children, and every other earthly belonging that he had. And he was a good servant to Columcille thenceforth. It was thus Columcille did reward Colman for the hospitality and the honor he had given him. And it is manifest to us from this history that great is the gain and profit a man hath, that hath a share with Columcille or giveth him honor or service.

287. There was a wicked man of royal blood in that land, and his wont was to steal and to plunder innocent folk. And in especial against the man that Columcille had saved from poverty as we have related afore in this history was he working great iniquity. And on a day that the reaver was bearing plunder and booty from the poor man's house to his ship, he met Columcille. And Columcille asked him to return the gear to his friend. But he gat not his

se aisecc dá caraid fen air, 7 ni fuair se sin, 7 ni raibe an droch-
duine misduama miglic sin acht ac fanámhud 7 ac scige fai, 7 do
cuaidh se n-a luing iarsin, 7 do lean C. C. conuice a gluinibh sa
bfhairge é, 7 do cuir se a tarcusne 7 a neimchin é, indus nach tucc
se freccra air. Acus do bi snechta mor 7 sic and an uair sin, 7
do bui eidhreóc ar an uisce, 7 do tóc C. C. a rusca 7 a lamha suas
docum an athur nemdha, 7 tuc moladh 7 buidechus mór dó
'n-a gnimharthaibh, 7 tainic a tir iar sin mar a rabutar a manuigh
naemtha fen, 7 do labuir co fáidhemail ríu 7 assedh adubairt:
'An droch-duine si tuc esonoír do Crísd in a serbfoghantaidhe fen,
ní ticfa docum an puirt se' ó a ndechaidh se,' [ar se], '7 ní mó
rachas docum puirt eli go brath arís; 7 ge ciuín an aimsir, 7 ge
mín an muir, docífí-si nell dorcha os cind na fairge, 7 do cuirfidh
na diabhuil ata sa nell sin combuaidredh 7 sdoirm mor uirre do
toil De, indus co mbaidfider é fen 7 a long con a fuil indte, 7
beruid na diabuil a anam leo a pianaib siraidhe suthaine ifrinn.'
Acus do fíradh sin a fiadhnuise caich uile ar in pongc sin fen
amail adubairt C. C., 7 as é inadh in ar baithedh an long sin itir
Muile 7 Colbasaíd; gur moradh ainm Dé 7 C. C. de sin.

288.[313]) Aroile aimsir do C. C. sa proibindse dána hainm
Pictora,[314]) 7 do bí duine uasal deorata faris an uair sin, 7 ruc
les é a cend duine saidhbir do bi as tir sin, 7 do athain de he 7
do gab-sumh as laimh C. C. é, 7 do ghell gach uile maith do
denumh dó. Acus fa aimsir girr íar sin, do marb an duine
saidbir se a fill 7 a meabhuil gránna an duine si do athain C. C.
de. Et iar na cloisdin sin do C. C., do labuir 7 assedh adubairt
nach do fen do gell an duine sen maith do denumh ar an duine
uassal ndeorata sin do marb se co holc acht do Día cumhachtach,
7 o nar comaill se a gelladh dó, gur scris Día a ainm sen as leabur
na beathadh. 'Et fos a n-aimsir deridh an t[s]amhraidh atamaíd
ag rádh na mbriathur sa,' ar C. C., '7 bídh a fhiss ag cach an
té-si dorinde an fell úd, nach íssa sé en greim d'feoil na muc fá
a fuil sé go curamach 7 dob ail les do beathughadh ar meass 7
ar thoradh an foghmair-se cucad, acht dogebha se bas faí sin.' Ar
na cluinsin sin don oclaech, do cuir se na briathar (sic) sa a tarcusne
7 do bi ag fanamhad 7 ac scige futha; 7 ar techt an foghmhair
cuicce, tucc se fa dera muc do marbudh dó 7 a bruith; oir dob
ail les faidhetóracht C. C. do brecnughadh; 7 ar cur na feola
in a fiadnaise do gerr sé grem dí, 7 sul rainic les a cur 'n-a bel,
do scar a anum ren a corp, 7 do cualatar a raibe do lathair andsin

[313]Source=Adamnan. See Reeves' *Adam.*, pp. 134-5.
[314]Correctly *Ilea insula* (now Islay) Adamnan.

asking; for in his folly the reckless wicked man went into his boat, jeering and mocking at him. And Columcille followed him, [wading] to his knees in the sea. But the man held him in disdain and disworship and gave him no answer. At that time there was much snow and frost in that place, and ice on the water. Columcille raised his eyes and his hands to his Heavenly Father and gave praise and great thanks to God for His powers. And then he came to land to his holy monks, and, speaking by the spirit of prophecy, he said:

"That evil wight that did dishonor Christ in person of us, His servant, shall not return to the port from whence he set out," saith he. "Nor shall he reach any other port from this day till Doom. And albeit the weather is calm and the sea is smooth, yet shall ye behold a black cloud over the water, and the devils that are in the cloud shall cause commotion and a great storm on her by God's will, so that the man shall be drowned, and his ship with all therein. And devils shall bear away his soul with them into everlasting pains of Hell."

And it came to pass in the sight of all on that very spot, as Columcille had said. And the place where that boat was sunk is betwixt Mull and Colbasaid. And thus God's name and Columcille's were magnified.

XXIII

OF THE MIRACLES OF COLUMCILLE IN PICTORA

288. Another time Columcille was in a province hight Pictora, and there was a noble exile with him at that time. And he took him to a rich man that was of that land, and he made him known to the rich man, and the rich man took him from the hand of Columcille, and promised to do him all kindness. And short while thereafter this rich man killed by treachery and wicked deceitfulness him that Columcille had commended to him. And when Columcille heard that, he spake, saying it was not to himself, but to mighty God the man had made the promise to befriend the noble exile that he had now killed treacherously. And since he had not yet kept his promise to him, God had torn his name from the Book of Life.

"And it is still in the late summer we are speaking these words," saith Columcille, "and wit ye well, the one that did that treachery shall not eat one morsel of the flesh of the swine he is tending dili-

na diabuil ag breith a anma docum ifrinn; gorab mar sin do fíradh Día gach ní adeireadh C. C.

289.[315]) Fechtus do C. C. 'sa proibindsi-se Pictora, 7 do bi se ag dul a luing tar an sruth dána hainm Neassa,[316]) 7 do condaic se moran dáine 'sa port remhe 7 corp aca ga breith da andlucadh; 7 do leicetar ar lár ar bruach na haband é ag feitheam ar arthrach d'fhaghaíl a mberdais tar an sruth é docum na hecluisi. Do labuir C. C. go faidheamail andsin 7 assedh adubairt: 'As se siud corp an droch-duine se dorinde an fheall ar in duine si do taebus-a ris,' ar se, '7 ní ced le Día an corp sa hanam do cuaidh a n-ifrenn 7 dorinde gnímh adhuathmar ar in saegul-sa a fíadhnuisi na ndaíne, d'indlocudh a reilicc coisrichta. Ar in ponge sin fen do condcatar peíst aduathmar ag erghe as an (fol. 42a) sruth 7 ag fúadach an cuirp le in a bel fon abaind; 7 do cuir C. C. fá aithne ar manach airidhe da manchuib naemta fen darbh'ainm Lugneus[317]) do bí faris an uair sin, capull[318]) do bí 'sa port do tabairt cuige. Acus nir cuir an manuch cairde ar an umlacht acht do cuir a edach uili de acht edach a seicreide amain, 7 do lecc ar snamh é, 7 do erich an péist cedna 7 do fhoscail a bel, 7 dob ail le an manach do slugadh den-ghrem in a craés 7 in a bragaid, 7 do cuir sí combuaidhredh 7 anfadh mor ar in bfairge, indus co raibe an long a raibe C. C. a nguasacht a baíte.[319]) Acus iar na faicsin sen do C. C., do cuir urnuidhe milis duthrachtach docum Dia d'fhagail fhurtachta don manach. Acus ar crichnughadh na hurnaidhte sin dó, do thócc a lamh 7 do bendaich 7 do coisric se uadha é, 7 do cuir fa aithne ar an péist gan digbail do denamh dó fen no do duine eli go brath aris. Acus do imthigh an péist go ciuin cendsa fón bhfairge le breithir C. C. iar sin, 7 tainic an manach slan tar a ais mar a raibe se. Acus ar faicsin na mirbul mor sin do na poiplechaib do bí sa port an uair sin, do creideatar uili do Día 7 do C. C. Acus fós as e adbhur far cuir C. C. fa aithne ar an manuch dul ar cend an capaill,[320]) do derbadh

---

[315]Source = Adamnan. See Reeves' *Adam.*, pp. 140-1.

[316]*necesse habuit fluvium transire Nesam* Adamnan. He was still on dry land.

[317]*Lug* (with a dash over *g*) MS. O'D. evidently meant it to be *Lugaidh*. Adamnan has *Lugneus*.

[318]Read *bád*. *Caupallum* (boat) Adamnan (Reeves' edition). But Codex D has *caballum* (horse), which evidently O'D. followed.

[319]Incorrect. C. C. was on dry land waiting for the boat that he ordered Lugneus to fetch him.

[320]Read *báid*.

gently and that he would fain fatten on the mast and the fruit of the coming harvest. And even then it is he shall die."

But the man, when he heard the words, disdained them. And he jeered and mocked at them. And when the harvest came he bade kill a pig and boil it, for he would fain belie the prophecy of Columcille. When the meat was set afore him, he cut a morsel thereof, but before he could put it to his mouth, his soul parted from his body, and those present heard the devils bearing his soul to Hell. Thus did God verify each thing that Columcille had said.

289. On a time that Columcille was in this province of Pictora, he was going in a boat across the stream that was called Neasa. And he saw much folk in the port that was before him, bearing a body to be buried. They let it down on the brink of the river awaiting a vessel to carry it across the stream to the church. Then spake Columcille by the spirit of prophecy and said:

"This is the body of that bad man that wrought the treachery against him I entrusted to him," saith he, "and God doth not permit to bury in holy ground the body whose soul hath gone to Hell and hath done a dastard deed in this world in the sight of men."

And at that same moment they saw a monstrous beast rising from the stream and carrying off the body with her in her mouth into the river.

Columcille had charged a certain one of his holy monks named Lungeus that was with him to fetch him a horse[1] that was in the port. And the monk had made no delay in obedience, but had stripped off all his garments save those on his loins only and set to swimming. And that beast rose up and opened her mouth. And she would fain have swallowed the monk with one bite into her belly and into her gullet. And she wrought commotion and great tempest on the sea, so that the boat wherein Columcille was, was in peril of sinking. And when Columcille saw that, he sent up to God a sweet fervent prayer for succour for the monk. And when he had done praying, he lifted his hand, and from where he was he blessed and sained him. And he commanded the beast to do no hurt to him nor to any other forever. And at the word of Columcille the beast went softly and gently through the sea, and the monk came back safe to Columcille. When the people that were in the harbor saw these great marvels, all believed on God and on Columcille. Now the reason why Columcille charged the monk to go for the horse was to prove his obedience and to the intent that those of the folk that had ere that no faith might believe when they saw the monk saved from the monster.

[1] *Cf.* note 318.

umlachta in manuigh fen, 7 docum co creidfidís an cuid nar creid
do na poiplechuib reimhe sin an uair docifidís an manach ga saeradh
ar an peísd.

290.³²¹) Aroile aimser do C. C. ag senmoír 'sa proibindse
adubramar romaind, 7 ni raibe tenga coitcend na talman sain
aige, 7 tainecc duine airidhe don popul d'estecht ris; 7 mar nar
tuic se na briathra adubairt C. C., do iarr se ar fher tenghta do
bui faris a minughadh do. Acus ar na tuicsin o'n fir tengthha
dó do gab se cuicce go gér in a croide 7 in a indtind íad, indus gor
creid sé fen 7 a bean posda 7 a cland 7 a muindtir do Dia 7 do
C. C., 7 do gabatar baisdedh uadha. Acus fa beccán do laithib
iar sin, tesda mac muirnech do bi ag an duine sin,³²²) 7 do cuatar
na draithe diabluide 7 gach duine da raibe a n-agaidh creidimh
as tír³²³) d'aírimaír³²⁴) air fa credemh Crist, ag nach raibe
cumhachta, do gabail ó C. C. fa na deiib cumhachtacha do bi
acu fén do trecean, 7 adubratar gorb íad na deie sin tuc bas dá
mhac tre diultadh doib fen. Ar na cloisdin sin do Col. C., do
cuaidh se go teg na carud sin do bi aige fen, 7 fuaír se fen 7 a
ben tuirsech dolásach fa bas a mic, 7 do labuir C. C. do briathraibh millse soláscha riu, 7 assedh adupairt: 'Bídh creideamh
daingen agaib,' ar se, '7 na heirgidh a midóchus ar trócuire 7 ar
cumhachta Dé.' Acus do fiarfuid ca raibe corp an macaímh sin
fuaír bás; 7 mar do hindissedh sin dó, do cuaidh os a cind 7 do
leicc ar a gluinib e, 7 do doirt a dera 7 do labuir go milis
duthrachtach re Día, 7 assedh adubairt: 'O a Tigherna, a Íssa Crist,
ar se, 'na léc an masla sa d'faghail damh-sa 7 dot creidemh fen,
7 nir mesde masla da fuighind-se tre mo midingbalacht fen,
muna benudh sin rib-se no re bur creidemh do cind mesi do beith
am serbfhogantaidhe aguib, 7 mo beith ag labuirt ris na cinedachaib as bur n-ucht, 7 na léic luthghair no solas docum na ndraith-
edh ndiabluidhe 7 docum na ndroch-daine ata a n-agaidh creidimh,
7 na lecc medughadh anma do na deib bodhra balba da creidind
síad tre bas an macaim se, 7 aithbeogaidh am onoir-se é; 7 gé
mídingbala mesi do labuirt rib, a Tigerna, no d'iarruidh a

---

³²¹In Adamnan, *ibid.*, pp. 145-6.

³²²There is a blot after *sin* and some words that do not seem to belong to the context.

³²³We should expect *'sa tir.*, But O'D. occasionally uses *as* for *sa*. Cf. §288, *as tir sin* in that country.

³²⁴*parentibus cum magna exprobratione coeperunt illudere* Adamnan. It is not likely that *aírimaír* is a mis-spelling for *airbiri*. See *oirbiri* § 38 *supra*.

290. Another time Columcille was preaching in the province we have aforementioned, and he had no knowledge of the native tongue of that land. And a certain one of the folk came to listen to him. And having no understanding of the words that Columcille spake, he asked a man of tongues that was with him to explain them to him. And when he understood them from the man of tongues, he took them eagerly to heart and mind, so that he believed on God and on Columcille, himself and his wife and his children and his folk. And they took baptism from him.

A short space of days thereafter a beloved son of that man died. And the diabolical druids and all that were opposed to the Faith in the land went japing at him for taking from Columcille the Faith of Christ that was without power, and abandoning the strong gods that they had. And they said it was those gods that had given death to his son for abandoning them. When Columcille heard this, he went to the house of those friends of his and he found the man and his wife heavy and sad by reason of the death of their son. And Columcille spake to them sweet words of solace and said:

"Let firm faith be in you," saith he, "and fall not into despair touching the mercy and the powers of God."

And he inquired where was the body of the dead youth. And when it was told him, he went thither and fell on his knees and shed tears. And he spake sweetly and fervently to God and said:

"O Lord Jesu Christ," saith he, "let not this shame fall on me and on Thy Faith. And however great the contempt I may get through my unworthiness, it is naught to me unless it touch Thee or Thy Faith by reason of my being Thy servant and speaking to the tribes in Thy name. Suffer not the fiendish druids and the evil folk that be against the Faith to exult and triumph. Suffer not the names of the deaf dumb deities they believe in to be exalted through the death of this youth. Restore him for my sake. And though unworthy I be to speak to Thee, O Lord, or to require such gift of Thee, yet have I desire and diligence to increase Thy name. Help me as Thou didst help the friends of Lazarus what time Thou didst restore him after his corruption in the tomb, and as Thou has holpen Thine own disciples oft ere this by restoring folk for their sakes."

leithéide so d'athcuinghid ort, ata mían 7 duthr*acht* agam dá bur
n-ainm-se do mhédughad, 7 furtaigh orum mar do furtaigheis
ar cairdib Lasaruis an uair do aithbeouighis é ar morgadh 'san
uaidh³²⁵) dó, 7 mar do furtaighis go minic reimhe so ar do
dhescibul³²⁶) fen fa dainib d'aithbeough*adh* 'n-a n-onoir.' Ar crichnugh*adh* na hurnaidthe-si do C. C., do labuir go laidir doch*us*-
ach a n-ainm Issa Crist ris an c*or*p, 7 ass*edh* adub*air*t. 'Eirigh
beo ar do cossaib fen', ar se; 7 do erigh an macamh a ced*ói*r le
breithir C. C., 7 ruc less ar laimh é mar a raibe a athuir 7 a
mathair; 7 an pop*ul* sin ga raibhe gairthe gola 7 tuirsi reme sin
fa bás an m*a*caimh se, do thogbat*ar* gairthe luthgara 7 solaís ar
na fhaicsin 'n-a beathaid doib, 7 tucat*ar* gloir 7 moladh 7 buidech-
us do Dia 7 do C. C. ar a son sein. Et as foll*us* duind as an
scel sin gor cuir Dia C. C. a cosmuiles ris na faidib naemtha .i. re
hEilias 7 re hEiles*eus*, 7 fos ris na heasbuluib .i. re Pedur 7 re
Pol 7 re hEoín bruinde, l*eth* re gach faidhetóracht da ndenadh
se do beith (*fol.* 42b) 'n-a firinde, 7 leth re siladh an creidimh, 7
re tathbeoughadh na marb, 7 re scris an tshechra*in*. Másedh o
do bi C. C. cosmhuil a n-oibrig*thibh* riu sin, is *d*emhin go fuil se
anois cosmail a ngloír 7 a subalt*aidh*ibh a flaithes De re gach
duine dib.

291.³²⁷) F*echtus* do cuaidh C. C. a crich Cruithnech do siludh
7 do senmoir breithre Dé, 7 do cuaidh go dorus na cúirti a raibe
ri an tíre sin .i. Bruidhe, 7 do iarr fosclud and, 7 nir leic an ri
astech é; oir do bi an ri fen dimsach doch*us*ach as a n*ert* 7 as a
cumhachtaib fen, 7 ni raibe an creidemh go himlan aige, 7 dob
í a doigh fen nach raibe 'sa mbith duine do claidhfedh e. Do
ch*uaidh* C. C. d'indsaighe an doruis 7 do ben comartha na croiche
'sa comluidh, 7 do scaíletar na glais íarnaidhe do bi uirre, 7 do
foscuil an dor*us* uada fen, 7 do cuaidh C. C. 7 a manuigh gan
toirmesc astech. Acus ar bfhaicsin na mirbul mor sin don righ,
do gab bidhg*hadh* 7 ecla imarcach é, 7 do cuaidh fen 7 a muindtir
a coinde C. C., 7 do gabatar cuca mailli re honoír 7 re raiuhíia*ns*
[raiverians] mor e, 7 do labuir an rí do briath*raibh* cendsaidhe
sithcanta ris, 7 rucc les da seomra fen é, 7 do gab creidemh uadha,
7 tuc é fen 7 a tir 7 a talumh ar a chom*us* o sin suas;³²⁸) gor
moradh ainm De 7 C. C. de sin.

---

³²⁵*leg.* uaigh.
³²⁶*leg.* dhescibuil.
³²⁷In Adamnan, *ibid.*, pp. 150-2.
³²⁸This is not in *Adamnan*.

When Columcille had finished those prayers, he spake in a strong hopeful voice in the name of Jesu Christ to the dead corpse and said:

"Rise up alive on thy feet," saith he.

And the youth rose up straightway at the word of Columcille. And he took him by the hand to his father and mother. And the folk that had erst been weeping and lamenting for the death of that youth now raised shouts of joy and gladness, seeing him alive. And they gave glory and praise and thanks to God and to Columcille therefor.

It is manifest to us from this history that God made Columcille like to the holy prophets; like to Elias and Elisha, and like to the apostles also, to wit, Peter and Paul and John of the Bosom, inasmuch as every prophecy he made was verified. And he was like to them touching sowing the Faith and restoring the dead to life, and stamping out heresies. And, since Columcille was like to them in works, it is certain that he is now like to every one of them in glory and in power in the Princedom of God.

291. On a time Columcille went to a Pictish land to sow and to preach the word of God. And he went to the door of the court where the King of that country was, even Bruide. And he asked entrance there. And the King suffered him not to enter, for he was orgulous and overweening of his might and power. And he was not yet wholly received into the Faith. And he thought there was none in the world that might undo him. Columcille went to the door and made the sign of the cross thereon. And the iron bolts thereon were loosed, and the door opened of itself. And Columcille and the brethren entered without hindrance. When the King beheld these great marvels he was affrighted and sore afeard. And he approached Columcille with his folk, and received him with great honor and worship. And the King spake to him soft and peaceful words and took him to his chamber and received the Faith from him. And he gave himself and his land and his country into the power of Columcille from that time. And thus God's name and Columcille's were magnified.

292.³²⁹) Fechtus do C. C. fáré righ an tire-si do raidhseamur remaind .i. Bruidhe a ainm, 7 do bi draí aige darb ainm Brocan, 7 fa he dob oide don righ fen. Et tarla inneilt Erindach a laímh agan draí sin, 7 do gab daendaigecht mor C. C. 'n-a timchell, 7 do iarr air a leicen uadha saer 'n-a onoir fen. Do eitigh an drai uimpe é. Ar na cloisdin sin do Col. C., do labuir go faideamhuil ris, 7 assedh adubairt: 'Bidh a fis agad a Brocáin,' ar se, 'muna leícir an indilt úd saer uaid sul fagbur-sa an tír se, co bfhuigheir bas go luath.' Do gab C. C. a ced ag an righ iar sin, 7 tainic conuice an sruth darb ainm Nesa, 7 do tócuib cloch ghel as an n-aphaind sin, 7 do benduigh í, 7 adubairt ris na manchuib do bi faris, go mbeith an cloch sin 'n-a hadbur slaínte ac morán d'eslaintibh cinedhach an tire sin a rabatar; 7 do labhuir ris,³³⁰) 7 assedh adubairt: 'Tainec aingel De do nimh anois,' ar se, 'do cum an druadh úd do eitigh mesi fa'n indilt, 7 do facuib sé a nguasacht bais é, 7 da derbadh sin, do bris se an soigthech gloine do bi 'n-a laimh as a raibe se ag ól dige, 7 ní fada go bfhaicfí-se dís marcach og techt ar mo cenn-sa on righ, indus go furtaighind air on guasacht bais a bfhuil sé.' Ar crichnughadh na mbriathar sin do C. C., tancutar techta and righ cuca, 7 do indisetar co raibe an drai a nguasacht bais, 7 cor brissedh an soighthech gloine do bui 'n-a laimh amail do indes C. C. da muindtir fen reme sin; 7 adubratar corb e an rí do cuir ar cend C. C. iad d'furtacht an druagh on guasacht bais sin a raibe se, 7 co leicfedh se an innilt saer uada dá cend sin. Do cuir C. C. dias manach da manchuib fen les na tec[h]ta sin an righ, 7 an cloch do togaib se reme sin a sruth Nessa leo, 7 adubairt riu da lecthi an indilt becc Erindach sin do bi fa daírse amach, uisce do chur timcell na cloiche 7 a tabairt ré a ól don draidh, 7 co mbeith se slan a cedoir, 7 muna lecthi amach hi, gan uisce na cloiche do tabairt do 7 go fuighedh bás iar sin. Do cuatar na manaigh mar a raibe an rig 7 an drai, 7 do indesitar doib gach ní da ndubairt C. C. leo. Acus ar na cloisdin sin don righ, do furail se an indeilt do lécen amach a n-onoír C. C., 7 do cuiretar na manuigh an cloch a soithech uisce; 7 gidh ingantach sin re radha, do erigh an cloch a fiadnaise caich uile a n-aghaidh a nadúire disli fen ar uachtar an uisce; oir nírb eidir bendacht C. C. do bi uirre do múchadh. Acus ar na fhaicsin sin don draidh, do ibh ní don uisce, 7 do bui slan a cedóir; cor moradh ainm De 7 C. C. de sin.

---

³²⁹§§ 292, 293 in Adamnan, ibid., pp. 146-8.
³³⁰leg. riu.

292. Whenas Columcille was with the King of this country aforementioned, to wit, Bruide, the King had a druid named Brocan that was his tutor. And it happed that the druid had an Irish bond-woman. And Columcille took great pity on her case. And he asked the druid to set her free for his sake. And the druid refused him concerning her. When Columcille heard this, he spake in manner of prophecy to him and said:

"Know, O Brocan," saith he, "save thou free that bond-woman ere I quit this land, thou shalt die in short space."

Anon Columcille took leave of the King. And he came to the stream by name Neasa. And there he took a bright stone from the river, and blessed it and told the brethren that were with him that the stone should be a cause of health to many of the sick of the land where they were, and he spake to them and said:

"But now there came from Heaven an angel of God," said he, "to the druid that refused me touching the bond-woman, and he left him nigh death. And for a sign hath the angel broken in the druid's hand the vessel of glass wherefrom he was drinking a draught. Nor shall it be long ere ye see two horsemen coming from the King for me to aid him in the peril of death whereas he is."

When Columcille had ended these words, the messengers of the King came to them. And they declared that the druid was in peril of death and that the glass vessel in his hand had broken as Columcille had told his household afore. And the messengers said the King had sent them for Columcille to save the druid from the danger of death whereas he was. And he would set free the bond-woman in return therefor.

Then Columcille sent back with the King's messengers two of his own monks, carrying the stone he had taken from the stream Neasa. And he charged them if the little Irish hand-maid that was in bondage should be set free, to put the stone in water and to give the water to the druid to drink. And he declared the druid should be whole forthwith. And if the King set her not free, he bade them withhold the water of the stone and he said that the druid would die thereafter. The monks went to the King and the druid, and they told them all that Columcille had charged them.

When the King heard that, he bade the maid be set free in honor of Columcille. Then the monks put the stone in a vessel of water. And albeit passing strange to tell, the stone rose up in sight of all in despite of its own nature. And it rose to the top of the water; for it were not possible to quench the blessing of Columcille that was thereon. When the druid saw that, he drank of the water and was

293. Do chuatar a manuigh mar a raibe C. C. iar sin, 7 do fosdó an ri an cloch-sa adubramar romhaind dib, 7 do cuir a coimhed 'n-a oircisde fen í, 7 do fóiredh an t-uisce do cuirthí timcell na cloiche sin gach duine do ibhedh ní de ó gach uile eslainte dá mbidh air, acht amhain an uair do íarradh duine do bidh a ngalur a baís a huisce, ni fhaghtai an cloch 'sa chofra in a mbidh si ga coimhed. Acus da derbhadh sin, ar techt criche a bethadh docum an righ sin oc á raibe an cloch ga coimhéd (*fol.* 43a) .i. Bruidhe rí Cruithnech, do linadh do galur 7 d'eslainte é, 7 do íarr sé uisce na cloiche dá fhurtacht, 7 ni frith an cloch 'san inadh a raibe sí a coimhéd; oir nírbh ail lé C. C. fad saegail d'fagail dó a n-agaidh toile De, go fuair bas a cedoir.

294.³³¹) A cind beccaín aimsire íar sin, tainic an draí-si, og a raibe an inailt a llaimh 7 do slanuigh C. C. re huisce na cloiche remhe sin, mar a raibe se; 7 ní do denamh buidechais air do cind a slanaighte tainic se *acht* do denumh diabluidechta 7 aibsereorachta air, ar na linadh d'aingidecht 7 d'imthnud[h] ris, 7 do fhíarfaigh de ca trath do fuicfedh se an rigacht sin a raibe se. Adubairt C. C. corb e bud triall dó maille re grasaib De, a fagbail an tres la on lá sin. Acus adubairt an drai nach fédfadh se a facbail an la sin, 7 go tiubradh se fen gaeth contrardha in a agaidh, 7 go toigebudh se sdoirm mor ar in bfairge 7 ceo dorcha, indus na budh eidir le C. C. imtecht 'san aimseir sin mar do gell se imthecht. Do frecoir C. C. é 7 assedh adubairt. 'Ata cumachta De os cind cumhscalta³³²) gach uile duile dar cruthaigh se féin,' ar se. Et ar techt don tres la cuca, teid C. C. d'indsaighe a luinge, 7 do lenutar moran do na poiplechaib docum puirt é, da fhis cindas do tecemhadh do fen 7 do na draithib do ghell gan imthect do lecen dó. Et ar na fhaicsin sin do na draithib, do tocbatar gaeth contrard[h]a in a agaidh, 7 sdoirm imarcach ar an bfairge, 7 ceó rodorcha uirre, indus nar leir d'en-duine í. Acus do gab luthgáir mor íad fen, oir do saeiletar go fedfidís C. C. do toirmesc, 7 a brecnughadh in a briathraibh, mar do gell se imtecht an la sin fen d'airithe as an righacht sin, 7 do saeiletar go creidfidís na poiblecha doib fen trid sen. Et fos na cuiredh nech ar bith a n-ingnadh go fuilngend Dia don diabul claechlódh 7 buaidhirt do chur ar an gaeith 7 ar an fairge 7 ar gach duil eli do mhedughadh luaigidhechta na ndaine maith creides co daingen dó fen, 7 do medughadh ecla 7 uamain na ndrochdaíne da filledh on a pecaíb, 7 do medughadh a anma fen 7 anma a descibuil.

³³¹§§ 294, 295 in Adamnan, *ibid.*, pp. 148-50.
³³²*cumhscata* (with a dash over first *a*) *MS*.

straightway whole, so that God's name and Columcille's were magnified.

293. Then the monks returned to Columcille. And the King kept the stone aforementioned, and put it in his own gold chest to guard. And the water wherein the stone was put used to heal every man that drank thereof from every malady that lay on him. Howbeit when any that was in sickness of death asked for the water, the stone could not be found in the coffer wherein it was kept. In proof whereof, when the King that had the stone in keeping, to wit, Bruide, King of the Picts, had come to the end of his life time, being filled with sickness and malady, he asked a drink of the water to heal him. And the stone was not found in the place where it was in keeping; for Columcille had no wish to get long life for Bruide against God's will. And so he died straightway.

294. Short while thereafter the druid that had held the maiden in bondage and that Columcille had healed with the water of the stone, came to Columcille. But it was not to thank him for his healing that he came, but to work evil and malice on him, because he was filled with envy and jealousy against him. And he asked him when he would leave that kingdom. Columcille said that with God's grace he thought to leave it on the next day thereafter. The druid said he might not leave it on that day, for he would raise against him a contrary wind and a great storm on the sea and a dark mist, so that Columcille might not be able to go at the time he had promised. Columcille made answer:

"The powers of God are above the motions of every creature that He hath made," saith he.

And on the coming of the third day Columcille went to his vessel, many of the folk following him to his ship to see how it would hap to him and to the druids that had sworn not to let him go. When the druids saw that, they raised an opposing wind in his face, and a great storm on the sea, and a very dark mist on her, so that she was not visible to any. And great joy seized them, for they thought to hinder Columcille and to belie his words, for he had promised to depart that same day out of the kingdom. And through this thing the druids thought that the folk would believe on them.

Let none wonder that God doth permit to the Devil the turning of the wind and the sea and every other element, [for it is] to increase the merit of good folk of steadfast faith, and the fear and dread of evil folk, that they may turn them from their sins. And moreover it is to magnify His name and the name of his disciple.

295. Et ata Adamhnan ga mebrug*hadh* go tarla a leithéid so do German Espog do bi ag dol on Frainc docum na Britaine do siladh breithre Dé, 7 co tancatar léighión do diabluib a timcell na luingi a raibe se, 7 co raibe sí a nguasacht a baíte uatha gor cuir an t-espog naemtha sin urnaidhe duthr*ach*tach docum a *Di*a fen d'faghail furt*ach*ta uadha. Acus ar crichnughadh a urnaidhe dó, cor benduigh an fhairge 7 cor techeatar na diab*uil* remhe, 7 go fuair aimser ciuin iar sin. Teid C. C. 'n-a luing mar in cedna 7 o'dcondairc an combuaidredh do cuiretar na d*rai*the diablaide sin ar an fhairge, do gair ainm Íssu Crist maille ré creidem daingen, 7 do fhurail a seolta do toc*bail* a n-agaid na gaithe draidechta sin. Acus dorindet*ar* an foirend amail adubairt C. C. ríu; ge do cuatar a midochus go mór nach fedfidís imtecht; 7 gidheadh do imt*igh*etar on purt 7 a seolta a n-airde aca amail do beith gaeth ger 'n-a n-diaidh go direch, 7 do bendaig C. C. an fhairce, indus cor imt*high* a sdoirm 7 a anf*adh* 7 an ceo d*rai*dhechta do bi uirre di. Acus do bí an t-imdecht sin C. C. 'n-a adbur míclu 7 dolaís do na draithib diabla*idh*i adubrumar romhainn, 7 'n-a hadbhur luthghára 7 solaís ag na daínibh do creid do Día 7 do C. C. reme sin, 7 'n-a adbur baisde 7 creidimh ag na dainib nar gab creidim remhe sin uadha. Et fos fech*eadh* gach nech da léghfa 7 da tuicfe an sdair-se, cá mhéd 7 ca mence uair tucc Día n*ert* 7 cumachta do C. C. leth ris na cinedhach*aibh* do tairring docum creidimh, 7 leith ris na droch-spiraduib do sc*ris*, 7 leath ris na daínib do aithbeoug*hadh*. Et as follus duínd as an scel-sa, cor chuir Día C. C. a cosmailes ré Pedur esp*ol* leith ris na draithib do claí an uair do clai se Simón Mághis neoch do bi ac tindtódh an creidim len a draid*echt* 7 len a diab*ul*dan*acht* fén.

296.³³³) Fechtus do C. C. a n-inadh airidhe a n-Albain, 7 do chuireatur na manaigh do bi uadha fen 'sa mainesdir darb ainm Mainisdir in Da Sruth techta ar a cend. Acus do cuaidh C. C. les na techta sin co humhal. Acus ar ndul don baile dó, do cuaidh se*a*chrán ecin ar eochrachuibh na ndoirrsech, induss narb eídir a lecen astech muna brisdí na glais do bi orra remhe; mar dob ail le Día medug*hadh* a anma fen 7 anma C. C. do thecht as sin. Teid C. C. docum an dorais iar sin, 7 do gab se na hairm lé a mberedh se buaidh do gnath cuige .i. creidemh daingen 7 umla 7 urnaidthe, 7 do ch*uir* bratuch Íssu Crist remhe .i. com (*fol.* 43b) artha na croiche, ris narb eidir sesam do denamh, 7 adubairt corb eidir le Día a serbfhoghantaidh fen do leccen astech gan eochracha. Ar crichnug*hadh* na mbriat*har* sin do, do scailetar na glais, 7 do

---

³³³ In Adamnan, *ibid.*, pp. 152-3.

295. Adamnan maketh mention that a like hap befell Bishop Gemman that was crossing from France to Britain to sow the word of God, and that a legion of devils surrounded the ship wherein he was, and that she was in danger of sinking by reason of them, till that holy bishop raised a fervent prayer to his God for aid. And when he had ended that prayer, he blessed the sea, and the devils fled afore him. And he had calm weather after that..

Columcille went into his ship in like manner, and when he saw the commotion the fiendish druids had put upon the sea, he invoked the name of Jesu Christ with right firm faith. And he bade hoist the sails against that magic wind. The crew did as Columcille charged them, albeit they had fallen into great despair lest they should be unable to depart. Natheless they set out from port with their sails unfurled as though there were a sharp wind behind them. Then Columcille blessed the sea, and her raging was stilled, and the magic mist that was on her left her.

That journey of Columcille's was cause of ill fame and grief to the fiendish druids whereof we have spoken; and cause of joy and solace to the folk that had already faith in God and Columcille. And it was cause of baptism and faith to the folk that afore had not the Faith from him. Moreover, let everyone that may read and ponder this history see how greatly and how oft God gave strength and power to Columcille in the matter of converting the heathen to the Faith, and in the matter of driving out evil spirits and restoring folk to life. It is manifest to us from this history that in respect of victories over druids God made Columcille like to Peter the Apostle when he defeated Simon Magus that had been perverting the Faith with his magic and his diabolical practices.

XXIV

OF THE MIRACLES OF COLUMCILLE IN ALBA

296. On a time that Columcille was in a certain place in Alba, the brethren that he had placed in the monastery hight Mainisdir An Da Sruth sent messengers for him. And Columcille went obediently with the messengers. And when they came to the place, the keys on the doors were lost in some wise, so that they might not enter except

fosclatar na doirrse uatha fen, 7 do cuaidh C. C. astech 'sa mainestir,
7 tucatar na manaigh do bi astigh reme buidechus 7 moladh mór
dó da cind mar do fhurta*igh* se an naíre mór do bi orra feín fa gan
eochracha d' faghail da lecen astech; cor moradh ainm De 7 C. C.
5 desin.

297[334]) Fechtus do Coluim C. a n-inadh áiridhe a n-Albain,
7 tainic duine daidhber don popul cuice, 7 do chuir a ceill dó
co raibe an uiret sin do bochtaine air indus co raibe se fen 7 a ben
7 a cland a nguas*acht* bais d'faghail d'uiresbuidh na beathad[h]
10 d'foighenad[h] doib, 7 nach raibe dul on bas acu muna furtaig*edh*
san orra. Do gab truaige C. C. do, 7 adub*airt* ris an ocl*aech* dul
fan coill bud goire do, 7 slat do buain 7 a tabairt cuige fen. Dorinde
an t-oclaech mar adub*radh* ris, 7 tucc an tshlat a laimh C. C. iar sin.
Dorinde C. C. rind uirre, 7 do benduig hí, 7 adubairt ris an
15 oclaech an bir sin do breith less 7 a sháthad[h] a talumh a n-inadh
a mbeith fiadhuch *no* énach no beath*adh*aigh egcialluide an
fáss*aigh* ac tathaig*e*, nó a sath*adh* a n-abuind no a loch *no* a
fairge, 7 nach rachadh se en uaír dá fech*ain* n*ach* bfhuighed se
a ri*ach*tanus a les fen 7 riachtanus less a mhuindt*ire* d'feoill no
20 d'íasc marb air. Acus adubairt C. C. n*ach* denadh an bir-sa
digbail do dhuine no d'ainmide cennsa ar bith an cein dobe*ith*
creidemh ag an duine daigbir sin dó *no* co ndechadh se a midóchus
air, 7 adubairt go faidhemail ris gan comairli a mna do gabail
air. Acus ar na cloisdin sin don óclaech, do gab luthgair mór
25 é, 7 ruc an bir sin les, 7 do saith a talm*ain* a n-inadh a mbidh
fiadhach ag tathaig*he* é. Acus teid ar na maruch da fhechain,
7 fuair fiadh mor barr marb air. Acus ni hedh amain a*cht* ní
dechaidh se en uair dá fechain n*ach* fuighed se fiadh barr no
agh[335]) no beth*adh*ach egcíallaide eli marbh air 7 an meíd nach
30 riged se fein nó a muindtir a les d'ithe don fiadach sin, do recadh
se íad, indus cor línadh do saidbres é. Gideadh, do gab tnudh
mór an diabul uime sin, indus narb ail less an oired sin do dul
a sochur do na dainib gan toirmesc do chur air. Et do cuir se
fa mnai an ocla*igh* sin buaidr*edh* do cur air fen ler bochtaigedh
35 é, mar do cuir se fá Ebha buaid[h]redh do chur ar Ádamh ler
bochtaigedh an cined daenna uile. Do labuir ben an ocláich sin
ar furailem an diabuil co glic dar le fen ren a fer, *acht* ger míglic
do labuir sí ris, 7 ass*edh* adub*airt*: 'Toc an bir úd co luath,' ar
sí, 'as an inadh a fuil se, no tuitfid daine no spréid ar comharsan
40 less in a tuitfem-ne 7 ar cland 7 ar n-airnés uli.' 'Ni to*í*ceb*ad*,'
ar an t-oclaech, 'oír adubairt C. C. rium an uair do beandaigh

---
[334]In Adamnan, *ibid.*, pp. 153-55.
[335]*cervus aut cerva* Adamnan. Cf. *fiadh barr* in § 163.

the locks thereon be broken. And sith it was pleasing to God that the magnifying of His name and the name of Columcille should result therefrom, Columcille went to the door. And he put upon him the arms whereby he did ever bear away the victory, to wit, Strong Faith and Humility and Prayer. And he put forth the standard of Jesu Christ, which is to say the sign of the cross, gainst the which none might make a stand. And he said that God had power to let in His servant without keys. And when he had said these words, the locks were unloosed, and the doors opened of themselves. And Columcille went into the monastery. Then the monks that were within gave him great thanks and praise, for that he had freed them from the great shame they had to be without keys to let them in. And thus God's name and Columcille's were magnified.

297. On a time that Columcille was in a certain place in Alba, there came to him a certain poor man of the folk. And he let him wit that he was in such sore poverty that he and his wife and babes were nigh death for lack of food whereof they had need. And they might not escape death but if he help them. Then was Columcille sore grieved for him, and he made the churl go into a wood fast beside, and cut a stake and bring it to him. Then did the churl as Columcille had charged him and gave the stake into Columcille's hand. Then Columcille made a point thereon, and blessed it. And he bade the churl take with him that stake and set it in the ground in a place whereas deer or wild birds or dumb beasts of the forest should come, or set it in a river or in a lake or in the sea. And not once should he come to see it that he should not find dead thereon what was needful for himself and his household of flesh or of fish. And Columcille said the stake should do no harm at all to man or to tame beast so long as the poor man believed in Columcille and lost not his faith in him. And he charged him in manner of prophecy not to heed the counsel of his wife touching it.

And when the churl heard this he made great joy. And he took the stake with him and stuck it in the ground in a place where deer were wont to come. And on the morrow he went to look, and he found a great stag dead thereon. And not that only, but he never went to look save he found a stag or a fawn or other wild beast dead thereon. And whatso he and his household needed not of the game, that he sold, so that he was filled with riches. Howbeit the Devil took great envy at this thing, for it liked him not that this should so much avail the folk without his hindrance. And he set the wife of the churl to tempting him, so that he was made poor once more, even as he set Eve to tempt Adam, whereby all mankind was made poor. Then spake

sé an bir nach denadh se dig[h]bail no urchoid do duine no
d'ainmhidhe cendsa ar bith an cein dobeith se a n-én-inadh da
ndubairt se fen a cur nó in cein dobeith creidemh agam do.' Agus
gidheadh, nir an an ben sin da mnaamhlacht no corb ecen dá
fer an bir do tabairt less as an inadh araibe se, 7 do íarr air a
gerradh no a loscadh. Do bi do grad[h] aige sen ar Col. C. 7 do
med an foganta dorinde an bir do remhe sin, narbh urussa les an
comhairli sin do gabail, 7 do cuir a n-airde a taeb a tighe fen é.
Acus a cind becain aimsire iar sin, tarla gadhar muirnech do bi
oc an oclaech fan mbir, co bfuair bás a cedoir. Et ar na faicsin
sin da mnaí, adubairt ris mana beiredh se an bir as in tigh co
luath co tibradh se bas do duine acu fen no do duine ecin da
claind. Rucc an t-oclaech an bir les ar comhairli a mná, 7 do
folaigh é ar coill ro-dluth rouaicnech nach bidh daíne no spreidh
ga tathaighe. Acus téid dá fhechain ar na marach, 7 fuair gabur
marb air. Acus do indeis sin da mnai, 7 adubairt sí ris, o nar
gab se a comairle fen ar an mbir do gerrudh no do losgadh, a
breith les as an inadh sin d'ecla go (fol. 44a) muirbfedh se
tuilleadh do spreidh a comarsan budh ecen doib d'íc. Ruc an
t-oclaech an bir les íar sin docum srotha aírithe darb ainm Dubdeca do bi laimh ren a toigh fen 7 do folaidh san uisce fa bruach
an tsrotha sin e. Acus do chuaidh da fhechain ar na maruch,
7 fuair íasc ro-mhór marb air. Acus do bi do mhed 'san iasc sin
gorub ar ecin tuc se fen 7 a muindtir docum a tighe é. Acus tucc
se an bir les íar sin, 7 do cuir a mulluch a tighe fen don taeb
amuigh e. Teit da fhechain arís, 7 fuair se fiach marb air. Ar
na fhaiccsin sin do mnai an oglaeich adubairt cor bir nimhe é,
7 nach ó ní maith do bi cumachta aige, 7 co raibe an oired sin
d'ecla uirre co tiubradh se bass di fen, 7 o nach raibe sesiun ag
gabail a comairle air, go fuicfedh sí é 7 nach beith sí fen 7 an bir
sin a n-enfhecht aige. Ar na cloisdin sin don oclaech, tuc se an
bir cuige, 7 do gearr go min le tuaidh é, 7 do loisc ar tenidh iar
sin é; 7 do melladh go mor é le comairle a mna, mar as minec do
melladh duine remhe le comhairle droch-mhna. Acus ar cur an
tindlaicthe díadha sin tucc C. C. dó a nemhchin 7 a tarcuisne mar
sin, do cuaidh se 'sa bochtaine cedna aris, indus co raibe se fen

the wife of the churl to her husband, aiding the Devil, wisely as her seemed, though it was folly she spake to him.

And she said, "Take away that stake swiftly," saith she, "from the place where it is, lest there fall thereon tame beast of our neighbors, and we fall, and our children and our gear."

"I will not," saith the churl, "for Columcille did promise me, when he blessed the stake, that it would do no harm to any, nor hurt, whether to man or tame beast, so long as it should be in any place where he bade put it and so long as I should have faith in him."

Howbeit the woman ceased not from her womanish arts until her husband must take the stake from the place where it was. And she required of him that he cut it or burn it. And such love had he for Columcille by reason of the service that stake had done him ere that time, that it was not easy for him to do her bidding. And he put it up beside his house. And short while thereafter there came by adventure a pet dog of the churl's upon the stake, so that it was killed forthwith. And when the wife perceived this, she said to him that save he bear away that stake from the house quickly it would bring death to one of them or of their children. The churl took away the stake at the counsel of his wife. But he concealed it in a passing thick wood and close, whereas no man came, nor tame beast. And he went on the morrow to look, and he found thereon a dead goat. And he related this to his wife, and she said to him, since he took not her counsel to cut the stake nor to burn it, that he should bear it away from the place lest it kill more of their neighbors' cattle for the which they must needs pay.

Then the churl took with him the stake to a certain stream hight Dubdeca, fast by the house, and hid it in the water at the edge thereof. And on the morrow he went to look, and he found a passing great fish dead thereon. And so great was the fish that it was needful he and his folk together should bear it to the house.

Then bare he the stake with him and set it on the top of his house without. And when he looked at it again he found a raven thereon dead. And when the wife of the churl beheld it, she said it was a stake of poison, and that it was from no good thing that it had power, and that so great was the fear upon her that it would bring her death, seeing that he would not take her counsel touching it, that she would leave him. And he should not have her and that stake both at the one time. And when the churl heard this, he took the stake and chopped it with an axe, and he burned it in the fire. And he was beguiled by the counsel of his wife as men have been beguiled by evil women oft ere this. And having thus despised and contemned that divine gift of Columcille, he fell again into the same poverty, so that he and his wife

7 a bean 7 a mhuindtir uile ag caínedh an beara do dul uatha,
co fuaratar bas do gorta dá dith; cor moradh ainm De 7 C. C.
de sin.

     298[336]) Fechtus do C. C. a n-inadh airidhe a n-Al-
bain,[337]) 7 tainec ben don pop*ul* 'gá raibe fúath ar a fer pósta
fen cuige, 7 do íarr air a delug*hadh* ris, 7 do gell co rach*adh* si
co mainist*ir* caillech ndub do bui'sa tir sin, 7 co coimhetfadh sí
a genmnaidhe*cht* do Dia 7 do san ar a shou sin. Freccruis C. C.
í 7 assedh adubairt: 'Bidh a fis agad,' ar se, 'gebe lanamhain
cenglus an ecluss re céle gan toirmeascc a hucht De, nach eídir le
duine 'sa mbith a scail*edh* co brath arís; 7 o ata sin mar sin,
tucthar hfer posta-ssa cugaind 7 denam ar tr*i*ur troscadh re Día
fan comairli as ferr do seoladh duinn.' Doronadh amluidh, 7 do
bí C. C. ag guidhe De co duthrachtach fa gr*adh* na mná sin do
tabairt ar a fer. Acus ar cric[h]nug[h]adh a troisce 7 a urn*ai*-
dhe do, do fhíarf*aigh* ar na mharach a fiadhnaise a fir fen narb
ail lé an indtind maith do bi aice remhe sin do coimlinadh .i. dul
a coim;thinol na cailleach ndub 7 a genmnaidhecht do coimhet.
Ar na cluinsin sin don mnai, assedh adubairt: 'Ó, a C. C., tuigim
7 creidim go fagand tú gach ní as ail l*et* o Día, óir do claechló
Día tre brigh hurnaighte-se 7 do troisce an fuath ro-mór do bi
ané am croide-si don fhir úd, a ngr*ad*[h] imarcach do tabairt
do, indus nach fuil ar bith fer is andsa lium ina é. Acus do
bat*ar* an lanamain sein go gradhach muindterach mar sin fa
cheli go a mbás; cor mor*adh* ainm De 7 Col. C. de sin.

     299.[338]) Fechtus do Coluim C. a mainist*ir* airidhe a Al-
bain,[339]) 7 tarla a adbur ecin dó dul a carbud do bend*aigh* se fein
remhe sin lé gnoaighhib an coimthinol (*sic*). Acus do bi an aít a raibe
se ag dul uimhir airidhe do mílt*ibh* uadha, 7 do bi Colman mac
Ech*ach* .i. funduír na mainistrech sin fen maille ris is an charp*ud*,
7 as se do bi ag sdiuradh an carb*aid* do, 7 do bui an Colman sin
fein naemtha fa deóigh. Et tarla do maindec*ht*naidhe na ndaine
do bi ag desug*hadh* an carb*aid*, nar cuimhnighet*ar* na tairrngedha
do cungbudh a rothadha gan scailed ó celi, do cur indta. Acus
nir mothaig cec*ht*ar dibh sen an uiresbaidh sin do bi ar an carbud
no go rancatar cend an uidhe. C*on*ad[h] amlaidh sin do coimheid
Día rothadha an carbaid sin a raibe C. C. gan scailed ó ceile, do
medughadh onora 7 anma a serbfoghant*aidh* diliss fen.

---

[336]In Adamnan, *ibid.*, pp. 164-6.
[337]Adamnan has *Rechrea* (either Lambay or Rathlin in Ireland).
[338]In Adamnan, *ibid.*, pp. 171-3.
[339]Adamnan has *in Scotia* (Ireland).

and all his household did mourn that the stake was lost to them. And for lack thereof they gat their death of hunger, and God's name and Columcille's were magnified thereby.

298. On a time whenas Columcille abode in a certain place in Alba, there came to him a woman of the folk that bare hatred to her husband. And she asked Columcille to part her from him. And she promised that she would go into a monastery of black nuns that was in the region, and that she would guard her chastity for God's sake and his in return therefor.

Columcille made answer to her and saith in this wise, "Wit thou well," saith he, "whatsoever twain Holy Church doth bind together without hindrance of God, no man may put them asunder forever. And since this is so, bring hither thy husband to us and let us three fast afore God for counsel what we should best do."

Thus it was done. And Columcille prayed God fervently that the love of that woman might be given to her husband. And when he had finished his fast and his prayer, he asked her on the morrow in presence of her husband if she would fain fulfill the good purpose that she had afore, to wit, to go into a convent of black nuns and keep her chastity.

And when the woman heard this, she said, "O Columcille, I do understand and believe that thou dost get from God all things thou dost desire, for by the power of thy prayer and thy fast God hath changed the exceeding hatred I did have in my heart for that man, into giving him passing great love, so that there is no man that is liefer to me than he."

And these twain were lovers in this wise of each other till their death. So that God's name and Columcille's were magnified thereby.

299. Whenas Columcille on a time abode in a certain monastery in Alba, it chanced that he rode for some cause on business of the household in a chariot that he had blessed ere then. And the place where he was going was some miles distant. And Colman, son of Eochaidh, that was the founder of that monastery, was with him in the chariot, and was guiding it. And that Colman was a saint at the last. And it befell through the carelessness of those that made ready the chariot, that they forgat to set therein the pegs that kept the wheels from disjoining. And neither of the holy men marked that lack in the chariot until they came to the end of their journey. Thus it was that God kept the wheels of that chariot wherein Columcille was from disjoining, to the increase of the honor and the name of His chosen servant.

300.³⁴⁰) Fechtus do C. C. nhÍ, 7 do bi manuch airidhe o
Bretain mailli ris,³⁴¹) 7 do gab esslaínte bais é, 7 do cuaidh C. C.
ar cuairt cuige. Do teccaisc 7 do benduigh e, 7 do cuaidh fen
amach iar sin, 7 do bi ag radh a trath 7 a urnaidhe ac techt
timcell na reilge; 7 fuair an manach-sa adubramar romaind bas
iaromh. Agus ar crichnughadh a urnaidhe do C. C., do fech óss
a cind san aiér, 7 do bi aimser fada mar sin ag fechain suas, 7 do
léic ar a gluinib é, 7 do chuir urnaidhe duthrachtach docum Dia.
Do (fol. 44b) eírigh 'n-a sesamh iar sin, 7 tucc gloir 7 moladh
do Dia cumachtach in a tidlaicib. Ar na faicsin sin do manach
airide darb ainm Aedhan do bi a fochuir C. C. an uair sin, do
tuic se cor tais[b]enadh³⁴²) mor ecin tucudh dó, 7 do leicc ar a
gluínib e, 7 do guidh se C. C. fa'n taisenadh sin d'foillsiughadh
dó fen. Do frecuir C. C. e 7 assedh adubairt, corub 'ad aingli
De 7 na droch-spiraid do condairc se ag cathughadh re celi
timchell anma an manuigh sin fuair bas, 7 co tainic do cumhach-
taibh na n-aingel 7 do brigh a guidhe fen, go rucatar na haingil
buaidh ar na droch-spiraduib, 7 go rucatar anam an manaigh leo
docum na cathrach nemdha do caithemh na gloíre suthaine. Et
do cuir fa aithne ar an manach sin dar indis se an radharc sin
do co ³⁴³) condaic se, gan a fhoillsiughadh air go a bás.

301.³⁴⁴) Fechtus do C. C. a nAlbain is in oilen áiridhi dana
hainm Scía, 7 do scar sé ren a manchuib, 7 do cuaidh se les fen
ar coill uaicnech do bi san oilen do rad a trath 7 a urnaidhe, 7
do condaic se torc romor alluidh cuige,³⁴⁵) 7 do gab graín 7 ecla
reme é, 7 do goir ainm De co duthrachtach, 7 do chuir urnaidthe
docum Íssu Crist d'fhaghail furtachta on péist granna sin. Acus ar
crichnughadh a urnaide dó, do cuir fa aithne uirre gan techt ni budh
ghoire ina sin dó, 7 bas d'faghail san inadh sin a raibe sí. Ar an
pongc sin fen, do tuit an torc a cend a choss 7 fuar bás fo cedoír.
Is mar sin do saer Dia a serbfoghantaidh diles fen gan buaidirt
do cur air in a urnaighte. Agus as follus duinn as an scel-sa go
cuiredh Día bethadhaigh egciallaidhe an fassaigh fa umla do Col.
Chilli.

302.³⁴⁶) Fechtus do C. C. cois srotha áiridhe a nAlbain, 7
fuair se iascairedha ag íascuirecht ar in sruth sin, 7 nir gabutar

---

³⁴⁰In Adamnan, ibid., pp. 202-3.
³⁴¹Incorrect. Adamnan has *quidam de suis monachis Brito*.
³⁴²*ni* written above the line in different handwriting.
³⁴³Omit *co*.
³⁴⁴In Adamnan, ibid., pp. 138-40.
³⁴⁵Adamnan has *mirae magnitudinis aprum .... obviam habuit*.
³⁴⁶In Adamnan, ibid., pp. 128-9.

300. On a time whenas Columcille abode in Iona, a certain monk was with him from Britain. And the sickness of death seized him. And Columcille went to him and instructed and blessed him. Then he went outside. And he was saying his hours and his prayers as he went around the churchyard. And then the monk we have aforementioned died. And when Columcille had finished his prayers he looked upward into the air. And he was for a long time in this wise gazing upward. Then he fell on his knees and sent up a fervent prayer to God. Thereafter he rose up and gave praise and glory to God Almighty in His gifts. And one of the monks hight Aedan, that was in the fellowship of Columcille at that time, when he beheld this, knew that it was some great vision that was given Columcille. And he fell on his knees and begged him to reveal it to him. Then Columcille made answer and said that he beheld angels of God and evil spirits striving with each other for the soul of the monk that had died. And it came to pass by the power of the angels and by virtue of his prayer that the angels overcame the evil spirits and bare the soul of the monk with them unto the holy city, to enjoy the glory everlasting. And Columcille charged the monk to whom he related that vision, that he should not betray it till his death.

301. On a time whenas Columcille was in Alba in a certain island hight Scia, he departed from the monks and repaired alone to a solitary wood on the island to say his hours and his prayers. And he beheld a wild boar exceeding great coming toward him. And he was sore affrighted and adrad thereof. And he called upon the name of the Lord right strongly, and sent up a prayer to Jesu Christ to get help from that dreadful beast. And when he had ended his prayer he put her under bonds to come no nigher to him, and to fall dead in the place where she was. And thereupon the boar fell forward and died straightway. Thus it was that God did save his chosen servant without disturbing him at his prayers. And it is clear to us from this history that God did put the dumb beasts of the wilderness under obedience to Columcille.

302. On a time whenas Columcille was hard by a certain river in Alba, he found fishers fishing in that stream. And they took but five fish. When Columcille saw this he bade them cast again their nets

acht cuíc eísc amhain. Ar na faicsin sin do C. C. adubairt ríu
a línta do chur amach 'n-a onoír fen arís 7 go ngebdaís íasc
romhar nar ghabha*tar* a leitheid riamh. Do chuiretar, iar*omh*,
a línta [amach] ar comairli C. C., 7 tarla íasc mór indta, indus corub
ar ecin do tairnge*tar* a tir é len a med; gor moradh ainm De 7 C. C.
de sin. Is follus duínd as na sceluib-se nach eadh amaín do cuir
Día betaduigh égciallaidhe an fhas*saigh* fa umla do C. C., *acht*
cor cuir se iascach na fairge fa umla dó.

303.³⁴⁷) Fechtus tainic manach áiridhe dá mhanchuib fein
dar ainm Laighnen³⁴⁸) mar a raibe C. C., 7 as e do bi 'n-a
uachtarán uadha 'sa mainisdir da ngairthí Elena, 7 do bi se
ga ecaine ris go raibe a sron ag teilgen fala méd airidhe do mísaib
7 nar fétud cosc di. Ar na cloisdin sin do C. C., do gab se srón
an mhanuigh itir a da mhér, 7 do iadh ar a ceile hi, 7 do leic
amach arís hí. Tainic do mirbuilibh De 7 C. C. nar teilcc an
tsron sin en-bráen fola o sin amach no co fuaír an manach bas;
gor moradh ainm De 7 C. C. de sin.

304³⁴⁹) Fechtus do C. C. a n-inadh airidhe a n-Albain, 7 do
cuaid oilithrech o Erinn ar cuairt cuice, 7 do labuir C. C. la
ecin ris 7 assedh adubairt, co faca se ar in pongc sin fen aingli
Dé ag breith anma clericch Erendaig sa hainm nach raibe aice
fen leo docum na cathrach nemhda. Et ar na cluinsin sin don
oilithr*ech,* do bi se ag radh anmand an meid dob aithn*idh* do fein
do clerchib na hErenn a fiadnaise C. C., 7 do fíarf*aigh* de nar
én ainm dib sin do bi ar an té sa hanam do cond*ai*c se les
na hainglib. Acus adubairt C. C. nárbh edh. Acus do bi an
t-oilithrech tamall 'n-a tost iar sin, 7 do labuir irís riss 7 adubairt
corb aithnidh dó fen nech naemtha áiridhe dar ainm Díarma*i*d do
bi aimser fada ac ridir*echt* do Crist, 7 co nderna se mainest*ir*,
'san inadh ina mbidh se fen 'n-a comn*uidh*e. Acus do fiarf*aigh*
do C. C. narb é a anam sin do *condairc* se ga breith docum
flaithi*usa* De an uair sin. 'Is e,' ar C. C., '7 as mor 7 an onórach
an coimide aingel do condarc-sa ar te*cht* a coinde a anma dá
breith (*fol.* 45a) leo a ngloir suthain. Agus gerb fada C. C. ó
an nech naemtha sin ó corp fuair bás, dob follus a fiadhnaisi a
spiraide gach ní dar imth*igh* ar a anam. Et ata Adamnan
naemtha ga mebrughhadh corub é adbur fa ndubairt C. C. nach
raibe fis anma an clerich sin aige, narb' ail les an tsheicréid do
foillsigedh Dia dó d'indesin do cach, gach en-uair comhsholass 7

---

³⁴⁷In Adamnan, *ibid.,* pp. 127-8.
³⁴⁸*Lugneus* Adamnan.
³⁴⁹In Adamnan, *ibid.,* pp. 204-5.

in his honor, and they should get a passing great fish such that its like they had caught never. Then they cast their nets according to the counsel of Columcille. And there came by adventure therein a fish so great that for its size unnethe might they bring it to land. And God's name and Columcille's were magnified thereby.

It is clear to us from these histories, not only that God did put the dumb beasts of the forest under obedience to Columcille, but that he put the fishes of the sea under obedience to him in like wise.

303. On a time there came to Columcille a certain one of his monks hight Laighnen that was in authority in the monastery that was called Elena. And he complained to Columcille that his nose had been a-bleeding for some months, and it could not be stopped. When Columcille heard this, he took the nose of the monk between his two fingers and shut it and freed it again. It came to pass by the miracles of God and Columcille that that nose shed not a drop of blood from that time. Nor did the monk die. And thus God's name and Columcille's were magnified.

304. On a time whenas Columcille was in a certain place in Alba, there came to him a pilgrim from Erin to visit him. And once Columcille spake to him and said that he beheld in that very moment angels of God bearing with them to the heavenly city the soul of an Irish cleric whose name he knew not. And when the pilgrim heard that, he rehearsed afore Columcille the names that he knew of the clerics of Erin, and asked him if it were one of those names he had whose soul Columcille had beheld among the angels. And Columcille said it was not. Then was the pilgrim for a while silent, and then he spake again to him and said there was a certain holy man hight Diarmaid that had been for long time in knightly service for Christ and had built a monastery in the place where he abode. And he asked Columcille if that was the soul that he had seen borne to the Kingdom of God in that hour.

"It is," said Columcille. "And great and worshipful the company of angels that I beheld coming to meet his soul and bear it to glory eternal."

And albeit Columcille was far distant in the flesh from that holy man, yet was all that had befallen his soul manifest to him in spirit. And holy Adamnan maketh mention that the reason wherefore Columcille did say he knew not the name of the cleric, was because he was loth to relate always to everyone with the like clearness that God revealed them to himself, the secrets that God did manifest to him. For he

do foillsighte dó fén í; oir dob ferr leis a cur a ceill doib co raibe
uiresbuid[h] gras 7 subaltaidhe air, ina sin do dul a moladh 7 a
n-onoir do fen. Acus as se dob'ail less do tuicsin do cách nach
raibe en-ní 'sa mbith gan uiresbuidh air acht Dia na n-uile
cumhacht, 7 nírb' ail leis gloir dimhain 'n-a tindlaiceadh do-
geibedh se o Día do beith dó fen.

305.³⁵⁰) Aroile la do C. C. a ní, 7 do cuaid se a n-inadh
uaicnech les fen do radh a trath 7 a urnaide 7 do denamh a dub-
trachta (sic) do Día. Acus ar crichnughadh a urnaide do, do condaic se sluaigh ro-mora diabul ag cruindiughadh faré celi, 7 siad
ga ndessugad fen docum cathaighte, 7 bera iarnaide 7 a lan do
droch-innstramaintibh eli in a lamaib. Et ar na faicsin sin do
C. C., do gab a culaidh cathaighte ime fen, .i. an culaid do bi ag
Pol apsdol³⁵¹) ag siladh an creidimh, .i. creideamh daingen 7
dóchuss laidir 7 urnaidhe glan duthrachtach, 7 do cuaidh do
cathughadh ris an sluag ndiabul sin. Acus ger mór íad san ó
uimhir, nir eídir leo buaid do breith ar C. C. 7 se 'n-a enur, le
daingne na culaidech sin do bi uime. Acus ni raibe dermad ag
an te donntaighed[h] in gach éicen remhe sin é air, .i. Dia na
n-uile cumhacht; oir do chuir se uimhir doairmidhe da ainglibh
fen do congnamh les an uair sin, indus gor scrisatar le cheli na
droch-spiraid as an oilen sin hí, 7 ni dernatar dith do na manchaib
nó don mainestir no do duine eli 'san oilen ó sin amach. Et tainic
C. C. tar ais iar sin don mainisstir, 7 do indis do na manchaib
gach ní dar imthigh air fen, 7 do indeis doib go rachadh an sluag
cedna sin na ndíabul 'sa mainestir do bi'san oilen dár ainm
Etica, 7 co fúigbheidís plaigh 7 galur indte, indus co fuighedh
moran do na manchaib 7 do na dainib eli do bí 'san oilen sin bas.
Agus do fíradh sin uile amhail do derbutar cuid do na manchaib
tainic as an mainestir sin fen d'indesin scel do C. C. Acus
adubairt se aris co rachdaeis na diabuil sin a cind dá lá iar sin
'sa mainestir a raibe Baithin a machairi Luighne,³⁵²) 7 co ndenadh
sesamh 7 riderecht ríu, induss nach dendaís do dith dó acht bas
do tabairt d'én-mhanach amain da coimhtinol. Agus do fíradh
sin do rér mar do indes Baithin fen do C. C. 7 da mhanchaib
iar sin.

---

[350] In Adamnan, *ibid.*, pp. 205-7.
[351] *Ephes.* VI, 13-17.
[352] *in Campo Lunge* Adamnan.

would liefer give them to wit that there was imperfectness of grace and virtue in him than that these things should bring him praise and honor. And what he were fain all should understand was that there was naught in the world without lack save Almighty God. And it misliked him to have vainglory of the gifts he gat of God.

XXV

OF THE MIRACLES OF COLUMCILLE IN IONA AND IN DIVERS PLACES

305. On another day whenas Columcille abode in Iona, he went alone to a solitary place to say his hours and his prayers and to make his devotions to God. And when he had finished his prayers he perceived an exceeding great host of devils assembling, and they making them ready for strife, bearing stakes of iron in their hands and much evil gear else. And when Columcille saw that, he girt on his armor of battle, that is to say the armor that Paul the Apostle had for sowing the Faith, to wit, Strong Faith and Stout Trust and Pure Fervent Prayers. And he went to do battle with that host of devils. And albeit they were many in number it was not possible for them to be victorious over Columcille, albeit he was alone, for the might of the armor that was about him. And he forgat not Him that had helped him in every need afore that, to wit, Almighty God; for He set round him a countless number of angels to aid him in that hour. And the fiends did no hurt to the brethren nor to the monastery nor to any else in the island from that time.

And Columcille went back then to the monastery. And he told the monks all that had befallen him. And he told them that same host of devils should go to the monastery that was in the island hight Etica, and they should leave plague there and disease, so that many of the brethren that were in that isle should die, and much folk. And all that was fulfilled, as certain of the monks bare witness that came from that monastery with tidings to Columcille.

And again he said that those devils should go within two days space to the monastery of Baithin in the plain of Luighen, and that he should make a stand and do stout service against them, so that they should do him no hurt save to slay one only of the brethren of his household. And thus it fell out, according as Baithin related to Columcille and his monks thereafter.

306.[353]) Fe*chtus* do C. C. a ní, 7 do labhair re nech airid[h]e darb ainm Colman[354] do bi a ngalur a bais an uair sin, 7 assedh adubairt, nar dimhain do cuaidh a shaethar don gabaind do bi 'sa Midhe a nErind; oír cor cendaigh se flaithes De ar saethur a lamh, 7 nach fuair sé en-ní do tarbha a cerde fén riamh, n*ach* tuc amach ar son Día e: 'Acus ataid aingli De ag br*eith* a anma leó docum nimhe anoss ar a son sin,' ar se. Gonadh mar sin do taisbenadh bas an gaband sin do bi a nErind 7 an luaídhidh*echt* fuair sé o Día ar son a deg-gnimharta do C. C. 7 é a nAlbain a n-oilen hí.

307.[355]) Fe*chtus* do C. C. a ní, 7 do ben se cluicín na caibidlech, 7 do cruindigh sé na manaigh uile faré celi, 7 do labhair ríu 7 assedh adubairt: 'As coir duínn cungnamh le hanmandaibh manach Comghaill do báithedh ar an fairge anoss,' ar se, '7 ataíd síad ag cathach*adh* ris na diabluib fá anam crisdaidhe do báitheadh ar en-slig*idh* ríu'. Do leic C. C. ar a gluínib a fiadhnaisi na haltora andsin é, 7 do chuir urn*aidh*e mileis duthr*acht*ach dochum Dia fa congnamh do t*a*b*air*t d'anmandaib na manach 'sa cathug*hadh* sin' a rabat*ar*. Et ar crichnughadh a urnaidhe dó, do eirigh da gluínibh, 7 tuc gloír 7 moladh do Día cumhachtach in a tindlaicib, 7 do indiss dá mhanchaibh fen gur (*fol.* 45b) chuir Dia móran d'ainglib nimhe do cungnamh les na hanmondaibh sin manach Comhgaill 7 do cathug*hadh* tar a cend, 7 co ruc*at*ar re celi anam an crisdaidhe sin leo go flaithess Dé; 7 adubairt C. C. gorub mogenair gá mbínd companaig maithe 'n-a diaidh sin.

308.[356]) Fechtus eli da raibe C. C. 'sa mBritaine ag dol t*ar* an sruth darb ainm Nisa, 7 do labuir ren a manchaib fen do bui faris mar do foills*igh* an Spirad Naeb dó, 7 assedh adubairt riu: 'As coir duind deithf*ir* do denamh anos,' ar se, 'a n-aircis na n-aingiul tainec a coinde anma dhuine geindtlidhi ata 'sa tir se, 7 ata síad ag fuirech rinde do coir an inaid a fuil se, 7 dob ail leo misi da baisd*edh* sul doghebadh se bas a pecadh Adaimh, 7 co mberdais a anam leo docum nimhe.' Ar crichnugh*adh* na mbriat*har* sin do C. C., do imdhigh reme mar dobeith eoluss maith aice docum an inaidh a raibe an t-ocl*aech*, 7 as demhin n*ach* raibe se and remhe sin riamh, 7 n*ach* raibe eol*us* aige and *acht* an t-eoluss do seol Día dó. Agus as aml*aidh* do bi an t-oclaech fen

---

[353]In Adamnan, *ibid.*, pp. 207-8.
[354]*Columbus* Adamnan. As a matter of fact Columbus was the name of the smith and Columcille did not speak to him but to his monks concerning him.
[355]In Adamnan, *ibid.*, pp. 213-4.
[356]In Adamnan, *ibid.*, pp. 214-15.

306. On a time whenas Columcille abode in Iona, he spake to one hight Colman that was then in sickness of death, and he told him how not in vain had been his labor for the smith that was in Meath in Erin, for the smith had bought the Kingdom of God with the labor of his hands. And naught had he got of profit from his trade but he had given it away for the sake of God. And for this cause angels of God are now bearing his soul with them to Heaven. And thus the death of that smith in Erin and the reward he gat of God for his good deeds were revealed to Columcille, and he in Alba in the island of Iona.

307. On a day whenas Columcille was in Iona, he struck the little bell of the chapter, and he brought all the monks together. And he spake to them and said in this wise:

"It beseemeth us to aid the souls of the brethren of Comgall, the which have but now been drowned in the sea," saith he, "and they are doing battle against the demons for the soul of a Christian [layman] that hath been drowned with them."

Then fell Columcille on his knees afore the altar and put forth to God a sweet fervent prayer to give aid to the souls of the brethren in their battle. And when he had finished his prayer, he rose up from his knees and he gave glory and praise to Almighty God for His gifts. And he told the brethren that God had sent many angels from Heaven to aid the monks of Comgall and to do battle for them. And together they had borne away the soul of that layman with them to the Kingdom of God. And then Columcille said that they be fortunate that do have good fellowship.

308. On another day whenas Columcille was in Britain, he was crossing a stream hight Nisa, and he spake as the Holy Spirit revealed to him, to the brethren that were with him. And he said in this wise:

"It beseemeth us now," saith he, "to hasten to the angels that come to meet the soul of a heathen of this land. And they wait for us there where he is, and they will that I baptize him ere he die in the sin of Adam, and they would bear his soul with them to Heaven."

When he had spoken these words he went forward, as one that knew well the way, to the place where the man was. And the man was

an uair sin, a richt egcruaidh 7 é a tendes a bais; 7 do senmoir
C. C. an creidemh do, 7 do gab san sin cuige co maith 7 do gab
baisdedh uada iar sin 7 fuair bás fo cédoir. Acus rucatar na
haingil tainic 'n-a coinde a anam leó docum nimhe. Acus do
fiarfaighetar a manaich fen do C. C. cred í an maith dorinde an
t-oclaech sin do bi a n-agaidh creidim conuice sin do Día an uair
nach raibe do toirmescc air fá gan a shlanughadh acht gan baisdedh do ghabail cuige. Adubairt C. C. corab í an maith nádurdha
do bí ar coimhét aicce indus nach derna sé en-ní ar duine eli
riamh budh mesde leis do denamh air fen.

309.[357]) Fechtus do C. C. ag scribneoracht in a duirrthigh
fen a nÍ, 7 tainic delradh imarchach da gnuís 7 da agaidh, 7 do
labuir do guth mór ard 7 assedh adubairt; 'ó furtacht, furtacht,
furtacht,' ar se. Acus do batar cupla manach da manchaib fen
a ndorus[358]) an duirrthighe ag estecht ris 7 ag feithem[h] an
claechlodha datha sin tainic de an uair sin .i. Colga 7 Laighnen a
n-anmonda; 7 do tuicetar corub taisbenadh tucadh do, 7 do guidhetar é imá a fhoillsiughadh doib fen. Do frecair C. C. iad 7
assedh adubairt, corub manach do condaic se ac tuitim do
mhullach tighe do bi se do cur fa dín a righacht na hErend san
inadh re n-aburtar Durmagh 7 cor íarr ar aingeal De do bi faris
dul da furtacht, 7 sul rainic an manach lár, co ruc an t-aingel
itir a dha laimh air, 7 cor leic se co min ar talmain é, gan digbail
ar bith do denam dó. Acus adubairt C. C. ren a manchaib fen
an uair sin corb ingantach an luas sin do bi is na hainglibh, .i. an
t-aingel do bi 'n-a fiadnaise fen a nÍ ag tuitim don manuch do
mullach an tighe san inadh adubramar romaind a n-Erind, breith
itir a dhá laimh air sul rainic se talamh 7 a saeradh o'n guasacht
mor sin a raibe se. Acus adubairt nar fhed se a indisin ca mhéd
budh tarbach 7 bud fogaintech do duine coimhet na n-aingel do
beith air, 7 cá mhet budh digbalach dó pecadh do denamh do
benfadh a cungnamh 7 a furtacht de.

310.[359]) Fechtus do Col. C. a n-Alpain 'san oilen ren aburthar
Imba, 7 do chuatar aithrecha naemtha o Erind ar cuairt cuige,
.i. Caindech 7 Comgall 7 Brenaind 7 Cormac. Acus ar mbreith
do shaíri an domnaigh orra, tucatar ar C. C. an t-aifrend do radha
doib. Acus do indeis Brenaind do na naemaib eli sin co bfaca se
fén nell tendtidhe ac techt os cind C. C. ag tindscnain aifrinn
dó, 7 co raibe an nell sin ar fas 7 ar bisech indus co ndernadh

---

[357]In Adamnan, *ibid.*, pp. 215-17.
[358]'in front of'.
[359]In Adamnan, *ibid.*, pp. 219-222. See § 102 for a similar story.

in this wise: in feeble state and in sickness of death. And Columcille gave him teaching in the Faith, and the man received it well. And he was baptized, and right so he died. And the angels that had come to meet him bare his soul with them to Heaven.

And the brethren inquired of Columcille what good service the man that had been against the Faith had done till that time for God, that there was naught to let his salvation save that he was without baptism. Columcille answered that he had kept a virtue natural, inasmuch as he had done naught to any that would mislike him to be done to him.

309. On a time whenas Columcille was writing in his oratory in Iona, a great light came into his countenance and his visage, and he spake with a great voice and high, and he said in this wise:

"Help! help! help!" saith he.

And twain of the brethren at the door of the oratory were listening to him, and they saw the change of hue that came upon him in that hour, to wit, Colga and Laighnen their names. And they understood that it was a vision that had been given him. And they prayed him to discover it to them. Then Columcille made answer to them and said in this wise, that he had seen a monk falling from a housetop that he was thatching in the Kingdom of Erin in the place that is called Durrow and he had asked an angel of God that was with him to go to his rescue. And ere the monk reached the ground, the angel caught him between his two hands, and let him down to earth softly, so that he suffered no hurt. Then said Columcille to his monks that marvellous was the celerity of angels, to wit, that the angel that had been with him in Iona what time the monk fell from the housetop in Erin in the place forementioned, should take him betwixt his two hands afore he reached the earth and save him from the sore peril he was in. And he said he might not tell how great was the profit and service to a man to have the ward of angels, and how great harm to do sin that cut him off from their aid and help.

310. On a time whenas Columcille abode in Alba in the island that is called Imba, there came holy fathers from Erin to sojourn with him, to wit, Cainnech, and Comgall, and Brenainn, and Cormac. And when it came the feast of the Lord's day they prevailed on Columcille to say the mass for them. Brenainn told the other saints that he beheld a cloud of fire above the head of Columcille at the beginning of the mass. And the cloud grew and waxed great, so that it made a fiery pillar

peiler tendt*idh*e de ó chend C. C. co mullach na h*e*claissi suas,
7 co raibe sé mar sin no cor c*ri*chnaig se an t-aifr*e*nd. Acus do
thuicetar na haithr*ec*ha naemtha sin corub é an Spir*a*d Na*em* do
bí sa peiler sin os cind C. C.

311.³⁶⁰) Fechtus eli do C. C. 'san oilen sin Imba, 7 do dóirt
an Spir*a*d Na*em* a grássa fen air an meide si innas co raibe sé.
tri la 7 teora haidhce 'n-a duirrth*igh* gan bíadh gan digh, 7
nar léc sé duine ar bith mar a raibe se ris an ré sin. Acus do bi an
duirrth*ech* lan do sh*o*l*us* 7 do delr*a*dh *in* a timchell, 7 an solus
ticedh t*ri*d polluib comhladh an duirrth*igh*e amach, dobeiredh
se soillse do lucht an oiléin uili *gach* n-oidhce amail (*fol.* 46a)
delr*a*dh na greíne a medhon-lai tsamr*aidh*. Acus do cuala manach
airidhe da mhanch*aibh* fen danár lecc ecla beith a fad ac éstecht ris
roind molta dorinde se do Día n*ach* closs riamh remhe sin uada
ga ngabail aicce. Et do cuireatar na manaigh techta ar cend
Baithin do bí a mainestir eli a fad uata ind*us* co fadhadh se scela
gach taisbenta da tucc*adh* do C. C. andsin ren a foillsiu*ghadh* 7
ren a scrib*adh* doibh fein; oir bad dalta 7 ba brathair geinel*aigh*
dos*om* Baithin, 7 do inds*edh* se *gach* seicr*éd* da mbidh aice dó
do ghn*ath*. Acus ní ruc Baithin orra an uair sin *no* co tainic
C. C. as in durrth*igh* 7 do innis se sc*e*la gach taisenta da tuc*adh*
dó do Baithin. Acus it*ir* *gach* ní dár indeis se dó, do indeiss co fuair
se eol*us* gach neich díamr*aigh* da raibe 'sa scribtuir, *acht* ge fuair se
eol*us* reimhe sin orra; 7 fós do indiss dó co bfuair se eolass ar a lan
do sheicreidib eli na diaghachta ar nach fuair se eolus remhe sin
riamh.

312.³⁶¹) Aroile oidhce geimhr*idh* do cuaidh nech naemtha
darb ainm Fergna docum ecla*i*si C. C. do rádh a trath 7 a urn*aidh*e,
7 do bi sé a sdella aíridhe 'sa coraidh.³⁶²) Acus nir cían dó and
an uair do c*o*nda*i*c se C. C. ac t*ech*t docum na h*e*claise 7 solus
7 delr*a*dh roimarcach gacha taeba de an meide si indus corbh
us*a* les beith ac feichemh na greíne an uair as mo a delr*a*dh 'sa
mbliadh*a*i*n* gan a shuile d'íaghadh ar a celi ina beith ac feichemh
an tsholais sin. Acus do línadh d'ecla 7 d'uamhan é, 7 do bi ga
folach fen mar as ferr gur fhet se, 7 do bí an oiret sin do nert
7 do laidir*ech*t 'sa delr*a*dh do c*o*nda*i*c Fergna an uair sin co
ndechaidh brigh 7 sbindadh a c*ui*rp uile ar cul 7 corub becc nach
deach*aidh* a spir*a*d uadha. Acus ar crichnu*ghadh* urnaidhe faide
do C. C., do cuaidh as an eclais amach, 7 do imdh*igh* an solus sin

---

³⁶⁰In Adamnan, *ibid.*, pp. 222-3.
³⁶¹In Adamnan, *ibid.*, pp. 223-5.
³⁶²*in quadam exedra, quae oratorii adhaerebat parieti* Adamnan.

from the head of Columcille to the top of the church. And it was thus until he had ended the mass. And those holy fathers understood that it was the Holy Spirit that was in that pillar above the head of Columcille.

311. On another day that Columcille was in that island of Imba, the Holy Spirit did so shed grace upon him that for three days and three nights he was in his oratory without food or drink. And he suffered none to come to him the while. And the oratory was filled with light and brightness round about. And the light that came through the holes of the door of the oratory without did enlumine each night the folk of the whole island, as it were the brightness of the sun in midst of a summer day. And a certain one of the brethren, albeit fear suffered him not to be long listening to him, did hear verses that from him were never afore heard, the which he made in praise of God.

And the monk sent messengers for Baithin that was in another monastery far from them, that he might learn the visions that were given to Columcille, touching the revealing of them, and touching writing them down. For this Baithin was his fosterling and kinsman by blood, and Columcille was wont to tell him all his secrets.

And Baithin reached them not until Columcille had come out of the oratory. And Columcille told Baithin all the visions that had been revealed to him. And among other things that he related to him, he told him that he had been given knowledge of all the mysteries of the Scriptures, of those also concerning the which he had had some knowledge afore that time. And he told him he had learned many other secrets of God concerning the which he had till then been ignorant.

312. Once also on a winter night there came a holy man hight Fergna to the church of Columcille to say his hours and his prayers. And he was in a certain stall in the choir. And he had not long been there when he beheld Columcille coming to the church. And there was light and exceeding brightness on every side of him. And so great was that brightness that it had been easier for him without closing his eyes to gaze on the sun in the time of the year that its brightness is greatest, than to gaze on that light. And he was filled with fear, and sore affrighted. And he hid him as best he might. And such was the strength and the might of the brightness that Fergna beheld in that hour, that the pith and sap of his whole body failed him, and well nigh did his spirit leave him.

And when Columcille had ended a long prayer, he went out of the church. And the light went with him. And at the coming of the day Columcille summoned Fergna to him, and he spake to him and said in this wise:

les. Acus ar te*ch*t an lai cuca, do ghair C. C. Fergna cuice 7 do
labuir ris 7 assedh adubairt: 'A mic gràdhaich,' ar se, 'as glic
a ndern*ui*s areír gan fechain an dara huair ar an tsoluss mor do
conncadhais; oir da bfechta, do dallfaidhe tú fo cedoir. Acus do
cuir fa aithne air gan an radarc sin d'indesin d'énduine eli an
céin do beith se fen 'n-a beath*aidh*. Acus do indis Fergna tar eís
bais C. C. é do shagart bud mac sethar dó darb ainm Coman. Acus
do indis an sagart sin d' Adhamhnan é.

313.³⁶³ F*ech*tus do cuaid C. C. oidhci airidhe docum na
h*ec*laisi reimhe na manch*aibh*, 7 do cuaidh manuch da manchaibh
fen darb ainm Colca 'n-a diaigh co dorus na h*ec*laise, 7 ni raibe
a fhis aice C. C. do beith reme astigh an uair sin. Acus do cond*ai*c
se an ec*lui*s uile ar n-a línadh do soillsi 7 do del*radh* imarcach.
Acus ar mbeith dó seol bec gerr ga feichemh, do ceiledh an soluss
air, 7 do impo aris maille re hecla moir da sella fen, 7 do bi ga
smuainedh 7 ga brethnug*hadh* 'n-a indtind cred í an tsoillse mor
sin do cond*ai*c se. Acus ar tec[h]t do na manch*aibh* docum an
medhoín oidhce,³⁶⁴) do goir C. C. an manach sin cuigi 7 do labuir
ris 7 assedh adubairt: 'A micc gr*ad*[h]aigh,' ar se, 'na bidh ac
scrúdadh *no* ag iarraidh na soillsi nach dingbala tú da faicsin,
7 da rabh*uir*, ni faicfe tu hí, 7 teichfedh sí romhad amail do teich
si o chíanaib romad an uair do bi tú a ndorus na h*ec*luisi.'

314.³⁶⁵) Fechtus do C. C. a mainestir aíridhe a n-Albain,
7 do labuir re nech airidhe b*udh* dalta dó fen do bidh ac denam
léighind maille ris darb ainm Berchan, 7 assedh adubairt: 'A
mic gr*a*duich,' ar se, 'na tarr anocht don tshella a mbím-se mar
ticce gach n-oidhce eli.' Gan fechain dó sin, an uair do batar na
manaich a ciun*us* san oidhce, do cuaidh Berchan co dor*us* an
tsella a raibe C. C., 7 do fech astech tr*ia* poll na comhladh, 7 do
cond*ai*c sé solass romhor 7 delradh imarcach gacha taeba de. Ar
na faicsin sin dó, do línadh d'ecla é, 7 nir fhed sé fechain an dara
huaír astech tre mhéd an del*raidh* sin, 7 do imd*igh* remhe on
tshella mailli re bidhg*adh* mor. Acus ar techt an laí cuca iar sin,
do goir C. C. Berchan cuice, 7 tucc aicept ger dó tre mar do bris
sé an aithne sin do chuir sé air 7 adubairt ris: 'Do pecaighis co
mór areir,' ar sé, 'oir do cuadhuis do scrudadh gras an Spirda
Naeimh 'san inadh nar toirmescas sa imad dul; 7 ge do saeilis
fen n*ach* faca enduine tú, do c*on*nac-sa ac te*ch*t 7 ac imth*ech*t
(*fol.* 46b) tú, 7 muna beith a luas do guidhes-a Día ar do shon,

---

³⁶³In Adamnan, *ibid.*, p. 225.
³⁶⁴Nocturns.
³⁶⁵In Adamnan, *ibid.*, p. 226.

"Beloved son," saith he, "it is wisely thou didst bear thee yesternight, not to look a second time upon the great light thou didst see, for hadst thou looked, thou hadst been blind straightway."

And he charged him to tell no man else of that sight, so long as he should be alive. And when Columcille was dead, Fergna told it to a priest hight Coman, that was his sister's son. And that priest related it to Adamnan.

313. On a certain night Columcille went to the church afore the monks. And afterward one of the brethren hight Colca went after him to the door of the church. And he knew not that Columcille was within before him. And he beheld the whole church filled with light and exceeding brightness. And when he had beheld it but for a short time, the light was hidden from him. And he returned to his cell in great dread. And he reflected and considered in his mind what was that great light he had seen. And when the brethren came to the matins, Columcille summoned to him that monk, and spake to him and said in this wise:

"Beloved son," saith he, "be not spying out and questioning the light thou art not worthy to behold. And if thou wert, yet would it flee thee as it fled a while since, when thou wast at the door of the church."

314. On a time that Columcille was in a certain monastery in Alba, he spake to one that was his foster-son that was studying with him, hight Berchan. And he said in this wise:

"Beloved son," saith he, "come not to my cell tonight as thou art wont on other nights."

But Berchan heeded not, and when the monks were at rest he went to the door of Columcille's cell, and peered in through the hole of the leaf. And he beheld a passing great light and exceeding brightness on every side of Columcille. And seeing it, he was filled with fear. And he was not able to look within a second time, for the greatness of the light. And he departed from the cell in great dread.

And when day came, Columcille summoned Berchan to him, and chid him sharply for that he had broken the commandment he had laid on him. And he said to him:

"Thou didst grievous sin yesternight," saith he, "for thou didst go spying upon the grace of the Holy Spirit in the place where I did forbid thee to go. And though thou didst deem none saw thee, yet I saw thee come and go, and were it not for the swiftness wherewith I prayed God for thee, thine eyes had fallen from thy head or thou hadst died forthwith. And I prevailed on God to give thee respite and not let the curse fall on thee."

do tuitfedh do suile as do cind nó do-gebtha bas ar in ponc úd
fen, 7 fuaras-sa o Día cairde do tabairt duit gan an t-indechadh
sin do denam[h] ort.' Ar crichnughadh na mbriathar sin adubairt
C. C. re Berchan, do labuir se co faidhemail ris na manchaibh
do bi maille ris an uair sin 7 assedh adubairt ríu. 'Rachaid an
nech-sa re rabus ag comradh costrasda .i. Berchan a n-Erind 'n-a
diaidh so, 7 do-bera se a betha co ro-olc ass maille re scandail
7 re miclu moír, 7 biaidh sé ac denamh adultrais[366]) 7 droch-
ghímartha eli co deiredh a saeghail. Gid[h]eadh chena do-geb-sa
ó Día, an meid as dalta damh fen é, co ticfidh a trocaire air,
indus co ndingna se aithrighe in a pecadh a crich a beathad, 7
co rachad a anum do caithemh na gloiri suthaine.' Acus do fíradh
sin uile amail adubairt C. C.

315.[367]) (T)innscantar andso dul C. C. a hAlbain a n-Erind
go mordail Droma Cet, airm a raibe rí Erend .i. Aedh mac
Ainmirech cethri mí 7 bliadhuin a bfoslongport co moirtinol fer
n-Erind ime itir laech 7 cleirech, ac ordughadh rechta 7 dligidh
etorra fen, 7 do coimhet Erend ar feruib Alban do bi a cogadh
riu am Dail Riada. Acus do cuid Aedhan mac Gabrain, .i. ri
Alban le C. C. a cend righ Erend, 7 do iarr sith no cairde do rig
Alban gan dul air da milledh, 7 ni tuc ri Erend cechtar aca sin
uadha. Fergaigter C. C. trid sin 7 adubairt co madh sidach
etorra, 7 co mbeith cairde co brath ac rig[h] Alpan uadha-somh
gan dul air da milledh. Do firadh an faidetóracht sin C. C.,
amail indeses an betha a n-inadh eli leth re sith do denamh itir
na rigaib sin, 7 ni dechaidh ri Erend a n-Alpain ó sin ille tre
breithir C. C. Acus ataid na roind-se gá derbudh co tainic ri
Alban leis a cend righ Erend 'sa mordhail sin Droma Cet. Et
fos corub ar a comairce tancatar na filedha indti mar an cedna :[368])

Dolotar for a laim deis   Colum, Aedhan, na hécis,
cus an comdail a m-bui Aedh   a nDruim Ceta suradh caemh.

---

[366]Adamnan has *luxuriose vivens*.
[367]See *R. C.*, XX, pp. 36 ff.
[368]See *ibid.*, p. 138.

When Columcille had said these words to Berchan, he spake by the spirit of prophecy to the brethren that were with him at that time; and he said to them:

"He to whom I have been speaking, to wit, Berchan, shall go to Erin hereafter, and he shall lead a life exceeding sinful, with ill fame and evil report. And he shall do adultery and other sins, till the last of his life. Howbeit I shall prevail on God to show mercy on him, sith he is my foster-son, so that he shall do penance for his sin at the end of his life, and his soul shall go to enjoy everlasting glory. And all that was verified as Columcille had said.

XXVI

OF COLUMCILLE'S GOING TO ERIN AND OF THE ASSEMBLY OF DRUIM CEAT

315. Here beginneth the journey of Columcille from Alba to Erin to the Assembly of Druim Ceat where the King of Erin, to wit, Aed son of Ainmire abode four months and a year encamped with a great gathering of the men of Erin, both laymen and clerics, making laws and dealing justice among them, and defending Erin against the men of Alba that were at war with them touching Dal Riada.

And Aedan son of Gabhran King of Alba went with Columcille to the King of Erin. And he asked peace or a truce for the King of Alba and begged the King of Erin not to go against him and destroy him. But the King of Erin would grant nor the one nor the other of them.

And Columcille waxed wroth thereat. And he said there should be peace between them notwithstanding, and the King of Alba should be given a lasting truce from Erin, and Erin should not go against him to destroy him.

And that prophecy of Columcille's was fulfilled, as the *Life* doth relate in another place touching the peace that was made betwixt these kings. And through the words of Columcille the King of Erin went never to Alba from that day.

And these be the verses that prove that the King of Alba came with Columcille to meet the King of Erin at that Assembly of Druim Ceat, and that the poets came under his protection there in like wise:

Ceith*r*i ri fo trí trena,   Aed[h] ainm gach fir airdsedha,³⁶⁹)
doruacht co d*r*uim naem na *n*dán³⁷⁰)   im Aedh 7 am Aedan.

Aodh f*o* a cethair fó t*ri*,   do Aedhuib an³⁷¹) a n-a*ird*r*í:*
a n-ainfe*cht* a baird na mbreth   a re ua aird Ai*n*mirech³⁷²)

Caeca n*aemh* am Col*u*m and   im dhá Ciaran, am Comgall.
Mobi, Caindech, Laisrén [b]ind,³⁷³)   dá Findén is da
                                                    [Brenaind.

Uile doib, ni trogdhal t*ra*,   a mordhail Droma Céta,
ac denam sithe, saér an dal,   it*ir* Aedh 7 Aedha*n*.

316. Is é so an t-adbur, im*orro,* fa ndechaidh C. C. a n-Erind
ar caithemh morain da aís 7 da aims*i*r a n-Albain do, do gab
cumha 7 dobron mor fir Erend 'n-a dhiaid, 7 do cuiret*ar* te*ch*ta
duthrachtacha ar a cend da iarraid cuca co mordail Droma Cet,
do bendu*ghadh* a laech 7 a clerech 7 a mban 7 a f*er* sul do facb*adh*
se an saeghal--sa; oir fa deiredh da aes 7 da aims*i*r an uair sin;
no as ar na hadburaibh-si eli do cuaid se indte amail asp*ert* an
file 'sa rand-sa:³⁷⁴)

Trí fotha f*ri*the don dail,   ar daig fuasluicthi Scandlain,
im Dail Ríada, rigdha an tres,   is am dichar na n-eces.

317. An ced adbur ar a ndechaidh C. C. a hAlbain a n-Er*ind*
go mordail Droma Cet .i. d'fhost*adh* na file*d* a nErinn, oir
do bat*ar* fir Erend oc a n-indarbadh ar a n-imad 7 ar
a ng*ere* 7 ar a ndoilge 7 ar a n-ainbreth*re*. Ee fos mar do aersad
Aedh mac Ainmirech ri Erend im set fine na rigraidhe, .i. an
delg oir bui aicce con a geim do lícc loghm*a*ir a cumdach and dia
mbó comsol*us* la 7 adh*aigh*, amail asb*ert* an file:

Batar bl*iadhain* a Clochur   do Daimhi*n*³⁷⁵) *acht* ger dochar;
gonadh ann do aersad Aedh   im an delg n-oir n-ilurchaemh.

---

³⁶⁹*ardsegda* R. C.
³⁷⁰*doruachtar druim na noeb n-an* R. C.
³⁷¹*leg.* am.
³⁷²*na dá Aed dec, aebda a ndrech,   im Aed n-ardmac nAnmerech* R. C.
³⁷³*leg.* laind 'eager' R. C.
³⁷⁴See *R. C.,* XX, p. 138.
³⁷⁵i. e. Daimin Dam-argait. See *Lis. Lives,* pp. 306-7.

> "Righthandwise went they—
> Colum, Aedan, the poets,
> To the meeting where Aed was,
> In Druim Ceat of fair heroes.
>
> Thrice four mighty kings,
> Aed the name of each high one,
> Came to holy Druim of poetry,
> Round about Aed and Aedan.
>
> Thrice four Aeds,
> Of Aeds round their High King,
> Including their judges,
> In the days of the descendants of High Ainmire.
>
> Fifty saints around Colum there,
> Around the two Ciarans and Comgall,
> Mobi, Cainnech, sweet Laisren,
> The two Finnens and the two Brendans.
>
> All those, in truth, no poor gathering,
> At the Assembly of Druim Ceat,
> Making peace, noble the cause,
> Between Aed and Aedan."

316. This is the reason, in sooth, why Columcille went to Erin, after he had spent much of his age and his time in Alba: Sorrow and exceeding longing seized the men of Erin for him, and they sent eager messengers for him to come to them to the Assembly of Druim Ceat to bless their laymen and their clerics and their women and their men, ere he should leave this world; for it was then the end of his age and his time.

Or it was for these other reasons that he went there, as the poet hath said in this quatrain:

> "Three reasons were found for the council:
> For the giving of freedom to Scannlan,
> For Dal Riada (royal encounter),
> And for the proscribing of poets."

317. The first cause wherefor Columcille did go from Alba to Erin to the great Assembly of Druim Ceat was this: to keep the poets in Erin. For the men of Erin were in point to banish them by reason of their multitude and their sharpness and their complaining, and for their evil words. And moreover because they had made satires against

318. In dara hadbur ar a ndechaidh C. C. a hAlpain, .i. do denamh sithe itir feruib Erend 7 Alban am Dail Riada; oir do batar fir Alban ga radha gor leo fen a mbu*n*adh*us*, 7 do bi sin (*fol.* 47a) 'n-a adbur imresna 7 cathaighe itir feruib Erind 7 Alpan a*cht* muna deach*aidh* C. C. do denamh sithe etorra.

319.[376]) In tres adbur ar a ndechaid C. C. a n-Erind .i. d'fhuaslagadh Scandláin moir mic Cinnfaeladh .i. mac righ Osruide, tuc a athair fen a laimh Aeda mic Ainmirech a mbraigdenass, 7 Col. C. a slanaidhe*cht* etorra fan a leicen amach a cind bliadhna 7 fa braghaid eli do gabail ar a shon. Acus mar tainec cend na bliadhna, nir lecedh Scandlan amach 7 nir gabadh braige eli uadha, 7 dorindeadh cro caelaidh[377]) gan dorus air 'n-a timchell, 7 ní raibe fuindeóg na inadh a ticf*edh* solus ar an cró sin *acht* poll becc a curthai becan d'feoil shaillte da indsaig*he* on t*ra*th go cheli, 7 ni fagadh se do digh in a diaidh sin a*cht* braen becc do lecthi as barr meoir cuice. Acus do budh mo bud metugh*adh* tarta sin na bud laghdug*hadh* *no* cosc tarta. Acus fos do bat*ar* da cuibrech decc itir glas 7 geibend 7 íarand air 'sa cro caelaigh sin, 7 do bat*ar* d*ei*ch*e*nbur 7 da XX don laechraidh dob fherr ag righ Erend a timchell an croi sin ga coimet. Acus rainic na scela sin C. C. go hÍ, 7 fa truag les, 7 do caí go mor r*e*n a cloisdin; 7 as se sin adbhur far mo a dheithfer a n-Erind.

320. Is ingnadh a radha co ndechaidh C. C. a n-Erind aris 7 gur gell se ac fagbail Er*end* dó, nach sailteoradh se uír Erend coidhce, 7 n*ach* faicfedh se a fir nó a mna coidhce, 7 nach caithf*edh* se a biadh nó a deoch go brath.

Do comaill C. C. co himlan sin; oir do bi fod d'uír na hAlpan fan a cossaib an fad do bi se a n-Erind, 7 do bi bréid cíartha t*ar* a suilib, 7 do bi a birrét ar a muin sin anúas, 7 do bi atan a cochaill tarrsa sin amuigh.[378]) Is amlaid sin nach b-faca se fir nó mna Erend mar do ghell se remhe sin am*ail* aspe*rt* an file:[379])

[376]See *ibid.*, p. 310.
[377]*leg.* caelaigh.
[378]That is a fairy tale. See Reeves' *Adam.*, pp. 23-6.
[379]See *Lis. Lives*, p. 310.

Aed son of Ainmire, King of Erin, touching the family jewel of the dynasty, to wit, the golden brooch he had, with a jewel of precious lustre set therein, that shone in the night as in the day. As the poet hath said:

> "They were a year in Clochur,
> Although it was damage to Daimin,
> And thus did they revile Aed there,
> About the gold brooch of great beauty."

318. The second cause wherefor Columcille did go from Alba was this: to make peace betwixt the men of Erin and the men of Alba, concerning Dal Riada. For the men of Alba were saying that to them belonged their foundation; and that had been a cause of strife and of battle betwixt the men of Erin and of Alba, if Columcille had not gone to make peace betwixt them.

319. The third cause wherefor Columcille did go to Erin was to release Scannlan Mor son of Cennfaeladh the son of the King of Ossory, that his father had given as a hostage to Aed son of Ainmire. And Columcille had been his surety that he would be released at the end of a year's space, and another hostage be taken in his stead. But the end of the year came and Scannlan was not released, and none other hostage was taken from the King of Ossory. And there was built around him a hut of wattles without a door. And there was nor window nor space where light might come into that hut, save a small hole wherein a little salt meat was set forth to him once daily. And of drink he gat thereafter but a small drop that was let down to him from the tip of a finger. And it did rather increase his thirst than minish or quench it. Moreover there were upon him in that hut of wattles twelve fastenings, both locks and fetters and iron, and there were ten and a score of the best heroes of the King of Erin round about that hut to guard it. And tidings of this thing came to Columcille in Alba, and he was grieved and wept exceedingly when he heard thereof. And for this cause most of all did he hasten to Erin.

320. Strange is it to tell that Columcille went again to Erin, notwithstanding he had vowed when he departed therefrom that he would not set foot upon the soil of Erin forever, nor look upon her men nor her women, nor taste her food or her drink till Doomsday. But Columcille did observe that fully, for there was a sod of the soil of Alba under his feet the while he was in Erin, and there was cere-cloth over his eyes, and his cap was over them in like wise, and the cape of his cowl was over them outside. And in this wise he beheld not man nor woman of Erin, as he had promised aforetime, according as the poet hath said:

> Ge tainic Colum Cille cain   anoir a n-ethor *tar* muir,
> ni fhaca ní a n-Er*ind* ain   iar toighect³⁸⁰) is an mordhail.

Et ruc lon bidh 7 dighe a hAlbain less ar cor nach caithead se biadh no deoch na hEirend an fad do beith se indte.

321. Ar triall do C. C. a hAlbain go mordail Droma Cet, teid ina luing, 7 do eirig peísd adbhul-mor ar an fairce do, 7 do combuaidir sí an fairce 'n-a timchell induss co raibe sí ac bathadh na luinge, 7 do tocaib si a cend as an fairce 'n-a fiadnaise, 7 do fosc*ail* sí a bel co haduathmur, 7 dob ail le an long *con* a foirind do sluc*adh* 'n-a braghaid. Gabais ecla mor muindter C. C. reme an p*éist*, 7 do íarra*tar* ar C. C. Dia do guidhe ar a son innas co fagdaeis furtacht on guasacht ro-mhór sin a rabatar. Frecruis C. C. íad 7 ass*edh* adub*airt*: 'Ní damh-sa ata a ndán f*ur*tacht d'fhagbail o Día daib aniugh,' ar se, 'acht do n*each* naemtha eli ata a n-íathuib Erend .i. Senach Sengabhai. Foillsighter an ní sin do Senuch, 7 as se inadh a raibe se an uair sin a nDoire Broscaidh os ur Locha hEirne, 7 é ag gaibnecht 'n-a cerdcha fen; oir ba sai gaband é, 7 do bi caér derg a mbel na tencuire do bi 'n-a laimh. Eirghiss Senach amach ass an cerdcha, 7 tuc urcor uadha don chaeir gor ben a mbel na piasda sin do bi ag bathud luinge C. C., gor marb a cedoir hí. Guidhiss C. C. Dia fa marb na pesde do chur cuige 'san inadh a tiucf*adh* a long a tír a n-Erind. Fuair C. C. an pesd marb iar sin reme ar tr*aig*h Locha Febuil, 7 do furail se a scolt*adh* 7 an caer sin adubramar romainn do búain esde 7 cuiris docum Senaich aris í. Acus dorinne Senach tr*i* cluic di .i. an Glu*n*an Senaigh 7 Gerr an Curuigh 7 an cloc tucc se do Naaile naemtha;³⁸¹) gor moradh ainm De 7 C. C. 7 Seanaich Sengabha de sin.

322. Do leic C. C. a long ar siubal as in loch sin tres in abuind tic as an loch re n-abur*tar* an Roa aniugh, 7 ni snaidhf*edh* long ele ar bith an aband sin fen o laighet a huisce 7 tre med a tanaige, muna snaidhed[h] long C. C. í tre grassaib Deí a*cus* tre mirbuilibh C. Ċ. fen.. Et fos, ni hedh amain do snaí si an abond sin, *acht* do snai sí mile nó a dó do tir o an abuind amail dobeith sí ac siubhal mara no fhairge da mbeith gaeth ger in a diaigh no gur gab comnaidhe do coir an in (*fol.* 47b) aidh re n-abur*tar* Druim

---

³⁸⁰*leg.* toidhect.
³⁸¹See § 141 *supra*.

> "Though fair Columcille did come
> From the east in a boat overseas,
> He beheld naught in noble Erin
> After coming into the great Assembly."

And he brought with him from Alba sufficient of food and of drink so that he ate not of the food nor of the drink of Erin the while he abode there.

321. When Columcille had set forth from Alba to the Assembly of Druim Ceat and had entered into his boat, an exceeding terrible monster rose up on the sea. And she stirred up the sea round about her so that she was sinking the boat. And she raised her head out of the sea afore him, and opened her mouth in fearsome wise, and fain had she swallowed the boat with its crew into her gullet. And the household of Columcille were seized with great fear afore the beast. And they called upon Columcille to pray God for them that they might get help out of the exceeding peril whereas they were. Columcille answered them and said in this wise:

"It is not for me to get help from God for you today," saith he, "but for another holy man that is in the land of Erin, to wit, Senach the old smith."

And this thing was made known to Senach. And the place where he was at that time was Doire Broscaidh on the brink of Loch Erne, at work at his forge. For he was a master smith. And there was red hot iron in the mouth of the tongs in his hand. And Senach left the forge and hurled the iron mass so that it entered the mouth of the monster that was sinking the boat of Columcille, and killed her forthwith.

Columcille prayed God to send the dead corpse of the beast to the place where his boat should come in Erin. And later he found it dead before him on the strand of Loch Foyle. And he bade it be split open and the iron mass we have aforementioned to be cut therefrom. And he sent it to Senach again, and Senach made three bells therefrom, to wit, the Glunan Senaigh, and Gerr an Curuigh, and the bell he gave to holy Naaile. And God's name and Columcille's and the name of Senach the old smith were magnified thereby.

322. Then Columcille let sail his boat out of that lake through the river that flowed therefrom yclept the Roa today. And no boat else might sail that river for the shallowness of its water and for its narrowness, save the boat of Columcille should sail it through the graces of God and the miracles of Columcille.

And not only did it sail that river, but it sailed a mile or twain of land from the river, as it were sailing the sea or main with a sharp wind

Cet, airm a raibe mordail b-fer n-Erend 7 Alban an uarr sin.
*Co*nadh Cabhan an Curuig ainm an inaidh sin inar gab in long
comnaidhe ó sin alle. Acus bendaighiss an t-inadh sin, 7 adubairt
comad andsin bud coir tossach oilethri an baile sin do denamh
co brath arís, gebe nech dogenad[h] oilithri and. Ticc C. C. remh*e*
iar sin docum na mordala in a raibe ri Erend. Mar do cual*aidh*
Aed mac Ainmirech, .i. rí Erend C. C. do beith ac dul d'indsaighe
na mordala, nir maith les a dul 'n-a cend; oir do bí fis na n-adbhur
fa raibe se ag dul 'n-a cend aige, 7 adubairt se re n-a sluagh, gebe
acu doberadh cadhuss no onoír do C. C., go cuirfedh se docum bais
é nó co mbenfadh a tigher*nus* de.

323. Do chuaid[h] C. C. d'indsaighe na mordala andsin, 7
as se lín cleirech do bi se,³⁸²) .i. uiret a ndechaidh leis a hErind
do clerchib .i. xx espog 7 da xx sagart 7 deich ndeochain xx, 7
dechenbur 7 da xx do maccuib leghind mar adubrum*ar* rom-
haind.³⁸³)

324.³⁸⁴) Is siad fo nessa do is an mordhail .i. Conall mac
Aeda, mic Ainmirech, gon a mhundt*ir*(sic), 7 fa mac dingbala don
righ 7 don rigain é, 7 fa hadbhur righ Erend gan imresain c*us* an
la sin é. Acus mar do condaic se C. C. d'indsaighe an oire*ch*tu*is*,
do greiss se daescursluagh a*cus* droch-daine a muindt*i*re a n-
ag*aidh* C. C. 7 a clerech, 7 do gabatar ga lecadh le cloch*aibh* 7 re
foidib an talman, indus cor lecatar moran do muindtir C. C., 7 do
léc an daescurs*luagh* gair mhór doib gá leccadh.

325. Is andsin do fiarf*aigh* C. C. da muindtir: 'Cia lécess
na gairthe fanamhaid-si fuinn *no* cia d'f*e*raib Erend do-beir an
esonoir se duind.' Do hindiss*edh* dó g*ur*b é Conall mac Aedha
mic Ainmirech .i. mac rig Erend do bi ag tabairt na hesonára
sin dó.

326. Is andsin do mallaigh C. C. Conall, 7 tuc se ar a mhuindt*ir* a cluic 7 a ceola*n* do buain a n-e*n*f*echt* d'escaine Conaill.
Gonadh uime sin aderar Conall clogach ris. Acus do ben se
rigacht 7 tigernus Erend de, 7 dorinde se oinmid gan cheill gan
cuimhne de, acht an fad do beith se ar an fialtech amhain. Gonadh
and dorinde an rann-sa:

Benaidh bur cluic ar Conall   doní aindlig*he* oraind;
corub oin*m*id 's narub ri,   co ndech*aidh* a brigh a ndeimb*ri*gh.

---

³⁸²A peculiar construction. Cf. § 157 *agus ba he so a lín*.
³⁸³See *R. C.*, XX, p. 38.
³⁸⁴See *ibid.*, pp. 426-7.

in its wake, until it abode in the place hight Druim Ceat, where was the great assembly of the men of Erin and Alba at that time. And thus the Field of the Coracle is the name to this day of the spot where the boat abode. And he blessed that place and said that it would be right for that spot to be the starting place of pilgrimage till Doomsday for all that should make there a pilgrimage.

Then Columcille came to the great assembly where was the King of Erin. And when Aed mac Ainmirech, to wit, the King of Erin, did hear that Columcille was on his way to the great assembly, he was loth to go to meet him, for he knew the reasons of his coming to him. And he charged the men of his host that whoso should show friendship or honor to Columcille, he would put him to death or take from him his domain.

323. Then went Columcille to the assembly, and this was the number of his clerics, to wit, the number that had gone with him to Erin, to wit, twenty bishops and two score priests, and ten and twenty deacons, and ten and two score sons of learning, as we have aforementioned.

324. And these were they that were nearest to him in the great assembly, to wit, Conall mac Aed son of Ainmire and his household. And this Conall was a worshipful son of the King and Queen. And he had been the makings of a king of Erin without contention till that day. And when he saw Columcille drawing nigh the assembly, he stirred up the rabble and evil folk of his household against Columcille and his clerics. And they took to pelting them with stones and sods of the earth, so that they felled many of Columcille's household. And the rabble gave a great shout as they struck them down.

325. And thereat did Columcille inquire of his folk: "Who is it that doth hoot and jeer at us, or who of the men of Erin doth us this dishonor?"

And he was told that it was Conall mac Aed son of Ainmire, which is to say the son of the King of Erin, that was doing him this dishonor.

326. Then it was that Columcille cursed Conall. And he bade his household strike their bells and their little bells all together, cursing Conall. And for this he is called Conall of the Bells. And Columcille cut him off from the kingship and dominion of Erin, and he made him a fool without wit or memory save only so long as he should be in the privy. And it was then he made this quatrain:

> "Strike ye your bells against Conall
> That hath done against us injustice;
> That he be a fool, not a king,
> That his strength may turn into weakness."

327.³⁸⁵) Is andsin rainic C. C. mar a raibe Domnall mac Aedha mic Ainmirech 'san oirechtass, 7 do erich Domnall remhe, 7 tuc pócc dó, 7 do fer failte ris, 7 do cuir 'n-a suide 'n-a inad fen e. Acus do bendaigh C. C. Domnall andsin, 7 do fagaibh buadha imgha air, 7 do gell se do a beith *deich* mbliadhna xx a rigacht Erend,³⁸⁶) 7 buaidh catha do breith ar a naimhd*ibh* an fad sin, 7 beith bliadhuin go leith dó a ngalur a bais, 7 corp Crist do caithem gacha domhnaig ar fedh a esslainte, 7 bas d'faghail aine an cesda, 7 a anam do dul a flaithes De.

328. Rainic Domnall a less an bendug*hadh* sin C. C.; oir do bi se ar meth *con*uice sin, 7 an banrig*an* ag cur a m*ic* fen oss a cind .i. an Conall sin do esscain C. C., oír nir isse máth*air* Domhnaill.

329. Is andsin do hindiss*edh* don righain 7 í a n-oirec*htus* ar leith tamall ó an inadh a raibe an ri 7 righna Erend 'n-a timchell, a mac fen do escaine 7 do mallug*hadh* 7 Domhnall do bendug*hadh*. Do cuir an rig*an* a hinailt a cend righ Erend da radha ris da bfaghadh an corr-clerech sin .i. C. C. cadhus no onoir uadha, n*ach* beith sí fen reidh ris coidhce. Do cuala C. C. sin, 7 do ghab f*erc* e, 7 adubairt: 'An masla sin tucc an righan d*am*-sa,' ar se, '.i. mo samhlug*hadh* re cuirr, as ced lem-sa isse do beith 'n-a cuirr ar an ath-sa this go brath.' Acus dorindedh corr don righ*ain* re breithir C. C. ar in pongc sin fen.

330. Do bi indailt na righna ag aithissiug*hadh* an cleirigh go mór imón ní sin 7 ga samlug*hadh* re cuirr mar an cedna, 7 adubairt C. C. cor ched leis isi do beith 'n-a cuirr a coimhide*cht* a baintig*her*na. Acus dorindedh corr don innailt andsin, 7 do ergheatar in da chuirr a n-airde a fiadhnaise fer n-Erend. Acus ar ndenamh gresi eitell*aige* doib, do luighetar ar an ath lethtis dib, 7 ataid in dá cuirr sin a nDruim, Cet o sin alle a comartha na mirb*ul* sin, amail aspert an file:³⁸⁷)

A hi*n*ailt as be*n* Aedh[a] laiter a corraibh léna:
ma*ir*id fos, don*í*ad cneta, a nD*ru*im Ceta g*an* tshéna.

331. Is andsin do íarr C. C. Domnall les a cend righ Erend, 7 (*fol.* 48a) do bi ecla ar Domnall fa dul a cend an righ, 7 adubairt C. C. na budh eccail dó en-ní, 7 co mbeith an Spir*ad*

---

³⁸⁵See *Lis. Lives,* p. 311.

³⁸⁶10 years according to *YBL*, col. 68². See *R. C.,* XX, p. 427. According to *A. U.,* he reigned from 628-42 A. D.

³⁸⁷See *R. C.,* XX, p. 40; *Lis. Lives,* p. 312.

327. Then Columcille came before Domnall mac Aed son of Ainmire in the assembly. And Domnall rose up afore him and kissed him, and bade him welcome, and made him sit in his own place. And Columcille blessed Domnall then, and left upon him a multitude of virtues, and promised him that he should be thirty years in the kingship of Erin and all that while be victorious over his enemies in battle, and that he should be for a year and a half in the sickness of death, and partake of the body of Christ each Sunday throughout his illness, and die on Good Friday, and his soul go to the Kingdom of God.

328. And Domnall had need of that blessing, for he had been a coward till that time. And the Queen had put her own son over his head, to wit, that Conall the which Columcille had cursed. For it was not she that was mother to Domnall.

329. Then it was told the Queen, whereas she abode in a group somewhat apart from the King, with the queens of Erin round about her, that curses and malisons had been laid on her son, and that Domnall had been given the blessing. And she sent her handmaid to the King of Erin to tell him that if that crane-cleric Columcille should receive friendship or honor from him, she would never be accorded with him again.

When Columcille heard this he waxed passing wroth and said:

"For the disworship the Queen hath put on me," saith he, "to wit, for likening me to a crane, I suffer her to be a crane at this ford below forever."

And by the word of Columcille the Queen was made a crane forthwith.

330. Now the handmaid of the Queen did upbraid the cleric exceedingly for this thing, and she also did liken him to a crane. And Columcille said that he did suffer her to be a crane in the fellowship of the Queen. And the handmaid was made a crane then. And the two cranes rose up in the sight of the men of Erin. And when they had been for a space flying, they alit on the ford below. And those two cranes are in Druim Ceat to this day in sign of that miracle, as the poet saith:

> "Aed's wife and her handmaid,
> Are changed into marsh-cranes.
> They still remain; they give groans
> In Druim Ceat without denial."

331. Then Columcille asked Domnall to go with him to the King of Erin, and Domnall feared to go. And Columcille bade him have no fear and the Holy Spirit would be his guard. Then he went

Naemh ga coimhet. Do cuat*ar* iar sin d'acall*adh* an righ, 7 do
gab ecla mor an ri re faicsin C. C. cuige, 7 tr*í*t na mirbuil*ibh*
mora dorinde sé reme sin 'san oire*ch*t*us*, 7 do éirigh an ri reime,
7 do f*er* failte fris. IS andsin adubairt C. C. n*ach* gebad se an
5 failte sin on righ muna faghadh se a breth fen uadha. Acus do
gell an r*i* sin dó.

332. 'Is hí breth beirim-se,—na filedha d'fosd*adh* a n-
Erind,' ar C. C. 'Ni hurassa lind a bfost*adh*,' ar an ri; 'oir is
mór 7 as imorcach iad, 7 as doi*lig* a frest*ul* re met a n-ainbreth.'
10 'Na hapuir sin,' ar C. C.; 'oir as buan 7 as marthanach na molta
do-ge*n*aid duit, mar as marthanach do Cormac mac Airt mic
Cuind na molta dorinde*tar* na file*dh*a do; uair mairid na molta
7 ní mairit na seoit *no* na ma*í*ne tuc*adh* ar a son.' Gonadh andsin
dorinde se an rosca-sa dana hainm an "Dublaidh" .i.

15 Cormac cain buich neoid, núa a molta, crín a seoid, 7
re*liqua*.³⁸⁸ 'Et as mar sin teicemhass duid-se a ri,' ar C. C.,
'mairf*idh* na molta do-gent*ar* duit do cend na filedh d'fost*adh*
a n-Erind, 7 ní mairf*idh* do maine t*ar* heis. Et bidh a fiss acat
nach beith an náire *no* an feile is na dainib muna beith daíne aca
20 da tiubraidís ní d'ecla a cai*n*te *no* a n-aertha mar ataid na file*dh*a;
mar nach beith trocaire no dérc and muna faghtai daíne bo*ch*ta
ar a ndingantaí trocuiri 7 da dtiubarthai d*erc* ar son De.' Gonadh
and dorinde an rand sa:

Ni beith d*erc* mun beith bo*ch*ta,   clamha tr*u*agha ta*rr*nochta;
25 ni beith feile tiar *no* toir   mun beith écse ag athcuingidh.

'Et fos bid a fiss agat gor cendaigh Dia fen t*ri caog*a salm molta
o Dáuith ri;' 7 dorinde na roind-se:

---

³⁸⁸See *R. C.*, XX, p. 44; *Lis. Lives*, p. 312; *Irish Liber Hym.*, I, p. 163.

to speak with the King. And the King was sore afeared when he beheld Columcille coming toward him, by reason of the great miracles that he had already done in the assembly. And he rose up afore him and bade him welcome. Then Columcille said he would not take that welcome save he get his own judgment from the King. And the King promised him this.

XXVII
OF COLUMCILLE AND THE POETS OF ERIN

332. "It is this, the judgment that I give, that the poets be kept in Erin," saith Columcille.

"It is no easy thing to keep them," saith the King, "for they are much folk and numerous, and it is hard to serve them, owing to the multitude of their unjust demands."

"Say not so," saith Columcille, "for lasting and enduring will be the praises they will make for thee, even as the praises they made for Cormac mac Airt, son of Conn; for the praises endure, and the treasure and riches that are given for them perish."

So he made this little poem that is called the *Dublaidh*, to wit:

> "Cormac of courtesy did conquer avarice.
> Fresh are his praises, withered his wealth."

et reliqua.

"And in like manner shall it be with thee, O King," saith Columcille, "the praises will live that shall be made for thee by reason of keeping the poets in Erin. But thy riches will not live after thee. And wit thou well folk would have no shame nor any largesse except they had those like unto the poets unto whom to give largesse for fear of their reviling and their scoffing verses, even as there would be no charity or almsgiving save there be found poor folk unto whom to do charity and give alms for God's sake."

And so he made this quatrain:

> "There were no alms if there were no poor folk,
> Lepers stark-naked and wretched;
> There were no largesse, westward nor eastward,
> If there were no poets making petitions."

Do cendaigh Dia fen go fír   tri caoga salm a Dauíth;
tuc dó rath ar talmain tigh,   as nemh da anmain ainglidh,

Nir diult Dia re dreich nduine   an fad do bi ar bith buidhe;
nir diultsatar 'n-a diaidh sin   a espoil no a desscipuil.

5   Nir diult Patraig puirt na clar,   nir diult Comgall no Ciaran,
ni diultus fen, ní saeb sin,   nir diult naem do na naemhaib.

Géin mairfes an diaghacht glan,   acus an daendacht idhan,
mairfidh an dérc dlightech   is an feile firdlightech.

Nir scribadh a lebraibh sin,   's nir ordaich canoin cubaidh,
10 go mbadh e budh naemhadh do nech   beith gan fheli, gan
            [einech.

'Et ar in adbur sin, as coir duit-se duana na filedh do cendach
7 íad fen d'fosdadh a n-Erind, 7 o nach fuil acht brecc 'sa saegal
uile, as diless duit-se an brec as buaine do cendach ar an mbreic
15 as dimbuaine.' Acus dorinde na roind-se:

"And wit thou also that God himself did buy thrice fifty psalms of praise from King David."

And he made these quatrains:

"Even God in truth made purchase,
Thrice fifty psalms he bought from David;
Gave him fortune in earth's dwelling,
To his Heaven-born soul gave Heaven.

God refused not human visage
Whilst he dwelt on earth the fruitful,
Nor did they refuse aught after,
His apostles or disciples.

Door nor board denied not Padraic;
Comgall, Ciaran withsaid nothing.
Nor have I denied,—no falsehood—
Nor hath saint to saint denied aught.

Whilst endureth still clean god-hood,
Whilst endureth still clean man-hood,
Righteous largesse shall continue,
Entertainment truly righteous.

Not in books hath it been written,
Nor have holy canons ruled it
That a man should be made holy,
Without bounty, without largesse."

And for this cause it were right for thee to buy the poems of the poets and to keep the poets in Erin. And sith all the world is but a fable, it were well for thee to buy the more abiding fable, rather than the fable that is less enduring."

And he made these quatrains:

"If poets' verses be but fables,
So be food and garments fables;
So is all the world a fable;
So is man of dust a fable.

For the fable more enduring
I shall give the one more transient;
With me in the grave shall not be
Blue nor red nor green the lovely.

God hath not made one of mankind,
Of the seed of fair-haired Adam,

Masa brec gach dan suad,   is brec brat 's as brec biadh,
's as brec an domhan uli,   's as brec fos an duinecriadh.

Do cend na breice as buaine   do-ber brec as dimbuaine;
ni bía leam cum na huaidhe   gorm no derg no deghuaine.

5 Nocha derna Dia duine   do sil Aduim foltbuidhe,
gan cerd ndaenna re dil bfir   no gan cerd ndiagha n-idhain.

Gach saer, gach gaba, gach cerd,   is gach liaigh luchair
[laimderg,
no ar ordaig Dia dil   a cerd d'fagbail a n-aiscid?

10   333. 'Ni ba mesi cuirfes a hErind iat festa,' ar in ri. Acus
do fostadh na filedha a n-Erind andsin ar comairli C. C.; 7 do
reidigh se etorra 7 fir Erend, 7 do ben a neimh don dan amail
aspert se fen sa rand-sa:

Benfad a nemh don dan   a nDruim Ceta na comdhal,
15 's cuirfed aicnedh na cliar   ag radh maithessa ar aenrían.

Oir do marbdais na daine lé a n-aeradh conuice sin, no do fássadh
bithainimh for a ngnuisib 7 for a n-aithchibh. Acus do cum
C. C. cert 7 dlige airide ar feruib Erend doib .i. ollamh gacha
tuaithe do coimet a ngenelaigh 7 a craeb coibnesa d'ecla a n-uaisli
20 7 a folaidecht do dul a mbathadh, amail aspert an file 'sa rand-
sa:[389])

Do saertha de na filedha   tre Colum an caimhdlighe;
file gach tuaithe, ni trom,   ise do ordaich Colam.

Et ní tuc se a ched d'file tuaithe eli a n-Erind dul d'iarruid
25 spreidhe no airnési a tuaith eli, no dán do denamh do tigherna
thuaithe ele gan ched dó fen; 7 dá madh chead les é dá denamh
dána do, a file fen do cur go hor criche in a coinde; 7 dá moladh
a dán a cenduch uadh, 7 muna moladh gan techt tairis sin acht
clodh dá tir fen. Et tuc a bendacht doib sen fa fuirech air sin, 7
30 tuc a bendacht d'fheruib Erend fán a comhall doib. Acus do
scaeil C. C. na filedha fó Erind iar sin, 7 nir leic doib beith ar en
slighidh o sin amach.

[389]See R. C., XX, p. 138.

> Without craft of man to fill him,
> Or of God a craft, a pure one.
>
> Wright and smith and every craftsman
> . . . .[1]
>
> Or hath then dear God ordained it,
> That their crafts should go for nothing?"

333. "It shall not be I that will banish them from Erin from this time," saith the King.

And the poets were suffered to remain in Erin by the counsel of Columcille. And he gave judgment between them and the men of Erin. And from their poetry he did take out the venom, as he hath said himself in this quatrain:

> "I shall take their sting from poems
> In Druim Ceat of the Assemblies;
> I shall set the minds of poets
> Saying goodness in one fashion."

For until that time they had been wont to do folk to death with their satire. Or there had sprung forth blisters upon their faces and their visages. And Columcille did lay a just and certain law upon the men of Erin concerning them, to wit, a chief bard of each tribe to keep its lineage and its ancestry lest the nobleness of its blood decay, as the poet hath said in this quatrain:

> "Thus the poets were delivered
> Through Colum the gentle law-giver,
> For each tribe a poet. Not heavy
> Was this that Colum ordained them."

And he suffered not the bard of one tribe in Erin to go into another tribe in quest of wealth or goods, nor to make a poem for a lord of another tribe without his leave. And if he should suffer him to make the poem for him, he should send forth his own bard to the border of his land to meet him. And if his own bard praised the poem, he should buy it from the other. And if he praised it not, the other should go back to his own land.

And Columcille gave the poets his blessing sith that they remained on those conditions, and he gave his blessing to the men of Erin sith that they fulfilled them. And then he sent forth the poets over Erin, and he suffered them not to be in one place from that time.

[1] And every bright red-handed leech. (?)

334. Mar do fost*adh* na filedha, 7 mar do reidigh C. C. (*fol.* 48b) eatorra 7 fir Erend, tucat*ar* duan gacha filedh 7 gacha hollaman aca leo do moludh C. C., 7 mar do cuala sesean na clíara uile ga adhmolad a n-enfhecht, tainic m[e]d menman 7 aicenta do indus gor linadh an t-aiér do droch-spir*adu*ib os a chind les sin. Acus do foillsig*hedh* sin do nech naemtha do bi maille ris darb ainm Bathin, 7 tuc se achmh*u*san trom do C. C., 7 adubairt se ris gor chóra dó a aire do tab*air*t do breithemhnus De ina don moludh saegalta sin; 7 do indeis se dó go raibe an t-aier lan do demnaib os a cend.

335. Is andsin do chuir C. C. a cend fan a choim 7 do cai go mór, 7 dorinde aithr*ighe* ger, 7 do thocuib a chend on a coim, 7 do eirigh detach mor da cend tr*í*t na cumhdaigt*ib* imdha do bi air, 7 do scáeil an detach sin a raibe do demhnaib os a cind san aiér. Acus do cond*aic* a raibe 'sa mordail sin, it*ir* laech 7 clerech, indam*ail*[390]) duin*e* a ndeilb ro-gr*a*nna ac tuitim in a fiadnaise as an aieór. Acus do bi se tamall a nell t*ar* eis tuitme do, 7 do eirig se iar sin, 7 tuc*adh* a fiadhnaise C. C. 7 righ Erend é 7 do fiarfuidhed[h] scela de. 'Sagart said*bhir* do cinel Conaill me,' ar se, '7 do cumdaig*edh* ecluss lium 7 do cuir me lecca loghmara 7 altóra gloinidhe san ecluis sin, 7 tuc me fo dera delb greine 7 esca do cur indte, 7 do gab dimus 7 med menman me trid sin, indus co tancatar na demhna cugam 7 gor tocbatar leo san aier a n-airde mhe, 7 ataim blia*dhain* 'com pia*n*udh aca mar s*i*n tre mo dímuss. Et an uair, u*morro*, dorinde C. C. an urnuidhe ud 7 do tocuib se a cend on a choim, do scaeilf*edh* an deth*ach* do erich da cenn an uair sin abfuil do demhnaib a n-ifrend dá mbeidís os a cend; 7 ger mor a raibe and, do scaeil sí íad, 7 do lecet*ar* mesi amach; oir nirb eídir leo mo congbail o do ch*uaidh* deth*ach* cin*d* C. C. futh*a*.' C*on*ad[h] da dherbadh sin adbert an file na ra[i]nd-sa:[391])

Mor a ferta an clerich caidh,   a nDruim Ceta 'sa mordhail,
deth*ach* a cind iar cr*a*budh,   dorad demhna a n-imgab*udh*.

Do bi an sagart, as derb de,   ria tuitim'n-a fiadhn*aise*,
bl*iadhain* ga pianadh, ni cel, itir diabl*uibh* an aiér.

---

[390]See §§ 355, 392 *infra* for the same word.
[391]See *R. C.*, XX, p. 42; *ibid.*, p. 428; Dinneen's *Keating*, III, p. 106.

334. When the poets had been suffered to remain, and when Columcille had given judgment between them and the men of Erin, each poet of them and each professor made a poem in praise of Columcille. And when he heard all the poets praising him in unison, there came upon him such exaltation of mind and heart, that the air above him was filled with evil spirits. And this was revealed to a certain holy man of his fellowship yclept Baithin, and he rebuked Columcille sharply, and said it were more fitting for him to give heed to the judgment of God than to worldly praise. And he told him that the air above him was filled with demons.

335. Then Columcille covered his head and wept sore. And he had sharp sorrow for his sin. And when he lifted his head from its cover, a great smoke rose up from his head through the many wrappings that were thereon. And that smoke did scatter the demons that were in the air above his head.

And those that were in the Assembly, both lay and cleric, did see fall out of the air before them a hideous semblance, as it were a man's. And it was a while in a cloud of smoke when it had fallen. And then it rose up. And it was brought before Columcille and the King of Erin. And they asked tidings of him.

"A rich priest I was, of the race of Conall," saith he, "and I built me a church and put therein precious colors and crystal altars, and I let put therein the form of the sun and the moon. And pride possessed me and vainglory by reason thereof, so that demons came to me and bare me with them into the upper air, and for a year's space I am in pain from them thus through my pride. Howbeit, when Columcille made that prayer and lifted his head from out its cover, the smoke that did rise up from his head in that hour had might to scatter all the demons of Hell above him. And albeit many they were that were there, natheless did it scatter them, and they let me from them, for they might not detain me what time the smoke from the head of Columcille came under them. And in proof thereof the poet hath made this quatrain:

> "Mighty his deeds, the chaste cleric's,
> In Druim Ceat in the Assembly.
> The smoke from his head after praying
> Did cause consternation to demons.
>
> The priest, it was manifest therefrom,
> Ere his falling there in their presence,
> Was a year in torment, I hide not,
> Mid demons above, of the welkin."

Do bendaigh C. C. an sagart iar sin, 7 ba hoclaech maith do Día 7 do C. C. é o sin amach.

336.³⁹²) Is andsin ro fiarfaigh cach do Dallán Forcaill .i. d'ard-ollamh na hErend, an raibe moladh aicce do C. C. Adubairt Dallan go raibe, 7 do tindscain se C. C. do mholadh. Adubairt C. C. re Dallan gan a moladh an fad do beith se 'n-a bethaidh, 7 cor ced les é da moladh a ndiaidh a bais. 'Tabuir-se dam-sa an uair ata tu ad bethaidh luach an molta,' ar Dallan, 'oir is ferr lim a íarraidh ort anoss no tar éis do bais.' 'Dogebha tu ba 7 capuill, ór 7 airget,' ar C. C. 'Ni geb,' ar Dallan; 'oir do-geb-sa sin o rigaib 7 o taissechaibh 7 o ard-mhaithibh Erend ar son a molta.' 'Do-ber-sa flaithes De duit,' ar C. C. 'Ni geb-sa sin uaid,' ar Dallan; 'oir ni furail lium flaithess De d'fagail ar mo deghgnimhartha fen.' 'Berad-sa anam a flaithess duit a n-agaidh an ruainde da fuil ad brat,' ar C. C. 'Ni geb,' ar Dallan. 'Do-ber-sa duit cill d'ainmniughadh uaid 7 nemh da gachaen adluicfidher indte,' ar C. C. 'Ni geb,' ar Dallan. 'Do-ber-sa nem dá gach aen mebreochuss an moladh,' ar C. C. 'Gebhat-sa sin,' ar an dall. 'As amhra an luach,' ar Baithin. 'Badh amra don ainm an molta,' ar C. C. Gonadh "Amhra" ainm an molta o sin alle. 'Ni fhuil andsin,' ar Baithin, 'acht dá nderna duine gach uile olc 7 mebruighedh se an moladh sa, go tibartai nemh do.' 'Olc sin a Baithin,' ar C. C., 'ni ba teirce ba maela odhra ina duine ga mbía an moladh ut; 7 gebe duine as demin do dam do damnadh, ni fedfa se a mebrughadh mar bus coir .i. con a ceill 7 gon a tuicsin.'

337. Et as minec do derbadh so; oir do mebraigh clerech uisce Arda Macha an ced leth don moladh-sa, 7 dobi dá olcus fen nar fet se an leath deigenach de do mebrughadh, 7 fos do troisc se ar tumba C. C. fan leith degenaich don "Amhra" do beith aice.

---

³⁹²See *R. C.*, XX, p. 134 ff.

Then Columcille blessed the priest, and he was a good servant to God and to Columcille from that time.

336. Then it was that all asked Dallan Forgaill, to wit, the High-bard of Erin, if he had praise for Columcille. And Dallan answered that he had. And he set to praising him.

But Columcille said to him that he should not praise him so long as he was living; howbeit he would suffer him to make praises for him after his death.

"But give to me the reward for the praise now while thou dost live," saith Dallan, "for I would liefer ask it of thee now than after thy death."

"Thou shalt have kine and horses, gold, and silver," saith Columcille.

"Such reward I will not have of thee," saith Dallan, "for I may have that from the kings and chieftans and nobles of Erin, in return for praising them," saith Dallan.

"I will give thee the Kingdom of God," saith Columcille.

"That reward I will not have of thee," saith Dallan, "for I must needs get me the Kingdom of God by mine own good deeds."

"I will bear a soul to Heaven for thee for every thread in thy cloak," saith Columcille.

"That reward I will not have of thee," saith Dallan.

"I will give thee a church to be called after thee, and Heaven to all that shall be buried therein," saith Columcille.

"That reward I will not have," saith Dallan.

"I will give Heaven to everyone that doth memorize the praise."

"That reward I will take," saith the blind man.

"The reward is a strange one," saith Baithin.

"Strange (*Amhra*) shall be the name of the praise," saith Columcille. And thus *Amhra* (*Strange*) is the name of that praise from that time

"This is naught save [to say] that if a man do every evil, yet hold in remembrance this praise, he will gain Heaven therefor," saith Baithin.

"That were an ill thing, O Baithin," saith Columcille. "[But] bald dun cows will not be scarcer than folk that can keep that praise in remembrance. And one that I know for a surety to be damned will not be able to hold it in memory duly, that is to say, with its sense and its signification."

337. And oft hath this been proved; for the water-clerk of Armagh did put in remembrance the first half of that praise. And such was his sinfulness that he could not put in remembrance the last half thereof. And he did fast at the tomb of Columcille for to have

Tuc C. C. sin do, oir adub*air*t se an leath degenach di do mebuir ar
maidin, 7 do ch*uaidh* an c*ed* leath do bi aige uadha, o nar tuill a
degh-gnimhart[h]a o Día a slanug*hadh,* 7 o nar guidh se C. C.
fan a cuimniug*hadh* dó re celi.

338.³⁹³) Is andsin adub*air*t Dallan Forcaill: 'Cind*us* do
b*eith* a fhiss agam-sa an uair do-gebtha-sa bas 7 tú a n-Albain 7
mesi a n-Erind?' 'Do-ber-sa com*ar*ta duid,' ar Col. C. .i. amarc
do tect duid an fad bias tú ag denamh an molta'; oir ni facaidh
Dallan en-ní reme sin riam. 'Comarta eli,' ol an dall. 'Do-bert*ar*,'
ol C. C.; 'oir benf*aidh*er an t-amharc ut dit an uair as mithigh
le Dia tu do cur criche ar an (*fol.* 49a) moladh.' 'Comartha eli,'
ar an dall. 'Do-berim,' ar C. C. .i. 'marcach eich bric d'indesin mo
bais duit ar maidin dia mairt 7 an ced focul adera sé, budh é sin
tossach an molta.' Gonadh da derbadh sin aspert an file na
roind-se:

 Marcach an eich aluidh aín, con echl*uisc* in a leth-laimh,
 ro indeis an scel co n*gr*aín bas C*oluim* C*ille* drechnair.

 Intan do cuaidh f*or* nemh nar Col*um* firbrethach fallan;
 doluidh Axul, aingel án dia indissin do Dallan.

339. Do scar C. C. 7 Dallan re cheli andsin, 7 do caith
Dallan a aimser iar sin no gor mit*high* le Día C. C. d'faghail
bais; 7 ar fagail baís do, do foillsig*hedh* do Dallan na comarth*a-sa*
do gell C. C. fen do .i. a amharc do techt cuice 7 marc*ach* eich bric
d'indisin a bais dó. Acus as se c*ed* foc*ul* adub*air*t se: 'Ni disceoil
do uíb Neill' .i. nocha beith gan scel do clanduib Neill naí-giallaigh
C. C. do écc. Acus as se sin toss*ach* an molta .i. 'Ni disceoil d'uib
Neill.' D*ixi*t an file:³⁹⁴)

---

³⁹³See *Lis. Lives,* pp. 314-15.
³⁹⁴See *R. C.,* XX, p. 134.

the last half of the *Amhra*. Columcille granted it to him, for he did repeat the last half thereof from memory in the morning, and the first part, the which he had, went from him, by reason that no good deeds of his did merit his salvation from God, and that he had not prayed Columcille that he might hold the two halves in remembrance together each with other.

338. Then said Dallan Forgaill: "In what manner of wise shall I have knowledge of the hour when thou art dead, thou being in Alba and I in Erin?"

"I will give thee a sign," saith Columcille, "to wit, thy sight to come to thee the while thou art making the praise."

For ere that time Dallan had never seen aught.

"Another sign," saith the blind man.

"I will give it thee," saith Columcille, "for thy sight shall be cut off in the hour God doth will thee to put an ending to the praise."

"Another sign," saith the blind man.

"I grant it," saith Columcille, "to wit, a horseman on a piebald horse to bring thee tidings of my death on a Tuesday morning. And the first word he shall say shall be the first word of the praising."

And thus it came to pass, as the poet hath said in this quatrain:

> "On a fair piebald horse a horseman,
> In one hand he held a horsewhip;
> He it was brought the ill tidings:
> Dead was Columcille the seemly.
>
> When he went to holy Heaven,
> Colum of the Righteous Judgments,
> Then went Axal, noble angel,
> To relate his death to Dallan."

339. Then departed Columcille and Dallan each from other, and Dallan passed his life-days thereafter until God deemed it time for Columcille's death. And when he died, the signs were shown to Dallan that Columcille had promised him, to wit, sight came to him and a horseman on a piebald horse with tidings of Columcille's death. And the first word that the horseman said was this:

"No trifling news to descendants of Niall"

that is, that he was not without news for the clan of Niall of the Nine Hostages, to wit, Columcille's death. And that is the beginning of the praising, to wit,

"No trifling news to descendants of Niall"

Dallan mac Colla m*i*c Erc   m*i*c Feradh*ai*g gan time,
airdeces Er*end* ga*n* on,   as se ro mhol Colum Cille.

340. Laibeoram anois mar do raidh C. C. 'sa mordhail se
Droma Cet ris an nech naemtha darub ainm Baithín mac Cuanach,
co *n*dechaidh a met 7 a sceimh os cend f*er* n-Erend uile; oir do
condcuss sin dó ina spir*ai*d, gin go faca sé o suilib corpardha e,
am*ai*l asp*ert* Baithin fen is na randuib-se:

Do raidh an Colaim go becht   rim-sa a mordail Droma Cet:
'As tu-ssa is airde gan fell,   do naemuib aibli Er*end*.'

'Is tu as ferr delb 7 drech,   a Baithin moir m*i*c Cuanach,
sect m*i*c imlesan atfil   in gach suil duid, a clerich.'

Ar na cloisdin sin do Baithin, do íarr ar Día a cur a n-isli 7
a delb do buain de; 7 fuair se sin o Día, indus gur leic an talumh
inad don leic, do bi fan a cossaib, an*d* fén sis gorb isli é na cach
eli no go ndub*ai*rt C. C. ris an talamh gor lór leis a fhad do bi se
ag lecen Baithin and, 7 do cuir se fa aithne air gan a lece*n* and
secha sin. Et dorinde an talumh a comarli air sin; oir do cuir
an tigherna fen .i. Íssa Crist gach uile duil fa umhla do, 7 do fhas
othar ar taeb Baithin an uair sin, 7 do fhúgaib a fhuil go mor e,
indus co ndechaidh a delbh ar cul co himarcach; 7 ni fhuair se
slainte on othar sin riam. *C*onadh de sin adertai "Baithín Ban"
friss; ut dixit Baithin ag a derbadh sin is na randaib-se:

O docuala messe sin,   do iarr*us* ar Crist cabair,
mo cur com ard f*ria* gach nech,   's tucad[h] dam o Dia
                                                              [duilech.

An lec do bi fam cossaiph,   do súidh*edh* síos[395]) cor fossaid;
co *n*debairt in Colaim caoin: 'Leor ticce anuas a Baoithin.'

---

[395]Cf. *Three Irish Glossaries* (1862) under *Coire Brecain* "co suidet siss," which Stokes translates in *Cormac's Glossary*, (1868) p. 41, "until they are sucked (down)." Read *co suigetar*.—Stokes.

The poet hath said:

> "Dallan mac Colla mic Erc,
> Son of Feradhach the Fearless,
> High poet of Erin the faultless,
> It is he that praised Columcille."

XXVIII
OF OTHER MIRACLES OF COLUMCILLE AT THE ASSEMBLY OF DRUIM CEAT

340. Now speak we of that which Columcille said in the Assembly of Druim Ceat to the holy man hight Baithin mac Cuanach, that did surpass all the men of Erin in stature and comeliness, for he beheld him there in spirit, albeit he saw him not with his bodily eyes, as Baithin himself hath said in these quatrains:

> "Then verily spake Columcille
> To me in Druim Ceat, the Assembly:
> 'Thou in sooth art the tallest
> Of the saints of Erin, the bright ones.
>
> The best in semblance and visage,
> Tall Baithin, son of Cuanaidh.
> Seven pupils there be
> In each of thine eyes, O cleric'."

And when Baithin heard that, he besought God to minish his stature, and to take from him his [fair] semblance.

And he did obtain that from God, so that Earth let down the place of the stone beneath his feet, so that he was lower than all others, until Columcille told Earth he thought it enough space she had let down Baithin. And he put her under bonds to let him down no farther. And Earth did his bidding, for the Lord Jesu Christ had put every element under obedience to him.

And an ulcer grew in that hour on Baithin's side, and much blood left him, so that his comeliness decayed exceedingly and he was not whole of that ulcer ever. So that he was called Baithin the Pale therefor; *ut dixit* Baithin in testimony thereof in these quatrains:

Do iarr*us* itche oile,   fuar*us* o C*ri*st gan coir e,
mo dealb do buain dím rem ré   an cein do beind ar bith-cé.

Do fhás utar ar mo taobh,   lochar dom righ cruthach caem;
o sin amach go tí an brath,   as se m'ainm-se "Baithi*n* Ba*n*."

Do raid Colaim re cloisdi*n*,   'caemh an taeb ro-fhuarusst*air*
becc lem a righ na ren*d* si*n*,   uair is ar cen*d* tuarusst*ail*.'

'Misi Baithin bind foghair,   truagh m'fhuirech ar druim
                               [domhain,
menic tar éis Colaim caimh   sruth dér ar adh*aidh*[396]) Baithín.

341. Ba ro-becc, im*orro,* an nech naemtha darbh ainm Caindech; 7 do fhoillsigh*edh* do C. C. gor nair less a beith mar sin amesc bfher n-Erend it*ir* laech 7 clerech, go tainic do mirbuil*ibh* De 7 C. C. 7 Caindigh fen, gor eirigh an talumh do bí fan a cossaib, cor comhard re cach e, *co n*dubairt C. C. ris an talumh gan eirghe ni budh mo. Acus da derbadh sin, mairid an cnocan sin do erigh fa Caindech and san inadh sin anuigh, a cui*m*niugadh na mirbal mor sin.

[396] *leg.* aghaidh.

"When I heard that thing,
I begged of Christ his assistance
To make me the stature of others.
It was granted by God the Creator.

The flagstone under my feet there
Was sucked (?) down until it was stable,
When spake there Colum the gentle,
'Enough hast thou shrunken, O Baithin'.

I made another petition;
I gat it from Jesu the sinless:
To take from me my fair semblance
The while I should be upon earth here.

An ulcer grew on my side then,
A light to my King fair and shapely.
From now until cometh the Doomsday,
Baithin the Pale shall my name be.

Then spake Colum on hearing,
'Fair is thy side, and right prudent!
O Star King, I deem it but little,
When it is for the sake of a guerdon!'

I am the sweet voiced Baithin,
Alas, that I tarry on earth's ridge!
Oft for Colum the gentle,
Streams of tears on the visage of Baithin."

341. Passing small of stature natheless was a certain holy man hight Cainnech. And it was shewn to Columcille that it was a shame to him to be in this wise among the men of Erin, lay and cleric, so that it came to pass, by miracles of God and Columcille and Cainnech himself, that Earth that was beneath his feet rose up, so that he was as tall as any. And Columcille bade Earth rise no farther. And in proof thereof that hillock still standeth today, that rose up under Cainnech. And it is for the keeping in remembrance of those great miracles.

342. Labrum andso mar dorinde C. C. sith idir feruib Erend
7 Alpan am Dail Riada; oir do bhatar fir Alpan ga radha corub ar
slicht Cairbri rig-fhoda mic Conaire do batar fen 7 uaisli Dal Riada,
7 nar coír do righ Erend imresain do denamh ríu 'n-a timchell, os
ar en-slicht do batar. Aderdis fir Erend gor leo fen an ferand
a rabutar 7 co caithfidis dliged a bferaind do tabairt doib fen.

343. Tainic Colman mac Coimhgellain mar a raibe C. C. an
uair sin; 7 as do dorinde C. C. an faidetoracht ag dul soir dó, 7
comadh e do-beradh an breth itir feraibh Erend 7 Alban am Dail
Riada, amail adubrumar romaind. Do híarradh (*fol.* 49b) ar Col.
C. an breth sin do breith, 7 adubairt C. C. nach dó fen do bui a
ndan a breith acht do Colman mac Coimghelláin.

344. Rucc Colman iaromh, an breth sin amlaidh so .i. a
cís 7 a cain 7 a n-erge amach ag feruib Erend; oir is a ndiaidh an
feruind ata an cís 7 eirge amach ut dixit Colman:[397])

Sloigedh la fondadh do gres,   coblach tar muir go mbith-bes:
mo breth belglic gan bine   as eruic la derbfhine.

Et tucc se a coblach d'feruib Alban 7 roind erca uatha da chele,
oir fa d'enfhine íad 7 gebe fecht no damh Albunach do ticfadh
a n-Erind, Dál Riada da mbiathadh 7 da n-indlocadh muna
faghdais treoir eli. Do mol C. C. 7 cach an breth sin ruc Colman
mac Coimgellain. Gonadh amlaidh sin, do firadh faidhetoracht
C. C. im gach ní dib sin; 7 ata an file ga derbudh sin 'sa rand-sa:

---

[397]See *Lis. Lives,* p. 314; *R. C.,* XX, p. 426; *Irish Liber Hym.,* I, p. 163; Dinneen's *Keating,* III, pp. 95-6.

XXIX
OF COLUMCILLE AND DAL RIADA

342. Speak we now of Columcille in what wise he made peace between the men of Erin and Alba concerning the Dal Riada, for the men of Alba said that they and the nobles of Dal Riada were of the seed of Cairbre Rigfoda son of Conaire, and that it beseemed not the King of Erin to quarrel with them concerning them, for they were of one kin. The men of Erin declared that the land they dwelt in belonged to them and they must pay tribute to them therefor.

343. At that moment there came to Columcille that Colman mac Coimgellan of whom Columcille had made the prophecy when he went eastward, that it should be he that should give judgment between the men of Erin and Alba concerning the Dal Riada, as we have aforementioned. They asked Columcille to give the judgment, and Columcille said that it was not he that was destined to give it, but Colman son of Coimgellan.

Then Colman gave judgment in this wise: The men of Erin should have rent and tribute and hosting; for rent and hosting be according to land, *ut dixit* Colman:

> "Hosting ever with territory,
> Ships across the sea with lasting tribute
> (My wise mouthed judgment without flaw)
> And compensation to kinsmen."

344. And to the men of Alba he adjudged their ships and a certain compensation from them to their fellows, because they were of one stock. And whatever hosting or expedition of the men of Alba should come to Erin, the men of Dal Riada should feed them and convoy them, except they gat other help.

Then Columcille praised the judgment that Colman mac Coimgellan had given, and all praised it. And thus the prophecy of Columcille was fulfilled, touching all these things. And the poet hath verified it in this quatrain:

> "Colman mac Comgaill, without concealment,
> Gave kingly judgment concerning the Dal Riada.
> For across the Irish (?) sea shall come
> To the King of Erin their tribute."[1]

[1] Prof. J. MacNeill's interpretation of the lines referring to this in the Old Irish *Life* (*Lis. Lives* p. 314) is cited by J. O'Keefe, *Adventures of Suibhne Geilt*, London, 1913, *Cf.* Skene's interpretation of the account in *Amra Columcille* and the O. I. *Life* in *Celtic Scotland* II 125.

Colma*n* m*a*c Comghaill gan cleith,　　ruc am Dal Ríada an
　　　　　　　　　　　　　　　　　　　　　　　　　　　　　[rigbreith,
uair dosia tar muir na men*d*　　a ndligedh do righ Erend.

345. Laibeoramaid anoss mar do shaer C. C. Scandlan mor mac Cind Faelad, do bi ar tuitim a mbraighden*us* ag righ Erend. Do iarr C. C. Scandlan ar Aedh mac Ainmirech. 'Ni fuight*er*,' ar Aedh, 'no go fagha se bas 'sa chro caelaidh a fuil se' 'Ni lenfa me ort *tair* eis sin,' ar Col. C., '*acht* masa thoil le Día é, gurub é berus mo bróga damh-sa ac erghe damh docum cluicc an medoin-oidhce[398]) anocht a nDoire.'

346. Do gluais C. C. andsin as an mordail, 7 tuc gradh Doire Calgaidh[399]) air gabail ar cuairt and sul do rachadh se a n-Albain. Acus ar n-imtect dó, 7 ar techt na hoidhce tainic lassair tend*tidh*e ar fedh an tsluaigh uile, 7 tainic nell mór sol*us* tait[h]nemach d'indsaighe an *c*ro*i* sin a raibe Scandlan, 7 do labuir an guth ris iss an nell 7 ass*edh* adub*airt*: 'Tarra amach, a Scandlain.' ol se. 'Cinduss do rachainn,' ar Scandlan; 'oir ata da cuibrech dec d'iarann aithlegtha orum, 7 atá cro dluith daingen gan en-dorus air am timchell, 7 ata dechenbur 7 da xx do trén-feruib an tsluaigh a timchell an *c*ro*i* fos ag am coimet.' Is andsin adub*airt* an guth cedna: 'A Scandlain,' ol se, 'fagaib do glais 7 do geibinn, 7 tarr amach as an cro in a bfuile 7 tabuir do lamh am laimh-se; oir is mesi aingel De ata gut gairm ar comairli C. C..' Do eirich Scandlan 7 do tuit a iarnach de mar nach beith se air riamh. Tainic Scandlan amach íar sin 7 ni fidir cind*us* tainic se as an cro sin do bi gan en dorus air, 7 do gluais se les an aingel, 7 do cualatar lu*cht* an coimeta an torand tarrsa, 7 do fiarf*aigh*etar cia do bi and. 'Scandlan ata and,' ar an t-aingel. 'Da madh tu, ni indeosta,' ar siad. Et ruc an t-aingel Scandlan uatha re filledh na sula aml*aidh* sin no go rainic go hairm a raibe C. C. sa duibrecles a nDoire.

---

[398]Incorrect. *Gurab se frithailes m'asa innocht iar n-iarmeirghe 'gidh be baili imbeth, Lis. Lives*, p. 313. See also Dinneen's *Keating*, III, p. 94.
[399]Read *Calgaigh*.

XXX

OF COLUMCILLE AND SCANNLAN

345. Now speak we of Columcille how he did free Scannlan Mor, son of Cennfaelad, that had fallen under the bondage of the King of Erin. Columcille asked the King of Erin for Scannlan.

"None shall get him," saith Aed, "till he gets death in the wattled hut where he is."

"I shall speak with thee no further concerning this thing," saith Columcille, "but if it be the will of God, it shall be he that will bring me my shoes when I rise up at the bell for matins this night in Derry."

346. Then Columcille left the Assembly, and by reason of his love for Derry he went to visit it ere he should go back to Alba. And when he had departed thither and night had fallen, there came a flash of lightning the length of the whole host, and there came a great cloud of shining light to the hut wherein Scannlan was. And a voice spake to him out of the cloud, and said in this wise:

"Come forth, O Scannlan," it saith.

"How should I come forth?" saith Scannlan, "for there be twelve chains of iron twice hardened upon me, and a straight strong hut round about me without a door. And there be ten and two score of the mighty men of the host round about my hut to guard me."

Then spake the voice again:

"O Scannlan," saith he, "leave thy chains and thy fetters, and come forth from thy hut, and put thy hand in my hand. For I am the angel of God that am summoning thee by the counsel of Columcille."

Then Scannlan rose up, and his chains fell from him as they had never been on him. And he went forth. And he knew not how he went out of that hut that was without a door.

And he fared forth with the angel. And the keepers heard the sound of his passing, and they asked who was there.

"It is Scannlan," saith the angel.

"If it were so, thou wouldst not say it," say they.

And the angel led Scannlan with him in the twinkling of an eye, and came to Columcille in the Black Church in Derry.

347. Is andsin do bi C. C. ag erge docum cluic an medhoin oidhce, 7 do iarr se a broga. 'Do-ber-sa duit iad', ol Scandlan. 'An tu Scandlan'? ar se. 'As me cena', ol Scandlan. Dixit C. C.:—

5 Frithail uaim na hass*u-s*a,   as mesi Col*uim* cuimnech;
   do cosa bad glassa-sa   ar toigec[h]t⁴⁰⁰) as do cuibrech.

'Nar celebhuir tu don righ'? al C. C. 'Deoch', ol Scandlan. 'Cindus tancaduis, a mic, as an cro a rabadhais'? ar C. C. . 'Deoch', ol Scandlan. 'Fagaim bailbe tengtha 7 cumgach uirighill ar do
10 sli*ch*t ad [d]iaidh go brath,' ol C. C. 'Na fagaib,' ol Scandlan; 'oir biaid a cis 7 a ndligedh duit-se go b*rath*'. 'Ni heidir an escaine ud do cur ar cul festa,' ar C. C., '7 facbhuim-se rigthe 7 esp*oig* ar do slicht-sa coidhce, 7 do-berthur deoch duid'. Tuccadh cuige iar sin dil trir do lind a n-en soidhech, 7 do ibh Scandlan
15 sin d'endigh; 7 tucad biadh cuice 'n-a diaid sin .i. nai mbairgena 7 secht cotchanda feola 7 aduaigh Scandlan sin uile d'en shaíth. Acus do coduil iar sin, 7 do bi tri la 7 teora hoidce 'sa codladh sin. Acus do eric Scandlan iar sin as a codladh, 7 do slecht se do Dia 7 do C. C., 7 tuc se hé fen 7 fer a inaidh in a diaidh fa
20 umhlacht 7 fa cís do Col. Chille.

348. Tocbais C. C. a lamh os cind Scandlain 7 adb*er*t an rand-sa:⁴⁰¹)

Slecht sis, a Scandl*ain*, dom reir,   as mesi Col*uim* o Neill;
ar dodechad t*a*r an lind,   ní raba ar cind Domnaill déin.⁴⁰²)

---

⁴⁰⁰Read *toidhecht*.
⁴⁰¹See *R. C.*, XX, p. 50.
⁴⁰²Distinguish from *děin* 'good', 'great'. Cf. *Saltair na Rann*, 1. 187. *cendolma ndein* 'without great delay'.

347. And then Columcille rose up for the bell of matins and asked for his sandals.

"I will bring them to thee," saith Scannlan.

"Art thou Scannlan?" saith he.

"I am in sooth," saith Scannlan.

Dixit Columcille:
>"Aid me to do off these sandals,
>Colum am I that remembereth;
>Thy feet must be livid,
>On thy coming out of thy fetters."

"Didst thou take leave of the King?" saith Columcille.

"A drink," saith Scannlan.

"How camest thou hither, O son, from the hut thou wast in?" saith Columcille.

"A drink," saith Scannlan.

"I leave stammering and stuttering on thy seed forever," saith Columcille.

"Do not so," saith Scannlan, "for thou shalt have tribute and thy due from them forever."

"The curse cannot be withsaid now," saith Columcille, "but I will leave kings and bishops on thy seed forever. And a drink shall be brought thee."

Then was brought to him in one vessel sufficient of ale for three. And Scannlan drank it at one draught. And food was brought to him thereafter, to wit, nine loaves and six portions of meat. And all that did Scannlan eat at one time. And he slept then, and was three days and three nights in that sleep. And then Scannlan rose up from his sleep, and did homage to God and to Columcille. And he put himself and his successors after him under obedience to Columcille and under tribute.

348. Columcille lifted his hand over Scannlan and uttered this quatrain:
>"Bow down to my will, O Scannlan,
>I am Colum, descendant of Niall.
>My coming across the waters
>Was not for the sake of fierce Domnall."

Dixit Scannlan:
>"I will bow to thee, descendant of Niall.
>And thy will shall my kindred do also.
>Whilst wind and sunlight continue
>From me thou shalt have thy desiring."

Dixit Scandlan:—

Slectfad-sa duid, a ua⁴⁰³) Neill is biaid mo (*fol.* 50a) cineth
             dot rer;
a n-edh maires gaeth is g*r*ian, rodbía do riar uaim budhdein.

5 Et an uair do bi ga bendugadh, do mothaig se ecla mor air, 7 do fiarf*aigh* de cred dob'ecail les. Adubairt Scandlán gorb ecail les Domnall mac Aedha mic Ainmirech 7 ocbaid cineoil Conaill 7 Eoghain do bi a foruire roime o Ess Ruaid go Banda, 7 nach raibe *con*air aice tarrsa muna dech*adh* se ar eitelluigh uasta.
10 Di*xi*t Sc*andl*an:

A Col*aim* Cille romcar, a m*i*c righ nimhe as talm*an!*
o ata Banda brectaid geill go hEss Ruaid ruibnech roreill.

Ro linsat sluaig imasech Aedha moir m*i*c Ai*n*mirech;
ni rogeb c*on*uir dom tigh *a*cht mu*n*a tias ar eitellaigh.

15 A Colaim Cille ced cland, cid dode*n*-sa⁴⁰⁴) re Domhnall?
cuindf*idh* Domnall form a réir a focus no a n-eidirchein.

Andess om tir trebnach tend dia raghba a righe nEr*end*,
rodusaircfe, mór an bet, oca robá gom coimet.

Oir is se Domnall bui ga coimet an oidhce rucc an t-aingel leis e.
20 'Ber-se mo bachull-sa let má ata ecla ort', ar C. C., '7 ni ba hecail duit duine no bethadhach no co soichir do tir duth*aigh* fen, amail asp*ert* is na randuib-se:

'Ber mo bachall lat ad laimh masad uaimnech, a Scand*l*ai*n*,
a hInnis Eog*ain* na n-ech go Magh Raigne ruadrindach.

25 Taisben a*cht* co t*í*s co tigh do Laisren m*a*c Feradaigh;
ni hághaidhther⁴⁰⁵) coin *no* dui*n*e no creich na cuairt na cuire.

Ni[t]tescfa fidh *no* faebur, cia do *t*ochra a ro-baeg*al*;
mebais ar cach red gnuis gil, biaidh Issu go*t* imdegail.

Fod goirid bia-sa ima alle, *acus* an bachull b*ere*;
30 a Scandla[i]n cia scel fot-ricc, impo deseal, eirg dot tigh?

---

⁴⁰³Read *ui.*
⁴⁰⁴Read *dogen-sa.*
⁴⁰⁵Read *áigther.*

And when he was blessing him, he perceived that he was sore afeared, and he asked him whereof he was adrad. Scannlan said that he feared Domnall mac Aed son of Ainmire and the men of the clan of Conall and Eogan that were in wait for him from Assaroe to the Bann. And he had no way to pass them save it be flying.
Dixit Scannlan:

> "O Columcille that hast loved me,
> O son of Earth's King and Heaven's.
> From the Bann with hostages speckled,
> To Assaroe spear-crowded and sparkling,
>
> The hosts are drawn up each in order,
> The hosts of great Aed mac Ainmirech;
> I shall find no path to my dwelling
> Save on wings I make my way thither.
>
> Columcille, that of clans hath a hundred,
> What may I do against Domnall?
> Domnall will seek to o'errule me,
> Nigh hand, mayhap, or far distant.
>
> From the south, from my . . . strong country,
> If he get him the Kingship of Erin,
> He will plunder it,—Great the disaster—
> He, the man that did guard me."

For it was Domnall that had guarded him the night the angel led him away.

"Take my staff with thee, if thou art afeared," saith Columcille, "and thou shalt fear no man nor beast till thou reach thine own land."

And he said in these quatrains:

> "Take my staff in thy hand,
> If thou art fearful, O Scannlan!
> From Inishowen of the Horses
> To Magh Raigne of the Red Spears.
>
> Show it, if home thou returnest,
> To Laisren son of Feradach;
> Fear none of wolf nor of mankind,
> Nor raid nor foray nor hosting.

Ar faesamh an Coimdhegh cain   dorossat nemh as talmain,
na tarairled⁴⁰⁶) Domnall dond   go lin crech 7 comland.

. . . .

Luag h'aistir tar loch alle,   as maith an aiscid bere.

⁴⁰⁷) Et fós beir deich mbliadna xx a tigernus a n-inad hathur. Et foiceortar aimser hecin as do tighernas tu, 7 cuirfidh lucht do tire fen fiss ar do cend aris, 7 beir tri haimsera gerra ad tigernus fen aris in a diaidh sin', [ar se]. Acus as iad tri haimsera adubairt C. C. tri mí, ge do saileatar na poiblecha gorub tri bliadhna adubairt se. Acus do firadh sin uile amail adubairt C. C. .

349. Is andsin ruc Scandlan an mor-bachall C. C. leiss; 7 gerb imdha foiriredha⁴⁰⁸) 7 bernadha baegail reme, do cuaidh tritha gan digbail do denamh dó no go raínic se a n-Ossruidibh tre mirbuilibh De 7 C. C. . Acus an la rainic Scandlan do baile a athur, as se sin la fuair a athair bas .i. Cend Faeoladh, ri Osruidhe; 7 as do cumaidh Scandlain fuair se an bas sin. Acus do righadh Scandlan a n-inadh a athur iar sin, 7 do bi se fen 7 a sil in a diaidh fa cís 7 fa canaidh do C. C. 7 d'fhir a inaid 'n-a diaidh o sin amach, amail aspert an file:⁴⁰⁹)

Do saeradh Scandlan, maith mor,   tre rath Colaim na caemh-slúagh;
conadh de dleaghar an cain   do claind sciatbuidhe Scandlain.

Dixit Scandlan ac tabairt na cánu-sa uadh:⁴¹⁰)

---

⁴⁰⁶Read nacha[t]tairle. See R. C., XX, p. 54.
⁴⁰⁷Taken literally from Adamnan. See Reeves' Adam., pp. 38-9.
⁴⁰⁸Cf. § 170 a bhfoirirechaibh remhe 'sa sligidh, also § 348 do bi a foruire roime, o Ess Ruaid go Banda.
⁴⁰⁹See R. C., XX, p. 138.
⁴¹⁰See ibid., p. 50.

Wood shall not cut thee, nor edges,
Through the grace of Colum of Fair Hosts.
All shall yield to thy bright shining visage.
Jesu shall be thy protection.

Late and soon I shall be in thy company;
And (my) staff, thou bearest (it) with thee.
O Scannlan, what doth delay thee?
Turn sunwise, arise, and go homeward.

In the beauteous Maker's safe-keeping,
That hath made the Earth and the Heaven,
Dark Domnall shall not come against thee
With fulness of hosts that seek plunder.

. . . .
. . . .
Thy fee of thy coming across the lake hither
A good gift it is that thou bearest.''

"And thou shalt be ten and a score years in lordship in place of thy father. And for a certain space thou shalt be cast out of thy lordship. But the folk of thy land shall send for thee again, and for three short spaces thou shalt be again lord."

And the three spaces whereof Columcille spake were three months, albeit men thought it was three years he said. And all this fell out as Columcille had said.

349. Then Scannlan took with him the great staff of Columcille. And albeit many were the snares and ambushments before him, he went through them without suffering hurt till by miracles of God and Columcille he came to Ossory. And on the day he came to his father's land, his father Cennfaelad, King of Ossory died. And it was of his grief for Scannlan that he died. And Scannlan was crowned in the stead of his father. And he and his seed after him were under tax and tribute to Columcille and to his successors after, as the poet hath said:

"Scannlan was freed, a great blessing,
Through the grace of Colum of Fair Hosts.
Therefore the tribute is owing
From Scannlan's sons yellow-shielded."

Dixit Scannlan on giving that tribute:

"My golden brooch, thou shalt have it
From the King in guerdon of service,
And homage for aye to thy household,
From my land from now until Doomsday.

Ro-m-bia⁴¹¹) mo delg-sa *co n*-ór   al-log do goire ond *rig*,
ríar do samtha in gach t*r*ath   *no* co tí an brath as mo tír.

Caeca ech *co n*-alluib oir,   *cae*ca bo bendach óm tír,
tidn*as*t*ar* uaim-se co cían,   budh é do riar ó gach righ.

5   Do riar om tuathuib om tigh;   go mbo lir luachuir is luib,
Screbull gacha hadb*a* sin,   a*n* mír o Bladhma co muir.⁴¹²)

Dixit C. C.:

Tidnaic do Laisren an cuairt,   do Durmuigh, ni duairc a*n* drec*ht*,
10 gach tres bliadhuin go tí an brath,   ass bend*acht* ar *cách* ro-slect.

350. Labrum anoss mar do crichnaigh C. C. gach toisc imo ndech*aidh* se co mordail Droma Cet leth re fost*adh* na fileadh 7 re fuasluc*adh* Scandl*ain*, 7 re sith do denamh it*ir* feruib Erend 7
15 Alpan am Dail Ríada, 7 leth re gan ri Erend do dul a n-Alpain da milledh[h], mar adubram*ar* romaind; 7 fos as mor d'fertaib 7 do mirbuil*ibh* dorinde a leth amuigh dib sin 'sa mordail cedna .i. mar do esscain se C*on*all clogach, 7 mar do bendaig se Domhn*all*, 7 mar do cuir se an righan 7 a hinailt a rechtaib corr, 7 mar do
20 fuasca*il* se an sagart o demnaibh, do rer mar derbuss an betha anuas.

351. Ar crichnugh*adh* gach tosca móa ndech*aidh* se a n-Eirind do C. C., 7 ar mbendach*adh* ban 7 fer n-Erend dó, do ceilebuir doib iar sin 7 do fagaib a bend*acht* aca, 7 do cuaid tar
25 muir go hÍ, 7 ni fuil scribtha cor fill se re n-a beó a n-Erend ó sin alle. Gededh tainic a corp go Dun Da Lethglass a n-Erind, amail indeo*sus* an betha a n-inadh eli.

---

⁴¹¹Read *rotbia*.
⁴¹²See Dinneen's *Keating*, III, p. 98.

> Fifty steeds with gold bridles,
> Fifty horned kine from my country,
> Shall be granted by me for a long time.
> From every king this shall thy claim be.
>
> Thy claims from my tribes, from my household,
> Though herbs and rushes outnumbering,
> A scruple for every dwelling,
> And the region seaward from Bladma."

Dixit Columcille:

> "Deliver the tribute to Laisren,
> To Durrow,—not poor is the portion,
> Every third year until Doomsday,
> And on each that hath bowed him a blessing!"

350. Speak we now of Columcille how that he brought to end every business for the which he went to the great Assembly of Druim Ceat, concerning the retaining of the poets, and the freeing of Scannlan, and the making peace betwixt the men of Erin and Alba concerning Dal Riada, and concerning the King of Erin not going to Alba to plunder it, as we have said afore. Great moreover were the marvels and wonders that were done besides in that same assembly, to wit, how that Columcille cursed Conall Clogach and blessed Domnall and turned the Queen and her handmaid into cranes and rescued the priest from the demons, according as the *Life* hath afore recorded.

XXXI

OF THE MIRACLES AND PROPHECIES OF COLUMCILLE AFTER HIS RETURNING TO IONA

351. When he had fulfilled all things for the which he had gone to Erin, Columcille blessed the women and the men of Erin and took leave of them. And having left his blessing upon them he went across the sea to Iona. And it is not written that he returned again to Erin the while he lived. Howbeit his body came to Dun da Lethglas in Erin as the *Life* will relate in another place.

352.⁴¹³) Dia mboi C. C. ag dul a n-Alba*in* iar mordhail [Droma Cet], gur eirigh coire Brecain re *n*-a ucht, g*ur* c*h*u*ir* cnam*h*a Brecain m*ic* Maine m*ic* Ne[i]ll *nai-giallaigh* f*a n*-a uacht*ur* ro baidh*edh* an*n* f*r*ia re ciana roi*m*e sin, g*ur* ro aithin C. C.
5 tre sp*i*raid fhaidhedo*ra*c*h*ta gurb iad cna*mh*a Breca*in* ro boi an*n*, c*o n*deab*ai*r*t*:
    'Is f*a* baid f*ri*m-sa si*n* at se*n* Bhreca*in*,'⁴¹⁴) or se;
    Acus ro guid C. C. annsin a*ir* Breca*n*, c*onus*fuair sochruidh[e] nimhe dó (*fol.* 50b).
10 353. F*ec*h*tus* do C. C. a n-Í, 7 do gab tendess 7 esslainte adbulmór e, indus co ndechaidh a aithne 7 a urlabra uada; no do reir morain do lebruib eli, a spirad uili do dealug*hadh* riss. Tainic an t-aidbirseoir a richt mna roscíamcha d'indsaighid na manach do bi ag denamh onóra an c*oir*p ro-naemtha, ro-bendaighte,
15 ro-coisrectha sin C. C., 7 leanub scíamhach 'n-a hucht, 7 adub*air*t cor Béda*in* a hainm, 7 gurub do mnaib na righachta sin fen na hAlpan di, 7 adubairt cor mac di fen 7 do C. C. an lenab sin, 7 do fiarf*aigh* do na manch*aibh* 7 go hairidhe do Baithin naemtha do bi do lathair an uair sin, nar chuimhn*igh* C. C. ria mbas d'faghail
20 dó, oigre*cht* ar bith d'facbail ga mac fen. 'A ben, na hab*air* sin,' ar Baithin, 'oír ata a deimin againd-e corub brecc cuires tú ar Col. C.; oir do togh Dia a mbroind a m*ath*ar mar serbfoghant*aid* diless do fen é, 7 do coimeit se 'n-a oigh ro-naemtha ro-bendaigthe ro-gloin o do ruc a mhath*air* é c*us* an ponc sin a bais gan truaill*edh*
25 a ógachda leth rit-sa na re mnai eli.' Is e adb*ar*, im*orro*, fa tainic an diab*ul* do denam na haibirseo*ra*c*h*ta-sa ar C. C. dés a bhais, mar nar fhet se buaidh no melladh do breith air re n-a beo, gorb ail les míclu d'fagbail 'n-a diaid 'sa saegal a cluassaib na ndaine air. An te do coiméit C. C. c*onu*ice si*n*, do taeb na ngras n-
30 imarcach tucc se dó gan a tect de fen a milled uime do coimet se andsin é leth ris in míclu moir sin do cur ar cul .i. Dia na n-uile cumh*ach*t, 7 tuc se aisec a spir*id*e 7 a urlabra fen dó andsin 7 do erigh 'n-a suide a fiadnaise caich uile, 7 do goir se an ben sain an lenib cuice 7 adubairt nar leiss fen a lenab, 7 adub*air*t dá cuirthi
35 agaidh oir ar an talamh uili do, 7 saegal d'faghail go la na breithe da caithem sin, nach tr*u*aillfed se a c*or*p fen ría-se na re mnai eli. Acus

---

⁴¹³This paragraph is written by a different hand in the MS. Notice the different style and language. It is clearly an interpolation. It is borrowed literally from the *Dinnseanchus.* See *Book of Lecan, fol.* 253ᵃ. See also Reeves' *Adam.,* p. 263.

⁴¹⁴"dia n-ebairt Col*um* Cil*li* c*on*dolb si*n* a sen-B*recain*" Book of Ballymote (*Fac*) 398ᵃ, 47.

352. When Columcille was on his way to Alba after the great Assembly, he came by adventure to the Gulf of Brecan, and it sent to its surface the bones of Brecan mac Maine son of Niall of the Nine Hostages, that had been drowned there long ere that time. And Columcille perceived through a spirit of prophecy that they were the bones of Brecan, and he said:

"Thou art friendly to me, O Brecan," saith he.

And Columcille prayed for Brecan, so that he obtained for him the peace of Heaven.

353. On a time whenas Columcille abode in Iona, pain and sore sickness seized him, so that understanding and speech went from him, or, as many other books make mention, his spirit departed from him wholly. Then came the Adversary in guise of a right comely woman to the brethren that were doing honor to the passing holy, blessed, and sanctified body of Columcille, and she had a beautiful child at her breast. And she said that her name was Bedain and that she was a woman of the Kingdom of Alba, and that the child was son to her and Columcille. And she inquired of the brethren, and in especial of holy Baithin that was there present, if Columcille had remembered before his death to bequeath any patrimony to his son.

"Speak not thus, O woman," saith Baithin, "for we know of a surety that it is a lie thou dost say of Columcille, for God chose him as His own true servant from his mother's womb. And he kept him a virgin passing holy, passing blessed, and passing clean, from the time his mother gave him birth to his death, without violating his virginity with thee or any other woman."

Now this is the cause why the Devil came to mischief Columcille in this wise after his death, because he could not outdo or deceive him in his life, and he was fain therefore to leave an ill report of him after his death in the ears of men.

But He that did guard Columcille till that time in respect of abusing not the exceeding great graces He had given him, did now guard him in respect of turning from him that great shame, to wit, the Allpowerful God. He gave back to him then his spirit and his speech, and he sat up before all, and called that woman with the child to him. And he said that her child was not his. And he said that if a face of gold were put over the whole earth for him and if he were given life to enjoy till Doomsday, he would not defile his body with her nor with any woman else.

And he made a *rithim* of poetry then, and it is called *Duan na Tuiledhach*. And he pronounced it before the woman. And she might not endure it, but rose up with her child into the air in the sight of all. And Columcille spake to her.

dorinde se rithim dána andsin, 7 "Duan na Tuiledhach" a hainm,
7 do gab se a bfiadnaise na mna sin hi, 7 nir fuilngedh sin les an
mnai acht do eirigh sí fen 7 a lenub a fiadnaise caich a n-airde san
aeieor ar cloisdin na duaíne dí, 7 adubairt C. C. fria: 'A diabuil,'
5 ar se 'imdigh romat a n-ifrend, 7 bidh and an fad bias Día in a
flaithemnus fen, 7 na déna aiberseoracht ar en duine co brath
aris.' Acus dob eigen don diabul sin do denamh ar furailemh
C. C. Is andsin adubairt C. C: 'An duan sa rer teich an ben
ud do bi ag cur an mic breice cucam-sa, fácaim-se mar buaduib
10 uirre gach ben bess ac cur lenib a mbréic docum fir go brath, dá
ngabtar os a cend í gan a bliadhain do comull do.⁴¹⁵) Acus do
derbudh sin co menic ó sin alle ar an duain sin. Acus do bi C. C.
'n-a beathaigh aimser ecin iar sin do reir mar tuicim-se é; oir as
demhin lem da madh a n-aimser a bais do imeochadh so air, go
15 mebrochadh Adamnan air é sa mbethaidh do decht se fen. Acus
as se tosach na Duaine sin na Tuileadhuch .i. 'Mac nach lem,
liter orm-sa,' 7 reliqua.⁴¹⁶)

354. Fechtus dia ndechaidh Congall claen mac Scandlain
Scíathlethain, ri Uladh, ar cuairt a cend righ Alban do bí 'n-a
20 bráthair aice, 7 do cuaidh Suibne mac Colmain Cuaír, ri Dal
Áraidhe, les, 7 do bi C. C. ar a cind a n-Albain an uair sin, 7 do
labhuir go faidhemhail re Suibne 7 assedh adubairt: 'Na bídh-se ag
cumdadh do Congall allmuruidh do breith a n-Erind,' ar se; 'oir da
mber, badh aithrighe le Congall 7 let-sa é, oír dobera an ri bes a n-
25 Erind an uair sin .i. Domnall mac Aedha mic Ainmirech, cath dib
7 muirbfider Congall 7 Ulaidh 7 allmuruidh and, 7 rachair-si fen, a
Shuibne, ar geltacht and,' ar se, '7 dá ngabthá-sa mo comairli-se
air sin,' ar C. C., '7 beith at oclaech maith do Dia ó so amach,
do-berainn-se flaithes saegalta duit 7 flaithius De fa deoigh.'
30 'Do-gen comairli Congail,' ar Suibne. Gan fechain do breithir
C. C., a cind aimsire airide iar sin, ruc Congall uimhir do-airmidhe
d'allmuruch les a n-Erind da milledh. Acus do bris Domhnall
mac Aeda mic Ainmirech, airdri Erend, cach Muighe Rath forra,
du in ar marbadh Congall 7 inar cuiredh derg-ár Uladh 7 all-
35 mharach, 7 a n-a ndechaidh Suibne ar geltacht, amail adubairt
C. C. Is lor do derbhadh an sceoil-se mar adubairt Domnall mac
Aeda mic Ainmirech re Suibhne an uair do condaic se a n-airde
a mbile Cille Riadhain a tir Conaill é a haithli an catha, gur
truagh les a bheith amlaidh sin, 7 corub olc do chuaidh dó gan
40 comairli C. C. do gabáil; 7 adubairt an rand-sa:

---

⁴¹⁵Cf. § 132 above *nach coimheolad sé a bliadain.* Read *di.*
⁴¹⁶Attributed to Cormac in *Book of Lecan.* See *Z. C. P.,* VIII, p. 561.

"Fiend," saith he, "be off with thee to Hell, and be in that place so long as God is in His princedom. And do thou none evil again to man till Doomsday."

And the fiend must needs do the command of Columcille.

Then Columcille said, "Upon that poem afore the which the woman fled that would have fathered upon me a son falsely, I leave such virtue that every woman that doth father a child upon a man falsely, if it be recited over her, she may not complete her year."

And of that poem this thing hath oft been proved.

And Columcille lived some while thereafter, as I understand it, for surely if it had been at the time of his death that this had befallen him, Adamnan would have made mention thereof in the *Life* that he did make himself.

And the beginning of that *Duan na Tuiledhach* is

"A son not mine is fathered upon me."

et reliqua.

354. On a time that Congall Claen son of Scannlan of the Broad Sword, King of Ulster went visiting the King of Alba his kinsman, Suibhne mac Colman Cuair, King of Dal nAraidhe went with him. And Columcille was awaiting him in Alba at that time, and spake prophetically to Suibhne, and said in this wise:

"Be not planning with Congall to bring foreigners to Erin," saith he, "for if thou do, it shall repent Congall and thee both; for the King that shall be ruling over Erin at that time, to wit, Domnall mac Aeda mic Ainmirech, shall do battle with thee, and Congall shall be slain there along with the Ulstermen and the foreigners; and thou thyself, O Suibhne, shalt go out of thy wits there. But if thou take my counsel therein," saith Columcille, "and be a good servant to God hereafter, I will give thee worldly dominion and the Kingdom of God at the last."

"I shall do the counsel of Congall," saith Suibhne.

But after a certain space, setting naught by the words of Columcille, Congall brought a countless number of foreigners with him to Erin to plunder it. And Domnall mac Aeda son of Ainmire won the battle of Magh Rath against them, and Congall was slain, and red slaughter was put on Ulstermen and foreigners. And Suibhne went out of his wits as Columcille had said.

Sufficient in proof of this history are the words that Domnall mac Aeda son of Ainmire said to Suibhne when he saw him above in a tree in Kilrean in Tirconnell after the battle, that it forthought him that Suibhne should be in this wise, and it had gone ill with him that he had not taken the counsel of Columcille. And he uttered this quatrain:

Tarccaidh Colum Cille deit   nemh 7 righe, a romheic![417])
dighair tancadhuis is an cath,   o primhfaidh nime is talman.

[(fol. 51a)

355. (A)r na tuicsin do Domnall mac Aeda mic Ainmirech,
5 d'airdrigh Erend, go mbeith cogadh no esaenta itir a cloind fa
n-a tighernus, da mbeith se fein gan beith aca, do reidigh se etorra
re n-a beo .i. do ordaigh se rige n-Erend do Dondchadh, 7
saermacánacht Erend 7 saerchuairt d'Fhíachra;[418]) 7 do orduig
ferand righdamhnachta do .i. Fir Roiss 7 Mugornn Maighen,
10 uar ni raibe ri diles aca, oir iss *edh* dognidis a righe duthaich do
mharbhadh. Gonadh airesin ro ordaich Dondchadh do Fhiachra
o Teamhraigh go hOilech. O ro siacht Fiachra dá soighidh, do
tinoil lucht an feraind cuice, 7 ro raid riu: 'Tabruid braighde
dam-sa, 7 dentar ratha righda ro-mhóra lib, 7 sondaidhe sithairde
15 7 foircenta fíraille fairsenga,' [ar se]. 'Do-denam-ne sin duid-se,'
ar iad san, 'gin co dernsamar riamh d'ar tigernadhuib fein he.'
Cidh tracht, doníad san na saethair sin, 7 do bi do méd a n-oibre
7 a saethair, conadh seiledha do cru 7 d' fhuil ro cuirdís amach
iar scís na hoibri moíre sin. Laa n-oen dia ndechutar do denamh
20 oireachtais, 7 do batar da rigdhamna do righaib duthaighe an
tíre aca and .i. Diarmaid Ollmar 7 Oilill: 7 ro raidhset riu: 'Messa
daib an ri comaidech ud[419]) oruib ina sind-e, doigh ni tucsad ar
sindser-ne docraide mar sud oraib-se cia ro marb sib íad.' 'Is fir
sin,' uar iat san. Do cinned[h] comairli leo .i. Fiachra do
25 marbudh. Do riacht Fiachra san oirechtuss iar sin. Nir cian
doib and go facatar an damh imdiscir alltaidhe[420]) cuca, 7 ro
lecetar a coin do, 7 ro-s-lenatar muinntir Fíachra an fíadh, 7 ro
facuibset é fen 'n-a aenar 'san oirechtus. Ro fell an lucht sin
air, 7 romarbhsat é, 7 do cuatar fen air sin, ar comairce Ronain
30 Fhind 7 Ronain mic Neill; uair dop iad sin dá ard-cumarce Erend
an tan sain. O'dcualaidh Donnchadh a brathair do marbudh, ro
thinóil morsluagh fo cedoir, 7 do cuaidh in a ndiaid do sharughadh
na naemh. 'Na saruigh sind-e,' ar siad, 'uair da ndernair, ni bia

---

[417]*ar omheic* MS. *O* is well separated from the preceding *r* and is written in larger character than is the usual *o*. It seems clear that O'D. understood *Omheic* to be the name of a place. Read perhaps *ar oimelc* = on St. Brigid's tide. See *oimelc* (O'Reilly). See also *Adventures of Suibhne Geilt*, ed. O'Keeffe, p. 18.
[418]*Fiacha* YBL. Domnall had no sons called Donnchadh and Fiachra.
[419]*in ri comaigthech ut.* Y. B. L., (fol. 86 b 49).
[420]Y. B. L. has *ad allaigh* (fol. 87a²) 'a stag'.

"To thee did Columcille offer
Heaven and kingship, O great son.
Eager thou camest to the battle,
Chief prophet of earth and of Heaven."

355. Domnall mac Aeda son of Ainmire High King of Erin, when he understood that there would be strife and war concerning his kingdom amongst his children when he would be no more with them, made a settlement amongst them whilst he was alive, to wit, he allotted the kingship of Erin to Donnchad and the "free ordering" of Erin and "free visiting" to Fiachra, along with the land of the crown-princedom, to wit, Fir Roiss and Mugdorn Maighen, since those had no rightful king. For it was their wont to kill their native king. And so Donnchad allotted to Fiachra the region from Tara even unto Ailech.

And when Fiachra came to them he assembled the folk of the land and said to them:

"Give hostages to me and let build royal, passing great forts and strong high palisades and gables truly beautiful and spreading."

"We will do it for thee," say they, "albeit never have we made such for our own lords."

Howso that may be, they built those works. And such was their labor and their toil that it was spittle of blood and of gore they spat out after the weariness of that great labor. And one day they held a council together, and two crown-princes of the native kings of the land were with them, to wit, Diarmaid Ollmar and Oilill. And Oilill said to them:

"The foreign king that is over you is worse to you than we. In sooth our forefathers put no such hardship upon you, and yet ye slew them."

"It is true," say they.

Then they took counsel together to put Fiachra to death.

And anon came Fiachra into the assembly. And not long after that they saw a very fierce stag coming toward them. And they set their dogs on him. And the household of Fiachra followed the stag and left him alone in the assembly. And the folk fell upon him and killed him. And then they sought sanctuary with Ronand Find and Ronan mac Neill, for those were the two chief protectors of Erin in that time.

When Donnchadh heard that his brother had been killed, he assembled forthwith a great host, and pursued them in violation of the sanctuary of the saints.

"Violate not our sanctuary," say they, "for if thou do, there will

comairce a n-Erind da éssi, *acht* do-béraim-ne mar adera C. C.
mac Feidlim*the* doid.' 'Gébhat-sa sin,' ar Dondch*adh*. Cuirid
techta íar sin co hÍ 7 indesid a scela ó tus go dereadh. Acus assí
breth ruc C. C., *tri* xx fer 7 *tri* xx ben do na dainibh dob uaisle
5   7 rob ferr ro bui ag denamh na finghaile *con* a cloind 7 *con* a
cinedh do chor t*ar* muir go nach ticdis a n-Erind go bráth aris,
7 an ferand in ar marbudh mac righ Erend, do tab*ai*rt do Dia
7 do Patruic. Acus do cuir C. C. dias clerech da muindtir, bud
daltaidhe do fein les an mbreith sin, 7 do faemh rig Erend sin.
10 Doronadh longa leo san, 7 do cuatar ar muir d'fagb*ai*l Erend,
am*ail* do cuiredh d'fhiach*ai*bh orra. Imthusa muin*d*t*ir*e C. C.,
do ceilebrat*ar* dond rig, 7 dob ail leo dul t*ar* a n-ais co hÍ, 7 atb*ert*
an righ ríu-san gan imtecht go dereadh erraich 7 co tos*ach* samr*aidh;*
7 as cuma do bi ga radh, 7 adub*air*t an laeid ann :[421])

15   Denaidh ai*n*mne as foisdine,   a clerche Col*uim* C*i*lle,
      go tí inam imramha,   gama lan-reid na linde.

      Glass, fuar, errach oighreta,   mór a tonda, 'sa tretha*in*
      imga cetha ag coimherge   f*a* an lind-fhairge lethain.

      Snamh t*ar* an rinn-muir rían*aigh*   fó sín tshamhraid
20   [shíralaind :
      gach re cuidechta acianaib,   budh coimhdhe dar curca*n*uibh.

      Snáaid eoi*n* ar indberuib;   bith a mblath ar gach mbuinde;
      lingid eiccne ilbreca   t*ar* drumcladh gacha tuinde.

      Géb*aidh* a clerche, ní ceilim-se,   reicles deirrid diamhaire,
25   a duara glana gla*s*a   aderim-se ribh denaidh. Denaidh.

[421]See *Miscellany pres. to K. Meyer,* p. 312 ff; *R. C.,* XXVI, p. 132 ff; *ibid.,*
IX, p. 14 ff.

be no more sanctuary in Erin hereafter. But we will yield thee the judgment of Columcille son of Fedlimid."

"I accept that," saith Donnchadh.

Then they send messengers to Iona and they relate the history from first to last.

And this was the judgment of Columcille: Three score men and three score women from them that were of highest rank and worthiest of those that had done the slaying to be banished overseas with their children and their kindred, so that they might never again come to Erin. And the land where the son of the King of Erin had been murdered to be given to God and to Padraic.

And Columcille sent twain of the clerics of his household that were fosterlings of his own to bear that judgment. And the King of Erin accepted it. And boats were built for them, and they went to sea, leaving Erin, as it had been charged them.

355[a] Touching the folk of Columcille, they took leave of the King, and they would fain have returned again to Iona. And the King told them they should not go till the end of spring and the beginning of summer. And sadly it was he said it, and he made this lay.

"Have ye patience, and tarry,
O clerics of Columcille,
Till a fitting time for sailing,
Till the sea be smooth.

Gray cold and frosty the spring-time!
Mighty its waves and its sea;
Many the mists that are rising
Over the wide wet main.

Sailing the smooth sea's pathway
In the time of beautiful summer,
Every other company
Would be to our boats a protection.

Birds swimming in mouths of rivers,
Every branch in blossom,
Speckled salmon leaping,
Across the ridge of each wave.

Ye shall have, O clerics, I hide not,
A cell secluded and secret,
. . . .
Do ye then as I tell you."

Doronsat na cleric an comairle sin, 7 do hindlaic*edh* go Cam*us* Comghaill bud thuaidh íat, 7 tucadh reicles derrid diamhair doib and, 7 ro fretl*edh* 7 do frithoil*edh* go maith íad on righ go táinec a cairde astech. Acus ro timnat*ar* ceilebr*adh* don righ iar sin,
5 7 tucsat a cur*ach* amach ar muir 7 ro impo an gaeth i n-a n-adh*aidh*,⁴²²) 7 do gabh íta adbulmhor íad no gor tuit tamh mor orra, cor codlat*ar* ass a haithli, gorub é ní do duísig iad, fuaim tuinde f*ria* tir. Is andsin fuarat*ar* oil*en* ferglass, fíraluind, 7 sruth linnglan leamhnochta ar a larmedhón. Acus do ibs*et* a
10 lor-daíthin ass, 7 ni fhuarat*ar* nech ro aicill*edh* íad and. Acus go gabat*ar* ga mol*adh* go mór; 7 raidhsed an laidh and:

Bend*acht* fort, a inis glan, tucais duínd digh dar sássadh;
fuaramur dil ar tarta, do minsruth lo*m*-lem*n*och*t*a.

Alaind do blath fo barr scoth, alaind do gria*n* mód
15 [glanloch,
suairc do níamh tall imat thuind, a glan barrglass bith-
[aluin*d*.

Da madh deoin le righ nimhe, le m*a*c Muiri inghene,
do budh mían lium⁴²³) beith mód caladh is mod caemport.
20 [aboss (*fol.* 51b)

Ni ceduight*e* duínd as daigh aitr*eb* an talm*an* tonnbaín
nídria olc na glere g*raf*,⁴²⁴) iss e Día fen rusbendach.
[Benda*cht*.

Ro lecet*ar* a cur*ach* ar muir 7 ar mor-fhairce. 'Lecem dar n-
25 imrumh,' ar siad, '7 seolf*aidh* an gaeth an leth bus ail le Dia sind'; 7 do bat*ar* co cend t*ri* la 7 téora n-oidhce mar sin go fucut*ar* oil*en* uath*a* 7 croind duillecha dosmora and, 7 so*n*nach airg*id* ar lar-medhon na hindse, 7 cora fir-éisc innte 7 sdiall airg*id* aenghil a tim*chell* na corudh sin; 7 ba meidight*ech* re colbt*aigh*
30 bliadhna gach br*adan* blaith ballcorc*ra* ac baethlem*n*igh suas f*ris* an coruich.⁴²⁵) 'Is derb lind,' ar síad, 'isat muindtir do Dia fil andso, 7 caithem ní don íasc, 7 beirem lind ar ndil de.' Acus doronsad aml*aidh* sin. Robat*ar* tri la 7 t*ri* hoidhce and, 7 doronsad an l*aeidh*:

---

⁴²²Read *aghaidh*.
⁴²³Read *linn*.
⁴²⁴*in ria olc na gleo galach* Mis. to K. Meyer, p. 314.
⁴²⁵Read *coraid*.

Then the clerics did as he counseled them and they were convoyed northward to the Bay of Comgall. And they were given a secret and secluded cell there, and were served and attended well by the King, until their time was out.

And they took leave of the King, and they put their coracle out to sea. And the wind turned against them. And sore thirst seized them; and then they fell on sleep. And what awakened them was the sound of the wave against the shore. Then found they a fair island and a clean stream of new milk through the midst thereof. And they drank their fill from that stream. And they found none that might hold speech with them. And they set to praising the island, and they made this lay:

> "A blessing on thee, O clean island,
> Thou hast given us our fill of drinking;
> Of our thirst we got us the stilling
> From the smooth stream of clean new milk.
>
> Fair thy bloom under flowery crown;
> Fair thy gravel strand round thy pure lakes;
> Fair thy shining yonder around thy wave,
> O pure, green topped, ever beautiful isle!
>
> If it were the will of the King of Heaven,
> The Son of Mary the Virgin,
> I would fain abide here,
> About thy harbor and gentle port.
>
> It is not suffered us, I deem,
> To dwell in the land of white surface.
> . . . .
> It is God himself that hath blessed it."

They put their coracle out to sea and upon the main.

"Let us leave off rowing," they say, "and the wind will guide us whither God willeth us to go."

They were three days and three nights thus, until they saw an island before them, and leafy bushy trees therein, and a silver palisade in the midst thereof, and a salmon weir therein, and a border of pure white silver encompassing that weir. And as big as a year old calf was every white purple-spotted salmon leaping up against the weir.

"We be sure," say they, "that it is the household of God that is here. Let us eat of the fish and take with us our fill thereof."

And thus they did. And they were three days and three nights there, and they made this lay:

Inis roglan rancamar, ni rancamar riam remhe,
aingil De dá dechcoimet 's ac forcoimhet a fledhe.

Cora alainn aircid ghil ar lar-medhon na hindse,
ecne breca ballcorcrai do lingdís os a cind-se.

5 A huisce sáer so-mhilis a hiasc a cnuas atcither;
ni faicem[426]) a hindamail noco roichem an riched.

A sirghnais a sir-aitreb ro badh mían ar a millse,
's na ceola do cualamar is fuarumar san inse. Inis ro.

A haitli na laide sin, tucsat a curach ar dromcladh na fairge re
10 fassenamh na gaithe gail-finne,[427]) go facatar a cind teora la 7
teora n-oidche, oilen ardglan ingantach uatha, 7 daine uathmara
and, go cenduib cat 7 co corpuib daine. Acus do gab ecla na
clerich rompo, 7 ro gabsat re taeb na hindse co tarla a cathraigh
iad, 7 fuarutar clerech is an cathraigh 7 casair fuilt find imme.
15 Benduigeis cách da celi dib, 7 fochtaid na clerich scela de, 7 ro
indiss doib a techt a tir n-Erend lucht curaigh, '7' [ar se], 'do
cosnamair leth na hindse si ris na caitcenduib, 7 as marb lucht an
curaich acht mesi am aenar.' 'Ticidh lium,' ar se, 'co tucar-sa
aeídighecht tri la 7 tri n-oidhce daeib, 7 dogebthai iasc 7 cruith-
20 necht, 7 fin.' Acus doronsat an laeidh and:

Innes duind a senoír sin, cuich do cinel, a clerich?
cred dorad tu cend a cend a comhaitreb na caitcend?

Raidhim-se rib, nocha chel, d'feruib Erend mo cinel,
indte famselbadh soladh[428]) romhoiledh romaltromadh.

---

[426]Read faicfeam, *ibid.*, p. 314.
[427]Cf. § 372 *find-muir*.
[428]*inti rom-selb 7 rom-solam*, ibid., p. 315.

"We have come to a very pure island,
Never before have we reached it;
Angels of God they that guard it,
That keep watch over its good things.

A beautiful weir of pure silver
There is in the midst of the island;
Salmon purple-spotted and speckled,
Go leaping over its waters.

In its very sweet water of virtue
Its fish are seen crowded together.
The like of it we shall not witness
Till we reach the Kingdom of Heaven.

To dwell and abide there forever,
Would be our desire, for its sweetness,
For what we have heard of its music,
And what there received on the island."

355[b] And when they had made that lay, they set their coracle on the ridge of the sea, before the rising of a fair wind, until they beheld at the end of three days and three nights a great island passing large and clear. And there were there monstrous folk with heads of cats and with bodies of men.

And the clerics were affrighted, and they skirted the island until they came to a city. And they found a cleric in the city, and a chasuble of white hair[cloth] upon him. And either saluted other, and the clerics asked tidings of him. And he told them that a boat-load had come from the land of Erin.

"And," saith he, "we did seize the half of the island from the Cat-heads, and the folk of the coracle are all dead save myself alone. Come with me," saith he, "and partake for three days and three nights of my hospitality, and ye shall get fish and wheat and wine."

And they made this lay:

"'Old man, of this give us tidings,
Where are thy kindred, O cleric?
What hath placed thee here shoulder to shoulder,
Dwelling together with Cat-heads?'

'I tell it thee, I conceal naught;
My race is the lineage of Erin.
There I was master of riches;
There I was fostered and nourished.

Foirend curaich, cumain lem,   tancamar a hiath Erend,
do sheíd gaeth an curuch cas   tar an lind-mhuir lethanglaiss.

Ro-m-dirich Día, as demhin lem,   cus an crich-se na caitchend;
ba hí ar n-obuir, nir suaill sin,   cocadh cruaidh re caitchen-
                                                    [daib.

Leth na hindse, tiar is toir,   ro lecsat duind 'n-a degaidh;
marb m'aes cumt[h]a ar nar ceis,   duinn-e fa hurchra aindeis
                                                    [Innes.

Ceilebruis cach dá cheli dib a cend tri la 7 tri n-oidce, 7 cuirid
na clerich a curach amach tar an muir meruallach acus tar trethan
tond, co facatar iar scís anfaidh, oilen alaind ingantach 7 bile
buadha ar a lar-medon, 7 cris aircid áingil in a urthimcell, 7
duillebur oír air, 7 ro leth a barr tar an oilén uile. Acus do bi
gach geg da raibe ar an crand sin lán d' enaib aille con eitib
airgid ainghil, 7 aen én mór ar uachtar an bile co cend oir 7 con
eitibh airgid. Acus assedh nocanadh an t-én sin o maidin go tert,
scela tossaich domain go gen Crist, o teirt go medhón-lai, genemaint
Crist 7 a macgnimharta 7 a baisdedh 7 a eiserghe, o medhon-lai
go noín, scela brigmara borrfadhacha an bratha ga n-indesin. An
tan do cluindís na heoín eli sin, rocrothidís a n-eitedha 7 rosbuaildis a nguilbne in-a taebaibh go mbendaís srotha fola esta re
cloisdin sceoil uathmair urbadaigh an laei sin. Iar sin tra, do
tuit a suan cotalta ar na clerchib ris an ceol sirechtach sirbind
rocandaeis na heoin aille sin do gegaib an bile os a cind, 7 roslecsat duille alaind ordha don crand orra anuas, cor folaidh uile
iad. Bá samalta re seiche doim riata ar med an duille sin. 'Beridh
lib an duille,' bar an t-én mor, '7 cuiridh ar altoír C. C. hí.' Acus
adbert an laeid and:

Beiridh lib an duillend sa,   a clerche blaithe binde.
d'foillsiughadh a mirbuile   ar altoir Coluim Cille.

The crew of a ship, I remember,
We came from the country of Erin;
Our nimble boat then the wind blew
Over the sea broad and green.

It was God that led me, I know it,
To this land where the Cat-heads were dwelling,
And our task it was,—no slight one surely—
Hard battle to wage against Cat-heads.

Half of the isle, west and eastward,
They left to us here behind them.
Dead are my comrades . . . . .
To us the loss was a sad one.' "

355[c] Then after three days and three nights they took leave each of other, and the clerics sent forth their coracle over the quick wilful sea, and across the high watered waves until when they were wearied with the storm they perceived an isle passing beautiful and wondrous, and a tree of virtue in midst thereof, and a girdle of shining silver encircling it, and a golden leaf thereon, and its summit spreading over the whole island. And every bough on that tree was full of beautiful birds with wings of shining silver. And from matins to tierce the bird sang the tidings of the world to the birth of Christ, and from tierce until mid-day the birth of Christ and His youthful deeds and His baptizing and His resurrection. And from midday till nones were recounted the mighty and moving tidings of Doomsday. And as the other birds listened, they flapped their wings and struck their beaks against their sides, so that they drew therefrom streams of blood when they heard the baneful fearsome tidings of that day.

And a while after that, sleep fell upon the clerics with the rapturous sweetness of the melody that those beautiful birds did sing from the boughs of the tree above them. And the birds let drop down upon them a beautiful golden leaf from that tree, and it covered them all. And like to the hide of a full-grown ox was the size of that leaf.

"Take with you the leaf" saith the great bird, "And lay it upon the altar of Columcille." And he uttered this lay:

"Take this leaf away with you,
O white sweet clerics,
That it may make known its wonder
On the altar of Columcille.

Ag cantain an buan molta,   adcluintí a aes caidh cumtha,[429]
ar an mbile buadhu-sa,   bemíd gan aeis gan urchrai.

Ar amus bur tigerna   Coluim Cille na ceilidh,
scela imdha (fol. 52a) ilardha,   inganta an betha[430]) beridh.
[Beridh.

Roergetar na cleirich ass a suan iar sin, 7 do cuatar in a curuch,
7 ní facutar an bile inaid na heoin. Atcondcatar a cend athaidh
iar sin oilen oili 7 croind duillecha dosmhóra and, 7 mil imdha
ac siledh da cranduib, 7 loch lind-glan lan-aluind ar a larmedon
con ngrianán ngloinidhe do margáret 7 do clochaibh uaisli eli.
Daine imda uathmara ardmora 'san indse go cendaib con 7 go
mongaib ech 7 gu corpuib daine. Rusgab ecla na clerich rompo
7 tucsat a curach re taeb na hindse, 7 do condcatar a taeb lan do
smeruib 7 d'airnedhaibh 7 dá gach cnuas ar cena, 7 do gabsat og
a cnuasacht 7 ag caithem a ndila do na toirtibh; 7 fuaratar ar an
traigh senoir 7[431]) sruith-ecna co cassair fuilt find ime.[432])
Bendaigis cach da celi dib, 7 fiarfaighis an senóir dib canus tancatar,
7 do innesitar do a techt a hErind. 'Anaid abuss,' ar se, '7
dogebthai betha gan aeis gan urcra am farradh-sa.' Roansad and
go cend tri la 7 teora n-oidhce, 7 timnaid ced 7 ceilebradh dó iar
sin, 7 tíagaid 'n-a curach 7 doronsat an laeidh:

Suairc an inis rancamar,   imga a cnuas, caemh a caingen;
oilen buadhu blath-solus   a mbi timthirecht aingel.

Do badh mían ler n-aicned-ne   beith is an indse mbarrglain,
sinn go buan da caidreb-se   ac túar nime dár n-anmain.

Maith ant inadh foistine   do neoch no biadh go sadhul;
maith ant inadh oilithre   ac nech do denamh crabhaidh.

---

[429]do cluinti a aés cumta, ibid., p. 316.
[430]an bracha, ibid.
[431]Omit.
[432]co casail ngil ime for a cind Y. B. L. (fol. 87ᵇ 10-11).

OF THE ISLE OF THE DOG-HEADS

> Chanting the praises eternal
> . . . . . noble companions,
> Upon this great tree of virtue,
> We shall be without age, without sorrow.
>
> For the surprise of your master,
> Columcille of the Guestings,
> Tidings many and varied,
> Strange tidings of life do ye carry."

355[d] Then the clerics rose up from their sleep and they entered their coracle. And they saw no more the tree or the birds. And within a while after they beheld another isle, and leafy thick branched trees there, and much honey dripping from those trees, and a right beautiful clear lake in midst thereof, with a crystal bower of pearls and other noble stones. Monstrous folk many and huge were in that island that had heads of dogs and manes of horses and bodies of men. And the clerics were afeared of them and they skirted the isle and they beheld its side full of berries and sloes and every kind of fruit. And they set to gathering them and ate their fill thereof.

And they found on the strand an old man passing wise that wore a chasuble of white hair [cloth]. Then either saluted other, and the old man asked them whence they came. And they told him they were come from Erin.

"Abide in this place," saith he, "and ye shall have life with me without age or sorrow."

They abode there three days and three nights. And they took their leave and departed from him then and they entered their coracle, and they made the lay:

> "Pleasing the isle we have come to;
> Many its fruits; its rule gentle;
> Isle of virtue, luminous, shining,
> Place where the angels visit.
>
> Pleasing it were to our nature
> To be in the isle clear and chosen;
> Ever to be there within it,
> For our souls awaiting there Heaven.
>
> That were a good place of resting
> For one that seeketh for solace;
> Of pilgrimage that were a good place
> For one that maketh devotions.

Colum Cille ar tigerna   nach bi re fand go fúachdha,
clerech ségda soidhelbha,   do-ber sind-e go suarca. Suairc.

Tiagaid ar muinchinn mara 7 mor-fhairge iar sin, 7 do tuit a
toirrcim suain orra, 7 as e ro duísich íad, fuaim tuinne fri tir.
5 Atrachtatar iar sin, 7 do condcatar oilen suthach siretrocht⁴³³) 7
methli ac buain arbha and do dainib do-delba duaibsecha, go
cendaib muc 7 go corpuib daine. O'tcondcatar an curach ag
mallfascnamh an mara da n-indsoighe, ro gabsat ga ndibhrucadh
do moírlechaibh na tragha. Ro impoiset na cleirich a curach re
10 taeb na hindse, 7 ro lensat na torathoir is an muir íad no cor
falchadh iad uile acht a cind. "A muindtir C. C.' ar siad, 'na
ticidh oraind, uair is do sil Caimh colaigh claeinbrethaigh sinn,
7 as si an muir as aitreb duinn, 7 an t-oilen-sa do trebadh⁴³⁴). Acus
doronsad an laeidh and:

15   A muindtir Choluim Cille,   da foghnann an fhírinde,⁴³⁵)
fágaidh an t-oilen atám,   uair ni cubhaidh ar comrádh.

Sinn-e ar slicht Caimh coluich,   miscnigh, molfa,
                                     [mallachtaich,
as hí ar n-aitreb an muir mor,   's nochan fhaicer ar n-urmor.

20   Is againn ata in gach tan   an t-oilen-sa ga aitreb,
na ticidh oraind alle,   a muindtir Coluim Cille.

Tancatar iar sin ar an ardmuir n-imdoinn 7 tar dromcladh na
dilend, 7 rocaised frasa firtruagha, 7 do muig tuirsi 7 dobron
orrtadh. Acus do batar ac imrádh C. C. go mor, 7 rocansad a
25 sailm; 7 nir cian doib and go facutar oilen uatha, 7 co cualutar
na mna 7 sianan sirbind aca gá canamhain. Acus tancatar cuca
do taeb an oilein 7 asedh no candaeís: 'Sen De donfe for don te
mac Muiri ronfelathar.'⁴³⁶) 'Canaidh sin duind, a mna,' ar na
clerich, 'oir is abhran ban Erend é.' Ro frecratar na mná íad

---

⁴³³Read sírétrocht.
⁴³⁴Perhaps meaning is 'to till'.
⁴³⁵See § 356 for similar construction.
⁴³⁶See Thes. Pal., II, p. 299; Irische Texte mit Wört, p. 6; R. C., XXVI, § 50,
p. 162.

> Columcille is our master;
> Not spiteful is he to the weaklings;
> A stately cleric and comely
> That doth bring us to places full fair.''

355[e] Then went they on the ridge of the sea and the great ocean, and a deep sleep fell on them, and it was this that awakened them, the sound of the wave against the land. Then they rose up and they saw a fruitful, delightful island, and a band of folk reaping corn there, men ill shaped and loathly, with heads of swine and bodies of men. When these beheld the coracle slowly sailing the sea toward them, they took to pelting it with the big stones on the shore. Then the clerics steered their bark along the coast of the island and the monsters pursued them into the sea until they were covered all save their heads.

"O household of Columcille," say they, "Come not unto us, for we be of the seed of shrewish Ham and the sea is our abiding place and we till this island." And they made the lay there:

> "O household of Columcille,
> Whom the truth serveth,
> Leave the isle we abide in;
> Our converse for thee is not fitting.
>
> Of the race of Ham are we, wicked,
> Odious, monstrous, accursed;
> Our dwelling place is the great ocean,
> And the most of us dwell unseen there.
>
> It is we it is that at all times,
> Have our dwelling here on this island.
> Come ye then not anigh us,
> Ye of Columcille's household!''

They went out then upon the great deep and upon the ridge of the waves, and they wept tears of true sadness, and grief and sorrow overcame them. And they set their thoughts right earnestly on Columcille, and they chanted their psalms.

355[f] And it was not long ere they beheld an island, and they heard women singing a melodious song. And the clerics came to the island. And it was this the women were singing:

> "May God's blessings guide us and help us,
> May the Son of Mary be round us!''

"Sing that for us, O women," say the clerics, "for it is a song of the women of Erin."

7 assedh no raidhsit ríu: 'Ticidh linde d'acalladh an righ.' Acus
do cuatar les na mnaib d'aculladh an righ. Feruis an ri failte
friu, 7 fochtus scéla dib canus tancatar no cía hiad fen. 'Do
muindtir C. C. sinde,' ar síad, '7 a hErind tancamur.' 'An fedu-
bhair ca lin mac do Domhnall mac Aeda mic Ainmirech as beo.'
'En mac,' ar iad san, '.i. Donnchadh, uair ro marbsat Fir Rois 7
Mughorn Maighen an mac eli .i. Fiachra, 7 ba hinmain lind an
lucht ler tuit .i. Diarmaid Ollmhar 7 Oilill, 7 ni fedamar a ndil
o sin ille.' 'Scela fire sin,' ol an ri, '7 as sinde ro marb mac righ
Erend, 7 atamíd gan aeis gan urcra andso, 7 bemíd no co tí Eli 7
Enoc do cathughadh fri hAntecrist, acus as beo rachmaid-ne 'sa
cath faríu, 7 dogebam bas. Acus as amlaidh atámíd 7 trillsi áille
ordae oraind, 7 da roichí-se go hErind, ataid da loch andso .i. loch
tenedh 7 loch uisce, 7 muna beith Martain 7 Pátraig, do roicfedh
gach loch dib tar Eirind o cíanuib.' 'Is saeth lind,' ar na clérich,
'nach faicmid Elí 7 Enóg con n--aicillmís iad.' 'Ni fuigthí-si iad,,'
ol se 'oír ataid a n-inad díamhair, 7 beid and sin no co tecaid do
cathughadh re hAntecrist. Do fobratar na clerich imtecht. Adubairt an ri ríu: 'Anaidh abus mar atamid-ne no co mben d'en
taeib; oir ni fhuaramar o do fhácbhamar Ere ní badh gairde lind
ina in fedh o tancabhair-se chucaind.' Acus as amlaidh do bi an t-
oilen sin 7 tibra in-a dorus. Acus do cuatar na clerich da fothrucadh
and, 7 fuaratar fon a mian í, itir tess 7 fhuacht, 7 an braén (fol.
52b) noferadh anuas indte, as se notéigedh an t-uisce. Is andsin
rocuirset a curach amach, 7 do batar fri re cian oc ascnámh docum
tire, 7 adbertatar.

Guidhium rí na righ,   dolai an duillend dund;
guidem Muire mhor,   naromcuire[r].

Then answered the women and said to them: "Come with us and have speech with the King."

And they went with the women to speak with him. And he welcomed them and asked tidings of them whence they came and who they were.

"We be of the household of Columcille," they say, "and we be come from Erin."

"Know ye what number of the sons of Domnall mac Aeda son of Ainmire there be still alive?"

"One son," say they, "to wit, Donnchad; for the Fir Roiss and Mugdorn Maighen slew the other son, Fiachra. And dear to us were those by whom they fell, Diarmaid Ollmhar and Oilill, and we know not their fate since then."

"These be true tidings," saith the King, "and we it was that slew the son of Erin's King. And we be here without age and without decay. And we shall be here till Elijah and Enoch come to war with Anti-Christ. And we shall fare forth living into that battle and there get our death. And it is in this wise we be, with beautiful tresses of gold upon us. And if ye reach Erin, [tell them] that there be two lakes here, to wit, a lake of fire and a lake of water, and were it not for Martin and Padraic those lakes were long since over Erin."

"It is a grief to us," say the clerics, "that we see not Elijah and Enoch, to hold converse with them."

"Ye may not come unto them," saith he, "for they be in a secret place, and they shall abide there until they come to fight with Anti-Christ."

And the clerics were in point to depart. But the King said to them: "Tarry with us till we be friends, for we have found not sith that we left Erin a time that passed more swiftly than the time since ye came to us."

And the island was in this wise, having a well at its entrance. And the clerics went to bathe therein. And they found it to their liking, both warm and cold. And the drop that poured down thereon did heat the water.

Then they put their coracle [upon the sea] and they were a long time sailing ere they came to land. And they said:

> "We pray to the King of Kings
> That did send down upon us the leaf;
> We pray to Mary the powerful
> That we may not be overcome.

Guidem Padraig naemh,   nach am-saruigh[i] sín;
guidem Findtan fial   go finntar ar ndíl.

Guidhium Petar [7] Pol   go rumlecar slan;
guidem ilar naemh   corup siubal samh.

Guidhem Colam caidh,   ar Colam d'ar ndín;
cuirem í go an,⁴³⁷)   guidem Ri na righ.
                                          Guidium.

Robatar co fada gan talamh d'faicsin no co facutar a cind trill
iar sin oilen uatha; 7 as amlaidh do bi an t-oilen sin 7 aitreb
aluind ilgresach ar a lar 7 dá cet dorus ar an tecdhuis sin, 7
altoir ar adhuig gaca doruis dib, 7 fer graid co n-ecusc n-orda ac
naemadh coirp Crisd ar agaidh gacha haltora dibh. Acus tancatar
muindter C. C. astech iar sin, 7 do feradh fir-chain failte friu. Acus
mar do batar and, do lecedh cochall alaind ordha anuas ar urlar
na peloide rigdha sin. Acus nír gab en-duine do lucht na tec-
dhaisi sech a celi é; uair ni fetatar cia dar deonaich Dia é.
Acus as í comairle doronsat a tabairt do muindtir C. C. Acus do
fretladh 7 do frithoiledh iad an oidhce sin, 7 ro dailedh lind sen
somesctha orra gur ba mesca medhairchain iad. Acus rucatar
ass an adhaig sin 7 do timnatar ceiliubradh do cach ar na márach,
7 tiagait ar muir, 7 do batar ag admoladh an oilein. Acus doronsat an laeidh:

Aitreb niamdha naem ainglidhe,   fuaramar íar scís fhairce;
mocen do Crist caem-chaingnech, maith do coraigh gach
                                              [taidbhse.

Da ced comla caem doruis   ar in cathraigh coir cúplaidh;
altóir senta saersholus   ar agaidh gacha dúnaidh.

Eídedh fa lor loghmaire   ar cach altoir 'sa caembrogh;
fer co n-ecusc nórdae,   corp Crisd aice ga náemhadh.

⁴³⁷*guidhim Isa án* (with acute accent over cap *I*). Mis. to K. Meyer, p. 319

> We pray to Padraic the holy,
> That the tempest may not defeat us,
> We pray to freehearted Findtan
> For the finding of our fortune.
>
> We pray to Paul and to Peter
> To suffer our passing in safety;
> We pray the saints in their numbers
> That we may have prosperous voyage.
>
> We pray to Colum the noble;
> Our Columcille for our protection;
> We call upon Jesu the Gentle;
> We pray to the King of Kings.''

355[g] For a long time they were without sight of land until at last they beheld an island. And in this wise was that island: a dwelling fair and well adorned in the midst thereof, having two hundred doors and an altar afore every door and a man in Holy Orders in golden apparel consecrating Christ's body afore every altar.

And the household of Columcille entered then, and a right courteous welcome was given them. And whilst they were there, a beautiful golden cowl was let down upon the floor of that royal hall. And not one of the folk of the house took it up rather than another, for they knew not for whom God willed it. And this is the counsel that they took, to give it to the household of Columcille. And they were richly served and had great cheer that night, and they were given well brewed ale so that they were drunken and merry. And they tarried there that night. And on the morn they bade farewell to all and went out upon the sea. And they praised the island. And they made the lay:

> ''A bright dwelling, shining and holy,
> We found after the wearisome sea;
> Welcome to Christ of rule gentle,
> Well hath he made every sight.
>
> Two hundred fair doors there
> In the righteous city—
> A blessed altar of noble light
> In front of every dwelling.
>
> A cloth of great price
> On every altar in the fair mansion;
> A man there in golden garments,
> The body of Christ consecrating.

Fir 7 mna ac sírguidhe   im gach altoir gó cheli;
ba hadbal a línmhaire,   's iat ac moladh righ greíne.

O taínic trath proindighte,   rucsat leo sinn cum loingthe,
'sa cuirt gresaich gloinide   dobo sochraid ar soillse.

5   Ga drem rind ba seimhidhe   no lucht frithoilte an tighe?
sind re fedh ar céilidhi,   gan esbaidh bidh no dighe.

Ga drem rind fa braithremla   no lucht cumaind facuibdhe?
gor tuit cochall caileamail,   cucaind ar lar na bruighne.

O nar fhidir en duine   cia dar deonaigh ri nemda,
10 nir ben nech don caemchuire   ris an cochall saer senta.

Do raidset tre oilemhain,   do briathruib blaithe binde:
'Beiridh an sed soinemail   co Colum craibtech Cille'.

Semidhe na saeraingil   do carsam tre n-a caidremh;
nir fedsam acht aen-adhaigh   anadh aca san aitrebh.
15   Aitrebh.

Do batar na clerich iar sin go dubach dobronach 7 siad ac imradh
C. C.; 7 ac rad na mbriathar sin doib, tainic sidhe gaeithe adhfuaíre
imluime da n-indsoighe no go riachtatar co hÍ. Is andsin do bi
C. C. ac tect timcell reilge Odhráin, 7 do gab an curach caladport.
20 Conadh "Port an Curaigh" ainm an inaidh in ar gab. Ro fiarfaigh C. C. scela dib, 7 do indesitar a fuaratar d'ulc 7 do maith
ó tus go deredh do. Acus tucadh an cochall 7 an duillend dó, 7
mairidh fos, an duillend a n-Í 7 ro scribadh an scél aca. Conadh
"Sechran clerech C. C."[438]) conuice sin. Et do cuir sé an cochall

---

[438]See *YBL* 86 B 29.

Men and women praying always,
From altar [proceeding] to altar;
Vast [in sooth] was their number,
Praising the King of the Sun.

When came then the hour of dining,
They took us with them to supper,
To the hall adorned and of crystal;
Our lights there were lights of beauty.

Where hath been to us folk more gentle
Than the serving-folk of that mansion?
We were some while at the banquet,
No lack there of food nor of drinking.

Where were there folk more like brothers
Or fellowship more concordant,
Till there fell a cowl of endowments
For us in the midst of the mansion?

Since no man there possessed knowledge
For whom Heaven's King had designed it,
None of these gentle folk took it,
The cowl that was noble and blessed.

Then spake they with gentle breeding,
With words that were sweet and full gracious,
Bear the treasure full precious
To Columcille that is pious.

Most gentle angels full noble,
That we have loved for their friendship,
For one sole night were we able
To tarry with them in their dwelling.''

Then were the clerics in sadness and heaviness, thinking on Columcille. And as they said those words there came a blast of wind right cold and bleak against them and drove them to Iona.

355[h] And Columcille was walking around the churchyard of Odran when the coracle entered the port. And so the Port of the Coracle is the name of the place where it took harbor.

Columcille asked tidings of them and they told him all that had befallen them, of bad and of good, from beginning to end. And the cowl and the leaf were given to him. And they still exist, the leaf in Iona. And they wrote down the history.

Thus far the *Wanderings of Columcille's Clerics*.

le haingl*ibh* De a n-Erind 7 adubairt ríu a breith co cill airidhe da
cell*aibh* fen da ngoirter Cill Mic Ne*n*a*in* aniugh, a *c*rich cineoil
Conaill Gulb*an*. Acus do facbatar na haing*il* ar leic cloiche do
bi uim*ir* áiridhe do mílt*ibh* on cill sin é. Conadh ''Lec an Cochaill'' ainm na leice íh sin. Acus ar na foillsiug*hadh* sin do nech
naemta do bi sa mbaile, do ch*uaidh* se ar cend an coch*aill*, 7 tuc
se leis é; cor cuir*edh* a cás onórach ar na c*umh*dach d'or 7 d'airced
é. Co*n*ad é as airmind do C. C. ag denamh f*er*t 7 mirb*aile* a Cill
Mic Nena*in* aniugh.

356.⁴³⁹) La airidhe do C. C. a ndége*n*ach a aimsire ag denam
urnaidhe ag tect timcell reilge a nÍ, 7 do cond*aic* ben boc*ht* ag
buain neandtoíge, 7 do fiarf*aigh* di cred dob ail le do denamh ria.
'Ni fhuil do beath*a* agam,' ar si, 'acht a nendtóc-sa do bruith ar
uisce 7 pra *(fol.* 53a) issech do denamh dí. Et ata en-bó a bfuil
laeg agam, 7 sailim í do breith an laigh sin gach la tic damh, 7
ata an doig sin a ta*n*⁴⁴⁰) agam as an mboin do breith laigh 7 an
praissech gom shasadh. 'Truag dam-sa,' ar C. C., '7 co saeilim
flaithes De d'fhagail n*ach* foghnann leitheíd na praisce sin do
beth*aidh* damh, 7 as deimhin nach caithfe mesi a haithe*rr*ach do
beth*aidh* ó so amach com bas.' Do-beredh C. C. fa dera an
praiss*ech* do denam 'n-a fiadnaise fen g*ach* laí ar ecla go cuirf*idhe*
en-réd indte *acht* nendtóc 7 uisce. Et mar do cond*aic* an serbfoghant*aidh* do bi ag denam na p*r*aisce .i. Diarmaid, nach caith*edh*
C. C. do beth*aidh* *acht* sin, do bi do gradh aicce dó, d'ecla go
fuighed[h] se bas go luath le c*r*uas na beth*adh* sin do bi aice, an
maide léa ngnath*aigh*e*adh* sé b*eith* ag mescadh na praisce, co
*n*derna se fedan an*d*, 7 do cuir*edh* se im 'sa bfedán sin docum go
leagadh an t-im ar fud na praisce. Do foillsigh an t-aing*el* sin do
C. C., 7 tuc se an serbfhoghantaighe sin cuice, 7 adub*air*t se ris
nach benfadh se nemh de trid sin 7 gan a denamh ó sin amach.
Acus do comhaill C. C. an gelladh sin tuc se, oir nir caith se do
biaidh an fad do bi se 'n-a beth*aidh* *acht* an p*r*aisech sin amháin.

357.⁴⁴¹) Fechtus do C. C. in a duirrth*igh* fen a n-Í, 7 do bi
dias da mhanch*aibh* fen an uair sin a ndorus an duirrth*ighe*,

---

⁴³⁹Same story in *F. O.*², p. 147; *LB* [236], col. 2.

⁴⁴⁰*at* (with a dash over *t*) MS. Perhaps for at*a*. Then translate 'and while
I am waiting for her to calve, I am living on the broth'. *LB, ibid.*, ll. 31-33, has
"aenbó fil ocu*m* 7 i*n*d laeg hi 7 iss*ed* so fognas da*m* oca hurnaige cian uad".

⁴⁴¹Taken literally from Adamnan. See Reeves' *Adam.*, p. 227 ff.

He sent the cowl by angels of God to Erin and bade them carry it to a certain one of his churches yclept Cill mic Nenain, in the domain of the clan of Conall Gulban. And the angels left it upon a flagstone that was some miles distant from that church, so that the Flagstone of the Cowl is the name of that flagstone. And when this was revealed to a holy man that was in the monastery, he went to get the cowl and brought it home with him. And it was put in a right worshipful shrine covered with gold and silver. And so it is a high relic of Columcille, working wonders and miracles in Cill mic Nenain to this day.

XXXII
OF THE LAST DAYS OF COLUMCILLE

356. On a certain day toward the end of his life Columcille was saying his prayers as he walked around the churchyard in Iona, and he saw a poor woman cutting nettles. And he asked her what she would do with them.

"I have no means of life," saith she, "save to boil these nettles in water and to make broth thereof. And my one cow is in calf, and I hope each day that passeth that she will bring forth the calf, and already for some time I have had that hope while subsisting on the broth."

"Alas for me," saith Columcille, "and I hoping to gain the Kingdom of God, that the like of that broth doth not suffice me for life. For a sooth I shall eat no other food save that henceforward."

And each day Columcille let make the broth in his sight lest aught be put therein save nettles and water. And when Diarmaid, the servant that made the broth, saw that Columcille ate no food save that, he had such love of him, and such fear lest he die soon with the hardship of the life he led, that he made a pipe in the stick wherewith he was wont to mix the broth, and he put butter therein, so that the butter flowed through the broth. And an angel made known this thing to Columcille. And he called his servant to him and said to him that for that thing he would not take Heaven from him, but he should do it no more from that time. And Columcille did fulfil his vow; for the while he lived he ate naught save that broth alone.

357. On a time whenas Columcille was in his oratory in Iona, and there were twain of the brethren at the door thereof, to wit, Laignen and Pilba, he lifted up his eyes and his hands and there came a right beautiful and shining light into his face, and he made signs of joy and de-

Laignen 7 Pilba a n-anmanda;⁴⁴²) 7 do thóg a rusca 7 a lamha
súas, 7 tainic delradh roalaind rologhmar in a, a⁴⁴³) agaidh, 7
dorinde comhartha mor gairdechais 7 solais an uair sin. Acus fa
aimsir girr iar sin, do claechlo an solas mor sin do bi air a tuirrse
7 a ndolás imarcach do. Acus ar na faicsin sin do na manchaibh
adubramar romhaind, do lin tuirse 7 dobron mór iad fén, 7 do
guidhetar C. C. im a fhis do tabairt doib cred ba cíall do na hair-
ghenaibh sin do condcatar fen ac imtecht air. Do frecair C. C.
íad 7 assedh adubairt: 'A cland gradhach,' ar se, 'ata do met mo
gradu ssa daeib nach eidir lem tuirse d'fulang oraib gan fis na
neichedh atathaí d'iarraid do tabairt dáeib; 7 denaid run oram an
cein mairfed fen.' Acus ar na gelladh sin doib-sean, do labair
C. C. ríu do briathraibh tuirrsecha dobronacha 7 assedh adubairt:
'Ataim deich mbliadna xx anos ar deoraighecht a fecmais Erend
a n-Albain 7 a mBretain, 7 fos ataím anois morán do laithibh ac
guidhe De fam anmain do breith on deoraighecht sa in a fuilim
docum na cathrach nemdha, 7 do condarc aingli De ag techt o
cianaib a n-aircis m'anma da breith leo ass an prisún-sa an cuirp
daenda in a bfuil se; 7 dob e sin adbar an tsolais do condcabhair-si
oram; 7 do connarc na haingil cedna ac denamh comhnaidhe a
port na hindse si in a bfuilim, 7 toirmesc ar n-a chur o Día orra
tria guidhe naemh Erend 7 Alban 7 na heclaissi a moran d'ina-
duibh eli do bi ac guidhe De fa gan mesi do breith uatha a
comluath sin. Et tainic do brigh a nguidhe, an ní sin do gnoaigh-
hes-sa o Día do cur ar cairde, 7 ceithri bliadhna eli do chur d'fhad
ar mo shaegal, 7 as hí an cairde sin do cuiredh oram dob adbur
tuirse acus dobroin damh.' Acus do bi C. C. ag dortadh a dér ag
indesin na scel sin do na manchaibh, 7 fos adubairt ríu, ar cur
criche ar na ceithri bliadhnaibh, go fuighedh se fen bas sochraidh
onorach gan tendess gan tshaéthar gan radharc na droch-spirad
d'fhaicsin dó, 7 co tiucfidis uimhir doairmide d'ainglibh nimhe a
coinde a anma. Do firadh sin uili amail adubairt C. C.

358.⁴⁴⁴) Aroile laithe do C. C. a n-I 'sa ced mí don tsham-
radh, 7 do bi se arsaidh an uair-sin, 7 do bi a corp anfand éccruaid
o cruas na bethadh do bi aice, indus nar fed se dul d'fhechain
an lochta oibre do bi ag na manchaibh 'sa cuid eli don oilen acht
a carbad. Acus do labair ris na manchaibh do bi maille ris an
uaír sin 7 assedh adubairt, corb e ba triall dó fen an saegal d'fagbail 7 dul do caithem na gloire suthaine fare Día na n-uile cum-

---

⁴⁴²*Lugneus* and *Pilu* Adamnan. (Reeves' ed.)
⁴⁴³Omit.
⁴⁴⁴§§ 358-64 follow Adamnan, *ibid.*, p. 228 ff.

light passing great. And short while thereafter the great joy was changed to exceeding heaviness and sorrow. And when the brethren aforementioned beheld this, they also were filled with grief and sorrow and they besought Columcille to let them wit what betokened the change that they saw coming upon him. Then Columcille answered and spake in this wise:

"Beloved children," saith he, "so great is my love for you that I cannot suffer you to be in sadness without discovering to you what ye seek. And promise me that ye will hold it secret the while that I live."

And when they had promised, Columcille spake to them with sad and heavy words, and said:

"Ten years and a score now am I an exile from Erin, in Alba and in Britain. And now for many days have I been praying God to bear away my soul to the heavenly city from this exile whereas I am. And a while since I beheld angels of God coming to bear it with them from this prison of the body whereas it abideth. And this was the cause of the joy ye beheld in me. And those same angels I beheld resting upon the port of this isle whereas I am, and delay put on them by God because of the prayers of the holy men of Erin and Alba and of the Church in many places else, the which were beseeching God to take me not so soon from them. And it befell by reason of their prayers that the thing I had begged from God was set back, and four years more were put to my life. And it is this delay that hath been laid upon me that doth cause me heaviness and sorrow."

And Columcille shed tears as he told these tidings to the brethren. And moreover he told them that at the end of the four years he should have a death beautiful and worshipful, without pain and without labor and without seeing a sight of evil spirits, and that a countless number of heavenly angels should come to meet his soul. And all this fell out as Columcille had said.

358. On another day Columcille was in Iona in the first month of summer, and he was passing ancient at that time, and his body passing weak for the hardness of the life he led, so that he might not go to see the laborers that the brethren had in the other part of the isle, save in his chariot. And he spake to the brethren that were with him at that time and said that it was his desire to leave the world and to go to enjoy the eternal glory with the God of all power. And he said further that they should take no heed thereof; for he suffered a certain delay to be put upon his life, lest his death destroy their joy in that season, for that time was a season of joy, to wit, the time betwixt the Resurrection of our Lord and the coming of the Holy Ghost upon His apostles. And when the brethren heard Columcille speaking of his

acht; 7 fos adubairt se ríu gan fechain dó sin cor ched les fen
cairde ecin do chur ar a shaegal d'ecla co millfedh a bás an solás
do bi aca san an uaír sin, oir dob aimsir sholais an aimser do bi
and an inbaid sin .i. itir eserghe an Tigherna 7 techt an Spirda
Naeim ar na hespulaibh. Acus mar do cualatar na manaich C. C.
ag labairt da bas fen, do línadh do thuirrsi 7 do dobrón íad. Ar
na faicsin sin do-san, do labair do briathraibh romhillse rogra-
dacha ríu, 7 do bi ac tabairt solais doib mar as ferr gorb eidir
les, 7 do bendaigh íad, 7 tainic timcell an oilein iar sin, (fol. 53b)
7 do bendaigh e; 7 ni dernatar naithrecha nimhe digbail do duine
no d'ainmidhe and ó sin alle. Gor morad ainm De 7 C. C. de sin.

359. Fechtus eli do Col. C. iar sin a mainistir hÍ ag estecht
serbísí De, 7 do condaic se an t-aingel ós cind na manach, 7 tainic
delradh imarcach 'n-a aghaid ar na fhaicsin dó; oir nirb eidir les
an soillse ro-mhoir ainglidhe do bi leth astigh in a croidhe gan
hí fen d'fhoillsiughadh don taebh amuigh in a aghaidh re faicsin
an aingil. Acus do fiarfuigetar manaigh airidhe do bi do lathair
andsin de, cred é an delradh mor sin táinic 'n-a agaidh. Do indeis se sin doib gur é an t-aingel docondaic se os cind na manach,
7 fos adubairt ríu gurb ingnadh an t-seimidhecht do bi is na
hainglibh; oir go faca se fen an t-aingel ac dul tria balla na mainestrech amach 7 astech gan truailledh, gan digbail dó fen na don
balla, 7 do indis doib gurub do bendughadh na manach tainic an
t-aingel andsin, 7 d'fechain taiscedha airidhe do bi aice 'sa mainistir do bi se ar tí do breith les. Acus nír tuicetar na manaich
cred í an taiscedh adubairt C. C. do beith ag an aingel; oir nír
minigh sé an bríathar sin doib an uair sin. Acus as í taiscedh
dar labuir C. C. an tan sin .i. da anam fen; oir fuair se bás fa
cend sé la iar sin adhaigh domnaich cincísse do sundradh.

360. Do cuaidh C. C. an satharn iarsin d'fhechain hagaird
na manuch, 7 fuair se da cruaich arbha and, 7 do bi a descibul
fen maille ris .i. Diarmuid; 7 ar n-a fhaicsin sin do, tuc buidechus mór do Día 7 do na manchaibh tre febhus an tigedhais dorindetar. Acus do bendaigh se fen na cruacha iarsin, 7 adubairt
o dob ecen dó a caidreb san d' fhacbail 7 dul do caithemh na
gloire suthaine mailli re n-a Tigerna, cor maith les lón na bliadhna
sain d'fhagbail aca san. Et do fíradh sin; oir do bí sáith an
coimtinoil go cend mbliadhna 'sa da cruaich becca sin tre mar
do bendaigh C. C. íad. Acus mar do cuala Díarmaid e sen ag
labairt da bas fen, do caí go ger tuirrsech, 7 adubairt gorub menic
tuc se dólás doib an bliadhain sin tria na mence do indessedh
doib go bfhuighedh sé bas. Ar na fhaicsin sin do C. C., do bi

death they were filled with heaviness and sorrow. And when he perceived this, Columcille spake to them passing sweet and passing loving words and he gave them solace as best he might, and he gave them his blessing. Then went he round about the island and blessed it. And venomous serpents have done no hurt to man nor to beast in that place to this day. And thus God's name and Columcille's were magnified.

359. Another time after that when Columcille was in the monastery in Iona listening to the service of God, he beheld an angel above the heads of the brethren. And exceeding brightness came into his face when he perceived this, for it might not be that the passing great angelic light that was within his heart should not show itself outwardly in his face when he beheld the angel. And certain of the brethren that were with him in that place asked him what was that great light that had come over his countenance. And he told them that it was an angel he had seen above the brethren. And he said further that wondrous was the subtilty of angels, for he had seen the angel passing through the walls of the monastery outward and inward doing no hurt nor harm neither to himself nor to the walls. And he told them that it was to bless the brethren that the angel had come thither, and to look upon certain treasures of his in the monastery the which he was in point to take away with him. And the brethren understood not what treasure Columcille had said the angel should have, for he construed not his words to them at that time. But the treasure whereof Columcille spake then was his own soul, for he died at the end of six days space right on the eve of Whit-sunday.

360. On the Saturday next following Columcille went to look at the haggard of the monastery and he found there two ricks of corn. And his disciple Diarmaid was with him. And when he beheld the corn he gave passing great thanks to God and to the brethren for the carefulness of their husbandry. And then he blessed the ricks and he said that sithen he must depart from their fellowship and go to have joy of the eternal glory in the fellowship of his Lord, he would fain leave to them a sufficiency for that year. And that word was verified, for there was enough for the household until the year's end in those two small ricks by reason that Columcille had blessed them.

And when Diarmaid heard him speak of his death he wept right bitterly and said it was oft that year he had caused them sadness by the many times he had told them that he was in point to die. And when

se ac tabairt sholais do Diarmaid marꝛ is ferr gor fhed, 7 do bi
se ga tecusc do briathraibh ro-bendaighte ro-naemtha. Et adubairt se ris go raibe secreid aice leth rena bás fen do indeosadh
se dó da madh ail les run do denamh air an cein do mhairfedh
sé fén. Acus ar n-a gelladh sin do Díarmaid, do labuir C. C. ris
7 assedh adubairt, gorb é an satharn do ba la ciunais no saeire
ac cach 'sa seanrecht 7 corub and dorinde Día ciunus ar crichnugadh an oibrighte se laithe dó, do reír mar adeir an dara caibidil
do Genesis .i. an ced leabar don Scribhtuír: 'Requievit ab omni
opere quod patrarat'⁴⁴⁵ .i. 'dorinde ciunus an sectmadh lá o gach
oibriughadh da nderna'. 'Acus do naemh 7 do bendaigh Dia an
la sin, 7 do gab se 'n-a la ciunaiss dó fén é; 7 da reir sin dob
ail le Día ciunus do tabairt damh-sa on michiunus a bfuilim ag
cathughadh ris an saeghal 7 ris an diabhal 7 ris an corp dháenda-
ssa ata umam. Et ó asse an domnach as lá ciunais anos is an
recht núa, dogeb-sa bás 'sa medhon-oidhce anocht indus co mbeinn
a ciunus na gloíre suthaine amarach dé domhnaigh.' Mar do
cuala an descibul sin .i. Diarmaid, do cai go gér 7 do tecaisc 7
do bendaigh C. C. é ar cor go raibe se naémtha fa deoigh trias
an mbendughadh sin C. C. . As follas dund as an scel-sa nach
edh amain do cuir Dia C. C. a cosmailes ris fen leth re hoibrigh-
thibh do bí os cind na naduire daenda do denamh é, acht cor
chuir se a cosmailes ris fén é leth re ciunus do denamh o gach
saéthar da nderna se comhainm an lai a nderna sé fen ciunus ar
crichnughadh an oibrighthe sé laithe dó.

361. A haithle na mbríathar sin adubairt C. C. re Díarmaid
'san agard, do tindscain dul ar ais docum na mainestrech; 7 ger
gerr uadha í, dob ecean dó suidhe do lethtaeib an bealaigh 7 scís
do lecen, oir do bi a corp eccruaidh anfand tría cruas na beathadh do bi aice conuice sin. Acus tainic gerran ban do bi ac tarraing bainde docum na manach cuice, 7 do cuir se a cend a n-ucht
C. C., 7 do sil frais do deruib fola tar a gruadhuibh; 7 do bi ac
cai 7 ac tuirrse aimser fhoda amlaidh sin, amail do beith duine
ag delughadh ren a companuch gradach, 7 gan suil aice a fhaicsin
go (fol. 54a) brath aris, acht corab mó do cuaidh an cumha do
bi ar an gerrán mban os cend cursa na náduire. Acus mar dob
fhada le Diarmaid do bi C. C. ag fuirech ag an gerrán, dob ail
les a cur uadha, 7 nir leic C. C. sin dó. Acus do labuir re Diarmaid 7 assedh adubairt, acht ge do bi se 'n-a duine 7 anam re-
súnta aice, corb ferr do bi fis a bais fein ac an ainmidhe mbruide-

⁴⁴⁵*Genesis*, II, 2.

Columcille heard that, he solaced Diarmaid as best he might, and gave him counsel with very blessed holy words. And he told him he had a secret touching his death that he would tell him if he would hold it hid the while he lived. And when Diarmaid had promised this, Columcille spake to him and told him that Saturday was the day of rest and repose for all in the Old Law, and God had rested on that day from completing his labor, according as saith the second chapter of Genesis, the first book of the Scripture: *Requievit ab omini opere quod patrarat,* to wit, "God rested on the seventh day from every labor he had done, and he hallowed that day and blessed it, and he took it to Himself for a day of rest." And thus God hath desired to give me rest from the restlessness whereas I am, doing battle against the world and against the Devil and against this human body that is round about me. And as the Sunday is now the day of rest in the New Law, so shall I die in midst of the night this night, that I may be in the restfulness of the everlasting glory tomorn, that is Sunday."

When his disciple, to wit, Diarmaid, heard this, he wept sore. And Columcille gave him teaching and his blessing, so that he was holy at the last through that blessing of Columcille. And it is manifest to us from this history, not solely that God set Columcille in likeness to Himself touching deeds that be above human nature to do, but he set him in likeness to Himself touching rest from every labor that he did on the same day that He Himself rested after completing the labors of the six days.

361. When Columcille had said these words to Diarmaid in the haggard, he turned him again toward the monastery. And albeit it was but a short space distant, he must needs sit down by the way and rest, for his body was feeble and passing weak for the hardness of the life he had led till then. And there drew toward him a white nag that brought milk to the monks, and laid his head on the bosom of Columcille and shed a shower of bloody tears upon his cheeks. And for a long time he wept and lamented in this wise, as a man that biddeth farewell to a beloved comrade and hath no hope to see him ever again. But the sorrow the white nag had did pass the bounds of nature. And when it seemed to Diarmaid that Columcille tarried too long with the nag, he would fain have sent the beast from him, but Columcille suffered it not. And he spake to Diarmaid and said that albeit he was a human being and had a reasoning mind, yet better knowledge of his death had that brute beast [than he], for God had willed him to have that knowledge rather than Diarmaid, save in the measure that Columcille had revealed it to him ere that. Then departed the white nag from them and Columcille blessed him. And it came to pass by virtue of that

amhail sin, mar do toilich Día dó a fhis do beith aicce iná ac
Diarmaid, acht an meid do foillsigh se fen roimhe sin dó é. Do
imthigh an gerran ban uadha iar sin, 7 do bendaigh C. C. e,
indus co tainic do brigh an bendaighte sin, corb ferr e 7 corub
5 mo donídh se do tarba do na manchaibh an cein do mair se aca
ina donidís uimhir mór do gearranuib eli. Do cuaidh C. C. íar
sin ar cnocán bec do bí laimh ris an mainestir, 7 do tócaibh a
lamha 7 a rusca suas docum nimhe, 7 do bendaich an maineistir
uadha, 7 do labuir co fáidhemail, 7 adubairt, cér becc deroil an
10 eclus sin, nach íad righthe na hAlban no a poiplecha amain do-
béredh onoir di acht co tiubraidís moran do rigibh 7 do cinedha-
chaibh eli an domain onoir di; 7 fos co tiubraidis naeimh 7 pa-
truin eclas Erend 7 Alban 7 iarthuir domain uile onoir mar an
cedna di. Acus do firadh sin uile amail adubairt C. C.; oir do
15 bí togha rigraidhe Alpan 7 coda do rigraidh Erend don mainistir
sin an cein do bí an t-ord 'sa sdaid in ar fhagaib C. C. íat.

362. Teid C. C. 'n-a duirrthigh fen íar sin, 7 do phuí ac
scribadh na saltrach and no co rainic se an deachmhadh salm di
in a bfhuil an fersa-sa scribtha .i. Inquirintes autem Dominum
20 non deficent omni bono⁴⁴⁶) .i. 'ni bi uiresbaidh na n-uile maithesa
ar lucht íarrata an Tigherna ó croidhi.' Acus do labuir C. C. go
fáidhemail andsin 7 adubairt, cor mithigh do fen scur dá
scribneoracht, 7 co m[b]adh e Baithin do scribhobadh an cuid
eli don tsaltair sin. Ata Adhamnan ga meabrughadh corub
25 imcubaidh an t-inadh inar scuir an t-athair naemtha sin .i. C. C.
do scribadh na saltrach .i. ag an fersa sin adubramar romhaind;
oir ní bia uiresbaid na n-uile maithessa co siraidhe suthain ar
C. C. Acus ata an fer cedna ga mhebrughadh corub imcubaidh
an t-inadh in ar tindscain Baithin an chuid eli don tsaltair do
30 scribadh .i. an tan raínic docum na fersa ata a ndiaigh na fersu-ssa
adubramair remaind .i. Venite filii, audite me timorem Domini
docebo vos⁴⁴⁷) .i. 'ticcidh a cland gradach, 7 éstigh frim, 7 teicceo-
scat-sa sib a n-ecla an Tigherna.' Acus is mar sin dob imcubaidh
tainicc and a fersa sin do Col. C. 7 do Baithin, mar athair 7 mar
35 mac spiridalta; 7 ar in adbhur sin, do fhacuib C. C. a timna
spiradalta ag Baithin an cuid eli don tshaltair do scribadh. Teid
C. C. am espartain don eclais iar sin; 7 ar crichnughadh na hoifice
sin do, do cuaidh docum a duirrthighe fen, 7 teit sa leabaidh a
ndenadh se an meid codulta donídh se. Acus ass í fa locais⁴⁴⁸)

---

⁴⁴⁶Psalm XXXIII, 11.
⁴⁴⁷Psalm XXXIII, 12.
⁴⁴⁸pro stramine Adamnan.

blessing that the nag mended and did more of service for the brethren the while he lived than did other nags a great number.

Then went Columcille up a little hillock that was beside the monastery, and he raised his hands and eyes upward to Heaven and blessed the monastery. And he spake prophetically and said that albeit small and mean was that church, not only would the kings and the peoples of Alba do it worship, but many kings and peoples of the world else. And the saints and patrons of the churches of Erin and Alba and all the Western World would do it honor in like wise. And all this was fulfilled as Columcille had said, for the choosing of the kings of Alba and some part of the kings of Erin was in that monastery the while the order lasted in the state that Columcille left it.

362. Then went Columcille into his oratory and there he was transcribing the psalter until he came to the thirtieth psalm thereof, wherein is written this verse, to wit, *Inquirintes autem Dominum non deficent omni bono,* to wit, "There shall be no lack of all good things to those that seek the Lord from the heart." And then Columcille spake prophetically and said it was time for him to give over writing, and Baithin should write the remnant of that psalter. Adamnan maketh mention that it was at a fitting place that the holy father Columcille left off transcribing the psalter, to wit, at that verse we have aforementioned, for Columcille shall have no lack of any virtue throughout eternity. The same man maketh mention that it was at a fitting place that Baithin began to write the remnant of the psalter, to wit, when he came to the verse that followeth that verse we have aforementioned, to wit, *Venite filii, audite me, timorem Domini docebo vos,* to wit, "Come beloved children, and hearken to me, and I will instruct you in the fear of the Lord." And it was in this wise that those verses fell to Columcille and to Baithin, as father and son in the spirit. And for this it was that Columcille left to Baithin as his bequest spiritual to write the remnant of the psalter.

dó .i. carruic cloiche, 7 as cloch eli fa cerchaill dó. Acus ata an
cloch sin do bidh imá chend gá tumba fein aniugh a n-Í mar
fíadhnuise corb' í fa cerchaill do. Acus do labair ren a serbhfo-
ghantaidhe fen .i. re Diarmaid 7 ris na manchaib eli do cuaidh ar
5 cuairt cuice an uair sin 7 assedh adubairt: 'A cland gradach,'
ar se, 'aithnighim dib, o ataim fen ga bur fagbail, gradh foirbthe
do beith agaib dá cheli in gach inadh a mbeithi, 7 da raibe so ar
congbail agaibh ar eisemplair na n-aithrech naemtha tainic rom-
haib, fuirteochaidh Dia oraibh and gach anshocair a mbeithí, 7
10 bet-sa ac guidhe Dé tar bur cend da nderntai mar adeirm ribh,
7 ní hedh amhain dobera Día bur riachtanas a less ar an saegal-sa
daibh ar a shon sin, acht dobera Dia flaithes Dé daeib.' Et
adubairt se "alleluia" tri huairi andsin. Acus focal ilcíallach
ebrae an focul sin. Cial da cialluib: 'Molaidh ainm an Tigherna'.
15 Ciall eli dó: 'A Tigherna slanaigh me.' Ciall eli do: 'An t-athair
7 an mac 7 an Spirid Naem.' Acus atáid a lan do cialluib eli aice.
Et cantaic uassal solássach é; 7 Eoin bruinde fuair ar tus o an
aingel é 'san oilén darub ainm Patmus, an tan do bí sé ar foccra
o Nera .i. on Impiri Romhanach. 'Tancamar ar a lan do comhradh
20 7 do briathraibh C. C. conici sin,' bar Adhamnan, '7 as ecen duin
crich do cur orra anos; oir nir labair C. C. en-fhocal o sin amach
no co fuar sé bás.'

363. Ar mbuain cluic an medoin oidhce iarsin do sacrisda
na manach, do cuaidh C. C. ría cach (fol. 54b) les fen docum na
25 mainestrech,[449] 7 do lec ar a glúinib a fiadhnuissi na haltora e, 7
do bi ac guidhe De co duthrachtach ó cridhe; gin gor fhéd sé a
guidhe o briathruib. Acus do len a descibul gradach fén é .i.
Diarmaid; 7 ar techt a ndorus na hecluise dó, do fech se astech 7
do condaic se an eclus uile ar comhlassadh do soillse 7 do delradh
30 imarcach a timcell C. C., amail tshoillse 7 delradh na grene an uair
as mo a delradh 'sa mbliadhain. Acus ar ndul do Diarmaid
astech iar sin, do teich an solus uadha, 7 do bi se ag iarruid an
athar naemtha fan a lamhaib 'sa dorchadus. Acus ar n-a faghail
dó, do suidh faris, 7 do cuir a cend 'n-a ucht. Acus nir cian do
35 amlaidh sin an uair tancatar na manuich cuca maille re móran
do choindlibh 7 do lochrannaib ar lassadh leo; 7 mar do condcatar
C. C. ag faghail báis daririb, do batar ag cai 7 ag toirrsi go

[449] *leg.* heclaise.

Then went Columcille about vespertide to the church, and when he had finished the office he went to his oratory and to his bed wherein he took what share of sleep he suffered himself. And this was his place to lie on, to wit, a stone. And another stone for his pillow. And the stone that was at his head is at his tomb today in Iona, in witness that it was his pillow. And he spake to his servant, to wit, Diarmaid, and to the rest of the brethren that had come to him at that time, and he said:

"Beloved children," saith he, "I charge you, since I am departing from you, to have perfect love one for another in whatsoever place ye be in. And if such love be abiding in you, after the ensaumple of the holy fathers that have come afore you, God will aid you in every affliction whereas ye be, and I shall be praying God in your behalf if ye do as I bid you. And not only will God fulfill your needs in this world by reason thereof, but He will bestow upon you the Kingdom of God."

And then he said thrice *Alleluia,* that is a Hebrew word of many significations, whereof one is, "Praise the name of the Lord," and another thereof "Save me, O Lord," and another: "The Father and the Son and the Holy Spirit." And many other significations hath it, and it is a canticle worshipful and of solace. And John of the Bosom it was that first gat it from the angel in the island that is called Patmos what time he was banned by Nero the Emperor of Rome.

"We have related much of the conversation and of the words of Columcille to this point," saith Adamnan, "and we must needs make now an end thereof, for Columcille spake no word after this till his death."

XXXIII

OF THE DEATH OF COLUMCILLE AND OF HIS BURIAL

363. When the sacristan of the brethren struck the bell of midnight, Columcille went alone afore all to the monastery and fell on his knees before the altar and he prayed God fervently from his heart, albeit he might not pray with words. And there followed him his beloved disciple, to wit, Diarmaid, and when he came to the door of the church he looked within and he saw the whole church blazing with light and with passing splendor round about Columcille, as it were the light and splendor of the sun in the time of the year when it is brightest. And when Diarmaid entered, the light fled before him, and he sought the holy father in the darkness with his hands. And when he found him

himarc*ach* in a thimchell. Et ata Adhamnan naemtha ga mebrughadh cor indisitar daeine naemtha airidhe do bi do lathair an
uair sin dó fen, cor fhoscail C. C. a suile andsin, 7 e 'sa mbas,
7 cor fech gacha taebha de ar na manchuib maille re delr*adh*
naemtha ainglidhe do beith in a aghaidh. Ar na fhaicsin sen
da descibul fein .i. do Diarmaid, cor glac sé lamh dess C. C., 7
cor tocuib í do bendu*ghadh* na manach; 7 an meid dob eidir le
C. C., go tuc cungnamh dó docum na laimhe do tocbail; 7 an ní
narb éidir less d'foillsiu*ghadh* o bríathra*ibh*, cor fhoillsigh ó
comharta he, indus cor tuicetar na manaich cor bendaigh se íad
fen. Tar éis in tuar*ustail* degenaich sin tuc se doib, cor scar a
spir*id* re a c*or*p ar in pongc sin fen, cor linadh an eclas uile don
bolltanad nemaidhe tainic de an uair sin, am*ail* tuis no mirr *no* spis-
rad*h*uib, *no* do luibenduib degbaluich an tsaegail uile ; 7 co raibe an
meide sin do ghile 7 do derge in a agaidh, nach cosmailes duine dogebadh bas do bi air, a*cht* cosmailes duine do beith 'n-a codladh. Do
crichnaig se aml*aidh* sin betha gerr aim*s*erdha temporalta an
tsaeghail-se, 7 do tindscain se an betha siraide suth*ain* marthanach
ar nach fuil crich na f*oir*cend, mara feicend Día na nDía 'na
díaghacht 7 'n-a daend*acht*, ata beo 7 do bi beó 7 bias beo, tria
saoghal na saeghal.

364. Ata an file .i. Dallan F*or*gaill ga mebr*ugha*dh 'sa lebur
re n-abart*ar* "Amhra C. C.," go tainic crith 7 cumhscach*adh* mor
7 delm dífulaing a n-Erind 7 a n-Alpain 7 a n-iart*ar* dom*ain* don
bas sin C. C. Acus fós ata se ga mebru*ghadh* nach a n-en-tir
ina a n-en-righacht do bi se ga ecaine, a*cht* in gach uile tir coruíce
an Indía, am*ail* asp*er*t Dallan :[450])

Easbaidh Col*uim* ar cloind *Q*uind,   ac sin an deilm difhulaing ;
fa bronach cach de gac día   ó ata Er*e* co hIndía.

365. Is follus duind as an c*ri*th 7 as an combuadr*edh* sa do
gabat*ar* na duile cuca le bas C. C., nar lor le Dia a cur a ̈cosmailes

---

[450]See *R. C.,* XX, p. 158.

he sat him down beside him and laid his head on his bosom. And they were not long thus when the brethren entered with many candles and lighted lamps. And when they perceived that Columcille was in very sooth in point to die, they fell to weeping and making great dole around him. And it is holy Adamnan that maketh mention that certain holy men that were with him in that hour related that Columcille opened his eyes then, and he dying, and that he gazed round him on the brethren, his face beaming with a holy angelic light. And when his disciple Diarmaid perceived this, he took the right hand of Columcille and lifted it to bless the brethren. And he gave aid to Columcille to lift his hand. And what Columcille might not manifest in words he made manifest by signs, so that the brethren understood that he gave them his blessing. And when he had given them this last gift, his spirit departed from his body straightway, and the whole church was filled with the heavenly fragrance that came from him in that hour, as it were from incense or myrrh or spices or sweet smelling herbs of the whole world . And such was the brightness and the ruddiness of his face that he seemed not one that was dead but as one asleep.

Thus ended he the brief space of the temporal life of this world and began the Life Eternal, Everlasting, and Enduring, that hath nor term nor ending, where he beholdeth the God of gods in his god-head and in his man-hood, Who liveth and hath been living and shall be living forever and ever.

364. The poet Dallan Forgaill maketh mention in the book that is called the *Praise of Columcille* that there came a trembling and great quaking and an intolerable tremor upon the land of Erin and of Alba and all the Western World at the death of Columcille. And moreover he saith it was not in one land nor in one kingdom that he was mourned, but in every land even to India. As Dallan saith:

> "The loss of Colum to Conn's clan,
> Thereat a tremor past bearing.
> Sad are all thereat, all days,
> From Erin even to India."

365. It is manifest to us from the trembling and quaking that seized the elements at the death of Columcille, that God thought it not

gnimharta ris fen ar an saegal-sa, gan a bas do cur a cosmailecht
re n-a bas, leth re cumscugadh na ndul, mar do dorchuidh an
grian, 7 mar do scoiltetar na cairrge, 7 mar do fosclatar na
húadhanda le bas an Tigerna.

366. Et ata Dallan Forcaill ga mebrughad[h] 'sa leabur
cedna, gor dai ar fhis 7 ar ecna 7 ar eolas cach en-duine coruice
an India a farradh C. C., 7 adeir se co tuiccedh sé glór enlaithe
an aieoir 7 piast na fairce; 7 da bfagadh se daine dogebadh
uadha e, co tiubradh se eolass doib ar suidiughadh grene 7 esca
7 na ndul uachtarach 7 ar gach cumachta da fuil ó Dia aca, 7 ar
gach cail a tucann grian soillse don ré, 7 do reltannaib an aieoir,
7 ar airem na retland 7 ar tragadh 7 ar linadh na mara 7 na fairce;
7 mar gabus sí na srotha 7 na huiscedha cuice, 7 mar lecess sí
uaithe íad, amail aspert Dallan ga derbad sin:[451])

  Rofidir Colum ua Neill   rith éssca, rith mara reill,
  is airemh retland go mbuaidh   's dofhidir runa Rochuaidh.

.i. píast ata 'sa fairce. Et adeir Dallan go bfoillsigedh se do cach
soinend no doinend na haimsire do bidh gan techt.. Gér mór,
umorro, an fis 7 an t-eolus do C. C. so, do ba mó (fol. 55a) 7 do
ba romo do eolass flaithis De 7 ifrind 7 an tsaegail-se do beith
aice ina sin, amail dearbus se fein 'sa rand sa:[452])

  Am eoluch for talmain teind,   ricim go hadbaidh ifrind,
  teighim gach dardaín for neamh,   fo gairm righ na tri maith.

Et fos ata an file cedna ga mebrughadh cor long can sdiuír, 7 cor
adbh cíuil gan crand glesta, 7 cor coland gan cend uirri, an ecluis
7 an tuath tar eís Coluim Cille, amail aspert sé sa rand sa:[452a])

  Coland gan cend ind da éis,   an doman as cruit gan ceis,
  long gan sdiuir an ecluis de   do bhas Coluim caidh Cille.

367.[453]) 'Ni coir duinn a dermad,' bar Adhamnan, 'no a lecen
toraind mar do taisbenadh do nech naemtha Erendach darb ainm

---

[451] See *R. C.*, XX, p. 256.
[452] See *ibid.*, p. 178.
[452a] *ibid.*, p. 165.
[453] In Adamnan. See Reeves' *Adam.*, p. 235 ff.

enough to make him like to Himself in works in this world, but he made his death in the likeness of His own death, touching the commotion of the elements, as when the sun darkened and the rocks split and the graves opened for the death of our Lord.

366. And Dallan Forgaill maketh mention in the same book that touching knowledge and wisdom and science every man even unto India is ignorant when he is likened to Columcille. And he saith that Columcille understood the voice of the birds of the air and of the beasts of the sea. And if he found those that might receive it from him, he would give them knowledge of the place of the sun and the moon and of the higher elements, and of every virtue they possess of God, and of all the properties whereby the sun giveth light to the moon and the stars of the firmament, and of the numbering of the stars and of the ebb and flow of the waters and the sea, and how she draweth to herself the streams and waters and how she doth let them from her. As Dallan saith in testimony thereof:

> "Colum descendant of Niall knew
> The course of the moon and the clear sea,
> The number of the stars, victoriously;
> And he knew the secrets of Rochuaidh."

That is a beast that is in the sea. And Dallan saith that he was wont to reveal to all the fairness or the foulness of weather that was not yet come. And albeit this were great knowledge and wisdom in Columcille, yet were it greater and still more great knowledge than this, that he knew of the Kingdom of God and of Hell and of this world. As he saith in this quatrain:

> "I have knowledge of Earth the unyielding;
> I go to the dungeon of Hell.
> I go every Thursday to Heaven,
> At the call of the King of Three Mercies."

Moreover the same poet maketh mention that a ship without a rudder, and a musical instrument without gear to attune it, and a body without a head thereon are the Church and the folk since the passing of Columcille. As he saith in this quatrain:

> "A body without head thereon, without him
> Is the world, and a harp without its key;
> A ship without rudder the church is
> From the death of pure Columcille."

367. "It behooveth us not to forget," saith Adamnan, "nor to be ignorant that to a certain holy man of Erin hight Lughaid was re-

Lughaidh anam C. C. ag dul a flaithes De.' Do bi an nech naemta sin a mainestir airidhe a n-Erind, 7 do bi se fein arsaidh an uair sin, 7 do indis se do manach eli darb ainm Ferghna do ba companach dó go bfaca se radharc a medón-oidhce an domhnaich a fuair C. C.
5 bas .i. oilen Ɫia; gen co raibe se fen o corp riamh and, lomnan do shoillse nach fetar a tuaruscbail d'indeisin 7 a lán d'ainglibh and fen 7 os a cend suas co flaithess De, 7 cor tuic se fen ass sin co fuair peiler eclaise De bas an uair sin .i. C. C., 7 corub a coinde a anma tancatar na sluaigh diairmidhe aingel sin. Acus do indeis sé don
10 manach cedna sin co cuala se fen an ceol ainglidhi 7 na cantaice molta do bi ac ainglibh De an tan do scar a spirid re C. C., 7 nach raibe cin aice ar ceol no ar aibnes an tsaegail iar sin acht oiret do bi do cin aice ar an ceol budh serbhe leis do cuala se 'sa saegal remhe sin. Acus da derbadh sin, do cuaid se fein and sna laithib
15 sin a n-oilen ro-uaícnech airidhe darb ainm Inda[454]) 7 do bi se ac ridirecht do Crist and no co fuair se bas. Et do bi an Ferghnu-sa, dar indiss Lughaidh an radarc sin,, da bliadhain dheag ac serbís 7 ac ridirecht do Crist 7 do C. C. 'san inadh airidhe dana hainm Bulcmar. 'Acus co firindech as se Ferghna do indiss scela
20 an radhairc sin duind-e,' bar Adhamnan.

368[455]) Laibeoram don taisbenadh tuccadh do nech naemtha .i. Maedog Ferna ar anam C. C. ag dul a flaithess De. La airidhe do bi Moedóc ag denam legind 7 foircetail do clereach ócc ba deiscibul dó fen, 7 do cuaid amach uadha, 7 do fagaib glas
25 air. Do fech an cleirech ar fuindeoig amach dia fhis cait a ndechaidh Maedhóc, 7 do condaic dreimire o talmain co nemh 7 é ga imtecht. Acus ar n-impodh do Maedóc, nir fhed an cleirech fechain air ar med a delraidh. 'Na hindiss en-ni da bfacadhuis an cein mairfed-sa,' ar Moedéc. 'Ní indeos dá faghar a fis uaid-se
30 cait a ndechadhais,' ar in cleirech, 'an uair do cuadhais amach o cíanaib uaim, 7 do facbuis fa glas me.' 'Festa 7 sollamain ro-mor ro-caithisech do bi a flaithes De aniugh' ar se, 're lind anma C. C. do chuaidh[456]) and, 7 do ba chara mór damh-sa C. C., 7 tainic do maithes De 7 C. C. mo lecen d'fechain an festa sin.'
35 As urusa a tuicsin as an scel-sa, nach edh amhain do ba tarba do na daínib saegaltai a cumand 7 a pairt do beith re C. C. acht cor tarba do na dainib naemtha cumand spiratalta do beith aca ris

---

[454]hinna Codex D. Reeves' *Adam.* has *Hinba*. It was Ferghna that went to Inda and then to Bulcmar. Adamnan has Muirbulcmar.

[455]See Plummer's *V. S. H.*, II, § 39, pp. 156-7.

[456]Peculiar construction. We should expect *do dhul and*. See § 80 *supra*, note on *do erigh dá chind*.

vealed the soul of Columcille on its way to the Kingdom of God." That holy man was in a certain monastery in Erin and he was passing ancient at that time. And he told another monk hight Fergna that was his companion that he had beheld a vision on the midnight of the Sunday that Columcille had died, to wit, the island of Iona, albeit he had never been there in the body, filled with light that it were not possible to tell of, and many angels therein and above it even unto Heaven. And he understood therefrom that the pillar of the Church of God had died in that hour, to wit, Columcille, and that it was to meet his soul that countless host of angels came. And he told that same monk that he heard the angelic music and the canticles of praise of the angels of God when the soul of Columcille departed, and from that time he had no more love for the music or pleasure of the world than for the harshest music that he had heard in his life ere that. And in proof thereof he went in those days to a certain passing solitary island hight Inda and there he did service for Christ until he died. And that Fergna to whom Lugaidh related that sight was twelve years in the service and soldiership of Christ in a certain place hight Bulcmar. "And in truth it was that Fergna that hath given us tidings of that sight," saith Adamnan.

368. Now speak we of a vision that was granted to a holy man hight Maedog Ferna, of the soul of Columcille on its way to the Kingdom of God. On a certain day that Maedog was teaching and instructing a young cleric that was one of his disciples, he went away from him and locked the door upon him. The cleric looked out from the window to see whither Maedog had departed, and he beheld a ladder from earth to Heaven, and Maedog departing thereby. And when Maedog returned, the cleric might not look upon him for the greatness of his shining.

"Tell naught of that thou hast seen, the while I live," saith Maedog.

"I will not tell it if I get knowledge from thee whither thou didst go," saith the cleric, "when thou didst depart from me a while since, and left the door locked."

"A feast and a passing great and joyous festival was held in the Kingdom of God today," saith he, "for the soul of Columcille that departed thither. And he was a friend dear to me. And it befell through the goodness of God and Columcille that I was suffered to behold that feast."

It is easy to see from this history not only that it was of profit to worldly men to be in communion and fellowship with Columcille, but it was of profit also to holy men to be in spiritual communion with him,

an uair tuc*adh* an tastáil mor sa na gloiri do Moedóc 'n-a onoír, amail derbuss betha Maedóic fen.

369.⁴⁵⁷) Et fos ata Adamhnan ga mebrughadh cor indiss manach naemtha eli darb ainm Iarnán do fein, 7 se 'n-a macaemh óc an uair sin, co bfaca se rad*arc* a medhon na hoidhce cedna a bfuair C. C. bás, 7 é ac iascaire*cht* ar sruth airidhe a rig[h]acht na hErind dara hainm an Fhind, 7 iascairedha eli faris .i. an t-aeieor d'fhaicsin lomnan do shol*us* 7 do delr*adh* imarcach, Acus ar na fhaicsin sen dó, do indis do na hiascuiribh eli é, 7 do fechatar uile soir don taib o tainicc an solas, 7 do condcat*ar* peiler tent*idhe* ag eirghe o hÍ 'san aier súas, 7 nir fétat*ar* beith ga feicemh ó mhed an delr*aidh* do bí de, 7 ní mo do fetatar tuar*uscbail* a dhelr*aidh* 7 a soillse do tab*airt* uatha, *a*cht amain cor brethnaichetar a raibhe do lathair andsin, nar mo dorchad*us* na hoidhce a ndiaid an laí as gile tainic riamh ina dorchad*us* an laei ar na maruch tar eís ama*irc* an peiléir do dul úatha as a fiadhn*uise* co fl*aithius* De. Acus do tuicetar san uile g*urb* e peiler do bí andsin .i. anam C. C. ag dul docum nimhe. (*fol.* 55b)

370.⁴⁵⁸) Rucatar na manaigh c*orp* C. C. leo as an ecl*uis* don proindtigh⁴⁵⁹) a mbidís fen faré C. C. remhe sin; 7 ger menic leo beith co subhac solásach fare cheli and, gan fech*ain* do cr*uas* a mbeth*adh* nó d'airde a fuirechruis, do b*a* dub*ach* dobron*ach* caidrebh na manach an uair sin ris. Gidhedh, do batar ac denamh onóra an c*oirp* ro-naemtha robendaicthe sin mar as caithis*ighe* 7 mar is onoruighe cor fetatar, 7 do bi se t*ri* la 7 teora hoidhce aca mar sin. Acus ar cor na haimsire sin tarrsa doibh, do cuiretar édach ro-ghlan ro-gleghel uime, 7 do cuiretar a comhr*aidh* iar sin é, 7 do indlaicetar co honórach a mainest*ir* hIi he. Acus ata Adamhnan ga mebrughadh cor indesitar cuid do na manchaibh n*ae*mta do bi do láthair an uair sin do fen corub mar sin dorindeth re c*orp* C. C. tar eis a bais.

371. Et, gidhedh, fos atá Berchan naemtha ga mebrughadh go fuil c*orp* C. C. i nDún da Lethglas a n-en-tumba re Patruic 7 re Brighid. Acus is mar so derb*us* sé a te*cht* and .i. a adluc*adh* a n-I, 7 Mandar mac righ Lochlann do te*cht* cobl*ach* cogaid[h] don baile, 7 síad do b*eith* ac milledh an baile 7 uadhann*a* an baile 7 a adluice do tochailt doib 7 a comr*adha* do tocbáil doib d'íarr*aidh* etala indta, 7 an comr*a* croind a raibe corp C. C. do tocb*ail* doib.

---

⁴⁵⁷See Reeves' *Adam.*, p. 237 ff.
⁴⁵⁸In Adamnan, *ibid.*, p. 239 ff.
⁴⁵⁹*hospitium* Adamnan.

since this great manifesting of glory was given to Maedog in his honor, as the *Life of Maedog* testifieth.

369. And moreover Adamnan maketh mention that another holy monk hight Iarnan did relate to him when he was a boy that he had seen a vision on the midnight of that same night that Columcille died, the while he was fishing in a certain river, that is called the Find, in the Kingdom of Erin, and other fisher-folk with him, to wit: he beheld the firmament full of light and great brightness. And when he had beheld it, he told tidings thereof to the other fishers. And all looked to the East, whence the light came, and they saw a pillar of fire rising from Iona to the heavens. And they might not look upon it for the brightness thereof, and no more might they give tidings of the light and brightness it gave forth, save only that they that were there deemed the darkness of night after the brightest of days to be less dark than the darkness of the morrow after the vision of the pillar on its way from them to the Kingdom of God. And all understood that the pillar that had been there was the soul of Columcille on its way to the Kingdom of Heaven.

370. The brethren bare the body of Columcille with them out of the church to the refectory where they had been wont to be in his fellowship. And albeit they had oft been merry and glad together there, recking not of the hardship of their life or of the greatness of their vigil, yet in great heaviness and sorrow was the fellowship of the brethren that were together with him in that hour. Howbeit they did such honor and worship as they might to that right holy and sanctified body. And they were with him for three days and three nights in this wise. And when they had been for that space thus, they put round him a cloth passing clean and passing white, and they put him in a coffin and buried him worshipfully in Iona. And Adamnan maketh mention that certain of the holy brethren that were there present at that time related to him that thus it was done with the body of Columcille after his death.

371. Howbeit, the holy Berchan doth relate that the body of Columcille is in Dun da Lethglas in the same tomb with Padraic and Brigid. And thus he beareth testimony of its coming thither: "It was buried in Iona. And Mandar son of the King of Lochlan came with a fleet of war to the monastery and plundered it and its graves, and tore up its tombs and lifted its coffins to search for booty therein. And they bare away with them the coffin of wood wherein was the body of Columcille. And they deemed it a coffer wherein was gold or silver or other treasure of the world, and they bare it away to their vessel on the sea and opened it not. And when they had put to sea, they opened the coffer. And when they found naught therein save the body of a man, they shut it again on the body and cast it in the sea. And it came to

Acus do sailetar cor cof*ra* a raibe or *no* aircet *no* maithes saegalta
eli é, 7 rucatar leo amach in a luing ar fairce gan fhoscl*adh* í.
Acus a ndiaidh dul ar an fairce doib, do fosclat*ar* an com*ra*, 7
mar nach fuaratar indti *acht* corp duine, do druidetar an comhra
aris fan c*or*p 7 do theilcet*ar* a fairce hí. Acus táinic do mirbuilibh
De 7 do grasaib an c*oir*p bendaighte sin do bi indte, nach derna
an comra comhn*uidh*e co rainic sí co Dun da Lethglas. Acus do
eirich ab Duín amach ar maduin, 7 do cond*aic* an com*ra* ar n-a
cur a tír don fhairce, 7 do foscail í 7 fuair se an c*or*p indte. Acus
do athain corb é corp C. C. é, 7 do tóc an t-ab an corp naemtha
sin ar n-a aithne dó, 7 do póc é, 7 tuc gloir 7 mol*adh* do Día do
cind a cor cuice mar sin. Acus do *t*onaich é iar sin, 7 do cuir
sa tumbai a raibe Patraicc 7 Brighid é; ut d*ixit* Bercan aga
derbadh sin:[460])

A ordan a n-Í gan ca*ir*e,   is a an*d*sa for Doire,
is a c*or*pan fon leic   fa ata Brig*hid* is Patr*aicc*.

Et do tairrngir Patraicc fein co mbeidis na triur a n-en-tumba;
amail derb*us* se fein sa rand sa:

Mesi *acus* Brig*hid* amne,   *acus* Col*um* caemh Cille,
maraen bes ar run malle,   a nDun bias ar n-eiseirghe.

372. Et fos do ta*irrngi*r Brig*hid* sin mar an cedna aml*aidh*
so .i. lá airidhe do bi sí ac fi*di* bruit 7 do lab*air* sí do spir*id*
faidhetor*acht*a re Patraicc 7 ass*edh* adubairt, co m*adh* é an brat sin
do bí sí d'fhidhe, do beith os cind an tumba a cuirf*idh*e hí féin
7 Patraicc 7 C. C., amail derbuss sí féin 'sa rand sa:

In blalín-se delbhai*m*-se,   go ngloine 7 *co* ng*ri*nde,
biaidh torum is torad-sa,   's tar Col*um* craibthech Cille.

373. Et léghter ar C. C. *co* nduba*irt* se ren a beo fein co

---

[460]See *Lis. Lives*, p. 317; Dinneen's *Keating*, III, p. 104.

pass by the miracles of God and by the graces of the blessed body therein, that the coffin made never a stay until it came to Dun da Lethglas. And the abbot of Down went out on the morrow and saw the coffin cast ashore by the sea, and he opened it and found the body therein. And he perceived that it was the body of Columcille. And when he perceived that, he took that holy body and kissed it and gave glory and praise to God for that He had sent it to him in such wise. He washed it then and put it in the tomb where Padraic was, and Brigid." *Ut dixit* Bercan in witness thereof:

> "In Iona without offence, his honor;
> His love upon Derry,
> And his body under the flag-stone
> Whereunder are Brigid and Padraic."

372. And Padraic himself prophesied that the three of them should be in the same tomb, as he beareth witness in this quatrain:

> "I and Brigid in this wise,
> And Columcille the gentle,—
> Our love shall be together,
> In Down shall be our uprising."

And Brigid prophesied this thing in like manner as followeth: On a certain day she was weaving a mantle, and she spake through the spirit of prophecy to Padraic, and said that the mantle she was weaving should be over the tomb wherein she was laid and wherein were laid Padraic and Columcille, as she beareth witness in this quatrain:

> "This linen sark I am making,
> In cleanliness and in beauty,
> Shall be across me and across thee,
> And across Columcille the pious."

373. And it is related of Columcille that he said while he was yet living that his body should be in the same tomb with Padraic and Brigid in Dun da Lethglas, as he beareth witness in these quatrains:

madh a n-en tumba re Patraicc 7 re Brighid do beith a corp a
nDún Da Lethglas; amail derbuss se fein is na randaibh se sis:

    Ticfidh Mandtar na cromluing   co hÍ, mar candtar cuindghim,
    béraid mo corp ar findmhuir,   ar daigh innmais mar tuirmhim.

5   Ticfidh Mandar gall go hÍ,   's béraidh mo cli óm shámadh;
    an tailgend do tairrngir sin,   a Baithin inmain airimh.

    Gid andlaicter misi a nÍ   do reir mo righ nach frithir,
    is a nDun anfad a nuadh   a ri na sluagh as mithigh.

    Ge andluicter mesi a nÍ,   bet a nDun do toil De bí,
10   's Patraicc is Brighid co mbuaidh   's ar cuirp ar triúr a
                                                        [n-enuáidh.

    Bíad a n-enuaidh[461]) 'sa tailgend,   as Brighid ban gan
                                                            [merbhall,
    no go roissiur mac De bí,   ó faghaim ní mar cuindgim.

15   374. Et fos ata an file .i. Dallan Forcaill gá dherbadh is na
randuib-se eli cor handluicedh C. C. a n-Íi 7 co ndechaidh[462]) a
corp co Dun da Lethglas mar an cedna:

    Saer in taide[463]) doriacht Í   fer ro adhnacht go fá dí,
    Colum Cille, cridhe glan,   mac Righ nimhe 7 talman.
20   hÍ con ilur a martra,   dia mbo Colum cumachta.[464])

    doluidh esde fá deredh,   conadh Dun a senneimedh.

    375. 'Et fos nir choir duinde a dermad,' bar Adham (fol.
56a) nan,[465]) 'mar adubairt manach da manchaibh fen fria C. C.
ria mbas d'fhaghail dó, 7 se ac labairt dá bás a bfiadnaise an
25 manaich, gurb ecail less nach fedfaidis fein onoir a cuirp sen do
denamh mar ba lor leo tar eis a bais o buaidredh 7 o míchiunus
lucht na talman sin uile, ar a mbeith tuirse 7 dobrón mor in a
diaid sen, 7 do ticfedh do denamh onóra dósomh.' 'Fetfaidhe,'
ar C. C., 'ni leceb-sa miciunus cucaib, oir ni ced lium duine 'sa
30 mbith do beith a timchel mo coirp con n-andluicter e acht mo
manaigh fen; 7 da derbadh sin, eirochaidh sdoirm mór 7 anfad

---

[461]Read en-uaigh. See Reeves' Adam., p. LXXIX.
[462]But Columcille's body was in Iona when Dallan composed the Amra.
[463]t-aegi in R. C., p. 280.
[464]coemdalta, ibid., p. 178. See also Lis. Lives, p. 317.
[465]See Reeves' Adam., p. 240.

> "Mandar shall come in his crooked ship
> To Iona, as it is sung, . . .¹
> He shall bear away my body on the white sea,
> For the sake of treasure, as I reckon.
>
> Mandar the Norseman shall come to Iona,
> And shall bear my ribs from my followers.
> The Adze-head² did make this prophecy,
> O beloved Baithin, take heed.
>
> Though buried I be in Iona,
> According to my King, not offended.
> In Down I shall dwell anew,
> O King of Hosts, in due season.
>
> Though buried I be in Iona,
> In Down I shall be, Live God willing.
> With Padraic and Brigid renowned,
> Our bodies three in one tomb.
>
> In one tomb shall I be with the Adze-head,
> And Brigid the Fair, without error,
> Till I reach the Son of the Live God,
> From whom I receive what I seek."

374. Moreover the poet, Dallan Forgaill, beareth witness in these further quatrains that Columcille was buried in Iona, and that his body went thus to Dun da Lethglas:

> "Noble the tide that reached Iona
> A man that was twice buried,
> Columcille, dear and pure,
> The son of the King of Heaven and Earth.
>
> Iona of numerous martyrs
> That belonged to Colum the Mighty,
> Therefrom at length he departed,
> So that Down is his joyous bright dwelling."

375. "Moreover it behooveth us not to forget," saith Adamnan, "how one of the brethren said to Columcille ere he died, when he was speaking of his death afore the brethren, that he was afeared they might not do worship sufficient to his body after his death, for the

---

¹ I seek?
² Padraic.

imarca̧ch ar an bfairce; indus nach biaidh ar cumus do dhuine sa
domhan techt 'san olen-so om bás-sa có m'andlucadh, 7 tiucfaidh
ciunus ánd íar sin.' Do fíradh sin amail adubairt C. C., oir na
tri la 7 na teora hoidchi do bi se gan andlucadh, do eirigh sdoirm
5 7 anfad mór ar an fairge, 7 nir lam enduine do na poiblechaib eli
dul don oilen no cor handluicedh é; amail adubrumar romaind.
Fuarattar soinend 7 aimser maith iar sin, amail do gell C. C. doib.

376. 'Is follus duind ass so 7 as gach ní eli dar labhrumar
ar fedh na bethad-sa anuas' bar Adamhnan, 'go raibe cin romhar
10 7 gradh imarcach ac Día ar a oclaech 7 ar a serbfhogantaidhe
diless féin .i. ar C. C., an uair do cuir se na cetri duile 7 gach
creatuír eli dar cruthaigh se fa umhla dó.' Acus dorinde C. C. an
t-adbur docum ar cruthaigh Día é .i. do denamh serbisi dó fen,
indus corub éidir a radha nach frith duine dorinde serbis do Día
15 no do coimeid recht an Tigerna mar dorinde C. C. Is ar an
adbur sin do cuir Dia gach uile creatuír do denamh umlachta dó
san: *Omnia subjecisti sub pedibus eius.*[466]) .i. 'do cuiris gach enní
fa umlacht don duine,' ar an faidh, ag labairt re Día 'sa saltair.
O do cuir Dia gach uile creatuir fa umlacht do na dainib uli mar
20 sin, as follus dund corub mo 7 corub romo ina sin do cuir se
d'fhiachaibh orra beith umal don te do chuaidh a ceim foirfidhechta os cind gach duine dá fhoirfe dá raibe ac serbis do Día 'sa
senrecht nó 'sa recht núa; do réir mar derbocham-ne ó resun 7
o údarás.

25 377. Ni coimes do rachadh a n-esonoír do na huassal-
aithrechaibh no do na faidib no do na hespulaibh no do na
suibescelaibh no do na mairtírechaibh no do coinfesoírib no do na
naemhaib eli no do na hóghaib, dob ail linn do denamh etorra
7 C. C. andso, acht nach ail linn na tindluicthe 7 na subáltidhe
30 roarda tuc Día da serbfhogantaidh fen a ceimib os cind gach
enduine, gan a foillsechadh do cach; 7 fos nach coir duind
oibrighthe De do muchadh gan a foillsiughadh 'sa té inar fhoillsich
se fen go himarcach íad.

---

[466]Psalm XXXVIII, 8.

trouble and turmoil of the folk of all that place that would be heavy and right sorrowful after him and would come to do him worship."

"Ye shall be able," saith Columcille, "I shall leave you in no turmoil, for I shall suffer none of the folk of the world to be near my body until it be buried, save mine own monks. And in fulfillment thereof a great storm shall arise on the sea, and a mighty tempest, so that it shall not be in the power of any man in the world to come to the island from the time of my death until my burial. And after that shall come a calm."

And this was verified as Columcille had said, for in the three days and the three nights that he was unburied, there arose a storm on the sea and a great tempest, and none other folk were able to come to the island until he was buried, as we have said before. And then they had sunshine and fair weather, as Columcille had promised them.

376. "It is manifest to us from this and from every other thing that we have related in this *Life* thus far," saith Adamnan, "that God had passing great affection and exceeding love for his servant and chosen follower Columcille, since he put under obedience to him the four elements and every other created thing that he had made." And Columcille did fulfill the end wherefor God created him, to wit, to serve Him. And it may be said that there hath been found none that hath served God or kept the law of the Lord as Columcille did. And for this it was that God put every created thing in subjection to him. *Omnia subjecisti sub pedibus ejus,* which is to say, "Thou hast put all things under subjection to man," saith the prophet, speaking of God in the psalter. Since God hath thus put all created things under subjection to all men, it is manifest to us that in greater and yet greater measure he hath put them under bonds to be subject to him that surpassed in perfection all men, howso perfect, that have been in the service of God in the Old Law or in the New, as we shall prove from reason and from authority.

XXXIV

A COMPARISON OF COLUMCILLE WITH OTHER HOLY MEN

377. It is not a comparison that would turn to the dishonor of the patriarchs or the prophets or the apostles or the evangelists or the martyrs or the confessors or the other saints or the virgins, that we would make betwixt them and Columcille in this place, but it misliketh

378. Da derbadh co tucc Día an foirfidhecht-sa adubrumar remaind do C. C., do bi se a cosmailes and 'sa senrecht ris an uassalathair .i. re hAbrahám mac Tara leth re n-a thir-duthaigh d'fhagbail 7 dul ar deoraidhecht a tírthibh ciana comaightecha. Et as follus duind cor tuic 7 gur gab se an comairli tuc Día fein d'Abrahám, amail mebraighes Moísi mac Amra a nGenisis rechta .i. an ced leabar don Bibla .i. Exi de terra tua 7 de cognacione 7 de domo patris tui et vade an terram quam tibi mostravero⁴⁶⁷) .i. 'Fagaib do tír 7 do talumh 7 do gael 7 t'atharda ndiless 7 eirigh 'sa tír fhoillseochad-sa duit.' Acus as eídir lind a radha go ndechaidh C. C. a ceim fhoirfechta os cind Abraham an méid corub serbus 7 dolás 7 anshocair fuair se do taeb a cuirp 'sa talmain a ndechaidh ar deoruidhecht, 7 corub aibnes 7 saidbress 7 gach uili maithess ar chena do ghell Día d'Abrahám 7 da slicht 'n-a diaidh 'sa talmhain a ndubairt sé ris dul.

379. Et fos do cuaid se a céim fhoirfechta os cind Aprahám, an meid cor fhacuib se a braithri 7 a comghael 7 a cairde uile do bi ro-linmhar ro-uassal ro-shaidbir 7 do bi grádach uime, 7 fa raibe se ro-gradhach, 7 co ndechaidh a braithri 7 a comghael 7 a cairde uili le hAbrahám ar an deoraidhect a ndechaidh se.

380. Do bi se fos a cosmailess re Maísse mac Amra leth re troiscthib faide 7 re huisce do buain as na cairrcib; 7 fetar a radha co ndechaidh se a cem foirbhfechta os cind Maisi an meíd nach edh amain do benadh se an t-uisce as (fol. 56b) na cairrcib acht co ndenadh fín de.

381. Do bi C. C. a cosmailes re hIsahias faidh leth re faidetóracht; 7 as eidir lind a radha go ndechaidh se a céim foirbfechta os cind hIsahias an med co mbidh a lan d'faidetoracht Isuhias dorcha dothuicsena, 7 an meid nar coimhlinadh an faidhetóracht dorinde se ar bas Esisias .i. ri cloinde Isralí, an uair adubairt se go fuigedh an rí bas ar na mharuch; 7 do cuir Día cuic bliadhna eli tairis sin ar a saeghal, amail adeir an fichetmadh caibdil don cethramadh leabar do leab[h]ruib na righ.⁴⁶⁸)

---

⁴⁶⁷Genesis XII, 1.
⁴⁶⁸IV Reg., xx.

us not to make manifest to all the gifts and right lofty virtues that God did bestow upon this His chosen servant in measure above every other. And it were moreover a wrong in us that the works of God should perish and be not revealed of him in whom He manifested them exceedingly.

378. In proof that God did bestow upon Columcille the perfection we have aforementioned, he was like unto the patriarch in the Old Law, to wit, Abraham, son of Tara, inasmuch as he left his native land and went into exile in distant foreign lands. And it is clear to us that Columcille understood and took the counsel that God gave to Abraham, as Moses son of Amram relateth in Genesis of the Law, to wit, the first book of the Bible, to wit, *Exi de terra tua et de cognacione et de domo patris tui et vade an terram quam tibi mostravero,* which is to say, "Leave thy land and thy country, and thy kinsmen and thy fatherland, and go to the land I shall show thee." And we may say that Columcille went a step of perfection above Abraham, inasmuch as it was bitterness and miscomfort and hardship he received touching his body in the land whither he went into exile, and it was delight and riches and every other good thing that God promised Abraham and his seed in the land whither he bade them go.

379. And he went a step of perfection above Abraham inasmuch as he left his brothers and his kinsmen and all his friends the which were right numerous, right noble, and of passing great riches, and loved him and were dear to him exceedingly, whereas his brothers and his kinsmen and all his friends went with Abraham into the exile the which he entered.

380. And moreover he was like unto Moses, son of Amram, touching his long fastings and touching the drawing of water from rocks, and it may be said that he went a step of perfection above Moses in this that not only did he strike the water from the rocks, but he made wine thereof.

381. Columcille was like unto Isaiah the prophet touching prophecy, and we may say that he went a step of perfection above Isaiah, inasmuch as many of the prophecies of Isaiah were dark and hard of understanding, and inasmuch as the prophecy was not fulfilled that he made of the death of Hezekiah, the King of the Children of Israel, when he said that the King should die on the morrow; and God put fifteen years more to his life, as saith the twentieth chapter of the fourth Book of Kings.

382. Ni hamlaidh soin, umorro, do bi fáidhetoracht C. C., acht do bi si solus sothuicsena, 7 do ticedh sí co firindech gan cairde ar bith do cur uirri 'san uair airidhe a ngelladh se fein a thecht.

383. Et fos as eidir a radh gor mo C. C. ina faidh amail adubradh re hEoin baisde, nach eadh amhain dorinde se fáidhetoracht ar techt an Tigherna, acht cor fhoillsich se do cach le n-a mer é, indus co facatar da suilib fen é ag rad na mbriathar-sa mebraighes Eoin suiphescel 'sa ced caibidil do lebraibh na soiscel air: Hic est de quo dixi vobis[469]) Hic est qui tollit peccata mundi[470]) .i. 'Ac so an tí do tairrngir mesi daeib, 7 ag so an tí tocbus pecadh an tshaegail.

384. Is mar sin do fhoillsigedh C. C. co follus a fiadhnaise na ndaine gach ní do gelladh se do techt in a spiraid faidhetorachta.

385. Do bi C. C. a cosmhailes re Solamh mac Dauid ar ecna 7 ar glicus; 7 do cuaidh se os cind Solaimh a nglicus; oir ger glic Solamh, do mellatar na mna é 7 rucatar buaidh ar a glicus. Acus do bi do glicus C. C. nar mhellatar na mna é 7 nach mo rucatar buaidh air.

386. Do búi C. C. a cosmhailes re hEoin bruinde leth re hóghacht; 7 fos as eidir lind a rádha go ndechaidh se a cem foirfechta os cind Eoin leth re coimhet a óghachta; (gen co tainic oigh ris nar comglan Eoin,[471]) an meid co rabatar a lan do neichibh ga brosdadh docum a óghachta do brisedh nach raibe ag brostadh Eoin da brissedh, mar ata uaisli 7 sceímh 7 oícce 7 saibhress; 7 gen gurbh urussa do C. C. a oghacht do coimhet itir gach guasacht dib so, do coimheid se hi gan a brisedh go becc no go mór ar feadh a bethadh go a bás. As follus duind ass so gur tuic C. C. an focul adubairt an feallsamh nadura .i. corub o neichib dochracha dodenta d'imchor, dogeibther an tsubaltaidhe ro-ard. Et as follus duind gor tuic se an focal adubairt Gridhoir naem, an meid as mo an cathughadh, gorub moide an luaididhecht é.

387. Fos, as eidir lind a radha corub mo an foirbfecht do C. C. a oghacht do coimhet 'sa corp daennu-sa a raibe se itir na guasachtaib adubrumar romhaind ina do na hainglibh a ngloine fen do coimhet, do reir mar adeir an doctuir naemtha .i. Ambros, corub mo an buaidh 7 an laidirecht do na daínib a ngloine 7 a n-oghacht do choimet ná do na hainglib a ngloine ata o naduír aca fein do coimhet.

[469] John I, 30.
[470] John, I, 29.
[471] See § 223 supra for a similar idiom. See also § 89.

382. But not thus was the prophesying of Columcille, for it was clear and easy of understanding, and it came to pass without any delay in the very hour that he promised it would come.

383. Moreover it may be said that Columcille was more than a prophet, as it was said of John the Baptist that not only did he prophesy the coming of the Lord, but he pointed Him out to all with his finger, so that they saw Him with their own eyes, when he spake the words whereof John the Evangelist maketh mention in the first chapter of the Books of the Gospels concerning him: *Hic est de quo dixi volis. Hic est qui tollit peccata mundi,* which is to say, "Behold Him that I promised you. Behold Him that taketh away the sins of the world."

384. And thus it was that Columcille did point out to all men all things that he had promised through the spirit of prophecy.

385. Columcille was like unto Solomon son of David in wisdom and shrewdness, and he went beyond Solomon in shrewdness, for albeit Solomon was shrewd, yet the women deceived him, and had the victory over his shrewdness. But such was the shrewdness of Columcille that the women did not deceive him, still less did they have the victory over him.

386. Columcille was like unto John of the Bosom touching virginity, and we may even say that he went a step of perfection above John touching his vigilance in virginity (albeit there was never virgin more pure than John), for there was much that tempted him to defile his virginity that tempted not John, as noble birth and beauty and youth and riches. And albeit it was difficult for Columcille to preserve his virginity in the midst of all these dangers, yet he preserved it undefiled in little or in much throughout his life till his death. It is clear to us from this that Columcille understood the word that the natural philosopher spake, to wit, that from suffering in things hard and difficult, very high virtue is attained. And it is manifest that he understood the word that St. Gregory spake: "The greater the struggle, the greater the reward."

387. Moreover it may be said that it was greater virtue in Columcille to preserve his virginity in the human body wherein he abode, midst the perils we have aforementioned, than for the angels to keep their purity. As saith the holy doctor Ambrose, "Greater is the victory and strength for those that keep their purity and virginity than for the angels to keep the purity the which they have of nature."

388. Do bi C. C. a cosmailes re Petor leth re gradh imarcach do tabairt da Tigherna fein .i. d'Issu Crisd; 7 fos as eidir lind a radha *co* *n*dech*aidh* se a ceim foirfechta os cind Petair a *n*gr*adh* a Tigherna ar an adbur-sa; oir do diult Petar fo t*ri* do Crisd a n-aimsir na paisi; 7 nir diult C. C. e⁴⁷²) o dó⁴⁷³) tindscain se serbís do denamh do *no* co fuair sé bas, *acht* do imchuir gach anshocair 7 gach t*ri*bloíd 7 gach dolás da bfuair se ar a shon.

389. Do bí se a cosm*ailes* re Pol apstal leth re siladh breithre De 7 ris na cinedhach*aibh* do tarraing docum creidmhe; 7 as eidir lind a radha *co* *n*dech*aidh* C. C. a ceim foirbfecta os cind Poil an meid go raibe Pol ar tús ag sc*ris* ecl*aise* De, 7 co raibe se ag congnamh les an lucht do chuir Sdefán mairtir docum báis, 7 go rabatar litrecha leis ó prindsadhuib I*rusalem* co Dam*usc* in a raibe sc*ri*btha cum*ach*ta do beith aice ar gach enduine dogebh*adh* se ac admhail anma Crisd do cur docum bais, *no* a mbreith a laimh les go hIrusalem an uair do gair Día é; mar derbh*us* an leab*ar* da ngoirt*er* "Gnimhartha na n-Apst*ol*."⁴⁷⁴) Ni hamlaidh sin, im*orro*, do bi C. C. a tossach nó a nderedh a beth*adh* *acht* gach duine ac nach fagadh se creidemh Crisd *no* admhail anma an Tigerna, do bidh se ag cathug*hadh* ríu 7 ac (*fol.* 57a) senmoir breith*ri* Dé doib d'ecla go fuighdis bas ar sechran creidimh *no* co tucadh docum Irusalem firindeidhe iad .i. docum flaithesa De.

390. Do bi fos C. C. a cosmailes re Sdefan mairtir ar mart*ra* d'imcar ar a corp fen 'sa saeghal-sa; 7 fedmaid a radha gorb ussa do Sdefan an mart*ra* fuair se fen d'fulang, le girri na haimsire a raibe sí ga tab*air*t do, ina do C. C. an mart*ra* do imchair se a croich an tsaegail re fed se mbliadhan ndecc 7 tri xx bliadhain ar a corp fen, leth re hurnaidhe fada 7 re codl*adh* gairid 7 re gorta toltanaig, 7 re tri c*aoga* salm do radha gach n-oidhce 7 se 'n-a sesamh a n-uisce gó a smeicc, 7 re hedach roindigh do beith im a cness iarsin, 7 corub carruc cloiche budh leba do, 7 corub cloch eli b*a* cerchaill do; am*ail* indeos*us* tuaruscbail a c*ra*baid fen a ndeired an leabhair-se.

391. Et da derb*adh* corub fír sin, do smuainedh C. C. go minic dul d'iarr*aidh* mart*ra* ar aithris na n-apsd*ol* 7 na mairtirech, co tainic aingel De cuice da rádha ris, cor pianamhla 7 cor mo a luaidhid*echt* co mor do a beith beo a fad ag imchor na banmartra do cuir sé ar a corp fen ina d*erg*-mart*ra* gerr d'fhag*ail* mar do fhuarat*ar* na mairtirigh.

---

⁴⁷²Read *do*.
⁴⁷³Read *do*.
⁴⁷⁴*Actus Apos.*, VII *et seq*.

388. Columcille was like unto Peter in the great love he bare his Lord Jesu Christ. And for this cause we may say that he went a step of perfection above Peter in his love for his Lord; Peter thrice denied Christ in the time of the Passion, but Columcille never denied Him from the time he began to serve Him till he died, but he bare every miscomfort and every trouble and every sorrow he received for His sake.

389. He was like unto Paul the Apostle touching the sowing of the word of God and in bringing the Gentiles to the Faith. And we may say that he went a step of perfection above Paul, inasmuch as Paul in the beginning persecuted the Church of God, and aided them that put to death Stephen the Martyr. And he had letters with him from the princes of Jerusalem (that he was bearing) to Damascus wherein was written the authority he had to put to death any that he should find confessing the name of Christ, or to bring them bound to Jerusalem, as witnesseth the book yclept the *Acts of the Apostles*. Not such was Columcille, neither in the beginning nor in the end of his life, but all those he found that had not the Faith of Christ or confessed not the name of the Lord, with them he strove and to them he preached the word of God lest they die straying from the Faith, until they were brought to the true Jerusalem, which is to say, to the Kingdom of God.

390. Moreover Columcille was like unto Stephen the Martyr in enduring martyrdom upon his body in this world. And we may say that the martyrdom that Stephen had to suffer was more easy by reason of the shortness of the time wherein it was given him than the martyrdom that Columcille did endure, with the cross of the world for seventy-two years on his body, with long prayers and short sleep and fasting of his own will, and saying thrice fifty psalms each night standing in water to his chin, and with haircloth next his skin, and a flagstone for his bed and another stone for his pillow, as the tidings of his piety in the last of this book will show.

391. And in witness that this is true Columcille oft thought to go seeking martyrdom after the manner of the apostles and the martyrs, until an angel of God came to him and told him that more painful and of greater merit would it be for him to live a long time enduring the white martyrdom that he laid upon his flesh than to have the brief red martyrdom that the martyrs had.

392. Do bi C. C. a cosmailes re Hioroinim*us* leth re *con*fisó-
racht; 7 as éidir a radha co *n*dech*aidh* se a ceim foirfechta os cind
Ioroinimus an meid co raibe Hioroinimus a toss*ach* a aeísi mailli
re hócanachaibh na Romha a cluiche 7 ag sug*r*adh 7 ag ol fina, 7 ac
raingce 7 ac damhsa; (gin gorb urusa duine b*a* ferr betha ina
é d'fhaghail fá deredh), 7 n*ach* derna C. C. a indam*h*ail no a
cosmhailes sin a n-aimsir a oíce *no* a arrsaidhechta; amail as follus
do lu*cht* leghtha na beatha-ssa aicce fen.

393. Gin corub dingbala sinde do tabairt a molta dilis fen
ar an athair naem|thu-ssa da fuilmid ag labairt, cind*us* bud eidir
duine do mol*adh* nísa mo ina corb eídir lind a radha go firindech
nach tainic uass*a*lath*air* no faidh no suibescel nó apst*ol* ina mairtír
no confissóir na oigh nach eidir lind C. C. do chor a coimes ris, *no*
a céim ecin foirfe*ch*ta os cind gach duine dib; mar as follus do
cach as gach ní da ndubram*ar* romhaind ar fedh an leabuir anuás.

394. Tr*i* c*ed* cell do cumdaigh C. C. a n-Erind 7 a n-Albain;
7 do bi c*ed* cell dib sin a n-aice mara aige; 7 fos tri c*ed* leabur do
scrib se; am*ail* asp*ert* an file:

Tri ced cell do cumhdaich Col*um;*   c*ed* cell a cois tuinde dib,
20   ac*us* tri c*ed* buadach trebhar   lebur solus saer ro scrib.[475])

Et da fhad do beith leabar da scribadh se fa uisce, ni baití en
litir and:

395. Laibeorum anois meid *h*eg*i*n do riagail C. C.,[476]) 7 do
cruas a c*r*abaidh .i. do gnath*aigh*eadh se beith 'n-a aenar 'n-a
duirrth*igh* fen *no* a n-inad uaícnech eli deis na t*r*ath 7 an aifr*ind*
do radha dó, ac denamh duth*r*a*ch*ta do Dia. Acus do gnáthaighedh
a c*or*p do no*ch*tadh 7 do sciúrsadh co menic 'sa sechtmhain, 7 co
hairide comhaim*ser*[477]) na huaire inar sciursadh Ih*s*u. Acus nirb
ail les tathaig*h*e daíne ar bith do beith cuice andsin, muna ticedh
becan do dainib c*r*aibthecha ecnaidhe a llaithibh sollamanta cuice,
do beith ga coimhn*er*tugadh a timma De 7 a mbriath*ar* an
Scribtuír. Acus na daine dobeiredh scela dímhainecha an tsae-
ghail cuice, ni gabadh 'n-a c*on*fersoíd íat. Acus nirb ail les
caidrebh na ndaine saeghalta a*cht* an uair do ticed d'entoisc do
senmoir doib, 7 nirb ail les a subalt*aidh*e d'foillsiugadh do duine

---

[475]*Three Homilies,* p. 112, has
    Tri cét doróraind cen mannair   *do chellaib cainib isfír*
    is trí cét buadach trebon   *lebor solas saer roscrib.*
[476]See *Regula Choluimb Chille* in Z. C. P., III, pp. 28-30.
[477]MS. has *comhaı̣m* which more likely stands for *comhainm.* Cf. § 360
supra, "comhainm an lai a nderna se".

392. Columcille was like unto Jerome touching confessorship. And we may say that he went a step of perfection above Jerome, inasmuch as in the first part of his life Jerome played and disported him with the youths of Rome, and drank wine and leaped and danced, albeit it were not easy to find one of better life than he at the last. But neither such things nor their like did Columcille; neither in his youth nor in his old age, as is manifest to those that have read this *Life*.

393. Albeit we be unworthy to give fitting praise to this holy father whereof we speak, yet how were it possible for one to have praise greater than that which we may say with sooth: There hath not come patriarch nor prophet, nor evangelist, nor apostle, nor martyr, nor confessor, nor virgin, that we may not liken Columcille to him or set him in some degree of perfection above all of them, as is manifest to all from what we have afore said throughout the book above.

XXXV

OF THE VIRTUES OF COLUMCILLE

394. Three hundred churches did Columcille found in Erin and in Alba; and a hundred of these were fast by the sea. And moreover he did write three hundred books, as the poet saith:

> "Three hundred churches did Colum build,
> A hundred of them near the sea;
> And three hundred, virtuous, skilful,
> Noble books of knowledge wrote he."

And a book that he had written, how long soever it might be under water, no letter thereof might be effaced.

395. Speak we now a little of the rule of Columcille and of the rigors of his piety: his wont it was to be alone in his oratory or in some other lonely place, after the hours and the mass were over, communing with God. And he was wont to bare his body and to scourge it often during the week and especially at the hour when Jesu was scourged. And it was displeasing to him that any should come to visit him save that a few wise and pious folk came to him on feast days to be strengthened in the word of God and in the words of the Scriptures. And the folk that brought to him the vain tidings of the world he received not into his conversation. And not pleasing to him was the company of the folk of the world save what time he came with intent to preach to them. And it was not pleasing to him that another should make

eli air, d'ecla a ndul a ngloir dimhain dó, muna foillsig*hedh* fen as adhburuib airidhe íad, da cur a tarbha do cach eli.

396. Do gnáthaigh*edh* C. C. obair do denamh gach en-la, 7 do roindedh se an obair sin a t*ri*; an c*ed* chuid di, do bidh ac senmoir timna De do chach, 7 do aithnighed[h] dib ecla De do beith orra 7 a gradh do beith aca os cind gach uile gradha, 7 grad do tabairt da com*a*rsai*n* amail doberdais doib fen, 7 guidhe go duthr*ach*tach ar a*n*main na marph. Do guidhedh fein 7 do aithnigh*edh* do cach mar an c*ed*na guidhe ar beoaiph 7 ar marbh*aibh* an ci*n*idh daenda, am*ail* budh cominmhain leis uile iad. In dara cuid di, do gnath*aigh*eadh beith ag s*cri*bhneor*acht* no ag fuaighel étaig na manach. In tress cuid di, doní*d*h obair eiccin do rech*adh* a tarbha shuth*ain* don mainistir 7 do na manchaibh, 7 ní scuiredh don obair (*fol.* 57b) sin no co ticed a allus.

397. Ní caithedh C. C. en-moimint da aimsir co dimhain gan beith ac denamh deghoibrighte h*ei*cin do rachad[h] a n-onoir do Dia 7 a tarbha anma dó fein 7 a n-esimplair do cach.

398. Teígheadh C. C. go menic re cois na fairge do cnuas*acht* 7 do dubhan*acht* da manch*aibh*; 7 do bidh sel eli ac roind bidh 7 dighe da lamaib bendaighti naemta fein ar boch*taibh* Dé; 7 do teigh*edh* se 'n-a diaid sin a carcair cumaing cloiche do tabairt pene da corp; amail asp*ert* se fen 'sa rand sa:

Trell ac buai*n* duilesc do carruicc,   seal ar a cluid,
sel ac taba*irt* bid do boc*ht*aib,   seal a carcair.

399. An uair, t*ra*, nach cuiredh C. C. seilens air fein, ní aigilledh duine eli gan adbur. As follus dúind cor tuic se an f*o*cal adub*ai*rt Matha suibescel .i. Rediture sunt hoimines recionem die iudicii de o*mn*i verbo ossiosa⁴⁷⁸) .i. Do-beraid na daine cund*us* 7 resún uatha la breithe in gach en f*o*cal dimain dar labratar ar an saeg*h*al-sa oir nir oibr*igh* C. C. do becc *no* do mór o breithir *no* o gnimh 'sa dimhaines, 7 ni mo tainec en-fhocal brege tar a bel an cein do bi se 'n-a bethaig; am*ail* asp*ert* an file b*a* naemtha 7 b*a* ferr betha tainic a n-Erind ríam .i. Dallan Forcaill ga mebrugh*adh* sin ar Col. C.:

Col*um* Ci*lle* a*r* nach rab buaidhirt,   mor a ecna, maith a chíall;
ni dub*ai*rt gai t*ar* a beluib,   is ní derna espa riamh.

.i. dimaines. Ut d*ixit* Brenaind Birra ga derb*adh* sin 'sa rand sa:

---

⁴⁷⁸Matth. XII, 36.

known his virtues, least he fall into vainglory, save he himself reveal them for certain reasons for the good of others.

396. It was the wont of Columcille to labor each day, and he divided this labor in three parts: the first part thereof he preached the word of God to all, and he bade them fear God and love Him above all love, and to love their neighbor as themselves, and pray earnestly for the dead. And he prayed and bade all in like wise to pray for the living and for the dead of human kind, as if they were all alike dear to them. In the second part thereof he was wont to be writing or weaving garments for the brethren. In the third part thereof he did some work that should be of lasting profit to the monastery and to the brethren, and he ceased not from the task till the sweat came.

397. Columcille used not an instant of his time vainly, without doing some good work that should redound to the honor of God and the profit of his own soul and be an ensaumple to all.

398. Columcille walked beside the sea right oft, beech-combing, and hooking [fish] for the brethren, and he passed another while sharing food and drink from his blessed holy hands with God's poor. And thereafter he went into a narrow cell of stone to put torment upon his body, as he saith in this quatrain:

> "A while at picking seaweed[1] from the rock,
> A while in his bed,
> A while giving food to the poor,
> A while in his cell."

399. Albeit in sooth Columcille laid not silence upon himself, he spake with no man save he had cause. It is manifest to us that he took to himself the words that Matthew said in the Gospel, to wit, *rediture sunt hoimines recionem die iudicii de omni verbo ossiosa*, which is to say, "Men shall render account and reason on the Day of Judgment touching every idle word they have spoken in this world." For Columcille wrought idleness neither in great thing nor small nor in word nor deed, and no more did lying word cross his lips the while that he was alive, as the poet hath said, the holiest and of most good life that ever lived in Erin, to wit, Dallan Forgaill, making mention thereof touching Columcille:

> "Columcille on whom was no trouble,
> Great his wisdom, good his understanding;
> A falsehood never passed his lips,
> And never did he do vanity."

[1] *Cf. Lismore Lives*, p. 340 n. 2331.

Colum Cille ar maighistir, bel nach dubhairt riamh goa;
ba he sin ar sendser-ne, ger uhó sesen ba soa.

400. Et donidh C. C. da ced dheg slechtan gach en-lo go n-oidhce acht a sollamnaib no a ndomhnaighibh; 7 ni scuiredh da slechtain no da urnaidhe no co ticdís a dera go himarcach. Et ni caithedh se bíadh no deoch no go coimheicnighedh gorta da caitemh é. Et ni caithedh C. C. do biad[h] no do digh sul tuc se moid nach caithfedh acht praissech nendta 7 uisce, (amail indises an lebar-sa a n-inadh eli mar adubramar romaind), acht arán 7 uisce; 7 trian a araín sin fen do gainemh; oir do ba craes mór less an t-aran d'ithe 'n-a cail fein gan ní drochblasda ecin do cur tríd da truailledh mar sin, 7 ni caithedh se de sin fen 'sa sechtmhain ní noshasfad bocht en-uair; amail aspert an fili cedna .i. Dallan Forcaill:[479])

Carais Colum caidh Cilli mac Feilimthe na naimhfert,
illadh re sectmhain 'n-a corp nocha sasfad bocht ainfhect.

401. Et do brethnuigedh aice fen cor craes mór 7 cor midingbála do a comhsóghamail sin do betaigh do tabairt da corp fen, 7 do labradh co bagrach ris 7 adeireadh co ndigeoladh se sin air. Acus do teighed a n-uisce les cóa smeicc, 7 adeiredh tri caega salm and amlaidh sin gach n-oidhce; amail aspert an file cedna:[480])

Na tri caega salm do radha dó cech n-oidhce, car mo pían?
is an ler re taebh Alpan resiu no-ardadh an grian.

402. Et ni bidh édach ba míne ina édach róinnich ren a cness do gnath, 7 carraic cloiche budh leba, 7 ni bidh edach itir se 7 hi acht an t-edach roinnich do raidhsimar romaind, 7 carruicc eli ba cerchaill do; 7 ni codladh co mbid ac tuitim ar ecin air. Acus ni denadh se do codladh ar an leabaidh sin fén acht an fedh do bídh Díarmaid .i. a descibul fen ac radh an cethrumadh cuid don Biaíd.[481]) Acus ar moscladh dó, caíedh co ger mar mnai mbáidh

---

[479]See *Z. C. P.*, I, p. 62, where it is ascribed to Cuimmin of Conneire; also *Z. C. P.*, IX, p. 173, where it is ascribed to Columcille:—
  Me Colum cille gu becht mac Feidlimidh na naoimfhert
   nir lág re sechtmuin am corp ní nosasadh bocht aoinfhect.
[480]See *Lis. Lives*, p. 316.
[481]See *ibid.*, p. 180.

Which is to say idleness. *Ut dixit* Brenainn of Birr in witness thereof in this quatrain:

> "Columcille our master,
> Ne'er did his lips utter falsehood.
> Older was he than we were,
> Yet he it was that was lucky."

400. And it was Columcille's wont each day afore night to make twelve hundred times obeisance, save on feast days and Sundays. And he ceased not from prostrating himself and praying until his tears came abundantly. And he ate neither food nor drink until hunger compelled him. And ere he took the vow to eat but broth of nettles and water, as this book doth relate in another place, he ate no food or drink save bread and water. And of that bread a third was sand, for him thought it great gluttony to eat bread in its own substance save he mix therewith some unsavory thing, to spoil it thereby. And even thereof he ate each week not so much as might be enough for a poor man for one meal, as the same poet hath said, to wit, Dallan Forgaill:

> "Pure Columcille did put,
> The son of Fedlimid of holy deeds,
> Into his body each week so much
> As would not sate a beggar at one meal."

401. And he deemed it great gluttony and unseemly for him to give his body so much of comfort, and he spake to it with threats and said he would visit punishment upon it. And therewith he waded into the water to his chin and there he repeated thrice fifty psalms each night, as the same poet hath said:

> "Thrice fifty psalms he repeated,
> Each night. What were more grievous?
> In the ocean fast by Alba,
> Before the sun had arisen."

402. And there was no garment more smooth than a hair shirt next his skin, and a rock of stone was his bed, and there was no cloth between him and it save the cloth of hair that we have aforementioned. And another stone was his pillow. And he slept not till it constrained him. And even in that bed he slept but so long as Diarmaid, his disciple, was saying the fourth part of the *"Beatus."* And when he awoke he wept bitterly as it were a loving woman bewailing her only son, by reason that so long he had neglected his Lord.

ag cainedh a henmic ar son an uiret sin d'faillidhe do denam fá n-a Tigerna.

403. Et, fos, do cuir se a corp fen a ndimbrigh mar sin, indus da curthai íarand gér tren a bragaid, nach ticfadh fuil as acht uisce no sughglas amail uisce, amail aspert an file:

Da tolltaí a cli gorm glas   d'iarand aith, étrom, amhnus,
nocha ticfadh ass, ní go,   cróchadh crotbaill na henchnó.

404. Et ata scribtha ar C. C. da loighedh sé ar traigh no ar gaineamh, go n-airemthai lorcc a asna trian a édach is an traigh ar truaidhe a cuirp, amail mebruighess an file cedna air .i. Dallan Forgaill:

Gle noloighed is an gainemh   in a lighe, ba mór sæth;
slicht a asna trén a edach,   ba leir and con[id]seídeadh
                                                    [gaeth.⁴⁸²)

405. Et do iarr C. C. ar Dia gan cruth a aighte do dul a ndochraidecht no a truaillidhecht le cruas crabaidh da ndingnedh se, indus co mbeith (fol. 58a) sí sochraidh subaltach a fíadnaise na ndaine aige.

406.⁴⁸³) Ata Adamhnan naemtha ga mebrughadh co fuair C. C. an athcuinge sin o Dia, indus co foillsighed se agaidh sochraidh subhaltach gradach naemtha do cach, amail do beith se ag ól no ag fleadhughadh gan fechain do crúas crabaidh no d'airde fuirechrais no d'imarcaigh treigenais da ndenadh se. Asse an t-adhbar e, oir nirb eidir le grasaib an Spiraid Naimh do bi go himarcach leth astigh in a croidhe gan iad fen d'fhoillsiughadh don taebh amuigh in a agaidh.

407. Ba ro-scíamhach ro-uassal, umorro, an corp sin do cuir C. C. a ndimbrigh 7 a tarcuisne co ro-mhor mar sin; oir ata scribta air nar chuir corp daenna uime riam, a fecmais daendachta Crist, corp bud sciamcha 7 ba feile 7 ba nairidhe, 7 as mo tuc d'airneis an tsaeghail-se do bochtaib De ina é, 7 fos, as mo tuc d'aeis eladhna 7 do lucht íarrata spreidhe d'ecla a cáinte no a aertha ina se.

---

⁴⁸²See *R. C.*, XX, p. 168; *Lis. Lives*, p. 316; *Irish Liber Hym.*, I, p. 166; Dinneen's *Keating*, III, p. 104.
⁴⁸³See Reeves' *Adam.*, p. 9.

403. And moreover so much did he hold his body in disdain that if any sharp iron were put through his throat, there would come forth naught save water and a greenish liquid like unto water, as the poet hath said:

> "If his bluish green side were pierced through,
> With a sharp iron, keen, not heavy,
> There would not come forth ('Tis no falsehood)
> The decaying saffron of a single nut (?)"

404. And it is writ of Columcille that when he lay on the strand or on the sand, the tracks of his ribs could be numbered on the strand through his garments by reason of the pitiful state of his body, as the same poet doth relate, to wit, Dallan Forgaill:

> "Clearly he lay in the sand,
> In his bed (Great was the toil);
> The track of his ribs through his raiment
> Was visible if the wind blew it."

405. And Columcille begged of God that his countenance should not become unsightly or uncomely to look on nor fall into corruption through the rigor of the piety he practiced, but be of good semblance and pleasing in the sight of men.

406. Holy Adamnan maketh mention that Columcille gat his prayer from God, so that he bare a comely, joyful, loving, holy face to all, right as he had been drinking or feasting, notwithstanding the rigor of his piety and the severity of his vigil and the much fasting that he did. And the reason thereof was this: it was not possible that the graces of the Holy Spirit that were passing great in his heart within should not show forth in his face without.

407. Passing comely and passing noble in sooth was that body that Columcille did hold thus in disdain and in passing great scorn; for it is writ of him that save the human body of Christ never afore was there body of man more comely and more noble and more chaste, nor one that gave more than he of worldly goods to God's poor. And to the folk of learning and to beggars also did he give, for fear of their vilifying and their satire.

408. Et anuair adeirthai cor saoghalta *no* cor gloir dimain do sin do denamh ris an aess eladhna, iss i frecra do-beredh se ar cach, corab ar a fidhair fen do cruth*aigh* Día e, 7 nach tuillf*edh* se scandail *no* naíre don fhidhair sin an fad do beith se 'n-a beth*aidh,* gan duillebhar dimbuan an tsaegh*ail* do tab*airt* amach ar a scath d'ecla a himd*er*gtha.

409. Et scribthar air 'na Leighindt*ib* fen, cor cosmail sdaid 7 faicsin a cuirp re Crisd fen. Et do bi an oiret-sa do coimed ac Día ar naire C. C., indus nach lecedh se aidhedha *no* coiccricha 'n-a cend gan aingel do chur dá indesin do co mbeidis cuice, ind*us* co mbeith se oircillech ar a cind.

410. Do bi an oired sin d'umla a C. C., gan fech*ain* da uaisli *no* da folaidh*echt* no do med a subhált*aidh*e o Dia, corub e fen do indl*adh* da mhanchaib 7 do benadh a mbrocca dib, am*ail* donidh an Tigerna .i. Issu Crisd da apsdal*aibh.* Et, fos, ata scribtha air corub minic do-beired se cuid arba an coimhtinoil ar a muin docum an muilind.

411. Ata an nech naemtha .i. Baithin mac Cuanach, ga mheabrugh*adh* go raibe an uired-sa do coimet ag C. C. ar a oghacht nar fhech se ar mnai ar bith riam, 7 fos nar fech se ar a mhath*air,* amail derbhus se is na randaib se:

Fa genmnaich Colum Cille,   flaith foss*adh* na firinde;
*noch*ar fhech ar mnai mi*n* moill   an fad do bi se a colaind.

Ge adeirthai ris beith gan cair,   ge fuair a fhis 'n-a trathaib;
adeirim-se go gr*ind* rib[h]   nochar sill ar a math*air.*

Mar ticced a mat[h]*air* fen   d'acallaim Col*uim* i Neill,
a hagaidh re Colu*m* ngle,   as cul Col*uim* re hEithne.

Et ata, u*morro,* C. C. fein ga derbadh sin sa rand-sa dorinde se fen:

Is inmai*n* lem-sa mo lec   ar nach denand deman glec,
mo druim-se rem math*air,* trath   aghaid mo math*ar* orm-sa.

408. And when men said that it was worldliness or vainglory in him to be thus toward the poets, he made answer ever that it was in His own image that God had created him, and he would not bring scandal or shame upon that image so long as he might be alive, but the fading leafage of the world he would bestow for His sake lest He be reproached.

409. And it is writ in the lectionaries concerning him that the state and the seeming of his body were like unto Christ's own. And so much of care did God have of the hospitality of Columcille and of his shamefastness that He suffered not guests nor strangers to come to him save He sent to him angels to tell him of their coming, that he might be prepared against their arrival.

410. Such was the greatness of the humility of Columcille, notwithstanding his noble blood and breeding and the many gifts he had of God, that he washed [the feet of] the brethren and took off their boots as the Lord Jesu Christ did for his apostles. And moreover it is writ of him that he did oft bear a share of the corn of the community to the mill on his own back.

411. Holy Baithin mac Cuanach doth make mention that Columcille did with so great vigilance guard his virginity that he looked not ever upon a woman. And moreover he never looked upon his mother, as it is proved in these quatrains:

> "Chaste was Columcille,
> A steadfast prince of truth.
> Never looked he on smooth, gentle woman
> The while he dwelt in the flesh.
>
> Though it be said of him he was faultless,
> Though his wisdom he gat in his Hours,
> Yet I tell thee right fairly
> Never looked he upon his mother.
>
> When his own mother came [hither]
> To talk with the seed of Niall, Colum,
> Her face was turned to bright Colum
> And the back of Colum to Ethne."

And moreover Columcille himself doth bear witness thereto in this verse that he hath made:

> "Dear to me is my flagstone;
> The demon thereon doth not wrestle,
> My back is turned to my mother, in sooth,
> The face of my mother to me."

412. Batar, imorro, da Baithin and re lind Coluim Cille .i. Baithin mac Cuanach 7 Baithin mac Brenaind. Baithin mac Cuanach, imorro, do cinel Enda mic Neill nai giallaig esidhe. Baithin mac Brenaind don, do cinel Conaill Gulban dó. Acus cland da derbrathar e fen 7 Colum Cille, amail aspert an file:

Baithin mac Brenaind don roind   mic Feargassa mic Conaill;
cland da derbrathar malle,   Baithin is Colaim Cille.

413. Et ba he an Baithin sin mac Brenaind nobidh do gnath a fochair Coluim Cille. Et ba ro-naemtha é 7 ní caithedh se en-moimint da aimsir go dímhain. Acus do bi an oired-sa do nemhfhaillide aige fa Dia, indus co ngabadh se orrtha 7 aintemhain itir gach da greim don meid proinde nocaithedh. Acus do tocbadh a rusca 7 a lamha suas ag guidhe De co duthrachtach do gnath mar an cedna. Acus nir lecc se en-focal da beathaidh nó da mirbuilibh do scribadh riamh, mar onoir do Colum Cille, indus go madh moide do beith aire caich ar mhirbhuilibh 7 ar beathaidh C. C. e. Acus, fos, do bi se 'n-a ab a nĩ aimser airidhe a ndiaidh Coluim Cille.

414. Do bi truaighe 7 compais mor acá mhanchaibh fen do C. C. an uair do gortaighedh se a corp go himarcach le troscadh no re hurnaidhe no re fuirechrus no re pianaib ro-mhora eli do tabairt do, amail adubramar remaind. Acus adeirdis ris corub mo 7 corub ro-mhó donídh se do na neichibh sin ina mar do athain Dia de a denamh.

415. Do frecradh san íad san 7 assedh adeiredh an briathar adubairt Matha suibescel: Ragnum Dei uim paititur et uiolenti rapiunt illud .i. 'Dogeibther 7 cosantar flaithemhnus De ar ecin 7 as síad na daine foiréccnecha fhuadaighess e' .i. na daine diultus da n-ainmíanaib fen 'sa saoghal-sa ar grad[h] Dé. Acus aderedh nac berthar buaid acht a cathughadh (fol. 58b).

416. Adeireadh fos ris na manchaibh nach corónfaidhe duine ar bith 'na codladh, 7 nach raibe sealbh flaithemhnais De co cindte ag nech do med a indilltaiss.

417. Adeireah an briathur adubairt an faidh mor .i. Dáuid: Filia Babilonis misera: beatos qui retribuit tibe retribucionem tuam[484]) .i. 'A ingen bocht na tribloide 7 na buaidirtechta, is

---

[484]*Filia Babylonis misera: beatus, qui retribuet tibi retributionem tuam, quam retribuisti nobis.*—Psalm 136, 8.

412. Two Baithins moreover were there in the time of Columcille, to wit, Baithin mac Cuanach and Baithin mac Brenainn. Baithin mac Cuanach was of the race of Enda son of Niall of the Nine Hostages, and Baithin mac Brenainn of the race of Conall Gulban. And children of two brothers were he and Columcille, as the poet hath said:

> "Baithin mac Brenainn of the Portioning,
> Son of Fergus mac Conaill,
> Children the twain of two brothers
> Baithin and Columcille."

413. And it was that Baithin that was son to Brenainn that was wont to be in the fellowship of Columcille. And he was passing holy and never did he use aught of his time vainly. And such was his diligence toward God that he recited prayers and antiphons between each two bites that he ate of his meal. And in like wise he was wont to lift up his eyes and his two hands in fervent prayer to God. And to honor Columcille he suffered not one word of his own life or miracles to be written down, so that men should give the more heed to the miracles and life of Columcille. And moreover he was abbot in Iona for a certain while after Columcille.

414. There was pity and passing compassion for Columcille among the brethren the time he did sore hurt to his body with fasting or prayers or vigils or with the other exceeding great pains he did put thereon, as we have aforementioned. And they were wont to say to him that more and passing more did he of these things than God commanded him to do.

415. Then he would make answer to them and say the words that Matthew the Evangelist said: *Ragnum Dei uim paititur et uiolenti rapiunt illud,* which is to say, "It is by violence that the Kingdom of God is taken and contested, and it is the folk of violence that bear it away, to wit, the folk that for the love of God deny their passions in this world." And he was wont to say that victory is not gained save by struggle.

416. And he was wont to tell the brethren that no man is crowned whilst sleeping, and no man hath of a surety obtained possession of the Kingdom of God, howso diligent his making ready.

417. He was wont to repeat the word of the great prophet David: *Filia Babilonis misera beatos qui retribuit tibe retribucionem tuam,* to wit, "Poor daughter of misery and woe, rich and of great substance

conaich saidbir anté tuc duit an ní tuc tú do.' Acus ass hi ingen bocht adubairt an faidh annso .i. an coland daénna. Acus as é ní do tuicc se do tabairt uaithe di [.i.] na peacaidh 7 na lochta marbuss an t-anam.

418. Do fhoillsigedh C. C. do na manchaib corub ar son peacaid an craéis 7 an dímaiss 7 na glóiri dímhaínche do scrisadh Adham a parthuss, 7 nach eidir dul and aris acht le ro-aibsdenens 7 le ro-umlacht 7 le neimchin do tabairt ar an soegal, 7 gebe dodenadh na tri neithe sin a n-agaidh na colla craesaidhe dímsaidhe ainmíanaidhe, corub duine bendaighte conaich é.

419. Et dobeiredh se esimplair 7 cosmalacht eli do na manchaibh narb eidir dul a parthuss acht ar mogaib[485]) contrardha do na hadburuib far cuiredh Adamh ass.

420. Et aderedh narb i an tslighe a tancatar na righte tainic les na haiscedhaib docum an Tigerna, do gabatar aris ac dul tar a n-ais da tír duthaig fen.

421. Mar sin 7 le hudarassaib mora eli do coiscedh 7 do toirmiscedh an t-uassal-athair .i. C. C., beoil 7 tengta na manach do bidh ga toirmese fan crabadh 7 fan cruaitech donidh se air féin.

422. Go deimin as eidir lind a radha co firinnech go raibe C. C. bendaighte fial firinnech trocairech do cach uile, 7 se cruaidh cumang ger gann gortach do fen. Mar sin do múch 7 do marb se na pecaid 7 na lochta 7 ainmiana an cuirp and fen. Donidh fos oibrigthe na trocuiri do cach uili, do truagh 7 do tren, do mnaib 7 d'fheraib, co spiridalta 7 go haimserdha, gan deithfer, gan delughadh itir persandaib na ndaine. Do benadh 7 do tógadh a biad 7 a deoch 7 a édach da corp fen da tabairt do bochtaibh Dé 7 da gach duine do riccedh a less é, 7 do bídh a muinel 7 a brollach lomnocht do gnath acht folach do croiceand beag deroil orra. Et an uair nach bidh deirc aige dobéradh sé do na bochtaibh, do cáiedh co gér do truaide 7 do compáis doib.

423. Et is deimin nach caithedh se fín na cuirm eli na bainde, 7 ata se fein ga derbadh sin is an rand sa:[486])

---

[485]Read modhaib.
[486]See Ériu, V, p. 13.

is He that hath given thee that which thou hast given Him." And this is the poor daughter whereof the prophet here spake, to wit, the body of man. And these are the things that he meant she gave, to wit, the sins and the flaws that destroy the soul.

418. Columcille was wont to set forth to the brethren that it was by reason of the sin of gluttony and pride and vainglory that Adam was driven from Paradise, and that men might not come again thither save by very great abstinence and lowliness and by despising the world. And whosoever did these three things against the gluttonous, proud, passionate flesh was a man blessed and of great substance.

419. And he was wont to give the brethren another ensaumple and similitude how it was not possible to go to Paradise save in manner contrary to the reasons wherefore Adam was cast forth therefrom.

420. And he was wont to say that the kings that came with gifts to the Lord went not back by the way they came, when they returned to their own land.

421. In this wise and by other great witnesses did the patriarch Columcille check and stop the mouths and tongues of the brethren that would have hindered him from his piety and from the hardships he visited upon himself.

422. In sooth we may truly say that Columcille was holy and princely, true and merciful to all, but hard and strait, sharp and niggardly to himself. Thus it was he quenched and killed the sins and weaknesses and passions of his flesh. And he did work of mercy to all, to weak and strong, to women and to men, in spiritual and in temporal things, without difference or distinction among the persons of men. He took away and bare off his food and his drink and his garments from his own body to give them to God's poor and to all that had need. His neck and breast were wont to be bare save for a small mean covering of skin upon them. And when he had no alms to give to the poor, he wept bitterly for sorrow and for pity of them.

423. And certain it is that he partook not of wine nor ale else, nor of milk. And he himself it is that beareth witness thereto in the quatrain:

Nímtorbha, ge beith nech ag ól corma,
an cein bias bainde a linde 7 minde nosnodra,
ferr lim comradh rem leabar cuiress ar deman doghra.

Et ní caithedh se im ina feoil do na huile feoil no ní méith no deghblasta ar bith; amail atbert Baithin 'sa rand sa:[487])

Feol no inmar blasda ar bith nir caith do min no do mor;
corp De do caithedh dar ndin, an fin do sechnadh a ól.

Et fos amail adbert Dallan Forcaill 'sa rand sa:[488])

Ceo ni cuirm, ceo ní sercoll saith sechnais beoil.

424. As follus do cach ass cech ní da ndubhramar ar feadh an liubuir si anuas conuice so, go tainicc an briathar adubairt Pol apstal ris fen do C. C.: Munduss mihi cruxifixus est et ega mundo .i. 'Do crochadh an saegal damh 7 do crochad mesi do tshaegal.'

425. Et co firindech ni raibe cin ag C. C. ar ór nó ar airget no ar airneis an tsaegail, acht a tabairt uadha ar son De 7 ar scath a aighthe amail dogeibeadh se o Día. Acus ata scribtha air gach ni do roichedh 'n-a laimh clí nach soichedh 'n-a laim deis gan a brondadh 7 gan a tidhlacadh, amail mebraighes Baithin is na rannaibh se:[489])

Ní da roichedh 'n-a laim cli Coluim Cille, fath gan gai,
nocha soichedh 'n-a laim des gan a brondadh gan esslis.

Ba maith da coindimh ré ré, ge beg do loinged ['n]a cli
as demhin nar cin o nai laech na naemh dob fherr amní.

Nochur taisced pingind riam do cisde ag Colum na cliar,
acht a brondadh da gach nech ar feili 7 ar enech.

[487]See *Z. C. P.*, VII, p. 304.
[488]See *Lis. Lives*, p. 316; *R. C.*, XX, p. 262.
[489]See *Z. C. P., ibid.*

> 'To me it availeth not
> Albeit one may be drinking the beer.
> So long as milk . . . . .
> . . . .
> Better to me converse with my book
> That putteth sadness on demons.''

And he ate not butter nor any meat nor aught fat or savoury in the world, as Baithin saith in his quatrain:

> "Of meat or any savoury condiment
> He ate nor little nor much,
> The body of God he took for our sake,
> The wine he shunned to drink of."

And moreover Dallan Forgaill saith in this quatrain:

> "[For him] naught of ale, naught of dainties,
> A full mouth he shunned."

424. It is manifest to all from what we have said throughout this book to this time that the word the Apostle Paul said of himself doth pertain to Columcille, *Munduss mihi cruxifixus est et ega mundo*, which is to say, "The world hath been crucified to me and I to the world."

425. In sooth Columcille had no love for gold nor silver nor for the treasures of the world, save to bestow for the sake of God and in defence of his honor such as he received from God. And it is written of him that what reached his left hand reached not his right without his bestowing it and giving it away, as Baithin doth relate in these quatrains:

> "The thing that came to the left hand
> Of Columcille, cause without falsehood,
> Came not into his right hand
> Without bestowal, without failure (?).
>
> Good in his time at quartering
> Though little his body did eat;
> 'Tis certain, ne'er sprang from any
> Hero or saint in aught better.
>
> He stored not a penny ever
> Of treasure, Colum of companies,
> But he gave it away to someone;
> In guesting [he gave] and in bounty."

Ut d*ixit* poéta ga derbadh sin:

Fe*rr* d'fheruib an fer rosfuair   *acht* an ri rogeluid gréin,
flaith gan clect gainde, gan cradh,   Col*um* cadh, n*er*t clainde
                                                                                                  [Neill.

426. Axal, im*orro* ainm an aingil coimhidh*echt*a do bi ag C. C., 7 Demal ainm an drochaingil do bidh 'n-a coimhidecht; am*ail* aspert an file .i. Dallan Forcaill:[490])

Crimthand ua Cuind, comhall ngle,   ai*n*m baisde Col*uim* C*ille;*
Axal a ainge*l* (*fol.* 59a) gan on   7 Deamal a demhon.

Et co firindech is eidir lind a rádha nar cuir C. C. dolas ar Axal riamh ag denamh a nemhthoili, 7 nach mo tuc se solas no gairdech*us* do Demál riamh ag denamh a toili go becc *no* co mor, o a bathais go a bas, o breith*ir* no ó gnim.

427. Mar do bidh, im*orro*, Uictor 'n-a aingel coimhidechta ac Patraig, as aml*aidh* sin do bidh Axal ag C. C., amail aspert an fili:

Uic*tor* aingel Patraig fén   ocár facbud geill gachaín;
Axul aingel Col*uim* caidh,   niruó rolond re daimh ndaír.

428. Go deimhin as eidir a radha co *n*dechaidh C. C. a ceim foirbf*echt*a os cind cumhachta na naduiri daenna o grass*aibh* an Spirda N*aimh* do bi go himarcach aice, 7 fos as eidir an focal ata scribtha 'sa Scribtuir do tuicsin dó .i. Non est in*u*entuss similis illi qui *con*seruaret legem excelsis .i. 'Ni frith nech bud cosm*ail* ris an te-si do coimet r*ech*ta an Tig*er*na.'

429. 'Sa sechtmhadh la do mí medoín an gemhr*idh* umorro, ruc*adh* C. C.; 7 an naemadh la do mí medoin an tshamhraid fuair se bas. Acus dob imcub*aidh* do beathaidh C. C. 'sa saeg*hal*-sa an aimsir a tainic se air; oir ba gemreta a betha leth re fuacht 7 re dorcadus, 7 re pein 7 re penduid, 7 re doirbes 7 re hanshocair d'imchar ar a c*or*p fen. Et fos, ba himcubaidh don beth*aidh* docum a *n*dech*aidh* se on tshoegal-sa an aimsir a fuair se bas .i. aimser as gloine 7 as teo 7 as mó soillse 7 delr*adh* 'sa mbl*iadhain* uili. Acus ba himcub*aidh* do cuir Dia na n-uile cum*acht* a n-esimplair duind tre beth*aidh* 7 tre bas a serbfogha*nt*a*idh*e dilis

---

[490]See *R. C.,* XX, p. 176; Dinneen's *Keating,* III, p. 100.

As the poet hath said, bearing witness thereto:

"Best of men the man that gat it (?),
Save the King that made the sunshine.
A prince of no miserly habit nor harshness,
Pious Colum, the prop of Clan Neill."

426. Axal was the name of the guardian angel that Columcille had, and Demal was the name of the bad angel that was with him, as the poet Dallan Forgail saith:

"Crimthann grandson of Conn, clear fulfilment,
Columcille was named in baptism.
Axal, his angel, the harmless,
And Demal [the name of] his demon."

And we may say in sooth that never did Columcille grieve Axal by doing aught contrary to his will, nor did he ever give solace or joy to Demal by doing his desire in things small or great from his baptism until his death, in word or deed.

427. And as Victor was guardian angel to Padraic, so was Axal to Columcille, as the poet hath said:

"Victor was angel to Padraic
. . . .
Axal to Colum the Pious;
He was not too fierce gainst a lowly band."

428. It may be said in sooth that by the graces of the Holy Spirit, the which he possessed abundantly, Columcille went a step of perfection above the powers of human nature. And the word that is written in the Scriptures may be understood of him, to wit, *Non est inventuss similis illi qui conseruaret legem excelsis,* which is to say, "There hath been found none like unto this man for keeping the law of the Lord."

429. On the seventh day of December Columcille was born, and on the ninth day of June he died. And fitting to the life of Columcille in the world was the season whenas he came hither, for wintry was his life in respect of cold and darkness and in respect of pain and penance and in respect of bearing adversity and hardships in the flesh. And fitting to the life into the which he entered from this world was the season whenas he died, to wit, the season that is purest and warmest and brightest and most shining of all the year. And it was a similitude that Almighty God gave us in the life and death of his chosen servant

fen .i. C. C., corub ó gemhred dubach dobronach gruamda a
bethadh 'sa soeghal-sa, ruc se leis e docum shamraidh delradhaig
glormhair na bethadh suthaine.

430. Dob i aes an Tigherna ac fagail bais do C. C. .i. se
bliadna decc 7 ceithri fichid 7 cuig ced bliadhain. Acus se bliadhna
decc 7 tri fichid aeis C. C. fen ag fagail bais do. Acus da bliadhain
7 da fhichid a aeis ag dul ar deoraidecht a n-Albain do 7 Molaisi
Daimh indse d'faghail bais an bliadhain sin. Acus dom doig is
do mirbuilibh De 7 C. C. tainic bas d'faghail dó an bliadhain sin
sech bliadhain eli tre mar do bi se ag cumhdach C. C. do chur a
n-Albain. Acus ceithri bliadhna dec ar fhichid do caith C. C. da
shaeghal a n-Albain. Conadh se bliadhna decc 7 tri fichid a
seoghal uili mar sin, amail aspert an fili:[491])

Teora bliadhna bai gan les   Colum ina duibreccles;
luid la hainglib ass an cacht,   iar se bliadnaib sectmhogad.

431. Do scrib messi a bfuair me do bethaigh C. C. conuice
sin; 7 ni coir a tuicsin co bfuil si uili annso. Acus do budh borb
ren a brethnugadh co madh tualaing a fhaisneis mona faisneidhedh
aingli Dé hí, le fad a soeghail, 7 le met a gras, 7 le himat a mirbhal
aca foillsiughadh gach lai.

432. Do labramar do bethaich C. C. conuice sin, as coir
duínd labairt anoss do meid ecin dá mhirbuilib tar eís a bais;
gen gorub eidir le hen-duine ar bith crich do chur orra on a
linmairecht 7 on a n-imat.

433.[492]) Do bi nech airidhe a n-Alpain[493]) a fad tar eis bais
C. C., ag dul ar sruth no tar apaind 7 mala leabur ar a muin, 7 do
ben escor don nech ar a raibe se, indus cor baithedh e. Acus
a cinn dá fhicid la iar sin, frith a chorp 7 an mala ren a tocbhail.
Acus, ní narb ingnadh, do truailletar 7 do lobhatar na lebair do
bi 'sa mala sin uili acht amhain duilleoc do scrib C. C. da laimh
coisrectha bendaighte fen do bi and, ge do cuaidh sin os cind
cumachta náduiri na duili sin an uisce. Ni derna an t-uisqui
dith no dighbail fris an ré sin di, acht mar do beith sí a cofra fa
íadhad no a n-inadh deiscreidech eli; cor moradh ainm De 7 C. C.
de sin.

[491]See R. C., XX, p. 168; Irish Liber Hym., p. 165; Dinneen's Keating, III, p. 104.
[492]In Adamnan, ibid., p. 114 ff.
[493]Read inEirinn.

Columcille, inasmuch as He took him from the dark and sad and gloomy winter of his life in this world to the shining glorious summer of Eternal Life.

430. This was the age of our Lord when Columcille died, to wit, seven and ninety and five hundred years. And sixteen and three score was Columcille when he took his death. And two and two score was his age when he went into exile in Alba, and Molaise of Devenish died that year. And methinks it was by miracles of God and Columcille that he gat his death in that year passing any other year, for it was he that helped to send Columcille to Alba. And fourteen and a score years of his life did Columcille pass in Alba, so that sixteen and three score years was thus the whole of his life, as the poet hath said:

> "Three years he was without light,
> Colum in his dark church.
> With angels he went from the body
> After six years and seventy."

431. Thus far have I writ what I have found touching the life of Columcille, but it should not be understood that it is all here. And it were pride indeed to deem that it were possible to declare it [all], save it were declared by the angels of God, by reason of the length of his life time and the abundance of his graces and the many miracles each day made manifest.

XXXVI

OF MIRACLES THAT COLUMCILLE DID AFTER HIS DEATH

432. Thus far have we spoken of the life of Columcille. It behooveth us now to speak of some of the miracles following his death, albeit it were not possible for any man in the world to set a term to them by reason of their number and multitude.

433. There was a certain man in Alba long while after the death of Columcille that was going on a stream or across a river bearing a satchel of books upon his back. And he fell and was drowned. And after the space of twenty days his body was found and when it was lifted, the bag also. And—no marvel—all the books that were in that bag were decayed and rotted, save one only, to wit, a leaf from a book that Columcille had written with his holy blessed hand; albeit it went

434.⁴⁹⁴) Do bi dair mor ar an magh a fuil Cenanndus a Midhe,
7 is fan a bun do bi C. C. 'n-a suidhe an uair fuair se an baili sin
o righ Erenn .i. o Diarmaid mac Cearbhaill. Acus do bendaigh
se hi, 7 do mair si san inadh sin go cend aim (fol. 59b) siri faide
5   tar eís bais C. C. ag denamh fert 7 mirbal, cor lecc gaeth mór
iarsin hi. Acus tainic fer denta brocc cuice, 7 do bean a croiceand
di do coirtedh an leathair da ndenadh se broca. Acus dorinde se
broga dó fen don leathar sin, 7 iar na cur uime do, dorindedh
lobur de; 7 do bi se amlaidh sin gó a bas trias an micadhass 7
10 trias an essonoír tucc se don crand sin do bendaich C. C.

435. Fechtass dar gabadh mac Taidg mic Toirrdelbaigh ua
Briain le righ Muman, ar slanaib maithe Leithe Mogha, 7 Turcaill
righ gall, 7 Ueinne .i. airdespoig na hErenn. Acus do eitig an righ
a lecen amach ar comairli na slana sin uili. Acus ar mbeith aimsir
15 fada a laimh do san amlaidh sin a prisun fa anshocair moír, 7 ar
mbuain a sul d'furtacht d'faghail do taeb eli do, as se smuaineadh
dorinde se 'n-a indtind fen .i. muindteruss do denamh ris in
diabhal, da fhis an saerfadh se on braighdenus sin e. Acus ar
crichnughadh an smuainthighe sin do, tainic an diabal cuige do
20 denamh a cuir riss. Et nír cian doib and iarsin, an uair tainic
C. C. o flaithes De anuas cuca 7 uimhir doairme d'ainglib nimhe
maille ris, 7 do labhuir ris an diabhul 7 assedh adubairt: 'Ni ced
duid óglachuss do gabail on duine sin,' ar se, 'oir is oclaoch dam-sa
e.' 'Cindus sin?' ol an diabal. 'Do mebraigh se an leabhar darub
25 ainm "Amhra Coluim Cille," '7 ni hail le Dia tu-ssa do gabail re
duine ar bith da ndena serbhis damh-sa,' ar se. 'Ni mesde,' ol in
diabal, 'má do saer tu-ssa a anam orm-sa, digheolad-sa ar a corp e.'
Tuc a anál fai iarsin, 7 dorinde lobhur ar an pongc sin fen de.
'As ced lium-sa an pian sin do beith ar a corp 'sa saegal-sa tria
30 mar do tucc a drochcreideamh fen air muindterus do denamh rit-sa,
a diabhail,' ar C. C., '7 mar do cuaidh se a n-amharus 7 a mídochus
ar Dia. Gidheadh, fos, legfidher as a braigdenas e 7 biaid se 'n-a
huachtarán os cind lobhur Lessa Moír Mochuda go a bas 7 dogeb-
sa flaithess De da anmain fa deoigh.' Do fíradh sin uile; cor
35 moradh ainm De 7 C. C. de sin (fol. 60a).

⁴⁹⁴In O. I. L. *Lis. Lives*, p. 176.

beyond the powers of the nature of that element of water [to spare it]. No hurt nor harm did the water to the book throughout that time, but it was as it had been in a coffer under cover, or in some secret place else, so that God's name and Columcille's were magnified thereby.

434. There was a great oak on the plain where Kells is in Meath. And Columcille sat at the foot thereof when he was given that place by the King of Erin, to wit, Diarmaid mac Cearbhaill. And he blessed it and it lived in that spot for a long space after his death, working marvels and wonders until a great wind felled it. And a cobbler came thither and cut off its bark that he might tan leather thereof to make shoes. And of that leather he made him shoes. And when he had put them on he became a leper. And in this wise was he until his death, by reason of the disworship and dishonor he had done to that tree the which Columcille had blessed.

435. On a time the son of Tadg mac Toirrdelbaigh grandson of Brian was seized by the King of Munster on the sureties of the nobles of Leth Mogha and Turcall King of the Norsemen and Ueinne Archbishop of Erin. And by the counsel of all those sureties the King refused to let him go. And when the son of Tadg had been for a long space thus in prison in great wretchedness, and had lost hope of getting help from any else, he thought in his heart to make fellowship with the Devil, to see if he might save him from that captivity. And when he had completed that thought, the Devil came to him to make the pact with him. And they had not been long thus when Columcille came down to them from the Kingdom of God, and a multitude of heavenly angels with him, and he spake to the Devil and said in this wise:

"It is not permitted thee to take service from this man," saith he, "for he is a servant to me."

"How it that?" saith the Devil.

"He hath committed to mind the book that is called the *Amra Coluim cille*, and it is not pleasing to God that thou shouldst take a man that doth serve me," saith Columcille.

"I care not," saith the Devil, "but if thou save his soul from me, I will avenge it on his body."

The Devil breathed on him then and made him a leper straightway.

"I suffer this pain to be on his body in this world by reason of his bad faith that led him to make a pact of fellowship with thee, O Devil," saith Columcille, "and by reason that he fell into doubt and despair of God. Natheless he shall yet be released from his captivity and he shall be in authority over the lepers of Lismore of Mochuda and I shall obtain the Kingdom of God for his soul at the last."

And God's name and Columcille's were magnified thereby.

[*Thus far the work of Manus O'Donnell.*]

GLOSSARY OF RARER WORDS

Numbers refer to pages and lines.

aball f. *apple-tree.* sg. gen. abhla 284, 5. voc. aball 92, 20.

aball-gort *applegarth.* sg. d. aballgort 92, 16. abullgort 92, 18.

abb m. *an abbot.* sg. gen. abbad 2, 2. dat. ab 64, 18.

accáinim *I wail, lament.* v. n. accáine. pass. pret. 3 sg. do hacainedh 72, 33.

acédóir (ad-cét-óir) *at once.* 56, 9. 86, 5. *etc.*

acht *doubt, uncertainty.* sg. acc. *id.* 42, 30. 198, 11.

adba *dwelling.* sg. g. *id.* 376, 6. acc. adbaidh 416, 22.

adbh cíuil *a musical instrument.* 416, 25. *Cf.* a(i)dben tool, instrument, *Contrib. s. v.*

ad-chi 138, 36. indic. pres. sg. 2 of adciú *I see.* atchim *I see* 260, 13.

ad-garim *I proclaim, cite, sue.* v. n. acra. accra 178, 6. fut. pl. 1 aigeóram 116, 33.

adhail 270, 19. meaning seems *presentiment, foreboding.*

adhnacht 158, 9. 10. 12. 16. 424, 18. passive perf. sg. 3 of adnacim *I bury.*

adhúathmhairecht f. *great dread.* 112, 29. 236, 11. sg. acc. *id.* 234, 25.

admhadair 108, 18. perf. pl. 3 of admhaim *I confess.*

aduaigh *he ate.* 370, 16, for -duaidh, used as pret. sg. 3 of ithim *I eat.*

aduara glana glasa 384, 25. or *read* atuara glana glana.

áe *liver, gall.* sg. gen. aéi 42, 9.

áeb f. *form, beauty.* sg. dat. áibh 168, 24.

aendacht *unity, loneliness* (in the sense of being alone). 46, 11.

aenurán *singleness, one person alone.* 180, 14.

1. áes f. *age.* sg. gen. aísi 86, 18.

2. áes m. *folk* 116, 6. aés martra *martyrs* 116, 6.

áes cum[m]tha *comrades* 390, 7. cummaid (com-buid) *partnership.* sg. d. aes cumtha 284, 4.

agaidh *face,* metaph. *honour.* 70, 34. sg. g. aigthe 70, 33.

agard, borrowed from Eng. *haggard* (hay-garth). sg. g. d'fhechain hagaird 406, 30. dat. agard 408, 27.

aghaidh do tabairt *to give countenance.* 120, 38. do tabairt aighti doib 120, 34. aibrisc dochum aighte do tabairt 120, 35.

áibell *a spark.* pl. n. aeibli 18, 6. gen. áibhell 18, 38.

aibrisce *brittleness,* deriv. of aibrisc *fragile,* 120, 33. 35. 122, 8. sg. acc. *id.* 120, 23.

aibstinens *abstinence.* 52, 26. sg. d. aibsdinians 230, 22.

aicenta 356, 4. seems sg. g. of aicned *nature, mind.* Gen. used as an adj. *natural.*

aicept *instruction, lesson, rebuke.* sg. g. aicepta 186, 39. sg. acc. aicept 170, 17.

aicned n. *nature, mind.* sg. acc. *id.* 354, 15. 392, 24.

aidbledh *vastness.* 46, 27. deriv. from adbul *vast, mighty.*

aidhberseóir *an adversary, the devil.* 222, 13. aibirseóir 222, 16. 25. sg. g. aiberseora 252, 9. pl. sg. aibirseoradh 224, 30.

aighne m. *a pleader, advocate.* 114, 28.

aimrid a. *barren.* 28, 26. 44, 19.

ain-eóil *unknown, foreign:* deriv. of aneol *ignorance.* sg. d. n. ainiuil 292, 5.

aindis (an-des) *untidy, awkward.* 166, 3. 220, 17.

aingidecht f. *wickedness, malice.* 42, 10. sg. a. *id.* 256, 18.

ainglide *bright.* 398, 21. acc. f. *id.* 406, 15.
ainmhne *patience.* sg. acc. ainmne 384, 15.
ainmindte *animals* (*leg.* ainminte). pl. acc. *id.* 194, 20.
aintemhan *antiphon.* (?) pl. acc. aintemhain 444, 11.
airc f. *greed, voracity; want, hardship* (Don), Dinneen. sg. acc. airc 282, 23.
airchel *a hiding-place, a retreat, lying in wait, expectation.* oircill 170, 15- sg. d. in phrase a n-oirchill an bais *in expectation of death* 122, 27. oirchill 206, 18.
airchess f. *meeting.* sg. d. aircis 266, 9. 12. 330, 30.
airchiss *commiseration.* (?) sg. g. aircissi 228, 11.
airdenu *sign, symptom.* pl. d. airghenaibh 404, 7.
air-er *coast, shore.* pl. dat. oireruib 294, 26.
áirimáir *act of mocking at.* (?) sg. d. *id.* 308, 14.
airm f. *place.* 90, 23. 338, 15. 346, 1. sg. acc. *id.* 368, 30.
áis *free will.* 284, 24.
aisce *a gift.* pl. gen. aiscedh 254, 24. acc. aiscedha 52, 33. 258, 24.
aisde *quality, nature.* 168, 22.
1. áith f. *a kiln.* 186, 28. dat. áith 186, 28. acc. áith 186, 4.
2. áith *keen, sharp.* sg. d. 440, 6.
aitherrach *change, an alternative.* 120, 1.
aithissiughadh *act of reviling.* sg. d. *id.* 348, 24.
aith-legtha *re-smelted, refined.* sg. d. *id.* 368, 18.
aithnidh as adj. *known* 326, 28.
aithrech *repentant.* sg. acc. n. *id.* 188, 5.
alad *piebald, speckled.* sg. g. mas. aluidh 360, 16.
all *a bridle.* pl. d. alluib 376, 3. ellaib R. C. xx, 52.
allmarach a. *transmarine, foreign, a foreigner.* deriv. from all-muir *ane from beyond the sea.* pl. n. allmaraidh 4, 37, for allmaruigh. pl. gen. allmharuch 114, 4.
alltan seems dim. of allt. f. *a wooded valley or glen.* See *Contrib. s. v.* allt. sg. acc. alltan 38, 7.
altaide *wildish.* dim. of allaid, *wild, savage, CCath.* Glossary. acc. m. alltaidhe 382, 26.
altrom *nurture.* 284, 23.
am-arus *unbelief, doubt, suspicion.* 52, 29. 62, 38.
amhnus *sharp, keen.* sg. d. *id.* 440, 6.
amne *thus.* 422, 19.
amos m. *a hireling soldier, mercenary.* pl. g. amhus 220, 3.
am-réid *rough, uneven.* pl. d. aimhreghib 124, 28, for aimhredhib.
am-ríar *disobedience.* sg. d. aimhréir 114, 25.
a^n infixed pron. sg. 3 mas. ronbia 12, 22, for rambia.
án adj. *noble* 12, 4. 360, 19. sg. d. fem. ain 344, 2.
an-áeb *distress, discomfort.* sg. acc. anaoibh 160, 11.
anaicim *I protect, save.* v. n. anacul 66, 32. 82, 9.
anba *vast, very great.* 194, 13.
ancaire *an anchorite.* sg. d. *id.* 144, 35.
ander f. *a woman.* pl. d. aindrib 194, 12.
an-dorus *before, in front of.* 56, 21. 94, 1. 112, 22.
anduthcasach *a non-native, stranger.* 38, 19.
an-fáilte *joylessness, a bad welcome.* anbfhailte 116, 35. sg. acc. anbfhailte 186, 4.
an-fine *a stranger or hostile tribe.* sg. dat. ainfine 194, 10.
anm-chara *a confessor.* sg. acc. anam carat 216, 19.
aoingel (lit.) *one bright, very bright.* sg. g. m. aenghil 386, 29. aingil 390, 12.
araile *alius, the other.* aroile 264, 26. 308, 4. re roile 210, 39.

arbor *any kind of corn.* sg. g. arbha 204, 4. 212, 38. pl. n. arbhunda 160, 18.

as-biur *I say.* (later form with infixed pronoun = atbiur). -t- pret. sg. 3 atbert 74, 19. fut. sg. 3 -eibéra 12, 20.

ass *a sandal, shoe.* 78, 12. 14. pl. acc. assu 370, 5.

at *thou art.* 378, 7. sg. 2 of copula.

atbath *he died.* 218, 21.

athaidh *a while, a space of time* 86, 18. 256, 26. athaigh 280, 40.

atharda f. *fatherland.* sg. g. *id.* 52, 25. dat. *id.* 124, 28.

ath-chuinge mic tshethar *the request of a sister's son.* 90, 11.

athimradh *backbiting.* sg. g. athimraidh 114, 5.

ath-le f. *track, remainder.* asa haithli *thereafter* 214, 27. as m'aithle *after me* 284, 19.

ath-ól *second drinking.* 290, 28. sg. d. *id.* 290, 27.

athtoirrse (attuirse) *great sorrow.* sg. acc. athtoirrsi 124, 19.

atráidhim *I declare.* 200, 2.

attán *a hood.* atan 342, 29.

bachall f. *a staff.* 134, 15. sg. gen. bachla 126, 16. 256, 24. 29. dat. bachaill 126, 4.

bachlach *a cleric.* 202, 35. co mbachaill na crub proves that *cleric* is the meaning rather than *rustic.*

bacudh *act of laming, hindering* (with dí de). v. n. of baccaim *I lame.* sg. d. bacudh 178, 15. acc. bachudh 226, 11 (gan a bachudh dít. Notice the "a" before bachudh).

bacús *a bake-house.* sg. g. bacúis 228, 6.

baeth-lemnech *reckless leaping.* dat. baethlemnigh 386, 30.

bághach *warlike.* bádhuch 284, 21.

báidh (1) adj. *affectionate.* dat. f. *id.* 438, 31.
(2) n. *affection.* sg. g. baide 6, 18.

bail *success, prosperity.* sg. acc. *id.* 88, 1. buil 302, 20.

bán *pale* 282, 29.

banais f. *a wedding-feast.* sg. d. *id.* 54, 37.

bán-martra f. *bloodless martyrdom.* sg. g. *id.* 432, 37.

bannaomh f. *a female saint.* sg. gen. bannaeimhe 106, 33. dat. bannaeimh 106, 37.

barr (lit.) *top; hair.* 282, 27.

barr-glass *green-topped.* 386, 16.

barr-scoth *a crown of flowers.* acc. *id.* 386, 14.

bathais f. *baptism.* dat. *id.* 450, 13.

bél m. *lip, mouth.* ar béluib *in preference to.* 246, 11.

benaim re *I touch, meddle with.* an coss do benad re lar aige 78, 13.

ben comarba (lit.) *a female successor.* sg. d. mnai comorba 42, 19.

bendachaim in *I make a holy habitation in* (a place). do bendaig se san inadh sin 84, 19. bendugadh ann 160, 27. bendeobadh 146, 28. fut. sec. sg. 3 of bendaigim *I bless.*

bengánuch *forked.* 190, 29. 192, 3. deriv. of bengán *a branch.*

bernán *anything gapped or indented.* Bernán Padruic 114, 18. a name for St. Patrick's bell.

berrad *tonsure, the hair of the head.* pl. nom. berrtha 282, 24.

bét *a deed, injury.* 372, 18.

betit *they will be.* a mid. Irish form, fut. pl. 3 of copula. beidíd 290, 12.

-bia 116, 1. 130, 22. fut. sg. 3 of substantive verb.

biáid f. *beatitude, blessing.* dat. biáid 438, 31. acc. biaid 292, 6.

bil *lucky, good.* 184, 16. bil also means *evil, bad.*

1. **bile** n. *a large or old tree, a sacred tree.* sg. g. *id.* 38, 20. 380, 38.
2. **bile** *rim, border.* sg. acc. *id.* 294, 3.

birrét *a hat.* 342, 29.

bith m. *world, age.* pl. g. bidhtó (for betha) 12, 3.

bith-beo *ever living.* 62, 17.
bith-ainimh *lasting blemish.* 24, 11. 354, 17.
bith-faith *Eternal Prophet.* 12, 22.
blad n. *fame, renown.* sg. d. blaidh 36, 12. bloidh 168, 21.
bláe *a cloak, cover.* bla-lín *linen cover* 422, 26.
blog f. *fragment.* sg. acc. bloidh (for bloigh) 4, 33.
boinin *a calf.* 178, 20. bóinín (*Contrib.*) boinín seems formed from boin and not from bó.
bol m. *a sage, poet.* 20, 21.
boltanad *smelling.* sg. d. bolltanad 414, 13.
bonn *a groat.* sg. g. buind 76, 22. 32. acc. bonn 76, 16.
borrfadach *fierce.* pl. acc. borrfadhacha 390, 19.
both f. *a hut* sg. acc. *id.* 56, 21. 22. 24. pl. n. botha 60, 13. acc. botha 60, 19.
brage f. *a hostage.* braighe 278, 23. 342, 11. sg. dat. acc. braghaid 342, 10. pl. acc. braighde 382, 13.
braine *front, edge.* sg. d. broine 294, 3.
brainech *edged, rimmed, prowed.* acc. f. broinigh 194, 15.
brat *a mantle.* sg. d. ina phrut 214, 9. brat 214, 12.
brathairse *brotherly love.* sg. g. brathairsi 6, 18.
bréid *a kerchief, cloth.* bréid cíartha *cerecloth* 342, 28.
breo n. *a flame, blaze.* 12, 4.
bró f. *a quern, a grind-stone.* sg. d. broin 56, 28.
bruighnechus *act of quarrelling.* sg. d. *id.* 268, 11.
bruinne *bosom, breast.* sg. acc. *id.* 50, 12.
buaid cathaige *victory in battle.* 248, 19. *Cf.* foillsighe 230, 28 = foillsiughadh. gortaighe = gortughadh, sg. g. gortaighe 288, 8. cathaighe then seems a sister form of cathughadh. See *Archiv. Celt. Lex.,* II, 35 s. v. cathu-ghadh. cathaige (sg. g.) 6, 33. 342, 4.
buaidh n-aénaigh. 156, 25. *Cf.* ruc trí lánbúada in óenaig, LL. 206 b 11 (cited in *Contrib. s. v.* buaidh).
búaidhred *trouble, worry.* 2, 8. v. n. of buaidrim *I trouble.*
búain amuigh *act of recovering.* 216, 27.
budechar f. *jaundice.* buidech 69, 9.
budein 22, 9 = féin. dhéin 170, 27. budhdein 372, 4.
buich *he broke.* 350, 15. pret. sg. 3 of bongim.
buidech condaill *the name of a plague.* 62, 9. 18. usually called buide Connaill.
buinde (1) *a branch.* (2) *a wave.* sg. acc. *id.* 384, 22.
bunadhus *origin, source.* 342, 3.

cabhán *a cavity, a hollow.* 346, 2.
cacht *imprisonment.* metaph. *body.* dat. *id.* 452, 15.
cadach *alliance.* 166, 21. sg. acc. *id.* 188, 23.
cádus m. *reverence.* sg. acc. *id.* 124, 31.
caeines comraidh *friendly converse.* 126, 25.
cáelach *wattling.* sg. g. caelaidh 342, 12. leg. caelaigh. caelaigh 342, 18.
caibidil f. *a chapter.* 58, 14. sg. d. *id.* 58, 15. 17. pl acc caibhdil 208, 11. 12.
caidriub *company, familiarity.* 106, 40. sg. acc. caidrib 106, 35.
cáil f. *quality.* dat. *id.* 438, 11. acc. *id.* 416, 11.
cáilidhecht f. *fame, reputation, character.* 234, 9.
caingen f. *business, contract, case.* 40, 16. 168, 29.
cair f. *fault, rebuke.* sg. d. *id.* 48, 28. acc. *id.* 44, 1. coir 364, 1. cair 442, 24. pl. d. cairthibh 58, 30.
cairdes *gossipred.* sg. d. *id.* 290, 13.
caire *a fault.* acc. *id.* 422, 15.
cairigim *I blame, rebuke, censure.* denom. of cair *blame.* v. n. cairiugad 114, 10.

cairthe 256, 35. coirthe *a pillar stone* (O'R.).

cáit *where*. 56, 21. 92, 15. 116, 3. 126, 21. 134, 15.

caithisech 418, 32, seems to mean *joyful*. compar. and super. caithisighe 420, 24. See cathais (caitheas) f. *affection, love*, Contrib. s. v.

cammas m. *a bend* (of a river), *a bay*. camass 146, 2. sg. acc camus 386, 1.

cantaic *a canticle*. 412, 17. pl. acc. cantaice 418, 10.

carais 438, 15. pret. sg. 3 of caraim *I love*. But see caradh *interring* (O'R.).

carcar f. *a prison, a prison cell*. dat. carcair 436, 21. 24.

carthanal *a cardinal*. pl. n. carthanail 206, 6.

cás m. *case, position, difficulty, sad plight*. sg. d. *id*. 54, 15. do bi se 'na cas mor orra *they were in a great predicament*. ibid., 14, 15. 72, 7.

casal *a chasuble*. casair (*leg.* casal) 388, 14. sg. d. cassair (*leg.* casail) 392, 16.

catar (1) *a set of four*, (2) *a quarter*. sg. d. cataír 118, 36. Here it means *quarter tense, ember days*. acc. catair 118, 29. 120, 5. catairech adj. 118, 25.

cé *this*. 364, 2.

cechtar *either of two, one or other of two*. 268, 7.

ced-labhra *first speech*. 36, 11. 168, 20.

céim (1) *step, pace*. (2) *degree, rank*. 2, 4. v. n. of cingim *I step, march, go*.

ceingeoltai 112, 34. pass. sec. fut. sg. 3 of cenglaim *I tie*.

ceis 390, 7.

céis *a small harp, a peg or key of the harp*. sg. acc. 416, 27.

celim *I conceal*. fut. sg. 1 ní chél 192, 21. cel 356, 34.

cena (O. I. cene) (lit.) *without it; anyhow, even so, already*. 124, 30.

ar chena *besides* 72, 17. 124, 38. 158, 18.

cenand *white-faced*. pl. n. cenanda 194, 18.

cendais *gentle, meek*. 284, 12.

cennadach f. *a province, district*. pl. d. cendadachaib 34, 2.

cennsa f. *gentleness, meekness*. the gen. used as an adj. *tame*. d'ainmide cennsa 318, 21. 320, 2.

cerchaill *a pillow, bolster*. 104, 32. 412, 1. 432, 32.

cess *niggardliness*. pl. acc. cessa 284, 6.

cethir *a quadruped*. sg. g. cethra 28, 32. pl. acc. cethra 156, 13.

cianaib 384, 21. gac re . . . a cianaib ibid. seems a plural form of cachlacéin *every other*. Distinguish from acían *ocean*.

cíartha *waxen, waxed*. 342, 28.

cibhir *a lid*. 300, 12. seems English *cover*.

cin *love, affection*. 60, 1. 29. sg. d. cin 110, 22. 112, 6.

cinedach *one of a race or nation* (cined). pl. g. cinedhach 312, 13. dat. cinedachaib 178, 16. 256, 33. 262, 22.

cinim *I am born, spring*. pret. sg. 3 cin 448, 23.

cistenach f. *kitchen*. sg. g. cisdenaidhe 264, 3.13, for cisdenaighe. dat. cisdenaigh 268, 29. 39.

cláirenech *flat-faced*. 60, 11.

clamh *a leper*. pl. n. clamha 350, 24.

cleth f. (v. n. of celim) *a hiding*. sg. acc. cleith 84, 16.

cli f. *body*. 440, 6. sg. d. *id*. 170, 11. acc. *id*. 138, 37. 424, 5.

clodh *act of returning*. 354, 29. seems v. n. of clodhuighim *I approach, draw near*. see O. R. s. v. clodhuighim.

clúid f. *a nook, corner*. acc. *id*. 436, 23.

cnaimhseach f. *a midwife* (Contrib.). sg. g. cnaimhsighe 148, 36.

cnedugud *act of wounding*. pret. sg. 3 cnedhaig 4, 28.

coblach cogaidh *a war fleet.* 420, 35. an interesting construction where the nominative is used instead of the acc. with *le.* *Cf.* tainec Brenainn ced eli 76, 2.

cobsud (from com-fossud), *stable, firm.* 48, 47.

cogús m. *conscience* 24, 28. from cocubus. sg. d. *id.* 70, 36.

coibnius m. *relationship.* sg. g. craeb coibnesa *a pedigree* 354, 19.

cóicedach *a pentarch.* pl. acc. coicedhaig 138, 14.

coill *a wood.* sg. acc. coillidh 174, 32. coill 320, 14.

coim *a cloak, covering.* sg. d. *id.* 80, 39. 356, 11. 12.

coimes *a judging between, comparing.* 60, 24. 78, 23. com-mess, v. n. of conmidiur.

coimh-écniughadh *act of compelling.* sg. d. *id.* 294, 10.

coimhdhe *security.* 384, 21.

coimsech *meet, suitable.* 292, 3.

coindem f. *quarterage, entertaining.* 206, 16. sg. d. coindimh 448, 22. pl. d. coindmhib 74, 22.

cointinn f. *contention.* sg. d. coindtind 300, 29.

cóir *justice.* 112, 5. sg. gen. córa 212, 25. acc. cóir 102, 2.

coirr-mhíoltog *a little fly, midge* (P. O'C.). sg. d. corrmiltoig 78, 26.

coirtim *I tan.* v. n. coirtedh 454, 7.

col *sin, blame.* sg. acc. *id.* 282, 13.

coléicc *now.* coleic 158, 20.

coloma f. *a column, pillar.* sg. acc. colamhan 98, 4.

colpthach f. *a heifer.* acc. colbtaigh 386, 29.

coma *a gift, bribe, condition.* cuma 100, 22. sg. d. comhaidh 196, 12.

comaidech *foreign.* 382, 23.

comairce *sign, signal.* (?) 126, 36. not identified. *Cf.* comarc *a signal,* Con-*trib. s. v.*-

comairghe *protection.* 30, 19. coimerghe 74, 7. sg. g. *id.* 30, 20. acc. *id.* 28, 4. 30, 32.

comairlech m. *a counsellor.* 24, 29.

com-arc *outcry.* sg. g. comarc (*leg.* comairc) 192, 7.

comartha *sign, character.* sg. d. comartha 140, 30. Here the meaning is somewhat obscure.

com-gháel *kindred.* sg. g. comghail 158, 27.

comhaighthech *foreign.* pl. d. comhaighecha 192, 29. comhaighthecha 196, 23.

comhall *fulfilment.* 450, 8.

comla *a door-valve, door.* sg. g. comladh 176, 33. acc. comlaidh 176, 25.

com-lán *complete.* 170, 12. 188, 31.

com-máin *a mutual favour, obligation.* cumain 192, 13. cumaín 270, 19.

com-mórad (1) *a glorifying,* (2) *a convening, assembling.* sg. d. comórad 86, 31.

comnaightech a. *continual, habitual,* for comnaidech. adv. go c. 4, 8. 12. go coimhnaitach 154, 30.

comramach *triumphant.* sg. g. m. comhromaigh 290, 25.

com-ríachtain *cŏïtus, union, meeting.* sg. acc. *id.* 238, 9.

comus *power, control.* 100, 13. sg. acc. comus 310, 36. cumus 426, 1.

con *pure, clear.* 196, 35.

conách *prosperity.* The gen. used as an adj. *prosperous, blessed.* as bendaighthe conáich 228, 3. *Cf.* do bi sé fíal degh-enigh 136, 24. duine ba deghenich na sé 164, 3. is conaich saidbir 446, 1.

conar f. *a way, road.* conair 372, 9. sg. acc. conuir 374, 14.

condailbe f. *kindliness, affection.* sg. d. *id.* 138, 13.

confersoid *conversation.* 48, 20. acc. *id.* 434, 33.

confisóracht *confessorship.* acc. *id.* 434, 1.

conid 160, 1. 168, 11. sg. 3 of copula with con-.

connlach *straw, stubble, hay*. sg. g. condlaigh 62, 10.
connud *firewood, fuel*. condadh 160, 29. sg. d. condadh 44, 12.
cor *a contract*. sg. g. cuir 454, 20. pl. acc. cuir 258, 27. 30.
cora f. *a weir*. 386, 28. 388, 3. sg. g. corudh 386, 29. acc. coruich 386, 31. *read* coraid.
córaid f. *a pair, couple*. sg. d. coraid 260, 15.
coraidh *choir* (?). sg. d. *id.* 334, 29.
coruice *until it reaches*. 252, 22. pres. sg. 3 of riccim *I reach*.
corr f. *a heron, a crane*. 196, 1. 268, 23. dat. cuirr 270, 4. 22. acc. corr 268, 38. 270, 7.
cosnam m. *a contending, contesting, defending*. 2, 7. 184, 12. v. n. of consním sec. fut. sg. 3 coiseónadh 160, 9.
cossáitim *I complain, accuse*. v. n. cossáit. sg. acc. cossaid 180, 21. pret. sg. 3 cosaid 180, 20.
cothugad *act of supporting, maintaining*. 50, 10. v. n. of cothaigim *I support*.
crábhadh m. *piety, devotion*. sg. g. crabaidh 4, 24. etc. acc. do chuaid a crabud 74, 10. Translate perhaps *he entered the religious state*.
cráes m. *maw, open jaws, gluttony*. sg. g. crais 66, 5.
cráibech *branches*. seems collect. of cráib *a branch*. Cf. én, énach, iasc, iascach. sg. d. *id.* 186, 7.
crand-ruaidh *lot of lordship, lordly lot?* sg. d. *id.* 284, 20.
crann m. (lit. *a tree*), *beam* (of a plough). sg. d. *id.* 62, 32. 64, 5.
crech-ól *imbibing plunder*. ar cuairt crechól 290, 27.
crédem *faith*. sg. g. credimh 8, 5. creidme 8, 9. 16, 34. 80, 6. creidim, creidme 96, 18.
críchnóbadh 148, 29. sec. fut. sg. 3 of críchnaigim *I end, finish*.

cró (crú) *gore, blood*. sg. dat. cru 110, 23. 186, 24.
crob *a hand*. sg. d. crub 202, 35.
cróchadh *redness, saffron*. 440, 7. seems deriv. of cróch *red*.
crod m. *live stock, cattle, chattels*. sg. g. cruid 28, 32. dat. crodh 72, 4. 282, 23.
cross-fhigell f. *cross vigil*. sg. d. croisfighill 182, 7. 16. 18. 19. 21. 24. 230, 16.
crottball *decay*. sg. g. crotbaill 440, 7.
cruadhach *steel*. sg. g. *id.* 264, 21.
cruaitech *hardness, cruelty*. dat. acc. *id.* 446, 19.
cruibhéd *cruet*. sg. acc. *id.* 54, 17. 23.
cruimther *presbyter*. cruimtheir 186, 2.
cú allaid *a wolf*. pl. n. coin allta 186, 25. 288, 8.
cúan f. *a pack or litter of hounds*. sg. n. cuan 30, 11. See Thur. *Handbuch*, p. 168.
cúanna *handsome, neat*. sg. d. *id.* 170, 2. 188, 31.
cúar *crooked*. sg. g. mas. cuaír 380, 20.
cubus *conscience*. 282, 13. sg. voc. cubhus, 196, 35.
cúich *who?* cuich 388, 21.
cuil f. *a fly*. 110, 26. sg. gen. cuile 112, 7. acc. cuil 110, 30. 112, 13.
cuindghim *I seek*. 424, 3. 14. fut. sg. 3 cuindfidh 372, 16.
cuing f. *a yoke*. sg. acc. *id.* 22, 18.
cuirebh 244, 33. fut. sg. 1 of cuirim *I put*.
culaidh tshairse (sg. acc.) 60, 25 *labouring suit*.
culpa Lat. *culpa, fault*, sg. g. *id.* 184, 20. acc. tuc se a culpa *he confessed*. 222, 11. a culpa do tabairt 222, 19. 30.
1. cuma (O. I. cumme) *equal, same*. 192, 23.
2. cuma *shape*. sg. acc. *id.* 108, 28.
cumal *bondmaid*. dual n. cumal 220, 2.
cumgach *narrowness*. acc. *id.* 370, 9.
cumgach uirighill *stuttering* 370, 9.

cumha *grief.* 102, 3. 5. 6. sg. g. cumadh 100, 30. dat. cumhaidh 192, 16. cumhaig 284, 14. pl. g. cumadh 102, 6.

cumhdach 380, 23. 452, 10. seems to mean *helping.*

cumhscal *a moving or stirring.* pl. g. (?) cumhscalta 314, 25. perhaps sg. g. which points to a sg. nom. cumhscaladh.

cumm-aim *I shape, I plan.* v. n. cuma 68, 11. 23.

cundlacht f. *constancy, steadiness.* sg. acc. *id.* 154, 32.

cúntas m. *an account, a reckoning.* pl. n. cundais 2, 20.

cúplaidh (sg. d. f.) 398, 24. (?)

cure *a band, host.* sg. d. caem-chuire 400, 10. acc. cuire 372, 26.

custrást *till now* 152, 3. custrásda 236, 31. 338, 6.

dabach f. *a vat, tub, a flax dam* (O'R. Supp.). 166, 2. dat. dabaig 42, 22. 166, 4. 6.

dáchair 132, 2. The author occasionally has "ch" for "gh". perhaps read daigher *a blast, gust of wind or fire.*

daghar *a pang.* 284, 19.

dáig in phrase ar dáig *because of.* 340, 18. 424, 4.

daigér *a dagger.* 264, 3. 8. sg. dat. *id.* 264, 23. acc. *id.* 264, 5. 13.

dainech (?) 12, 4.

dainim f. *a fault, blemish.* 194, 12.

dairgech *planted with oaks.* sg. acc. dairgech 194, 9.

dair-mhes *noble mast.* sg. g. dairmhesa 284, 6.

dair-thech n. (lit.) *oak-house, an oratory.* duirrthech 82, 14. sg. gen. duirrtige 84, 6. dat. duirrtech 82, 27. duirrthigh 216, 3.

dál f. *a case, matter, event.* 36, 11, dail 168, 20. 26. 170, 3. sg. acc. dail 108, 38. 110, 3.

dalb *a lie, falsehood, guile.* sg. acc. dalb 40, 14, for dailb.

dam allaid *a stag.* sg. d. *id.* 26, 26. acc. *id.* 64, 7.

damhain 126, 31. The contert requires it to be pret. sg. 3 of damnaim *I damn, condemn.* I can't explain the aspiration of "m". v. n. damnadh 210, 17. sec. fut. pass. 3 sg. daimeóntai 210, 7.

danar *a Dane.* pl. n. danair 4, 37.

dardaín mandail *Maundy Thursday.* 166, 13.

debech *strife, conflict.* sg. acc. deibech 140, 5.

dech 212, 18. subj. sg. 1 (corresponding to the perf. -dechud) of tíagu *I go.*

dechmad (1) *tenth.* 84, 11. (2) f. *a tenth part, tithe.* 86, 37. 88, 1. 11. sg. gen. dechmaide 88, 3. acc. dechmad 88, 9. 10. pl. n. dechmaidh 88, 13. acc. dechmaidh 88, 15.

dechtaim *I dictate, I compose.* v. n. dechtadh 4, 34. -t- pret. sg. 3 decht 6, 14. 58, 10. pass. perf. sg. 3 dechtagh (for dechtadh) 6, 21.

dedail *act of separating.* degail 194, 31. v. n. of dedlaim *I separate.* sg. d. deghail 192, 32. acc. dedail 8, 8.

dee adhartha *gods of worship.* 78, 15. pl. d. 78, 18.

i ndegaid n- prep. with gen. *after, behind.* am deaghaid *behind me.* 192, 19. am deghaid 194, 30. ad degaidh *behind thee* 220, 17.

deilm (delm) n. *a noise, din.* 44, 24. 28.

deirrid *secret.* 386, 2. acc. m. *id.* 384, 24.

deisgridech a. *discreet.* 32, 32. adv. go descreidech 228, 7.

delbaim *I shape, frame, ordain.* -s- pret. and perf. sg. 3 rodelbusdair 74, 23. *Cf.* O. I. rolabrastar, perf. sg. 3 of labrur *I speak.*

delg *a pin, brooch.* 214, 12. sg. g. deilg 214, 26. acc. delg 214, 13.

demhes *a pair of shears or scissors.* sg. acc. demhes 244, 31. deimhes 244, 32.

demhin adj. *certain, sure.* 232, 15. used substantively = *certainty.* demhin 254, 6. sg. acc. deimhin bais 228, 27. tucc a demhin doib 230, 4.
denta 138, 22. fá nach denta duit olcus uime *why you should not do ill concerning it.* ibid.
deoch *drink.* sg. acc. digh 386, 12.
derb-fhine *kindred, relatives.* sg. acc. *id.* 192, 32.
dercu *an acorn.* pl. n. dercain 120, 7.
des adj. *neat, ready.* adv. co des 232, 11.
deochain *minister, deacon.* 96, 11. sg. g. *id.* 198, 8.
dessel *sunwise, righthandwise.* desiul, 68, 16. 182, 37. 190, 21. 23.
dethach f. *smoke, fume.* 356, 26. detach 356, 13. sg. acc. *id.* 70, 28.
dethide *care, concern.* sg. d. deithide 50, 15.
diabhuldánacht *necromancy.* 80, 16. sg. acc. *id.* 316, 28.
díamair (1) *hidden, concealed, secret.* (2) *a hidden thing or place, secret, mystery.* sg. acc. díamhair 122, 22. 270, 28. pl. d. diamraib 54, 4.
diamrach *hidden, secret.* an adj. formed from the adj. diamair. sg. d. diamrach 68, 20. pl. d. díamhracha 78, 28. 208, 3.
dias, f. *a couple, two persons.* 234, 7. dís 240, 7. sg. g. dēsi 220, 2. acc. días 242, 11.
díbhrucadh *act of casting.* for diburcad. sg. d. *id.* 394, 8.
díchell *neglect, negligence.* 116, 34.
didhnad *a comforting, consoling.* 12, 23. v. n. of do-donaim *I console.*
dí-fhulaing *intolerable.* 414, 24. 28.
dí-gaind *stout, firm.* pl. g. dighainn 198, 26.
dighair *vehement.* 382, 2. *leg.* daghar(?)
díl (1) *sufficiency.* 144, 19. sg. g. dila 392, 15. acc. dil 76, 9. 144, 16. 204, 22. (2) *fate.* 398, 2. acc. *id.* 396, 8.
dílim *I satisfy.* v. n. díl 68, 1. 3. 8. pret. 3 sg. 68, 3. pass. pret. 3 sg. 68, 6.

dimdha (from dim-buide) *ingratitude, displeasure.* corruptly dimgha 58, 5. 110, 6. sg. acc. dimdha 154, 34.
dimdhach *displeased.* corruptly dimghach 124, 2. 138, 27.
dind *a height, hill.* 292, 16.
dingbála *fit, equal, worthy.* 8, 31. 228, 35. gen. of dingbál (v. n. of do-ingbaim *I ward off*).
dinite *dignitas, dignity.* 64, 17. pl. g. dineteadh 2, 9.
dí-sceóil *without a story, newsless.* 360, 24. 26.
dísert Lat. *dēsertum, hermitage.* sg. d. *id.* 216, 30.
disliugud *act of appropriating.* 66, 13, for dílsiugud, v. n. of dílsigim *I appropriate,* a denom. of dílse.
díth *destruction, ruin.* 218, 20. 22. *absence, want.* sg. d. do dith bidh 230, 23.
dítiu f. *act of protecting, protection.* v. n. of do-emim *I shelter.* sg. dat. díden 212, 18 (*leg.* dídin).
dítnim *I protect.* fut. sg. 3 rel. diteónus 212, 15.
dliged *a tax, due, tribute.* 368, 3. 370, 11.
dlús *closeness.* sg. acc. *id.* 84, 2.
dno = dono, q. v. (*Contrib.*). 12, 25. 26, 14. 176, 1.
dobiur *I give, I bring.* protot. tabur. v. n. tabart. past subj. 3 -tibradh 14, 13. 1 perf. sg. 3 dorad (to-ro-dad) 14, 15. pass. sg. 3 doradadh 170, 3. 2 perf. sg. 1 -tucas 14, 16. 2 perf. sg. 3 -tucc 14, 18. 2 perf. pass. sg. -tucadh 16, 41.
dochraidecht *ugliness.* acc. *id.* 440, 16.
dochumhscanta *immoveable.* 158, 5.
documscaigthe *immoveable, steadfast.* 48, 22.
dodaing adj. *difficult, dangerous.* sg. acc. doghaing 36, 11. 168, 20. 26.
doghena 16, 3. O. I. dogéna fut. sg. 3 of dogníu *I do.* dodéna 20, 13.
doghra *sadness.* acc. *id.* 448,

doghraing *hardship, affliction.* sg. d. *id.* 8, 11.
dogníu *I do.* indic. pres. sg. 3 doní 104, 36. 106, 32. 108, 10. O. I. dogní. pass. sg. 3 doníther 108, 28. indic. past sg. 3 donídh 104, 35. O. I. dogníth. pl. 2 donithí 28, 18. O. I. dogníthe. fut. sg. 1 -dingen (protot.) 218, 3. O. I. digen. sg. 2 dingnair 240, 24.
doinmhe *ill-success. Cf.* soinmhe. sg. acc. doinnmhe 74, 22.
domblas (do-mblas) (lit.) *evil taste, bitterness.* 42, 9. from do + mlas (the original form of blas). sg. gen. domblais 126 8. acc. domblas 160, 11. 13.
don = dan *also, besides, now.* 444, 4.
don *misfortune.* 218, 21.
donntaighed[h] 328, 19. (?).
do-riacht *uenit* (to-ro-shiacht). 382, 25. 424, 18.
do-sia 368, 3. -s- fut. sg. 3 of dosagim *I reach.*
dosmor *bushy.* pl. n. dosmhóra 392, 8. acc. dosmora 386, 27.
drécht *portion.* 376, 9.
drenn *quarrel.* pl. g. drend 184, 15.
dreollan *a wren.* 110, 26. 30. sg. gen. dreollain 112, 8. acc. *id.* 110, 30. 112, 8. 13.
dromchla *a ridge, surface.* sg. acc. drumcladh 384, 23. 388, 9. 394, 22.
dron ? sg. acc. 40, 14. Henebry in *Z.C. P.,* III, 558 translates 'bend', evidently equating it with dronn.
druighecht *magic.* 80, 15.
du *a place.* 380, 34.
duadh *trouble, sorrow.* sg. acc. *id.* 80, 34.
dub duaibsech 130, 26. 31. a name for St. Columba's bell.
dubhánacht *fishing* (?) deriv. from dubhán *a fishing hook.* sg. d. *id.* 436, 19.
dub-reclés *nigra cellula, the black cell.* A name for Columcille's oratory in Derry. sg. g. duibreicléis 190, 7. dat. duibreicles 190, 13. *Cf.* duibrecles *cellula nigra, LB,* 237, col. 1, l. 3.

dúilech *elemental, creative.* 170, 4.
duma *mound.* pl. d. dumhachaib 144, 23.
dúnadh *a fort.* sg. g. dúnaidh 398, 25. dat. dúnadh 66, 1.
dutchas *heritage.* deriv. from duthaig. sg. g. duthcais 52, 25. dat. duthcus 60, 26. 124, 27.
duthcasach *a native.* pl. d. duthcasachaibh 38, 17.
duthaig *heritage, land, estate.* sg. gen. duthaidhe 140, 9, for duthaighe.
duthchusa adj. *native.* sg. acc. *id.* 194, 26.
duthracht *gratuity, bounty.* in the phrase a nduthracht 134, 1.

ealchuing *a rack* (for books). sg. d. *id.* 218, 13. *Cf. Z. C. P.,* I, 359, *s. v.* ealachain.
-ébert pret. sg. 3 (prototonic) of asbiur *I say.* condébert 188, 26.
ebrae *Hebrew.* 412, 14.
echlasg *horsewhip* (ech-flesc). sg. d. echluisc 360, 16.
écne *a salmon.* pl. eiccne 384, 23. ecne 388, 4.
ecusc *dress.* 28, 15. sg. d. *id.* 398, 10. 398, 27.
ed n. *a space.* 372, 4. fed 396, 21.
édaigh *ugly, hateful.* 284, 8. éidig, *Cath Cathardha* 1700.
égcruth *deformity, disfigurement.* do cuaid se a n-égcruth romhor 92, 9. Translate *he became very much deformed.* do cuaidh se a truas 7 a n-écruth 302, 6.
eidhreóc *ice.* 304, 6.
éighim *I cry aloud.* pret. sg. 3 do eigh 80, 28.
éiliughadh *act of accusing.* 282, 13.
eislis *mistake, neglect.* acc. esslis 448, 21.
eite *feather, wing, winged creature.* pl. n. ethaidedha 34, 1.
eiteóg *a wing, act of flying* (Donegal). sg. g. eiteóige 268, 25. pl. nom. eiteóga 280, 6.

GLOSSARY OF RARER WORDS

énach birds. 34, 1. 194, 21. seems collect. of én *a bird.* sg. acc. énuch 194, 20. 270, 30.

enech (lit.) *face;* metaph. *honour, hospitality.* 140, 5. the gen. used as an adj. *generous, hospitable.* do bi se fíal degh-enigh 136, 24. duine bú drochenigh 138, 18. duine ba degh-enich na sé 164, 3.

eo-derg *red-eared.* pl. n. eoderga 78, 33.

eolas (1) *way, direction.* sg. acc. eolass 234, 23. eolas 234, 26. 36. (2) *knowledge.* sg. acc. eolass 234, 40.

eolchaire *lamentation, home-sickness.* 292, 13. *Cf.* éulchaire, *Voyage of Bran,* I, 41. sg. d. eolchuire 192, 11. 19. 286, 6. acc. *id.* 292, 12. 13.

erlumh m. *a patron.* 210, 33.

eruic f. *fine, ransom.* 28, 28, for éric. sg. g. érca 218, 34. dat. eraic 94, 10. 210, 29. acc. eraic 28, 32.

esbadach *deficient, defective.* 22, 33. deriv. from esbaidh *loss.*

esca *the moon.* 34, 9. 12. 18.

escert 186, 31. *Cf.* eiscir *a ridge of mounds or mountains* (Dinneen).

escor *a fall.* 452, 27.

esidhein 250, 37.

esimlair *exemplum, example.* 8, 3. 20, 17. 32, 8. sg. d. *id.* 20, 29. 100, 2.

espach adj. *vain* 66, 13.

espartu *Vespers* (*Ériu,* III—Part I, p. 116). sg. g. espartan 186, 34. dat. espart 186, 36. espartain 232, 16. acc. espartain 410, 37.

ethar *a ferry-boat.* sg. d. *id.* 14, 31. 132, 14. 344, 1.

fadás antal 158, 20. This is evidently corrupt.

fáemaim *I accept.* pret. sg. 3 do faemh 384, 9.

faesamh *protection.* sg. acc. *id.* 374, 1.

faidhide *patience.* 4, 17. O. I. foditiu *toleratio.* foidhide 4, 21. 22. 25.

faiside *confession.* sg. acc. *id.* 128, 3.

faitech *timid, fearful.* go f. 176, 25.

fallan a. *sound.* 360, 18. *Cf.* mod. Ir. folláin *sound, healthy.*

faris *along with him.* 108, 4. a contraction of i farrad fris. as a preposition governing the acc. faris an easpoc *along with the bishop.* 58, 15.

farradh *company.* sg. d. a farrudh *in the company of* 164, 32.

fascnam (with prosthetic f) *advancing.* sg. d. oc ascnámh 396, 25. sg. acc. fasscnamh 388, 10.

fastaim *I detain, I hold back.* v. n. fostadh 340, 21. pret. sg. 3 do fasdó 214, 26. fasdó is really indic. pres. sg. 3. The particle do proves that O'D. intended it to be preterite. fosdó 314, 2.

fedaim *I lead, I bring.* -s- subj. sg. 3 don fe 394, 27.

fedán *a pipe.* acc. *id.* 402, 27.

fedh *a space* (for edh). 72, 15. 100, 4. 104, 6. an fedh *during* 112, 17. feadh radairc *as far as the eye can see.* 104, 6.

féghaim *I see.* 198, 27.

feidhm *need* (Donegal). sg. d. *id.* 132, 16.

féil *a feast.* sg. gen. feili 134, 40. acc. féil 114, 27.

feithemh *act of observing, watching.* sg. d. *id.* 198, 23. 270, 26. 332, 15. feichemh 334, 32. 336, 14.

félaim *I veil, I cover.* pres. subj. pass. sg. 3 ron-felathar 394, 28.

fer-chú *a male dog.* sg. g. ferchon 142, 8.

fern m. *the alder tree.* sg. g. ferna 186, 7.

fersad f. *club, spindle, axle* (O'Donnell). pl. n. feirsde 12, 30.

fetigim *I calm.* impv. sg. 2 feithigh 220, 31.

fiadh barr *cervus, a stag.* sg. acc. *id.* 174, 13. 318, 27. 28.

fialtech *privy.* sg. acc. *id.* 346, 34.

fích *anger, wrath.* 286, 2.

fidbad *forest* (deriv. of fid). 70, 21.

fidh *a wood.* 194, 11.

fidhach *shrubs, copse.* seems collect. of fid *a wood.* sg. g. fidhaigh 68, 36. sg. acc. fidhach 70, 4.

finda *hair.* sg. d. *id.* 186, 5.

fingal f. *the slaughter of a kinsman.* sg. d. finghail 124, 22. acc. fingail 94, 14. 17.

finnaim *I know, examine.* go finda sib 62, 28.

fír-íasc *a salmon.* sg. g. firéisc 386, 28.

fochtaim *I ask.* pres. sg. 3 fochtus 396, 3. pl. 3 fochtaid 388, 15.

fod goirid *long* (or) *short.* 372, 29. Cf. fat gairit 7186, *Irische Texte* 4, part 1.

fódhord *murmuring.* 114, 9.

fo-ga *javelin, a small spear.* 104, 4. 9.

fo-garim *I proclaim.* fograim a (ess) *I expel.* sec. fut. sg. 3 foigeoradh 118, 10.

foghar *sound.* sg. acc. *id.* 112, 33.

fognamh *service.* sg. g. foganta 320, 7. The gen. foganta is used as an adj. in mod. Irish. adj. fogaintech 332, 30. d'foighenad[h] 318, 10. fut. sec. sg. 3 of foghnaim *I serve.* The form is interesting as being the only instance in the *Life* of elision of the verbal particle *do*, except possibly donntaighedh 328, 19.

foirfe adj. *complete, mature.* for foirbthe 256, 22. part. from for- benim *I complete, I end.* adv. go foirfe 8, 33. 32, 35. 50, 4. sg. d. fem. foirbthe 234, 16.

foirfidhecht f. *perfection.* sg. g. foirfidhechta 36, 18. foirbfhidhechta 256, 1.

foistine *rest,* deriv. of foss. sg. g. *id.* 392, 26. acc. foisdine 384, 15.

folaidhecht f. *right by blood, noble blood.* 2, 12. 6, 32. 10, 1. 48, 16.

folaightech a. *secret, hidden.* 148, 9. go folaightech 146, 36. pl. d. folaightecha 146, 40.

folt *hair.* sg. acc. leth-folt 150, 4.

fonn Lat. *fundus, a base, soil.* sg. acc. fonn 236, 33. pl. acc. fonnadh 366, 16. *Cf.* fonnuibh, *Lis. Lives,* p. 314.

for-aire *watching, sentry.* sg. d. foruire 572, 8. pl. d. foirirechaibh 180, 8. (?)

forbtighect *perfection.* 8, 6. deriv. from forbe *completion*, v. n. of forbenim.

for-coimhet *act of guarding.* sg. d. *id.* 388, 2.

for-lethan *very broad.* sg. g. mas. forlethain 78, 9.

for-tíagaim *I help.* -s- subj. sg. 3 fordon-te 384, 27.

fossaid *stable, firm.* 362, 26. fossadh 442, 22.

frithir *sore, peevish.* (?) 424, 7.

fuachdha *perverse.* go fúachdha 394, 1.

fuarusstair *prudent, judicious.* 364, 5.

fuigeabh 116, 23. fut. sg. 1 fagbaim.

fuil f. *blood.* sg. g. fala 326, 12. fola 326, 16.

furtaigheoir *helper.* 48, 31.

ga *a spear.* 104, 4. sg. g. *id.* 202, 26.

gabaim do laim *I undertake.* pret. 3 sg. 66, 37.

gabhsatar 170, 23 *they went.* -s- perfect pl. 3 (dep. ending) of gaibim.

gabustar 142, 6. -s- pret. (dep. ending) sg. 3 of gaibim *I take, I receive.*

gaeth adj. *wise.* 282, 22.

gairid adj. (1) *short.* 122, 16. (2) *short distance* 106, 29.

gairm *crowing.* sg. d. *id.* 120, 7.

galar m. *sickness.* pl. d. galruib 4, 25.

ganiur *I am born.* fut. sg. 3 geinfid 10, 30. 12, 19. gidhnither for gignithir 12, 3. fut. pass. sg. genter 14, 2. 20, 19. geinfidhir 20, 1. genfes 22, 30. geinfider 24, 18.

-gēb 258, 24. -ē- fut. sg. 1 of gaibim *I take.* fut. sg. 3 rel. gēbas 22, 15. pass. sg. 3 gēbt[h]ar 22, 14. pl. 3 gēbaid 22, 18.

gelltanas *pledge, promise.* sg. g. gelltanais 212, 33.

genelach m. *pedigree.* sg. g. genelaig 6, 19. 78, 5. 122, 10. 134, 13. acc. geinelach 10, 4.

gengairi (lit.) *cheerfulness of laughter, a cheerful laugh*. 94, 22. Cf. golgaire *lamentation*.
  gengairi must not be confused with árd-gaire *a loud laugh*. cen ard-gaire boeth *without a loud foolish laugh* *Fél.*, p. cxlv. When Deirdre was in mourning after the death of her lover, it is said of her *"risin re sin ni ro thib gen ngairi I. Texte mit Wörter.* 77, 6. This latter example clearly excludes the meaning *loud laughter* for gengairi.
gerrughadh *act of shortening*. 214, 7. sec. fut. sg. 3 gerreochadh 212, 34.
giall *a hostage*. pl. n. geill 372, 12.
gingora 152, 37 = gen gor ab.
glac f. *the fist half open, a clutch*. dual nom. glaic 104, 33.
glacach *a hand-stone*. 104, 31.
glainide *crystalline*, deriv. of glaine *glass, crystal*. pl. acc. gloinidhe 356, 21.
glassan, name for St. Columcille's bell; also called glassan Findbharr 156, 33. 36. sg. gen. glassain 156, 38.
gleic *wrestling*. acc. glec 442, 30.
gléire *choice, purity*. sg. g. gleri 286, 3.
glere graf 386, 22. (?)
glé-thend (lit.) *bright and strong*. adv. go g. 138, 13.
1. gné f. *a kind or sort, a species*. 122, 2. sg. d. *id*. 122, 4. 7.
2. gné *a favour*. sg. d. *id*. 138, 11.
goibhnecht f. *the work of a blacksmith*. acc. *id*. 86, 9. 12.
goire f. *piety*. sg. g. *id*. 376, 1.
goiste *a halter, snare*. sg. d. gaisde 112, 34.
go nuice *as far as*. 12, 29. 18, 1. with acc. gonuice an abhainn 62, 4.
gradh ecmaisi *absent love*. sg. acc. *id*. 106, 4.
gréss *adornment*. grés 190, 13.
grían *gravel*. 386, 14.

iachdaim *I bewail, I howl*. pass. pret. 3 sg. do hiachtadh 72, 33.

iarand (lit. *iron*), *coulter*. 64, 5. 86, 7. sg. g. íarainn 86, 11. acc. *id*. 62, 32. 86, 10.
iarmerge *matin*. sg. g. *id*. 60, 15.
iarnach *irons*. 368, 24. collect. of iarann *iron*.
íascach *fish*. a collective of íasc. sg. acc. *id*. 68, 32. 326, 8.
ícaim *I pay, atone for, fulfil, perform*. v. n. íc 222, 37. sec. fut. sg. 3 ícfedh 238, 14. 20.
idhan *pure*. 352, 7. sg. voc. m. idhain 192, 31. 290, 24.
idón *id est, that is*. 204, 39.
illadh 438, 16. seems collect. of il *many, much*.
ilrad *multitudes*. 32, 12. collect. of il *many*. sg. acc. *id*. 120, 25.
ilrugad *act of multiplying*. 8, 18. seems formed from ilar *multitude* on the analogy of ilugud, v. n. of ilaigim *I multiply*.
imagallamh *act of conversing with, colloquy*. 186, 21. sg. d. imagallaimh 168, 18.
imann *a hymn*. 100, 20.
imargae *falsehood*. 12, 20. *Lis. Lives* 770 has imarbhe *falsehood*. Thurneysen in his *Handbuch*, p. 510, says "immurgu vielleicht aus im-ro-gáu 'grosse unwahrheit!"
imasech *in turn*. 372, 13. sech *a turn*.
im-degail *act of protecting*. sg. d. *id*. 372, 28.
im-díscir *very fierce*. sg. acc. m. *id*. 382, 26.
imdoinn *very deep*. (?) acc. *id*. 394, 22.
imeclaighim *I terrify*. pret. sg. 3 do imeclaig 48, 29.
im-gábud *great terror*. sg. dat. *id*. 356, 32.
imlochta (sg. g.) 240, 13. sg. g. imlochtaidh (Franciscan copy, Dublin). Cf. lochd, lochdain *a nap, slumber, a wink of sleep* (*O'Reilly*).
immalle *simul, together*. imaalle 372, 29.
impidech *an intercessor*. 24, 29.

impobudh 190, 22. fut. sec. sg. 3 of impóim (prototonic), deuterotonic im-sóim *I turn*. pret. sg. 3 do impó 190, 21. 214, 25.

impodhbhad 286, 9. fut. sg. 1 of imsóim intr. *I turn*. *Cf*. fut. sg. rel. impóbas, *B. Colmáin m. Lúacháin* 66, 5.

imretar 234, 32. pret. pl. 3 of imraim *I row*.

imroll *error, blunder*. sg. acc *id*. 40, 14.

in-am *a fitting time*. 384, 16.

inathar *bowels*. sg. g. inathair 34, 2.

inbaid *time*. 406, 4.

in-banna *female, womanly*. 90, 3.

inbher *estuary*. 134, 38. sg. acc. *id*. 108, 16, 24. pl. d. indberuib (*sic*) 384, 22.

inbuana *ripe for the sickle*. 70, 14.

1. indamail (int-shamail) *semblance*. sg. acc. *id*. 356, 16. 434, 6.

2. indamail *similar*. 42, 26. 50, 36. 388, 6.

indechad *vengeance*. 124, 3. v. n. of indechaim *I avenge*. sg. gen. indighthe 178, 35. Phonetically indighthe pron. indihe) = indiche (pron. indihe) of *O'Davoren's* Glossary. O'Davoren's indich should probably be indechad, and then his glosses on the word would be intelligible. sg. acc. indechadh 338, 2.

indell *attire*. 28, 15. ionnal (O'R.). sg. acc. ar an indell sin *in that wise* 176, 26.

indilltas *preparedness*, (?) *readiness*. sg. g. indilltaiss 444, 33.

indlad *act of washing*. 28, 13. sg. g. indluidh 190, 18. 20.

indracus *integrity*. 12, 14.

ingaibim *I protect, guard*. pret. sg. 3 do ingaib 50, 13.

(do) ingantar *they marveled*. 12, 32. denom. of ingna *wonder*.

in-mar *smeary, Cath Catharda* Index s. v. acc. inmar *condiment* 448, 6.

inne *entrail, a bowel*. sg. d. *id*. 44, 5.

-isadh 112, 1. -s- fut. secondary sg. 3 of ithim *I eat*. pl. 3 ísdais 130, 37.

isat *they are*. 386, 31. pl. 3 of copula.

íssa 304, 32. -s- fut. sg. 3 of ithim *I eat*.

íta *a devouring thirst*. 108, 3.

itche *a request*. sg. acc. *id*. 364, 1.

iubhor m. *a yew tree*. 190, 6. 10. 12. sg. dat. iubhar 190, 8.

laim *I throw, I deposit*. pret. sg. 3 do lai, 396, 27.

laech *a layman*. sg. acc. *id*. 90, 23. 164, 13.

laithe *a day*. sg. d. *id*. 116, 25.

lámaim *I dare*. pret. sg. 3 lam 426, 5. fut. sec. sg. 3 lémhadh 180, 1.

lasán *a frog*. *Cf*. loscán *a frog* (Dinneen) pl. gen. *id*. 280, 6.

leabar *book*. sg. gen. leabair 126, 9. liubair 126, 12. liubuir 448, 11.

leabhair *long, lanky*. 284, 7.

lebar oiris *a history*. pl. n. lebair oiris 4, 40.

lebhrán (lit.) *little book, copy, transcript*. 140, 20. 178, 20.

leceb 424, 29. fut. sg. 1 of lecim.

leighión *a legion*. 230, 17.

leoargnímh *reparation, satisfaction*. sg. acc. *id*. 122, 20. 274, 38.

lesbairi *light*, for lésspaire. 12, 20.

lesc *loth, unwilling*. 188, 25.

les[s] *coxa* (hip) Adamnan. See Reeves' ed., p. 112. sg. g. cnaimh a lesi *her hip-bone* 272, 27. cnáim lessi *thigh-bone*, Contrib. s. v. cnáim.

less *light*. acc. les 452, 14.

liaigh *a leech*. 354, 7. See Derg-liaigh, Contrib. s. v.

lígh *colour*. sg. d. lícc 340, 25. pl. acc. lecca 356, 20.

linde 448, 2.

lir *much, numerous*. 376, 5.

liter 380, 17. for lithir, pres. pass. sg. 3 of liim *I fasten on, charge*.

locais *a couch*. 410, 39.

lochar *a light*. 364, 3.

loghad *venia, pardon.* 8, 4. v. n. of logaim *I forgive.*
loghmar *precious.* ro-loghmar *very bright* 404, 2. sg. d. f. loghmair 340, 25.
lógmaire f. *costliness.* sg. g. *id.* 398, 26.
lomnán *quite full.* 44, 37. 280, 2. by dissimilation from lom-lán.
lond *impetuous.* 116, 12.
luaighill *act of moving, motion.* 268, 26. luadhail, Dinneen *s. v.*
luaigidhecht *act of rewarding, merit.* 58, 21. 64, 24. s. gen. luaigidhechta 2, 7.
luchair *a glittering colour, brightness,* (O'R.). adj. *clean, bright.* 354, 7.
lucht a coimleabair *classmates.* 48, 10.
lúdacán *the little finger.* sg. g. lúdacáin 288, 7.
luib *plant.* pl. luibenda 92, 27.
luid *he went.* pret. sg. 3 of tíagu *I go.* doluidh 360, 19. 424, 21. luid 452, 15. pl. 3 do lotar 338, 30. laiter 348, 32.

m infixed pron. sg. 1, romcluin 112, 12. romfes 290, 12. romlín 292, 3. (conumtarla 292, 5). romcar 372, 11. famselbadh soladh, romhoiledh, romaltromadh 388, 24. romdirich 390, 3. nimtorbha 448, 1.
mac imlesan *pupil of the eye.* pl. nom. mic imlesan 362, 11.
mac medha *son of the mead, son of the scales.* sg. g. mic medha 142, 5.
mac ochta (lit.) *son of the breast, darling.* 12, 13. 40, 2. 82, 9. 170, 7.
mad-genair *well-born, lucky.* from madh *good* and genair perf. dep. sg. 3 of ganiur *I am born.* mogenair 74, 11. madhngenair 114, 25. 26. mogenar 114, 24. 140, 21.
maeich *dejection.* 290, 19. maích 292, 3.
maidhm *defeat, rout.* v. n. of maidim. sg. acc. *id.* 182, 21.
maindechtnaige *negligence.* Cf. *Lis. Lives,* 1418. sg. d. maindechtnaidhe 332, 32.
mainistir *a monastery.* pl. g. mainesdrech 62, 3. The context here demands the meaning *shrine* rather than *monastery.*
maithemh *forgiveness.* sg. g. maithmhe 188, 8.
mal *a prince.* 22, 19.
malle *simul, together.* 422, 20. 444, 7.
mall-fascnamh *slowly advancing.* sg. d. *id.* 394, 8.
marg *a mark.* 76, 25. 30.
margarét *a pearl.* sg. d. margáret 392, 10.
masad *if thou art.* 372, 23.
mebais 372, 28 *it will break,* for memais. redupl. -s- fut. sg. 3 of maidim *I break,* maidim for *I defeat.*
mebul f. *deceit.* sg. acc. mebuil 74, 21.
meidightech *as big as.* 386, 29.
mencomharc 282, 26. Cf. menmarc (menm-sherc) *desire.*
mer-uallach *wild and wilful.* sg. acc. n. *id.* 390, 10.
mes-te from messa de *the worse.* misde 132, 7. mesti 158, 32. mesde 160, 5.
meth-ól *a failing drink.* 290, 28.
miadh *honour.* 286, 16.
micadhus *dishonour, irreverence.* sg. d. *id.* 124, 24.
mídhingbala *unworthy.* 50, 31. 308, 34.
mí-dingbálacht *unworthiness.* sg. acc. *id.* 308, 27.
míl mor *a whale.* sg. acc. *id.* 78, 26.
mímodh *disrespect.* sg. acc. mimogh 118, 27.
minde 448, 2.
minn *a diadem, a relic.* 14, 22. pl. g. minn 62, 3. dat. mindaib 74, 7. acc. minda 96, 2.
mír *a bit, piece.* 376, 6.
miscnech *odious.* sg. g. m. miscnigh 394, 17.
misduaim *intemperance,* 52, 17. 18. beatha maith sodhamail of 52, 20 proves that *intemperance* is the meaning of misduaim in 52, 17. 18. sg. acc. misdúaim *imprudence* 216, 13.
misúr *measure.* sg. acc. *id.* 68, 24.
mithigh *opportune.* 220, 11. 250, 38. 252, 5.

mnaamhlacht *womanishness. Cf.* banamla (*Contrib.* p. XIX). sg. d. *id.* 320, 4.
mocha *earliness.* 8, 15. deriv. of mach *early.*
mochen *welcome.* 156, 38. 188, 22.
modh *measure.* in phrase tar modh *beyond measure* 224, 25.
molad na hecluisi *rites of the church.* 106, 23. 126, 6.
molfa *great.* sg. g. m. *id.* 394, 17.
monmar m. *a murmuring,* for monbar. sg. g. monmair 114, 5. dat. monmar 58, 17. 184, 17. 204, 17.
morán *many.* sg. gen. morain 118, 11. 148, 27.
morgadh *act of corrupting.* sg. acc. *id.* 310, 3.
mortlaith *mortalitas.* 68, 30. 32.
múad a. *noble, good.* sg. gen. m. muaid 36, 13. mac rig Caisil Muman muaid *prince of noble Cashel in Munster, ibid.*
much-ól *early drinking.* pl. g. *id.* 290, 28. (?)
-muidh 174, 14. 21. 33. pret. and perf. sg. 3 of maidim *I break forth.* do muig 394, 23.
muincenn *surface* (of the sea). sg. acc. muinchinn 394, 3.
muinidhin f. *confidence, trust,* for muinighin. sg. d. *id.* 26, 30.
muirfider 110, 23. pass. fut. sg. 3 of marbaim *I kill.* As to f for bf see Thurn. *Handb.,* § 135.
muir na mend 368, 3.

naemhadh *act of consecrating.* dat. *id.* 398, 11. 27. acc. *id.* 150, 37.
namá (nammá) adv. *only.* 254, 5.
naoi *a person.* dat nai 448, 23.
neimedh *a sanctuary* (*O'R. Supp.*). 424, 21.
nenaid *nettles.* gen. nendta 438, 8.
neoch *which* 58, 23. *anyone* 72, 6.
neóid *niggardliness.* sg. acc. *id.* 350, 15.
ni *a thing.* sg. g. neich 32, 14. 88, 10.

pl. g. neichedh 124, 7. dat. neichib 122, 22. acc. neithinna 150, 25. neiche 178, 14.
nibdar *they were not.* 66, 8.
nídria = nítria *will not reach thee* (?) 386, 22.
nirsat *they were not.* 290, 28. pret. pl. 3 of copula. nirsat methol a n-athól, *ibid.* Here meth-ól and ath-ól must be regarded as plural.
nocha = ní. 114, 9. 180, 15. 186, 40. nochon 188, 31.
nómaide *a space of three days and three nights* (Glossary to *Fianaigecht*). nomad *a period of nine days* (*B. Laws,* Glossary). sg. gen. nomhaidhe 84, 9.
nosnodra 448, 2.
nuall *sound, ripple.* 282, 16.

ocbad *youth, youths.* ocbaid 372, 7.
oide faisidnech *confessor.* sg. d. *id.* 252, 34. 35.
oide foircetail *instructor.* 170, 14.
oifig f. *office, officium.* sg. g. oifice 268, 18. dat. oifiged 2, 14.
oil f. *reproach.* sg. acc. *id.* 282, 14.
oirbiri f. *reproach, taunt.* 22, 22. for airbire.
oirches (airchess) *proper, meet.* 122, 25.
oircillech *ready, prepared.* 442, 11.
oireamh m. *a ploughman.* 62, 27. pl. d. oireamhnaib 86, 8.
oirecht *clan, party.* 284, 21.
oirne *on us.* 136, 19
oirnech seems collect. of orda *a piece,* but formed from pl. n. oirdne. sg. gen. oirnigh 108, 28. dat. oirnech 108, 18.
oll adj. *great, grand.* sg. g. m. uill 292, 9. sg. acc. f. uill 22, 8.
on *fault.* 20, 22. on *hurt* 218, 19. sg. acc. *id.* 362, 2. 450, 9.
ón *this, that.* 72, 33. 156, 9. 244, 17.
onfaise *diving* (*C. Cath.*). sg. d. onfaisi 152, 11.
or *border, edge, brink.* 12, 30. sg. dat. ur 72, 25. 78, 9. acc. or 218, 22.

ord *death.* See *O'Reilly s. v.* ord. sg. acc. *id.* 284, 21.
orda *a piece* 76, 6. pl. n. oirdne 76, 4. 10.
ordan *rank.* 422, 15.
ordu *thumb, great toe* (*Wörterbuch*). sg. acc. ordain 36, 14.
ortha *a prayer, collect.* pl. acc. orrtha 444, 11.
othar *an ulcer.* 362, 19. uthar 364, 3.

painter *a net, snare, gin.* sg. d. *id.* 112, 34.
peilér *a pillar.* 418, 8. sg. g. peilér 420, 16. acc. peler 58, 35. peilér 420, 10.
pelait f. *a palace.* in phelait rígda, LL. 256a, 45. sg. g. peloide 398, 14.
póc *a kiss.* borr. from Lat. *pācem.* sg. d. poicc 58, 17.
popal m. *populus, people.* pl. n. poiplecha, 116, 9. gen. poiplech 2, 27. poiblech 20, 28. dat. poiplechaib 8, 35.
posda *a post, a prop.* 24, 24.
prefaid sg. dat. 228, 37 *Preface* (of the mass).
proibhindse *province.* sg. d. *id.* 256, 28. acc. *id.* 256, 23.
pubull *tent.* 186, 35.
pudhar *harm.* 222, 12.
pultadh 16, 29.

rāna borrowed from Lat. rāna *a frog.* 280, 6.
rath n. *grace.* sg. g. raith 136, 19. acc. rath 140, 14. 17.
rathughadh *act of noticing.* 20, 22.
red *a thing.* sg. g. réda 242, 21. sg. d. droch-raed 28, 33. acc. red 42, 12.
régles m. *cell.* reicles 386, 2. sg. d. *id.* 100, 15. acc.(?) reicles 384, 24.
reidhechadh *act of levelling.* sg. d. *id.* 132, 25.
reighidhon *a region.* sg. d. reidighón 266, 24. pl. nom. reighidhoin 52, 15.
réil *clear.* 46, 27.
ríadaim *I break in.* pass. part. riata. sg. g. m. riata 390, 26.

riagul Lat. *regula, rule.* sg. g. riagla 106, 6. 158, 14.
ríar *will.* sg. d. réir 114, 24. do réir *according to* (with gen.).
ríarach *obedient, submissive.* 116, 38.
riched n. *heaven.* sg. g. richid 40, 17. acc. riched 388, 6.
rigend a les *needs.* 12, 34. from riccim *I come.*
righnaide *royal.* sg. d. n. *id.* 244, 16.
righ-tech (lit.) *a royal mansion, Heaven.* sg. gen. rithoighe 168, 29.
rith *a course.* acc. *id.* 416, 15.
rithim *rhythm.*(?) sg. acc. *id.* 380, 1.
roimh *a cemetery.* rúam is an older form, "borrowed from Roma" (*F. O.*[2] Glossary). roimh adhlaicthe *a burial place* 160, 14.
roind *act of sharing, dividing, division, share.* 138, 26. 150, 38. v. n. of roinnim *I share.* impv. sg. 2 roind 152, 1.
róinde *a hair.* sg. acc. *id.* 100, 6.
róinnech *hairy.* deriv. of róin, roinne *hair.* róinnich 438, 25. acc. roindigh 432, 30. pl. n. róindigh 114, 3.
roissiur 424, 14. subj. sg. 1 of ro-sagim *I reach.*
romh *early, soon.* 20, 22.
rónach *seals* 242, 17 collect. of rón *a seal.*
ro-shochim *I reach, I come.* sec. fut. pl. 3 soichfidís 132, 19. past indic. sg. 3 soichedh 132, 26.
ruad-rindach *red-speared, red-pointed.* acc. *id.* 372, 24.
ruaig *a pursuit.* sg. d. *id.* 56, 4.
ruibnech *spearful, strongly guarded.* deriv. from ruibhne *a lance.* sg. acc. *id.* 372, 12.

s infixed pron. sg. 3, nosadrann 156, 37. nodusdoirtfe 202, 38. conusfúicfe 202, 38. rodusaircfe 372, 18. conusfuair 378, 8. roslenatar 382, 27. rusbendach 386, 22. roslecsat 390, 24. rosfuair 450, 2.
s infixed pronoun pl. 3, rustogaib 176, 5. rosbuaildis 390, 20. rusgab 392, 12.

sacrista *sacristan*. 216, 9. sg. d. *id*. 412, 23. acc. *id*. 216, 2.
sádail *easy*. go sadhul 392, 26.
sáeb *false*. 352, 6.
saei gabonn *a master smith*. 86, 13.
saerclannacht f. *noble breeding*, deriv. of clann *offspring*. sg. acc. *id*. 56, 31.
sagart crábuid seems to mean, in the present context, *a religious* in contradistinction to a secular priest. Hence translate *a priest in religion* (not *a pious priest*). sg. d. 64, 18.
saí clerigh *sage--cleric*. 100, 9.
saill muice *salt pork*. 118, 26.
sailmchétal *psalmody*. sg. acc. *id*. 198, 11.
saíri *a feast, festival*. 54, 12. 148, 1. for saíre.
sairse *a sieve*. 16, 29.
saith *bad*, opp. of maith *good*. is oth lium in modern Irish, for is saith lium. pl. acc. saithe 84, 9.
sal *dirt, defilement*. 218, 26.
samhadh *congregation, community*. sg. g. samtha 376, 2. dat. sámadh 424, 5.
scáilim *I scatter, I dissolve*. . fut. sg. 3 scailfid 84, 21. pret. sg. 3 do sgail 62, 11. do scaeil 84, 28.
scandail comraidh *abusive language*. sg. acc. *id*. 102, 21.
scainder *an attack*. 58, 21. scáinnear *a sudden irruption or unexpected attack* (*O'R*.).
scannail (lit.) *scandal, offense*. sg. acc. *id*. 118, 28. 276, 15.
sceathaim *I spew, I vomit*. pres. indic. sg. 3 sgeithes 68, 27. 29. 31.
scís *weariness*. sg. acc. *id*. 106, 10. 382, 19.
scol *school*. 8, 1. pl. n. scola 186, 26.
scolaidhe *a schoolboy, a scholar*. sg. dat. *id*. 112, 28.
screboll *a scruple*. 24, 35. Lat. *scripulum*.
scredach *act of screaming*. sg. d. -aigh 194, 22. 270, 14.
scribeóbha me 126, 11. fut. sg. 1 of scribhaim *I write*. fut. sec. sg. 3 scribhobadh 410, 23.

scribtur, Lat. *scriptura, writing, Scripture*. pl. acc. screbtra 4, 39.
scrín, Lat. *scrinium, shrine*. 150, 2. 17. sg. d. scrin 150, 7. 14. pl. acc. scrine 4, 39.
sdella *stall*.(?) sg. d. *id*. 334, 29.
sduidéar *a study, meditation*. sg. d. 6, 16.
sech *beyond*. 20, 21. 36, 36. sech is 20, 21. *Cf.* sechis *Thes. Pal*., I, 639. *Cf.* also mod. Ir. seochas é sin.
ségda *stately*. 394, 2. sg. g. m. airdsedha 340, 1.
seimidhecht *subtilty*. 406, 20.
seisrech f. *a team*. 62, 33. 64, 5. sg. g. seisrighe 62, 24. 17. sg. d. seisrigh 64, 6. 9. sg. acc. sesrech 64, 11.
sella *cell*. sg. d. *id*. 218, 9. 11. 250, 23. 270, 11.
sēnta *sained*. 398, 25. acc. *id*. 400, 10.
seol *a while*. 336, 14. seal 436, 23. sel 436, 24.
seoladh *act of directing, guidance*. sg. d. *id*. 322, 13. acc. *id*. 162, 30.
seolaim *I direct*. pret. sg. 3 do sheol 256, 36.
sercoll *a delicacy, dainty*. 448, 9.
sét *journey*. 180, 14. sg. a. séd 190, 23.
sían *a cry*. sg. acc. *id*. 212, 38.
sianán *a plaintive song*. 392, 26.
sighnum, Lat. *signum, sign*. sg. acc. *id*. 104, 20.
simhin *a rush* (*O'R*.). pl. n. sibne 66, 8. for simne.
sír-étrocht *very shining*. acc. *id*. 394, 5.
sír-rechtach *ever-enrapturing, -entrancing*. sg. acc. m. sírechtach 390, 23.
sísana *below*. 222, 4. *Cf.* anallana *hitherto, formerly*, Cath Catharda 5036.
sithbrugh *fairy mansion*. pl. d. sithbrogaib 80, 15. (This form [brog] is very common in M. poetry and is, no doubt, equivalent to brugh. Dinneen.)
slán *bail, guarantee, protection*. pl. d. slánaib 164, 26. 184, 10.

slán-chíall *sound sense.* sg. d. go roissidh slán-cēill. 270, 32.
slechtan *genuflection.* dat. slechtain 438, 5. pl. g. slechtan 438, 3.
sméidim *I beckon, nod.* v. n. smeideadh 112, 25. pret. sg. 3 do smeid 112, 22.
snéróidech 18, 6. seems collect. of sméróid (smér-fhoit) *ember.* sg. g. sméroidigh 18, 30. 38.
snoidhe for snoighe *hewing, cutting.* 4, 19. v. n. of snoighim *I hew.*
so *here* 128, 4, for annso..
soa 438, 2. perhaps = sóagh *happy, lucky* (O'R.).
socenelaighe *noble lineage,* deriv. of cenél n. *a race, lineage, kindred.* sg. acc. id. 56, 31.
sochaide *a multitude.* sochaidhe 136, 20.
sochraidh *stately, handsome.* 254, 1. 400, 4. 440, 17.
soiches 186, 16. indic. pres. sg. 3 (relative form) of ro-shochim *I reach, come.* soich 188, 28.
soinemail *illustrious.* acc. id. 400, 12.
soirbes *prosperity:* deriv. of soirb *prosperous.* sg. acc. id. 88, 1. 298, 16.
soirbhiughadh *act of solving, settling* (a quarrel). sg. d. id. 224, 17. acc. id. 224, 17.
soir gach ndírech *directly eastward.* 82, 15. Cf. súass cech direch, B. Colmáin m. Lú. 70, 17.
soithech *a vessel.* dat. soightech 240, 34. acc. soithech 96, 5. pl. n. soithighe 72, 16.
soladh *profit.* 388, 24. opp. of dolod *loss.*
sologha a. *venial.* 58, 12.
son, Latin sŏnus, *sound.* 46, 26.
sonnach *a wall, palisade.* 386, 27. pl. sondaidhe 382, 14. for sondaighe.
sop *a wisp of hay.* sg. acc. id. 186, 12.
so-réidh *smooth.* 180, 14. soraidh 290, 23.
speclair *speculum, mirror.* 8, 3.
spreighim *I disperse, I scatter.* past part. spreite, for spreighte 6, 13.

sraibtine 116, 3. meaning obscure.
sreb *a stream, rill.* 134, 21. 136, 1. etc. pl. n. srebha 108, 8. 9.
sruith *old, venerable.* sg. acc. id. 392, 16.
suaill adj. *small, insignificant.* 390, 4.
subaltaige *joy.* 94, 22. sg. gen. id. 94, 23.
suidhiugad ar *attributing to.* 58, 2.
sundrad (old Ir. sain-red) *a particular thing.* sg. d. do sundradh 406, 29.
sundradach a. *special, particular.* adv. go s. 6, 4. do sundrách 268, 19.
suthach *fruitful.* acc. id. 394, 5.

t infixed pron. sg. 2, rodbia 372, 4 fotricc 372, 30.
tabairt taeba *relying on, depending on, trusting to.* sg. dat. ag tabairt taeba ris 296, 38. Hence mod Ir. ag tabhairt taoibh, corruptly i dtortaoibh. See Dinneen s. v. taobh.
taebhaim (ri) *I entrust.* indic. past sg. 3 taebudh 218, 7. pret. sg. 1 taebus 306, 10.
taemadh *act of bailing out boat.* sg. d. ac taemadh na luinge 294, 29.
tagaill 146, 32. Cf. tailgim *foveo* (Wörterbuch).
taibhghedh 112, 13. impv. sg. 3 of toibgim *I demand, claim, recover.*
taidhen (tóiden) *a troop.* pl. g. id. 220, 11.
taidhiúir *tearful, mournful.* 292, 5.
taidlidhfe 202, 36. fut. sg. 3 of taidlim *I visit.*
taigeorach 198, 20.
tailgend *adzehead.* 424, 6.
-taircim *I offer, I undertake.* v. n. taircsin 212, 25. pret. and per. sg. 3 tairc 232, 23. 268, 40. tarccaidh 382, 1. pl. 3 taircetar 258, 22.
tairm-thecht *transitus, journeying beyond.* tairimthecht 186, 36.
tairn-gire *act of foretelling, prophesying.* 10, 18. v. n. of tairngirim (doair-con-garim).

taisidther 10, 25, *let (it) be put by.* ro taisich *he put by, stored* 186, 20. *Cf.* taisigh *do thou put by, Lis. Lives,* 755. These forms point to a form taisighim *I store.*

tál *a cooper's axe or adze.* sg. acc. tal 60, 23.

tallann *a talent.* 70, 31. sg. acc. *id.* 70, 32.

támh *repose, trance.* tamh 386, 6.

taob *a side.* sg. gen. taeibhe 134, 33. taebha 154, 1. 414, 4. taeba 298, 15.

tarachar *an auger, gimlet.* sg. acc. tarathar 60, 23.

tastáil 420, 1 seems borrowed from English *tasting. Cf.* tástáil *a trial, an examination, a testing,* Dinneen, *s. v.*

tathaighim *I frequent.* v. n. tathaige 112, 17. 318, 17.

tegsa, *text.* 2, 14.

teimhel *darkness.* 220, 11.

teinne *severity.* 114, 8. deriv. of tenn *stiff.*

teinteach *lightning.* sg. d. teindtigh 66, 33.

teli 196, 36. dale póic dam, *R. C.,* XX., 132. See *Thes. Pal.,* I, 89. 719.

tendtighe for tentide *fiery.* deriv. from tene *fire.* 4, 11. 44, 37. 60, 35.

tenga *a clapper.* sg. acc. tenga 132, 7. tengaidh 132, 8.

termonn *sanctuary, protection.* 28, 3. sg. acc. *id.* 126, 3. pl. d. termonnaib 28, 1.

tes[s]-moladh *ardent praise.* sg. g. tesmolta 284, 13.

test *testimony, recommendation.* 80, 8.

testa 148, 23. tesda 210, 10. 14. 308, 12. *deest, it is lacking, he dies:* v. n. testáil. Mod. I. teastuighim *I am wanting.*

tibra, tobar *a well.* 126, 4. 396, 22. pl. n. tobair 126, 17. pl. gen. toibrech 126, 15. 17.

tí *design, intention.* sg. acc. ar tí báis do tabairt do 268, 3. ar tí do breith leis 406, 24.

tidnastar 376, 4. fut. pass. of tidnacim *I deliver, I offer up.*

tigh = tiugh *thick, solid, plentiful.* sg. d. fem. tigh 352, 2.

time *fear.* sg. acc. *id.* 362, 1.

timsaigim *I collect.* pret. sg. 3 timsaig 6, 13.

tindlacad *act of bestowing, gift.* pl. n. tindluicthe 2, 20. pl. acc. tindlaicthe 2, 18.

tír n. *land.* sg. g. an tire 266, 31. 310, 24.

tír dúthaig *native land.* sg. d. *id.* 62, 12. 446, 16.

tir mor *mainland.* 104, 8.

tiugh s. (1) *the end.* (2) adj. *last.* 286, 19. tiugh-dhál *last condition, event, state. ibid.*

tlás *weakness, defeat.* sg. acc. *id.* 284, 24.

tóicebad 318, 40. fut. sg. 1 of tócbaim *I take.*

tóirndim *I measure out, define, signify.* fut. sg. 3 toiridnid 12, 4. for tóirindfid.

toirnidhfidh 207, 37. fut. sg. 3 of tairnim *I stoop, I descend.*

toirrces *foetus.* 36, 5. deriv. from torrach. sg. d. *id.* 32, 33.

toirrcim *deadness, numbness (O'R.).* toirrcim suain *a deep sleep.* 394, 4.

toisc *purpose, intention.* 194, 14. sg. acc. *id.* 118, 23. pl acc. tosca 106, 19.

tond f. *surface, skin.* glac toindghel (tonngel) *a clear skinned palm* 170, 7.

tonuch (do-nigim) *I wash.* pret. sg. 3 tonaich 422, 12.

torathar *a monstrosity.* pl. torathoir 394, 10.

torrach a. *pregnant.* 32, 12. 36, 3. 36, 17. 144, 8.

torrumha *act of visiting.* 46, 18.

tosach *beginning..* sg. d. tossach 214, 19. pl. n. tossaighe 214, 16.

trá *therefore.* 172, 9.

traethad *act of subduing, exhausting.* 62, 1.

trág *strand.* sg. gen. trágha 268, 27. acc. traigh 144, 17.
tráth *a time, a canonical hour.* pl. acc. tratha 2, 9.
treb *homestead, household.* sg. acc. *id.* 220, 11.
trebar *skilful.* pl. gen. *id.* 434, 20.
treidhe *three things.* sg. acc. *id.* 292, 15.
trell *a while.* 436, 23. sg. g. trill 398, 17.
trethan *a wave.* pl. trethain 384, 17.
treoraigteoir *a guide.* sg. d. *id.* 32, 39.
tres *one of three.* 140, 2.
tres[s] *a stroke, a skirmish, contest.* 340, 19. sg. acc. tuc se tres mor admolta 282, 19. 292, 10. Here tres probably = dreas *a bout. Cf.* ar tabairt an tesmolta moir sin 284, 12.
trilis *tress.* pl. n. trillsi. 396, 12.
trom-damh f. (lit.) *a heavy company, a band of poets.* 162, 9. 11. 164, 17. sg. g. tromdaimhe 162, 14. dat. tromdhaimh 163, 33. 162, 24.
troscadh *fasting.* sg. g. troiscthi 116, 29. acc. troscad 116, 29.
trostán *a long staff or pole.* 104, 11. sg. acc. 104, 2. 4. 7. 9. pl. n. trostain 100, 7. acc. trosdain 104, 1.

trúaighe f. *misery, pity.* 102, 1. sg. voc. truaidhe 84, 24.
tuidchim *I come.* v. n. toigecht 220, 28, corruptly for tuidecht. gan toigecht adrud 's do rath, *ibid. Cf.* tiachtain etarru *Lis. Lives,* 2102.
tuirmhim *I reckon.* 424, 4.
túr *searching, seeking.* sg. d. túar 392, 25.
turcbál, turcbáil *uprising, ascension.* sg. d. *id.* 12, 3.

úamh f. *a cave.* sg. d. uamhaigh 242, 16. corruptly for uamhaidh. uamhaid 242, 19.
uasta *from them.* 372, 9.
uidhe (ude) *journey.* sg. g. *id.* 332, 36.
ula f. *a stone-station.* 102, 27. 174, 15. sg. gen. ulaidhe 108, 29. acc. **ulaidh** 108, 26. pl. gen. uladh 114, 2.
ur-chra *deficiency, ruin.* 390, 7. sg. acc. urchrai 392, 2. urchra 392, 19. 396, 10.
ur-fuigell *judgment, decision.* sg. acc. uirighell 116, 22.
ur-labra *eloquence, speech.* sg. acc. urlapra 110, 27. urlabhra 194, 24.

INDEX OF PLACES AND TRIBES

Numbers refer to sections.

Acaill, 156, Achill Island (Onom)?
Achad Bó, Aghaboe, Queen's co., 282.
Aillend, seat of the Kings of Leinster, 5 m. E. of t. of Kildare, 126.
Aird, now Ardmagilligan, co. Derry, 146.
Alba, 1, 21, 22, 23, 35.
Albanaig, 24, 32, 208.
Albunach, Scottish, 344.
Allmurach, foreigner, 8, 127.
Ara na Naomh, Aranmore in Galway Bay, 155, 156.
Ard Macha, Armagh, 27, 119, 120, 166, 337.
Ard Sratha, Ardstraw, co. Tyrone, 40, 220, 250.
Ath [Droma Ceat], at Druim Cet, 330.
Ath an Carbaid, a ford on the river Dell in Tirconnell, 26.
Ath Imlaise; now p. Ahamlish, co. Sligo, 181.
Ath Lunga, now Aghanloo, co. Derry, 146.
Ath na hOrdoige, near Aghanloo, co. Derry, 146.

Babylon. Filia Babilonis, 417.
Baile Guaire mic Colmain, 157.
Banda, r. Bann in Ulster, 197, 348.
Belach an Adhraidh, 111.
Belach Damhain, in Glencolmkill, co. Donegal, 42.
Belach Duínbolg, at Rathbran chapel in par. of Baltinglas (Onom.), 94.
Bendchor; Bangor in co. Down, 223.
Bir, now Moyola river, which flows into L. Neagh on the N. W., 75.
Birra, now Birr, King's co., 72, 399.
Bladhma, Slieve Bloom, co. Tipp., 349.
Boinn, r. Boyne, which flows into the Irish Sea, about 4 miles below Drogheda, 131, 149.
Both Brain, 93.
Bregha, a plain in East Meath, 99, 137, 170.
Bretain, Britain, 100, 236, 295, 300, 308, 357.
Bretanach, British, 208.
Brethfne, Brefny, the counties of Leitrim and Cavan, 152.
Buill (a dat. form, the nom. is Búall); Boyle, co. Roscom., 29, 30, 152.
Bulcmar, (Muirbulcmar in Reeves' *Adam.*, p. 237), 367.
Bun Lindedh, 115.
Bun Sentuinne, 90.

Cabhan an Curuig, 322.
Cairpre Connucht, usually called C. Droma Cliab, 94.
Cairthe Snamha, east of Loch Foyle, 164.
Caissel Mumhan, Cashel, co. Tipp., 141.
Camass Comghaill, on the river Bann, 3 m. below Coleraine, 142, 355.
Carrac Eolaircc, at L. Foyle, 82, 83, 87, 159.
Cedimtecht Colaim Cilli, 55, 56.
Cell Garadh, in the north of Ossory, 221.
Cell mac nEoin = Cell mic Nenain, 54.
Cell mic Nenain, Kilmacrenan in co. Donegal, 53, 93, 115, 117, 150, 355.
Cell Mór Dithruimhe, Kilmore, co. Rosc., 161.
Cell Mudáin, 182.
Cell Riadhain, Kilrean, co. Donegal, 354.
Cell Rois, now Magheross, c. of Monaghan, 238.
Cell Sciri, Kilskeery in Meath, 98.

Cianachta Glinde Gemhin, now b. Keenaght, co. Derry, 95, 142, 146.
Cinel Conaill = Tirconnell, 26, 38, 169, 173, 275, 335, 412.
Cinel Énna mic Neill Naigiallaig, 116, 412.
Cinel Eogain mic Neill, 212, 275, 277, 278.
Cland Cnaimhsighe, 146.
Cland Conaill on Gulpain geir = Clanda Conaill, 275.
Clanda Conaill, 219, 275.
Clanda Cuind, 219, 364.
Clann Dálaig, 116.
Clann Echach Buide, 243.
Clanna Eogain, 219.
Clann Israli, Israelites, 381.
Clann Luighdech Laimhdheirc, 222.
Clann Maeil Colaim mic Dondchada, 93.
Clann Maicne Oililla, 154.
Clann Néill, 191, 339.
Clanna Rugraide, 179.
Clann Sciathbuidhe Scandlain, 349.
Cloch Ruad, at Ráith Cno, Gartan, 52.
Clochur, home of St. Maugina, 267, 317.
Cluain Deochra(ch), now Clondara, co. Longford, 106.
Cluain Foda, Clonfad, in Farbill, W. Meath, 76.
Cluain Iraird, Clonard, in Meath, 121, 219.
Cluain mic Nois, Clonmacnois, on the Shannon, King's co., 48, 106, 108, 120.
Cluain Mor bfher n-arda, Clonmore p., in b. of Ferrard, co. Louth, 99.
Cluaine, 90.
Cnoc an tShuide, 159.
Cnocan na n-Aingel, 229.
Coire Brecain, the whirlpool off Rathlin Island, now called Sloghnamara, 352.
Colbasaid, probably the larger Colonsay, in Scotland, 287.
Colunsa, Isle of Colonsay, Scotland, 239.
Connachta, npl.; gpl. Connacht; Connaught and the people of C., 94, 136, 139, 146, 157, 168, 169, 172, 173, 250.

Conullaigh, 172, 188, 189.
Corann, b. of Corann, co. Sligo, 153.
Corrsliabh, Curliew Hills between cc. Sligo and Roscommon, 153.
Crich Bregh = Bregha, 137.
Crich Ceneoil Conaill = Tir Conaill, 114, 115, 132, 141, 178, 355.
Crich Cruithnech, 291.
Cruithnech, g. pl., Picts, 291, 293.
Crosa Cail a Mide, Crossa-Keele in b. upr. Kells, co. Meath, 120.
Cross Mor Colaim Chilli, in Tory Island, 215.
Cruach = Cruach Patraic, 120.
Cruach Patraic. See Cruachan Aigle, 132.
Cruachan Aigle = Cruach Patraic, Croaghpatrick Mt., co. Mayo, 120, 132.
Cruachu, palace of the Kings of Connaught, in co. Roscommon, 126.
Cuailgne, Cooley in co. Louth, 157.
Cuiged Laigen, Leinster, 93, 108, 161, 228.
Cuil Dremne, in bar. of Carbury, co. Sligo, 139, 159, 172, 176, 177, 179, 182.
Cuil Fedha, not identified, 179.
Cuil Rathain, Coleraine, co. Derry, 179.
Cúiged Connacht, Connaught, 138.

Dael, river Dale, now Burndaley, in Tirconnell (Onom.), 26.
Daingen Mór, 266.
Dal [n]Áraidhe, the region extending from Newry, co. Down, to Slemmish, co. Antrim, etc., 354.
Dál Riata, now the Route, co. Antrim, 197, 315, 318 342, 343, 344, 350.
Damh-liac, Duleek in co. Meath, 158.
Dam-innis, Devenish, an island in Loch Erne, 122, 180, 430.
Damusc, *Damascus,* 389.
Danair, Danes, 8.
Disert Garuidh, to the north of Ossory, 221.
Doire Broscaidh, Derrybrusk near Inniskillen, 321.

Doire (Calgaigh), Derry, 76, 77, 78, 79, 80, 81, 82, 83, 84, 85, 86, 87, 88, 89, 90, 101, 13, 184, 218, 279, 345, 346, 371.

Doiri Eithne = Cill mic Nenain, 53, 117.

Domnach Mor Muige hÍthe, Donaghmore in b. Raphoe, 26.

Drobés, the river Drowes which flows into Donegal Bay, 133.

Druim Cet, now the Mullagh or Daisy Hill in Roe Park, near Newtownlimavady, 95, 136, 142, 143, 157, 197, 315, 316, 317, 321, 322, 330, 333, 335, 340, 350, 352.

Druim Cliab a Cairpri Connucht, Drumcliff, co. Sligo, 94, 172, 279.

Druim Colaim Chilli = Druim na Macraidhe, 154.

Druim Find, 168.

Druim na Lebur, 163.

Druim na Macraidhe, now Drumcolumb p. in Tirerrill b., Sligo, 154.

Druim Túama, Drumhome, co. Donegal, 279.

Dubdeca (Nigra Dea, Reeves' *Adam.*, p. 155), 297.

Duibregles, Columcille's oratory in Derry, 88, 89, 185, 346, 430.

Duirrthech, Columcille's oratory in Iona, 251, 284, 309, 311, 357, 362.

Dun = Dun da Lethglas, 371, 373, 374.

Dun Cuillin, Dunkeld, in Scotland, 120.

Dun Cruin, in co. Derry, 146.

Dun da Lethglas, Downpatrick, 36, 166, 351, 371, 373, 374.

Durlas, in co. Galway, 157.

Durmagh, Durrow, in King's co., 94, 96, 97, 271, 275, 276, 279, 280, 309, 349.

Eas Ruaid, falls of Assaroe at Ballyshannon, 31, 108, 133, 134, 348.

Ebra, Hebrew, 362.

Edail, *Italy*, 237.

Eibgheit, Eigheibht, Egypt, 17, 203.

Ela, a river near Tullamore, in King's co. (Reeves' *Adam.*, p. 124), 219, 249.

Elena, an island in Scotland, 303.

Emain Macha, Navan Fort, co. Armagh, 126.

Eoganaigh, 172, 188, 189.

Eorthanan, the Jordan, 34, 53, 214.

Erennaig, 24, 32, 82, 120, 181, 208, 235, 265, 277, 292, 304, 367.

Ériu, 1, 8, 11, 21, 22, 23.

Erne, Loch Erne, 134, 321.

Escert na Trath, 182.

Ess Finan, 114.

Ess Mac nEirc, now Assylin, co. Roscommon, 30, 152, 153.

Etica, the island Tiree, in Scotland, 233, 283, 305.

Fánaid, (dat. sg.) = Glend Fanad according to O'D., 163.

Ferna, Ferns, co. Wexford, 219, 368.

Fidbad, a wood near Derry, 80.

Find, the river Finn co. Donegal, 369.

Fir Bili, Farbill, Westmeath, 76.

Fir Roiss (*bis*), embraced a portion of the bar. of Farney, co. Mon., and some of Meath and Louth, 355.

Fochain, the river Faughon, co. Derry, 165.

Frainc, *France*, 237, 295.

Fuindsendach, river north of Assaroe, according to O'Donnell, 133.

Gaidil *Gaels*, 8, 21, 118, 127, 222, 275, 278.

Gaill, Norsemen, Englishmen, 8, 90, 127, 156, 373, 435.

Galile, 69.

Garad, see Cell Garadh, 221.

Gartan, Columcille's birthplace, in Tirconnell, 44, 51, 52, 54, 57, 58, 108, 109, 110, 159.

Glacach, 112.

Glais an Indluidh, 186.

Glais (*Facs.* Glend) Naiden, Glasnevin, near Dublin, 73.

Glan, "the well of Swords", according to O'Donnell, 103.

Glend an Scail, not identified, 157.

Glend Colaim Cilli, Glencolumkill, in Tirconnell, 42.
Glend Fanad, not identified, 163.
Glenn Gemhin, see Ciannachta G. G., 95, 142, 146.
Gort an Cochaill, 156.
Gort na Leci a nGartan, 109.

Í, Iona, 24, 161, 192, 202, 207, 211.
Í Colaim Chilli, see Í, 202.
Imba, supposed to be Oransay, Scotland, 243, 262, 310, 311.
Imlech Foda, in b. of Corann, co. Sligo, 153.
Impódh Dessiul, on the west side of Derry, according to O'Donnell, 218.
Inber Naaili, the estuary of Donegal, in Tirconnell, 141.
Inda, island in Scotland = Imba, 367.
India, *India,* 113, 364, 366.
In(n)is Eogain, Inishowen, co. Donegal, 348.
Inis Mór Locha Gamhna, probably Inchmore or Inishmore in L. Gawna, co. Longford, 152.
Irusalém, 155, 389.
Israel *Israel,* 135.
Iubhala, Jews, 72.

Lacc an Fogha, in Tory Island, 111.
Laíghes, Leix, a district in the Queen's co., 249.
Laigin, Leinstermen, 94, 219, 249.
Land, Lynn, bar. Delvin, W. Meath, 219.
Lec an Cochaill, 355.
Lec na Cumadh, *Flag of the Sorrows,* 109.
Leim an Eich, not identified, 179.
Leth Cuinn, 38, 121, 141, 219.
Leth Mogha, 435.
Lind Ingine Aeda, 94.
Lios Mor Mochuda, Lismore, co. Waterford, 435.
Loch Bethach, L. Veagh, near Gartan, co. Donegal, 110.
Loch Cé, L. Key in co. Roscommon, 147.

Loch Derg, L. Derg, in co. Donegal, 37.
Loch Eirne = Erne, 321.
Loch Febhail, L. Foyle, co. Derry, 82, 83, 87, 90, 164, 186, 188, 189, 192, 197, 279, 321.
Loch Gamhna, L. Gownagh, co. Longford, 152.
Lochlainn, Danes, Swedes, Jutes, Finns, 43, 371.
Loch mic Ciabain, in Gartan, co. Donegal, 51, 58.
Lugmad, *Louth,* 24.

Machuire Luighne, in Tiree, Scotland, 283, 305.
Magh Bile, probably in co. Down, 69.
Magh Coscain, probably Macosquin, co. Derry, 142.
Magh Lifi, plain near r. Liffey, in Leinster, 107.
Magh Raigne, a plain in the barony of Kells, co. Kilkenny, 348.
Magh Rath, Moyra, co. Down, 243, 359.
Mainistir Buide, Monasterboice, co. Louth, 170.
Mainistir Cailleach nDub, 298.
Mainister in da Sruth, in Scotland, 296.
Maith, name of a well, 81.
Maithe Lethe Cuind, 219.
Maithe Leithe Mogha, 435.
Methenach, river at Drumcliff, co. Sligo, 94.
Mic Israel, 135
Mic Luighdech Laimdheirc, 222.
Midhe, *Meath,* 76, 99, 120, 137, 219, 271, 275, 306, 434.
Moirtempall Petair, *St. Peter's,* Rome, 88.
Mug[d]ornai Maighen (*bis*), the baronies of Cremourne and Farney, co. Monaghan, 355.
Muili, Isle of Mull, Scotland, 214, 236, 239, 287.
Muindter Gualan, 115.
Muinnter Padruic, 120.
Muma, *Munster,* 50, 141, 148, 238, 435.

Neassa, Nisa, the river Ness in Inverness, Scotland, 289, 292, 308.
Neim, the r. Blackwater in Munster, 121.

Oilech (Ailech) na Righ, Greenan Elly, co. Derry, 81, 355.

Oilen Ia = Í, 367.
Oilen na Naemh, one of the Western isles of Scotland, 273, 274.
Oirgialla, *Oriel*, 94.
Orca, the Orkneys, 272.
Osruide [Osruighe], Ossory, 94, 221, 319, 349.

Patmus, Patmos, 362.
Pictoria, Pictora, the land of the Picts, 252, 253, 270, 288, 289.
Port an Curaigh, Portawherry in Iona, 355.
Port an Moirsheser, 113.
Port na hIndse, the landing place at Iona, 262, 357.
Port na Long, on the east side of Derry, 218.
Port na tri namat, Lifford, 13.
Port Toraidhe, 114.
Purcadoir Patruic, St. Patrick's Purgatory on L. Derg, 37.

Rachra, Lambay Island, 99.
Raith Both, Raphoe, co. Donegal, 91, 92, 279.
Raith Cno, 51, 52, 109.
Raith Enaigh, now Rathmochy, co. Donegal, 61.
Raith na Fleidhe, 81.
Rathen *Rahen,* in King's co., 121.
Reilec Odhrain, in Iona, 207, 355.
Reilec Patruic, 120.
Reileg an Duibregleis, in Derry, 88.
Reilg Árand, 155.
Roa, river in Donegal, 322.
Rómh *Rome,* 40, 88, 140, 157, 215, 216, 218, 219, 237, 250, 255, 256, 392.
Romhanach, Roman, 215, 362.

Ros Torathair, not identified, 179.

Sacsanach, *a Saxon,* 208, 210.
Saxa, England, 43.
Saxain, npl.; gpl. Saxan, Saxons, English, 21.
Scía, Isle of Skye, in Scotland, 301.
Scrin Colaim Cille, Columcille's Shrine, 146.
Sen-glend Colaim Chilli, Glencolumkill in co. Donegal, 42, 132, 133.
Sirie, Syria, 214.
Sith Aeda, now Mullashee at Ballyshannon, co. Donegal, 25.
Slaine, *Slane,* co. Meath, 121.
Sliab Bregh, near Monasterboice, 170.
Sliab Oiliféd, Mt. Olivet, 120.
Sliab Sioín, Sion Hill, 120.
Sliabh Cúa, Slieve Gua, in par. of Seskinan, co. Waterford, 121.
Sligech, *Sligo,* 172.
Sord, *Swords,* near Dublin, 102, 103, 107, 279.
Srath na Circe, 132.
Suidhe Colaim Chilli, 175.

Teach na n-Aidhedh, the guest-house at Iona, 222.
Tefa (tethbe), Teffia, in co. W. Meath, 96.
Tempul an Moirshesir, 113.
Tempull Mor na Romha, St. Peter's, Rome, 218.
Temair, Tara Hill, co. Meath, 43, 126, 129, 139, 168, 355.
Termond Arda Meg Gillagain, 146. See Áird.
Termond Cluana hIraird, at Clonard, co. Meath, 219.
Termonn Cille mic Nenain, 93. See Cell mic Nenain.
Termonn Cumainigh, now Termon Maguirk, co. Tyrone, 128.
Tibra an Laeich Leisc, not identified, 43.
Tír Conaill, Tirconnell, 75, 108, 354.
Tír Énna, in co. Donegal, 61.

Tír Eogain, *Tyrone*, 128.
Tír Fergna, not identified, 93.
Tir in Charna (Tirmcharna A. U., 560; F. M., 555), 168, 173; not identified.
Tír Luighdech, in Tirconnell, 279.
Tír Oililla, b. Tirerill, co. Sligo, 154.
Tobar Colaim Chille, in Derry, 86.
Tobar Colaim Chilli, at Glend Fanad, 163.
Tobar Eithne, in Kilmacrenan, co. Donegal, 117.
Tobar na Conalluch, in Termonn Cumainig, co. Tyrone, 128.
Tobur an Deilg, 164, 165.
Tobur na Duibhe, 165.
Toirinis Martain = Torón, 101, 257.
Tonda Cenanda, 192.
Torach, Tory Island, 111, 112, 113, 215.
Torón, Tours, 255, 256.
Traigh Eothaile, Trawohelly in co. Sligo, 279.
Trefhóid, now Trevet, co. Meath, 145.

Tuatha Toraidhe, not identified, 111.
Tuilean, now Dulane near Kells, co. Meat, 158.
Tulach Dubglaisi, Temple Douglas, co. Donegal, 54, 55, 159.
Tulach na Salm, 150.
Tulach Seghsa, in Corann, co. Sligo, 153.

Úi Ainmirech, 315.
Úi Cennselaigh, 161.
Úi Briain, 435.
Úi Fiachrach, 223. See Úi Fíathrach.
Úi Fíathrach, read *Fiachrach;* in Connacht, desc. of Fiachra, son of Eochaid Muigmedon, K. of Ireland, 223.
Úi Liathain, 271.
Úi Mhaine Condacht, 173.
Úi Neill, 339, 348.
Ulaid, Ulster, Ulstermen, 87, 93, 157, 179, 197, 243, 354.

INDEX OF PERSONAL NAMES

Numbers refer to sections.

Abrahám mac Tara, *Abraham son of Terah,* 378, 379.
Adamnan, 8, 46, 63, 72, 158, 192, 225, 238, 243, 269, 275, 280, 295, 304, 312, 353, 362, 363, 367, 369, 370, 375, 376, 406.
Adham, Adam, 21, 22, 72, 89, 297, 308, 332, 418, 419.
Aedh, twelve of the name, 315.
Aedh, f. of Manus O'Donnell, 10.
Aedh mac Ainmirech, k. of Ireland, 77, 94, 95, 128, 136, 142, 146, 243, 315, 317, 319, 322, 324, 325, 327, 345, 348, 354, 355.
Aedh mac Bric, 248.
Aedh mac Echach, 168, 173.
Aedh Ruad, grand-f. of Manus O'Donnell, 10.
Aedh Slaine mac Diarmada, 98, 121, 136.
Aedhan, a monk, 300.
Aedhan mac Gabhrain, k. of Scottish Dalriada, 240, 241, 242, 243, 315.
Aibel, son of Adam, 72.
Ailbhe Imlech Iubair, St. Ailbhe of Emly, 120.
Ainmire, f. of Aedh, 77, 94, 95, 128, 136, 142, 146, 243, 315, 316, 319, 322, 324, 325, 327, 345, 348, 354, 355.
Ainmire mac Setna, 173.
Ambros, St. Ambrose, 387.
Amra, f. of Moses, 378, 380.
Ananias, *Ananias* husband of Saphira, 70.
Annadh mac Duibhindse, 124, 125.
Antecrist, 355.
Aonghas mac Nadfraich, 141.
Art mac Cuind, 131, 332.
Augustin, St. Augustine, 3.
Axal, C. C.'s guardian angel, 64, 65, 338, 426, 427.

Baedan, f. of Fiachna, 179.
Baedán, f. of Maelumha, 212.
Báedan, f. of Oilill, 111.
Baedan mac Nindedha, 179.
Baithin Ban, namely, Baithin mac Cuanach, 275, 341.
Baithin mac Brenaind, 27, 55, 56, 98, 105, 120, 123, 137, 149, 151, 155, 161, 212, 215, 221, 222, 234, 236, 240, 241, 246, 278, 283, 305, 311, 334, 336, 353, 362, 373, 412, 413.
Baithin mac Cúanach, 83, 138, 340, 411, 412, 423, 425.
Barran mac Muiredhaigh, 133.
Bec mac De, a prophet, 98, 129.
Bédain, name of a woman, 353.
Beglaech o Beclaidhe, 110.
Bera, a monk, 233.
Berchan, a fosterling of Columcille, 314.
Berchán, B. of Clúain Sosta, 371.
Bernard, *St. Bernard,* 5, 6, 7.
Blathmac, son of Aed Sláine, 121.
Bonaventura, 17, 18.
Bran, name of Finn's hound, 42.
Brandubh mac Echach, 219.
Brec, f. of Aedh, 248.
Brecan, f. of Oilill Mar, 22.
Brecan mac Maine, 352.
Brenaind, f. of Baithin, 412.
Brenaind, an uncle of C. C., 93.
Brenainn, 84, 227, 275, 310. See Brenainn Birra.
Brenainn, 39, probably Brenainn of Birr. See Brenainn Birra.
Brenainn Birra, 72, 399.
Brígid, 28, 35, 36, 107, 127, 138, 159, 371, 372, 373.
Brocan, a druid, 392.
Brónach, f. of Buite, 41, 99.
Brugach mac nDegadh, 61.
Brughach, a saint, 137, 151.

INDEX OF PERSONAL NAMES

Bruidhe, k. of the Picts, 272, 291, 293.
Buide mac Bronaigh, 41, 99.
Cael mac Luighdech, 222.
Caibhdenach mac Enna, 124.
Caiin, *Cain,* 72.
Caillín naemtha, 38, 157.
Cailtean, a monk, 247.
Caindech mocua Daland, 120. See Reeves' *Adam.,* p. 220.
Cainnech = Caindech mocua Daland, 73, 75, 102, 104, 137, 213, 220, 229, 275, 282, 310, 315, 341.
Cairbre mac Luighdech, 222.
Cairbre mac Neill Naigiallaig, 31, 133.
Cairbre Rigfoda mac Conaire, 342.
Cairnech Tuilen, Cairnech of Dulane near Kells, 158.
Camh, *Ham,* son of Noah, 355.
Cathair Mor, f. of Daire Barrach, 22.
Cathrand, C. C.'s uncle, 93.
Ceannfaeladh, f. of Scandlan Mor, 319, 345, 349.
Cerball, f. of Diarmaid, 98, 129, 168, 182, 432.
Cerc .i. gilla Colaim Cilli, 132.
Cerd Connla, *Connla the Artificer,* 146.
Cíanán Daimhliac, Ciánan, bp. of Duleek, 158.
Ciaran, 332. See Ciaran mac an tSaeir.
Ciaran Cluana, 108, 157 = Ciaran mac an tSaeir.
Ciaran mac an tSaeir, St. Kiaran of Clonmacnois, 48, 73, 74, 75, 120, 123, 130, 225.
Coimghellan, f. of Colman, 197, 343, 344.
Coinchend, d. of Aedhan, 241.
Colaim Cilli, 1, 2, 7, 9, 15, 16, 17, 18, 19, 20, 21, *etc.*
Colaim mac Crimthain, 275.
Colga, Colca, a monk, 309, 313.
Colla mac Erc, f. of Dallan, 340.
Colman, a poor man whose cattle C. C. blessed, 286.
Colman, a poor man whose milk pail C. C. blessed, 284.
Colman, a smith, 306.

Colman, f. of Guaire, 136, 138, 157.
Colman, 225. Adamnan has *Columb Crag.* See Reeves' *Adam.,* p. 19.
Colman [mac Beognai], 231. *filius Beognai* Adamnan. See Reeves' *Adam.,* p. 29. Also called Colman Ela.
Colman Cuar, f. of Suibne, 354.
Colman Deochain, 99.
Colman Ela, 219, 249, 283.
Colman Espog 228, (249). Adamnan has *C. Mocu Loigse,* C. son of ui Loigse. See Reeves' *Adam.,* p. 210.
Colman Lainde mac Luacháin, 219.
Colman Liath (*recte* Cu), 238.
Colman mac Aedha, 144.
Colman mac Coimgellain, 197, 343, 344.
Colman mac Comghaill [Coimgellain], 344. See C. mac Coimgellain.
Colman mac Echach, 299.
Colman Mor mac Diarmada, 96, 179.
Colum ua Neill, namely, Columcille, 366, 248, 411.
Coman, a priest, nephew of Fergna, 312.
Comghall, St. Comgall of Bangor, 73, 75, 102, 137, 140, 142, 161, 179, 275, 307, 310, 315, 332.
Comhgall Bendchair, 223. See Comghall.
Conaire, f. of Cairbre Rigfoda, 342.
Conall, a holy bishop of Coleraine, 144.
Conall Clogach, namely, Conall mac Aedh, 350.
Conall Gulban, 21, 25, 35, 37, 38, 39, 40, 44, 93, 115, 116, 117, 133.
Conall mac Aedha, 324, 325, 326, 328.
Condla, 275.
Congall Claen mac Scandlain Scíathlethain, 354.
Conghalach mac Maeilmithidh, 149.
Conn, f. of Art, 219, 332, 364, 426. See Conn Ced-cathach.
Conn Ced-cathach, 43, 131.
Corb File, f. of Eithin, 22.
Cormac mac Airt, 131, 332.
Cormac ua Cuinn, 42 = Cormac mac Airt.

Cormac ua Liathain, 271, 272, 273, 274, 275, 276, 310.
Crimthan, f. of Colaim, 275.
Crimthand mac Luighdech, 222.
Crimthand ua Cuind, 426.
Crimthann, Columcille's baptismal name, 53, 159.
Crimthann ó Coinneannta, 110.
Crisd, *Christ,* 5, 6, 17, 40, 53, 72, 80, 81, 120.
Cruithnechan mac Cellachain, 53, 54, 59, 60, 61, 62, 68.
Cuanaidh, f. of Baithin (mac Cuanach), 83, 138, 340, 411, 412.
Cuculainn, 138.
Cuimín, 275, the *Cummeneus Albus* of Adamnan, according to Reeves. See Reeves' *Adam.,* p. 199.
Cul re hErind, *Back to Erin,* 201, a poetic name for Colum Cille.
Cumaín Fada mac Fiachna, 243.
Cumaine mac Colmain Moir, 179.
Curnan mac Aedha, 168.

Dabheoog, St. Dabheog, 37.
Daconna, a monk, 152.
Daimhin, 317. See Daimhín Daimh-airgid.
Daimhín Daimh-airgid rí Oirgiall, 94.
Daire Barrach, f. of Brecan, 22.
Dalach, 116, 117, Chief of Cenel Conaill, d. 869.
Dalann (gen. sg.), ancestor of Cainnech, 120.
Dallan Forgaill, 159, 179, 198, 336, 338, 339, 364, 366, 376, 399, 400, 404, 423, 426.
Dauith Ri, *King David,* 332, 385, 417.
Dé (sg. gen.), f. of Becc, 98, 129.
Degadh (sg. gen.), f. of Brugach, 61.
Demal, a fallen angel, 426.
Dhá Brenaind, namely, of Clonfert and of Birra, 315.
Dhá Ciaran, namely, of Saiger and of Clonmacnois, 315.
Diarmaid, a disciple of Columcille, 227, 236, 244, 246, 260, 261, 281, 356, 360, 361, 362, 363, 402.
Dha Findén, probably of Mag Bile and of Clonard, 315.
Diarmaid, f. of Colman Mor, 96, 179.
Diarmaid, founder of a monastery, 304.
Díarmaid mac Cerbaill, 98, 129, 139, 168, 182, 434.
Diarmaid Ollmar, 355.
Díma, f. of Cormac ua Liathain, 276.
Dima, f. of Eithne, 22.
Domnall mac Aedha, 95, 128, 136, 142, 243, 327, 328, 329, 331, 348, 350, 354, 355.
Domnall mac Muirchertaigh, 173.
Dondchadh, son of Domnall mac Aedha (*sic*), 355.
Donn, son of Milidh of Spain, 38.
Donnchad mac Aeda Sláine, 136, 137.
Dub na Cat, name of a cow, 165.
Dubhinnis mac Caibhdenaig, 124, 125.

Ebha, *Eve,* 297.
Echaid, f. of Colman, 299.
Echaidh, f. of Brandubh, 219.
Echaidh mac Conaill Gulban, 133.
Echaidh Muighmhedhon, 154.
Eilias, Eli, Elias the prophet, 290, 355.
Eithin, f. of Nae, 22.
Eithne, mother of Columcille, 22, 35, 37, 39, 40, 46, 47, 51, 52, 411.
Elisdabed, m. of John the Baptist, 50, 77.
Eliseus, Eileseus, *Elisha* the prophet, 214, 290.
Énde Arand, St. Enda of Áran, 155, 156.
Énna mac Neill Náigiallaig, 116, 412.
Enna mac Nuadain, 153.
Enoc, *Enoch,* 355.
Eochaidh Buide mac Aedhain, 243, 245.
Eochaidh Tir in Charna, 168, 173.
Eogan Arda Sratha, Bishop Eogan of Ardstraw, 40, 220, 250, 255, 256.
Eogan mac Neill Naigiallaig, 173.
Eoin baisde *John the Baptist,* 50, 53, 383.

INDEX OF PERSONAL NAMES

Eoin Bruinde, *John of the bosom,* namely, John the Evangelist, 290, 362, 386.
Eoin Suiphescel, John the Evangelist, 383.
Erc ingen Loairn, 22.
Erc mac Feradhaig, grand-f. of Dallan, 339.
Ercus, a robber, 239.
Ernan Toraidhe, Ernan of Tory, 111.
Esisias, *Hezekiah,* k. of Israel, 381.

Feilimidh, f. of Columcille, 1, 21, 35, 37, 39, 40, 48, 53, 93, 141, 215, 355, 400.
Felimid Rechtmar, 43.
Feradach, f. of Laisrén, 348.
Feradhach, greatgrand-f. of Dallan, 339.
Feradhach mac Duach rí Osruidhe, 94.
Ferghna, a monk, 367.
Ferghus mac Muirchertaigh, 173.
Ferghuss mac Róich, 157.
Fergna, a monk, uncle of Coman, 312.
Fergna (saei gabonn), 92.
Fergna mac Rig Caisil, 50, 159.
Fergus Cendfada mac Conaill Gulban, 21, 25, 40, 173, 412.
Ferudhuch mac Luighdech, 222.
Fiachaidh, C. C.'s uncle, 93.
Fiachna, f. of Cumaín Fada, 243.
Fiachna, f. of Mochonna, 250.
Fiachna, f. of Mongan, 87.
Fiachna mac Baedain, 179.
Fiachra, son of Domnall mac Aedha (*sic*), 355.
Fiachra, son of Eochaid Muigmedon, 223.
Fiachra, son of Lugaid, 40.
Fidruidhe, C. C.'s uncle, 93.
Finan Lobar, 102.
Findachta mac Dunadha (*recte* Dunchadha), 136, 137.
Findbharr, a monk, 154.
Findcaemh, mother of Mochonna, 250.
Findchan, owner of a wood in Derry, 79.
Finden, a monk of the monastery of Magh Coscain, 142. Adamnan has *Finan of Durrow* (Reeves' *Adam.,* p. 95).
Finden, probably Finden Muighe Bile, 48, 100.
Finden, 139. See Findén Droma Find.
Finden Cluana hIraird, St. Finnen of Clonard, 71.
Findén Droma Find, 168, 176.
Finden Muighe Bile, 69.
Finden, 225, *recte* Fintan, more commonly known as Munda mac Tulchain. Adamnan has *Fintenus* (Reeves' *Adam.,* p. 18).
Findia mac ua Fiathruch, 223.
Findtan Fial, 355.
Findtan mac Gaibrein, 160, 249.
Finn mac Cumaill, 42.
Fíonán Ratha, 114.
Fraech the Presbyter, 182.

Gabhran, f. of Aedhan, 240, 241, 243, 244, 315.
Garb mac Ronain, 175.
Gemman (MS. German), one of Columcille's teachers, 70.
Generifebus, a monk, 226.
German Espog, 295.
Gerran Ban, name of a horse, 361.
Gridoir Beil-oir, *Pope Gregory,* 2, 40, 88, 157, 215, 216, 219, 250, 255, 256.
Guaire, a man whose manner of death C. C. foretold, 264.
Guaire mac Colmain, k. of Connaught, 136, 138, 157.
Hieroinimus, *St. Jerome,* 392.
Iarnán, a monk, 369.
Iarnán Cluana Deochrach, 106.
Ihsu, *Jesus,* 34, 50, 77.
Ihsu Crisd, 49, 63, 65, 72, 81, 82, 91, 113.
Iohannes, 77. See Eoin baisde.
Irial, 225. Adamnan has *Erneneus filius Craseni* (Reeves' ed., p. 25).
Isahias, *Isaiah the prophet,* 381.
Laighnen, Lugneus, a monk, 289, 303, 309, 357.

Laisrén, abbot of Durrow and afterwards of Iona, 315.
Laisrén Ab Durmhaigh, abbot of Durrow, 276, 280, 348, 349. See Laisrén.
Lasarus, g. Lasaruis, 290.
Liathan, ancestor of Cormac (ua Liathain), 271.
Loarn, C. C.'s uncle, 93.
Loingínus *Longinus*, 182.
Lon = Longarad, 221.
Longarad, a scholar, 221.
Luachán, f. of Colman, 219.
Lugaid mac Sedna, mic Ferghosa Cennfada, 40.
Lugaidh, 275. Tír Luighdech named from him.
Lugaidh mac Setna, f. of Ronan, 116.
Lughaidh, 367, a monk of Cluain Finnchoill which Reeves identifies as the modern Rossnarea (Reeves' *Adam.*, p. 235).
Lughaidh, a monk of Iona, 235, 236, 237, 238, 239, 267.
Lughaidh Lamhdherc, 222.

Mac Díma, namely, Cormac ua Liathain, 276.
Mac Medha, a millionaire, 140.
Mac Taidg, 435.
Macarius = Mochonna, 250, 251, 252, 253, 254, 255, 256, 257.
Macrith, servant of Mochta of Louth, 24.
Maedóg Ferna, 219, 368.
Maelcabha mac Aedha mic Ainmirech, 82.
Mael Colam, 93.
Maelmithidh, f. of Conghalach, 149.
Maelumha mac Baedáin, a relative of Columcille, 212.
Maelumha mac Baódain, 87.
Maghnas o Domhnaill, 10, Chief of Tirconnell, etc., died 1563.
Maine mac Neill, 352.
Mandar mac Righ Lochlann, 371, 373.
Marban, King Guaire's brother, 157.
Martain, St. Martin of Tours, 34, 101, 120, 228, 255, 256, 257, 355.

Matha, *St. Matthew,* 4, 399, 415.
Mauricius, 250, 255. See Mochonna.
Michel, *Michael the Archangel,* 174, 175.
Mobi Clairenech, 73, 75, 77, 315.
Mocaemhóg Comruire (*leg.* Mocholmóc), 219.
Mochonna, a disciple of Columcille, 40, 250, 251, 252, 255.
Mochta, bishop of Louth, 24.
Mochuda Lessa Moir, 435 = Mochuda Rathain.
Mochuda Rathain, 121.
Mogh, 435. Leath Mogha called after him.
Moisi (Maise) mac Amra, *Moses son of Amram,* 120, 135, 378, 380.
Molaisi Daimh-indse, 122, 180, 430.
Mongan mac Fiachna, 87, 159.
Mor (*recte* Moghain), a holy woman, 267.
Motharen Droma Cliab, 94.
Mudán, 182.
Muirchertach mac Muirethaich, 173.
Muire, *Mary,* 19, 50, 146, 275, 277, 355.
Muiredhach mac Echach, 133.
Muirethach mac Eogain, 173.
Munda mac Tulchain, 120, 161.
Mura, saint and poet (d. 650), 50, 53, 54, 159.

Naail, son of Aongus, k. of Munster, 141, 321.
Nadfrach, f. of Aonghas, 141.
Nae, f. of Dima, 22.
Naman, *Naaman,* 214.
Nera, *Nero,* 362.
Niall, f. of Ronan, 355.
Niall Garb, great grand-f. of M. O'Donnell, 10.
Niall Naigiallach, † 405, 21, 133, 173, 339, 352, 412.
Nicól Bastún, 90.
Nindidh, f. of Baedan (K. Ire.), 179.
Nindigh, C. C.'s uncle, 93.

Odhran, a monk, 190, 206.
Oilill, b. of Diarmaid Ollmar, 355.

Oilill inbanna ri Connacht, 94.
Oilill mac Báedain, 111.
Oilill mac Echach, 154.
Oilill Mar, f. of Corb File, 22.
Oissin mac Cellaig, 99.

Patruic, *Patrick,* 25, 26, 27, 28, 29, 30, 31, 32, 33, 36, 37, 120, 127, 133, 138, 141, 146, 152, 158, 159, 166, 332, 355, 371, 372, 373, 427.
Petar, *Peter,* 70, 72, 88, 100, 257, 290, 295, 355, 388.
Pilba, a monk, 357.
Pól, *Paul,* 120, 238, 290, 305, 355, 389, 424.

Róch (Rogh), m. of Ferghus, 157.
Rochuadh, name of a sea-monster, 78, 366.
Ronan, f. of Garb, 175.
Ronan, slain by Colman Liath, 238.
Ronan Find, 355. See *The Adventures of Suibhne Geilt* (ed. O'Keeffe), p. 161.
Ronán mac Luigech (*read* Luigdech), 116.
Ronan mac Neill, 355.
Ruadhan, St. Ruadhan, 139.

Scandlan Mor mac Cinnfaeladh, 316, 345, 346, 347, 348, 349, 350.
Scandlan Sciathlethan, f. of Congal Claen, 243.

Sdefán, *Stephen,* 389, 390.
Sedna, C. C.'s uncle, 93.
Sedna, f. of Lugaid, 40.
Segenus, 225. Segineus (Reeves' *Adam.,* p. 26).
Senach Sengabhai, 321.
Senchan Senfhile, 157.
Sersenach, a rich man, 140.
Setna mac Fergusa, 173.
Sillan, a monk, 239, 266.
Simón Mághis *Simon Magus,* 295.
Solamh mac Dauid, *Solomon,* 385.
Suibne mac Colmain Cuair, 354.
Suibne mac Colmain Moir, 98.
Suidemhain mac Samhain, 87.

Tadg mac Toirrdelbaigh, 435.
Tailgend, *Adzehead,* a nickname of St. Patrick, 373.
Tara, *Terah,* f of Abraham, 378.
Ternóc, St. Ternóc, 137, 151.
Tice, a holy man of Ath Lunga, 146.
Toirrdelbach an Fina, f. of Niall Garb, 10.
Toirrdelbach ua Briain, 435.
Tulchan, f. of Munda, 120.
Turcall Ri Gall, 435.

Ua Neill, descendant of Niall, namely, Colum Cille, 73.
Úeinne, 435.
Uictor, Patrick's guardian angel, 427.

INDEX RERUM

Numbers refer to sections.

abbot, Cc 1, 76, 78, 208.
abbot, of Jerusalem 155, of Down 371.
absolution, validity doubted 223.
abstinence, ember 122, 418.
adultery 119, 314.
advance checked by curse 111, 219, 301.
adventurous voyage 355a.
Adze-head, name for Padraic 373.
age of Cc, forty-two on leaving Ireland 199, in Alba thirty-four years 199, 357, 430,
  at death, seventy-two 390, seventy-six 430
  death delayed four years 357.
age, old 67.
agriculture. See reapers, grain, farmyard, ricks, haggard wheat, corn.
ale 347, 355g, 423.
aliases of Irish saints: Crimthann, Columcille 53, Mochonda, Macarius, Maurísius 250, 255.
alleluia, significance of 362.
almoner, refuses alms to Christ 78.
alms, duty of giving 138, given in state of sin 144, given unwillingly 149, given for fear of satire 407.
almsgiving, impossible without poor 332; 425.
alphabet on cake 59. *Cf.* H. Gaidoz, *Les gâteaux alphabétiques*, Paris, 1886, and Horace, *Sat. I.* i. 25.
altars, prepared 227, 335
altar, cruet upon 69, in east of church 89.
altar-cloth 227, 355g.
ambushes, against Cc 170, against Scannlan 348-9.
Amra Choluimchille 336-339, 435. See Dallan Forgaill *Index Nominum*.
anchor 204.

angel, appears to Padraic 33, prophecy of Cc 43, announcing birth to mother 45, 46, 51, naming Cc 53, Axal, the helper appears to Cc 64, 65, 67, three maidens 66, makes peace 74, reveals goblets to Cc 81, greets Cc 87, in company of Cc 100, directing Cc to Tory 111, reveal demons 132, worship cross 154, advise Cc 155, 166, 219, Michael, the Archangel 174-175, like leaves 183, ten hundred guard 185, returns staff 213, let down cross 215, come to hear clerics sing 216, saves souls 220, announce guests 222, bearing souls to heaven 226, 228, 304, meet soul 227, 367, attend Cc at prayer 229, with book 243, guides 250, breaks glass vessel, token of death 292, vision of 300, guard Cc 305, aid monks 307, 309, leads Scannlan 346, visit island 355c, come for Cc 357, go through wall 359, guardian 426, 427, multitude of 435, in Patmos 362.
angelic radiance 310-14, causes blindness 312, at death of Cc 367-9. See also light.
animals. See cat, wren, fly, cow, nag, ox, deer, wolf, monster, fawn, stag, pig, hog, swine, horse.
animal language 118, 366.
antenatal miracle. See prenatal.
appetite, enormous 212, 347.
apple tree 275.
apples of ill-taste made sweet 97. *Cf.* Plummer, *V. S. H.*, I, cliv.*
archangel 174-5.

*Plummer, *V. S. H.*, I, refers to C. Plummer, *Vitae Sanctorum Hiberniae*, Vol. I.

armor 132, of Cc 305.
arrival of Cc at Iona 202.
arbitrator, Cc, between sons of Lughaidh 222, among saints 223, between man and woman 224, between Finnen and kinsmen 225, regarding Easter 225, between Erin and Alba 315, 342, between poets and king 332-5, between Donnchad and Fir Roiss 355.
assembly, of Druim Ceat 315-351.
ascetic practises of Cc 17, 67, 229, 390, 392, 395, 398, 400, 401, 402, 403, 404, 406, 414, 417, 418, 422, 424. See also psalms, water, hair-cloth, stone, flag-stone, scourging, silence, prostrating, vigils, weeping.
austerities. See ascetic practises.
author's observations 10-14, 20, 431. See prayer, elements, comparisons.
automata, staff 133, vat 158, bells 218, bolts 291, doors 296, wheels of chariot 299, boat 322, chains 346, coffin 371. *Cf.* Plummer, *V. S. H.*, I, clxxxvi.
avarice 332.
axles, of chariot 26. See pegs.

back, on Erin 201, on mother 411. *Cf.* Fowler, lxvii.
backsliding caused by death of son 217, 290.
bacon. See pig.
bailing 281.
bakehouse 226.
baker, notes words of Cc 226.
ban, put on Cc 72, on fishers 115.
banishment 121, 180, 203, 332-3, 355, of druids 204.
ball-playing 168.
baptism, of Cc 54, of skull 131, of Irish 162, of old man 259, of child 269, of converts 295, to death 426.
bards. See poets.
bark for tanning 434.
Banquet, Barrow of the 81.
barley, sown late yields harvest 79.

bath 158, 230, hot and cold 355 f.
"Battler" 178, 275.
battle, of Belach Duinbolg 94, of Cuil Dremhne 159, 173-179, of Cuil Fedha 179, of Cuil Rathain 179, of Magh Rath 354.
beast 78, gives up youth 196, 253, subservient to Cc 301. See monster.
beauty, danger to chastity 386.
bed, things kept above, books 221, salt 267.
beach combing 398.
beer 423. See ale.
bees 105.
beggar, Christ in guise of 78.
bell, noonday 120, broken upon demons 120, 132, ring of selves 156, 218; 220, made by Senach 321, used for cursing 326, poem made on 182, struck 244, for matins 73, 345, 347, midnight 363. *Cf.* Plummer, *V. S. H.*, I, clxxvi.
berries 355d.
bestiary 78.
bilge water 281.
birds, bearing vitals of woman 47, grieve 192, 265, 355c, language 355c, 366, love Cc 192, 265, sing hours 355c. See crane, seagulls. *Cf.* Plummer, *V. S. H.*, I, cxlvi.
birth on stone 51. *Cf.* Plummer, *V. S. H.*, I, cxxxix.
birthday 429.
bishop, Finnen 69, bans Cc 72, gives orders to Cc 76, prepares banquet 144, pretends to be priest 148, twenty 198, sham 204, 248, Moconda made 252, 255, Gemmán 295, accompanies Cc 323, 347. See Eoghan Arda Sratha.
blessing 25, of Padraic on Assaroe 31, completed 133, of God on tribe of Conall Gulban 38, of Eoghan 40, of Axal on Cc 64, of Pope 218.
blessing by Cc 74, 93, 96, 97, 103, 109, 132, 136-138, 140, 144, 152, 212, 214, 218, 223, 224, 233, of sea 234, 244, 260, 268, 270, 277, 278, 281, 285, 289, 292, 297, 327, 358, 434.

blindness, healed 143, 268, temporarily healed 338; fish stricken blind 132, caused by miraculous light 312, 314, averted by prayer 314.
blisters raised by satire 333.
blood, color of milk 285.
blood, defiles well of Ethne 117, of Comgall 142, given as milk 285, like water 403.
blood-shed atoned for by fine 43.
blue 332.
boar, falls dead 301.
boat. See ship.
body, rises from grave 113, kept without decay 120, 158, beauty of 158, of Cc honored 353, 370, drifts to shore 371, protected by storm 375, disdained 418. See corpses, dead.
bolts, loosened 291. See locks.
bondage 345. See bondwoman, hostage.
bond-woman, delivered by Cc 292. Cf. Plummer, *V. S. H.*, I, cvii.
bone, broken, cured by letter in water 267.
bones take on flesh, of man 146, of ox 212, rise to surface 352.
book, treasured by Cc, St. Martin's Gospel 28, 34, 101, 256, copied by Cc 103, 394, Finnen's 168, 178, saved from fire 182, writing of 221, of crystal 243, by Mochonda, son of Kilgarrow 221, last psalter by Cc, completed by Baithin 362, miraculously preserved 433. See writing.
booksatchel 433.
boots 345, 410. See also sandals, shoes.
bothy, position of 71, 73. Cf. Plummer, *V. S. H.*, I, cxiii.
bread 122, 182, 239, increased 215, heals of plague 266.
────── and water, penance 223, 400.
brooch, golden, Aed's 317, Scannlan to Cc 349, exchange of 219.
broth, nettle 356, 400.
brothers, 93, 113, 157.
buidech connaill 75.

burial, delayed 289, preparation for 370.
burial place revealed by Cc, of Buide 99, of Martin 34, 101, 256, of abbot of Jerusalem 155.
burning of town by Cc 77.
butter 182, in stirring stick 356, 423.

cairn. See stone-station.
cake, alphabet on 59.
calf, red 87, salmon, size of 355a.
calvary 218.
candles, of faith 33, lighted of themselves 156, miraculous 251.
canonical hours. See hours.
captivity of Scannlan 319.
carpentry 74.
casket, containing written blessing 267.
cat, pet of Cc 118, milk for 165.
Cathach, s. v. "Battler" 178, 275.
cat-heads 355b.
cattle, miraculous increase of 286, 336, as tribute 349. Cf. Plummer, *V. S. H.*, I, clxxiv. See ox, cow.
Cattle Raid of Cualnge, related by Fergus 157.
cauldron miraculously mended 182.
cell. See hut.
chair 123.
character of Cc 123, diligent 397, his speech 399, his food and drink 400, ascetic practises 401-4, 414-24, beauty 405-9, respect for poets 408, humility 410, chastity 411, generosity 425, good and bad angels 426, birthday and death day 429, age at death 430.
chariot, serviceable without pegs, aged Cc in 358. Cf. Plummer, *V. S. H.*, I, civ, clxxxvi.
chastity 66, 223, 224, 225, 298, 407. See virginity.
chasuble 355b, 355d.
chieftain, of the people of Erin 38.
child at breast 353.
choir of angels 257.
choir-stall 312.
church, prophesied by Padraic 30, to be

filled with books, distempers, or gold 75, power of 72, 277, persecution of 389.
churches, built by Cc 79, 80, 90, 94, 99, 102, 108, 111, 146, 153, 154, 162, in Iona 207, 208, 253, 394, named after Ciaran 130, enumerated 279.
────── by followers of Cc 254.
church-yard, dead naked in 120, place of prayer 300, of Odran 355h.
churl borne to heaven in bishop's company 248.
churlishness of Guaire 138.
circuitous route recommended 186, 233.
clairvoyance 148, 155, 204, 223-4, 226-238 *passim,* explanation of Cc's 239; 256, 280, 307, 321. *Cf.* Plummer, *V. S. H.,* I, clxx. See also prophecy, guests, visions.
clapper of bell 132.
clay, helpful to pregnant women 51, flees into tree 51.
cleric 37, 62, 106, 114, 119, 159, 161, 215, 216, 275, 315, 316, 323, 335, 355, *et passim.*
cloak, many colored, seen in a vision 45, as measure of land 111.
cloud, pestiferous 266, devils in 287.
cloud of fire 60, 310. See light, angelic radiance.
club 187.
cobbler 434.
coffin, robbed 370-1.
cold 280.
colony of Dal Riada 318.
colors, in church 335. See also blue, red, green, dun, grey, purple.
compact with devil 435.
companions of Cc 100, 323. See followers.
companionship on journey to heaven 248.
comparison, of Padraic to a mill 32, sinners to stinging bees 105, Cc's piety to chair, etc. 123, Cc's exile to Jesus' in Egypt 203, druid to Simon Magus 295, to Paul 238, 389, 425, to proph-

ets and apostles 266, 290, to God 360, to Abraham 378-9, to Moses 135, 380, to Isaiah 381, to Solomon 385, to John 386, to Peter 70, 295, 388, to Stephen 390, to Jerome 392, to Christ 51, 364, 395, 407,
compensation for bloodshed 43, 222.
concelebration 148. *Cf.* J. T. Fowler, *V. S. C.,* xliii.
concessions. See pilgrimage, *Altus,* prerogative.
confessor, seen in vision appointed 249.
congregation 285-6.
contests with druids 87, regarding curse 240, regarding ox 285, regarding bondmaid 292, regarding wind 294-5. *Cf.* Plummer, *V. S. H.,* clxvi.
contrition. See repentance.
convention. See assembly.
conversions, of Mongan 87, of druid 129, 154, of many 254, of old man 259; 290, 291, 295, 308.
convoy 344.
cooking 212.
coracle 191, 192, 200, 271, 276, 355-6.
corn 212, 219, 355e, 410, 360.
corpse rises from burial place 113, shaved 158. See also body.
coulter 76.
courtesy 122. See also guests, hospitality, kiss.
covenant between Odhran and Cc 206.
covetousness 144.
cow, lost and found 165, "to every cow her calf" 168, dung as fuel 156, dun 157, 336, multiplied 286, ready to calve 356, in calf 356.
cows, white and red 87, multiply 286, dun-colored 336.
cowl given by Cc to Aed, son of Ainmire 94, to Aed Slaine 98, left 275, over Cc's eyes 320, golden 355g, h.
coward 328, 331.
craftsman. See smith.
crane, pet, plucks out eye of spy 168, comes to visit Cc in Alba 192, 265, transformed woman 329-30. *Cf.*

Plummer, *V. S. H.*, I, cxlvi.

crane-cleric, Cc 329.

cross, on flagstone 52, set in church 154, let down upon altar 215, memorial of Cc's uncle 262. See sign of.

crosses, left by Cc 103, erected in Iona 207.

cross-vigil 175, 176, 229. *Cf.* Plummer, *V. S. H.*, I.

crowds undesirable, coming to sanctuary 132, wake 375.

crown 72.

crozier touches glass vessel 99.

crystal, vessel 99, chair 123, book 243, altars 335, hall 355g. See glass.

curse, south side of Assaroe cursed by Padraic 31; of Bishop Eoghan 40, put upon fishers and bay 115, indicated by bell in rock 132, laid on Diarmaid 139, on man with forked club 187, for inhospitality 182, on Saxon 210, on Brandubh 219, on books 221, changed to blessing 240, on Conall mac Aeda 326, on Queen 329, on handmaid 330, stammering 347, 350. *Cf.* Plummer, *V. S. H.*, I, clxxiii. See also vindictiveness.

customs, Thursday sacred to Cc 159, *Cathach* borne round the army 178. See also sunwise.

damnation, for neglecting *Altus* 217.

dancing 392.

dark-red sea 279.

day, divided for labors 396, 398.

days of week. See Monday, Tuesday, *et seq.*

deacon 198, 323.

dead, seen naked save sarks 120, prayed for 352, body drifts 371. See also body, death, corpse.

dead, speak. See skull.

deaf healed 143.

death, choice of 67, by accident 222, thought of 224, voluntary 248, averted 261, 314, not to be warded off 293, caused by miraculous light 314, announced by piebald horseman 338-9, delayed four years 357, postponed from Easter to Pentecost 358, of Cc announced 360, of Cc 363.

death foretold, of youth 232, of Caíltean 247, of Moconda 257, of monks 258, of kinsmen 262, manner of 264, of Cormac 271, of druid 292, of Domnall mac Aeda 327, of Cc 356, 358, 360.

decay prevented, of books 221, 433, of body 120, 158.

December 52, 429.

deer, spared by hounds 42, 44, ploughs instead of horse 76, carries books 163; (*cf.* Plummer, *V. S. H.*, I, cxliii); spear aimed at 222, impaled on stake 297, followed 355.

defence of poets 332.

deisel 178. *Cf.* Plummer, *V. S. H.*, I, cxxxv. See *sunwise*.

deliverance, miraculous 346.

demon, guardian of Cc, Demal 426.

demons, 70, 149, 219, 220, 223, 284, 287, 295, 305, 334-5, enter rock 132, changed to fish 132, threaten ship 295, flee blessing 270, struggle for soul 300, attack Cc 305, driven from Iona to Etica to Luighen 305, wrestle on flagstone 411.

departure from Erin 100, 180-202, 219, delayed 355a.

deputy 219.

despair, induced by the Devil 223.

destruction of man's home known to Cc 263.

devil, messenger unmasked 119, in milk pail 284, tempts woman to ruin husband 297, in form of woman 353, named Demal 426, compact with 435. See demon.

diet of Cc 423.

diligence 396-400, 413, 416.

disciples of Cc. See followers.

disease 128, 275. See leprosy, paralysis, plague, ulcer, *buidech Connaill, jaundice.*

disfigurement, caused by magic 285.
disobedience 229, 243, 314.
dispraise of Alba 275, 278.
dispute concerning Easter 225.
dog, pet 297.
dog-heads 355d.
dogs. See hound.
Doomsday 87, 151, 355c, Ireland to be flooded before 120. *Cf. Tripartite Life*, p. 116, 118.
door shut on Cc 98, 291; doors, hundreds of 355g. *Cf.* Plummer, *V. S. H.*, I, cxxxix. See locks.
doublets, many colored cloth prefigurement of Cc 45, 46, flesh-meat transformed 122, 182; 86 and 269, 94 and 98, 100 and 198; old man of natural virtue baptized 259, 308. *Cf.* Plummer, *V. S. H.*, xc.
dove 53.
dream, symbolic 141. See vision.
drifting of corpse to Dun da Lethglas 371.
drink 144, 251, on tip of finger 319. See ale, milk, beer, wine, water.
drowning 94, 149, 231, 352.
druids 129, pretend to be bishops 204, curse becomes blessing 240, contest of 270, draw milk from ox 285, refuse bondwoman 292, explanation of power 294. *Cf.* Plummer, *V. S. H.*, clviii ff. See also contests with druids.
Duan na Tuiledhach, poem composed by Cc 353.
drunkenness 355g. *Cf.* Plummer, I, ci.
Dublaidh, poem composed by Cc 332.
dun cow, hide of 157, 336.

earthquake 364-5.
earth, fertilized by blood 205, struck by Cc 259, the fruitful 332, rising 159, 341, sinking 340.
earthly paradise 355 f.
eggs 122.
eight 238.
elements 97, 216, 283, 340, 365-6, 376, powerless to injure belongings of Cc 77, 268, 433. See earth, winds, fire, water, waves, storms, sun, moon, stars.
eleventh 117
emaciation of Cc 404.
enigmatical prophecy 264.
envy 47, 251, 252.
episcopal institutions. See bishop.
escape of Scannlan 346.
etymologies, Crimthann 53, Columcille 53, Axal 64, Maurisius 255.
eucharist. See mass, sacrament.
exile, of Cc 174-198, 203, 277-8, 378, lasts thirty-four years 357; befriended by Cc 287.
———, vow of 250, virtue of 378-9. See also banishment.
eye, plucked out 168, grey 201-2. See also pupils.
eyesight regained by sprinkling with salt water 268, token of approaching death 338-9, spiritual 340.

fable, the world a 332.
failings of Cc 123.
fair-haired Adam 332.
fairy mansions 87.
falsehood 399.
fame of Cc 113.
farmyard 360. See haggard.
fasting 173, 298, 311, 337, 380, 400. *Cf.* Plummer, *V. S. H.*, I, cxiv.
fat 423.
father of Cc 35, 37, 39, 40, 48, 250, 348, 355, 400; 66, 95, 116, 245.
fathering a son falsely 353.
fawn. See deer.
fear, caused by angelic radiance 312, 314; 348.
feast of Pentecost 204, in heaven 368, given by Conall 144, of Easter 225, 358.
feeding of hungry 83, 212, multiplying of loaves and fishes 84. See guests, generosity.
feet, kissed 211, washed in well cause

disease 270, livid from fetters 347, washed 410.
fetters 319, loosed 345. *Cf.* Plummer, *V. S. H.,* I, cxxxix.
feud caused by chance death 222.
fields unplowed yield harvest 156.
fiend, as woman 353. See demons, Devil.
fiery cloud over Cc's face 60, 310.
fiery stream 132.
fifty, boys 198, saints 315; 73, 332, 346.
——— thrice, islands 87, psalms 332, 390, 401, master bards 157, prentice-bards 157.
fines, exacted instead of corporal penalties. See compensation.
finger, from living hand as relic 276, drink on tip of 319. See thumb.
fire, spares grove 77, in guest-house 222, in Italy 237, spares Cc's salt 268, lake of 355 f.
fires, method of laying 156. See flames, light, pillar.
first, flames of faith in Erin 33, speech of Cc 50, 159; walk of Cc 55-6, 159.
fish, abundant because of Padraic's blessing 29, declared a help to Cc by Padraic 30, bidden to come from lake 83, red and blind 132, become stones 115, demons 132, plentiful on north side of Assaroe 133, impaled on stake 297, under obedience to Cc 302, miraculous cast 302, hooked 398, as food 141, 182, 355a-b, *et passim. Cf.* Plummer, ci. See trout, salmon.
fishing, miraculous cast 302. See nets, hooks.
fishers behold pillar of fire 369.
five, of his seed 40, marks 85, youngest of 116, pentarchs of Erin 137, cows 286.
flagstone from lake whereon Cc was born 51, opens to receive Cc 52, whereon Cc was baptized 54, cast away by warden 54, of chastity 58, lifted by Cc 101, yields water to quench sorrow 109, sinks 340, of the Cowl 355h, for bed 390, demons wrestle on 411.
flames, of symbolic significance 24, 33, 37. See Plummer, *V. S. H.,* cxxxv-cxli.
flesh, restored to bones 146, 212.
flour 32, 51, 141.
fly, pet of Cc 118.
fog, surrounding demons 132. See mist, cloud, rain.
followers of Cc 198, 225, 226, 250, 275, 313, 323.
food. See ale, apples, bacon, butter, honey, meal, milk, ox, salmon, salt, seaweed, wine, pork.
fool, prince made 326.
ford 329, 330.
foreigners in Erin 90, 118, 127, 354.
forge 321.
forgetfulness 163, 182.
forked staff, cursed by Cc 187.
fornication 223, 224, 353. See also incest, adultery.
forts 355.
forty, priests 198, sons 198.
fosterer, of Cc 54, 59-63, 68, resuscitated 62; 95, 160, 250.
fosterling of Cc 114, 314.
foundation laid with human sacrifice 205, 206. *Cf.* Plummer, *V. S. H.,* I, clxxxvii; Stokes, *Lis. Lives,* 309, *n.* 1007.
fountains. See wells.
four 98, saints 120, months 157, 315, fragments of heart 191, sons 222, four and twenty 262, kings 38.
fourteen 199, 274. See seven.
fragrance from dying saint 363.
"free ordering" of Erin 355.
"free visiting" of Erin 355.
freedom of Erin, prophesied by Cc 118, 127.
Friday 232, Good 327.
friendship with saints. *Cf.* Meyer, *Colman,* XI-XII. See Index of Persons.
frost 287, 355a.
fruit 46. See apples, sloes, berries.

gables 355.
gambler, given a groat 85.
game, impaled on miraculous stake 297.
garment, trips Cc 149.
genealogy 21-2, 116, 243.
generosity, of Guaire 138, of Cc 425. See poets, alms, almsgiving, hospitality, guests.
———, stimulated by poets 332, essential to holiness 332.
genuflexions 400. See obeisance.
geography, marvellous 87. See science, marvellous lands, adventurous journey.
gestures 363.
ghost, in churchyard 120, returns to warn comrade 217.
giant 212.
gifts 68, 77, 94, 96, 98, 111, 141, 355.
girdle of Mobi as token 77.
glass of purity 25.
glass, vessel broken omen of death 99, 292. See also crystal.
gluttony 418.
goat 297.
goblets, found in barrow 81.
gods of idolatry 87.
gold, made from sweat 80, chest 293, as reward 336, cannot tempt Cc 256, tresses 355f, coffin, believed full of 371.
golden, adj., -tongued 40, chair 123, brooch 317, leaf 355c,f,h; apparel of priests 355g, cowl 355g, h.
golden rule 259, 308.
goldsmith, restored to life 146. See also craftsman, smith.
gospel, on Martin's breast 34, 101, 256. See also missal, writing. Cf. Reeves, p. 324.
gospels, copied 130, 168. See writing.
gossip avoided by Cc 395.
grain, miraculous growth of 79. Cf. Plummer, *V. S. H.*, I, cxxxix. See corn, wheat.
grave 332.
graveyard 120.

graves open 365.
gravel 355a.
green 332, 355a, b, stone 132, blood 403.
grey 201, 355a.
grinding 71. Cf. Plummer, *V. S. H.*, I, xcvii.
groat 85.
ground sinks 340.
grove cut down by Cc 79, 80, spared 89. Cf. Plummer, *V. S. H.*, I, cliii.
guardian angel 426, 427, Axal to Cc 64, 65, 338-9, 426, Victor to Padraic 426. See demon, guardian.
guests, their coming foretold 160, 215, 265, by Pope 218, 222, 230, preparation for 230. Cf. Plummer, *V. S. H.*, I, cxiv.
guest-house ill provisioned 122, prepared by Cc 222. Cf. Plummer, *V. S. H.*, I, cxiii.

hair, pulled from coat by lad 106, fair-haired Adam 332, next skin 390.
hair shirt 402.
haircloth 355b.
hairy pig 182.
haggard 361.
half, year 257, 327; name 34, 53, kingdom 38, northern, of Erin 35.
hall, royal 355g.
halves 337.
handicraft 332. See craftsman, smith, wright.
handmaid 329, cursed 330.
"hand-stone" 112.
hand stretched from tomb 158. See thumb.
harp, comparison with 366.
heads, of cats 355b, of dogs 355d, of swine 355e.
healing. See water; bread, salt, writing, stone submerged in water; well.
———, conditioned upon obedience, 292.
heaven 87, 159, 219, offered poet 336, knowledge of 366, visit to 368.
height altered 340, 341. Cf. Plummer, *V. S. H.*, I, clxxiv.

hell 70, 87, 89, 204, dungeon of 366.
hem of Cc's garment 143.
herbs 349.
heresy in regard to penance 223.
hermit 271, 272, 355b.
hermitage, island, sought 271-3, 276.
high bard 157, 336, 338-9.
hillock, of Angels 229, rises miraculously 341; 361. See mound.
hills 33.
hipbone broken 267.
hogs 275. See swine, pig, pork, salt-pork.
hole, used for spying 168, 314, to let in food 319.
holly-rod, hurled by devil 132.
holy father 105, 310, 363.
holy man 50, 56, 105, 137, 145, 146, 152, 153, 154, 158, 159, 212, 321, 243, 249, 250, 271, 367, 368. See saint.
holy men 155, 197, 205, 218, 223, 225.
Holy Spirit 67-8.
holy woman 113. See woman.
homesickness of Cc for Erin 201, 265, 275, 277, 278, 279, 316.
honey, in water 156, dripping from trees 355d.
honor, to Cc 27, 71, 80, *et passim*.
hood as measure of land 156. See *mantle*.
hooking, fish 398. See fishing.
horse, mane of 355d, brought by monk 289.
horsemen as messengers 292, 338.
horses 336.
hospitality 137, 138, 157, 222, 230, 286, 332, 355b, 409, 425.
host, goes to meet guest 218, fails to meet guest 322.
hostages 345, with Bruide 272, Scannlan 319, son of Tadg mac Toirrdelbaigh 435. *Cf.* Plummer, *V. S. H.*, I, cv.
hound, venomous 111, symbolic of child 141, pursues deer 355.
hounds, venerate Cc's birthplace 42, 44.

hours, chanted by Cc 61, 114, 150, 155, 156, 185, 207, 301, 305.
human sacrifice, man given to propitiate monster 195, man to be put beneath clay to sanctify Iona 205-6. *Cf.* Plummer, I, clxxxvii.
humility of Cc, bails water 281, yields place 282, 410, of Baithin 413.
hundred years 34, 101, cows not more than 286, Conn of the — Battles 43, poor men fed 78, holy folk 84, doors 355g.
hunger. See appetite.
hunting 42, 44, 222. Plummer, *V. S. H.*, I, cix.
hut, location transferred by miracle 73, wattled 319, 345.
hymn composed by Cc 77, 108, 216, 311. See lay.

ice 287.
idolatry 254.
illegibility of books, caused, by curse 221, by water 433.
immortality, on island 355d, 355f, of fame 332.
incense 363.
incest 236.
inclusus (person walled up), Scannlan 319.
indulgence to poets 123, to pilgrims 218.
inheritance 222.
inkhorn upset by zealous pilgrim 211.
interpolations, made by clerics in Cc's hymn 216.
interpreter 259, 290.
interruption, by bell 120, of psalter 362.
intrigue 119.
introductory paragraphs 1, 23, 167, 203, 432.
invasions by Danes 8, by Vikings 371.
invocation, against fires and thunder 77, by Finnen and Irial 225, by woman 267, by Cormac 276, by O'D. 277.
invulnerable, Scannlan 348.
iron, stakes borne by demons 305, molten, thrown at monster 321, chains 346, sharp 403.

iron, blessed by saint incapable of wounding 260. *Cf.* 96 and Plummer, *V. S. H.,* clxxxv.

island, with river of milk 355a; of salmon 355a; of Cat-heads 355b; of Golden Leaf 355c; of Dog-heads 355d; of Swine-heads 355e; of Elijah and Enoch 355f; of Golden Cowl 355g.

island hermitage sought 271-4, 276.

javelin miraculously blunted 210.
jaundice of the color of stubble 75.
jealousy 251. See envy.
jeering 285, 287, at convert 290, at Cc 325, 332.
jewel Cc 36, makes night day 317.
journey of Cc, to Britain 100, around Erin 162, miraculous, through mountain 171, to Dal Riada 197, to Iona 198-204, from Iona to Tours 256-7, to Rome 218, to Druim Ceat 315, 321-3, *et passim.*
judgment, of God 2, of Irish by Padraic on Doomsday 120, by Diarmaid concerning transcript 168, prophesied by Cc 197, of Cc upon sons of Lughaidh 222-3, concerning Dal Riada 344. See arbitrator.
June 429.

keys, of church 72, of monastery 296.
killing the king, native custom 355.
killing, accidental 40, 168, 222.
kings, ill behavior to Cc, Oillil sets hound on 111, King of Erin refuses alms 149, Bruide denies entrance to palace 291, Aed refuses hospitality 322.
kingship, declined 1, prophecies concerning 38, 93, 327, of Erin given to Finnachta 137, awarded to Cairbre 222, to Aedan 243, hereditary 222, Conall cut off from 326, allotted to Donnchad 354, awarded in Iona 361.
kinsman 98, 124, 133-4.
kinsmen 93, 109, 124, 127, 133, 142, 170, 173, 179, 189, 190, 196, 342, 343.
kiss, given by Brenainn to Cc 72, by child 197, of welcome 218, 258, 327, presages kingship 245, of farewell 262.
kisses, refused by Cc 66.
kissing, feet 211, dead body 371.
kitchen 260.
"Kluge Bauernmädchen," analogue 180, 320.
knife, blunted by blessing 260, causes owner's death, 264. *Cf.* Plummer, *V. S. H.* I, clxxxv. See also iron.

labor conditions 280, 355.
labors of Cc 396, 397, 398, 410.
ladder to heaven 368.
lady 284.
lake of fire 355f.
lame to walk 143.
lamp, Cc likened to 25.
lampoon 332. See also satire, poets, jeering.
land, gifts of, "his own place" given Cc by Patrick 28, Derry given Cc by Aed 94, Druim Cliab given Cc by Aed 94, Kells given Cc by Aed 94, Tory given Cc by Oilill 111, Land of the Height given Cc by Aed mac Ainmirech 146, Druim na Macraidhe given Cc by Ailill mac Echach Muigmedoin 154. *Cf.* Plummer, *V. S. H.* ciii.
languages, known by Cc, "Latin and Irish and every tongue" 108, of animals 118, Latin and Irish only 259, no knowledge of Pictish 290, of birds and beasts 366. *Cf.* Plummer, *V. S. H.,* I, cxlv.
largesse, virtue 332.
laugh, leading to disclosure 231.
laws 43, for poets 333.
lay, sung by clerics 355d. See also hymns, poets.
leaf, golden, 355c, 355h, size of ox 355c.
leaping 392.
leather tanned by bark of Cc's oak 434.
lectionaries 409.

leech 332.
legal issues 168, 172, 222. See also laws, compensation, tax.
length of life foretold 232, 261, 267, 269. See death.
lepers 214, 332.
leprosy 214, 434, caused by water 270, of Lismore 435. *Cf.* Plummer, *V. S. H.*, I, cx.
life of Cc, his lineage 21-23; birth 51-52; baptism 53-54; childhood 55-63; youth and studies 63-75; ordination 76; labors in Derry 77-95; death of father 93; labors in Meath 96-99; missionary journeys 99-108; labors in Tirconnell 109-117; miracles, visions, and prophecies 118-133; blessings and curses 133-141; miracles, prophecies, and clairvoyance 141-150; prophecies, foundations, and topographical legends 150-166; the transcript of Finnen's book 168; quarrel with Diarmaid, King of Erin 169-172; battle of Cuil Dremhne 172-178; commanded by angel to go into exile 174; advised by Molaise 180; departs for Iona 181-201; age on going into exile 199; arrival in Iona 202-204; foundations and activities in Iona 204-214; relations with Pope Gregory 215-218; labors in Iona 221-227; prophecies and miracles in Iona 227-249; relations with Mochonda 250-258; miracles and prophecies in Iona 258-271; relations with Cormac 271-278; love of Ireland 278-284; miracles in Iona 284-288; in Pictora 288-296; in Alba 296-304; in Iona 305-8; in divers places 308-315; visit to Ireland to Assembly of Druim Ceat 315-332; relations with bards 332-335; with the poet Dallan Forgaill 336-339; other miracles 340-2; concerning Dal Riada 342-5; relations with Scannlan 345-351; return to Iona 351-3; miracles in Iona 353-356; falsely accused of fleshly sin 353; eats only broth of nettles 356; approaching death 357-364; death 364, 366; quaking of earth 364-5; miracles attendant upon his entrance into heaven 367-70; burial 370, 375; body transported to Dun Da Lethglas 371-5; his character and habits 391-431; miracles after death 432-5.
life, prolonged four years 357. See death, length of life.
light miraculous, Dabheooc sees a great light 37, in face 60, 237, 357, 359, 363; into huts 346, surrounds dead Cc 363, 367. See flames, miracles.
lightning flashes, sign of grace 220, 346.
limit, put on wealth 286.
linen 227, 372.
lineage, of Cc 21-2. See genealogies.
livid 347.
loaves multiplied 84, eaten 347.
locks, loosened 291, 296, for Scannlan 319. *Cf.* St. John xx. 19, 26; also J. B. Bury, *Life of St. Patrick*, p. 108. See bolts.
lord 284.
love of Cc, for Derry 186-192, 279; for dumb creatures of Erin 265; for Erin 266, 275, 279; for kinsmen 189, 277-8, 259, 275, for Irish crane 265, for Kells 279, for Swords 279, for Raphoe 279, for Drumhome 279, for Durrow 279, 280, for Tir Luighdech 279, for companions 357, for Christ 388.
love, Cc's like Christ's 5.
———, from hearsay 113; intrigue 119; purified 224; restored 298.
——— for Cc, God's 27, *et passim*, Cormac's 275, Moconda's 250, Irish 316, companions 357, 363.
lust universal 3, 241.

madness, of Suibhne 354.
magic object. See sword, stone, cowl.
maiden, saved by Cc 70, maidens, three virtues 66.
mantle, Cc's shelter for maiden 70, shelter for vision 87, spreads over

island 111, fastened for flying 219, woven by Brigid 372.
marriage 66, indissoluble 298. See wife.
marsh 330.
martyrdom 7, for seventy-two years 390, white and red 391.
marvellous lands 87, 156, 216, 355-355f. See science, natural history
mass 69, 88, 131, 135, 145, by bishop 148; 215, 228, 310, 395.
matins 313, 345, 347, *et passim*.
meal, miraculously ground 71.
meat 122, 182, 239, 288, 319, 347, 423. See also pork.
melody, sleep inducing 355c.
memory of clerk 337.
memorizing, *Praise of Cc* 336-8, 435.
merchants 237.
messengers 79, 93, 292, 311, 338-9.
metamorphoses 87, 329-330.
metaphors. See similes.
mill (Padraic) 32; 91.
milk, taste of upon lake water 83; because of hound 141, vessel blessed 284, given by ox 285, flowing like river 355a; 423.
miracle, trout revived 57, position of bothies changed 73, ploughing with deer 76, goblets found in barrow 81, sweat of shame becomes gold 80, Fergna learns smith-work 92, bitter apples made sweet 97, drink of forgetfulness 109, cloak magnified 111, hound killed 111, wrought by Handstone 112, pork made acorn, egg, meat 122, levelling of water at Assaroe 133, staff approaches 133, sand yields flour 141, poetic gift withheld 157, vat without bottom holds water 158, earth rises under Cc 159, thorn extracted by water 164, crane plucks out eye 168, Finnen restores it 168, Cc made invisible 170, caldron mended 182, pork becomes fish, fish becomes blood 182, book saved from fire 182, flesh re-covers bones of ox 212, bells ring of themselves 218, falling books signify death 221, gift of prophecy obtained 225, curse changed to blessing 240, poison extracted from drink 251, burial place of Martin revealed 256, broken bone healed 267, wind in opposite directions 283, devils driven from milk pail 284, ox restored, druids confounded 285, number of cows multiplied 286, iron bolts loosed 291, health-giving stone 293, St. German and Cc save ship from druidic storm 295, locks loosened 296, game impaled on stake 297, hatred changed to love 298, chariot 299, to be wrought by Senach 321, monster drifts to Loch Foyle 321, ship sails on land 322, coward becomes brave 328, queen and handmaid changed to marsh-cranes 329-30, ground sinks 340, ground rises 341, fiend departs 353, serpents no longer poisonous 358, following Cc's death 432-5.

——— analogous to scriptural miracles; thumb through womb 50, water turned to wine 69, 81, man struck dead 70, plague stopped 75, 266, seed sown late yields harvest 79, guests fed 83, five thousand fed, nine loaves and fishes 84, water from rock 86, 114, 269, sea yields fish 141, healing 143, 261, 266-9, corpse without decay 158, monster gives up youth 196, bones assume flesh 212, angels sent by Cc 213, lepers healed 214, wine and bread multiplied 215, tidings brought by dead 217, angels solace Cc 229, weather calm amid storm 230, 276, 282, blindness healed 270, changed to pillar of stone 253, sea calmed 281-2, youth raised to life 290, demons banished 305, demons defeated 307, great fish caught 302, bleeding healed 303, prince becomes fool 326, bonds loosened 346, rustic taken to paradise 248, two ricks of corn suffice 360. See also resuscitation.
mirror of purity, Cc 25, 123.

misers of learning, Finnen 168, Longarad 221.
missal 102, 256. See also gospel, writing.
missionary journey, to Britain 100.
mist, raised by druid 294. See cloud.
monastery 27, 40, 73, 208, 296, 303, 314, 359, 361, 363.
Monday 182.
monk, black 1, 78.
——, 100, 124, 127, 161, 208, 210, 220-1, 223, 228, 229, 230, 231, 233, 235, 239, 247, 251, 260, 262, 265-7, 271, 274, 280, 283, 289, 292, 293, 300, 301, 303, 307, 308-9, 311, 313, 314, 353, 357, 358-9, 363, 369, 370, 375, 398, 414, 416, 418-19, 421, *et passim*.
monkhood, exacted by Cc 258.
monster, poisonous 253, cat-heads 355b, dog-heads 355d, swine-heads 355e. See also sea-monsters, beasts.
moon, knowledge 366.
moon worship 335. *Cf.* Plummer, *V. S. H.*, cxxxiii.
moons, seen in vision 48.
mother 45-8, 50-2, 262, 268, 411.
mound 259. See hillock.
mourners, troublesome 375.
murder, unwitting, see killing; treacherous 287.
murderer, punished by Cc 70, 210.
music lulls to sleep 87, angelic 248, 367.
myrrh 363.

nag prophesies death 361. See also horse.
naked, dead in church-yard 120, king 149, lepers 332.
names, various ones for same person 250. See aliases.
napkin, manycolored, seen in vision 46.
natural history, unnatural 216, 233. See also marvellous lands.
natural virtue 259, 308.
nephew 93, 98, 262.
nettle-pottage 356, 400.
nets, miraculous cast 302.

night made day 311, by jewel 317.
nine, hostages 21, 31, 38, 44, 35, 173, nine and fourscore generations 21, days 40, persons 77, loaves 84, hierarchies of heaven 120, men 157, waves 184, loaves 347.
nobility of birth, danger to chastity 386.
nobleman, young 138.
none 182, 220, *et passim*.
nose-bleeding healed 303.
number, countless, of angels 305. See three, four, five, six, etc.
nuns, black 62, 298.
nuts 24.

oak 275, 434.
oaken, planks 201.
obedience 247, 271, 275, 289, 292.
obeisance, of beasts 134; 400. See also genuflexions.
ocean 201. See sea.
oriental personages, children of King of India 113, abbot of Jerusalem 155.
ordination, of Cc as priest 76, 78.
orisons 114, 120, 246, 247, 281. See also prayers.
ox, slaughtered 260, leaf, size of 355c, gives milk 285, eaten by one man, resuscitated by Cc 212. *Cf.* Plummer, *V. S. H.*, I, cxliii.

pact with devil 435.
pagans come to Cc by sea, children of King of India 113, old man 259; of land 308.
palisades 355.
parables of Cc, bees in glove 105, strong pets swallow weaker 118, return by different route 419-20, *et passim*.
paradise, earthly 355f.
paralysis, caused by water 270.
paternity denied 353.
patriarch 1, 69, 421, *et passim*.
patron 218.
peace, between Erin and Alba 342.
peace-making by Cc. See arbitrator.

peculiar sanctity of Cc 238.
peg, axle 299.
penance, necessary for salvation 94, slight but sufficient 223, of twelve years 236, for disobedience 271, wins heaven 314.
penny 85.
Pentecost 204, 358.
persecution, of church 389.
perils on sea. See sea.
personal remarks of O'D. 8-14, 20, 365-8, 376, *et passim*.
petrifaction, fish transformed to stone 115, beast to stone 253.
pets, of Cc 118, of poor man 297.
philosopher, natural 386.
physical signs of emotions, shame 80.
piebald horseman brings tidings of death 338-9.
piety 225, 390, 395.
pig, hairy 182; 288.
pilgrim, awkward 211, two become monks 258.
pilgrimage, to Cc's first walk 56, to Rome 140, 255, to Glais an Indluidh 186, to Alba 190, Pope allows Cc to choose place 218, on the sea 271, 273, to Field of the Coracle 322, to island of Dog-head's 355d. *Cf.* Plummer, *V. S. H.*, cxxii-iii.
pillar of fire over Cc 72, 102, 310, 369.
——— of stone, transformed beast 253.
pillow, of stone 112, 362.
pipe in stirring stick 356.
plague, yellow jaundice 75, caused by rain 266, by demons 305.
plain, bestowed in thought 107.
poesy, value of 332, poison in 333.
poets, threaten to satirize Cc 80, 81; 147, 157, threatened with banishment 316, 317, 332, retained in Erin 333, conditions on which tolerated 333-4, treated with generosity 408 *Cf.* Plummer, *V. S. H.*, I, cii ff.
poison, made harmless 251, well made healing 270, poetry 333, serpents 358.
ploughing 76, 92.

plunder 287, 373.
pope 88, 157, 215-20. *Cf.* Plummer, *V. S. H.*, cxxiii.
poor, fed by Cc to the number of a hundred 78, given money 85, given costs of pilgrimage 140, erstwhile robber fed 239, relieved by stake 297, cows multiplied 286, no alms without 332, fed 398, served by Cc 422.
pork 122, 182, causes death 288. See swine, salt pork, hog.
portion, enormous 212, 347.
possession, by cloak 111, by hurling rod 132, by hood 156.
pottage 356, 400.
postponement of death 356, 358. See also death.
praise, of Erin 183-6, 191, 275, 278, 279, of Cc by poets 333, by Dallan Forgaill 334, 336, 364.
prayer, of O'Donnell 15, 20, 277, of Cc 81, 82, 87; 150, 155, 196, 274 281, 298, 300, 301, 305, 352, 400, to Cc must be prefaced by prayer to Odhran 206-7, of Cainnech in church 282, of Cc quoted 290, Baithin at meals 413.
———, position during. See cross vigil.
preaching 154, 290, 291, 395.
precocity, of Cc, recites psalm 61, 62.
———, of Mochonda 250.
prenatal miracle 50, 159. *Cf.* Plummer, clxxxvii n.
prerogative, of Odhran 205-6.
presence of sinner disastrous 271.
preservation. See decay.
prevision. See clairvoyance.
pride attracts demons 334, punished 335; 431, *et passim*.
priest 145, 335.
priesthood, order of 78. See ordination.
priests 198, 323.
procession on Doomsday 120.
prophecy concerning Cc's birth
Mochta prays with face to north 24, Padraic honors Cc's grandfather 25, of land of Cc's birth 26, Padraic un-

willing to forestall Cc's blessing 27, 31, Padraic's bequests to Cc 28, Padraic makes water shallow and full of fish 29, 30, in vision of Padraic 33, by Brigid 35. by Dabheooc 37, by Caillin 38, by Brendan 39, by Eoghan of Ard Sratha who makes peace with Lugaid 40, by Buide mac Bronaigh 41, by Finn mac Cumaill when Bran spares the deer 42, by Fedlimid Rechtmar, who is promised issue 43, by druids when hounds of Conall Gulban spare deer 44. See *visions* to 48.

―――― concerning Cc church of 30, gospel in Martin's tomb 34, 101, Brigid promises blossoming sapling 35, Padraic promises Cc shall be in same tomb 36, Dabheooc promises light from the north 37, Cc's power 42, fosterer promises career from alphabet 59, as to the time of taking holy orders 75, death 357.

―――― made by Cc concerning young man 70, his priesthood 76, beast Rochuaidh 78, palace not completed 90, kings of Erin and Alba 93, Clan Conall 94, Domnall 95, Kells 98, Aed Slaine 98; from wave 104, of lad Iarnân 106, birth of Daluch 116, bloody well 117, Erin freed from foreign yoke 118, day of doom 120, resurrection of Mochuda 121, length of life 124, 125, ruin of Tara, Cruachan, Aillend, and Emain 126, misfortunes and sins of Erin 127, Domnall and tribe of Conall 128, false prophecies of druid Bec mac De 129, churches named for Ciaran 130, stream 132. in reward of hospitality 137, coming of Nâail 141, bloody water 142, death of poet 147, island withheld from Cc 156, coming of guests foretold by Fintan 160, greatness of Munda 161, Erin 181, lad 197, kings to be buried in Iona 207, inkhorn to be upset by pilgrim 211, coming of guests 215, sacrament promised before death 219, coming of guests 222, of Colman 231, age of sons 232, monsters of sea 233-4, arrival of sinner 235-6, penance 236, flame in Italy 237, duel in Erin and coming to Iona 238, death of robber 239, Aedan and heir 243-5, sinner 246, death of Cailtean 247, death of Bishop Aed 248, confessor of Colman Eala 249, attempted poisoning 251, river shaped like staff 252-3, death of two noblemen 258, heathen to be baptized 259, Diarmaid's recovery from illness 261, never to see kinsman in life 262, manner of death 264, coming of Irish crane 265, child 269, failure and death 271, Cormac's coming to Orca 272, Cormac's return 273, 274, Adamnan 275, body to be devoured by wolves 276, feud between Kinel-Connell and Kinel-Owen 267, Cainnech will calm sea 282, death of Colman 283, number of cows 286, death of robber 287, treacherous friend will not live to eat swine 288, death of Brocan 292, poor man will lose stake through wife's counsel 297, plague in Etica 305, Berchan's wickedness 314, help from Senach 321, Domnall, son of Aed 327, death 338, Colman 343, Scannlan 345, 348, 353, 354, Cc's death 357, church 361, three in one tomb 372, 373. Dun da Lethglas 373; 381-4. *Cf.* Plummer, *V. S. H.,* I, clxiii, clxx.

――――, concerning others, by Caillin 38, by druid 98, by Cairnech 158, by Finnen 225, by Eoghan of Moconda's birth and third name 250, 255, by Moconda of own death 257.

―――― Cc given power of 65.

―――― See also clairvoyance.*

―――――

*Prophecy and clairvoyance are not clearly differentiated.

propitiatory sacrifice 195, 205-6. See human sacrifice.
prying into divine secrets 229. See secrecy.
psalter, Cc's 168, 178, interrupted 362. See *cathach*, battler.
psalm, priest breaks down in 61.
psalms, sung in heaven 219, recited 390, 401.
pupils, seven in each eye 340.
pun 336.
purple 355a.

quatrains. See Index of first lines of quatrains.
queen 330.
quern 71.

radiance of face. See light, angelic radiance.
rain 266.
raven 297.
reading 238.
reapers, 212, 219.
rebuked, Cc 334.
recording of visions 311. See writing.
red, stone 52, ears of cow 87, fish 132, dark-red sea 279, color 332.
refectory 251, 370.
regicide, ritual 355, 355f.
relics, of Buide, enshrined by Cc 99.
———, Angel's Gospel 28, 166, Gospel of Martin 34, 101, 256, clay in Gartan 51 (*Cf.* Reeves, lxviii), Red Stone in Gartan 52 (*Cf.* Reeves, 281, 330), flagstone of birth 52, of baptism 54 (*Cf.* Reeves lxviii), flagstone of chastity in Gartan 58, Hand-stone, pillow of Cc 112, Shrine of Columcille 146, bell of the testament, goblet 166; Cc's psalter 178, great cross at Tory 215, Pope Gregory's brooch 219, finger tip of Cc 276, golden leaf at Iona 355c, golden cowl in Cill mic Nenain 355g, h. *Cf.* Plummer, *V. S. H.*, cxxvii; Reeves, 318-330 (thirty relics mentioned).

rent 343.
repentance, more valued than sinlessness 182, relation to penance 223, false 236, true 246, of Cc 335.
resurrection, place of 271. See death foretold.
resuscitation of persons, fosterer 62, fosterling 82, drowned wright 91, daughter of Aed 94, youth on sod of death 110, children of King of India 113, of Connla's bones 146, of Fergus 157, youth swallowed by monster 196, man killed by serpent 209, Brandubh 219, convert's son 290, bones of Brecan 352.
——— of animals, trout 57, ox 212. *Cf.* Plummer, *V. S. H.*, I, cxliii.
reward for repeating the *Altus Prosator* 217, for poems 333, 337, proportional to struggle 386.
ribs 404.
rich man, treacherous 288.
riches, gained by stake 297, danger to chastity 386.
ricks of corn 360.
right hand, to Fergus 25.
righthandwise 315. See also sunwise.
ring, bishops' 252.
ripening of grain, miraculous 79.
river, (Boyle) blessed by Padraic 29; *et passim*.
robber 287, Cc's kindness to 239. *Cf.* Plummer, *V. S. H.*, I, cii, civ.
Rochuaidh 78, 366.
rocks, abased at Assaroe 134, floating 51, split 365.
roof, falling from 309.
rudder 366.
rudderless voyage 355a.
ruse, of Padraic to save the Irish 120, of Cc to prevent sinner's gaining heaven. See *kluge Bauernmädchen*.
rushes 349.
rustic 248.

sacrifice, human 195, 205, 206. See human sacrifice.

sacrament 129, 148, 355g.
sacristan 220, 363.
safeguard 168, *et passim*.
saffron 403.
saint, king becomes 82; 299, 332.
saints 27, 42, 45, 49, 71, 123, 127, 131-2, 141, 151, 155, 185-7, 274, of Erin 157, 161, 180, 186, 340. See holy men.
salmon 115, 355a.
salt, healing 268. *Cf.* Plummer, I, cxxxviii.
salt meat, sole diet 319.
salt-pork made acorn 122.
sanctuary, maiden seeks Cc 70; 128.
—— violated 219, 355.
sand, made flour 141, mixed with bread 400.
sandal, alternately on one and another foot 87; 347. See shoes, boots.
sapling, blossoming (Cc.) 35.
satchel of books 433.
satire of poets, avoided 80, raises blisters 332-3, feared 407.
Saturday 182, 232, formerly day of rest 360.
scourging, by angel in vision 243, by Cc of self 395.
scholar, intrigue of 119, dead 221.
schooling 68, 73, 87, 161, 366. *Cf.* Plummer, *V. S. H.*, I, cxv. See studies, teacher.
science 216, 233, 366. See skill.
Scriptures, studied by Cc 68-9, 70-1, knowledge of 197, mysteries revealed 311; 428.
scruple, tax of 40, 349.
sea 192-5, 280-1, 295, 297, 344, 355-6, 371. See ocean.
sea-monster 78, 193, 233, 234, 274; devours traitor, spares monk 289, threatens Cc's boat 321. See also monsters.
seagulls 192.
seaweed 398.
seals, preserve for 239.
second sight. See clairvoyance. *Cf.* Plummer, *V. S. H.*, clxx-clxxii.

secrets revealed 144-5, divine 311. See also clairvoyance.
secrecy, of Cc regarding miraculous manifestations 229, 312, virtues 395; of Baithin 413.
—— enjoined 229, 238, 312.
see, episcopal 255, 256.
sentence, laid upon Cc 180. See also arbitrator, judgment.
separation of husband and wife 298.
serfdom 292.
serpent, attacks man 209, no longer poisonous 358. See poison.
servants 222, of God 126, of Cc 132, 355g.
seven, battalions 38, temple of 113, at death of father 116, bishops 120, years before Doomsday 120, times bathed 214, and twenty 240 years, in fosterage 250, twice 258, 274, -fold 278, pupils 340, and two score 240.
seventh, day of December 52.
seventy, 98, 323.
sex, opposite avoided 66, 113, 411 (*Cf.* Plummer, *V. S. H.*, cxxi), sins of 224, 241, 314.
shaving a corpse 158.
shears, temptation to vainglory 242.
ship 29, sinks 105, sails on land 322, *Cf.* Plummer, *V. S. H.*, cxlvii; 186-7, 231, robber's 287, with tribute 343, crooked 373.
shirts, dead naked save 120, 402.
shirt, as gift 213, made by Brigid 372.
shoes, one off, one on 282, brought to Cc 345. See also sandals, boots.
short man wants to become tall 341. *Cf.* Plummer, *V. S. H.*, I, clxxxiv.
shout, signal of arrival 211, 238, 258.
shrewdness of Cc 385.
shrine, made for Padraic and Cc 146, of Cc's psalter 178.
sickness, cured by Cc 143, 261, prevented by miracle 181, of Cc's uncle 262, of Irish 266, impossible to heal by stone 293. See disease.

INDEX RERUM

sign, of cross 86, 91, 94, 111, 209, 269, 284, 296, of death 338.
silence, enjoined 229, 238, 312, not vowed by Cc 399. See also secrecy.
silver 123, 425, as reward 335, -winged birds 355c, border encompassing weir 355a, coffin believed full of 371.
similes, coals 5, flame 24, lamp 25, 37, sieve 32, water 32, mill 32, flour 32, 51, wheat 32, light 33, 168, 251, 340, 363, sparks 33, tree 35, sage 35, jewel 36, gold 40, 275, diadem 40, moon 48, flour 51, dove 53, milk 83, wine 83, bees 105, chairs 123, leaves 183, soul parting 190, mountain 193, 233, roots 205, swiftness 257, storm 275, blood 285, sun 311, crane 329, calf 355a, silver 48, 355c, hide 355c, showers 361, sun 363, spices 363, harp, ship, body 366, Adze-head 373.
similitude. See parables.
sin, of one visited upon many 105, secret 144-5, 271, of Cc 334, prevents memorizing 337, none done by Cc 72, 426.
six, 79, 113, 137, 266, 347.
sixty 166, hundreds 171.
skill, Cc's and Mongan's 87. See also science.
skull speaks 131.
sleep 87, long 347; 402, melody induces 355c.
sloe 275, 355d.
smile, leading to disclosure 231.
smoke of repentance disperses demons 335.
smith, raised from dead 146, melts knife 260, borne to heaven 306, every 332, kills sea monster 321. *Cf. Rev. Celt.,* X, p. 53. See goldsmith, wright.
smith-craft learned by miracle 92. *Cf.* Plummer, *V. S. H.,* I, clxxxv.
snow 287.
sod, of death, birth, burying 110, of Alba 320, thrown at Cc 324.
soles stuck to ground 156. *Cf.* Plummer *V. S. H.,* clxviii.

solitude for prayer 87, 237, 305, 367, 395.
son 39, 54, 93, 95, 141, 168, 222, 245, 290, 313, 353, 355f.
soul, delivered from torment 131, parted from body is parting from Erin 190, tormented by demons 219, of dead helped 226, demons struggle for 300, borne to heaven 300, 304, 306-8, dropped by demons, departs for heaven 367-370, of Cc returns to earth 435.
sorrow, forgotten 109, at departure of Cc 189, 191-2, of Cc for kinsman 275.
soul-friend. See confessor.
sparks, belched forth by monster 253. See flame.
spear 222.
spear-thrust 70.
speckled 355a.
speech. See language.
spewing of sea beasts interpreted by Cc 78. See *Rochuaidh.*
spices 363.
spirits, evil 119, 132, 226, 285.
spittle of blood 355.
spy loses eye 168, condemned 313-4.
staff, cast to claim ownership becomes spear 111, ground struck with 128, 259, man with 187, summoned by Cc 133, forgotten 213, bishop's 252, river shaped like 252-3, permits miraculous journey 348. *Cf.* Plummer, *V. S. H.,* clxxv. See also club, stake.
stag. See deer.
stake, miraculous, to impale game 297. *Cf.* Plummer, *V. S. H.,* I, clxxv. See also staff, club.
stakes of iron borne by demons 305.
stammering 347.
standing, in sign of reverence 216, 327, 331, in water to chin 229, 401.
"*Starker Hans*" 212.
stars, properties of 366.
starvation 297.
stature, altered 340, 341.

sterility, miraculously induced by flagstone 58.
sting, taken from poetry 333, of bee 105.
stipulation, healing if bondmaid freed 292, welcome accepted if boon granted 331. See also *Altus, Amra,* human sacrifice, monster, *et passim.*
stone station 115, 207.
stone, red, wonder-working 52, as pillow 112, 362, 390, giving forth water 114, 135, with magic powers 132, large 155, as pier 186, healthgiving, on surface of water 292-5, sinks 340, sleeping place of Cc 362. See flagstone, Hand-stone, relic. *Cf.* Plummer, *V. S. H.,* clv.
stoning of Cc 324.
storm, calmed for Cainnech 230, for Colman 231, for Cc 274, 295, 281, on land 280, by prayer of Cainnech 282, destroys robber's boat 287, raised by druid 294, calmed for German 295, prevents pilgrimage to dead Cc 375. See wind, waves, sea.
strand 404.
struggle with demons 149, 219, 220, 226, 300, 305, 307, 415. See also demons.
study of the Scriptures. See Scriptures.
stuttering 347.
submerging of Erin before Doomsday 120.
subtilty of angels 359.
summaries 49, 159 (Thursday), 317-19, 350, 376, 393, 394-411, 413-28.
summer, departure delayed until death-day of Cc 358, 429.
sun, worship 335, 355g (*Cf.* Plummer, *V. S. H.,* cxxxvi), mentioned in oath 348, properties of 366. See also sunwise.
sunwise 178, 186, 348. *Cf.* Plummer, *V. S. H.,* cxxxv. See also righthandwise.

superiority of Cc 393.
superstitions. See magic, human sacrifice, sword, cowl, *cathach,* flame, womb, wave, monsters, Doomsday, water; reciting *Altus, Amra.*
surety 319, 435.
Sunday 145, 182, 249, 258, 310, 327, now day of rest 360; 400.
sweat, turns to gold 80; 396.
swimming 149, 289.
swine 288. See hog, pork.
swine-heads 355e.
swineherd 157.
swoon 285.
sword blessed by Cc, owner may not die 96. *Cf.* Plummer, *V. S. H.,* I, clxxxvi.

tales mentioned, *Departing of the Importunate Company, Cattle Raid of Cualnge, Voyage of Columcille's Clerics.*
tall saint, wants to become short 340. *Cf.* Plummer, *V. S. H.,* I, clxxxiv.
tanning, shoes 434.
taxes, nuts to be put by for Cc 24, annual tax paid by Padraic's successor in Armagh to Cc 27, triennial, by Lugaid to Eoghan 40, annual, by Maelcabha to successors of Cc 82, tithes by Sedna and Loarn to Cc 93, on Cc's feast day, fishing of Assaroe to his successors 134, adjudged at Druim Ceat 343, triennial, by Scannlan to Cc 349.
tanistry 222.
teacher of Cc 68-76, 100. See tutor.
tears, shed by Cc 189, 357, induced by prayer 400, *et passim.*
ten, years 82, hundred angels 185.
tenth, generation 42, degree 131, hour 274.
tent 182.
tenuousness of angels 359.
test, of truthfulness 241, of humility 242.

thirst 319.
thorns extracted 164.
thought as good as deed 107.
three, men in a vision 43, daughters 62, wives 66, maidens 66, sisters 66, sods 110, streams 114, pets 118, chairs 123, causes 124, strokes of staff 128, things 139, gifts of God 150, fifties 157, score 166, 171, women 197, chapters 216, *Altus* three times a day 218, holy men 218, thousand 237, commands 243, slain 244, oldest sons 245, names of Macarius 255, years 257, days and nights 265, 355a, 355b, 355c, 355d, 370, things left 279, reasons 316, causes 319, spaces 348, hundred 394, parts 396. See multiples of three (9, 12, 30).
third, a scruple every third year 40, generation 44, reason 53, book 72, day 78, man 138, heaven 238, night 243, day after 265, day 294, years 349, of bread 400.
thirty, years 41, 327, kine, cloaks, and cattle 82, masses 131, deacons 198, years 348, 357. See three.
thrice 82, four kings 315, fifty 87, 157, 390, 401. See fifty.
thumb thrust through mother's womb 50, 159, acquired as relic 146; *See* finger. Cf. Delahaye, *Legends of the Saints*, 52.
Thursday 43, 50, 53, 124, 366, summary of 158-9.
tide, properties of 366, bears body 374.
tierce 355c.
tithes 93. See taxes.
token of death 338, 339.
tomb, of Martin 34, of Cc at Downpatrick 34, 370-5, of the children of India's King 113, of abbot of Jerusalem 155, of Cianan 158, of Cc 337, of Cc in Iona 362, of Padraic, Brigid, and Cc 371-5.
tongs 321.
tongue 40. See language.

tonsure 275.
topographical legends, Ath an Carbaid ar Dail 26, Ess mac n-Eirc 30, Belach Damhain 42, Elend Colaim Cilli 42, flagstone of birth 52, of baptism 54, of chastity 58, Cedimtecht Colaim Cilli 55, Termonn Cille mic Nenain 93, Lind Ingine Aeda 94, Belach an Adhraidh 111, An Glacach 112, Port an Moirsheser 113, Tempul an Moirshesir 113, Ess Finan 114, Tobar Eithne 117, Tobair na Conalluch 128, Ath na Hordoige 146, Port an Moirsheser, Port of the Seven, west end of Tory 113, Tempul an Moirshesir, Temple of the Seven, in Tory 113; Ess Finan, Waterfall of Fianan, in Tory 114, cairn of petrified fish 115, Tobar Eithne, Well of Ethne, in Doire Eithne 117, Tobair na Conalluch, Well of the Conalls in Termon Cumainig, in Tir Eogain 128, Ath na Hordoige, Ford of the Thumb, in Ath Lunga 146, Gort an Cochaill 156, Druim na Lebur 163, Well of Columcille 163, Tobur an Deilg 164, Tobur na Duibhe 165, Glais an Indluidh 186, Reilec Odhrain 206, Cnocan na n-Aingel 229, mound of old man's baptism 259, high cross over grave in Iona 262, Cabhan an Curuig, Field of the Coracle 322, cranes at ford in Druim Ceat 330, hillock that rose under Cainnech 341, Port an Curaigh 355h, Lec an Cochaill 355h.
track, of child on flagstone 52, of cow in stones 165, of ribs in sand 404.
transcribing of books 168, 211, 251. See writing, books.
transference of task of working miracle 321.
transitoriness of all save poesy 332.
treachery punished 287-289.
tree, refuge of clay 51, man in 354, girdled with silver, gold leaves 355c,

dripping honey 355d. See grove, apples.
treasures, of Padraic 166, of Cc 215, alluding to Cc 359, of world 425.
tresses 355f.
tribal poets 333.
tribute 82, 343-4, 348-9.
Trinity 216.
trout, restored to life by Cc 57.
truthfulness 399.
tub. See vat.
tuning-gear 366.
tutor of Bruidhe 292. See also teacher, fosterer.
twelve, and a score years 13, kings 38, men 41, 182, apostles 41, monks 100, lepers 214, companions of Moconda 252, thrice four 315, fastenings 319, chains 346, years 367, genuflexions 400.
twelfth, generation 43.
twenty, hundreds 87, bishops 198, 323, and four paces 262, days 433.

ulcer, miraculous, destroys beauty 340.
uncle, maternal 262. See nephew.

vainglory 242, 304-5, 312, 335, 395, 408, 418.
vat without bottom 158.
vehicles, chariot of Padraic 26.
vengeance of God, feared 169, 235, by wolves 276.
venom taken from poetry 333, taken from serpents 358.
verses made by Cc *passim*, in secret 311.
vespers 362.
vessel, lacking 81, of glass 99, 292, for milk 284.
vestments 69.
vigil 402. See cross-vigil.
vikings, carry off coffin 371.
vindictiveness of Cc, toward Ara 156, Erin for exile 181, man with forked stick 187, Niall's clan 191, Cormac 278, Scannlan for delay 347; of Padraic toward Cairbre 31.
virgin, dies in hour of conversion 113. *Cf.* other examples, J. P. Bury, *St. Patrick,* pp. 141, 307.
virginity 64, 65, 67, 113, 241, 353, 386-7, 411. See chastity.
virtue, 5, 66, of Moconda 257, tree of 355c, attained through suffering 386.
———, natural 259, 308.
visions, Faith rekindled by Cc 33, light of north 37, many-colored cloak 45, napkin 46, birds with vitals of Ethne 47 (*Cf.* Plummer, clviii), two moons 48, birth of Cc 51, Virginity, Prophecy, and Wisdom 66, heaven and hell 87, Gregory saying mass 88, chairs of crystal, etc. 123, whelp 141, end of world 151, treasures of Padraic 166, angels depart during interpolations 216, two souls 226-7, confessor 249, angels and demons 300, angels bear soul to heaven 304, 306-8, monk falling from housetop 309, Brennan sees cloud of fire 310, revealed to Baithin by Cc 311, Iona filled with light 367, soul of Cc going to heaven 368, fisherman sees pillar of light 369. See clairvoyance, prophecy.
visit of Cc to heaven 158-9, to Rome 218; of Maedog to heaven 368. See "free visiting".
vitals borne by birds 47.
voice of Cc heard a mile off 62. *Cf.* Plummer, *V. S. H.,* I, clxxii.
volcanic eruption 237.
voyage, of Cc in search of hermitage 271-4, to Druim Ceat described 321-3, of Cc's clerics 355, delayed till summer 355a, *et passim.* See exile, journey.
vow, of exile 180, 250, breaking of 217, of sinner 236, fulfilled 320, to eat nettle broth only 356.

wake 239, of Cc 367-75. *Cf.* Plummer,

V. S. H. I, cix.
walking, Cc learns 55-6, 159.
warden casts away miraculous flagstone 54.
Wars of the Gaidhil with the Gaill 8.
water, made shallow 29, 30, turned to wine 69, 81, 83, 380, to milk 83, forgetfulness of sorrow 109, struck from rock 114, 135, from ground 128, tastes of honey 156, to chin 229, 309, 401, bread in, heals of plague 266, writing in, heals of plague 267, salt in, heals of blindness 268, miraculously furnished 269, bilge 281, restores ox 285, stone in, heals of sickness 292, hot and cold 355f, does not harm belongings of Cc 433. *Cf.* Plummer, *V. S. H.*, cxxxviii.
———, holy 51, 143.
water-clerk 337.
wattles, hut of 319, 345.
wave, prophecy from 104. *Cf. Lis. Lives,* cx. See storms, sea.
weather, properties of 366.
weaving, of mantle by Bridget 372, 396.
weakness caused by angelic radiance 312.
wedlock 66, 298.
weeping of Derry folk 191. See tears.
weir full of giant salmon 355a.
well, vision seen at 42, from rock for baptism 86, 269, becomes bloody, prophesying death 117, from ground 128, from rock 133, struck by Cc 163-6, heals lepers 214, poisonous becomes healing 270. *Cf.* Plummer, *V. S. H.*, cxlix.

werewolves 182.
wheat 355b, people like 32.
white 87, 355a, b, 373.
wife 119, 141, 226, 263, 287, 296, 298. See woman.
wind, power over 281, 283, 294-5, 355g, mentioned in oath 348. See storms.
window 368.
wine, water changed to 69, 81, 83, increased 215; 355b, from rocks 380, of revelry 392, 423. *Cf.* Plummer, *V. S. H.,* ci.
winter, birthday of Cc 429.
wisp to mend cauldron 182.
wolves, clerics become 182, destroy Cormac 276.
woman, rises from grave 113, tempts religious man 223, used to tempt Cc 224, 241, soul of 226, healed 267, ruins husband 297, hates husband 298, really she-devil 353, deceitful 385, regarded as temptation 411.
womb 23, 50, 159, 353.
wood, cut for Cc 79-80, casket of 267, stake cut from 297, shall not cut 348.
wren, pet of Cc 118.
wright 74, 91, 332. See smith.
writing 211, 219, 221, 251, healing by means of 267, psalter completed by Baithin 362, 396, uninjured by water 394, miraculously preserved in water 433. See transcribing.

yew-tree 185.
youth, saved from death by Cc 116, eternal 355d, danger to chastity 386.

INDEX OF FIRST LINES OF QUATRAINS

Numbers refer to pages

A Baithin anum coleic, 158.
A chubhus con, 196.
A Colaim Cille ced cland, 372.
A Colaim Cille romcar, 372.
A fir teid a n-Erind síar, 290.
A henailt as ben Aedh[a], 348.
A huisce sáer so-mhilis, 388.
A muindtir Choluim Cille, 394.
A ordan a n-Í gan caire, 422.
A sirghnais a sir-aitreb, 388.
Act gidh ecail lem, gan fhell, 84.
Ag cantain an buan molta, 392.
Áille a mberrtha, buidhe a fuilt, 282.
Aitreb niamdha naem ainglidhe, 398.
Alaind do blath fo barr scoth, 386.
Am aenurán damh 'sa sliab, 180.
Am eoluch for talmain teind, 416.
An lec do bi fam cossaiph, 362.
An uair bui a Carraic Eolairc, 74.
Andess om tir trebnach tend, 372.
Annsin adubrad on cill, 40.
Aodh fo a cethair fó tri, 340.
Ar amus bur tigerna, 392.
Ar faesamh an Coimdhegh cain, 374.
As aibhind sin 's as aibind, 294.
As tíar ata Brenaid bind, 282.
Asse sin iub[h]ar na naemh, 190.
Atbath Lon, 218.

Ba maith da coindimh ré ré, 448.
Bachlach isan purt, 202.
Baithin mac Brenaind don roind, 444.
Batar bliadhain a Clochur, 340.
Beiridh lib an duillend sa, 390.
Bendacht fort, a inis glan, 386.
Benaidh bur cluic ar Conall, 346.
Benfad a nemh don dan, 354.
Ber mo bachall lat ad laimh, 372.
Bíad a n-enuaidh 'sa tailgend, 424.
Bid sai acus bid craibtech, 12.

Breth leabair C. c., 140.

Caeca ech co n-alluib oir, 376.
Caeca naemh am Colum and, 340.
Carais Colum caidh Cilli, 438.
Cath Cula Dremne na ndrend, 184.
Ceathracha sagart a lín, 198.
Ceo ni cuirm, ceo ní sercoll, 448.
Ceithri ri fo trí trena, 340.
Cinel Conaill comhromhaigh, 290.
Coland gan cend ind da éis, 416.
Colman mac Comghaill gan cleith, 368.
Colam cilli, a ainm do nimh, 40.
Colum Cille ar maighistir, 438.
Colum Cille ar nach rab buaidhirt, 436.
Colum Cille ar tigerna, 394.
Cora alainn aircid ghil, 388.
Cormac cain buich neoid, 350.
Cred fa m-bíadh galar no greim, 44.
Crimthand ua Cuind, comhall ngle, 450.
Cris Mobi, 66.

Da ced comla caem doruis, 398.
Da madh deoin le righ nimhe, 386.
Dá madh uile Alba uile, 294.
Da tolltaí a cli gorm glas, 440.
Daghar leam gan a n-aithne, 284.
Dallan mac Colla mic Erc, 362.
Dardaein cedlabhra Colaim, 36.
Dardain baisded Colum caimh, 168.
Dardaín breith Coluim Cille, 168.
Dardaín cedimthecht Coluim, 168.
Dardaín cedlabra Coluim, 168.
Dardaín do cuaid isan cnoc, 170.
Dardain doradadh an cath, 170.
Dardain, nochar caingen cle, 168.
Dardain nochar chaingen cle, 40.
Dena, a Guairi, maith imni, 138.
Denaidh ainmne as foisdine, 384.
Díadardaín tainic gan meirg, 168.

INDEX OF FIRST LINES OF QUATRAINS 513

Do badh mían ler n-aicned-ne, 392.
Do bi an sagart, as derb de, 356.
Do cend na breice as buaine, 354.
Do cendaigh Dia fen go fír, 352.
Do fhacbus ag cloind Conaill, 286.
Do fhás utar ar mo taobh, 364.
Do Gaidhealuib mé fene, 292.
Do iarrus itche oile, 364.
Do raid Colaim re cloisdin, 364.
Do raidh an Colaim go becht, 362.
Do raidset tre oilemhain, 400.
Do riar om tuathuib om tigh, 376.
Do saeradh Scandlan, maith mor, 374.
Do saertha de na filedha, 354.
Dochím hÍ, 200.
Dogén eolchuire truagbind, 292.
Dolotar for a laim deis, 338.
Domnall dorinde oirne maith, 136.
Dorad Patruic, daingen fir, 14.

Easbaidh Coluim ar cloind Quind, 414.
Eídedh fa lor loghmaire, 398.
Eirigh a Baithin uaim síar, 290.

Fa genmnaich Colum Cille, 442.
Fagbuidh duínd Doire dairgech, 194.
Failenda Locha Febhail, 194.
Feithig, a C[h]rist, an muir mall, 220.
Feol no inmar blasda ar bith, 448.
Ferr d'fheruib an fer rosfuair, 450.
Findachta go condailbe, 138.
Fir 7 mna ac sírguidhe, 400.
Fir Erend nach dual d'athól, 290.
Fod goirid bia-sa ima alle, 372.
Foirend curaich, cumain lem, 390.
Frithail uaim na hassu-sa, 370.
Fuil suil nglais, 198.

Ga drem rind ba seimhidhe, 400.
Ga drem rind fa braithremla, 400.
Gach saer, gach gaba, gach cerd, 354.
Gaeth a clerigh, bind a heoín, 282.
Gaidhel Gaidhel, inmain ainm, 282.
Ge adeirthai ris beith gan cair, 442.
Ge andluicter mesi a nÍ, 424.
Gé maith adeir tussa sin, 192.

Ge tainic Colum Cille cain, 344.
Ge tshire an doman uile, 286.
Gébaidh a clerche, ní ceilim-se, 384.
Gebtar uada fa dodhec, 22.
Géin mairfes an diaghacht glan, 352.
Geinfid macam dia fine, 12.
Gid andlaicter misi a nI, 424.
Glass, fuar, errach oighreta, 384.
Gle noloighed is an gainemh, 440.
Guairi mac Colmain aníar, 140.
Guidem Padraig naemh, 398.
Guidhem Colam caidh, 398.
Guidhium Petar [7] Pol, 398.
Guidhium rí na righ, 396.

hI con ilur a martra, 424.

Imdha tiar toradh abhla, 284.
In blalín-se delbhaim-se, 422.
IN gnimh-sin doronsatar, 112.
Inis roglan rancamar, 388.
Inmain fidh, 194.
Inmain oirect bias gan ord, 284.
Inmhain Druim Cliab mo croidhe, 292.
Inmhain Durmagh as Doire, 292.
Innes duind a senoír sin, 388.
Intan do cuaidh for nemh nar, 360.
INte timcellus gan chair, 44.
Is againn ata in gach tan, 394.
Is amluidh roindim-se sin, 292.
Is anba luas mo curaidh, 194.
IS é Dia rodelbhusdair, 74.
Is imdha abhus laech leabhair, 284.
Is inmain lem-sa mo lec, 442.
Is inmain lium-sa an t-iubar, 190.
Is marb Lon, 218.
Is mesi Colum Cille, 170.
Is sí mo cubus gan col, 282.
Is tu as ferr delb 7 drech, 362.
Is uimme caraim Doire, 188.

Leth na hindse tiar is toir, 390.

Mac bearar do Feilimid, 24.
Macam Ethne taeb-foda, 20.
Macam gidhnither atuaid, 12.

Maith ant inadh foistine, 392.
Mar do fer failte re Ferghna, 36.
Mar ticced a mat[h]air fen, 442.
Marcach an eich aluidh aín, 360.
Masa brec gach dan suad, 354.
Me as ferr ina n-altrom fein, 284.
Mesi acus Brighid amne, 422.
Misi Baithin bind foghair, 364.
Mithigh tene a tech n-aidhedh, 220.
Mo bendacht ar cloind Eogain, 290.
Mo bendacht ort indis tiar, 292.
Mo bendacht-sa ar cloind Eoghain, 290.
Mo bendacht-sa ar in cloind, 290.
Mo bendacht-sa leo da tigh, 290.
Mo choss am churchan ceoluch, 198.
Mo cros a n-Druim mocroide, 156.
Mo delughadh re Gaidhealaibh, 192.
Mo radharc tar sal sínim, 198.
Mo thruaidhe, 84.
Moch trath is am noín caínim, 200.
Mona beith briathra Molaisi, 184.
Mor a ferta an clerich caidh, 356.

Na tri caega salm do radha, 438.
Ni beith derc mun beith bochta, 350.
Ni ceduighte duind as daigh, 386.
Ní da roichedh 'n-a laim cli, 448.
Ní faghaid inudh ar tir, 190.
Nímtorbha, 448.
Nir diult Dia re dreich nduine, 352.
Nir diult Patraig puirt na clar, 352.
Nir scribadh a lebraibh sin, 352.
Ni[t]tescfa fidh no faebur, 372.
Nocha derna Dia duine, 354.
Nochon fhuil duilleog ar lár, 188.
Nochur taisced pingind riam, 448.

O docuala messe sin, 362.
O fhuícfed mo braithri fen, 192.
O nar fhidir en duine, 400.
O taínic trath proindighte, 400.
Ona gaírthib-se adcluinim, 194.

Raidhim-se rib, nocha chel, 388.
Re sirlenmhain co Condla, 286.
Reilec bec don taeb atuaidh, 42.

Rí na n-uile, ri na naemh, 288.
Righe duid, a Cairpri cain, 220.
Ro linsat sluaig imasech, 372.
Rofidir Colum ua Neill, 416.
Ro-m-bia mo delg-sa co n-ór, 376.
Ro-m-dirich Día, as demhin lem, 390.
Ro-m-lín maích a nfhécmhuis Erend, 292.
Rugad a nGartan da deoin, 42.

Saer in taide doriacht Í, 424.
Semidhe na saeraingil, 400.
Sesiur duind do muinnter De, 138.
Sinn-e ar slicht Caimh coluich, 394.
Slecht sis, a Scandlain, dom reir, 370.
Slectfad-sa duid, a ua Neill, 372.
Sloigedh la fondadh do gres, 366.
Snáaid eoin ar indberuib, 384.
Snamh tar an rinn-muir rianaigh, 384.
Son a gotha Colaim cille, 46.
Suairc an inis rancamar, 392.

Taisben acht co tís co tigh, 372.
Tan nac beid os Erinn uill, 22.
Tarccaidh Colum Cille deit, 382.
Teighe[dh] Colum gach dardain, 170.
Teora bliadhna bai gan les, 452.
Ticfaid tar mh'eis Colam caid, 22
Ticfidh Mandar gall go hÍ, 424.
Ticfidh Mandtar na cromluing, 424.
Tidnaic do Laisren an cuairt, 376.
Toirnidhfidh sís, 202.
Treidhe as dile leam ro facbus, 292.
Trell ac buain duilesc do carruicc, 436.
Tri caéca eces nach mín, 160.
Tri ced cell do cumhdaich Colum, 434.
Tri fodain nach sechantar, 102.
Tri fotha frithe don dail, 340.
Tri ní do ben dím mo rath, 140.
Triallaim uaíd, a Ghuaire gloin, 162.
Truag lem-sa na gaírthe guil, 192.
Truagh mo saethur-sa, a mic De, 286.
Tu-ssa siar is mesi abhus, 290.

Uchan! a Crist, a mhic De, 284.
Uictor aingel Patraig fén, 450.
Uile doib, ni trogdhal tra, 340.

LIST OF CHAPTERS IN THE ENGLISH TRANSLATION.

CHAPTER		PAGE
I	Of the Making of this Life and of the Lineage of Columcille	1
II	Of Prophecies concerning Columcille Made before his Birth	11
III	Of Visions Foretelling the Birth of Columcille and of Marvels before his Birth	31
IV	Of Marvels Following his Birth and of the Childhood of Columcille	41
V	Of the Studies of Columcille	53
VI	Of the Labors of Columcille in Derry and Tirconnell	65
VII	Of the Labors of Columcille in Meath	93
VIII	Of the Journeys of Columcille in Sundry Places to sow the Faith and in Especial of his Labors in Leinster	96
IX	Of the Labors of Columcille in Tirconnell and in Tory Island	101
X	Of Sundry Miracles and Prophecies of Columcille in Erin and of Certain Visions	111
XI	Of the Virtue of Columcille's Blessing and of his Curse	133
XII	Of the Miracles and Prophecies of Columcille and of his Revealing of Secret Things	143
XIII	Of the Labors of Columcille in the West of Erin and of Sundry Matters	155
XIV	Of the Exile of Columcille from Erin	177
XV	Of the Labors of Columcille in Iona	201
XVI	Of Columcille and Pope Gregory of Rome	207
XVII	More of the Labors of Columcille in Iona	217
XVIII	Of Columcille and Mochonda	255
XIX	More of the Miracles and Prophecies of Columcille in Iona	261
XX	Of Columcille and Cormac	277
XXI	Of Columcille's Love for Erin and of the Miracles he Did for the Folk There	289
XXII	More of the Miracles of Columcille in Iona	301
XXIII	Of the Miracles of Columcille in Pictora	305
XXIV	Of the Miracles of Columcille in Alba	317
XXV	Of Visions and Miracles of Columcille in Iona and in Diverse Places	329
XXVI	Of Columcille's Going to Erin and of the Assembly of Druim Ceat	339
XXVII	Of Columcille and the Poets of Erin	351
XXVIII	Of Other Miracles of Columcille at the Assembly of Druim Ceat	363
XXIX	Of Columcille and Dal Riada	367
XXX	Of Columcille and Scannlan	369
XXXI	Of Columcille's Returning to Iona and of the Voyage of Columcille's Clerics	377
XXXII	Of the Last Days of Columcille	403
XXXIII	Of the Death of Columcille and of his Burial	413
XXXIV	A Comparison of Columcille with Other Holy Men	427
XXXV	Of the Virtues of Columcille	435
XXXVI	Of Miracles that Columcille Did after his Death	453

ERRATA.

page 15, § 27, a true matter, *for* a true bond
page 17, § 30, the waterfall of, *for* Ess
page 25, § 40, not one of his race, *for* not one of his seed
page 28, l. 15, ecuse, *for* ecusc
page 30, l. 1, doirtid, *for* doirtfid
page 30, l. 26, creidemn, *for* creidem
page 31, § 44, and be safeguard, *for* it shall be safeguard
page 32, l. 16, audbairt, *for* adubairt
page 37, § 50, Prince of Cashel, etc., *for* Prince of noble Cashel in Munster
page 40, l. 19, tiufad, *for* tiucfad
page 44, l. 2, baegan, *for* baegail
page 44, l. 12, soightig, *for* soightib
page 44, l. 22, Cruithnechna, *for* Cruithnechan
page 46, l. 10, sargartacht, *for* sagartacht
page 50, l. 38, maigdhenaib, *for* maighdenaib
page 53, § 67, misery of old age, *for* intemperance (bis)
page 68, l. 8, dierce, *for* deirce
page 69, § 78, he should provide not, *for* he should plan not
page 88, l. 12, *ar, for* ar
page 167, l. 23; 189, l. 30, friendship *for* alliance
page 185, l. 25. *Delete* of
page 217. Chapter *heading* XVII *should precede* § 220
page 295, l. 18, center *for* edge
page 299, l. 2, to yield place to, *for* relying on
page 317, l. 2, Gemman, *for* German
page 367, § 344 *should stand at the head of the paragraph above*
page 377, l. 27, add AND OF THE VOYAGE OF COLUMCILLE'S CLERICS
page 389, l. 33, where, *for* who
page 437, l. 15, beech, *for* beach

We wish here to record our appreciation of the accuracy and intelligence of Mr. Staley, the type setter of this work.

G. S., A. O'K.